THE FOOD HISTORY
READER

THE FOOD HISTORY READER

PRIMARY SOURCES

Edited by Ken Albala

B L O O M S B U R Y
LONDON · NEW DELHI · NEW YORK · SYDNEY

Bloomsbury Academic

An imprint of Bloomsbury Publishing Plc

50 Bedford Square	1385 Broadway
London	New York
WC1B 3DP	NY 10018
UK	USA

www.bloomsbury.com

Bloomsbury is a registered trade mark of Bloomsbury Publishing Plc

First published 2014

© Ken Albala, 2014

British Library Cataloguing-in-Publication Data

A catalogue record for this book is available from the British Library.

ISBN:	HB:	978-0-85785-412-4
	PB:	978-0-85785-413-1

Library of Congress Cataloging-in-Publication Data

A catalog record for this book is available from the Library of Congress.

Typeset by Apex CoVantage, LLC
Printed and bound in India

CONTENTS

Part Four: Imperial China

Part Five: Ancient India

Part Six: Ancient Hebrews

Part Seven: Early Middle Ages

Part Eight: Medieval Islam

Part Nine: Late Medieval and Renaissance Europe

Part Ten: The Americas

Part Eleven: Era of Nation-States 1500–1650

EDITOR'S NOTE

The citations and internal notes in the modern editions of these primary documents have been mostly removed, since they usually refer to parts of the text not replicated here or specialized secondary sources that would probably not be of interest to the general reader. For pedagogical reasons, I thought it best to leave interpretation entirely to the student rather than depend on extensive annotations by modern editors. Thus, what is presented here is essentially the original texts as faithfully as they can be replicated. Original spellings, punctuation, and author's quirks have been left as originally published.

GENERAL INTRODUCTION

For the past dozen years I have been teaching a Global History of Food class for under-graduates at the University of the Pacific and more recently for graduate students at Boston University. Since the very beginning I have lamented the absence of a good reader of primary documents to accompany the lectures and stimulate discussion. So let me admit from the out-set that my motive for gathering this book has been entirely self-serving. But the very fact that there is now demand for such a reader beyond my classroom walls attests to the phenomenal growth of interest in food studies and food history in particular. Courses like mine are now sprouting up like mushrooms across college campuses everywhere.

Although this volume is meant to be used in a classroom, the readings are truly fascinating and will interest anyone who enjoys food history. There are recipes going back centuries; gas-tronomic texts; agricultural and botanical writings; and religious, philosophical, and scientific texts. There is food just about everywhere, of course; everyone has to eat. A surprising array of people wrote about food in the past as well. It is hardly a peripheral concern for us as a species, and I have gathered readings that I think reflect how important a topic it has always been.

I have tried to give a representative sampling of as many types of literature as possible while offering good-sized selections that students can really sink their teeth into. This is not a collection of little pithy snippets or literary references to food—there are anthologies like that. These are texts meant to illustrate attitudes and practices of the past, drawn from a broad range of sources and multiple vantage points. They are meant to stimulate ideas, conversation, comparison to the present, and, for the intrepid historian who so chooses, an opportunity to cook and taste recipes from the past.

Some of these texts are expensive or hard to find. To amass the books from which these readings have been gathered would take an enormous amount of time and energy, so I have done the work for you. The readings may be familiar, from the Bible or a literary classic, though you may not have thought of these as directly concerned with food. I have deliberately not chosen sources that can be found only in rare book rooms or have never been translated, simply because I hope you will want to read these works in their entirety. Many are online or can be found in a good library. The introductions for each section and the brief introductions to each selection set the readings in context, prod you with ways to think about the author, audience, motives for writing, and the mental framework of the culture that produced it. To paraphrase historian E. H. Carr, history is a matter of interpretation, not an assemblage of facts. These texts all invite multiple interpretations, and my introductions are merely intended to stimulate your own thought; they are by no means definitive.

The range of sources represented here does not try to cover every place on earth, because many culinary traditions are purely oral and without written texts. Nor have I tried to cover the full historical range of each tradition. In other words, Judaism is covered in ancient times but not in the present, the United States in modern times but not Native American cuisine. Rather, this book touches down in some of the great culinary moments in world history. So we have medieval Islam, Tudor England, France of Louis XIV. For some traditions I have chosen texts spanning several hundred years simply because these have been translated, as with the Chinese excerpts. For other sections the choices are more narrow, covering perhaps just a century. The idea is to cover major themes that explain why the world's cooking and eating habits turned out the way they did.

Many places with a rich culinary culture, which I do cover extensively in class, are not included here. The logic is a matter of focus and clarity. I have found that providing readings for every geographic location and time period is simply overwhelming for students, and it makes more sense to spend about a week with focused readings on one culture. Within each week I might also lecture on Japan, or Africa, or immigrant cuisines in the United States, but the readings focus on only one culture for the week. For students, and I think for general readers also, this makes for a more coherent text with themes that carry over clearly from section to section rather than a maze of tiny snippets that make discussion, let alone manageable assignments and examinations, very difficult. Again, this is not meant to be an anthology, but a reader.

I have also chosen to include only primary sources, because there are many excellent secondary sources in print, surveys of food history, specialized texts, and a spate of encyclopedias. But now it is time to return to the original texts and comment on them anew. Hopefully this reader will help inspire a new generation of food historians with fresh new perspectives on the past. Ultimately what we need is less rehashing of what we already know and new investigation of lesser known texts across many cultures. I hope this reader will serve as a stepping-stone for future scholarship—and especially translations from the numerous food texts that remain relatively unknown.

In my experience teaching, using primary sources is the way to make a classroom come alive. Otherwise history can become a random collection of facts, names, and dates. While those are important, it is the active interpretation of texts that makes history exciting. I've provided a bibliography of secondary sources in the event that you are writing a research paper or simply want to learn more about a particular period or individual featured here. But you should read the primary sources first, form your own opinions about them, and then turn to the secondary sources. In fact, it might be a good idea to read the introductions *after* you've read the original text.

THEMES OF THIS READER

The readings selected cover history of the interaction of humans with food resources from the earliest societies to the present. They illustrate how and why civilizations have been shaped by geography, native plants and animals, and technological developments that have enabled humans to exploit their natural resources. Feeding people has always been the primary concern of our species, and more than any other factor, finding, growing, and trading food products has been the prime catalyst in human history. In fact, from the earliest civilizations to the present, the movement of peoples, plants, and animals has increasingly connected one part of the world to another. Globalization is nothing new, nor is the dominance of some people over others who produce food for them.

Beyond the larger economic and social issues, the selections also cover the culture of food, why humans made the food choices they have, and what their food practices tell us about them and their world outlook. In other words, food practices are used as a window for viewing culture as a whole, much as one might study painting or literature. Foodways reveal much more because not only must all humans eat but we all make conscious choices about food within a cultural milieu. These choices reveal not only who we are and where we fit in socially but often our political, religious, and philosophical bent as well. For example, a vegetarian of the twentieth century (or from any century) makes food choices that reveal a great deal about the individual, perhaps the dominant food culture which is rejected, and a host of other concerns: animal welfare, a thin physique, religious taboos, and so on. By studying what humans have thought and written about food, I hope that history will become alive and direct in a way that the stories of great kings and epic battles sometimes cannot. Whenever possible, we will try to capture the experience of ordinary people in the readings, even if it is through the eyes of elites.

It is also important to remember that the past is a strange place, and many of the foods people liked, the animals (or humans) they sacrificed, and even the perfectly delicious things they wouldn't eat may strike us as strange. Often it is the matter out of place, what is considered unclean and abominable, that reveals the most about people through history, including us.

The readings will enable you to examine in detail why different people make different food choices, why they sometimes go to extraordinary lengths to find rare or exotic items while refusing to eat foods that are cheap and plentiful, why individuals from certain social classes will avoid or esteem particular foods, and in general how food is the most important factor of self-definition. In other words, food helps define identity and helps people situate themselves in society and, in terms of culture, nationality, or ethnicity, all of which are expressed through food and cuisine. Of course, what a particular food or dish may mean differs dramatically from place to place, from one time to another, and from one generation to another, and even in the mind of one individual depending on the context. So this reader will help you to see not only how and why other cultures shape what people eat but how your own choices are ultimately determined by your own culture and are often equally bizarre and arbitrary to outsiders.

Naturally taste changes over time, and, as you will see, the taste preferences of the past were radically different from our own. The purpose of studying them is not to gawk or marvel at their oddity but to understand why people made the choices they did. A particular ingredient may have conferred status because of its rarity or cost, like spices in the Middle Ages. A certain food may have been taboo simply because it didn't fit into a certain system of thinking, like pork to Jews and Muslims. Moreover, who eats with whom and the rituals that surround eating with others, like perhaps the formal Roman dinner or a modern wedding banquet, all reveal the ideals and aspirations of a given culture. The texts included here all supply ample material for speculation.

Last, because this is a history reader, we will examine the way the interaction of cultures and their destruction, transformation, and assimilation are all hastened by the human drive to feed and titillate the gullet. For example, the demand for sugar and spices in the late Middle Ages was not only the impetus for discovering the New World, but it also transformed the economy of both Old and New Worlds and involved massive migrations; the spread of human pathogens; and biological interaction of flora, fauna, and humans among several continents. All this literally changed the world—so Europeans could have sugar in their tea.

LEARNING OBJECTIVES

This reader is designed to help you master a significant body of information about food in history. Of particular interest is the origin of ingredients, where they travel, how and why, as well as how they are transformed through processing and cooking in different contexts. These selections will help you understand how culinary cultures develop over time. By the end I anticipate that you will have a firm grasp of the history, geography, social structure, religion, technology, and agriculture of the cultures covered and be able to relate these to eating habits, aversions, manners, and a variety of topics.

Most importantly, the reader is designed to help you develop critical thinking skills. First, you should not believe everything you read, and being able to assess an argument, point out its strengths and weaknesses, and offer constructive criticism is one of the goals of this text. Unfortunately, popular food history is rife with mistakes, exaggerations, and fallacies, so returning to the original primary sources I think should in some measure help to redress much of the nonsense and fakelore that circulates regarding food history. I hope these readings will help you hone your ability to discern sound from unsound arguments.

I also hope to instill in you the value of thinking objectively about people in the past and around the world. You will find many of the topics covered here are strange and sometimes disturbing. I hope that by the end of the readings you will not only understand why people eat the way they do but gain a measure of respect for the diversity of the human species, and maybe even broaden your own tastes.

I want you to see the value of thinking about what you eat and how it has been shaped by history. Understanding the consequences of what you put in your body in terms of aesthetics, health, and sociability is not simply a concern of the present, but, as we will see, is perennial. I also would like you to have a greater appreciation for the environmental, social, and economic consequences of your diet, and I hope this reader will help you make informed choices. Remember, eating is the only thing everyone on this planet must do and about which we make conscious choices.

HOW TO READ THESE TEXTS

Interpreting primary sources in food is essentially the same as any historical document. The only challenge they present is that we are not generally accustomed to looking at recipes and gastronomic writings as sources for history, but they certainly are.

First, it is important to establish *who* wrote the document. The author might be known, but even if not, try to make a general assessment of the person who composed the work. Can you determine the author's sex or social class? This will take reading between the lines, and might involve some sleuthing. For example, if the author instructs you to purchase a chicken, that might indicate an urban setting with butchers; instructions to first kill a chicken might suggest a farm or estate. One cannot be certain of these details, but educated guesses can be useful nonetheless.

Next consider *who this was written for*, which is sometimes easier than establishing authorship. A book may specifically be addressed to a housewife or to the lady of the house, who was then expected to pass on the information to a servant. Again, reading between the lines will suggest the social class of the projected reader. If comments anticipate spending large amounts of money on rare ingredients, one can assume it is an elite audience, though not necessarily. People do, for example, read travel magazines about exotic places with no intention of ever visiting. Likewise, people may read recipes as simply an aspirational exercise, to imagine what it would be like to throw a grand party or cook elaborate meals.

Consider also *what* the advice entails, and the content of the message. It might be a formal set of food rules; it might be an entertaining satire, an advertisement, a shopping list, a last will and testament, or a food column for a newspaper. It might simply be a menu. The form of the message is equally important and will probably reveal more information about the readership. In other words, a recipe is probably intended for someone who cooks, a poetic discourse on the pleasures of tea most likely has an erudite audience, and a government policy statement is meant for wide distribution and application. The form of the historical text need not be a written document. A painting depicting food, a film about food, a song extolling the virtues of a food—like Bach's *Coffee Cantata*—all can be profitably used by historians.

When the text was written will naturally offer all the contextual clues, and anything you know about the period and culture that produced it will enrich your interpretation. For example, if you knew a text was written for homesteaders on the U.S. frontier, it might explain the presence of advice for preserving food or keeping it from wild predators. If you knew that there was great social mobility at a certain time following a period of upheaval, it might explain why books of manners proliferate: to teach the newcomers how to pass in polite society. Dating a text based on linguistic usage is essential to the historian's trade, but it also can be done with ingredients. For example, if a European recipe purports to be medieval but includes potatoes, you know it's a fake.

The setting, or *where* question, concerns not only the geographical setting—perhaps a particular city, state, or specific locale—but also where physically this text was meant to be used. Is it a kitchen manual or intended to be read in a library or used in practice in a doctor's office? Perhaps it's meant for classroom use or to teach neophyte priests a particular form of ritual practice. Many food texts are clearly meant for professional academics in a scholarly setting, or to be used in the field by scientists, or as evidence in a legal proceeding. Imagine the details of a court trial of a baker arrested for selling underweight bread. This suggests not only a state sophisticated enough to enact such rules and enforce them but a public weary of being regularly cheated and concerned enough about prices and the supply of food to have officials spend time inspecting bread. Imagine the exact opposite—a culture such as ours that routinely allows the weight of mass-produced packaged bakery items to be lowered and yet offered at the same price. Clearly, either bread is not such an important staple that life depends on it, or the state does not have the power to enforce uniform standards, or simply doesn't listen to the public, who perhaps doesn't make such an issue of it. Larger issues are indeed at play in weight of bread.

The most important question, and sometimes the most difficult to answer, is *why*. We must never assume, for example, that a cookbook records the meals that people actually ate. Sometimes they are written simply for entertainment. And even when they do purport to give an actual record of a meal, one must interrogate the source. Is the author simply flaunting his or her knowledge of a subject? Is the author trying to inspire the reader to try something new or learn a new technique? Is there a hidden agenda within the text? For example, a set of published menus from an aristocratic court might be competitive, one ruler trying to outdo another with opulence and sophistication. A report on the food practices of a newly discovered land might seem to be objective and ethnographic, but the information may have been intended to suppress a native religion and food practices associated with it. Or it may have been used to open up a new market and sell new products.

There are many other questions you might ask of these texts, and certainly do not feel restricted to these basics. They will at least get you started thinking critically about these sources and the stories they tell. You might simply begin by listing the ingredients in a cookbook to see what was available and was used most often. You might look only at the technology and implements to get a sense of the physical labor expended by the cook, or even at the range of dishes and cutlery called for to determine the social class of the household. These are only a few questions to ask of cookbooks; other food-related literature, of course, suggests many more.

Keep in mind that ultimately what you are trying to learn is only partly about what people cooked and ate. You are also trying to discern larger historical questions about gender roles, conceptions of class or caste, how food is used to denote ethnicity or status, or how nationhood is expressed through foodways and how that consciously excludes outsiders. There are even the larger questions of world outlook, conceptions of purity and corruption, and the relation of humans to the divine.

Finally, in certain places I've suggested that you look at an online image to accompany a text. This might be a medieval banquet scene, a picture of a plant from an herbal, an illustration in a cookbook, or perhaps a still-life painting showing the ingredients in the selection. Or it might be a simple cooking scene. These are also excellent sources for food history. I have hesitated to give specific website addresses since they tend to change or links become broken, but if you do a simple search for an image, you should find many choices. Also, a search for any author will bring up an image and more background information should you desire.

PART ONE

Sumer and Egypt

For the vast majority of our time on this planet, our species has survived as hunters and gatherers, moving from place to place, with limited possessions and a comparatively simple level of culture. We tend to think of the lives of our prehistoric forebears as brutal, but, in fact, they were taller than our civilized ancestors, enjoyed better health, and had much more free time. This was partly because they left behind refuse, never lived in close proximity with animals whose diseases can mutate into human pathogens, and ate an extremely varied diet. Wild animals were plentiful, and, ironically, toward the end of the last ice age, the herds and wild grasses were confined to a narrow band in the warmer parts of the globe. This made the nomadic life fairly easy.

All this changed with the advent of civilization, which took place separately and at different times around the world, but usually with the same basic result: Humans moved into cities and villages, cultivated staple crops, and lived with animals. This resulted in a more narrow diet based largely on grains, a lot more time spent in laborious farming tasks, as well as diseases caused by lack of sanitation and living close to other people and domesticated animals. On the other hand, it did make possible larger populations and eventually surpluses of food that could sustain them. Although it is easy to exaggerate the pace of these changes—and there were definitely intermediary economies for many centuries—the invention of farming forever changed our lives and the species on which we depend.

The earliest civilizations on earth were located in the Fertile Crescent, an arc that stretches across what is today Iraq, Syria, Turkey, Lebanon, Jordan, and Israel. They existed only because of the change in how food was produced about 10,000 years ago. Archaeologists argue about how and why this change took place, whether sedentary living came first or domestication of plants and animals. Domestication—as the Latin root of the word *domus,* or house, implies—means not only cultivating plants and rearing animals but actually changing them slowly to benefit humans. That is, we carefully selected grains for replanting that would have more seeds per stalk or bean pods that would not shatter, leaving the beans on the ground for vermin. Likewise, cattle were chosen for size or milk production. Elsewhere around the world, other species played a major role—rice in China, for example, corn in Mexico. In all cases, we transformed the plants and animals to get traits that made them more efficient for food, traction, wool, and other uses.

Whatever the precise motivating factors, the Neolithic Revolution completely changed human life. We were forced to cooperate with many more people for basic needs, especially irrigation. These required more organized governments, armies to defend or attack neighboring cities, and a priestly class for maintaining social mores. This led directly to the invention of writing, which is why this history reader begins here, as does human history itself. Not coincidentally, among the first recorded words were cuneiform symbols impressed into clay representing head of cattle, sheaves of wheat, and tax records.

Although we don't have specifically culinary texts from the earliest civilized cities of Sumer, Ur, and Lagash, which flourished about 3,500 B.C., Mesopotamia was later conquered by the Akkadians from the north. Although they spoke a Semitic language, they used Sumerian cuneiform, and they recorded the earliest recipes to have survived on three clay tablets, excerpted below.

Egyptian society, sometimes included in the Fertile Crescent, is nearly as old as the Sumerian, and, unlike Sumer, was for much of its history relatively peaceful. The deserts bordering the Nile provided a natural defense, and this led not only to long prosperous dynasties and great material wealth but a rich and varied culinary tradition. The fecundity of the Nile and the Egyptians' dependence on its regular flooding are attested to in Herodotus.

Despite what appears to be an obsession with death, the Egyptians were generally happy people who clearly loved their food and especially beer, which was brewed in vast quantities. Unlike almost every other civilization, we have an exact record of what many Egyptians ate, because they often buried the dead with complete meals to be enjoyed in the afterlife. Archaeologists have examined the stomach contents of mummies in scrutinizing detail, and common practices such as butchering animals, hunting wild fowl, and milking cows are all detailed in tomb paintings and carvings. Kitchen implements, especially pottery, have survived, and recent scrapings and molecular analysis have revealed their contents. We also know a great deal about Egyptian bread baking, which used ground emmer—a relative of wheat—baked in conical clay molds using a natural yeast leavening. The molds and the bread itself have been excavated.

It is surprising, therefore, that gastronomic literature has not survived—not a single true recipe—but the closely related medical and dietary texts do offer a glimpse of the ingredients and techniques used in the kitchen. Religious texts, and in particular sacrificial practices, also reveal a great deal about Egyptian foodways.

ONE

Cuneiform Recipes

Three cuneiform tablets survive in the Akkadian language recording recipes from Mesopotamia. They are the oldest recipes on earth dating from about 1600 B.C., slightly after the reign of the great lawgiver Hammurabi. It is generally known as the Middle Babylonian period. From the recipes one can get a decent sense of the technology used, the domesticated and wild animals, and people's flavor preferences. Although many of the terms have still not been adequately translated, many of these recipes can be cooked today. If you search online for "cuneiform recipes," you'll find images of these tablets.

Tablet A (*YOS II 25*) is of average size: 118 × 164 × 37 mm. It is rather well preserved, deteriorating here and there only on its obverse side; but it is often possible to reconstruct what had probably been written there. It contains, as is indicated by its summary (lines 74ff):

Twenty-five recipes: 21 (kinds of) meat broth and 4 (kinds of) vegetable (broths).

Each recipe covers only a few lines, between two and five. And each is preceded by a sort of heading, no doubt the technical name by which it was known and which served as a reference.

1   (*1*) **Meat broth.** Meat is used. Prepare water; add fat [ ], (*2*) mashed leek and garlic, and a corresponding amount of raw *šuḫutinnû.*

2   (*3*) **Assyrian style.** Meat is used. Prepare water; add fat [ ], garlic, (*4*) and *zurumu* with . . . blood (?), and (mashed) leek and garlic. It is ready to serve.

Jean Bottéro, ed. and trans. *The Oldest Cuisine in the World.* English translation by Teresa Lavender Fagan. Chicago: University of Chicago Press, 2004, pp. 26–35.

3 (5) **Red broth** (?). Fresh meat is not used. Prepare water; add fat [ ], (6) salt, [as desired, cake crumbs (?)], intestines or stomach; (7) onion, *samidu;* cumin; coriander; and mashed leek and garlic [ ]. (8) Soak the meat in the reserved blood, and assemble all the ingredients in a pot.

4 (9) **Clear broth** (?). Meat is used. Prepare water; add fat [ ], milk (?); (10) cypress (?) as desired, and mashed leek and garlic. It is ready to serve.

5 (11) **Venison broth.** Other meat is not used. Prepare water; add fat (12) some crushed dodder, salt to taste; cake crumbs (?) [ ]; (13) onion, *samidu;* cumin (?); coriander (?); leek; garlic and *zurumu* [ ]. (14) Soak the meat in the reserved blood, assemble all the ingredients in a pot.

6 (15) **Gazelle broth.** Other meat is not used. Prepare water; add fat [ ]; (16) salt to taste; onion, *samidu,* leek and garlic [ ].

7 (17) **Kid broth.** Singe the head, legs, and tail. Other meat is used. (18) Prepare water; add fat; onion, *samidu;* leek and garlic, bound with (?) blood [ ], (19) mashed (?) *kisimmu.* Then, a corresponding amount of raw *šuḫutinnû.*

8 (20) **Bitter broth** (?). Meat is used. Prepare water; add fat [ ]; milk; cypress [ ]; (21) onion, *samidu;* leek, garlic, and *zurumu.* Bring to a boil, remove the cooked meat; (22) and stir leeks, garlic, *šuḫutinnû,* and mint into the broth in the pot; then add (?) *zurumu.*

9 **Broth with crumbs** (?). Meat is used [there is probably an error by the copier here, who writes "meat is not used"]. Prepare water; add fat, *šuḫutinnû;* coriander; (24), salt to taste; leek and garlic. Crush and sift spiced grain cakes, (25) sprinkle into the pot before removing it from the fire.

10 (26) **Zamzaganu.** Scatter cut-up pieces of meat in a kettle and cook. Clean some *bâru* and add to the kettle. (27) Before removing the kettle from the fire, strain the cooking liquid and stir in mashed leek and garlic, and a corresponding amount of raw *šuḫutinnû.*

11 (28) **Dodder broth.** Not fresh meat but rather "salted" meat is used. Prepare water; add fat; (29) some crushed dodder; onion, *samidu;* coriander; cumin; leek and garlic. (30) With the pot resting on the heat, the broth is ready to serve.

12 (31) **Lamb broth.** Other meat is used. Prepare water; add fat; salt, to taste; (32) cake crumbs (?); onion, *samidu.* Also add some milk, and some mashed [ ].

13 (33) **Ram broth** (?). Other meat is not used. Prepare water; add fat; some [ ]; (34) dodder as desired; salt to taste; onion, *samidu* [ ]; (35) coriander; leek and garlic. Put the pot on the stove (36) and, after removing it, mash in *kisimmu.* It is ready to serve.

14 (37) *Bidšud* (?) **broth.** Other meat is not used. Prepare water; add fat. [ ] (38) dill; crushed dodder; onion, *samidu;* cumin [ ]; leek and garlic, (39) bound with blood. It is ready to serve.

15 (40) **Spleen broth.** Other fresh meat is not used. Prepare water; add fat [ ] (41) Scatter pieces of "salted" stomach and spleen in the cooking vessel and add milk to it; (42) Some crushed dodder; cake crumbs, (?), salt to taste; onion, *samidu* [ ]; (43) bits of roasted *qaiiâtu*-dough *šuḫutinnû;* high-quality mint; mashed leek and onions, bound (?) with blood, (44) It is ready to serve.

16 (45) **Elamite broth.** Meat is used. Prepare water; add fat; dill; *šuḫutinnû;* (46) coriander; leek and garlic, bound (?) with blood; a corresponding amount of *kisimmu;* and more garlic. The (original) name of this dish is *zukanda.*

17 (47) *Amursânu-***pigeon broth.** Split the pigeon in two; (other) meat is also used. Prepare water; add fat; (48), salt, to taste; bread crumbs, (?); onion, *samidu;* leek and garlic. (49) (Before using), soak these herbs in milk. It is ready to serve.

18   (50) **Leg of Mutton broth** (?). With fresh meat from the leg of mutton. Other meat is also
       used. Prepare water; add fat; (51) salt, to taste; onion, *samidu;* leek and garlic, mashed
       with *kisimmu.*

19   (52) *Ḥalazzu* **in broth.** Meat is used. Prepare water; add fat; salt, to taste; onion, *samidu;*
       (53) leek and garlic, mashed with *kisimmu.* Crush the corolla (?) of some of the cultivated
       plant called *Ḥalazzu,* (54) Assemble all the ingredients in a pot.

20   (55) **Salted broth.** Leg of mutton (?), but no (other) meat is used. Prepare water; add fat;
       (56) dodder as desired; salt to taste; cypress; onion, *samidu;* cumin; coriander; (57) leek
       and garlic, mashed with *kisimmu.* It is ready to serve.

21   (58) **Francolin broth.** Fresh leg of mutton is also used (?). Prepare water; add fat. Trim the
       francolins, (59) add salt, to taste; cake crumbs (?); onion, *samidu,* leek and garlic mashed
       with milk (?). (60) Once the francolins have been cut up, put them into the broth in the
       pot, but they should first be cooked in a kettle [ ]. (61). Then return them to the pot. It is
       ready to serve.

22   (62) *Tuḥ'u* **beet broth.** Lamb meat is used (?). Prepare water; add fat. Peel the vegetables.
       Add salt; beer; onion; (63) arugula; coriander, *samidu;* cumin, and the beets. Assemble all
       the ingredients in the cooking vessel. (64) and add mashed leeks and garlic. Sprinkle the
       cooked mixture with coriander, and *šuḥutinnû.*

23   (65) *Kanašû* **broth.** Leg of mutton (?) is used. Prepare water; add fat; [ ]; (66) *samidu;* cori-
       ander; cumin, and *kanašû.* Assemble all the ingredients in the cooking vessel, and sprinkle
       with crushed garlic. (67). Then blend into the pot *šuḥutinnû* and mint [ ].

24   *Ḥiršu* **broth.** Leg of mutton (?) and "salted" meat are used. Prepare water; add fat; [ ] (69)
       onion; arugula, the best chopped coriander, and *Ḥiršu* [ ]. (70) Assemble all the ingredients
       in the pot, and sprinkle leeks and coriander on top. It is ready to serve.

25   (71) **Garden turnips broth.** Meat is not used. Prepare water; add fat [ ]; (72) onion; aru-
       gula; coriander and cake crumbs (?), bound with blood; (73) add mashed leeks and garlic
       [ ] (?). (74) 21 meat broths (75) 4 vegetable broths

Tablet B (no. 26 of *YOS II*) is physically the largest: its text, spread over four columns, two on
the obverse and two on the reverse, must have originally contained close to 240 lines. There
remain somewhat fewer than 220, and a certain number of them are incomplete or damaged:
some parts have completely disappeared, in particular at the beginning of column iii and at
the end of columns ii and iv. The recipes—there are seven in all, numbered 1 to 7—are much
more detailed, filled with minutiae, and quite different from the rapid and brief style of A.
They are separated from each other by two horizontal lines. In two passages we can note the
curious alternation of speech style (i: 53–ii: 15 and iv: 32–end): most often, the one who
is speaking uses a familiar form of address with the one who is listening, as is generally the
case elsewhere, but then suddenly speaks in the first person, presenting himself thus more as
a *model* than as an *instructor.* We will return to this peculiarity. At the bottom of the fourth
column, over two lines, there is a sign on each line that appears to initiate some invocation of
the copyist to two known divinities.

━● ●━

1   **Bi:** *1–49;* (1) To prepare a [ ] of [ ] or "small birds," (2) you remove the heads, necks and
       legs; (3) you open their bellies, and remove (4) gizzards and pluck. Then you split and peel

the membrane from the gizzards. (5) You then wash the birds and chop the pluck. In a clean kettle (6), you place the birds, gizzards and entrails. After heating it, you remove the meat, (7), and wash the contents well in cold water [ ].

In a clean pot, (8) you add water and milk, and put it on the stove. [N.B.: this last passage was smudged by the distracted copyist]

(9) You wipe carefully the birds, gizzards, and entrails and sprinkle (10) with salt, and put everything into the pot. You add a piece (11) of fat, from which the gristle has been removed. You also add (12) pieces of "(aromatic) wood," as desired, (13) and stripped rue leaves.

When it comes to a boil, you add (14) a little onion, *samidu,* leek and garlic, (15) mashed with onion. You also add (16) a small quantity of cold water. Meanwhile, you wash some *sasku*-flour; soak it in milk, and (17) once it is wet, knead it with *siqqu*-brine, and, being careful that it remains pliant, add *samidu,* leek, garlic, (18) milk, and pot juices. (19) While kneading it you must watch it carefully. You divide the dough into two equal parts. (20) You let one half rise and keep in a pot; (21) from the other half, bake shaped *sebetu*-rolls of 2? grams each in the oven, (22) and remove when done.

You knead more *sasku*-flour soaked and saturated with milk, (23) and add some oil (?), leek, garlic, and *samidu.* (24) Then, you take a platter that can hold the cooked birds, (25) and line it with the dough, allowing some (of it) to overlap (the rim) by a few centimeters [literally: four fingers].

(26) You then take the large container (in which half of the previous dough was reserved), (27) set that dough onto another platter and line it with the dough. You choose the platter (28) so that it covers the space taken up by the birds. (29) You sprinkle the dish with mint, then, (30) to make a "lid," (31) you cover it with the dough that you reserved in the large container. (32) You then remove the top cover from the stove, (33–34) and replace it by two (baking sheets?), on which you place the two dishes covered with their pastry dough. (35) When it has all been cooked, you remove (36) from the serving dish only the piece of pastry that will serve as a "cover," (37) and rub it with oil. While waiting for the meal, (38) you keep [a distraction by the copyist, who wrote: "you do not keep" . . .] this piece in its dish. (39) When the birds and the broth are cooked, (40–41) you chop and mash leek, garlic and *andahšu* together and add them to the mixture.

(42) Just before serving, you take the platter prepared with a lining of crust and (43) place the cooked birds on it carefully; (44), you scatter over it the pluck and (45) the cut-up gizzards that were being cooked in the pot, (46) as well as the (little) *sebetu* rolls that were baked in the oven.

(47) You set aside the fatty broth in which the meat was cooked in the pot. (48) You cover the serving dish with its (pastry) "lid" and (49) bring it to the table.

2   (i: 50). To prepare *amursânu*-pigeon in broth, (51) after slaughtering the pigeon, you heat some water (52) and pluck the bird. Once plucked (53) [here the instructor begins to alternate between "I" and "you," sometimes teaching what he knows to the student, and sometimes presenting himself to him as a model to follow] (53), you wash it with cold water. (54) I skin its neck, and you cut out the ribs, (55) (56) I open its underbelly and remove the gizzards and pluck; (57) I wash the body and (58) you soak it in cold water. (59) Then I slit and peel the membrane from the gizzard; I slit and chop the intestines.

(*60*) When I am ready to prepare the broth, (*61*) you place the gizzard and pluck into a kettle, (*62*) with the [red] intestines, and the head, (*63*) as well as a piece of mutton, (and you place everything on the fire). (*64*) After removing meat from the fire, you wash it well in cold water, (*65*) and I wipe off the skin. (*66*) I sprinkle the meat with salt and I assemble all ingredients in the pot.

(*67*) I prepare water; I add a piece of fat, (ii: *1*) after removing the gristle. I pour in vinegar to taste [ ]. (*2*) You mash together *samidu*, leek, and garlic (*3*) with onion; (*4*) you also add water, if necessary. (*5*) When these are cooked, mash together some leek, garlic, (*6*) *andaḫšu,* and *kisimmu;* (*7*) if there is no *kisimmu*, you mash (*8*) *bâru,* and add it.

(*9*) After removing the *amursânu*-pigeon from the pot, (*10*) you wipe it off. Then you [ ] the stove, (*11*) and stoke the fire [ ]. (*12*) I then roast the legs at high heat (?) (*13*); I wrap them in dough, (*14*) and I place the *amursânu*-pigeon filets on [the dish?]. (*15*) When it is all cooked, I remove the pot from the fire, (*16*) and before the broth cools, you rub the meat with garlic, add greens (*17*) and vinegar. (*18–19*) The broth may be eaten at a later time. (*20*) It is ready to serve.

3   (ii. *21*). To prepare a bird slaughtered for a *timru* ceremony, (*22*) once it has been decapitated, you pluck the animal; (*23*) you wash it in cold water; you slit its throat (*24*) and take out its ribs. (*25*) Open its belly carefully, (*26*) and remove its gizzard and pluck, (*27*) wash them in cold water, (*28*) and soak the bird in cold water.

(*29*) I then split and peel the membrane from the gizzard; (*30*) I split and chop the pluck; (*31*) you disjoint legs and wings.

(*32*) The broth should be prepared the same way as that of the *amursânu*-pigeon. (*33*) Meanwhile, (*34*) you soak *sasku*-flour in milk, and knead with *siqqu*-brine, (*35*) with leek, garlic and cooking juices. (*36*) I then allow this mixture to rise. I place (what is needed) into a pot; (*37*) I also put in the gizzard, and the bird resting on its back.

(*38*) When the bird is cooked, you remove it from the fire.

(*39*) I then spread the dough kneaded with brine onto a platter (*40*) big enough to hold the bird, (*41*) and you place the platter covered with the dough in the oven.

(*42*) You remove the platter from the fire, and onto the platter you place (*43*) the cooked bird. You disjoint (*44*) the thighs [ ] (*45*) and [ ]; and, (*46*) using a string, (*47*) you truss the legs to the sides, (*48*) and tie the neck to the body, (*48*) so that [ ] doesn't [ ]; (*49ff*) [in a damaged passage there is mention of "roasted barley" *qalîtu;* then the word "pot" reappears. A dozen lines are lost, or unintelligible].

4   [From the end of column ii, through the beginning of iii, over some forty lines, nothing coherent or intelligible can be read. The discernable vocabulary is known: "pot"; "kettle"; various condiments; fat; gristle removed; one "stokes the fire" (*13*); "when it is cooked" (*14*); "filet" (?) (*20*) . . . This concerns (*21ff*) the preparation of a bird called *agarukku* (*211*) to which the following recipe refers (*30*).]

5   (iii: *38*). To prepare *kippu* birds in broth, (*39*) the same method is used as for *agarukku*-birds.

(*40*) You open the birds (to empty them and carve them), and wash them in cold water; (*41*) then put them in a kettle. (*41b*) After removing from the fire, (*42*) you wash them well in cold water; (*43*) sprinkle with vinegar, (*44*) and rub all over with crushed mint and salt, (*45*) . . . (*46*) You clean a kettle, place water and mint in it (*47*) and (the bird itself). When you have removed everything from the fire, wash (the meat) well in cold water. (*48*) Then you place everything into a pot. It is ready to serve.

6   (iii: 49–end of column iii): [over only some fifteen lines, there remains only the initial rec-
     ipe heading:] (49) To prepare *kamkam*-birds in broth, (50) the same method is used as for
     agarukku-birds. (51–57); [a few incoherent words].

7   (iv:1) To prepare a francolin for a . . . (2) You split the bird open, wash it well in cold water,
     (3) and place it in a kettle. (4) You remove it from the fire, and wash it again in cold water;
     (5) sprinkle with vinegar; combine mint and salt (6), and rub bird with mixture thoroughly.

     [Variant:] (Or) you scrub a kettle (7), place beer and fat in it; wash the bird well in cold water,
         and (8) combine all ingredients (needed) in the kettle. (9) When the kettle is hot, you
         remove from fire, sprinkle the contents with vinegar, and rub (10) with mint and salt.
         [Another variant:] (Or yet), you clean a kettle, (11) put clear water and the bird in it, and
         place on the fire. You remove from the fire, (12) clean the contents well in clear water,
         and, when dry, (13) rub well with garlic. (14) [Another variant, for the preparation of
         the broth] You prepare a kettle; singe the "white" meat of the francolin, clean it well
         with water, (15) and place it in the kettle. You remove it from fire, wash it well with cold
         water, (16) and wipe off the "skin." [Another variant:] (Or) (17), wash a piece of beef or
         mutton. You remove it from fire, wash it well in water, (18) and wipe off the "skin."

     (19) You place all ingredients in a pot, with water, (20) and add a piece of fat with the
         gristle removed. (21) You carefully measure some vinegar (which you sprinkle onto it),
         (22) and add, as desired, pieces of "(aromatic) wood," (23) and stripped rue leaves.
         When it comes to a boil, you add (24) *samidu*, leek, and garlic mashed with onion,
         (25) and put it in the pot. You then place the bird in the pot, and cook.

     (26) When the francolin meat is cooked, (27) you crush together leek, garlic and [ ], and
         kisimmu, (28) and sprinkle mint onto the leg. (29) With these herbs [ ], (30) as the first
         time [ ] (31) with water [ ].

     (32) [Another alternation of the "I" and the "you," from here to the end of the tablet] I
         then wash some *sasku*-flour, (33) and I soak it in cold water (34) and knead it with
         siqqu-brine. I mix [ ] in a mortar, (35) I sift it with a sieve, and I separate on the one
         hand (36) the larger particles; on the other, the smaller ones. (37) [Variant:] (Or) I
         combine in a mortar some [ ], with its *ridu* and its *egasilimmu* [ ] (38–39) like (?) to
         grind the roasted seeds; I sift them with a sieve, (40) and I separate, on the one side,
         the larger particles, (41) on the other, the smaller ones. (42) [Another variant:] (Or)
         (I take) some coarsely-ground *sasku*-flour, with its *ridu* and its *egasilimmu*, (43) which
         I sift and put aside. (44) [Another variant:] (Or) some coarsely-ground white flour,
         with its *ridu* and its *egasilimmu*, (45) which I sift and set aside. (46) [Yet another vari-
         ant:] (Or) I take, some light *buṭumtu*, or husked lentils, (47) which are milled for me:
         I sift everything with a sieve, (48) separating the larger and smaller particles.

     (49) I cook these porridges slowly, each one (50) in an *assallu* platter, with beer in which
         "(aromatic) wood" has been soaked, in order later to add the porridge (to the meat on
         the dish). (51) [Variant?:] (Or [?] I knead coarsely ground *ziqqu*-flour with buttermilk.
         (52) I "butter" an *assallu* platter (53) and I cook the dough (thus layered) in it, spread
         very thin.

     (54) When it is cooked, I rub it (with oil?) and set it aside. (55) Then I mix together
         tiktu-flour with beer in which pieces of "(aromatic) wood" have soaked, (56) and
         I pour everything into an *assallu* platter. I also add leek, garlic, (57) *samidu*, honey,
         clarified butter, and one of the above mentioned porridges, and (58) I put the bird on
         the same *assallu*-platter. (59) Before removing from the fire [ ].

The following five lines are unintelligible and convey nothing to us; again they deal only with "porridge" (to accompany the main dish upon serving?).

At the foot of the column, one finds traces of the first words of (66) and (67), that is, two divine names:

(66) Nisaba [ ]
(67) Ḫaia [ ]

Tablet C *(YOS II, no. 27)* is the smallest of the three (89 × 137 × 37 mm), the shortest, and the most damaged. It contains only three recipes 1–3, separated by two horizontal lines after the first, and a single line after the second. It is impossible to restore the complete text, but what is left of its contents connects it closely to the other two tablets, especially B.

⚬⟋　⟍⚬

1　(1) To prepare a *nin*-bird [ ], (2) you split open the bird, (3) detach its [ ] larynx, and (4) [ ], place it in a kettle.

　　(5) After removing it from the fire, you wash it well in cold water. (6) You sprinkle with clean salt. Then you take a pot, (7) add water; (8) and add a piece of fat with its gristle removed. (9) You also add some vinegar, as required; some crushed "(aromatic) wood," (10) stripped rue leaves. (11) Then you mash together *samidu,* leek and garlic, with onion.

　　(12) When it comes to a boil [ ] meat and beer (13) [ ] a lot [ ]. (14) You sprinkle (everything) with leek, garlic and *andaḫšu.* (15) Then you clean *sasku*-flour [ ] (16) and add to the meat that has been cut up and [ ] (17) pour it into the pot. It is ready to serve.

2　(18) To prepare (a porridge) of clear *buṭumtu* [an unidentified grain], (19) you take either a *sabiltu*-container or (20) a pot. In addition [ ], (21) you put [ ] (22) cold water in.

　　(23–29) [are lost].
　　(30) [ ] the pot [ ], (31) will be present [ ] (32) in the water and oil.
　　(33) You put (into the pot?) water and oil, (34) and, when removed from the fire, (35–36) [ ], (37) [ ] some oil over the mixture.
　　(38) As desired, you add (39) *tiktu*-flour, [ ] in the *tiktu*-flour of [ ]; (40) as desired, (41) immediately after pouring (the mixture) into the pot, (42) you pour it back into the kettle. And just before serving (43) you put it back in the pot.

3　(44) To prepare a [ ], for a *tamqîtu* sacrifice (45) after slaughtering it (the animal) and (46) removing the legs, wash it well in water (47) and assemble (all ingredients) in a pot.

　　(48) As soon as you have put the cut-up meat into the water, (49) before the cooking juices have cooled ("rested"), you stir in *šuḫutinnû* and [ ].
　　(50) When the cooking juices have clarified, with some *šuḫutinnû,*
　　(51) you (mix) blood and garlic, (53) which you scatter in the pot. Then you add some [ ] (53) into the pot.
　　These are the "recipes" we have recovered out of the long history of ancient Mesopotamia. They touch upon only a tiny number of categories of food: grain and flour products; an armful of vegetables, and quite a few meats—cattle, sheep, and fowl, both domestic and wild.

We possess no further documentation concerning the preparation and eating of any other foods, that is, just about anything in that land and its surrounding areas that could be eaten: fruits; fungi; eggs, even ostrich eggs; certain seasonal game and insects, such as grasshoppers; and, especially, the vast river and marine world of fish, shellfish, turtle, mollusks, cephalopods, to which it would seem—a curious but unprovable exception—the Mesopotamians were rather indifferent, at least at times, although we have evidence that they appreciated them and traded them in the thousands.

We don't really know, at least not explicitly, whether they had any true dietary taboos (perhaps only on certain dates); we do know, however, that there was never any question of eating horses or dogs, much less snakes! There is no known ban on pork: it was raised and eaten. But it was considered dirty, according to a Babylonian maxim:

The pig is not clean: it dirties everything behind it,

It dirties the streets, it fouls houses.

Perhaps that is what discouraged those rather fastidious people, if not from eating pork, then at least from flaunting their consumption of it.

TWO

Egyptian Book of the Dead

This text is essentially a handbook, meant to be carried by the dead on their journey to the underworld, so they can successfully pass through various obstacles. In the process, their hearts would be weighed, they would have to explain their actions in life, and various spells would have to be recited to appease the gods. The Egyptians had a clear sense of justice in the afterlife. Thus, this text would have been buried with the mummy, along with food, furniture, and anything else needed in the afterlife. This particular version was written for Ani, a court administrator, in the eighteenth dynasty of the Middle Kingdom, about 1500 B.C. Although cryptic, and a literal translation from the hieroglyphics following their original grammar, these scattered selections and prayers do show how important food was to the Egyptians in life and in death. There are countless online images of this text as it was written on papyrus as well as images of food preserved in tombs for use in the afterlife and scenes of food preparation painted on tomb walls.

O givers of cakes and beer to souls perfected in the house of Osiris, give ye cakes and beer at the double season to the soul of Osiris Ani, victorious before the gods all of Abydos, victorious with you.

   An adoration of Osiris, lord of Re-stau and of the cycle of the gods great which is in Neterxert. Osiris, the scribe Ani, he saith: Homage to thee, president of Amentet, Un-nefer within Abydos! I have come to thee, and my heart possesseth right and truth. Not is there sin in my body, not have I spoken lies with knowledge, not have I acted with a motive double. Grant

E. A. Wallis Budge, ed. and trans. *The Book of the Dead: The Papyrus of Ani.* 1895. Reprint by New York: Dover, 1967, excerpted from throughout text.

thou to me cakes, and a coming forth in the presence at the altar of the lords of right and truth, and a going in and coming out from Neter-khert, not being driven away my soul from the sight of the dish, the sight of the moon forever: twice.

Grant to me a vessel of milk, cakes, loaves, cups of drink, and meat of flesh in the temple of Anubis.

May I sit down among the gods those great ones of Nut. Is placed for me a field, and offerings are before me; may I eat in it, may I be glorious in it; may I be filled according to what wisheth to receive my heart. May be given to me divine wheat for my mouth; may I obtain power through myself over the keeper of my head.

Not have I caused pain. Not have I made to weep. Not have I killed. Not have I made the order for killing for me. Not have I done harm to mankind. Not have I taken aught of the oblations in the temples. Not have I purloined the cakes of the gods. Not have I carried off the offerings of the blessed dead. Not have I fornicated. Not have I defiled myself. Not have I added to, not have I diminished the offerings. Not have I stolen from the orchard. Not have I trampled down the fields. I have not added to the weight of the balance. Not have I diminished from the weight of the balance. Not have I carried off the milk from the mouth of the babe. Not have I driven away the cattle which were upon their pastures. Not have I captured the birds of the preserves of the gods. Not have I taken fishes with bait of their own bodies. Not have I turned back water at its seasons. Not have I cut a cutting in water running. Not have I extinguished a flame at its hour. Not have I violated the times for the chosen offerings. Not have I driven back the cattle of divine things. I have not repulsed God in his manifestations. I, even I, am pure. Times four.

See Osiris Ani, triumphant, girt about is he with raiment, shod with sandals white, anointed with the finest oil of anta unguent. Have been offered to him a bull, vegetables, incense, ducks, offerings of flowers, beer, and vegetables. Behold thou must make the image of a table of offerings, in writing upon a tile pure, with colour pure, and bury it in a field which not hath trodden a pig upon it. If be made writing this upon it he shall rise, and shall flourish the children of children his, as flourisheth Ra without intermission; he shall be in . . . of heart the king among his chiefs, shall be given to him cakes, and vessels of water, and joints of meat upon the table of the god great. Not separated is he from door any of Amentet, shall go along he with kings, he shall be with the followers of Osiris near Un-nefer in unbroken regularity, millions of times.

The beginning of the chapters of the Sekhet-hetepu, and the chapters of coming forth by day and of going in and of coming out from the underworld, and of arriving in the Sekhet-Aanru, and of being in peace in the town great, the lady of winds, Let me have power there. Let me be strong there that I may plough there. Let me reap there. Let me eat there. Let me drink there as they are done all upon earth.

Saith Osiris Ani, triumphant: Homage to thee who are the lord, the lord of right and truth, the One, the lord of eternity, the maker of everlastingness, I have come to thee, O my lord Ra. I have made food offerings to the lord of the cows seven together with the bull belonging thereto. O ye who give cakes and ale to the shining ones, grant ye to my soul to be with you. May he come into being upon your thighs. May he be like one of you for ever and for ever.

THREE
Ebers Papyrus

The Ebers Papyrus, dating to about 1550 B.C., is one of the oldest medical texts on earth. As you can see from the brief excerpts below, much of the materia medica of the Egyptians was composed of common foods and could be prepared easily at home. There were also professional physicians, though, as well as magical incantations only they could recite to effect cures.

The Beginning of the Remedies to Drive Away Indigestion

Green Onions: Put in water in a new hunnu-glass and take for four days.

Onions: Cook in Sweet beer and drink the third part thereof for four days.

Another: Take a Casserole, half-filled with Water, half with Onions. Let it stand for four days. See that it does not become dry. After it has stood moist, beat to a froth one-fourth of the third-part of the contents of this vessel, and let him who suffers from the vomiting drink it for four days so that me may become well immediately.

Another: Date-meal Make into a dough in a hennu-vessel, put into two earthenware jugs, and set up in the fire so that the dough cracks. When this has happened, put the pap in Fat and Olive Oil. To be eaten hot by the patient so that he may become well immediately.

To Kill the Round Worm: Bark of the Pomegranate root 1, water 1/2, keep moist, strain, and take for a day.

Another: Inner of the Fruit of the Castor Oil Tree 1/3, yeast 1/3, water 1/2. Keep moist, strain, and take for a day.

Cyril P. Bryan, trans. *Ancient Egyptian Medicine: The Papyrus Ebers*. 1930. Reprint by Chicago: Ares, 1974, pp. 50–58.

FOUR
History

HERODOTUS

Herodotus is widely recognized as the father of history. Although he often repeats fanciful tales and hearsay, he did attempt to verify his findings, and his travels throughout the ancient world certainly made him a reliable reporter and a good storyteller. Many of his statements have been confirmed by modern archaeologists. His comments about ancient Egypt are probably the most detailed by any outsider. Egypt was at the time under Persian rule, but earlier rites and customs were still being practiced, and thus we have a detailed glimpse of foodways in the home and in sacrifice. The following passages are excerpted from Book II. Do look at a map of Upper and Lower Egypt to get a sense of the geography Herodotus describes.

I give credit to those from whom I received this account of Egypt, and am myself, moreover, strongly of the same opinion, since I remarked that the country projects into the sea further than the neighbouring shores, and I observed that there were shells upon the hills, and that salt exuded from the soil to such an extent as even to injure the pyramids; and I noticed also that there is but a single hill in all Egypt where sand is found, namely, the hill above Memphis; and further, I found the country to bear no resemblance either to its borderland Arabia, or to Libya—nay, nor even to Syria, which forms the seaboard of Arabia; but whereas the soil of Libya is, we know, sandy and of a reddish hue, and that of Arabia and Syria inclines to stone and clay, Egypt has a soil that is black and crumbly, as being alluvial and formed of the deposits brought down by the river from Ethiopia.

Herodotus. *The History of Herodotus*. Book 2. Translated by George Rawlinson. Available at http://en.wikisource. org/wiki/History_of_Herodotus/Book_2 under a Creative Commons Attribution/Share-Alike License.

But now let me tell the Egyptians how the case stands with themselves. If, as I said before, the country below Memphis, which is the land that is always rising, continues to increase in height at the rate at which it has risen in times gone by, how will it be possible for the inhabitants of that region to avoid hunger, when they will certainly have no rain, and the river will not be able to overflow their cornlands? At present, it must be confessed, they obtain the fruits of the field with less trouble than any other people in the world, the rest of the Egyptians included, since they have no need to break up the ground with the plough, nor to use the hoe, nor to do any of the work which the rest of mankind find necessary if they are to get a crop; but the husbandman waits till the river has of its own accord spread itself over the fields and withdrawn again to its bed, and then sows his plot of ground, and after sowing turns his swine into it—the swine tread in the corn—after which he has only to await the harvest. The swine serve him also to thrash the grain, which is then carried to the garner.

Now the Nile, when it overflows, floods not only the Delta, but also the tracts of country on both sides the stream which are thought to belong to Libya and Arabia, in some places reaching to the extent of two days' journey from its banks, in some even exceeding that distance, but in others falling short of it.

Concerning Egypt itself I shall extend my remarks to a great length, because there is no country that possesses so many wonders, nor any that has such a number of works which defy description. Not only is the climate different from that of the rest of the world, and the rivers unlike any other rivers, but the people also, in most of their manners and customs, exactly reverse the common practice of mankind. The women attend the markets and trade, while the men sit at home at the loom; and here, while the rest of the world works the woof up the warp, the Egyptians work it down; the women likewise carry burthens upon their shoulders, while the men carry them upon their heads. They eat their food out of doors in the streets, but retire for private purposes to their houses, giving as a reason that what is unseemly, but necessary, ought to be done in secret, but what has nothing unseemly about it, should be done openly.

All other men pass their lives separate from animals, the Egyptians have animals always living with them; others make barley and wheat their food; it is a disgrace to do so in Egypt, where the grain they live on is spelt, which some call zea. Dough they knead with their feet; but they mix mud, and even take up dirt, with their hands.

They consume none of their own property, and are at no expense for anything; but every day bread is baked for them of the sacred corn, and a plentiful supply of beef and of goose's flesh is assigned to each, and also a portion of wine made from the grape. Fish they are not allowed to eat; and beans—which none of the Egyptians ever sow, or eat, if they come up of their own accord, either raw or boiled—the priests will not even endure to look on, since they consider it an unclean kind of pulse. Instead of a single priest, each god has the attendance of a college, at the head of which is a chief priest; when one of these dies, his son is appointed in his room.

Male kine are reckoned to belong to Epaphus, and are therefore tested in the following manner: One of the priests appointed for the purpose searches to see if there is a single black hair on the whole body, since in that case the beast is unclean. He examines him all over, standing on his legs, and again laid upon his back; after which he takes the tongue out of his mouth, to see if it be clean in respect of the prescribed marks (what they are I will mention elsewhere); he also inspects the hairs of the tail, to observe if they grow naturally. If the animal is pronounced clean in all these various points, the priest marks him by twisting a piece of papyrus round his horns, and attaching thereto some sealing-clay, which he then stamps with his own signet-ring. After this the beast is led away; and it is forbidden, under the penalty of death, to sacrifice an animal which has not been marked in this way.

The following is their manner of sacrifice: They lead the victim, marked with their signet, to the altar where they are about to offer it, and setting the wood alight, pour a libation of wine upon the altar in front of the victim, and at the same time invoke the god. Then they slay the animal, and cutting off his head, proceed to flay the body. Next they take the head, and heaping imprecations on it, if there is a market-place and a body of Greek traders in the city, they carry it there and sell it instantly; if, however, there are no Greeks among them, they throw the head into the river. The imprecation is to this effect: They pray that if any evil is impending either over those who sacrifice, or over universal Egypt, it may be made to fall upon that head. These practices, the imprecations upon the heads, and the libations of wine, prevail all over Egypt, and extend to victims of all sorts; and hence the Egyptians will never eat the head of any animal.

The disembowelling and burning are, however, different in different sacrifices. I will mention the mode in use with respect to the goddess whom they regard as the greatest, and honour with the chiefest festival. When they have flayed their steer they pray, and when their prayer is ended they take the paunch of the animal out entire, leaving the intestines and the fat inside the body; they then cut off the legs, the ends of the loins, the shoulders, and the neck; and having so done, they fill the body of the steer with clean bread, honey, raisins, figs, frankincense, myrrh, and other aromatics. Thus filled, they burn the body, pouring over it great quantities of oil. Before offering the sacrifice they fast, and while the bodies of the victims are being consumed they beat themselves. Afterwards, when they have concluded this part of the ceremony, they have the other parts of the victim served up to them for a repast.

The male kine, therefore, if clean, and the male calves, are used for sacrifice by the Egyptians universally; but the females they are not allowed to sacrifice, since they are sacred to Isis. The statue of this goddess has the form of a woman but with horns like a cow, resembling thus the Greek representations of Io; and the Egyptians, one and all, venerate cows much more highly than any other animal. This is the reason why no native of Egypt, whether man or woman, will give a Greek a kiss, or use the knife of a Greek, or his spit, or his cauldron, or taste the flesh of an ox, known to be pure, if it has been cut with a Greek knife. When kine die, the following is the manner of their sepulture: The females are thrown into the river; the males are buried in the suburbs of the towns, with one or both of their horns appearing above the surface of the ground to mark the place. When the bodies are decayed, a boat comes, at an appointed time, from the island called Prosopitis, which is a portion of the Delta, nine schoenes in circumference, and calls at the several cities in turn to collect the bones of the oxen. Prosopitis is a district containing several cities; the name of that from which the boats come is Atarbechis. Venus has a temple there of much sanctity. Great numbers of men go forth from this city and proceed to the other towns, where they dig up the bones, which they take away with them and bury together in one place. The same practice prevails with respect to the interment of all other cattle—the law so determining; they do not slaughter any of them.

The pig is regarded among them as an unclean animal, so much so that if a man in passing accidentally touch a pig, he instantly hurries to the river, and plunges in with all his clothes on. Hence, too, the swineherds, notwithstanding that they are of pure Egyptian blood, are forbidden to enter into any of the temples, which are open to all other Egyptians; and further, no one will give his daughter in marriage to a swineherd, or take a wife from among them, so that the swineherds are forced to intermarry among themselves. They do not offer swine in sacrifice to any of their gods, excepting Bacchus and the Moon, whom they honour in this way at the same time, sacrificing pigs to both of them at the same full moon, and afterwards eating of the flesh. There is a reason alleged by them for their detestation of swine at all other seasons, and their use of them at this festival, with which I am well acquainted, but which I do not think it proper to mention. The following is the mode in which they sacrifice the swine to the Moon—As soon as the victim is slain, the tip of the tail, the spleen, and the caul are put together, and having been covered with all the fat that has been found in the animal's belly, are straightway burnt. The remainder of the flesh is eaten on the same day that the sacrifice is offered, which is the day of the full moon: at any other time they would not so much as taste it. The poorer sort, who cannot afford live pigs, form pigs of dough, which they bake and offer in sacrifice.

FIVE
Papyri on Food in Daily Life

*These two brief snippets give us a glimpse of daily life of food workers through their inter-
action with the government and legal system. From it one gets a vivid sense of the degree to
which the state controlled the food supply and managed labor. They date from a time when
Greek was the language spoken in Egypt under the Ptolemys and even later under the Romans. Egypt, and in particular the city of Alexandria, was one of the busiest, wealthiest, and
most learned places in the ancient world.*

266. PETITION OF A LENTIL-COOK

Middle of 3rd cent. B.C.

   To Philiscus greeting from Harentotes, lentil-cook of Philadelphia. I give the product of 35
artabae a month and I do my best to pay the tax every month in order that you may have no
complaint against me. Now the folk in the town are roasting pumpkins. For that reason then
nobody buys lentils from me at the present time. I beg and beseech you then, if you think fit,
to be allowed more time, just as has been done in Crocodilopolis, for paying the tax to the
king. For in the morning they straightway sit down beside the lentils selling their pumpkins
and give me no chance to sell my lentils.

A. S. Hunt and C. C. Edgar, trans. *Papyri on Food in Daily Life—Select Papyri*. London: William Heinemann, 1956,
    pp. 229, 377–79, 455–57.

331. SWORN DECLARATION BY AN EGG-SELLER

A.D. 327.

To Flavius Thennyras, logistes of the Oxyrhynchitenome, from Aurelius Nilus son of Didymus, of the illustrious and most illustrious city of Oxyrhynchus, egg-seller by trade. I acknowledge, swearing the august, divine oath by our masters, both Emperor and Caesars, that I am to carry on the retailing of eggs in the market-place publicly, for the supply in retail of the said city, every day without intermission, and that it shall not be lawful for me in the future to sell secretly or in my house. If hereafter I should be detected selling in my house, . . . [In the consulship of . . .] the most illustrious, Tubi 21. (Signed) I, Aurelius Nilus, have sworn the divine oath as aforesaid. I, Aurelius Dius, wrote for him, as he is illiterate.

364. SURETY FOR A SAUSAGE-MAKER

A.D. 566.

In the 1st year of the reign of our most godlike master Flavius Justinus the eternal Augustus and Imperator, the 25th year after the consulship of the most honourable Flavius Basilius, Phamenoth 21, . . . To the administration of the market through you, Philemon, chief assistant at Antinoe, from Flavius Sarapammon also called Colluthus, of Antinoe. I acknowledge voluntarily and of my own accord that I accept at your hands the charge of and responsibility for Aurelius . . ., sausage-maker, of Antinoe, engaging that he shall remain here in Antinoe pursuing his trade of sausage-making without fault, and shall devote himself to it from the holy Easter day of the present 14th indiction to the time of taking over in the (D.V.) 15th indiction, and shall in no circumstances leave his work. If he should leave his work, and I shall fail to bring him when he is wanted and deliver him to you in a public place, debarred from the protection of sacred precincts and sacred images and Sundays and holidays, I as his surety will pay you for his evasion 1 gold solidus. This deed of surety is valid and guaranteed, and in answer to the formal question I have given my assent on every point. (Signed) I, Flavius Sarapammon also called Colluthus, accept the charge and I agree to everything as aforesaid. I, Aurelius Stephanus son of Horus . . ., of Antinoe, wrote for him by request, as he is illiterate. (Subscribed) Executed by me, Cosmas, private notary.

PART I
Study Questions

1. Considering the evidence provided in the recipes, what was the state of cooking technology among the Mesopotamians; what kinds of ingredients did they eat; and why, if the basic staples were cultivated grains, did they still eat wild animals?
2. How does Egyptian geography explain its long and flourishing history? Consider how this land was both fertile with predictable floods yet also surrounded by deserts, serving as a natural barrier.
3. What did the Egyptians commonly eat, and were there distinctions based on social class or profession? Why were priests forbidden to eat certain foods?
4. Did the Egyptians have a sense of justice in the afterlife, and how do they conceive of rewards awaiting the virtuous? If one passed all the interrogations, what was the afterlife like?
5. Can Herodotus be considered a reliable witness to Egyptian culture and foodways? Do you suppose he understood everything he said or heard about?

PART TWO

Ancient Greece

Ancient Greek society is the unique product of its geography. The peninsula is mountainous, making land travel difficult; settlements are scattered across the Aegean Sea, which means that the Greeks were from an early date a maritime people. The lack of abundant arable land led to the founding of colonies that could supply grain, while the hillsides at home were largely left for grapes, olives, and animals such as goats and sheep. Luckily, these all provide foodstuffs that can be preserved, stored, and traded long distance: wine, oil, and cheese. The colonies stretching the length of the Mediterranean and into the Black Sea remained connected to their mother cities. The mercantile nature of the Greek city-states also meant that wealth was relatively evenly spread among the populace. Although they did have rich and poor, and even slaves, the elite class was large enough to patronize the arts, study philosophy, participate in politics, and hire professional cooks. It is no surprise, therefore, that they were highly literate and also produced the earliest cookbooks.

All this was in the later classical age, but earlier elite Greeks were warriors. Life in this period, known as the Mycenaean Era, was recorded several centuries later by the great poet Homer in *The Iliad* and *The Odyssey*, and the feasts of the Trojan War, with huge steer roasting before sacrifice, give a good idea of the gastronomic values of this civilization. Here strength and manliness were equated with a prodigious appetite for flesh. The other side of the coin, the simple farming tasks back home, are recounted in Hesiod's *Works and Days*, also written around the 800s B.C.

The ancient Greeks also took animal sacrifice seriously, and large communal feasts were a way to strengthen bonds between people and to the state, as was the theater and athletic competition. Opting out of these feasts, by being vegetarian, was a form of social protest. Pythagoras, the great mathematician, founded a commune in the colony of Magna Graeca.

Although his motives have been hotly debated for centuries, he was the first and best known vegetarian of ancient times.

The communal worship of Dionysus developed into a unique practice among the Greeks. It was a kind of ecstatic rite in which supplicants would become intoxicated by consuming the blood of the god, in the form of wine. Most civilizations incorporate intoxicating substances into their worship—in particular *entheogens,* through which one was said to achieve union with the deity. Not all drinking among the Greeks was so serious, though. They also held what were by most accounts raucous parties with naked flute girls, dancing, and storytelling. Plato's Symposium is the only very serious one. Normally participants would drink from a large, flat, stemmed vessel called a *kylix*. When you reached the bottom, you would fling the dregs at a target on a stand, a game called *kottabos*.

Plato's attitude toward the body and physical tasks left a lasting influence on Western civilization. In his dialogue *Gorgias,* he compares the job of a physician, who thinks about food in the context of diet, which is largely an intellectual pursuit, with the job of the cook, which is merely to feed so as to maintain the body. He finds the former far more valuable, as he does all mental pursuits. This made physical tasks, especially those performed by women, of lesser status than mental tasks. Eating, in a sense, reminds of us our base animal nature, and it is abstract thought and possession of a soul that separates us from animals. One might easily see this dualism as the root of much Western thought that denigrates cooking as unimportant.

Other philosophical attitudes existed toward food. Plato's pupil Aristotle could not have been more different and spent most of his time categorizing animals as well as devising systems of logic, analyzing political systems, and so forth. He would be extremely influential on later scientists—many of whom wrote about food, as we will see in the Middle Ages. Other schools include the Stoics, who adopted a position of detachment from worldly things and people, so as not to suffer when they are taken away. Only with inner strength can one cultivate virtue. Food and bodily pleasures, as might be expected, are not high on the Stoics' list of priorities. Neither was it among the Epicureans, even though that label had come to mean exactly that in later centuries. The original followers of Epicurus decided that all life is a matter of maximizing pleasure and avoiding pain. But it turns out that luxuries actually cause dependence and in the end cause greater suffering than they're worth. So the original Epicureans, ironically enough, were abstemious.

A major food preoccupation among the Greeks was dietary health and the tradition founded among the Hippocratic authors and continuing especially to Galen of Pergamon, who dominated Western medical thought well into the modern era. The system they devised is known as humoral physiology, which posits that every body is composed of four humors: blood, phlegm, yellow bile (or choler), and black bile (or melancholia). These humors can be described in terms of basic qualities, so blood is hot and moist, phlegm cold and moist, yellow bile hot and dry, and black bile cold and dry. Likewise, all foods can be described in these same terms. So diet is largely a matter of counteracting bodily imbalances with foods of the opposite temperature. Thus, if you are feeling hot on a summer day, a qualitatively cold and moist drink—sour milk—would act as a counterbalance. As you will see in the selections, the Greeks were also obsessed with the digestibility of food and thought of diet holistically, taking account of sleep patterns, physical activity, season, age, and a range of other factors.

Greek cuisine was raised to a high art, as shown in the surviving fragments of Archestratus's cookbook. It is not mere quantity or profusion or even complexity of technique, but knowing where the best ingredients come from, getting them in the right season, and cooking them simply to perfection. One could easily argue that the gastronomic tradition in the West begins right here.

Greek culture changed considerably after the conquests of Alexander the Great. Not only were trade routes to the East opened and new ingredients flowing in, making Greek cooking considerably more luxurious, but Greek culture spread to such places as Egypt, Syria, and as far as India as Alexander's generals founded their own dynasties. This was Greek or Hellenistic culture and language spread far and wide. It is probably in this context that Archestratus's comments about eschewing extravagance make the most sense. It was also this culture with which Rome interacted when it conquered the Eastern Mediterranean.

SIX

The Iliad

HOMER

The following feast follows a fight between Hector and Ajax, which neither wins, and, although the feeding seems incidental to the war between the Greeks and Trojans, their attitudes toward food and drink are plainly evident. It is not only an opportunity to rest after battle but a time to regather as a people and communicate with the gods, especially through sacrifice. Homer, who flourished about the eighth century B.C., *was the greatest poet of antiquity, and the stories he tells describe an earlier heroic age in Greece when the city of Mycenae dominated and led other Greek cities to war with Troy four or five centuries before Homer.* **Achaeans** *here refers to the Greeks.*

Then Hector said, "Ajax, heaven has vouchsafed you stature and strength, and judgement; and in wielding the spear you excel all others of the Achaeans. Let us for this day cease fighting; hereafter we will fight anew till heaven decide between us, and give victory to one or to the other; night is now falling, and the behests of night may not be well gainsaid. Gladden, then, the hearts of the Achaeans at your ships, and more especially those of your own followers and clansmen, while I, in the great city of King Priam, bring comfort to the Trojans and their women, who vie with one another in their prayers on my behalf. Let us, moreover, exchange presents that it may be said among the Achaeans and Trojans, 'They fought with might and main, but were reconciled and parted in friendship.'"

On this he gave Ajax a silver-studded sword with its sheath and leathern baldric, and in return Ajax gave him a girdle dyed with purple. Thus they parted, the one going to the host

Homer. *The Iliad*. Book 7. Translated by Samuel Butler.
Available at http://en.wikisource.org/wiki/The_Iliad_%28Butler%29/Book_VII under a Creative Commons Attribution/Share-Alike License.

of the Achaeans, and the other to that of the Trojans, who rejoiced when they saw their hero come to them safe and unharmed from the strong hands of mighty Ajax. They led him, therefore, to the city as one that had been saved beyond their hopes. On the other side the Achaeans brought Ajax elated with victory to Agamemnon.

When they reached the quarters of the son of Atreus, Agamemnon sacrificed for them a five-year-old bull in honour of Jove the son of Saturn. They flayed the carcass, made it ready, and divided it into joints; these they cut carefully up into smaller pieces, putting them on the spits, roasting them sufficiently, and then drawing them off. When they had done all this and had prepared the feast, they ate it, and every man had his full and equal share, so that all were satisfied, and King Agamemnon gave Ajax some slices cut lengthways down the loin, as a mark of special honour. As soon as they had had enough to eat and drink, old Nestor whose counsel was ever truest began to speak; with all sincerity and goodwill, therefore, he addressed them thus:

"Son of Atreus, and other chieftains, inasmuch as many of the Achaeans are now dead, whose blood Mars has shed by the banks of the Scamander, and their souls have gone down to the house of Hades, it will be well when morning comes that we should cease fighting; we will then wheel our dead together with oxen and mules and burn them not far from the ships, that when we sail hence we may take the bones of our comrades home to their children. Hard by the funeral pyre we will build a barrow that shall be raised from the plain for all in common; near this let us set about building a high wall, to shelter ourselves and our ships, and let it have well-made gates that there may be a way through them for our chariots. Close outside we will dig a deep trench all round it to keep off both horse and foot, that the Trojan chieftains may not bear hard upon us."

Thus he spoke, and the Princes shouted in applause. Meanwhile the Trojans held a council, angry and full of discord, on the acropolis by the gates of King Priam's palace; and wise Antenor spoke. "Hear me," he said, "Trojans, Dardanians, and allies, that I may speak even as I am minded. Let us give up Argive Helen and her wealth to the sons of Atreus, for we are now fighting in violation of our solemn covenants, and shall not prosper till we have done as I say."

He then sat down and Alexandrus husband of lovely Helen rose to speak. "Antenor," said he, "your words are not to my liking; you can find a better saying than this if you will; if, however, you have spoken in good earnest, then indeed has heaven robbed you of your reason. I will speak plainly, and hereby notify to the Trojans that I will not give up the woman; but the wealth that I brought home with her from Argos I will restore, and will add yet further of my own."

On this, when Paris had spoken and taken his seat, Priam of the race of Dardanus, peer of gods in council, rose and with all sincerity and goodwill addressed them thus: "Hear me, Trojans, Dardanians, and allies, that I may speak even as I am minded. Get your suppers now as hitherto throughout the city, but keep your watches and be wakeful. At daybreak let Idaeus go to the ships, and tell Agamemnon and Menelaus sons of Atreus the saying of Alexandrus through whom this quarrel has come about; and let him also be instant with them that they now cease fighting till we burn our dead; hereafter we will fight anew, till heaven decide between us and give victory to one or to the other."

[. . .]

As he spoke he upheld his sceptre in the sight of all the gods, and Idaeus went back to the strong city of Ilius. The Trojans and Dardanians were gathered in council waiting his return;

when he came, he stood in their midst and delivered his message. As soon as they heard it they set about their twofold labour, some to gather the corpses, and others to bring in wood. The Argives on their part also hastened from their ships, some to gather the corpses, and others to bring in wood.

The sun was beginning to beat upon the fields, fresh risen into the vault of heaven from the slow still currents of deep Oceanus, when the two armies met. They could hardly recognise their dead, but they washed the clotted gore from off them, shed tears over them, and lifted them upon their wagons. Priam had forbidden the Trojans to wail aloud, so they heaped their dead sadly and silently upon the pyre, and having burned them went back to the city of Ilius. The Achaeans in like manner heaped their dead sadly and silently on the pyre, and having burned them went back to their ships.

[. . .]

Thus did they converse, and by sunset the work of the Achaeans was completed; they then slaughtered oxen at their tents and got their supper. Many ships had come with wine from Lemnos, sent by Euneus the son of Jason, born to him by Hypsipyle. The son of Jason freighted them with ten thousand measures of wine, which he sent specially to the sons of Atreus, Agamemnon and Menelaus. From this supply the Achaeans bought their wine, some with bronze, some with iron, some with hides, some with whole heifers, and some again with captives. They spread a goodly banquet and feasted the whole night through, as also did the Trojans and their allies in the city. But all the time Jove boded them ill and roared with his portentous thunder. Pale fear got hold upon them, and they spilled the wine from their cups on to the ground, nor did any dare drink till he had made offerings to the most mighty son of Saturn. Then they laid themselves down to rest and enjoyed the boon of sleep.

SEVEN

Works and Days

HESIOD

Hesiod was a contemporary of Homer who lived between 750 and 650 B.C. His poems tell of Greek mythology and lofty issues but also of simple farming tasks around the year. These selections do both. The excerpts begin with an account of the corruption of mortals through successive ages in history, from the Golden Age to the Iron Age. The passage parallels the expulsion from Eden in interesting ways, especially the punishment of labor. The latter selections are about farming and keeping honest and thriving and paint an excellent picture of daily life in this era of ancient Greece. Consider also the context of these verses—this was just about the time the Greeks were forced to found far-flung colonies to supply them with grain.

First of all the deathless gods who dwell on Olympus made a golden race of mortal men who lived in the time of Cronos when he was reigning in heaven. And they lived like gods without sorrow of heart, remote and free from toil and grief: miserable age rested not on them; but with legs and arms never failing they made merry with feasting beyond the reach of all evils. When they died, it was as though they were overcome with sleep, and they had all good things; for the fruitful earth unforced bare them fruit abundantly and without stint. They dwelt in ease and peace upon their lands with many good things, rich in flocks and loved by the blessed gods. But after the earth had covered this generation—they are called pure spirits dwelling on the earth, and are kindly, delivering from harm, and guardians of mortal men; for they roam everywhere over the earth, clothed in mist and keep watch on judgements and

Hesiod. "Works and Days." In *The Homeric Hymns and Homerica*. Translated by Hugh G. Evelyn-White. Cambridge, MA: Harvard University Press; London: William Heinemann, 1914. http://www.perseus.tufts.edu/hopper/text?doc=Perseus%3Atext%3A1999.01.0132%3Acard%3D109.

cruel deeds, givers of wealth; for this royal right also they received;—then they who dwell on Olympus made a second generation which was of silver and less noble by far. It was like the golden race neither in body nor in spirit. A child was brought up at his good mother's side a hundred years, an utter simpleton, playing childishly in his own home. But when they were full grown and were come to the full measure of their prime, they lived only a little time and that in sorrow because of their foolishness, for they could not keep from sinning and from wronging one another, nor would they serve the immortals, nor sacrifice on the holy altars of the blessed ones as it is right for men to do wherever they dwell. Then Zeus the son of Cronos was angry and put them away, because they would not give honor to the blessed gods who live on Olympus.

But when earth had covered this generation also—they are called blessed spirits of the underworld by men, and, though they are of second order, yet honor attends them also— Zeus the Father made a third generation of mortal men, a brazen race, sprung from ash-trees; and it was in no way equal to the silver age, but was terrible and strong. They loved the lamentable works of Ares and deeds of violence; they ate no bread, but were hard of heart like adamant, fearful men. Great was their strength and unconquerable the arms which grew from their shoulders on their strong limbs. Their armor was of bronze, and their houses of bronze, and of bronze were their implements: there was no black iron. These were destroyed by their own hands and passed to the dank house of chill Hades, and left no name: terrible though they were, black Death seized them, and they left the bright light of the sun. But when earth had covered this generation also, Zeus the son of Cronos made yet another, the fourth, upon the fruitful earth, which was nobler and more righteous, a god-like race of hero-men who are called demi-gods, the race before our own, throughout the boundless earth. Grim war and dread battle destroyed a part of them, some in the land of Cadmus at seven-gated Thebes when they fought for the flocks of Oedipus, and some, when it had brought them in ships over the great sea gulf to Troy for rich-haired Helen's sake: there death's end enshrouded a part of them. But to the others father Zeus the son of Cronos gave a living and an abode apart from men, and made them dwell at the ends of earth. And they live untouched by sorrow in the islands of the blessed along the shore of deep-swirling Ocean, happy heroes for whom the grain-giving earth bears honey-sweet fruit flourishing thrice a year, far from the deathless gods, and Cronos rules over them; for the father of men and gods released him from his bonds. And these last equally have honor and glory. And again far-seeing Zeus made yet another generation, the fifth, of men who are upon the bounteous earth Thereafter, would that I were not among the men of the fifth generation, but either had died before or been born afterwards. For now truly is a race of iron, and men never rest from labor and sorrow by day, and from perishing by night; and the gods shall lay sore trouble upon them.

But they who give straight judgements to strangers and to the men of the land, and go not aside from what is just, their city flourishes, and the people prosper in it: Peace, the nurse of children, is abroad in their land, and all-seeing Zeus never decrees cruel war against them. Neither famine nor disaster ever haunt men who do true justice; but light-heartedly they tend the fields which are all their care. The earth bears them victual in plenty, and on the mountains the oak bears acorns upon the top and bees in the midst. Their woolly sheep are laden with fleeces; their women bear children like their parents. They flourish continually with good things, and do not travel on ships, for the grain-giving earth bears them fruit.

But do you at any rate, always remembering my charge, work, high-born Perses, that Hunger may hate you, and venerable Demeter richly crowned may love you and fill your barn with food; for Hunger is altogether a meet comrade for the sluggard. Both gods and men are angry with a man who lives idle, for in nature he is like the stingless drones who waste the labor of the bees, eating without working; but let it be your care to order your work properly, that in the right season your barns may be full of victual. Through work men grow rich in flocks and substance, and working they are much better loved by the immortals. Work is no disgrace: it is idleness which is a disgrace.

So soon as the time for ploughing is proclaimed to men, then make haste, you and your slaves alike, in wet and in dry, to plough in the season for ploughing, and bestir yourself early in the morning so that your fields may be full. Plough in the spring; but fallow broken up in the summer will not belie your hopes. Sow fallow land when the soil is still getting light: fallow land is a defender from harm and a soother of children. Pray to Zeus of the Earth and to pure Demeter to make Demeter's holy grain sound and heavy, when first you begin ploughing, when you hold in your hand the end of the plough-tail and bring down your stick on the backs of the oxen as they draw on the pole-bar by the yoke-straps. Let a slave follow a little behind with a mattock and make trouble for the birds by hiding the seed; for good management is the best for mortal men as bad management is the worst. In this way your corn-ears will bow to the ground with fullness if the Olympian himself gives a good result at the last, and you will sweep the cobwebs from your bins and you will be glad, I think, as you take of your garnered substance. And so you will have plenty till you come to grey springtime, and will not look wistfully to others, but another shall be in need of your help.

But when the House-carrier [snail] climbs up the plants from the earth to escape the Pleiades, then it is no longer the season for digging vineyards, but to whet your sickles and rouse up your slaves. Avoid shady seats and sleeping until dawn in the harvest season, when the sun scorches the body. Then be busy and bring home your fruits, getting up early to make your livelihood sure. For dawn takes away a third part of your work, dawn advances a man on his journey and advances him in his work,—dawn which appears and sets many men on their road, and puts yokes on many oxen. But when the artichoke flowers, and the chirping grass-hopper sits in a tree and pours down his shrill song continually from under his wings in the season of wearisome heat, then goats are plumpest and wine sweetest; women are most wanton, but men are feeblest, because Sirius parches head and knees and the skin is dry through heat. But at that time let me have a shady rock and wine of Biblis, a clot of curds and milk of drained goats with the flesh of a heifer fed in the woods, that has never calved, and of firstling kids; then also let me drink bright wine, sitting in the shade, when my heart is satisfied with food, and so, turning my head to face the fresh Zephyr, from the everflowing spring which pours down unfouled, thrice pour an offering of water, but make a fourth libation of wine. Set your slaves to winnow Demeter's holy grain, when strong Orion first appears, on a smooth threshing-floor in an airy place. Then measure it and store it in jars. And so soon as you have safely stored all your stuff indoors, I bid you put your bondman out of doors and seek out a servant-girl with no children;—for a servant with a child to nurse is troublesome. And look after the dog with jagged teeth; do not grudge him his food, or some time the Day-sleeper may take your stuff. Bring in fodder and litter so as to have enough for your oxen and mules. After that, let your men rest their poor knees and unyoke your pair of oxen.

EIGHT

Regimen II

Although there was an actual historical figure named Hippocrates (ca. 460–370 B.C.), well known for his skill in healing, he was probably not the author of the author of the entire Hippocratic corpus that has survived. A mass of medical writings were probably collected years later and labeled as "Hippocrates." These dietetic texts are typical of the corpus as well as the dietary tradition that follows from this, and the tendency to list foods and give their specific properties was the model right down to modern times; you might argue that we are still in the habit of declaring foods good or bad for various reasons. Notice that he uses the humoral system but also specific medicinal virtues of each food with special attention to digestibility.

LIV. The qualities of vegetables are as follows. Garlic warms, passes well by stool and by urine, and is good for the body though bad for the eyes. For making a considerable purgation of the body it dulls the sight. It promotes stools and urine because of the purgative qualities it possesses. When boiled it is weaker than when raw. It causes flatulence because it causes stoppage of wind. The onion is good for sight, but bad for the body, because it is hot and burning, and does not lead to stool; for without giving nourishment or help to the body it warms and dries on account of its juice. The leek warms less, but passes well by urine and by stool; it has also a certain purgative quality. It moistens and it stops heartburn, but you must eat it last. The radish moistens through melting the phlegm by its sharpness, but the leaves do so less. The root is bad for arthritis, and it repeats and is hard to digest. Cress is heating and melts the

---

Hippocrates. *Hippocrates*. Vol. 4. Loeb Classical Library, Vol. 150. Translated by W.H.S. Jones. Cambridge, MA: Harvard University Press, 1967, pp. 329, 331, 333, 335, 337, 339.

flesh; it congeals white phlegm, so as to produce strangury. Mustard is hot and passes well by stool; it too passes hardly by urine. Rocket also has effects like those of mustard. Coriander is hot and astringent; it stops heartburn, and when eaten last also causes sleep. Lettuce is rather cooling before it has its juice, but sometimes it produces weakness in the body. Anise is hot and astringent, and the smell of it stops sneezing. Celery passes better by urine than by stool, and the root passes by stool better than does the stalk. Basil is dry, hot and astringent. Rue passes better by urine than by stool, and it has a certain congealing quality, while if drunk beforehand it is a prophylactic against poisons. Asparagus is dry and astringent. Sage is dry and astringent. Night-shade cools and prevents nightly pollutions. Purslane when fresh cools, when preserved it warms. Nettles purge. Catmint warms and purges. Mint warms, passes easily by urine, and stops vomiting; if eaten often it melts the seed and makes it run, preventing erections and weakening the body. Sorrel warms and passes well by stool. Orach is moist without passing well by stool. Blite is warm without passing well by stool. Cabbage warms, passes well by stool and evacuates bilious matters. Beet juice passes well by stool, though the vegetable itself is astringent; the roots of beet are rather more aperient. The pumpkin warms, moistens, and passes easily by stool though not by urine. The turnip is heating, moistening, and disturbing to the body; but it does not pass easily, either by stool or by urine. Pennyroyal warms and passes easily by stool. Marjoram warms, and also evacuates bilious matters. Savory acts in a similar way. Thyme is hot, passes easily by stool and urine, and evacuates phlegmatic humours. Hyssop is warming and expels phlegmatic humours. Of wild vegetables, those that are warming in the mouth, and of a sweet smell, warm and pass more readily by urine than by stool; those that have a moist, cold and sluggish nature, or a strong smell, pass more easily by stool than by urine; those that are rough or harsh, are binding; those that are sharp and of a sweet smell pass easily by urine; those that are sharp and dry in the mouth are drying; those that are acid are cooling. Diuretic juices are those of samphire, celery, garlic (in infusions), clover, fennel, leek, maiden-hair, nightshade. Cooling are hart's tongue, mint, *seseli*, endive, bur-parsley, hypericum, nettles. Juices that send to stool or purge are those of chick-pea, lentils, barley, beet, cabbage, mercury, elder, carthamus. These help stools rather than urine.

LV. The following are the qualities of fruits. Fruit generally is rather relaxing, more so when fresh than when dry. The properties of fruits shall now be given. Mulberries warm, moisten and pass easily by stool. Pears when ripe warm, moisten and pass easily by stool, but when hard they are binding. Wild winter pears when ripe pass easily by stool and purge the bowels; when unripe they are binding. Sweet apples are indigestible, but acid apples when ripe are less so. Quinces are astringent, and do not pass easily by stool. Apple juice stops vomiting and promotes urine. The smell too of apples is good for vomiting. Wild apples are astringent, but when cooked they pass more easily by stool. For orthopnœa their juice, and the apples themselves when a draught is made of them, are beneficial. Service berries, medlars, cornel berries and such fruit generally are binding and astringent. The juice of the sweet pomegranate is laxative, but has a certain burning quality. Vinous pomegranates are flatulent. The acid are more cooling. The seeds of all are astringent. Unripe gourds are indigestible; ripe gourds pass easily by urine and stool, but are flatulent. Grapes are warming and moist, passing easily by stool; white grapes are especially so. Sweet grapes are very heating, because by the time they are sweet they have absorbed much heat. Unripe grapes are less warming, but a draught made from them is purgative. Raisins are burning, but pass well by stool. The green fig moistens, passes well by stool and warms; it moistens because it is juicy, warms and passes well because of its sweet juice. The first crop of figs is the worst, because such figs have most juice; the latest are the best. Dry figs are burning, but pass well by stool. Almonds are burning but nutritious; burning because they are oily, and nutritious because they are fleshy. Round nuts are similar. Flat nuts are nutritious when ripe, pass easily by stool when peeled, and cause flatulence. Their skins, however, are binding. Ilex nuts and acorns are binding when raw, but less so when boiled.

LVI. Rich meats are burning, but pass well by stool. Meats preserved in wine are drying and nutritious; drying because of the wine, and nourishing because of the flesh. When preserved in vinegar they are less warming because of the vinegar, but they are quite nutritious. Meats preserved in salt are less nutritious, because the brine has deprived them of their moisture, but they attenuate, dry, and pass by stool quite well. The powers of foods severally ought to be diminished or increased in the following way, as it is known that out of fire and water are composed all things, both animal and vegetable, and that through them all things grow, and into them they are dissolved. Take away their power from strong foods by boiling and cooling many times; remove moisture from moist things by grilling and roasting them; soak and moisten dry things, soak and boil salt things, bitter and sharp things mix with sweet, and astringent things mix with oily. All other cases judge in accordance with what has been already said. Foods grilled or roasted are more binding than raw, because the fire has taken away the moisture, the juice and the fat. So when they fall into the belly they drag to themselves the moisture from the belly, burning up the mouths of the veins, drying and heating them so as to shut up the passages for liquids. Things coming from waterless, dry and torrid regions are all drier and warmer, and provide the body with more strength, because, bulk for bulk, they are heavier, more compact and more nutritious than those from moist regions that are well-watered and cold, the latter foods being moister, lighter and colder. Accordingly, it is necessary to know the property, not only of foods themselves, whether of corn, drink or meat, but also of the country from which they come.

NINE

Gorgias

Plato's dialogue Gorgias, *written in 380* B.C., *is designed to distinguish true rhetoric, or the art of persuasion based on philosophy, from mere sophistry and wordplay, which is just a skill. To prove his point, he uses the example of cooking as a mere routine, flattering diners into believing certain things are good for the body. It is contrasted with medicine, which truly does know. Inadvertently he reveals much of the prejudice against cooking in Greek society and perhaps in the entire Western tradition.*

Soc. Will you ask me, what sort of an art is cookery?

Pol. What sort of an art is cookery?

Soc. Not an art at all, Polus.

Pol. What then?

Soc. I should say an experience.

Pol. In what? I wish that you would explain to me.

Soc. An experience in producing a sort of delight and gratification, Polus.

Pol. Then are cookery and rhetoric the same?

Soc. No, they are only different parts of the same profession.

Pol. Of what profession?

Soc. I am afraid that the truth may seem discourteous; and I hesitate to answer, lest Gorgias should imagine that I am making fun of his own profession. For whether or no this is that art of rhetoric which Gorgias practises I really cannot tell: from

Plato. *Gorgias*. Translated by Benjamin Jowett. 1871.
Available at http://en.wikisource.org/wiki/Gorgias under a Creative Commons Attribution/Share-Alike License.

what he was just now saying, nothing appeared of what he thought of his art, but the rhetoric which I mean is a part of a not very creditable whole.

Gor.   A part of what, Socrates? Say what you mean, and never mind me.

Soc.   In my opinion then, Gorgias, the whole of which rhetoric is a part is not an art at all, but the habit of a bold and ready wit, which knows how to manage mankind: this habit I sum up under the word "flattery"; and it appears to me to have many other parts, one of which is cookery, which may seem to be an art, but, as I maintain, is only an experience or routine and not an art: another part is rhetoric, and the art of attiring and sophistry are two others: thus there are four branches, and four different things answering to them. And Polus may ask, if he likes, for he has not as yet been informed, what part of flattery is rhetoric: he did not see that I had not yet answered him when he proceeded to ask a further question: Whether I do not think rhetoric a fine thing? But I shall not tell him whether rhetoric is a fine thing or not, until I have first answered, "What is rhetoric?" For that would not be right, Polus; but I shall be happy to answer, if you will ask me, What part of flattery is rhetoric?

Pol.   I will ask and do you answer? What part of flattery is rhetoric?

Soc.   Will you understand my answer? Rhetoric, according to my view, is the ghost or counterfeit of a part of politics.

Pol.   And noble or ignoble?

Soc.   Ignoble, I should say, if I am compelled to answer, for I call what is bad ignoble: though I doubt whether you understand what I was saying before.

Gor.   Indeed, Socrates, I cannot say that I understand myself.

Soc.   I do not wonder, Gorgias; for I have not as yet explained myself, and our friend Polus, colt by name and colt by nature, is apt to run away.

Gor.   Never mind him, but explain to me what you mean by saying that rhetoric is the counterfeit of a part of politics.

Soc.   I will try, then, to explain my notion of rhetoric, and if I am mistaken, my friend Polus shall refute me. We may assume the existence of bodies and of souls?

Gor.   Of course.

Soc.   You would further admit that there is a good condition of either of them?

Gor.   Yes.

Soc.   Which condition may not be really good, but good only in appearance? I mean to say, that there are many persons who appear to be in good health, and whom only a physician or trainer will discern at first sight not to be in good health.

Gor.   True.

Soc.   And this applies not only to the body, but also to the soul: in either there may be that which gives the appearance of health and not the reality?

Gor.   Yes, certainly.

Soc.   And now I will endeavour to explain to you more clearly what I mean: The soul and body being two, have two arts corresponding to them: there is the art of politics attending on the soul; and another art attending on the body, of which I know no single name, but which may be described as having two divisions, one of them gymnastic, and the other medicine. And in politics there is a legislative part, which answers to gymnastic, as justice does to medicine; and the two parts run into one another, justice having to do with the same subject as legislation, and medicine with the same subject as gymnastic, but with a difference. Now, seeing that there are these four arts, two attending on the body and two on the soul for their highest good; flattery knowing, or rather guessing their natures, has distributed herself into four shams or simulations of them; she puts on the likeness of some one or other of them, and pretends to be that which she simulates, and having no regard for men's highest interests, is ever making pleasure the bait of the unwary, and deceiving them into the belief that she is of the highest value to them. Cookery simulates the disguise of medicine, and pretends to know what food is the best for the body; and if the physician and the cook had to enter into a competition in which children were the judges, or men who had no more sense than children, as to which of them best understands the goodness or badness of food, the physician would be starved to death. A flattery I deem this to be and of an ignoble sort, Polus, for to you I am now addressing myself, because it aims at pleasure without any thought of the best. An art I do not call it, but only an experience, because it is unable to explain or to give a reason of the nature of its own applications. And I do not call any irrational thing an art; but if you dispute my words, I am prepared to argue in defence of them.

Cookery, then, I maintain to be a flattery which takes the form of medicine; and beautification, in like manner, is a flattery which takes the form of gymnastic, and is knavish, false, ignoble, illiberal, working deceitfully by the help of lines, and colours, and enamels, and garments, and making men affect a spurious beauty to the neglect of the true beauty which is given by gymnastic.

I would rather not be tedious, and therefore I will only say, after the manner of the geometricians (for I think that by this time you will be able to follow)

beautification : gymnastic :: cookery : medicine; or rather,
beautification : gymnastic :: sophistry : legislation; and
as cookery : medicine :: rhetoric : justice.

And this, I say, is the natural difference between the rhetorician and the sophist, but by reason of their near connection, they are apt to be jumbled up together; neither do they know what to make of themselves, nor do other men know what to make of them. For if the body presided over itself, and were not under the guidance of the soul, and the soul did not discern and discriminate between cookery and medicine, but the body was made the judge of them, and the rule of judgment was the bodily delight which was given by them, then the word of Anaxagoras, that word with which you, friend Polus, are so well acquainted, would prevail far and wide: "Chaos" would come again, and cookery, health, and medicine would mingle in an indiscriminate mass. And now I have told you my notion of rhetoric, which is, in relation to the soul, what cookery is to the body.

TEN

Oeconomicus

XENOPHON

Xenophon lived from about 430 to 354 B.C. in Athens at the same time as Socrates. He is mostly remembered as a historian and philosopher, but in this Socratic dialogue he discusses household management and agriculture. In it we get an idea of social relations among Athenians, the status of women and slaves as well as the running of a typical farm. Managing a farm in this case may be a metaphor for managing other things in life. Incidentally, Xenophon also wrote a Symposium, which is considerably more raucous than Plato's.

"'Oh, I will tell you, Socrates. It is not knowledge nor want of knowledge on the part of farmers that causes one to thrive while another is needy. You won't hear a story like this running about: The estate has gone to ruin because the sower sowed unevenly, or because he didn't plant the rows straight, or because someone, not knowing the right soil for vines, planted them in barren ground, or because someone didn't know that it is well to prepare the fallow for sowing, or because someone didn't know that it is well to manure the land. No, you are much more likely to hear it said: The man gets no corn from his field because he takes no trouble to see that it is sown or manured. Or, The man has got no wine, for he takes no trouble to plant vines or to make his old stock bear. Or, The man has neither olives nor figs, because he doesn't take the trouble; he does nothing to get them. It is not the farmers reputed to have made some clever discovery in agriculture who differ in fortune from others: it is things of this sort that make all the difference, Socrates. This is true of generals also: there are

Xenophon. *Memorabilia and Oeconomicus.* Vol. 4. Loeb Classical Library, Vol. 168. Translated by E. C. Marchant. Cambridge, MA: Harvard University Press, 1923, pp. 511, 513, 515, 517, 519, 521.

some branches of strategy in which one is better or worse than another, not because he differs in intelligence, but in point of carefulness, undoubtedly. For the things that all generals know, and most privates, are done by some commanders and left undone by others. For example, they all know that when marching through an enemy's country, the right way is to march in the formation in which they will fight best, if need be. Well, knowing this, some observe the rule, others break it. All know that it is right to post sentries by day and night before the camp; but this too is a duty that some attend to, while others neglect it. Again, where will you find the man who does not know that, in marching through a defile, it is better to occupy the points of vantage first? Yet this measure of precaution too is duly taken by some and neglected by others. So, too, everyone will say that in agriculture there is nothing so good as manure, and their eyes tell them that nature produces it. All know exactly how it is produced, and it is easy to get any amount of it; and yet, while some take care to have it collected, others care nothing about it. Yet the rain is sent from heaven, and all the hollows become pools of water, and the earth yields herbage of every kind which must be cleared off the ground by the sower before sowing; and the rubbish he removes has but to be thrown into water, and time of itself will make what the soil likes. For every kind of vegetation, every kind of soil in stagnant water turns into manure.

"'And again, all the ways of treating the soil when it is too wet for sowing or too salt for planting are familiar to all men—how the land is drained by ditches, how the salt is corrected by being mixed with saltless substances, liquid or dry. Yet these matters, again, do not always receive attention. Suppose a man to be wholly ignorant as to what the land can produce, and to be unable to see crop or tree on it, or to hear from anyone the truth about it, yet is it not far easier for any man to prove a parcel of land than to test a horse or to test a human being? For the land never plays tricks, but reveals frankly and truthfully what she can and what she cannot do. I think that just because she conceals nothing from our knowledge and understanding, the land is the surest tester of good and bad men. For the slothful cannot plead ignorance, as in other arts: land, as all men know, responds to good treatment. Husbandry is the clear accuser of the recreant soul. For no one persuades himself that man could live without bread; therefore if a man will not dig and knows no other profit-earning trade, he is clearly minded to live by stealing or robbery or begging—or he is an utter fool.

"'Farming,' he added, 'may result in profit or in loss; it makes a great difference to the result, even when many labourers are employed, whether the farmer takes care that the men are working during the working hours or is careless about it. For one man in ten by working all the time may easily make a difference, and another by knocking off before the time; and, of course, if the men are allowed to be slack all the day long, the decrease in the work done may easily amount to one half of the whole. Just as two travellers on the road, both young and in good health, will differ so much in pace that one will cover two hundred furlongs to the other's hundred, because the one does what he set out to do, by going ahead, while the other is all for ease, now resting by a fountain or in the shade, now gazing at the view, now wooing the soft breeze; so in farm work there is a vast difference in effectiveness between the men who do the job they are put on to do and those who, instead of doing it, invent excuses for not working and are allowed to be slack. In fact, between good work and dishonest slothfulness there is as wide a difference as between actual work and actual idleness. Suppose the vines are being hoed to clear the ground of weeds: if the hoeing is so badly done that the weeds grow ranker and more abundant, how can you call that anything but idleness?'

" 'These, then, are the evils that crush estates far more than sheer lack of knowledge. For the outgoing expenses of the estate are not a penny less; but the work done is insufficient to show a profit on the expenditure; after that there's no need to wonder if the expected surplus is converted into a loss. On the other hand, to a careful man, who works strenuously at agriculture, no business gives quicker returns than farming. My father taught me that and proved it by his own practice. For he never allowed me to buy a piece of land that was well farmed; but pressed me to buy any that was uncultivated and unplanted owing to the owner's neglect or incapacity. "Well farmed land," he would say, "costs a large sum and can't be improved"; and he held that where there is no room for improvement there is not much pleasure to be got from the land: landed estate and livestock must be continually coming on to give the fullest measure of satisfaction. Now nothing improves more than a farm that is being transformed from a wilderness into fruitful fields. I assure you, Socrates, that we have often added a hundredfold to the value of a farm. There is so much money in this idea, Socrates, and it is so easy to learn, that no sooner have you heard of it from me than you know as much as I do, and can go home and teach it to someone else, if you like. Moreover, my father did not get his knowledge of it at secondhand, nor did he discover it by much thought; but he would say that, thanks to his love of husbandry and hard work, he had coveted a farm of this sort in order that he might have something to do, and combine profit with pleasure. For I assure you, Socrates, no Athenian, I believe, had such a strong natural love of agriculture as my father.'

"Now on hearing this I asked, 'Did your father keep all the farms that he cultivated, Ischomachus, or did he sell when he could get a good price?'

" 'He sold, of course,' answered Ischomachus, 'but, you see, owing to his industrious habits, he would promptly buy another that was out of cultivation.'

" 'You mean, Ischomachus, that your father really loved agriculture as intensely as merchants love corn. So deep is their love of corn that on receiving reports that it is abundant anywhere, merchants will voyage in quest of it: they will cross the Aegean, the Euxine, the Sicilian sea; and when they have got as much as possible, they carry it over the sea, and they actually stow it in the very ship in which they sail themselves. And when they want money, they don't throw the corn away anywhere at haphazard, but they carry it to the place where they hear that corn is most valued and the people prize it most highly, and deliver it to them there. Yes, your father's love of agriculture seems to be something like that.'

" 'You're joking, Socrates,' rejoined Ischomachus; 'but I hold that a man has a no less genuine love of building who sells his houses as soon as they are finished and proceeds to build others.'

" 'Of course; and I declare, Ischomachus, on my oath that I believe you, that all men naturally love whatever they think will bring them profit.' "

ELEVEN

The Life of Luxury

ARCHESTRATUS

The surviving fragments of Archestratus's cookbook, mostly about fish and bread, are included in Athenaeus's voluminous compendium on ancient food practices composed many centuries later, The Deipnosophists. *Athenaeus is not always nice to Archestratus, calling him sarcastically the Daedalus (i.e., inventor) of dainty dishes. The work is sometimes known as the* Hedypatheia *or* Life of Luxury *and was composed in the fourth century* B.C. *If anything, the title is a misnomer, since the book is more about connoisseurship, knowing where to find the best ingredients, and how to serve them without much fuss or ostentation. One could very well argue that Archestratus was the first gastronome in the very modern sense of that word. The text was probably meant to be recited aloud during a symposium.*

FRAGMENT 4

[Athenaeus 111e]

Archestratus in his Gastronomy discourses on barley meal and breads as follows: First then I will list the gifts of Demeter of the fair tresses, my dear Moschus: keep it safe in your heart. Now the best to get hold of and the finest of all, cleanly bolted from barley with a good grain, is in Lesbos, in the wave-surrounded breast of famous Eresos. It is whiter than snow from the sky: if the gods eat barley groats then Hermes must come and buy it

---

Archestratus. *The Life of Luxury.* Translated by John Wilkins and Shaun Hill. Totnes, UK: Prospect Books, 1994, pp. 41–45, 72–73, 93–97.

for them from there. In seven-gated Thebes too it is reasonably good, and in Thasos and some other cities, but it is like grape pips compared with Lesbian. Get that idea clearly into your head. Get hold of a Thessalian roll, rounded into a circle and well pounded by hand. They themselves call this roll *krimnitas*, but others call it *chondrinos* bread. Then I praise the son of fine wheat flour from Tegea, ash-bread. Bread made in the market, famous Athens provides for mortals, of an excellent quality. In Erythrae which bears clusters of grapes a white bread comes out of the oven, bursting with the delicate flavours of the season, and will bring pleasure at the feast.

FRAGMENT 5

[Athenaeus Fragment 112b]

After this [i.e., fragment 4] *the chef Archestratus advises that you have a breadmaker from Phoenicia or Lydia, unaware of the fact that breadmakers from Cappadocia are the best:* Get yourself a man from Phoenicia or Lydia in your house, a man who will know how to make every kind of bread product on a daily basis, whatever you order.

FRAGMENT 6

[Athenaeus 64a]

Archestratus: Bulbs. I bid farewell to vinegar-dishes of bulbs and plant stalks, and to all the other side-dishes.

FRAGMENT 7

[Athenaeus 56c]

Archestratus in his Gastronomy: Let them serve you wrinkled and tree-ripened olives.

FRAGMENT 8

[Athenaeus 298e]

Concerning the eel Archestratus records this: Eels. I praise all eels, but by far the best is the eel caught from the sea off the straits of Rhegium. There, citizen of Messina, in being able to put such food to your lips, you are richer than all other mortals. Of course, the eels of Copais and Strymon have a great reputation for excellence. They're huge and amazingly fat. All in all I believe the eel lords it over everything else at the feast and is a guide to pleasure, though it is the only fish that has no scrotum.

FRAGMENT 9

[Athenaeus 285b]

Archestratus, the Daedalus of tasty dishes, says: Small fry [*aphue*]. Value as shit all small fry except the Athenian kind. I'm speaking of *gonos* which the Ionians call foam. Get it when fresh and caught in the beautiful bay of Phaleron, in its sacred arms. It is also of good quality in wave-girt Rhodes, if it is local fish. And if perhaps you desire to taste it, you should buy at the same time [sea] nettles, nettles with long locks. Mix them together and bake them on a frying pan, grinding the fragrant flowers of the greens in oil.

FRAGMENT 34

[Athenaeus 301f]

Now around holy Samos with its wide dancing places you will see the great tuna enthusiastically caught: they call it *orkus,* others call it the monster-fish. In summertime you must buy such cuts of the fish as are appropriate swiftly, with no fighting [?] over the price. It is good at Byzantium and Carystus; and in the famous island of Sicily the Cephalodian and the Tyndarian shores breed much better tuna than these. If you ever go to Hipponium in holy Italy, make your way to the garlands of the waters [?]: there are the very best [tuna] of all, by a long way, and they have the culmination of victory. The tuna in these waters are those that have wandered from there after travels over many seas through the briny deep. As a result we catch them when they are out of season.

FRAGMENT 35

[Athenaeus 278a]

Archestratus the Daedalus of tasty dishes in his Gastrology (for such is its title according to Lycophron in his books on comedy, just as the work of Cleostratus of Tenedos is titled Astrology) says this about the amia: The *Amia.* Prepare it by every method, in the autumn, when the Pleiad is sinking. Why recite it to you word for word, for you could not do it any harm even if you wished to? But if you desire to learn this too, my dear Moschus, the best way to present this fish I mean, then in fig leaves with not too much origano is the way. No cheese, no fancy nonsense. Simply place it with care in the fig leaves and tie them with rush-cord from above. Then put into hot ashes and use your intelligence to work out the time when it will be roasted: don't let it burn up. Let it come from lovely Byzantium if you wish to have the best, though you will get a good one if it is caught near here. The further from the Hellespont, the worse the fish: if you travel over the glorious salt ways of the Aegean sea, it is no longer the same fish at all; rather, it brings shame on my earlier praise.

FRAGMENTS 59–60

[Athenaeus 29b]

from Archestratus the writer on banquets then when you have drawn a full measure for Zeus the Saviour, you must drink an old wine with a really grey old head, its moist locks festooned with white flowers, born in Lesbos with the sea all around. I praise Bybline wine from Phoenicia, though it does not equal Lesbian. If you take a quick taste of it and are previously unacquainted, it will seem to you to be more fragrant than Lesbian, for this lasts for a very long time. When tasted though it is very inferior, and the Lesbian will take on a rank not like wine but like ambrosia. If some scoff at me, braggarts, purveyors of empty nonsense, saying that Phoenician has the sweetest nature of all, I pay no attention to them . . . [.] Thasos also produces a noble wine to drink, provided it is aged over many good seasons down the years. I know too of the shoots dripping with grape clusters in other cities. I could cite them, praise them, and indeed their names are well known to me. But the others are simply worthless beside the Lesbian wine. Some people of course like to praise products from their own locality.

FRAGMENT 61

[Athenaeus 4d]

Archestratus from Syracuse or Gela says: All should dine at a single table set for an elegant meal. In all the diners should be three or four, and certainly no more than five. Otherwise it would be a tentful of soldiers, mercenaries and looters of foodstuffs.

FRAGMENT 62

[Athenaeus 101b]

Archestratus the Daedalus of cooking speaks of sow's womb after the dinner and the toasts and the anointing with perfumes: always festoon the head with all kinds of garland at the feast, with whatever the fruitful floor of the earth brings into flower; dress your hair with fine distilled perfumes and all day long throw on the soft ashes myrrh and incense, the fragrant fruit of Syria. And while you are drinking, let these tasty dishes be brought to you: the belly and boiled womb of a sow in cumin and sharp vinegar and silphium; the tender race of roasted birds, whatever may be in season. Have nothing to do with those Syracusans who drink only in the manner of frogs and eat nothing. No, do not be taken in by them, but eat the foods I set forth. All those other *tragemata* are a sign of wretched poverty, boiled chickpeas, broad beans, apples and dried figs. I do though applaud the flat-cake born in Athens. If you cannot get one there, go and get one elsewhere and seek out some Attic honey, for that is what makes it flaunt itself proudly. That is how a free man should live: the alternative is to go beneath the earth and the bottomless pit and Tartarus to destruction and be dug down countless stades deep.

TWELVE
The Moral Theory

EPICURUS

Although the name Epicurus and the word epicurean have come down through the ages as meaning excessively luxurious and overly concerned with pleasures of the palate, the histori-cal figure who lived from ca. 341 to 271 B.C. was actually abstemious and frugal. This miscon-ception sprung from Epicurus's claim that human actions can be very simply understood as an attempt to maximize pleasure and minimize pain. Maximizing pleasure, however, might mean forgoing luxuries to which we are all too easily attached, or which in the end cause greater suffering than they're worth. The basic logic of his approach to pleasure is outlined here.

A. PLEASURE AS THE MOTIVE

The necessary desires are for health of body and peace of mind; if these are satisfied, that is enough for the happy life.

You must consider that of the desires some are natural, some are vain, and of those that are natural, some are necessary, others only natural. Of the necessary desires, some are necessary for happiness, some for the ease of the body, some for life itself. The man who has a perfect knowledge of this will know how to make his every choice or rejection tend toward gaining health of body and peace (of mind), since this is the final end of the blessed life. For to gain this end, namely freedom from pain and fear, we do everything. When once this condition is

Epicurus. *Epicurus: Letters, Principal, Doctrines, and Vatican Sayings.* 1st ed. Translated by Russell M. Geer. New York: Macmillan, 1964, pp. 55–57.

reached, all the storm of the soul is stilled, since the creature need make no move in search of anything that is lacking, nor seek after anything else to make complete the welfare of the soul and the body. For we only feel the lack of pleasure when from its absence we suffer pain; (but when we do not suffer pain,) we no longer are in need of pleasure. For this reason we say that pleasure is the beginning and the end of the blessed life. We recognize pleasure as the first and natural good; starting from pleasure we accept or reject; and we return to this as we judge every good thing, trusting this feeling of pleasure as our guide.

B. PLEASURES AND PAINS

Pleasure is the greatest good; but some pleasures bring pain, and in choosing, we must consider this.

For the very reason that pleasure is the chief and the natural good, we do not choose every pleasure, but there are times when we pass by pleasures if they are outweighed by the hardships that follow; and many pains we think better than pleasures when a greater pleasure will come to us once we have undergone the long-continued pains. Every pleasure is a good since it has a nature akin to ours; nevertheless, not every pleasure is to be chosen. Just so, every pain is an evil, yet not every pain is of a nature to be avoided on all occasions. By measuring and by looking at advantages and disadvantages, it is proper to decide all these things; for under certain circumstances we treat the good as evil, and again, the evil as good.

C. SELF-SUFFICIENCY

The truly wise man is the one who can be happy with a little.

We regard self-sufficiency as a great good, not so that we may enjoy only a few things, but so that, if we do not have many, we may be satisfied with the few, being firmly persuaded that they take the greatest pleasure in luxury who regard it as least needed, and that everything that is natural is easily provided, while vain pleasures are hard to obtain. Indeed, simple sauces bring a pleasure equal to that of lavish banquets if once the pain due to need is removed; and bread and water give the greatest pleasure when one who is in need consumes them. To be accustomed to simple and plain living is conducive to health and makes a man ready for the necessary tasks of life. It also makes us more ready for the enjoyment of luxury if at intervals we chance to meet with it, and it renders us fearless against fortune.

D. TRUE PLEASURE

The truest happiness does not come from enjoyment of physical pleasures but from a simple life, free from anxiety, with the normal physical needs satisfied.

When we say that pleasure is the end, we do not mean the pleasure of the profligate or that which depends on physical enjoyment—as some think who do not understand our teachings, disagree with them, or give them an evil interpretation—but by pleasure we mean the state wherein the body is free from pain and the mind from anxiety. Neither continual drinking and dancing, nor sexual love, nor the enjoyment of fish and whatever else the luxurious table offers brings about the pleasant life; rather, it is produced by the reason which is sober, which examines the motive for every choice and rejection, and which drives away all those opinions through which the greatest tumult lays hold of the mind.

THIRTEEN

The Deipnosophists

ATHENAEUS

Athenaeus should be considered the first food historian in the Western tradition. He was a Greek from Naucratis in Egypt who lived in the second to third century A.D., when Egypt was under Roman rule. In this huge work, he sets out to recount and comment on every single snippet of food, eating practice, and revelry mentioned in classical literature. Many works survive, even if only in fragment, because preserved by Athenaeus. The title literally means The Dinner Sophisticates, and it was meant to be a dialogue, though Athenaeus often strays from his intended form. In either case, it is certainly the most detailed source about food from ancient times, as shown in this selection on cooks.

36. But the whole tribe of cooks are conceited and arrogant, as Hegesander says in his Brothers. For he introduces a cook, saying—

> A. My friend, a great deal has been said already
>   By many men on the art of cookery,
>   So either tell me something new yourself,
>   Unknown to former cooks, or spare my ears.
> B. I'll not fatigue you; know that I alone
>   Of present men have sounded all the depths
>   Of culinary science and invention;
>   For I have not been just a short two years
>   Learning my art with snow-white apron girt,

Athenaeus. *The Deipnosophists*. Translated by C. D. Yonge. London: Bohn, 1854, pp. 455–60, 593–603.

But all my life I have devoted anxiously
To the investigation of each point
Of moment; I have inquired into all
The different kinds of herbs and vegetables;
I know the habits of the bembrades,
I know the lentils in their various sorts;
In short, this I can say—Whene'er I am
At a funereal feast as minister,
As soon as men come back from the funeral,
Clad in dark garments, I take off the lids
Of all my saucepans, and the weeping guests
I clothe with smiling faces in a moment;
And such a joy runs through each heart and frame
As if they were a marriage feast attending.

A. What! serving up lentils and bembrades?

B. These are some accidental dishes only;
But when I've got my necessary tools,
And once have properly arranged my kitchen,
That which in old time happen'd with the Sirens
You shall again behold repeated now.
For such shall be the savoury smell, that none
Shall bring themselves to pass this narrow passage;
And every one who passes by the door
Shall stand agape, fix'd to the spot, and mute,
Till some one of his friends, who's got a cold
And lost his smell, drags him away by force.

A. You're a great artist.

B. Do not you then know
To whom you speak? I do declare to you
I have known many of the guests, who have,
For my sake, eaten up their whole estates.

Now, I beg you, tell me, in the name of all the gods at once, in what respect this man appears to you to differ from the Celedones in Pindar, who, in the same manner as the Sirens of old, caused those who listened to them to forget their food through delight, and so to waste away?

37. But Nicomachus, in his Ilithyia, himself also introduces a cook, who in arrogance and conceit goes far beyond the artists on the stage. This cook then speaks to the man who has hired him in this way,—

A. You do display a gentlemanlike taste
And kind; but one thing still you have omitted.

B. How so?

A. You never have inquired it seems
How great a man I am. Or had you heard it

From some one else who was acquainted with me,
And so was that the reason you engaged me?

B. By Jove I never heard or thought about it.

A. Perhaps you do not know how great the difference
Is that exists between one cook and another?

B. Not I, but I shall know now, if you tell me.

A. To take some meat that some one else has bought,
And then to dress it tolerably, is
What any cook can do.

B. O Hercules!

A. A perfect cook is quite another thing.
For there are many admirable arts,
All of which he must master thoroughly
Who would excel in this. He first must have
A smattering of painting; and indeed
Many the sciences are which he must learn
Before he's fit to begin learning cookery,—
And you should know them ere you talk to me,—
Astrology, and Medicine, and Geometry.
For by these arts you'll know the qualities
And excellences of the various fish.
You'll learn to guide your dishes by the seasons;
And when this fish is in, and this is out,
For there is great variety in the pleasures
That from the table spring. Sometimes, for instance,
A boax will be better than a tunny.

B. Perhaps; but what on earth has that to do
With your geometry?

A. Why this. We say
The kitchen is a sphere; this we divide,
And take one portion, as may suit our art,
Borrowing the principles of mensuration.

B. I understand; that's quite enough of that.
Where does your medical skill display itself?

A. Know there are meats hard, indigestible,
Pregnant with flatulence, causing only torture
To the unhappy eater, and no nourishment.
Yet those who sup at other folks' expense
Are always greedy and not temperate.
For these and similar viands, remedies
Must come from the resources of our art;
And how to marshal everything in order

With wisdom and propriety, we learn
By borrowing from the science of the General.
To count the guests requires arithmetic.
And no one else has all these parts of knowledge
Except myself.
B. Now in your turn, awhile
Listen to me.
A. Say on.
B. Give no more trouble
To me nor to yourself: but just keep quiet,
And rest yourself all day for all I care.

38. And the cook in the Younger Philemon wishes to be a sort of tutor, and speaks in this fashion—

There, let things be as they are. Only take care
The fire may not too small be or too slow
To roast the joints. (As a fire like that
Makes meat not roast but sodden.) Nor too fierce,
(For that again does burn whate'er it catches,
And yet is far from cooking the meat through.)
It is not every one who has a spoon
And knife about him that we call a cook,
Nor every one who puts his fish in a pan;
There is more wit and reason in the business.

39. And the cook in Diphilus's Painter tells us also to whom he thinks it worth his while to hire himself saying—

A. I will not use your meat, nor give my aid
Unless I'm sure that I shall have all means
Which needful are to make a proper show;
Nor do I e'er go anywhere till first
I know who 'tis who makes the sacrifice,
Or what the cause may be which prompts the banquet,
Or who the guests are who have been invited.
For I have got a regular list at home
Of where I choose to go, and where I don't.
As first, to speak of the commercial class;
Some captain of a ship may make a sacrifice
Just to discharge some vow, made when he lost
His mast, or broke the rudder of his vessel,
Or, having sprung a leak, threw overboard
His cargo. I'll have nought to do with him;

    For he does nothing willingly, but only
    Just so much as he thinks he cannot help.
    And every time a cup is fill'd with wine,
    He makes a calculation of the sum
    Which he can charge his owners or his passengers,
    And thinks that what his guests do eat and drink
    Is his own flesh and blood. Another came,
    But three days since, from the Byzantine port,
    Safe and successful; joyful in a profit
    Of ten or twelve per cent; talking of nothing
    But freight and interest, spending all his love
    On worn-out panders. Soon as he did quit
    The ship and set his foot upon the land,
    I blew my nose, gave him my hand, and utter'd
    Audible thanks to saving Jupiter,
    And hasten'd forth to wait on him. For this
    Is always my way; and I find it answer.
    Again, an amorous youth will feast and squander
    His sire's estate; to him I go at call.
    But those who feast in shares, and throw together
    Into one dish their petty contributions,
    Though they may tear their clothes, and cry aloud,
    "Come, who will cook us our new-purchased supper?"
    I let bawl on. For if you go to them,
    First there is language hard and blows to bear;
    Secondly, one must slave the livelong night;
    And when at last you ask them for your pay,
    "First bring the pot," say they. "There was no vinegar
    In all that salad." Ask again. "Aye, you
    Shall be the first to be well beaten here."
    I could recount ten thousand facts like this.
B. But where I take now is a rich brothel,
    Where a rich courtesan with other friends
    Desires to celebrate with great abundance
    A joyous feast in honour of Adonis,
    And where you may enjoy yourself in style.

40. And Archedicus, in his Treasure, another philosophical cookling, speaks in this way—

    In the first place the guests invited came
    While still the fish lay on the dresser raw.
    "Give me some water." "Bring the fish up quick."

Then placing all my pans upon the fire,
I soak'd the ashes well with oil, and raise
A rapid heat. Meantime the fragrant herbs
And pleasant sharpness of the seasonings
Delight my master. Quickly I serve up
Some fish exactly boil'd; retaining all
His juice, and all his unextracted flavour;
A dish which any free-born man must know
How to appreciate rightly. In this manner
At the expense of one small pot of oil
I gain employment at full fifty banquets.

And Philostephanus, in his Delian, gives a catologue of the names of some celebrated cooks in these lines, and those which follow them—

In my opinion you, O Dædalus,
Surpass all cooks in skill and genius,
Save the Athenian Thimbron, call'd the Top.
So here I've come to beg your services,
Bringing the wages which I know you ask.

41. And Sotades, not the Maronite poet, who composed Ionian songs, but the poet of the middle comedy, in the play entitled The Shut-up Women, (for that was the name which he gave to it,) introduces a cook making the following speech,—

First I did take some squills, and fried them all;
Then a large shark I cut in slices large,
Roasting the middle parts, and the remainder
I boil'd and stuff'd with half-ripe mulberries.
Then I take two large heads of dainty grayling,
And in a large dish place them, adding simply
Herbs, cummin, salt, some water, and some oil.
Then after this I bought a splendid pike,
To boil in pickle with all sorts of herbs.
Avoiding all such roasts as want a spit,
I bought too some fine mullet, and young thrushes,
And put them on the coals just as they were,
Adding a little brine and marjoram.
To these I added cuttle-fish and squills.
A fine dish is the squill when carefully cook'd.
But the rich cuttle-fish is eaten plain,
Though I did stuff them all with a rich forced meat
Of almost every kind of herb and flower.
Then there were several dishes of boil'd meats,

And sauce-boats full of oil and vinegar.
Besides all this a conger fine and fat
I bought, and buried in a fragrant pickle;
Likewise some tench, and clinging to the rocks
Some limpets. All their heads I tore away,
And cover'd them with flour and bread crumbs over,
And then prepared them as I dress'd the squills.
There was a widow'd amia too, a noble
And dainty fish. That did I wrap in fig-leaves,
And soak'd it through with oil, and over all
With swaddling clothes of marjoram did I fold it,
And hid it like a torch beneath the ashes.
With it I took anchovies from Phalerum,
And pour'd on them one cruet full of water.
Then shredding herbs quite fine, I add more oil,
More than two cotylæ in quantity.
What next? That's all. This sir is what I do,
Not learning from recipes or books of cookery.

19. And once when a pig was served up before us, the half of which was being carefully roasted, and the other half boiled gently, as if it had been steamed, and when all marvelled at the cleverness of the cook, he being very proud of his skill, said—And, indeed, there is not one of you who can point out the place where he received the death wound; or where his belly was cut so as to be stuffed with all sorts of dainties. For it has thrushes in it, and other birds; and it has also in it parts of the abdomens of pigs, and slices of a sow's womb, and the yolks of eggs, and moreover the entrails of birds, with their ovaries, those also being full of delicate seasoning, and also pieces of meat shred into thin shavings and seasoned with pepper. For I am afraid to use the word [isíkia] before Ulpian, although I know that he himself is very fond of the thing. And, indeed, my favourite author Paxamus speaks of it by this name, and I myself do not care much about using no words but such as are strictly Attic. Do you, therefore, show me now how this pig was killed, and how I contrived to roast half of him and to boil the other side.—And as we kept on examining him, the cook said,—But do you think that I know less about my business than the ancient cooks, of whom the comic poets speak? for Posidippus, in his Dancing Women, speaks as follows—and it is a cook who is represented as making the following speech to his pupils—

20. My pupil Leucon, and the rest of you,
   You fellow servants—for there is no place
   Unfit to lecture upon science in;
   Know that in the cookery no seasoning
   Is equal to the sauce of impudence.
   And, if I must confess the whole o' the truth,
   You'll find this quality of great use everywhere.
   See now, this tribune, who displays a breast-plate

All over scales, or dragon wrought in steel,
Appears some Briareus; but when th' occasion
Calls for his might, he proves a very hare.
So when a cook with helpers and attendants
Comes to some stranger, and his pupils brings,
Calling the servants of the house mere humbugs,
Mere cummin splitters, famine personified;
They all crouch down before him: but if you bear
Yourself with honesty and spirit towards him,
He'll fly half flay'd with fear. Do you remember,
And, as I bade you, give fair room for boasting,
And take you care to know the taste of the guests;
For as in any other market, so
This is the goal which all your art should seek,
To run straight into all the feasters' mouths
As into harbour. At the present moment
We're busied about a marriage feast—
An ox is offer'd as the choicest victim;
The father-in-law is an illustrious man,
The son-in-law a person of like honour;
Their wives are priestesses to the good goddess.
Corybantes, flutes, a crowd of revellers
Are all assisting at the festival.
Here's an arena for our noble art.
Always remember this.

And concerning another cook (whose name is Seuthes) the same poet speaks in the following manner—

Seuthes, in the opinion of those men,
Is a great bungler. But I'd have you know,
My excellent friend, the case of a good cook
Is not unlike that of a general.
The enemy are present,—the commander,
A chief of lofty genius, stands against them,
And fears not to support the weight of war:—
Here the whole band of revellers is the enemy,
It marches on in close array, it comes
Keen with a fortnight's calculation
Of all the feast: excitement fires their breasts,
They're ready for the fray, and watch with zeal
To see what will be served up now before them.
Think now, that such a crowd collected sits
To judge of your performance.

21. Then you know there is a cook in the Synephebi of Euphron; just hear what a lecture he gives—

When, Carion, you a supper do prepare,
For those who their own contributions bring,
You have no time to play, nor how to practise
For the first time the lessons you've received.
And you were yesterday in danger too;
For not one single one of all your tenches
Had any liver, but they all were empty.
The brain was decomposed too.—But you must,
O Carion, when at any future time
You chance a band like this to thus encounter,
As Dromon, Cerdon, and Soterides,
Giving you all the wages that you ask'd,
Deal with them fairly. Where we now are going
To a marriage feast, there try experiments.
And if you well remember all my rules,
You are my real pupil; and a cook
By no means common: 'tis an opportunity
A man should pray for. Make the best of it,
The old man is a miser, and his pay
Is little. If I do not find you eating up
The very coals, you're done for. Now go in;
For here the old man comes himself, behold
How like a skin-flint usurer he looks!

22. But the cook in Sosipater's Liar is a great sophist, and in no respect inferior to the physicians in impudence. And he speaks as follows—

A. My art, if you now rightly do consider it,
    Is not, O Demylus, at all an art
    To be consider'd lightly;—but alas,
    'Tis too much prostituted; and you'll find
    That nearly all men fear not to profess
    That they are cooks, though the first principles
    Of the great art are wholly strange to them;
    And so the whole art is discredited.
    But when you meet an honest, genuine cook,
    Who from his childhood long has learnt the art,
    And knows its great effects, and has its rules
    Deep buried in his mind; then, take my word,
    You'll find the business quite a different thing.
    There are but three of us now left in Greece;

    Boidion, and Chariades, and I;
    The rest are all the vilest of the vile.
B. Indeed?
A. I mean it. We alone preserve
    The school of Sicon: he was the great teacher
    Of all our art: he was the first who taught us
    To scan the stars with judgment: the great Sicon!
    Then, next to this he made us architects:
    He open'd too the paths of physical knowledge;
    And after this he taught us all the rules
    Of military science; for all these
    Were but preliminaries accessory
    To the preeminent, god-like art of cooking.
B. I think you mean to choke me, my good friend.
A. Not I; but till the boy comes back from market
    I'll stir you up a little with some rules
    About your art, since we can never have
    A more convenient time for talking of it.
B. Oh, by Apollo, you're a zealous man.
A. Listen, my friend. In the first place, a cook
    Must the sublimer sciences have learnt:
    He must know when the stars do set and rise,
    And why. Moreover, when the sun returns,
    Causing the long and short days on the earth;
    And in what figures of the zodiac
    He is from time to time. For, men do say
    All fish, and every meat and herb we eat,
    Have different qualities at different seasons
    Of the revolving year; and he who knows
    The principles and reasons of these things
    Will use each meat when it is most in season;
    And he who knows them not, but acts at random,
    Is always laugh'd at most deservedly.
    Perhaps, too, you don't know wherein the science
    Of th' architect can bear on this our art.
B. Indeed I wonder'd what it had to do with it.
A. I'll tell you:—rightly to arrange the kitchen,
    To let in just the light that's requisite,
    To know the quarter whence the winds blow most,
    Are all of great importance in this business—
    For smoke, according to which way it goes,
    Makes a great difference when you dress a dinner.

B. That may be; but what need is there, I pray,
   For cooks to have the science of generals?
A. Order is a prevailing principle
   In every art; and most of all in ours:
   For to serve up and take away each dish
   In regular order, and to know the time
   When quick t' advance them, and when slowly bring,
   And how each guest may feel towards the supper,
   And when hot dishes should be set before him,
   When warm ones, and when regular cold meat
   Should be served up, depends on various branches
   Of strategetic [sic] knowledge, like a general's.
B. Since then you've shown me what I wish'd to know,
   May you, departing now, enjoy yourself.

23. And the cook in the Milesians of Alexis is not very different from this, for he speaks as follows—

A. Do you not know, that in most arts and trades
   'Tis not th' artificer who alone has pow'r
   O'er their enjoyment? Those who use them too
   Contribute all their part, if well they use them.
B. How so? Let me, O stranger, understand.
A. The duty of the cook is but to dress
   And rightly season meat; and nothing more.
   If, then, the man who is to eat his meat,
   And judge of it, comes in proper time,
   He aids the cook in that his business.
   But if he come too late, so that the joint
   Already roasted must be warm'd again,
   Or if he come too soon, so that the cook
   Is forced to roast the meat with undue haste,
   He spoils the pleasure which he might have had
   From the cook's skill by his unpunctuality.
   I class a cook among philosophers;
   You're standing round; my fire is alight;
   See how the numerous dogs of Vulcan's pack
   Leap to the roof; . . .
   . . . You know what happens next:
   And so some unforeseen necessity
   Has brought on us alone this end of life.

24. But Euphron, whom I mentioned a little while ago, O judges, (for I do not hesitate to call you judges, while awaiting the decision of your sense,) in his play called the Brothers,

having represented a certain cook as a well-educated man of extensive learning, and enumerating all the artists before his time, and what particular excellence each of them had, and what he surpassed the rest in, still never mentioned anything of such a nature as I have frequently prepared for you. Accordingly, he speaks as follows—

I have, ere this, had many pupils, Lycus,
Because I've always had both wit and knowledge;
But you, the youngest of them all, are now
Leaving my house an all-accomplish'd cook
In less than forty weeks. There was the Rhodian
Agis, the best of cooks to roast a fish;
Nereus, the Chian, could a conger boil
Fit for the gods: Charides, of Athens,
Could season forcemeat of the whitest hue:
Black broth was first devised by Lamprias;
Sausages rich we owe to Aphthonetus;
Euthunus taught us to make lentil soup;
Aristion made out whole bills of fare
For those who like a picnic entertainment.
So, like those grave philosophers of old,
These are our seven wisest of all cooks.
But I, for all the other ground I saw
Had been pre-occupied by former artists,
First found out how to steal, in such a way
That no one blamed me, but all sought at once
T' engage my aid. And you, perceiving too
This ground already occupied by me,
Invented something new yourself—'tis this:—
Five days ago the Tenians, grey old men,
After a tedious voyage o'er the sea,
Did hold a sacrifice: a small thin kid:
Lycus could crib no portion of that meat,
Nor could his master. Yon compell'd the men
To furnish two more kids. For as they long
And oft survey'd the liver of the victims,
You, letting down one unperceived hand,
Were impudent enough to throw the kidneys
Into the ditch: you raised a mighty tumult:
"The victim has no kidneys," they exclaim'd,
And all look'd downcast at th' unusual want.
They slew another, and again I saw
You eat the heart from out this second victim.
You surely are a mighty man; you know it—

For you alone have found a way to hinder
A wolf (λύκον) from opening his mouth in vain.
And I yesterday you threw some strings of sausages
(Which you had sought all day) into the fire,
And sang to the dichordon. And I witness'd
That play of yours; but this is merely sport.

25. I wonder if it was any of these second seven wise men who contrived this device about the pig, so as to stuff his inside without cutting his throat, and so as to roast one side of him and boil the other at the same time. And as we now urged and entreated him to explain this clever device to us, he said,—I will not tell you this year, I swear by those who encountered danger at Marathon, and also by those who fought at Salamis. So when he had taken such an oath as that, we all thought we ought not to press the man; but all began to lay hands on the different dishes which were served up before us. And Ulpian said,—I swear by those who encountered danger at Artemisium, no one shall taste of anything before we are told in what ancient author the word παραφέρω is used in the sense of serving up. For as to the word γεύματα, I think I am the only person who knows anything about that. And Magnus said, Aristophanes in his Proagon says—

Why did you not desire him to place
The goblets on the board (παραφέρειν)?

And Sophron, in his Female Actresses, uses the word in a more general sense, where he says—

O Cocoas, bring (παράφερε) me now a goblet full.

And Plato, in his Lacedæmonians, says—

Let him bring forward (παραφερέτω).

And Alexis, in his Pamphila, says—

He laid the table, then he placed on it (παραφέρων)
Good things in wagon loads.

But concerning the word γεύματα, meaning anything which is tasted, food, the exclusive knowledge about which you have claimed for yourself, it is time for you now to tell us, O Ulpian, what you do know. For as to the verb γεῦσαι, we have that in Eupolis, in his Goats, where he says—

Take now of this, and taste (γεῦσαι) it.

And Ulpian said, Ephippus in his Peltastes says—

There there were stations for the horses and asses,
And wine to drink (γεύματα οείνων).

FIFTEEN
Geoponika

This farming text is essentially a compilation from older authors, many of whose writing would have otherwise disappeared. It was compiled in the tenth century in the Byzantine Empire, when scholars preserved many ancient Greek and Latin texts. Nonetheless it is a good working manual for farm work, and its recipes, including those for the ancient fish sauce garum, can be followed today.

19. *MAKING UNRIPE OLIVE OIL.* **APULEIUS.**

As may be seen from the name, unripe olive oil is made from unripe berries.

When you see them begin to turn colour, tell the children or the workers to collect them from the trees by hand, being careful not to drop any. Pick as many each day as can be worked on overnight or on the following day. After picking, spread them out on rush or cane matting so that the watery element in them can be exuded and so that they are not damaged by one another's heat. Remove any leaves or twigs: if these remain they will reduce the keeping quality of the oil. In the evening take the olives, sprinkle them with salt, put them in the mill (which must be clean) and mill them gently by hand. The olive stones must not be smashed, because the *ichor* from them will infect the oil. Turn the millstone gently and lightly so that only the flesh and skin of the olives are crushed. After milling take the crushed olives in

Andrew Dalby, trans. *Geoponika: Farm Work*. Totnes, UK: Prospect Books, 2011, pp. 194–95, 252–53, 303–6, 348–49.

small tubs to the press and add wickerwork mats (willow contributes significantly to the oil); then press, employing light weight and no force. The oil that flows first, after light pressure, is pleasantest and smoothest; collect it in clean vessels and keep it separate. Then press the olives remaining under the press with a little more force, and again keep [the oil] separate; it will be not quite so good as the first but better than what follows. As soon as these first two products have run off add a little salt and natron to them and stir with an olive-wood stick; then leave them alone till they have settled, and you will find the watery element, that is, the *amorge,* lying underneath and the oiliest part floating on top. This must be taken off, separating it from the *amorge,* and stored in a glass vessel. Glass is best for storing olive oil because it is cold by nature; by its nature, olive oil likes cold. If you have no glass vessels, put the oil in new earthenware vessels whose insides have been covered with gypsum or *amorge.* Store them in a north-facing, dry room. Oil likes to rest in a dry and cold place; warmth and moisture are in opposition to oil.

20. *MAKING AROMATIC OIL.* DIOPHANES.

Take 8 pints of grape juice, or must as it is called, 2 pints olive oil, and a good quantity of pounded iris bulbs, tied in a bunch, and put in a jar for 10 days. After this, strain off and use the oil. The wine will be suitable for women to drink.

21. *HOW TO MAKE OLIVE OIL CLEAN.* TARANTINOS.

Roast salt over a fire and, while still hot, drop into the oil.

Pine cones, burned and dropped in while still fiery hot, have the same effect; also citron root dropped in; also roasted lees of oil.

22. *TREATING RANCID OIL.* TARANTINOS.

Boil white wax in good olive oil, and add it while still liquid.

Roast salt and add it while still very hot.

It is worth knowing that any olive oil keeps better in an underground room; also that fire or sun will clean any olive oil, or boiling water if placed in the oil in a bronze or otherwise unbreakable vessel.

Rancid olive oil is also cured by adding anise seed. If you add the anise in advance it will not go rancid.

13. *LETTUCE, ITS MEDICINAL USE, AND HOW TO GROW IT WHITE AND SHAPELY.* FLORENTINUS.

Lettuce is a wet and cold vegetable; for this reason it is helpful with feverish ailments. It is a food that suppresses thirst and induces sleep; it also encourages lactation. When boiled it becomes more nourishing; it also suppresses libido, which is why Pythagoreans call it *eunouchos* "castrato" and women call it *astytis* "impotent."

If you want to have shapely lettuce, tie around their hair (their upper parts, that is) two days before you pick them. This will make them white and shapely. Sand poured over them also whitens them.

Lettuce gives appetite for food; clears phlegm; inhibits sexual acts; when taken with sweet wine or vinegar, tempers bile; with hyssop and vinegar, is good for the hypochondria; cooked in rose oil and swallowed, stops cholera. Its juice reduces swollen bowels; rubbed on with woman's milk, it heals erysipelas. Its seed, ground and drunk, cures a scorpion sting; it helps with pain in the chest.

Lettuce induces sleep in healthy subjects when eaten; also in those who are sick, if without their knowledge it is placed under them, and particularly if with the left hand, before sunrise, one picks from the earth a whole lettuce with the roots and places it under the patient's bedding. Its juice, rubbed on the face of one who cannot sleep, will put him to sleep.

If you want to grow saucer-shaped lettuces with many leaves and with no stalk, remaining close to the ground, transplant them and water them; then, when they are palm-sized, dig around them to expose the roots, smear fresh cow dung on them, then earth them up and immediately irrigate them. When they are full-grown divide each plant with a very sharp knife and place [in the cut] an unpitched potsherd, so that they will continue their growth outwards and not upwards.

Eating lettuce frequently, especially if sweet, hinders the dimming of sight and produces sharp-sightedness.

Eating plenty of lettuce relaxes the bowels; eating a little constipates them.

They soothe a cold.

Travellers will not be upset by frequent changes of water if they eat lettuce at breakfast before any other food. Drunkenness will also be prevented if one eats lettuce first.

Aromatic lettuce will be produced if a lettuce seed is inserted in a citron seed and sown.

The seed, drunk, inhibits ejaculation; it is thus prescribed to those who have frequent wet dreams. 5 or 3 leaves or a single leaf of lettuce will induce sleep in one who is confined to bed, if the lettuce is secretly placed under the mattress in such a way that the ends broken off the stalk point towards the foot and the outer ends towards the head.

3. *BEES*. DIDYMOS.

The bee is the wisest and cleverest of all animals and the closest to man in intelligence; its work is truly divine and of the greatest use to mankind. Its social life resembles that of the best-regulated cities. In their excursions bees follow a leader and obey instructions. They bring back sticky secretions from flowers and trees and spread them like ointment on their floors and doorways. Some are employed in making honey and some in other tasks. The bee is extremely clean, settling on nothing that is bad-smelling or impure; it is not greedy; it will not approach flesh or blood or fat but only things of sweet flavour. It does not spoil the work of others, but fiercely defends its own work against those who try to spoil it. Aware of its own weakness, it makes the entrance to its home narrow and winding, so that those entering in large number to do harm are easily destroyed by the guardian bees. This animal is pleased by a good tune: when they are scattered, therefore, beekeepers clash cymbals or clap their hands rhythmically to bring them home. This is the only animal that looks for a leader to take care of a whole community: it always honours its king, follows him enthusiastically wherever he goes, supports him when he is exhausted, carries him and keeps him safe when he cannot fly. It particularly hates laziness; bees unite to kill the ones who do no work and use up others' production. Its mechanical skill and near-logical understanding is shown by the fact that it makes hexagonal cells to store honey.

4. *TO STOP BEES FLYING AWAY.* DIDYMOS.

The bees would not fly away if you smeared the mouths of their hives with the dung of a cow that has calved once.

When the swarm has settled and taken up residence, take the king gently and cut off the extremities of his wings; if he stays inside the others will not move elsewhere.

Bees will not fly away if you grind together leaves of wild and cultivated olive and rub this on the hives in the evening.

Or smear the walls and interior structures with honey-water.

[Seasonal care of bees.]

As food for young bees put out wine mixed with honey, in basins, and in these place leaves of many-flowered savory so that they do not drown. To feed your swarms in the best possible way whenever they stay at home because of wintry weather or burning heat and run out of food, pound together raisins and savory finely and give them this with barley cakes. When the first ten days of spring are past, drive them out to their pastures with the smoke of dried cow-dung, then clean and sweep out their hives: the bad smell of dung disturbs them, but cobwebs are an obstacle to them. If there are many combs in the hives, take away the worst, so that they are not made unhealthy by overcrowding. Do not take more than two swarms from any hive: they will be underfed and weak.

5. *WHEN TO HARVEST HONEY.* DIDYMOS.

The best time to harvest honey and combs is at the rising of the Pleiades—according to the Roman calendar, at the beginning of May; the second harvest is at the beginning of autumn; and the third, when the Pleiades set, around October. It is not done on fixed days, however, but according to the completeness of the combs; if you harvest before they have finished making them the bees are angry and stop working. They do the same if you take all the produce away, leaving the hives empty. You should leave one tenth for them in the spring and summer; in the winter you should take one-third, and leave two-thirds for them, so that they will not be discouraged and will have food. Before harvesting drive them off with the smoke of cow-dung.

Or the harvester should be smeared with the juice of the male wild mallow known as tree-mallow, against the stings.

Lemon-balm smeared on, and lentisk flower, are also helpful.

6. *TO AVOID BEING STUNG WHEN GATHERING HONEY. PAXAMOS.*

Take flour of roasted fenugreek, add the decoction of wild mallow with olive oil so that it has the consistency of honey; anoint the face and bare skin with this thickly, take it into the mouth and blow into the beehive three or four times.

Set fire to cow-dung in a pot, place it at the entrance to the beehive and leave the smoke to penetrate for half an hour; then lift and hold the pot outside so that there is plenty of smoke outside, and harvest [the honey].

If you want to get rid of young wasps use the same preparation [as above] but mix flour of lentil with the rest.

7. *HONEY AND ITS IMPROVEMENT.* DIOPHANES.

The best honey is Attic; the best Attic honey is from mount Hymettos. Island honey is also good: the best Sicilian is from Hybla, the best Cretan is *Akramanmorion,* the best Cyprian is *Chytrion,* the best Koan is Kalymnian. It should be translucent and pale yellow in colour, smooth to the touch, remaining in a long string when pulled, readily raised to a point and slow to sink back, thick when it reluctantly separates; and it should have a good aroma. All honey solidifies over a long period; Attic, however, remains liquid, but darkens in colour.

Cook poorer honey, because that will improve it; eat the best honey raw. It is not only pleasant to those who eat it, but prolongs their lives, so that those who in old age eat nothing but bread with honey live the longest. It also keeps the senses active.

Demokritos, asked how men could be made healthy and long-lived, said: apply olive oil outside and honey inside.

Is honey unadulterated? Dip and touch it. If it is unadulterated, it will touch more cleanly.

8. *TO PREVENT ENCHANTMENT OF BEEHIVES, FIELDS, HOUSES, ANIMAL SHEDS AND WORKSHOPS. LEONTINOS.*

Bury the hoof of the right foreleg of a black donkey under the threshold of the entrance, and pour on liquid unburnt pine resin (this is found in Zakynthos, thrown up from a lagoon, just as asphalt is thrown up from a pool at Apollonia near Dyrrhachion), salt, Heracleotic oregano, cardamom and cumin. Each month bring bits of bread, squill, a twist of white or red wool, chaste-tree, vervain, brimstone, pine torches, and amaranth, pile them up, throw on a *panspermia,* and leave it all there.

41. *GREY MULLET, CEPHALUS.*

Bread from spring wheat, goat's milk cheese, unslaked lime: mix, pound, add seawater, make lumps from this, use as bait.

42. *OCTOPUS.*

Fasten bogues, mormes and *aradoi* to some stiff object and use as bait.

43. *CUTTLEFISH ONLY.*

Wine lees, dry, pounded in olive oil. Go to the place and throw this into the sea. They will notice this, emit their ink, come to the place where they saw the oil, and you can catch them.

44. *CRAYFISH, MORME.*

[. . .] tied to some strong object. Pound 10 purple-shells with olive oil and a little laver. Spit this on to the rock and you will catch them.

45. *OBLADE.*

Take goat liver and put it on your hook.

We may have found another way to get a great number of fish: bait with a goat's or a donkey's hoof.

46. *MAKING GARA.*

The so-called *liquamen* is made thus. Fish entrails are put in a container and salted; and little fish, especially sand-smelt or small red mullet or mendole or anchovy, or any small enough, are all similarly salted; and left to pickle in the sun, stirring frequently. When the heat has pickled them, the *garos* is got from them thus: a deep close-woven basket is inserted into the centre of the vessel containing these fish, and the *garos* flows into the basket. This, then, is how the *liquamen* is obtained by filtering through the basket; the residue makes *alix*.

The Bithynians make it thus. Take preferably small or large mendole, or, if none, anchovy or scad or mackerel, or also *alix,* and a mixture of all these, and put them into a baker's bowl of the kind in which dough is kneaded; to one *modios* of fish knead in 6 Italian pints of salt so that it is well mixed with the fish, and leaving it overnight put it in an earthenware vessel and leave it uncovered in the sun for 2 or 3 months, occasionally stirring with a stick, then take [the fluid], cover and store. Some add 2 pints of old wine to each pint of fish.

If you want to use the *garon* at once, that is, not by ageing in the sun but by cooking, make it thus. Into pure brine, which you have tested by floating an egg in it (if it sinks, the brine is not salty enough) in a new bowl, put the fish; add oregano; place over a sufficient fire, until it boils, that is, until it begins to reduce a little. Some also add grape syrup. Then cool and filter it; filter a second and a third time until it runs clear; cover and store.

A rather high quality *garos,* called *haimation,* is made thus. Take tunny entrails with the gills, fluid and blood, sprinkle with sufficient salt, leave in a vessel for two months at the most; then pierce the jar, and the *garos* called *haimation* flows out.

PART II
Study Questions

1. What is the purpose of sacrifice? Apart from feeding the gods, what social role could it have served to kill animals publicly and distribute their flesh?
2. Why does Hesiod think men fell from a Golden Age, and in what ways were his ideas similar to the biblical account?
3. Where did the Hippocratic authors get their ideas about the various qualities of food and how they interact with the body, and why do you suppose this system made sense to them?
4. Consider how a bias against women may have informed Plato's conception of cooking as mere maintenance, while medicine is art.
5. In what ways were the motivations for a vegetarian diet in the ancient world similar to our own?
6. Was life stable or tumultuous in a society where ideas like those of Epicurus could flourish?

And Antiphanes, in his Twins, says—

Now he drinks wine (*οἰνογευστεῖ*) and walks about in splendour,
Wreathed with flowery garlands.

26. On this the cook said—I, then, will relate to you now, not an ancient contrivance, but a device of my own, in order that the flute-player may escape being beaten; (for Eubulus, in his Lacedæmonians or Leda, says—

But I have heard of this, I swear by Vesta,
That when the cook at home makes any blunder,
The flute-player is always beaten for it.

And Philyllius, or whoever the poet may have been who wrote the play of The Cities, says—

Whatever blunders now the cook may make,
The flute-player receives the stripes for them.)

And I mean the device about the pig half-roasted, half-boiled, and stuffed, without having had any apparent incision made in him. The fact is, the pig was stuck with a very short wound under his shoulder; (and he showed the wound.) Then when the greater part of the blood had flowed from it, all the entrails, with the intestines, I washed (and the word *ἐξαίρεσις*, O you revellers who think so much of words, means not only a taking out, but also the entrails themselves) carefully in wine several times, and hung the pig up by his feet. Then again I washed him in wine; and having boiled up beforehand all the seasonings which I have spoken of with a good deal of pepper, I pushed them in at his mouth, pouring in afterwards a quantity of broth very carefully made. And after this I plastered over one-half of the pig, as you see, with a great quantity of barleymeal, having soaked that in wine and oil. And then I put it in an oven, placing under it a brazen table, and I roasted it at a gentle fire, so as not to burn it, nor, on the other hand, to take it away before it was quite done. And when the skin began to get roasted and brown, I conjectured that the other side was boiled enough. And so then I took off the barleymeal, and brought it up in that condition and set it before you.

27. But as to the word *ἐξαίρεσις*, my excellent friend Ulpian, Dionysius the comic poet, in his drama called Things having the same Name, speaks thus, representing a cook speaking to his pupils—

Come now, O Dromon, if you aught do know,
Wise or accomplish'd in your, business,
Or fit to charm the eyes, reveal it straight
To me your master. For I ask you now
For a brief exhibition of your skill.
I'm leading you into an enemy's country;
Come gaily to the charge. They'll weigh the meat
And count the joints they give you, and they'll watch you:

But you, by boiling them to pieces, will
Not only make them tender, but confuse
The number of the pieces, so as quite
To upset all their calculations.
They bring you a fine fish;—his trail is yours.
And if you filch a slice, that, too, is yours.
While we are in the house: when we've got out
It then belongs to me. Th' ἐξαιρέσεις,
And all the other parts, which can't be counted,
In which you cannot easily be found out,
Which may be class'd as parings and as scrapings,
Shall make a feast for you and me to-morrow.
And let the porter share in all your spoils,
That you may pass his gate with his good-will.
Why need I say much to a prudent man?
You are my pupil, I am your preceptor,
Remember this, and come along with me.

28. And so when we had all praised the cook for the readiness of his discourse, and for the exceeding perfection of his skill, our excellent entertainer Laurentius said—And how much better it is for cooks to learn such things as these, than as they do with one whom I could mention of our fellow-citizens, who having had his head turned by riches and luxury, compelled his cooks to learn the dialogues of the incomparable Plato, and when they were bringing in dishes to say, "One, two, three, but where is the fourth, O most excellent Timæus, of those who were guests yesterday, but who are hosts to-day?" Then another made answer, "An illness has overtaken him, O Socrates,"—and so they went through the whole dialogue in this manner, so that those who were at the feast were very indignant, and so that that all accomplished man was laughed at and insulted every day, and that on this account many most respectable men refused all invitations to his entertainments. But these cooks of ours, who are perhaps just as well instructed in these things as he was, give us no little pleasure. And then the slave who had been praised for his cleverness as a cook, said,—Now what have my predecessors ever devised or told us of a similar kind to this? and is not my behaviour moderate enough, since I do not boast myself? And yet Corœbus the Elean, who was the first man who ever was crowned as victor in the Olympic games, was a cook; and yet he was not as proud of his skill and of his art as the cook in Straton in the Phœnicides, concerning whom the man who had hired him speaks thus—

29.'Tis a male sphinx, and not a cook, that I
Seem to have introduced into my house.
For by the gods I swear there's not one thing
Of all he says that I can understand,
So full is he of fine new-fangled words.
For when he first came in, he, looking big,

Ask'd me this question—"How many μέροπες now
Have you invited here to dinner? Tell me."—
"How many μέροπες have I ask'd to dinner?"—
"You're angry."—"Do you think that I'm a man
To have acquaintance with your μέροπες?
It is a fine idea, to make a banquet
And ask a lot of μέροπες to eat it."
"Then do you mean there'll be no δαιτύμων (guest)?"
"No Dætymon that I know of."—Then I counted—
There'll be Philinus, and Niceratus,
And Moschion, and this man too, and that—
And so I counted them all name by name;
But there was not a Dætymon among them.
"No Dætymon will come," said I. "What! no one?"
Replied he in a rage, as though insulted
That not a Dætymon had been invited.
"Do you not slay that tearer up of th' earth,"
Said he, "the broad-brow'd ox?" "In truth, not I;
I've got no ox to kill, you stupid fellow."
"Then you will immolate some sheep?" "Not I,
By Jove; nor ox, nor sheep, but there's a lamb."
"What I don't you know, said he, that lambs are sheep?"
"Indeed," said I, "I neither know nor care
For all this nonsense. I'm but country bred;
So speak more plainly, if you speak at all."
"Why, don't you know that this is Homer's language?"
"My good cook, Homer was a man who had
A right to call things any names he pleased;
But what, in Vesta's name, is that to us?"
"At least you can't object when I quote him."
"Why, do you mean to kill me with your Homer?"
"No, but it is my usual way of talking."
"Then get another way, while here with me."
"Shall I," says he, "for your four dirty drachmas,
Give up my eloquence and usual habits?
Well, bring me here the oὐλόχυται." "Oh me!
What are oὐλόχυται?" "Those barley-cakes."
"You madman, why such roundabout expressions?"
"Is there no sediment of the sea at hand?"
"Sediment? Speak plain; do tell me what you want
In words I understand." "Old man," says he,
"You are most wondrous dull; have you no salt?

That's sediment, and that you ought to know;
Bring me the basin."—So they brought it. He
Then slew the animals, adding heaps of words
Which not a soul of us could understand,
Μίστυλλα, μοίρας, δίπτυχ', ὀβελοΰς—
So that I took Philetas' Lexicon down,
To see what each of all these words did mean.
And then once more I pray'd of him to change,
And speak like other men; by earth I swear,
Persuasion's self could not have work'd on him.

30. But the race of cooks are really very curious for the most part about the histories and names of things. Accordingly the most learned of them say, "The knee is nearer than the leg,"—and, "I have travelled over Asia and Europe:" and when they are finding fault with any one they say, "It is impossible to make a Peleus out of an Œneus."—And I once marvelled at one of the old cooks, after I had enjoyed his skill and the specimens of his art which he had invented. And Alexis, in his Caldron, introduces one speaking in the following manner—

A. He boil'd, it seem'd to me, some pork, from off
  A pig who died by suffocation.
B. That's nice.
A. And then he scorch'd it at the fire.
B. Never mind that; that can be remedied.
A. How so?
B. Take some cold vinegar, and pour it
  Into a plate. Dost heed me? Then take up
  The dish while hot and put it in the vinegar;
  For while 'tis hot 'twill draw the moisture up
  Through its material, which is porous all;
  And so fermenting, like a pumice-stone,
  'Twill open all its spongy passages,
  Through which it will imbibe new moisture thoroughly.
  And so the meat will cease to seem dried up,
  But will be moist and succulent again.
A. O Phœbus, what a great physician's here!
  O Glaucias!—I will do all you tell me.
B. And serve them, when you do serve them up,
  (Dost mark me?) cold; for so no smell too strong
  Will strike the nostrils; but rise high above them.
A. It seems to me you're fitter to write books
  Than to cook dinners; since you quibble much
  In all your speeches, jesting on your art.

31. And now we have had enough of cooks, my feasters; lest perhaps some one of them, pluming himself and quoting the Morose Man of Menander, may spout such lines as these—

No one who does a cook an injury
Ever escapes unpunish'd; for our art
Is a divine and noble one.

FOURTEEN

On Abstinence from Animal Food

PORPHYRY

Porphyry was a neo-Platonist philosopher who espoused vegetarianism. He is one of the principal sources for our knowledge about Pythagoras, founder of the sect of vegetarians many centuries before. He lived from 234 to 305 A.D., was born in Tyre in what is now Lebanon, and eventually went to Rome. He is firmly in the Greek philosophical tradition and thus included in this chapter. Note the many similarities of his arguments to those of modern-day vegetarians, but also some features that are conspicuously absent.

1. Hearing from some of our acquaintance, O Firmus, that you, having rejected a fleshless diet, have again returned to animal food, at first I did not credit the report, when I considered your temperance, and the reverence which you have been taught to pay to those ancient and pious men from whom we have received the precepts of philosophy. But when others who came after these confirmed this report, it appeared to me that it would be too rustic and remote from the rational method of persuasion to reprehend you, who neither, according to the proverb, flying from evil have found something better, nor according to Empedocles, having lamented your former life, have converted yourself to one that is more excellent. I have therefore thought it worthy of the friendship which subsists between us, and also adapted to those who have arranged their life conformably to truth, to disclose your errors through a confutation derived from an argumentative discussion.

2. For when I considered with myself what could be the cause of this alteration in your diet, I could by no means suppose that it was for the sake of health and strength, as the vulgar

Porphyry. *On Abstinence from Animal Food.* Translated by Thomas Taylor. 1823. Published online by the Tertullian Project, 2007. http://www.tertullian.org/fathers/porphyry_abstinence_01_book1.htm.

and idiots would say; since, on the contrary, you yourself, when you were with us, confessed that a fleshless diet contributed both to health and to the proper endurance of philosophic labours; and experience testifies, that in saying this you spoke the truth. It appears, therefore, that you have returned to your former illegitimate conduct, either through deception, because you think it makes no difference with respect to the acquisition of wisdom whether you use this or that diet; or perhaps through some other cause of which I am ignorant, which excited in you a greater fear than that which could be produced by the impiety of transgression. For I should not say that you have despised the philosophic laws which we derived from our ancestors, and which you have so much admired, through intemperance, or for the sake of voracious gluttony; or that you are naturally inferior to some of the vulgar, who, when they have assented to laws, though contrary to those under which they formerly lived, will suffer amputation [rather than violate them], and will abstain from certain animals on which they before fed, more than they would from human flesh.

15. But why should any one abstain from animals? Is it because feeding on them makes the soul or the body worse? It is, however, evident, that neither of these is deteriorated by it. For those animals that feed on flesh are more sagacious than others, as they are venatic, and possess an art by which they supply themselves with food, and acquire power and strength; as is evident in lions and wolves. So that the eating of flesh neither injures the soul nor the body. This likewise is manifest, both from the athletae, whose bodies become stronger by feeding on flesh, and from physicians, who restore bodies to health by the use of animal food. For this is no small indication that Pythagoras did not think sanely, that none of the wise men embraced his opinion; since neither any one of the seven wise men, nor any of the physiologists who lived after them, nor even the most wise Socrates, or his followers, adopted it.

16. Let it, however, be admitted that all men are persuaded of the truth of this dogma, respecting abstinence from animals. But what will be the boundary of the propagation of animals? For no one is ignorant how numerous the progeny is of the swine and the hare. And to these add all other animals. Whence, therefore, will they be supplied with pasture? And what will husbandmen do? For they will not destroy those who destroy the fruits of the earth. And the earth will not be able to bear the multitude of animals. Corruption also will be produced from the putridity of those that will die. And thus, from pestilence taking place, no refuge will be left. For the sea, and rivers, and marshes, will be filled with fishes, and the air with birds, but the earth will be full of reptiles of every kind.

17. How many likewise will be prevented from having their diseases cured, if animals are abstained from? For we see that those who are blind recover their sight by eating a viper. A servant of Craterus, the physician, happening to be seized with a new kind of disease, in which the flesh fell away from the bones, derived no benefit from medicines; but by eating a viper prepared after the manner of a fish, the flesh became conglutinated to the bones, and he was restored to health. Many other animals also, and their several parts, cure diseases when they are properly used for that purpose; of all which remedies he will be frustrated who rejects animal food.

18. But, if as they say, plants also have a soul, what will become of our life if we neither destroy animals nor plants? If, however, he is not impious who cuts off plants, neither will he be who kills animals.

19. But some one may, perhaps, say it is not proper to destroy that which belongs to the same tribe with ourselves; if the souls of animals are of the same essence with ourselves. If, however, it should be granted that souls are inserted in bodies voluntarily, it must be said that it is through a love of juvenility: for in the season of youth there is an enjoyment of all things. Why, therefore, do they not again enter into the nature of man? But if they enter voluntarily, and for the sake of juvenility, and pass through every species of animals, they will be much gratified by being destroyed. For thus their return to the human form will be more rapid. The bodies also which are eaten will not produce any pain in the souls of those bodies, in consequence of the souls being liberated from them; and they will love to be implanted in the nature of man. Hence, as much as they are pained on leaving the human form, so much will they rejoice when they leave other bodies. For thus they will more swiftly become man again, who predominates over all irrational animals, in the same manner as God does over men. There is, therefore, a sufficient cause for destroying other animals, viz. their acting unjustly in destroying men. But if the souls of men are immortal, but those of irrational animals mortal, men will not act unjustly by destroying irrational animals. And if the souls of brutes are immortal, we shall benefit them by liberating them from their bodies. For, by killing them, we shall cause them to return to the human nature.

21. If, however, some one should, nevertheless, think it is unjust to destroy brutes, such a one should neither use milk, nor wool, nor sheep, nor honey. For, as you injure a man by taking from him his garments, thus, also, you injure a sheep by shearing it. For the wool which you take from it is its vestment. Milk, likewise, was not produced for you, but for the young of the animal that has it. The bee also collects honey as food for itself; which you, by taking away, administer to your own pleasure. I pass over in silence the opinion of the Egyptians, that we act unjustly by meddling with plants. But if these things were produced for our sake, then the bee, being ministrant to us, elaborates honey, and the wool grows on the back of sheep, that it may be an ornament to us, and afford us a bland heat.

54. Hence also, in simple and slender food, repletion is to be avoided, and every where we should consider what will be the consequence of the possession or enjoyment of it, what the magnitude of it is, and what molestation of the flesh or of the soul it is capable of dissolving. For we ought never to act indefinitely, but in things of this kind we should employ a boundary and measure; and infer by a reasoning process, that he who fears to abstain from animal food, if he suffers himself to feed on flesh through pleasure, is afraid of death. For immediately, together with a privation of such food, he conceives that something indefinitely dreadful will be present, the consequence of which will be death. But from these and similar causes, an insatiable desire is produced of riches, possessions, and renown, together with an opinion that every good is increased with these in a greater extent of time, and the dread of death as of an infinite evil. The pleasure however which is produced through luxury, does not even approach to that which is experienced by him who lives with frugality. For such a one has great pleasure in thinking how little he requires. For luxury, astonishment about venereal occupations, and ambition about external concerns, being taken away, what remaining use can there be of idle wealth, which will be of no advantage to us whatever, but will only become a burden, no otherwise than repletion?—while, on the other hand, the pleasure arising from frugality is genuine and pure.

PART THREE

Ancient Rome

The Romans began as a stern, God-fearing agricultural people who happened to be masters at engineering and conducting war. The growth of their empire was only possible because of their ability to harness the energy of slaves on what were eventually large *latifundia*, a kind of plantation, which supplied grain to feed the armies. Characteristic of the early republican era is the statesman Cato the Elder, who wrote an agricultural manual about how to start up a business once you've inherited money or retired from military service. It contains detailed instructions on how to manage vineyards, olive groves, and other profit-making crops. It also contains recipes, especially for sacrificial cakes and such.

After they conquered Greece and the Hellenistic world, the Romans both adopted Greek culture and, according to some commentators, went soft. There is no doubt that great fortunes could be made and lost, especially speculating in grain and foodstuffs, and that extravagance at the table was a way to flaunt one's wealth. Whether it was pepper from India, the finest *garum* (a kind of fish sauce) from Spain, or exotic ingredients like flamingo tongues, some Romans enjoyed a truly profligate existence. Social mobility was bound to create tensions, though. The newcomers naturally threatened the status of the old patrician class who had been born into wealth, and they tried to show that merely spending a fortune or serving wildly complex dishes is not a way to gain respect. Petronius was exactly this sort of person; he served as arbiter of taste at the court of Nero and for some unknown insult was disgraced and killed himself. *The Satyricon* he composed only makes sense when one realizes that the lead character in one story, Trimalchio, is a slave who bought his freedom, rose to wealth in grain speculation and is now trying to impress guests at a banquet. Of course, he fails miserably, the details of which are presented in the selection below. The types of foods that are served are also important, and many of them will appear in the first full cookbook, attributed to Apicius.

There is much debate about who Apicius was and when he lived. There were several figures of this name, though most likely Marcus Gavius Apicius is the one about whom stories circulated. He was said to have taken a boat all the way to Africa when he heard about the largest shrimp in the world being sold there. After seeing them, unimpressed, he turned back for home without ever going ashore. When his vast fortune began to dwindle, he is said to have committed suicide rather than face the disgrace of having to live simply. Whether these stories are true is beside the point, the name Apicius came to be associated with perverse extravagance. Several centuries later the name was attached to a cookbook, which includes some ordinary dishes that most Romans might have known well, but also some seriously complex ones with such a wide array of flavors and exotic ingredients that one wonders what they could have tasted like.

The formal dinner was not merely an eating experience; it was also a time to express your status and the dependency of others. Who got invited and what they were served was just as important, and as the selection from Juvenal suggests not everyone was treated equally—in fact, exactly the opposite. Juvenal also suggests that there is another way of dining: with good friends; using fresh country produce; simple, honest, and healthy fare. Clearly this was a different kind of aesthetic, more akin to country folk, and certainly not trying to imitate the urban sophisticates. Nor was it like the diet of the urban masses, though. Juvenal said that the common people could be pleased today merely with "bread and circuses"—meaning chariot races, not circuses with clowns. He was really criticizing the lack of civic engagement of the Romans more than anything else, a critique of the powerful who believed mere distraction was good enough.

There were other ways to directly criticize the antics of the great and powerful, and Aelius Lampridius's life of Heliogabalus does exactly that. It is meant to be a warning to other would-be rulers that some kinds of behavior simply go too far. You have to admit, though, the emperor had a sense of humor, even though he did wind up murdered and thrown in the sewer.

Other ways of thinking about food flourished among the Romans. Eating to maintain health appears in many of the writings of Galen of Pergamon, the fullest expression of humoral theory. The Stoic approach to food is also expressed succinctly by Seneca. In many respects, the classical approach to dining continues through to the fall of the Roman Empire. Thereafter, it would be replaced, at least in the Western half of the empire, by an entirely different aesthetic, more based on wild plants and animals, deriving from Germanic culture.

SIXTEEN

De Re Agricultura

MARCUS PORCIS CATO

Cato the Elder was a Roman statesman and official censor who lived from 243 to 149 B.C. He is best known for pounding his hand on the rostrum in the senate demanding that Carthage be destroyed, which it was in the third Punic War. But he is far more important for the agricultural text he composed. It is exactly the kind of manual one would need if one suddenly inherited money and wanted to make a safe investment, or perhaps retired from the army with a nice pension and a piece of land. It is clear that this is primarily farming for profit, because the owner appoints a steward while he is away and makes sure that there is good transportation to cities to carry the crops—such as olives for oil, grapes for wine, and vegetables. Like most Romans during the republic, he is stern, very religious, and perhaps harsh toward his slaves. His De Re Agricultura *is nonetheless among the most important and earliest works in Latin prose.*

INTRODUCTION: OF THE DIGNITY OF THE FARMER

THE pursuits of commerce would be as admirable as they are profitable if they were not subject to so great risks: and so, likewise, of banking, if it was always honestly conducted. For our ancestors considered, and so ordained in their laws, that, while the thief should be cast in double damages, the usurer should make four-fold restitution. From this we may judge how much less desirable a citizen they esteemed the banker than the thief. When they sought to commend an honest man, they termed him good husbandman, good farmer. This they rated

Marcus Porcis Cato. *Roman Farm Management. The Treatises of Cato (De Agricultura) and Varro (Rerum Rusticarum Libri Tres).* Translated by a Virginia Farmer [Fairfax Harrison]. New York: Macmillan, 1918, pp. 19–26, 48–49.

the superlative of praise. Personally, I think highly of a man actively and diligently engaged in commerce, who seeks thereby to make his fortune, yet, as I have said, his career is full of risks and pitfalls. But it is from the tillers of the soil that spring the best citizens, the staunchest soldiers; and theirs are the enduring rewards which are most grateful and least envied. Such as devote themselves to that pursuit are least of all men given to evil counsels.

And now, to get to my subject, these observations will serve as preface to what I have promised to discuss.

Of Buying a Farm

(I) When you have decided to purchase a farm, be careful not to buy rashly; do not spare your visits and be not content with a single tour of inspection. The more you go, the more will the place please you, if it be worth your attention. Give heed to the appearance of the neighbour-hood,—a flourishing country should show its prosperity. When you go in, look about, so that, when needs be, you can find your way out.

Take care that you choose a good climate, not subject to destructive storms, and a soil that is naturally strong. If possible, your farm should be at the foot of a mountain, looking to the South, in a healthy situation, where labour and cattle can be had, well watered, near a good sized town, and either on the sea or a navigable river, or else on a good and much frequented road. Choose a place which has not often changed ownership, one which is sold unwillingly, that has buildings in good repair.

Beware that you do not rashly contemn the experience of others. It is better to buy from a man who has farmed successfully and built well.

When you inspect the farm, look to see how many wine presses and storage vats there are; where there are none of these you can judge what the harvest is. On the other hand, it is not the number of farming implements, but what is done with them, that counts. Where you find few tools, it is not an expensive farm to operate. Know that with a farm, as with a man, how-ever productive it may be, if it has the spending habit, not much will be left over.

Of the Duties of the Owner

(II) When you have arrived at your country house and have saluted your household, you should make the rounds of the farm the same day, if possible; if not, then certainly the next day. When you have observed how the field work has progressed, what things have been done, and what remains undone, you should summon your overseer the next day, and should call for a report of what work has been done in good season and why it has not been possible to complete the rest, and what wine and corn and other crops have been gathered. When you are advised on these points you should make your own calculation of the time necessary for the work, if there does not appear to you to have been enough accomplished. The overseer will report that he himself has worked diligently, but that some slaves have been sick and others truant, the weather has been bad, and that it has been necessary to work the public roads. When he has given these and many other excuses, you should recall to his attention the program of work which you had laid out for him on your last visit and compare it with the results attained. If the weather has been bad, count how many stormy days there have been, and rehearse what work could have been done despite the rain, such as washing and pitching the wine vats, cleaning out the barns, sorting the grain, hauling out and composting the manure, cleaning seed, mending the old gear, and making new, mending the smocks and hoods furnished for the hands. On feast days the old ditches should be mended, the public roads worked, briers cut down, the garden dug, the meadow cleaned, the hedges trimmed and the clippings collected and burned, the fish pond cleaned out. On such days, furthermore, the slaves' rations should be cut down as compared with what is allowed when they are working in the fields in fine weather.

When this routine has been discussed quietly and with good humour and is thoroughly understood by the overseer, you should give orders for the completion of the work which has been neglected.

The accounts of money, supplies and provisions should then be considered. The overseer should report what wine and oil has been sold, what price he got, what is on hand, and what remains for sale. Security should be taken for such accounts as ought to be secured. All other unsettled matters should be agreed upon. If any thing is needed for the coming year, it should be bought; every thing which is not needed should be sold. Whatever there is for lease should be leased. Orders should be given (and take care that they are in writing) for all work which next it is desired to have done on the farm or let to contract. You should go over the cattle and determine what is to be sold. You should sell the oil, if you can get your price, the surplus wine and corn, the old cattle, the worn out oxen, and the cull sheep, the wool and the hides, the old and sick slaves, and if any thing else is superfluous you should sell that.

The appetite of the good farmer is to sell, not to buy.

(IV) Be a good neighbour. Do not roughly give offence to your own people. If the neighbourhood regards you kindly, you will find a readier market for what you have to sell, you will more easily get your work done, either on the place or by contract. If you build, your neighbours will aid you with their services, their cattle and their materials. If any misfortune should overtake you (which God forbid!) they will protect you with kindly interest.

Of Cakes and Salad

(LXXV) This is the recipe for cheese cake (*libum*): Bray well two pounds of cheese in a mortar, and, when this is done, pour in a pound of corn meal (or, if you want to be more dainty, a half pound of flour) and mix it thoroughly with the cheese. Add one egg and beat it well. Pat into a cake, place it on leaves and bake slowly on a hot hearth stone under a dish.

(CXIX) This is the recipe for olive salad (*epityrum*): Select some white, black and mottled olives and stone them. Mix and cut them up. Add a dressing of oil, vinegar, coriander, cumin, fennel, rue and mint. Mix well in an earthen ware dish, and serve with oil.

(CXXI) This is the recipe for must cake (*mustaceus*): Sprinkle a peck of wheat flour with must. Add anise, cumin, two pounds of lard, a pound of cheese and shredded laurel twigs. When you have kneaded the dough, put laurel leaves under it and so bake.

Of Curing Hams

(CLXII) This is the way to cure hams in jars or tubs: When you have bought your hams trim off the hocks. Take a half peck (*semodius*) of ground Roman salt for each ham. Cover the bottom of the jar or tub with salt and put in a ham, skin down. Cover the whole with salt and put another ham on top, and cover this in the same manner. Be careful that meat does not touch meat. So proceed, and when you have packed all the hams, cover the top with salt so that no meat can be seen, and smooth it out even. When the hams have been in salt five days, take them all out with the salt and repack them, putting those which were on top at the bottom. Cover them in the same way with salt and press them down.

After the twelfth day remove the hams finally, brush off the salt and hang them for two days in the wind. On the third day wipe them off clean with a sponge and rub them with (olive) oil. Then hang them in smoke for two days, and on the third day rub them with a mixture of (olive) oil and vinegar.

Then hang them in the meat house, and neither bats nor worms will touch them.

SEVENTEEN

The Satyricon

PETRONIUS

Petronius (27–66 A.D.) was official arbiter of taste during the reign of Nero, although for some unknown offense he was disgraced and committed suicide. The spectacle, and joke, of an upstart making a complete fool of himself only makes sense when one realizes that Petronius came from old money and the patrician class. In this era when fortunes could be made easily, upstarts such as Trimalchio might have the wealth to throw lavish parties, but certainly not the sophistication to do it properly. So rather than a picture of how actual Romans dined, take this as intended—a satire to warn other newly wealthy people not to attempt to pretend they have taste. On the other hand, compare some of the dishes served to the recipes that show up in Apicius's cookbook. As an interesting exercise, look at modern images of Trimalchio and consider why, through history, he has stood as the example of gastronomic perversity.

Then came a sumptuous antepast; for we were all seated, but only
Trimalchio, for whom, after a new fashion, the chief place was
reserv'd. Besides that, as a part of the entertainment, there was set
by us a large vessel of metheglin, with a pannier, in the one part of
which were white olives, in the other black; two broad platters
covered the vessel, on the brims of which were engraven Trimalchio's
name, and the weight of the silver, with little bridges soldered

---

Petronius. "The Feast of Trimalchio." In *The Satyricon*. Translated by William Burnaby. Harmondsworth, UK: Penguin, 1984. http://www.gutenberg.org/dirs/etext04/7pasw10a.txt.

together, and on them dormice strew'd over with honey and poppy: There
were also piping-hot sausages on a silver gridiron, and under that
large damsons, with the kernels of pomegranats.

In this condition were we when Trimalchio himself was waddled into the
consort; and being close bolster'd with neck-cloaths and pillows to
keep off the air, we could not forbear laughing unawares: For his bald
pate peep'd out of a scarlet mantle, and over the load of cloaths he
lay under, there hung an embroidered towel, with purple tassels and
fringes dingle dangle about it: He had also on the little finger of
his left hand, a large gilt ring, and on the outmost joint of the
finger next it, one lesser, which I took for all gold; but at last it
appeared to be jointed together with a kind of stars of steel. And
that we might see these were not all his bravery, he stripp'd his
right arm, on which he wore a golden bracelet, and an ivory circle,
bound together with a glittering locket and a meddal at the end of it:
Then picking his teeth with a silver pin, "I had not, my friends,"
said he, "any inclination to have come among you so soon, but fearing
my absence might make you wait too long, I deny'd myself my own
satisfaction; however suffer me to make an end of my game."

In the mean time while he was squandering his heap at play, and we
were yet picking a relish here and there, a cupboard was brought in
with a basket, in which was a hen carved in wood, her wings lying
round and hollow, as sitting on brood; when presently the consort
struck up, and two servants fell a searching the straw under her, and
taking out some peahens eggs, distributed them among the company: At
this Trimalchio changing countenance, "I commanded my friends," said
he "the hen to be set with peahens eggs; and so help me Hercules, am
afraid they may be half hatcht: however we'll try if they are yet
suppable."

The thing we received was a kind of shell of at least six pounds
weight, made of paste, and moulded into the figure of an egg, which we
easily broke; and for my part, I was like to have thrown away my
share; for it seemed to me to have a chick in it; till hearing an old
guest of the tables saying, it was some good bit or other, I searched
further into it, and found a delicate fat wheatear in the middle of a
well-pepper'd yolk: On this Trimalchio stopped his play for a while,
and requiring the like for himself, proclaim'd, if any of us would
have any more metheglin, he was at liberty to take it; when of a
sudden the musick gave the sign, and the first course was scrabled
away by a company of singers and dancers; but in the rustle it
happening that a dish fell on the door, a boy took it up, and
Trimalchio taking notice of it, pluck'd him by the ears, and commanded

him to throw it down again; on which the groom of the chamber came with a broom and swept away the silver dish, with whatsoever else had fallen from the table.

When presently came in two long-hair'd blacks, with small leather bottles, such as with which they strew sand on the stage, and gave us wine to wash our hands, but no one offered us water. We all admiring the finicalness of the entertainment, "Mars," said he, "is a lover of justice, and therefore let every one have a table to himself, for having more elbow-room, these nasty stinking boys will be less troublesome to us"; and thereupon large double-eared vessels of glass close plaistered over, were brought up with labels about their necks, upon which was this inscription:

Opimian Muscadine of an Hundred Years Old.

While we were reading the titles, Trimalchio clapped his hands, and "Alas, alas," said he, "that wine should live longer than man! Wine is life, and we'll try if it has held good ever since the consulship of Lucius Opimius, or not. 'Tis right Opimian, and therefore make ready; I brought not out so good yesterday, yet there were persons of better quality sup'd with me."

(The next course) it was a large charger, with the twelve signs round it; upon every one of which the master cook had laid somewhat or other suitable to the sign. Upon Aries, chick-pease, (a pulse not unlike a ram's head); upon Taurus a piece of beef; upon Gemini a pair of pendulums and kidneys; upon Cancer a coronet; upon Leo an African figg; upon Virgo a well-grown boy; upon Libra a pair of scales, in one of which was a tart, in the other a custard; upon Scorpio a pilchard; upon Sagittary a grey-hound; upon Capricorn a lobster; upon Aquarius a goose; upon Pisces two mullets; and in the middle a plat of herbs, cut out like a green turf, and over them a honey-comb. During this, a lesser black carry'd about bread in a silver oven, and with a hideous voice, forced a bawdy song from a buffoon that stunk like assa foetida.

When Trimalchio perceived we look'd somewhat awkwardly on such course fare, "Come, come," said he, "fall to and eat, this is the custom of the place."

Nor had he sooner said it, than the fourth consort struck up; at which the waiters fell a dancing, and took off the upper part of the charger, under which was a dish of cramm'd fowl, and the hinder paps of a sow that had farrowed but a day before, well powdered, and the middle a hare, stuck in with finns of fish in his side, that he look'd like a flying horse; and on the sides of the fish four little images, that spouted a relishing sauce on some fish that lay near them, all of them brought from the river Euripus.

EIGHTEEN
De Re Coquinaria

APICIUS

The name Apicius, from ancient times down to recent times, has been a byword for luxury and extravagance. His name could be both a term of abuse or of refinement, depending on the context. Whether the recipes actually came from the pen of the historical figure Apicius is less important than what they reveal about Roman taste and power. Consider how far flung are the sources for his ingredients, how exotic and perhaps even perverse. What does this reveal about Roman taste? On the other hand, some very simple dishes also are included. Cooking and tasting them yourself will reveal that they aren't so strange after all. Two surviving copies that were made in the eighth century in Fulda are housed at the New York Academy of Medicine and the Vatican Library. These are the oldest complete cookbooks in the world. These manuscripts and images of versions printed in the Renaissance are easily found online.

Conditum Paradoxum (Spiced Wine)

Put fifteen pounds of honey into a bronze vessel along with four cups of wine, so in cooking the honey and wine mix. On a small fire of dry twigs heat the vessel, stirring with a stick while it cooks. If it starts to boil, sprinkle in some wine, or remove from the fire so it settles. When it cools, heat again a second or third time, then it is finally removed from the fireplace. Skim it the day after, then add four ounces of crushed pepper, three scruples of mastic, a dram each of bay leaf and saffron, five toasted date pits, and the dates themselves softened in wine, the same kind used before, then ground up smooth. When all this is prepared, add in fourteen bottles of fine wine, strain through charcoal.

Apicius. *De Re Coquinaria*. Translated by Ken Albala. 2013.

(Two sextarii in the original text is about a liter or a little over four cups, a fourth more than in a standard U.S. bottle. Thirty-six cups is about ten and one-half liters or fourteen standard wine bottles. Since few people are likely to make this on such a massive scale, use roughly one jar of honey to start per bottle of wine added in the end. The mastic can be purchased in a Greek grocery store; it is a resin of the lentisk tree and should be ground up before using. The text says merely leaves, which may be bay leaves that work very nicely. It is also not clear if the wine is filtered at the end or if charcoal is merely placed in, though the former seems more likely.)

Liver Meatballs Are Made Like This

Roast pork liver and remove the veins. But before that crush pepper, rue and garum, and pour over the liver, pound and mix to make meatballs, and wrap one bay leaf around each and suspend over the smoke as long as you like. When you want to eat them, remove from the smoke and roast them afresh.

(These are not meatballs as we know them, but closer to a kind of liverwurst in flavor and texture. The garum is the ubiquitous fish sauce used by ancient Romans, a southeast Asian fish sauce works fine. Rue is a very bitter herb, so use sparingly and fresh, but the flavor is alluring. The bay leaves must also be fresh and should stick to the liver paste. Smoking on a rack over smoldering fruit wood chips is ideal, though the use of the word suspend here suggests that they might have been tied up and hung over the smoke.)

Stuffed Womb Make Like This

Ground pepper, cumin and the white part of two leeks, pared down to the soft parts, rue and garum. Mix with thoroughly beaten and pounded meat so it's completely combined. Add pepper corns and pine nuts and stuff the well washed womb, and thus poach in water, oil and garum, with a bunch of leeks and dill.

(This is essentially a big sausage stuffed into a sow's uterus, though any kind of large casing would work, providing it is sewn up so the contents don't leak.)

Sala Cattabia

Put together in a bowl: pepper, mint, celery, dried pennyroyal, cheese, pinenuts, honey, vinegar, garum, egg yolks, fresh water. Then soak bread in diluted vinegar and squeeze out, add cow's milk cheese, and cucumbers. Among this strew pinenuts. Add chopped capers and little chicken livers. Pour the dressing over. Set the pot in a bowl of cold water and thus serve.

(This is a kind of bread salad or panzanella, still common in Italy. It's an ingenious way to use up stale bread, which is best torn into little mouthfuls. Toss everything together and let everything soak up the dressing while it chills. If you can't find dried pennyroyal, use dried spearmint, it is similar.)

Another Sala Cattabia à La Apicius

Add in a mortar celery seed, dried pennyroyal, dried mint, ginger, dried coriander, seedless raisins, honey, vinegar, oil and wine. Pound it. Add in a bowl bits of Picentine bread, among it chicken, goat sweetbreads, Vestine cheese, pine nuts, cucumbers, finely chopped dried onions, pour over the dressing, set the bowl in snow about an hour, sprinkle on pepper and serve.

(The Romans fetched snow from mountain tops and stored it for cooling drinks and salads such as these. A light, fluffy bread approximates the Picentine, and the cheese was probably a sheep's milk cheese like pecorino)

Apician Patina Make Like This

Bits of cooked udder, fish, chicken flesh, figpeckers or thrush's breast cooked and whatever is the best. Chop all this carefully except the figpeckers. Beat raw eggs with oil. Crush pepper with lovage, and moisten with garum, wine, raisin wine and put in a pot so it's heated and thicken with wheat starch. Before this however, put in all the chopped meat and boil. Then when it's cooked lift out with its juices and put in another platter and garnish with peppercorns and pine nuts, layering twice over like you do lagana. For each laganum you lay down add another ladleful on top. Then poke a hole in one laganum and place on top. Sprinkle with pepper. Before this though, you should mix the eggs with the meat and put in the pot with the rest. The kind of bronze platter you should have is shown here.

(If the word lagana here reminds you of lasagna, that's because it's the ancestor. This was more of a thin, crisp baked sheet of dough, often used broken up to thicken stews, but here in layers. The final effect is much like a lasagna even though they are not boiled noodles. Also the order of steps has been muddled by the author as he keeps reminding you of things you should have done before. To clarify, take the meat, add the seasonings and boil, then add starch to thicken, and then finally add eggs before making the layers. The whole figpeckers would presumably be added in too at some point, though feel free to just use chicken. To make laganae, simply roll thin sheets of dough and bake in a low oven until hard.)

Minutal of Apricots

Place in a pot oil, garum, wine, chopped dry shallots, chopped cilantro, and pork shoulder cut into cubes and already cooked. All this cook with crushed pepper, cumin, dry mint, dill, moisten with honey, garum, raisin wine, vinegar and some of its own juices to temper. Add in pitted apricots, and let it simmer until they are cooked. Break in tracta, so it's thickened, sprinkle on pepper and serve.

(Although the riot of flavors here might suggest something strange tasting, in the end it is a very familiar kind of thick sweet and sour sauce with fruit that one would not be surprised to find in an Asian restaurant.)

For Ostrich

For boiled ostrich: pepper, mint, toasted cumin, celery seed, dates or caryota dates, honey, vinegar, raisin wine, garum and a bit of oil. Put all this in a pan and boil. Thicken with starch, and put over the ostrich pieces in a dish, and sprinkle with pepper. If however you want to cook it in this mixture, add spelt.

(Ostrich might sound very exotic, but it is fairly mild and lean meat, hence this complex sauce. It is not clear if the spelt, a kind of grain, is cooked whole in the sauce or crushed like grits.

Obviously the latter will cook more quickly, and in either case the sauce will flavor the grain, making this like a pilaf.)

For Flamingo

Pluck, wash and gut your flamingo and put in a pot, add water, salt, dill and a bit of vinegar. When half cooked, add a bunch of leeks and coriander to cook. Close to being cooked, add defrutum, to color it. Put in a mortar pepper, cumin, coriander, silphium root, mint, rue and pound. Moisten with vinegar, add dates, and pour in some of its own broth. Pour this into the same pot, thicken with starch, pour over the sauce and serve. You can do the same with parrot.

(Silphium or laser is a plant from northern Africa whose strong aromatic sap was used in cooking. At some point in ancient times it went extinct and was replaced with asafoetida, an extraordinarily strong-smelling spice still used in India.)

Dormice

Stuff the dormice with ground pork along with the meat from every part of the dormouse chopped with pepper, pine nuts, silphium, garum. Sew up the dormice and place in a clay casserole and put in the oven or stuffed cook under a domed clay pot.

(The clibanus is like a clay pot lid or cloche which you use to cook in the fireplace. Food is placed on a flat clay dish and the dome is placed on top which radiates the heat inward.)

NINETEEN

Satires V and XI

JUVENAL

These two satires, better than probably any other writing of ancient times, reveal what the social experience of dining was like. Who threw a dinner party, who got invited, and what they were served were matters of prime importance, and, as you will see, equality was not a particularly Roman value. But Juvenal reveals an entirely different aesthetic approach to food as well: the rustic, natural, homegrown and simple. This goes to show that not all food was wildly extravagant; many people enjoyed the simpler pleasures of food as well.

SATIRE V

IF you are not yet ashamed of your course of life, and your feeling is still the same, that you consider living at another man's table to be the chief good; if you can put up with such things as not even Sarmentus or Galba, contemptible as he was, would have submitted to even at the unequal board of Cæsar himself; I should be afraid to believe your evidence though you were on oath. I know nothing more easily satisfied than the cravings of nature. Yet even suppose this little that is needed to be wanting, is there no quay vacant? is there no where a bridge, and a piece of mat, somewhat less than half, to beg upon? Is the loss of a supper so great a matter? is your craving so fierce? when, in faith, it were much more reputable to shiver there, and munch mouldy fragments of dog-biscuit. In the first place, bear in mind, that when invited to dinner, you receive payment in full of your long-standing account of service. The sole result of

Juvenal. "Satires V and XI." In *The Satires of Juvenal, Persius, Sulpicia and Lucius*. Translated by Lewis Evans. London: George Bell & Sons, 1904, pp. 33–39, 123–35.

your friendship with the great man is—a meal! This your patron sets down to your account, and, rare though it be, still takes it into the calculation. Therefore, if after the lapse of two months he deigns to send for his long-neglected client, only that the third place may not be unoccupied in one couch of his triclinium—"Let us sup together," he says; the very summit of your wishes! What more can you desire? Trebius has that for which he ought to break his rest, and hurry away with latchet all untied, in his alarm lest the whole crowd at his patron's levee shall have already gone their round of compliments, when the stars are fading, or at the hour when the chill wain of sluggish Bootes wheels slowly round.

But what sort of a supper is it after all? Wine, such as wool just shorn would not imbibe. You will see the guests become frantic as the priests of Cybele. Wranglings are the prelude of the fray: but soon you begin to hurl cups as well in retaliation; and wipe your wounds with your napkin stained with blood; as often as a pitched battle, begun with pitchers of Saguntine ware, rages between you and the regiment of freedmen. The great man himself drinks wine racked from the wood under some consul with long hair, and sips the juice of the grape pressed in the Social war; never likely, however, to send even a small glass to a friend, though sick at heart. Tomorrow, he will drink the produce of the mountains of Alba or Setia, whose country and date age has obliterated by the accumulated mould on the ancient amphora; such wine as, with chaplets on their heads, Thrasea and Helvidius used to drink on the birth-days of the Bruti and Cassius.

Virro himself holds capacious cups formed of the tears of the Heliades and phialæ incrusted with beryl. You are not trusted with gold: or even if it is ever handed to you, a servant is set as a guard over you at the same time, to count the gems and watch your sharp nails. Forgive the precaution: the jasper so much admired there is indeed a noble one: for, like many others, Virro transfers to his cups the gems from off his fingers, which the youth, preferred to the jealous Hiarbas, used to set on the front of his scabbard. You will drain a cup with four noses, that bears the name of the cobbler of Beneventum, already cracked, and fit to be exchanged, as broken glass, for brimstone.

If your patron's stomach is overheated with wine and food, he calls for water cooled by being boiled and then iced in Scythian snow. Did I complain just now that the wine set before you was not the same as Virro's? Why, the very water you drink is different. Your cups will be handed you by a running footman from Gætulia, or the bony hand of some Moor, so black that you would rather not meet him at midnight, while riding through the tombs on the steep Latin way. Before Virro himself stands the flower of Asia, purchased at a greater sum than formed the whole revenue of the warlike Tullus, or Ancus—and, not to detain you, the whole fortunes of all the kings of Rome. And so, when you are thirsty, look behind you for your black Ganymede that comes from Africa. A boy that costs so many thousands deigns not to mix wine for the poor. Nay, his very beauty and bloom of youth justify his sneer. When does he come near you? When would he come, even if you called him, to serve you with hot or cold water? He scorns, forsooth, the idea of obeying an old client, and that *you* should call for any thing from his hand; and that you should recline at table, while he has to stand. Every great house is proportionably full of saucy menials.

See, too, with what grumbling another of these rascals hands you bread that can scarce be broken; the mouldy fragments of impenetrable crust, which would make your jaws ache, and give you no chance of a bite. But delicate bread, as white as snow, made of the finest flower, is reserved for the great man. Mind you keep your hands off! Maintain the respect due to the cutter of the bread! Imagine, however, that you have been rather too forward; there stands over you one ready to make you put it down. "Be so good, audacious guest, as to help yourself from the bread-basket you have been used to, and know the colour of your own particular bread." "So then! it was for this, forsooth, that I so often quitted my wife, and hurried up the steep ascent of the bleak Esquiline, when the vernal sky rattled with the pelting of the pitiless hail, and my great coat dripped whole showers of rain!"

See! with how vast a body the lobster which is served to your patron fills the dish, and with what fine asparagus it is garnished all round; with what a tail he seems to look down in scorn on the assembled guests, when he comes in raised on high by the hands of the tall slave. But to you is served a common crab, scantily hedged in with half an egg sliced, a meal fit only for the dead, and in a dish too small to hold it. Virro himself drowns his fish in oil from Venafrum; but the pale cabbage set before you, poor wretch, will stink of the lamp. For in the sauce-boats you are allowed, there is served oil such as the canoe of the Micipsæ has imported in its sharp prow; for which reason no one at Rome would bathe in the same bath with Bocchor; which makes the blackamoors safe even from the attacks of serpents.

Your patron will have a barbel furnished by Corsica, or the rocks of Tauromenium, when all our own waters have been ransacked and failed; while gluttony is raging, and the market is plying its unwearied nets in the neighbouring seas, and we do not allow the Tyrrhene fish to reach their full growth. The provinces, therefore, have to supply our kitchen; and thence we are furnished with what Lenas the legacy-hunter may buy, and Aurelia sell again. Virro is presented with a lamprey of the largest size from the Sicilian whirlpool, for while Auster keeps himself close, while he seats himself and dries his wet pinions in prison, the nets, grown venturesome, despise the dangers even of the middle of Charybdis. An eel awaits you—first-cousin to the long snake—or a coarse pike from the Tiber, spotted from the winter's ice, a native of the bank-side, fattened on the filth of the rushing sewer, and used to penetrate the drain even of the middle of Suburra.

"I should like to have a word with Virro, if he would lend an attentive ear. No one now expects from you such presents as used to be sent by Seneca to his friends of humble station, or the munificent gifts which the bountiful Piso or Cotta used to dispense; for in days of old the glory of giving was esteemed a higher honour than fasces or inscriptions. All we ask is that you would treat us at supper like fellow-citizens. Do this, and then, if you please, be, as many now-a-days are, luxurious when alone, parsimonious to your guests."

Before Virro himself is the liver of a huge goose; a fat capon, as big as a goose; and a wild boar, worthy of the spear of the yellow-haired Meleager, smokes. Then will be served up truffles, if it happen to be spring, and the thunder, devoutly wished for by the epicure, shall augment the supper. "Keep your corn, O Libya," says Alledius, "unyoke your oxen; provided only you send us truffles!" Meanwhile, that no single source of vexation may be wanting, you will see the carver capering and gesticulating with nimble knife, till he has gone through all the directions of his instructor in the art. Nor is it in truth a matter of trifling import with what an air a leveret or a hen is carved. You would be dragged by the heels, like Cacus when conquered by Hercules, and turned out of doors, if you were ever to attempt to open your mouth, as though you had three names. When does Virro pass the cup to you, or take one that your lips have contaminated? Which of you would be so rash, so lost to all sense of shame, as to say, "Drink, sir!" to your patron lord? There are very many things which men with coats worn threadbare dare not say. If any god, or god-like hero, kinder to you than the fates have been, were to give you a knight's estate, what a great man would you, small mortal, become all at once from nothing at all! What a dear friend of Virro's! "Give this to Trebius! Set this before Trebius! My dear brother, will you take some of this sweet-bread?"

O money! it is to thee he pays this honour! it is *thou* and he are the brothers! But if you wish to be my lord, and my lord's lord, let no little Æneas sport in your hall, or a daughter more endearing than he. It is the barrenness of the wife that makes a friend really agreeable and beloved. But even suppose your Mycale should be confined, though she should even present you three boys at a birth, he will be the very one to be delighted with the twittering nest; will order his green stomacher to be brought, and the filberts, and the begged-for penny, whenever the infant parasite shall come to dine with him.

Before his friends whom he holds so vile will be set some very questionable toadstools— before the great man himself, a mushroom—but such a one as Claudius eat, *before* that furnished by his wife, *after* which he eat nothing more. Virro will order to be served to himself and his brother Virros such noble apples, on whose fragrance alone you are allowed to revel; such as the eternal autumn of the Phæacians produced; or such as you might fancy purloined from the African sisters. You feast upon some shrivelled windfall, such as is munched at the ramparts by him that is armed with buckler and helmet: and, in dread of the lash, learns to hurl his javelin from the shaggy goat's back.

You may imagine, perhaps, that Virro does all this from stinginess. No! his very object is to vex you. For what play, what mime is better than disappointed gluttony? All this, therefore, is done, if you don't know it, that you may be forced to give vent to your bile by your tears, and gnash long your compressed teeth. You fancy yourself a freeman—the great man's welcome guest! He looks upon you as one caught by the savour of his kitchen. Nor does he conjecture amiss. For who is so utterly destitute as twice to bear with his insolence, if it has been his good fortune, when a boy, to wear the Tuscan gold, or even the boss, the badge of leather, that emblem of poverty.

The hope of a good dinner deludes you. "See! sure he'll send us now a half-eaten hare, or a slice of that wild-boar haunch. Now we shall get that capon, as he has helped himself!" Consequently you all sit in silent expectation, with bread in hand, untouched and ready for action. And he that uses you thus, shows his wisdom—if you *can* submit to all these things, then you *ought* to bear them. Some day or other, you will, present your head with shaven crown, to be beaten: nor hesitate to submit to the harsh lash—well worthy of such a banquet and such a friend as this!

SATIRE XI

If Atticus sups extravagantly, he is considered a splendid fellow: if Rutilus does so, he is thought mad. For what is received with louder laughter on the part of the mob, than Apicius, reduced to poverty?

Every club, the baths, every knot of loungers, every theatre, is full of Rutilus. For while his sturdy and youthful limbs are fit to bear arms, and while he is hot in blood, he is driven (not indeed forced to it, but unchecked by the tribune) to copy out the instructions and imperial commands of the trainer of gladiators. Moreover you see many whom their creditor, often cheated of his money, is wont to look out for at the very entrance of the market; and whose inducement to live exists in their palate alone. The greatest wretch amongst these, one who must soon fail, since his rain is already as clear as day, sups the more extravagantly and the more splendidly. Meanwhile they ransack all the elements for dainties; the price never standing in the way of their gratification. If you look more closely into it, those please the more which are bought for more. Therefore they have no scruple in borrowing a sum, soon to be squandered, by pawning their plate, or the broken image of their mother; and, with the 400 sesterces, seasoning an earthen dish to tickle their palate. Thus they are reduced to the hotchpotch of the gladiator.

It makes therefore all the difference, who it is that procures these same things. For in Rutilus it is luxurious extravagance. In Ventidius it takes a praiseworthy name, and derives credit from his fortune.

I should with reason despise the man, who knows how much more lofty Atlas is than all the mountains in Libya yet this very man knows not how much a little purse differs from an iron-bound chest. "Know thyself," came down from heaven: a proverb to be implanted and cherished in the memory, whether you are about to contract matrimony, or wish to be in a part of the sacred senate:—(for not even Thersites is a candidate for the breastplate of Achilles: in which Ulysses exhibited himself in a doubtful character:)—or whether you take upon yourself to, defend a cause of great moment. Consult your own powers; tell yourself who you are; whether you are a powerful orator, or like a Curtius, or a Matho, mere spouters.

One must know one's own measure, and keep it in view, in the greatest and in most trifling matters; even when a fish is to be bought. Do not long for a mullet, when you have only a gudgeon in your purse. For what end awaits you, as your purse fails and your gluttony increases: when your patrimony and whole fortune is squandered upon your belly, what can hold your money out at interest, your solid plate, your flocks, and lands?

By such proprietors as these, last of all the ring is parted with, and Pollio begs with his finger bare. It is not the premature funeral pile, or the grave, that is luxury's horror; but old age, more to be dreaded than death itself. These are most commonly the steps: money, borrowed at Rome, is spent before the very owners' faces; then when some trifling residue is left, and the lender of the money is growing pale, they give leg-bail and run to Baiæ and Ostia. For now-a-days to quit the forum is not more discreditable to you than to remove to Esquiline from hot Suburra. This is the only pain that they who flee their country feel, this their only sorrow, to have lost the Circensian games for one year. Not a drop of blood remains in their face; few attempt to detain modesty, now become an object of ridicule and fleeing from the city.

You shall prove to-day by your own experience, Persicus, whether all these things, which are very fine to talk about, I do not practise in my life, in my moral conduct, and in reality: but praise vegetables, while in secret I am a glutton: in others' hearing bid my slave bring me water-gruel, but whisper "cheese-cakes" in his ear. For since you are my promised guest, you shall find me an Evander: you shall come as the Tirynthian, or the guest, inferior indeed to him, and yet himself akin by blood to heaven: the one sent to the skies by water, the other by fire.

Now hear your bill of fare, furnished by no public market. From my farm at Tibur there shall come a little kid, the fattest and tenderest of the whole flock, ignorant of the taste of grass, that has never yet ventured to browse even on the low twigs of the willow-bed, and that has more milk than blood in his veins: and asparagus from the mountains, which my bailiff's wife, having laid down her spindle, gathered. Some huge eggs besides, and still warm in their twisted hay, shall be served up, together with the hens themselves: and grapes kept a portion of the year, just as they were when fresh upon the vines: pears from Signia and Syria: and, from the same basket, apples rivalling those of Picenum, and smelling quite fresh; that you need not be afraid of, since they have lost their autumnal moisture, which has been dried up by cold, and the dangers to be feared from their juice if crude. This would in times gone by have been a luxurious supper for our senate. Curius with his own hands used to cook over his little fire pot-herbs which he had gathered in his little garden: such herbs as now the foul digger in his heavy chain rejects with scorn, who remembers the flavour of the vile dainties of the reeking cook-shop. It was the custom formerly to keep against festival days the flitches of the smoked swine, hanging from the wide-barred rack, and to set bacon as a birthday treat before one's relations, with the addition of some fresh meat, if a sacrificial victim furnished any. Some one of the kin, with the title of "Thrice consul," that had held command in camps, and discharged the dignity of dictator, used to go earlier than his wont to such a feast as this, bearing his spade over his shoulder from the mountain he had been digging on. But when men trembled at the Fabii, and the stern Cato, and the Scauri and Fabricii; and when, in fine, even his colleague stood in dread of the severe character of the strict Censor; no one thought it was a matter of anxiety or serious concern what kind of tortoise floated in the wave of ocean, destined to form a splendid and noble couch for the Trojugenæ. But with side devoid of ornament, and sofas of diminutive size, the brazen front displayed the mean head of an ass wearing a chaplet, at which the country lads laughed in wantonness.

The food then was in keeping with the master of the house and the furniture. Then the soldier, uncivilized, and too ignorant to admire the arts of Greece, used to break up the drinking-cups, the work of some renowned artists, which he found in his share of the booty when cities were overthrown, that his horse might exult in trappings, and his embossed helmet might display to his enemy on the point of perishing, likenesses of the Romulean wild beast bidden to grow tame by the destiny of the empire, and the twin Quirini beneath the rock, and the naked image of the god coming down with buckler and spear, and impending over him. Whatever silver he possessed glittered on his arms alone. In those days, then, they used to serve all their furmety in a dish of Tuscan earthenware: which you may envy, if you are at all that way inclined.

The majesty of temples also was more evidently near to men, and a voice heard about midnight and through the midst of the city, when the Gauls were coming from the shore of ocean, and the gods discharged the functions of a prophet, warned us of these.

This was the care which Jupiter used to show for the affairs of Latium, when made of earthenware, and as yet profaned by no gold. Those days saw tables made of wood grown at home and from our native trees. To these uses was the timber applied, if the east wind had chanced to lay prostrate some old walnut-tree. But now the rich have no satisfaction in their dinner, the turbot and the venison lose their flavour, perfumes and roses seem to lose their smell, unless the broad circumference of the table is supported by a huge mass of ivory, and a tall leopard with wide-gaping jaws, made of those tusks, which the gate of Syene transmits, and the active Moors, and the Indian of duskier hue than the Moor; and which the huge beast has deposited in some Nabathæan glen, as now grown too weighty and burdensome to his head: by this their appetite is whetted: hence their stomach acquires its vigour. For a leg of a table made only of silver is to them what an iron ring on their finger would be: I therefore cautiously avoid a proud guest, who compares me with himself, and looks with scorn on my paltry estate. Consequently I do not possess a single ounce of ivory: neither my chess-board nor my men are of this material; nay, the very handles of my knives are of bone. Yet my viands never become rank in flavour by these, nor does my pullet cut up the worse on that account. Nor yet will you see a carver, to whom the whole carving-school ought to yield the palm, some pupil of the professor Trypherus, at whose house the hare, with the large sow's udders, and the wild-boar, and the roe-buck, and pheasants, and the huge flamingo, and the wild goat of Gætulia, all forming a most splendid supper, though made of elm, are carved with the blunted knife, and resounds through the whole Suburra. My little fellow, who is a novice, and uneducated all his days, does not know how to take dexterously off a slice of roe, or the wing of a guinea-hen; only versed in the mysteries of carving the fragments of a small collop.

My slave, who is not gaily dressed, and only clad so as to protect him from cold, will hand you plebeian cups bought for a few pence. He is no Phrygian or Lycian, or one purchased from the slave-dealer and at great price. When you ask for any thing, ask in Latin. They have all the same style of dress; their hair close-cropt and straight, and only combed to-day on ac-count of company. One is the son of a hardy shepherd, another of a neat-herd: he sighs after his mother whom he has not seen for a long time, and pines for his hovel and his play-mate kids. A lad of ingenuous face, and ingenuous modesty; such as *those* ought to be who are clothed in brilliant purple. He shall hand you wine made on those very hills from which he himself comes, and under whose summit he has played: for the country of the wine and the attendant is one and the same.

Gambling is disgraceful, and so is adultery, in men of moderate means. Yet when rich men commit all those abominations, they are called jovial, splendid fellows. Our banquet to-day will furnish far different amusements. The author of the Iliad shall be recited, and the verses of high-sounding Mars, that render the palm doubtful. What matter is it with what voice such noble verses are read? But now having put off all your cares, lay aside business, and allow yourself a pleasing respite, since you will have it in your power to be idle all day long. Let there be no mention of money out at interest. Nor if your wife is accustomed to go out at break of day and return at night, let her stir up your bile, though you hold your tongue. Divest yourself at once of all that annoys you, at my threshold. Banish all thoughts of home and servants, and all that is broken and wasted by them—especially forget ungrateful friends! Meantime, the spectacles of the Megalesian towel grace the Idæan solemnity: and, like one in a triumph, the prey of horses, the prætor, sits: and, if I may say so without offence to the immense and overgrown crowd, the circus to-day encloses the whole of Rome: and a din reaches my ears, from which I infer the success of the green faction. For should it not win, you would see this city in mourning and amazement, as when the consuls were conquered in the dust of Cannæ. Let young men be spectators of these, in whom shouting and bold betting, and sitting by a trim damsel, is becoming. Let our skin, which is wrinkled with age, imbibe the vernal sun and avoid the toga'd crowd. Even now, though it wants a whole hour to the sixth, you may go to the bath with unblushing brow. You could not do this for five successive days; because even of such a life as this there would be great weariness. It is a more moderate use that enhances pleasures.

TWENTY

The Life of Antoninus Heliogabalus

AELIUS LAMPRIDIUS

This biography of the emperor Heliogabalus is taken from a larger work known as the **Augustan History,** *covering the Roman emperors from 117 to 284* A.D., *compiled probably in the reign of Constantine. The identity of the author is unknown and Aelius Lampridius may even be a made-up name. Whatever the provenance, this biography is certainly meant to provide a negative case example and may be largely untrue. Nonetheless, it is an excellent example of how an author can write a character assassination by describing the food preferences and perversities of an individual.*

Concerning his life many filthy anecdotes have been put into writing, but since they are not worthy of being recorded, I have thought I ought to relate only such deeds as illustrate his extravagance. Some of these, it is said, were done before he ascended the throne, others after he was made emperor; for he himself declared that his models were Apicius among commoners and, among emperors, Otho and Vitellius. XIX. For example, he was the first commoner to cover his couches with golden coverlets—for this was lawful then by authorization of Marcus Antoninus, who had sold at public auction all the imperial trappings. Also, he gave summer-banquets in various colours, one day a green banquet, another day an iridescent one, and next in order a blue one, varying them continually every day of the summer. Moreover, he was the first to use silver urns and casseroles, and vessels of chased silver, one hundred pounds in

Aelius Lampridius. *The Scriptores Historiae Augustae.* Vol. 2. Translated by David Magie. Loeb Classical Library, Vol. 140. Cambridge, MA: Harvard University Press, 1924, pp. 143, 145, 147, 149, 151, 153, 155, 157, 159, 161, 163, 165, 167, 169, 171, 173.

weight, some of them spoiled by the lewdest designs. He was also the first to concoct wine seasoned with mastich and with pennyroyal and all such mixtures, which our present luxury retains. And rose-wine, of which he had learned from others, he used to make more fragrant by adding pulverized pinecone. In fact, all these kinds of cups are not met with in books before the time of Elagabalus. Indeed, for him life was nothing except a search after pleasures. He was the first to make force-meat of fish, or of oysters of various kinds or similar shell-fish, or of lobsters, crayfish and squills. He used to strew roses and all manner of flowers, such as lilies, violets, hyacinths, and narcissus, over his banqueting-rooms, his couches and his porticoes, and then stroll about in them. He would refuse to swim in a pool that was not perfumed with saffron or some other well-known essence. And he could not rest easily on cushions that were not stuffed with rabbit-fur or feathers from under the wings of partridges, and he used, moreover, to change the pillows frequently.

XX. He often showed contempt for the senate, calling them slaves in togas, while he treated the Roman people as the tiller of a single farm and the equestrian order as nothing at all. He frequently invited the city-prefect to a drinking-bout after a banquet and also summoned the prefects of the guard, sending a master of ceremonies, in case they declined, to compel them to come. And he wished to create a city-prefect for each region of Rome, thus making fourteen for the city; and he would have done it, too, had lie lived, for he was always ready to promote men of the basest character and the lowest calling.

He had couches made of solid silver for use in his banqueting-rooms and his bed-chambers. In imitation of Apicius he frequently ate camels-heels and also cocks-combs taken from the living birds, and the tongues of peacocks and nightingales, because he was told that one who ate them was immune from the plague. He served to the palace-attendants, moreover, huge platters heaped up with the viscera of mullets, and flamingo-brains, partridge-eggs, thrush-brains, and the heads of parrots, pheasants, and peacocks. And the beards of the mullets that he ordered to be served were so large that they were brought on, in place of cress or parsley or pickled beans or fenugreek, in well filled bowls and disk-shaped platters—a particularly amazing performance.

XXI. He fed his dogs on goose-livers. Among his pets he had lions and leopards, which had been rendered harmless and trained by tamers, and these he would suddenly order during the dessert and the after-dessert to get up on the couches, thereby causing an amusing panic, for none knew that the beasts were harmless. He sent grapes from Apamea to his stables for his horses, and he fed parrots and pheasants to his lions and other wild animals. For ten successive days, moreover, he served wild sows' udders with the matrices, at the rate of thirty a day, serving, besides, peas with gold-pieces, lentils with onyx, beans with amber, and rice with pearls; and he also sprinkled pearls on fish and truffles in lieu of pepper. In a banqueting-room with a reversible ceiling he once overwhelmed his parasites with violets and other flowers, so that some of them were actually smothered to death, being unable to crawl out to the top. He flavoured his swimming-pools and bathtubs with essence of spices or of roses or wormwood. And once he invited the common mob to a drinking-bout, and himself drank with the populace, taking so much that on seeing what he alone consumed, people supposed he had been drinking from one of his swimming-pools. As banquet-favours, he gave eunuchs, or four-horse chariots, or horses with saddles, or mules, or litters, or carriages, or a thousand aurei or a hundred pounds of silver. XXII. At his banquets he would also distribute chances inscribed on spoons, the chance of one person reading "ten camels," of another "ten flies," of another "ten pounds of gold," of another "ten pounds of lead," of another "ten ostriches," of another "ten hens-eggs," so that they were chances indeed and men tried their luck. These he also gave at his games, distributing chances for ten bears or ten dormice, ten lettuces or ten pounds of gold. Indeed he was the first to introduce this practice of giving chances, which we still maintain. And the performers too he invited to what really were chances, giving as prizes a dead dog or a pound of beef, or else a hundred aurei, or a hundred pieces of silver, or a hundred coppers, and so on. All this so pleased the populace that after each occasion they rejoiced that he was emperor.

XXIII. He gave a naval spectacle, it is said, on the Circus-canals, which had been filled with wine, and he sprinkled the people's cloaks with perfume made from the wild grape; also he drove a chariot drawn by four elephants on the Vatican Hill, destroying the tombs which obstructed the way, and he harnessed four camels to a chariot at a private spectacle in the Circus. It is also said that he collected serpents with the aid of priests of the Marsic nation and suddenly let them loose before dawn, when the populace usually assembled for the more frequented games, and many people were injured by their fangs as well as in the general panic. He would wear a tunic made wholly of cloth of gold, or one made of purple, or a Persian one studded with jewels, and at such times he would say that he felt oppressed by the weight of his pleasures. He even wore jewels on his shoes, sometimes engraved ones—a practice which aroused the derision of all, as if, forsooth, the engraving of famous artists could be seen on jewels attached to his feet. He wished to wear also a jewelled diadem in order that his beauty might be increased and his face look more like a woman's; and in his own house he did wear one. He promised a phoenix to some guests, it is said, or in lieu of the bird a thousand pounds of gold, and this sum he handed out in the imperial residence. He constructed swimming-pools filled with sea-water in places especially far from the coast, and would hand them over to individual friends who swam in them, or at another time he would fill one with fish. One summer he made a mountain of snow in the pleasure-garden attached to his house, having snow carried there for the purpose. When on the sea-coast he never ate fish, but in places most remote from the sea he regularly served all manner of sea-food, and the country-folk in the interior he fed with the milt of lampreys and pikes.

XXIV. The fish that he ate were cooked in a bluish sauce that preserved their natural co-lour, as though they were still in the sea-water. He supplied swimming-pools that he used for the moment with essence of roses and with the flowers themselves, and when he bathed with all his courtiers he would furnish oil of nard for the hot-rooms; he also furnished balsam-oil for the lamps. He never had intercourse with the same woman twice except with his wife, and he opened brothels in his house for his friends, his clients, and his slaves. He never spent less on a banquet than one hundred thousand sesterces, that is, thirty pounds of silver; and sometimes he even spent as much as three million when all the cost was computed. In fact, he even outdid the banquets of Vitellius and Apicius. He would take fish from his ponds by the ox-load, and then, as he passed through the market, bewail the public poverty. He used to bind his parasites to a water-wheel and, by a turn of the wheel, plunge them into the water and then bring them back to the surface again, calling them meanwhile river-Ixions. He used

Lacedaemonian stone and porphyry to pave the open spaces in the Palace, which he called Antonine; this pavement lasted down to within our own memory but was lately torn up and destroyed. And he planned to erect a single column of enormous size, which could be ascended inside, and to place on its summit the god Elagabalus, but he could not find enough stone, even though he planned to bring it from the district of Thebes.

XXV. When his friends became drunk he would often shut them up, and suddenly during the night let in his lions and leopards and bears—all of them harmless—so that his friends on awakening at dawn, or worse, during the night, would find lions and leopards and bears in the room with themselves; and some even died from this cause. Some of his humbler friends he would seat on air-pillows instead of on cushions and let out the air while they were dining, so that often the diners were suddenly found under the table. Finally, he was the first to think of placing a semi-circular group on the ground instead of on couches, with the purpose of having the air-pillows loosened by slaves who stood at the feet of the guests and the air thus let out.

When adultery was represented on the stage, he would order what was usually done in pretence to be carried out in fact. He often purchased harlots from all the procurers and then set them free. Once during a private conversation the question arose as to how many ruptured people there were in the city of Rome, and he thereupon issued an order that all should be noted and brought to his baths, and then he bathed with them, some of them being men of distinction. Before a banquet he would frequently watch gladiatorial fights and boxing matches, and he had a couch spread for himself in an upper gallery and during luncheon exhibited criminals in a wild-beast hunt. His parasites would often be served during dessert with food made of wax or wood or ivory, sometimes of earthenware, or at times even of marble or stone; so that all that he ate himself would be served to them too, but different in substance and only to be looked at, and all the while they would merely drink with each course and wash their hands, just as if they had really eaten.

XXVI. He was the first of the Romans, it is said, who wore clothing wholly of silk, although garments partly of silk were in use before his time. Linen that had been washed he would never touch, saying that washed linen was worn only by beggars. He would often appear in public after dinner dressed in a Dalmatian tunic, and then he would call himself Fabius Gurges or Scipio, because he was wearing the same kind of clothing which Fabius and Cornelius wore when in their youth they were brought out in public by their parents in order to improve their manners.

He gathered together in a public building all the harlots from the Circus, the theatre, the Stadium and all other places of amusement, and from the public baths, and then delivered a speech to them, as one might to soldiers, calling them "comrades" and discoursing upon various kinds of postures and debaucheries. Afterward he invited to a similar gathering procurers, catamites collected together from all sides, and lascivious boys and young men. And whereas he had appeared before the harlots in a woman's costume and with protruding bosom, he met the catamites in the garb of a boy who is exposed for prostitution. After his speech he announced a largess of three aurei for each, just as if they were soldiers, and asked them to pray the gods that they might find others to recommend to him.

He used, too, to play jokes on his slaves, even ordering them to bring him a thousand pounds of spiders-webs and offering them a prize; and he collected, it is said, ten thousand pounds, and then remarked that one could realize from that how great a city was Rome. He also used to send to his parasites jars of frogs, scorpions, snakes, and other such reptiles, as their yearly allowance of provisions, and he would shut up a vast number of flies in jars of this sort and call them tamed bees.

XXVII. He often brought four-horse chariots from the Circus into his banqueting-rooms or porticoes while he lunched or dined, compelling his guests to drive, even though they were old men and some of them had held public office. Even when emperor, he would give an order to bring in to him ten thousand mice, a thousand weasels, or a thousand shrew-mice. So skilful were his confectioners and dairymen, that all the various kinds of food that were served by his cooks, either meat-cooks or fruit-cooks, they also would serve up, making them now out of confectionery or again out of milk-products. His parasites he would serve with dinners made of glass, and at times he would send to their table only embroidered napkins with pictures of the viands that were set before himself, as many in number as the courses which he was to have, so that they were served only with representations made by the needle or the loom. Sometimes, however, paintings too were displayed to them, so that they were served with the whole dinner, as it were, but were all the while tormented by hunger. He would also mix jewels with apples and flowers, and he would throw out of the window quite as much food as he served to his friends. He gave an order, too, that an amount of public grain equal to one year's tribute should be given to all the harlots, procurers, and catamites who were within the walls, and promised an equal amount to those without, for, thanks to the foresight of Severus and Trajan, there was in Rome at that time a store of grain equal to seven years' tribute.

XXVIII. He would harness four huge dogs to a chariot and drive about within the royal residence, and he did the same thing, before he was made emperor, on his country-estates. He even appeared in public driving four stags of vast size. Once he harnessed lions to his chariot and called himself the Great Mother, and on another occasion, tigers, and called himself Dionysus; and he always appeared in the particular garb in which the deity that he was representing was usually depicted. He kept at Rome tiny Egyptian snakes, called by the natives "good genii," besides hippopotami, a crocodile, and a rhinoceros, and, in fact, everything Egyptian which was of such a kind that it could be supplied. And sometimes at his banquets he served ostriches, saying that the Jews had been commanded to eat them.

It seems indeed a surprising thing that he is said to have done when he invited men of the highest rank to a luncheon and covered a semi-circular couch with saffron-flowers, and then said that he was providing them with the kind of hay that their rank demanded. The occupations of the day he performed at night, and those of the night in the daytime, and he considered it a mark of luxury to wait until a late hour before rising from sleep and beginning to hold his levee, and also to remain awake until morning. He received his courtiers every day, and he seldom let any go without a gift, save those whom he found to be thrifty, for he regarded these as worthless.

XXIX. His chariots were made of jewels and gold, for he scorned those that were merely of silver or ivory or bronze. He would harness women of the greatest beauty to a wheelbarrow in fours, in twos, or in threes or even more, and would drive them about, usually naked himself, as were also the women who were pulling him.

He had the custom, moreover, of asking to a dinner eight bald men, or else eight one-eyed men, or eight men who suffered from gout, or eight deaf men, or eight men of dark complexion, or eight tall men, or, again, eight fat men, his purpose being, in the case of these last, since they could not be accommodated on one couch, to call forth general laughter. He would present to his guests all the silver-plate that he had in the banqueting-room and all the supply of goblets, and he did it very often too. He was the first Roman emperor to serve at a public banquet fish-pickle mixed with water, for previously this had been only a soldier's dish—a usage which later was promptly restored by Alexander. He would propose to his guests, furthermore, by way of a feat, that they should invent new sauces for giving flavour to the food, and he would offer a very large prize for the man whose invention should please him, even presenting him with a silk garment—then regarded as a rarity and a mark of honour. On the other hand, if the sauce did not please him, the inventor was ordered to continue eating it until he invented a better one. Of course he always sat among flowers or perfumes of great value, and he loved to hear the prices of the food served at his table exaggerated, asserting it was an appetizer for the banquet.

XXX. He got himself up as a confectioner, a perfumer, a cook, a shop-keeper, or a procurer, and he even practised all these occupations in his own house continually. At one dinner where there were many tables he brought in the heads of six hundred ostriches in order that the brains might be eaten. Occasionally he gave a banquet in which he would serve twenty-two courses of extraordinary viands, and between each course he and his guests would bathe and dally with women, all taking an oath that they were deriving enjoyment. And once he gave a banquet in which one course was served in the house of each guest, and although one lived on the Capitoline Hill, one on the Palatine, one beyond the Rampart, one on the Caelian Hill, and one across the Tiber, nevertheless each course was served in order in one of the houses, and they went about to the homes of all. It was difficult, therefore, to finish the banquet within a whole day, especially as between the courses they bathed and dallied with women. He always served a course of Sybariticum, consisting of oil and fish-pickle, which the men of Sybaris invented in the year in which they all perished. It is further related of him that he constructed baths in many places, bathed in them once, and immediately demolished them, merely in order that he might not derive any advantage from them. And he is said to have done the same with houses, imperial headquarters, and summer-dwellings. However, these and some other things which surpass credence, I believe to have been fabricated by those who wished to vilify Elagabalus in order to curry favour with Alexander.

XXXI. He purchased, it is said, a very famous and very beautiful harlot for one hundred thousand sesterces, and then kept her untouched, as though she were a virgin. When some one asked him before he was made emperor, "Are you not afraid of becoming poor?" he replied, so they say, "What could be better than that I should be my own heir and my wife's too?" He had abundant means besides, bequeathed to him by many out of regard for his father. Furthermore, he said that he did not wish to have sons, lest one of them should chance to be thrifty. He would have perfumes from India burned without any coals in order that the fumes might fill his apartments. Even while a commoner he never made a journey with fewer than sixty wagons, though his grandmother Varia used to protest that he would squander all his substance; but after he became emperor he would take with him, it is said, as many as six hundred, asserting that the king of the Persians travelled with ten thousand camels and Nero with five hundred carriages. The reason for all these vehicles was the vast number of his procurers and bawds, harlots, catamites and lusty partners in depravity. In the public baths he always bathed with the women, and he even treated them himself with a depilatory ointment, which he applied also to his own beard, and shameful though it be to say it, in the same place where the women were treated and at the same hour. He shaved his minions' groins, using the razor with his own hand—with which he would then shave his beard. He would strew gold and silver dust about a portico and then lament that he could not strew the dust of amber also; and he did this often when he proceeded on foot to his horse or his carriage, as they do today with golden sand.

XXXII. He never put on the same shoes twice and never, it is said, wore the same ring a second time. He often tore up costly garments. Once he took a whale and weighed it and then sent his friends its weight in fish. He sank some heavily laden ships in the harbour and then said that this was a sign of greatness of soul. He used vessels of gold for relieving himself and his urinals were made of murra or onyx. And he is said to have remarked: "If I ever have an heir, I shall appoint a guardian for him, to make him do what I have myself done and intend to do." He was accustomed, furthermore, to have dinners served to him of the following kind: one day he would eat nothing at all but pheasant, serving only pheasant-meat at every course; another day he would serve only chicken, another some kind of fish and again a different kind, again pork, or ostrich, or greens, or fruit, or sweets, or dairy-products. He would often shut up his friends in halting-places for the night with old hags from Ethiopia and compel them to stay there until morning, saying that the most beautiful women were kept in these places. He did this same thing with boys too—for then, before the time of Philip that is, such a thing was lawful. Sometimes he laughed so loud in the theatre that no one else could be heard by the audience. He could sing and dance, play the pipes, the horn and the pandura, and he also performed on the organ. On one single day, it is said, he visited every prostitute from the Circus, the theatre, the Amphitheatre, and all the public places of Rome, covering his head with a muleteer's cap in order to escape recognition; he did not, however, gratify his passions, but merely gave an aureus to each prostitute, saying as he did so: "Let no one know it, but this is a present from Antoninus." XXXIII. He invented certain new kinds of vice, even going beyond the perverts used by the debauchees of old, and he was well acquainted with all the arrangements of Tiberius, Caligula, and Nero.

The prophecy had been made to him by some Syrian priests that he would die a violent death. And so he had prepared cords entwined with purple and scarlet silk, in order that, if need arose, he could put an end to his life by the noose. He had gold swords, too, in readiness, with which to stab himself, should any violence impend. He also had poisons ready, in ceraunites and sapphires and emeralds, with which to kill himself if destruction threatened. And he also built a very high tower from which to throw himself down, constructed of boards gilded and jewelled in his own presence, for even his death, he declared, should be costly and marked by luxury, in order that it might be said that no one had ever died in this fashion. But all these preparations availed him nothing, for, as we have said, he was slain by common soldiers, dragged through the streets, contemptuously thrust into sewers, and finally cast into the Tiber.

TWENTY-ONE

On the Properties of Foods

GALEN

*Galen of Pergamon (a town on the west coast of what is today Turkey) was the most pro-
lific author of all classical antiquity. That is, more survives by Galen than any other writer,
volumes upon volumes of writings on medicine. He had what was arguably the best job in
the Roman Empire: physician to the emperor himself, Marcus Aurelius, and his successors.
Obviously he had enough time for private practice and for writing as well. His works range
on every imaginable topic related to medicine—surgery, physiology, pharmacy, and even
philosophy. In a nutshell, he was the medical authority of the era, summing up or criticizing
everything that went before and setting the stage for everything that followed. His ideas
were reigning medical orthodoxy for fifteen centuries after his death, and his ideas about
diet lasted even a little longer. There is a simple reason: humoral physiology is simple, easy
to understand, and eminently logical. Although his ideas about food may sound strange to
us today, think of the many random and arbitrary things we are told today by nutritionists.*

PASTRIES

Now is the opportune moment to elaborate on the other sorts of pastries that are made with
wheat flour. What are called griddle cakes by the Athenians, but girdle cakes by Greeks like
me from Asia, are cooked in olive oil. The olive oil is poured into a frying pan which is placed
over a smokeless flame. When the oil is hot, wheat flour kneaded with lots of water is spread

Galen. *Galen on Food and Diet*. Translated by Mark Grant. London: Routledge, 2000, pp. 82–85, 132–34, 188–90.

on top. Fried quickly in the oil, this mixture becomes as firm and thick as the soft cheese that sets in wicker-work baskets. Then the cooks turn it, making what was the top the bottom, so that it comes into contact with the frying pan. When it has been sufficiently fried, they turn it so that the underside is now upperside, and when this has set they turn it two or three times more, until it is certain that the whole cake has been evenly cooked.

This food is, of course, full of thick juices, blocks the bowels and produces undigested fluids. So some people mix in honey with the dough, others sea salt. This is one sort or type (whatever term you want to use) of flat cake which, along with lots of other flat cakes, those living both in the country and the city make in a rough and ready way. All thin cakes that contain no yeast and which are baked in an oven, should be taken out and dipped at once in hot honey so as to saturate them. These are one sort of flat cake, as are all the honey cakes made with wafer biscuits.

WAFER BISCUITS

There are two sorts of wafer biscuits: the superior is called *ryemata,* the inferior *lagana.* Everything made with wafer biscuits and finest wheat flour has thick juices, is slow to pass and liable to obstruct the passages for food in the liver, exacerbates a weak spleen, produces stones in the kidneys, and yet is reasonably nourishing, if it is digested and converted into blood properly. All those things made with honey have a mixed power, since the honey itself has a fine juice and comminutes everything with which it comes into contact.

Understandably everything that absorbs a lot of honey in its manufacture, and which is subjected to longer baking, is less slow to pass, produces a juice that is a combination of thick and thin, and is better for the liver, kidneys and spleen—provided that these organs are in good health—than whatever is prepared without honey. But if these organs are at the initial stage of a blockage, either through inflammation or induration, then the cakes made with honey are no less harmful than those without honey. There are even occasions when they are more harmful, especially with those cakes whose flour is rather sticky. The juice derived from these cakes is not only prevented from moving on because of its thickness, but also furs up the narrow limits of the vessels and causes blockages that are difficult to shift. When the spleen is affected in this way, a feeling of weight is created, which requires the help of attenuating foods and drink. This has been discussed elsewhere in my book *On Attenuating Diet.*

It certainly does not harm the chest or lungs when prepared like this. But I have in turn written about the foods which produce thick and viscous juice. My present argument asks you to commit to memory the other matters which I have gone through up to this point, and especially about the powers of breads, since we use bread all the time. In fact there is nothing wrong in reviewing the main points of what was said about breads.

The best bread in terms of health for someone who is neither young nor does physical exercise is that which contains a lot of yeast, a lot of salt, and has been kneaded for as long as possible by the baker, before being shaped and baked. It is cooked in a moderately hot oven, as has been stated before. Its flavour should be your test as to whether it has too much yeast and salt, because the distress caused by too liberal a mixing of these ingredients means bad bread. So as long as one's taste does not register any unpleasantness from the mixing, it is better to increase the quantities of the ingredients.

REFINED BREAD

Those who have devoted thought to the preparation of refined bread have discovered a food with little nourishment, but it does avoid, as far as is possible, the harm that comes from blockages. This bread is the least thick and viscous, since it is more airy than earthy. Its lightness is observed from its weight and from it not sinking in water, but rather bobbing on the surface like a cork.

Although the people who live in the countryside around me cook large quantities of wheat flour with milk, it should be understood that this food causes blockages. All such foods that contain good juices and are nourishing, harm those who use them constantly, by creating blockages in the liver and generating stones in the kidneys. For when the raw juice acquires viscosity—whenever the passages through the kidneys are in some people by nature rather narrow—whatever is very thick and viscous is ready to generate the sort of scale that forms on pots in which water is heated, and is deposited around stones in many of the waters that are naturally hot. The temperament of the kidneys is a contributory factor, especially when its heat is fiery and sharp.

In this category lies the scale that forms in diseased joints. For everything superfluous always flows into the weakest areas and causes whatever condition is appropriate to the nature of the individual. There will shortly be a discussion on its complete use in the section about milk, just as there will be one on fattening foods, since there are some other foods that contain the same power.

GROATS

Groats are made from a type of wheat. They are fairly nourishing and contain a viscous juice, whether, after being boiled in just water, they are eaten with honey mixed with wine, or with sweet wine or with astringent wine (for each is used at a given time); or whether, they are eaten after being stirred about with olive oil and salt. Sometimes vinegar is also added. Doctors call this recipe groats, adding that the seasoning belongs to barley soup; some suggest that soup from groats nourishes anyone who is ill. But a few of the doctors in the past, like Diocles and Philotimus, gave the name of wheat soup to groats prepared in this way. This is why the term is rarely found in these ancient authors, as for the same reason "spring wheat," because they referred to it by the common term of wheat.

It is stated in the work *On Diet* by Hippocrates that breads made from groats are extremely nutritious, but pass through the body less well; but it is also stated that fine wheat flour and boiled groats are strong and nourishing. So it is right to guard against their excessive use, especially with those whose liver is prone to blockages or who have kidneys that are inclined to generate stones.

It is particularly important to keep an eye on those thin soups made with what are called refined groats. For the juice of groats, when mixed with water, requires considerable boiling. Those preparing it can be deceived: although they think they have boiled it enough, it does in fact cause no little harm to the patients for whom it has been made, because it quickly con-geals and thickens through being glutinous. So it must be mixed with plenty of water, boiled over charcoal and stirred frequently, until it has been properly cooked, at which point some salt should be added. Olive oil does no harm, if it is added at the beginning. But this subsidiary discussion is appropriate for therapy, not for the task now at hand.

Whenever at any time those in good health need a drink for severe stomach ache or the passing of much bile, boil groats for a long time until it becomes soft, then stir it and blend it, so that it resembles strained barley juice, and finally give it to drink. The seasoning is the same as for washed groats.

WHEATS BOILED IN WATER

If I had not at one time eaten wheat boiled in water, I would never have considered there to be any purpose in eating it. For no one, even during a food shortage, would arrive at such a practice, since bread can be made if there is a good supply of wheat. And although chickpeas are eaten at dinner as a side-dish either boiled or fried, as are other seeds prepared in the same way, nobody serves boiled wheat. I would never have expected anyone to have eaten boiled wheat for the following reason.

Once, when I was walking in the countryside far from any city with two young men the same age acting as guides, I came across some peasants who were at that moment making their supper. Their wives were about to make some loaves because they had run out of bread. One of them straightaway poured some wheat into a pot and boiled it. Then, after it was seasoned with a little salt, we were invited to eat. Since we had travelled far and were hungry, it was quite reasonable that we should decide to do this.

So we ate a lot of it, and felt a heaviness in the bowels, as if clay was lying there. Even by the following day it was not digested, so we passed that whole day without food, unable to eat anything because of flatulent bloating, headache and blurred vision. For nothing was passing downwards, which is the sole remedy for indigestion. So I asked the peasants if they ever ate boiled wheat and how they coped with it. They replied that they often ate it through necessity, as we too had been forced on that occasion, and that wheats prepared like this were a heavy and indigestible food.

NUTS

Some people use the term "royal nuts" for the nuts which everyone else today calls simply "walnuts." There are some other nuts called filberts that some people refer to as hazelnuts; they are far smaller than walnuts. Both sorts of nut possess a great deal that is useful, although they do not afford much by way of nourishment to the body, even if there is more nutrition in hazelnuts than in walnuts, since their substance is more compressed and less oily, whilst the walnut is spongier and has more oiliness in it.

For a short time it has a share of astringency, although as time passes this fades away as the whole of its substance changes to an oily juice, until eventually it becomes completely inedible as a result of its oiliness taking on a similar appearance to old olive oil. When green and moist, the walnut has no evident share of astringency or oiliness, but is perhaps rather inert, or what is usually termed watery as I have already said.

The walnut is more digestable than the hazelnut and is better for the stomach, especially when it is eaten with dried figs. Many doctors have written that if both these nuts are eaten with rue before any other food, no great harm will come from noxious drugs.

Clearly whatever is moist is more appropriate for evacuation, whilst whatever is dry is less appropriate. Quite a few people eat these nuts with fish-sauce to help relax their bowels. They are better for this purpose when green, as they then have less of a share of astringency, but when dried and then soaked beforehand in water, as some people do, the power is similar to those that are green.

Almonds

These nuts do not possess much by way of astringency. A cleansing and attenuating quality is prevalent in them, by means of which they purge the inwards and act towards the expectoration of moist matter from the lungs and chest. Some of them have such an overriding power of cutting through thick and viscous moisture that they cannot be eaten because of their bitterness.

They have an element of the fatty and oily quality, just like walnuts, so they too become oily, just like walnuts. This quality in them is less than that of walnuts, so it is only after a longer period of time that they seem to be as oily as walnuts. From these facts it is clear that they are not as useful for purging the stomach, and they afford little nourishment for the body. All nuts that contain a sufficient amount of that overpoweringly bitter quality are extremely useful for the spitting up of matter and of thick and viscous moisture from the lungs and chest.

Among those who do nothing useful in life, but call themselves speakers of Attic Greek, some think it is correct to call this nut feminine, whilst other reckon it is neuter, not realising, as they pit their energies against each other, that both words are written by the Athenians.

Pistachios

These grow in famed Alexandria, but much more so in Beroea in Syria. They do not contain much nourishment, but they are useful for strengthening the liver, as well as purging the juices that block its passages, for they have a quality that is simultaneously bitter, astringent and aromatic. I know that there are many other similar things besides that are good for the liver, as I have shown in my treatise *On Simple Medicines*. I must point out that they offer next to no help or harm to the stomach, just as they neither relax nor constipate the stomach.

PLUMS

When fully ripened this fruit is rarely found to be astringent, sharp or, in short, with any unpleasant quality. Before they reach this state, some display sharpness, others harshness, others bitterness.

The body derives very little nourishment from this fruit, but it is useful for anyone who chooses deliberately to cool and moisten the stomach to a moderate degree, for it relaxes (through being moist and sticky), just like some of the other items I have already mentioned. They can be used even when dried, like figs, and it is the general consensus that the best plums grow in Syria around Damascus; second to these are those that are grown in the Iberian peninsula, otherwise known as Spain. But the Spanish plums reveal no astringency, whilst some Damascus plums exhibit a lot.

The best plums are those that are moderately astringent, large and spongy; any that are small, hard and astringent are bad to eat and bad for the evacuation of the stomach, a characteristic especially of Spanish plums. Boiled in honeyed wine (use a lot of honey for this) they loose the bowels sufficiently, both if eaten on their own, and even more so if the honeyed wine is taken too. It is obvious that drinking sweet wine after eating plums contributes to the evacuation of the bowels, provided that an elapse of time is allowed and lunch is not taken immediately after them. This should be remembered as a basic rule with everything that relaxes the bowels, and just as with rules that are common to other ideas, it should be assumed that there is no need to hear a repeated explanation of them.

JUJUBES

I do not have any information about jujubes that testifies either to their preserving health or to their curing diseases. They are a food for women and little children, since they provide little nourishment, and are at the same time both hard to digest and not very good for the stomach. It is obvious that they furnish the body with hardly any nourishment.

CAROBS

The carob (*ceration*), whose third syllable is spoken and written with the letter t, looks nothing like the cherry (*cerasia*) with an s, since it is a food that is woody and full of bad juices; consequently it is difficult to digest, for nothing that is woody is easy to digest. Since it does not pass through the body quickly, it is furnished with considerable bad qualities. So it would be better if these fruits were not exported from the areas in the east where they are grown.

CAPERS

These are shrubby plants that grow mainly in Cyprus. Their power is generally composed of fine particles, with the result that they afford hardly any nourishment to those who eat them, as is the case with all the other foods that are made up of fine particles. I use the fruit of these plants more as a medicine than as a food. These fruits are brought to where I live sprinkled with salt because they rot when left on their own.

So they evidently contain more nourishment when still green and not yet pickled, for in the pickling process they become completely neutralised and devoid of nutrition (unless the salt is rinsed off), but they do relax the bowels. When used as a food—after being washed and soaked until the salt has gone completely—they furnish very little nourishment; but as an accompaniment to bread and as a medicine they are ideal for whetting a jaded appetite, cleansing the stomach and bringing up phlegm, and for purging blockages of the spleen and liver.

In these instances they should be taken before all other foods, with vinegar and honey or oil and vinegar. The tender shoots of the caper plant are also eaten in the same way as terebinth shoots when still green, seasoned with vinegar and brine like terebinth shoots.

WINE

Everyone agrees that wine is among that which nourishes; and if everything nourishing is a food, it must be said that wine too should be classed as a food. Some doctors, however, state that there is no need to call wine a food; certainly drink, which also goes under the name of beverage, is distinguished logically in speech from food, just as food is also called victuals, provender and edibles. These are therefore the reasons why they do not think it correct to call wine a food, although they do agree that it is nutritious, which is all I need at the moment.

If they believe that certain other substances are nourishing, but refuse to call them foods, I could summarise all their learning in just one book. But as it is only wine that they are unhappy about calling a food, although it is nutritious, they allow me to add to this work on foods a brief note about wines, because those powers that Hippocrates mentioned in his book *Diet in Acute Diseases* belong to medicine rather than food. I in fact explained those powers in the third part of my commentary on that book and in my *On the Therapeutic Method* and *Hygiene*. In this present work I am going to talk about the differences in their nutrition, beginning as follows.

Of all the wines the red and thick are most suited for the production of blood, because they require little change before turning into it, whilst after these come wines that are dark, sweet and thick, then those that are red and dark in colour, but thick in consistency and containing something of an astringent quality. White wines that are at the same time thick and astringent are less able to nourish than these. The least nourishing of all are wines that are white in colour, but thin in consistency and almost resembling the water that is needed for what is called honey-water.

That thick wines are more nutritious than thin wines is revealed by their natural quality and reinforced through experience of them. Sweet wines are digested more easily in the stomach and are better assimilated than harsh wines because they are hotter in power. Thick wines are digested very much more slowly, and the same is true for their assimilation, but if they meet with a stomach strong enough to digest them properly, they furnish the body with plenty of nourishment. It is obvious that their superiority in nutrition over thinner wines is matched by their inferiority in micturition.

PICKLED FOODS OMITTED FROM THE PREVIOUS BOOK

I have put off talking about pickled and average foods until the end of this book. So in case these should be omitted, it is the right moment now to run through each of their powers.

Animal carcasses are suitable for pickling, provided they have hard, and at the same time excrementitious, flesh. What I mean by "excrementitious" is, as I said in the previous book, flesh that has phlegmatic moisture diffused in it. The greater the quantity and thickness of this moisture, the better the flesh becomes when pickled.

Anything which has a constitution that is either completely soft or is absolutely dry and without superfluity is not suitable for pickling. For the power of salt, as has been shown in my treatise *On Simple Medicines,* is such as to dissipate, through attenuation and absorption, excessive moisture in those bodies with which it has contact. Whilst nitron-foam and porous sodium-carbonate have the ability to attenuate and disperse, they are unable to draw together or make firm.

So all bodies that are naturally dry become inedible when sprinkled with salt for preserving. Anyone can test this by pickling hare and producing what looks like preserved weasel. The flesh of plump pigs in their prime is ideal for pickling, but two extremes should be avoided, namely the dryness of old pigs and the excessive moistness of sucking pigs; for just as dry bodies become like leather when pickled, so the opposite is true, that when too much moisture is flowing, the meat dissolves and resembles salt.

It is for this reason, then, that all fish with soft flesh and without anything excrementitious—such as those called rock fish and the poutassou from a clean sea—are suitable for pickling. Corb, grey mullet and tuna, as well as pilchard, sardine and what are called Spanish mackerel are suitable for pickling. Sea creatures like whales are better for pickling since they have excrementitious flesh. The worst for pickling are red mullets because their flesh is dry without anything superfluous.

It is clear from this that anything hard, sinewy, resembling skin and leathery is very difficult to digest when pickled. Whatever possesses the opposite composition is made up of fine parts and thins thick and glutinous juices. The best of these in my experience are the pickled fish which were called Sardinian by doctors in the past, but which people now call "sardine," and grey mullets which are exported from the Black Sea. In second place after these come corb, tuna and Spanish mackerel.

AVERAGE FOODS

In each of the categories of foods that I have said exist, there are some foods that are average. For among those that have hard flesh and those that have soft flesh one can find some midway between those that have neither soft nor hard flesh, and the same is true for foods which are thinning and fattening, heating and cooling and drying and moistening.

Foods that are suitable for animals to eat to maintain their natural temperament without any problem are all those which match their constitution, whilst useful nutrition for animals with a bad temperament either at the outset or from subsequent acquisition, is not what matches their temperament, but what is contrary to their temperament. For whatever is by nature faultless is safeguarded by what is like, whilst whatever is poorly composed is led to its proper state by what is opposite. So there will be a special balance in the nature of every animal, for example one for humans, one for dogs and one for each of the other animals. For humans there is, in turn, a particular balance according to the time of life and another—especially with the contrasts in the way of life—according to race and the place where they have for most part lived.

PART III

Study Questions

1. Judging from Cato, what were Romans like in the early republican period? What kind of reader was he addressing?
2. How did Romans flaunt their wealth and sophistication through food, and when was this seen as something distasteful?
3. Do you think Apicius's recipes were merely intended for shock value, or are we merely judging them with modern eyes and palates?
4. Compare Juvenal's simple, rustic aesthetic with present-day advocates of natural, local, and even Slow Food. Why do preferences like these appear both then and now?
5. If Aelius Lampridius's biography of the dissolute emperor is a kind of political slander, consider how reports of what rulers eat can be used to promote or tarnish the reputation of a leader.

PART FOUR

Imperial China

Chinese civilization and its food traditions are the longest lived on earth, stretching from the advent of agriculture to the present. Only slightly after the Neolithic Revolution occurred in the Middle East, the Chinese had domesticated the pig, millet, and eventually rice as civilization sprung up around the Yangtze and Yellow Rivers. Later, water buffalo were used for traction, and chickens arrived from the south. During the Zhou Dynasty, starting around 1000, China became a proper empire, iron was used for farming and cooking implements, and the soy bean was cultivated on a wide scale. Perhaps most importantly, the Zhou built up a bureaucracy of administrators who connected the imperial court to outlying feudal dependencies. This way court culture and its arts, music, and cooking were spread throughout the empire.

Around 500 B.C., K'ung Fu Tzu (known in the West as Confucius) introduced a novel philosophy of maintaining order and harmony that also directly influenced Chinese manners and eating habits. The key to peace is that every individual knows his or her place in a rigid hierarchy. All inferiors obey their superiors, and the powerful take care of their dependents. This occurs at the level of the state but also within each household; children obey parents, and younger sons obey the older. This is the principle of filial piety. Confucian thought also stipulated that as a way to avoid misunderstanding or conflict, life would be governed by strict rules of protocol and deference. The proper way of addressing superiors was important, as were rules for eating politely in ways that are not threatening. Hence, knives were banished from the table, and people ate with chopsticks. Food was cut into manageable portions, and elders were served before subordinates. This deference to elders and extended households was probably also key to the longevity of this culinary tradition.

There is a practical reason for cutting up food before cooking: it cooks much faster. To facilitate this kind of cooking, the wok was invented. Although the earliest iron ones have disintegrated, clay copies survive that attest to the great antiquity of this technology. It was during the Han Dynasty, roughly concurrent with the Roman Empire, that the empire truly expanded; it was, in fact, connected to Rome via trade. Feeding its cities required enormous levels of organization as well as what might be called a kind of agricultural extension service. New crops were consciously tested, manuals and agricultural guidebooks were published, public irrigation works were initiated, and relief systems were created to mitigate famine. The manual of Sheng-Chih describes multiple cropping, irrigating rice fields with recirculating water to keep them cooler in the summer, and cultivating hillsides with ridges.

New food technologies were also developed, such as fermenting soy to create *jiang*, a paste from which soy sauce is derived. Its importance is that soy becomes more nutritious when fermented, and, with a grain staple, provides a nutritious diet that need not be based on meat. Gun powder, compasses, and porcelain are just a few of the other technologies invented during this period.

Chinese medicine also flourished at this time, as recorded in the *Yellow Emperor's Classic*. Superficially similar to the humoral system, the Chinese system begins with two fundamental interdependent forces in the universe—yin and yang—and food can be described as increasing one or the other. There are also five, not exactly elements, but rather phases that explain transformations in nature and within the body. These are earth, fire, wood, metal and water. They are described as phases because one becomes another, as when water makes trees grow, wood burned creates fire, fire creates ash, ash is like earth, earth is the source of metals, and metals flow like water when heated. These five phases govern metabolic processes, as does chi, a force that can be heightened or decreased by particular foods, medicines, or activities. The proper flow of chi is also essential to health, and acupuncture essentially opens up the internal pathways to facilitate its flow. In any case, diet is central to the holistic conception of health in the Chinese system, and a remarkably complex pharmacopoeia accompanies it should the body fall out of balance.

Chinese civilization also flourished under the Tang Dynasty from the 600s to 900s, when extensive contacts were made with the Abbasid court in Baghdad. Foods such as grapes, spinach, lettuce, almonds, pistachios, figs, and dates traveled along the silk routes. These were also written about in the *Food Canons*, which describe the plants grown in imperial gardens and their properties. Wine, milk products, and flatbreads were consumed as curiosities, but it was during this period that tea became the drink of choice, and elaborate rituals were devised for its consumption. Lu Yu's *Book of Tea* is the classic.

Following a long period of Mongol overlordship, the Ming Dynasty (1348–1644) reasserted control of the empire and revived forms of etiquette and classic Chinese cookery. Beijing became the new capital, and a huge Forbidden City was built housing palace servants, eunuchs, and, of course, cooks to feed the court. Yuan Mei's *Suiyuan Shindan* and the Gao Lian's *Discourse on Food and Drink* were both composed in this era.

TWENTY-TWO

The I-Li (Yili) or Book of Etiquette and Ceremonial

The I-Li *is a classic Confucian etiquette manual prescribing proper behavior in all circumstances, from within families to state occasions. This selection describes merely one part of a formal banquet held by a duke, and every single move is orchestrated. It was compiled during the Han Dynasty, though it may date back several centuries earlier. Consider the purpose of formally prescribing every move, especially in a society prone to warfare, but trying to preserve peace within. Deference to superiors is intended to maintain tranquility at every level of society.*

THE BANQUET

At the conclusion of an audience the Duke sends a retainer to apprise those who are invited to take part in the banquet. The court steward prepares all the viands for the use of the various officials, to the east of the private apartments. The musicians suspend the bells and the musical stones. The used-water jar and cup-basket are set to the south-east of the east steps, and abreast the eastern rain-gutter. The jar of water is placed to the east of it, and the cup-basket to the west, all squarely south. The Duke's cup-basket is placed to the north of them, and faces west.

The keeper of the sacrificial vessels places the wine-holder to the west of the eastern pillar. This consists of two square-mouthed vases, in the left of which is the "dark wine," and they are graded from the south. The wine-holder for the Duke consists of a pair of earthenware

John Steele, trans. *The I-Li or Book of Etiquette and Ceremonial*. London: Probsthain, 1917, pp. 122–49.

pots, with stands covered with fine or coarse cloth, according to the season. These covers are placed to the south of the wine-holders, and graded from the south. The holder from which the wine for the ordinary officers and that to be used at the general feasting is taken is placed to the west of the door, and consists of a pair of round-necked vases.

The keeper of the vessels then lays the mat for the principal guest to the west of the door of the room, with its head to the east, but with no second mat on it. The captain of the archers announces that all is ready. Then a retainer lays the Duke's mat at the head of the eastern steps, facing westward, spreading it in several layers. Then the Duke ascends the steps, and goes to his place on the mat, sitting with his face westward.

Then a retainer receives the ministers and great officers, who all enter by the right of the door, and stand inside it, with their faces north, and graded from the east. The ordinary officers stand in the western part, facing east, and graded from the north. The liturgist and the recorder stand to the east of the door, and east also of the others, facing north, and graded from the east. One of the retainers takes his stand below the eastern side hall, facing south, and the ordinary officers who are to take part in the general feasting stand west of the door and face north, graded from the east.

The Duke then descends, and, standing to the south-east of the eastern steps, and looking south, invites the ministers to draw near, whereupon they move round and settle themselves, facing west, and graded from the north. Then the Duke does the same to the great officers, and they all advance a little.

Appointing the Principal Guest and the Manager

Then the captain of the archers invites the Duke to name the principal guest, and he says: "Let So-and-so have the honour." This appointment the captain of archers conveys to the principal guest, and he, advancing a little, formally declines, this being reported to the Duke. Then the captain recommunicates the Duke's appointment, and the guest kowtows twice and accepts, this being reported to the Duke by the captain. Then the principal guest goes out the door and stands, facing east.

Thereafter the Duke salutes the ministers and great officers, who all ascend the steps and go to their mats. Then the retainer, standing below the east steps and facing north, asks the Duke to name the men who shall be the cover-holders, and thereafter to say who shall act as the Duke's waiter. He then gives orders to the cover-lifters, and they, going up by the west steps, stand to the south of the wine-holder, facing north, and graded from the east. Thereafter the Duke's steward invites the Duke to name those who shall serve the dainties to the feudal Dukes and ministers.

[The Principal Guest arrives next.]

The Master of Ceremonies Offers Wine to the Principal Guest

The Master of Ceremonies goes down to wash a cup, and stands, facing north-west, to the south of the used-water jar. Then the principal guest descends, and, at the west of the western steps, faces east. The Master of Ceremonies excuses himself the honour of his company, and the guest replies suitably. Then the Master of Ceremonies, facing north, washes his hands, and, sitting down, takes the drinking-cup and washes it. The guest advances slightly and declines the honour, and the Master of Ceremonies, sitting, places the drinking-cup in the cup-basket, and, rising, responds in suitable fashion, whereupon the guest returns to his place. Then the Master of Ceremonies finishes the washing, and the guest, with a salute, ascends, the Master of Ceremonies ascending also. The guest bows in acknowledgment of the washing, and the Master of Ceremonies, at the guest's right side, lays down the drinking-cup and responds with a bow.

Then the Master of Ceremonies descends and washes his hands, the guest descending also, and the Master of Ceremonies excusing himself the honour, the guest making a suitable reply. When the washing of hands is finished, the guest salutes and ascends, the Master of Ceremonies following him, sitting down, and taking the drinking-cup. Thereupon the cover-holder lifts the cover, and the Master of Ceremonies ladles out the wine from the Duke's wine-holder, the cover-holder replacing the cover.

Then the Master of Ceremonies, in front of the guest's mat, offers wine to him, and he, at the top of the western steps, bows, and, going forward, receives the cup in front of his mat, and returns to his place. The Master of Ceremonies, to the right of the guest, bows, inviting him to drink. Then the court steward brings forward the dried flesh and hash, and, when the guest has gone to his mat, the steward sets out the stand of dismembered joints.

Whereupon the guest sits, and, taking the cup in his left hand, makes an offering of the relishes with his right, afterwards laying down the cup to the right of the relishes. He then gets up, takes the lung for sacrificing, and, sitting down, cuts off the end and offers it, thereafter tasting the lung, rising and placing it on the stand. Then he sits, wipes his hands, and, taking the cup, pours a libation of the wine, gets up, sits at the end of the mat, and sips the wine, leaves the mat, and, sitting, lays down the cup, and bows in acknowledgment of the excellent quality of the wine, takes the cup, and rises, the Master of Ceremonies replying to him with a bow.

Then the guest sits down at the top of the western steps, with his face to the north, and washes the cup, rises, sits again, and, laying down the cup, bows, the host responding likewise.

The Guest Toasts the Host

The guest takes the empty cup down to wash it, and the Master of Ceremonies goes down also. The guest sits to the south of the used-water jar, and, laying down the cup, rises, and, going forward a little, declines the honour of his company, the host facing east and responding suitably. The guest then sits down, and, taking the drinking-cup, lays it at the foot of the cup-basket, and, after washing his hands, washes it. The Master of Ceremonies excuses himself the honour of this washing, and the guest sits, laying the cup in the basket, rises, replies, and finishes the washing. When he gets to the foot of the steps in going up again, he salutes the Master of Ceremonies, and ascends. The Master of Ceremonies then ascends and bows, acknowledging the honour of the washing with the same ceremonial that the guest used.

Then the guest descends and washes his hands, the Master of Ceremonies descending also, and the guest declining the honour. When the hand-washing is finished, the guest salutes, ascends, ladles out wine from the Duke's holder, the cover-holder lifting the cover as before. He then takes the cup and toasts the Master of Ceremonies at the head of the western steps.

The Master of Ceremonies, facing northward, bows as he receives the cup, and the guest, at the left side of the Master of Ceremonies, bows as he invites him to drink.

The Master of Ceremonies sits and pours a libation, but neither tastes the wine nor bows his thanks for it nor praises its quality, but finishes off the cup, rises, sits, lays down the cup, bows, takes the cup, and rises. The guest replies with a bow, but the Master of Ceremonies does not acknowledge the honour done to the wine, and, taking the empty cup, goes down and lays it in the basket. The guest then descends and stands to the west of the western steps. Then the captain of the archers takes the guest up again, and he ascends and stands at the inner side of the west inner wall, with his face to the east.

[The Banquet continues with many more drinking ceremonies, toasts, music, and further formalities involved in drinking wine, plus slaughtering and cooking a dog.]

TWENTY-THREE

Book of Rites

LI JI

Li Ji's Book of Rites *is also a text on etiquette, but it goes into much greater detail about specific dishes that would have been served at formal meals of the Zhou Dynasty. In a period of turmoil, the original texts were burned (in 213 B.C.) along with many other classics, but they were recompiled from memory and later formed a regular part of the material required to be known for state examinations well into the modern era.*

21. Of grain food, there were millet, the glutinous rice, rice, maize, the white millet, and the yellow maize, cut when ripe, or when green.

Of prepared meats, there were beef soup, mutton soup, pork soup, and roast beef; pickle, slices of beef, pickle and minced beef; roast mutton, slices of mutton, pickle, and roast pork; pickle, slices of pork, mustard sauce, and minced fish; pheasant, hare, quail, and partridge.

22. Of drinks, there was must in two vessels, one strained, the other unstrained, made of rice, of millet, or of maize. In some cases, thin preparations were used as beverages, as millet gruel, pickle, with water syrup of prunes, and of steeped rice; clear wine and white.

Of confections, there were dried cakes, and rice-flour scones.

23. For relishes, snail-juice and a condiment of the broad-leaved water-squash were used with pheasant soup; a condiment of wheat with soups of dried slices and of fowl; broken glutinous rice with dog soup and hare soup; the rice-balls mixed with these soups had no smart-weed in them.

Li Ji. *Li Chi: Book of Rites*. Hyde Park, NY: University Books, 1964, pp. 59–64, 468–707.

A sucking-pig was stewed, wrapped up in sonchus leaves and stuffed with smart-weed; a fowl, with the same stuffing, and along with pickle sauce; a fish, with the same stuffing and egg sauce; a tortoise, with the same stuffing and pickle sauce.

For meat spiced and dried they placed the brine of ants; for soup made of sliced meat, that of hare; for a ragout of elk, that of fish; for minced fish, mustard sauce; for raw elk flesh, pickle sauce; for preserved peaches and plums, egg-like suet.

24. All condiments for grain food were of a character corresponding to the spring; for soup, to the summer; for sauces, to the autumn; and for beverages, to the winter.

In all attempering ingredients, sour predominated in the spring; bitter, in the summer; acrid, in the autumn; and salt, in the winter:—with the due proportioning of the unctuous and sweet.

The glutinous rice (was thought) to suit beef; millet, to suit mutton; glutinous millet, to suit pork; maize, to suit dog; wheat, to suit goose; and the broad-leaved squash, to suit fish.

25. Lamb and sucking-pig were (thought to be) good in spring, fried with odorous (beef) suet; dried pheasant and fish, in summer, fried with the strong-smelling suet (of dog); veal and fawn, in autumn, fried with strong suet (of fowl); fresh fish and goose, in winter, fried with the frouzy suet (of goat).

26. There were dried beef, and dried stalks of deer's flesh, of wild pig's, of elk's, and of the muntjac's. Elk's flesh, deer's, wild pig's, and muntjac's, was (also eaten uncooked; and) cut in large leaf-like slices. Pheasants and hares were (made into soup) with the duck-weed. There were sparrows and finches, partridges, cicadas, bees, lichens, small chestnuts, the water-caltrops, the hovenia dulcis, the zizyphus, chestnuts, hazel-nuts, persimmons, cucumbers, peaches, plums, ballaces, almonds, haws, pears, ginger, and cinnamon.

27. If a Great officer, at his ordinary meals, had mince, he did not have, at the same time, dried slices of meat; and if he had the latter, he did not have the former. An ordinary officer did not have two kinds of soup, or sliced flesh. (But) old men of the common people, did not eat their meat alone without accompaniments.

28. Mince was made in spring, with onions; in autumn, with the mustard plant. Sucking-pig was used in spring, with scallions; in autumn, with smart-weed. With lard they used onions; with fat, chives. With the three victim-animals they used pepper, and employed pickle as an accompaniment. For wild animals' flesh they used plums. In quail soup, fowl soup, and with the curlew, the condiment was smart-weed. Bream and tench were steamed; pullets, roasted; and pheasants, (boiled), with fragrant herbs and no smart-weed.

29. Things not eaten were the turtle, when hatching; the intestines of the wolf, which were removed, as also the kidneys of the dog; the straight spine of the wild cat; the rump of the hare; the head of the fox; the brains of the sucking-pig; the yî-like bowels of fish; and the perforated openings of the turtle.

30. (Bones and sinews) were taken from the flesh; the scales were scraped from fish; dates were made to appear as new; chestnuts were selected; peaches were made smooth; kâ and pears had the insects drilled out of them.

31. When an ox lowed at night, its flesh was (considered) to be rank; that of a sheep, whose long hair showed a tendency to get matted, to be frouzy; that of a dog which was uneasy and with (the inside of) its thighs red, to be coarse; that of birds when moulting and with their voices hoarse, to be fetid; that of pigs, when they looked upwards and closed their eyes, to be measly; that of a horse, black along the spine and with piebald fore-legs, to smell unpleasantly.

A pullet, whose tail could not be grasped by the hand, was not eaten, nor the rump of a tame goose, nor the ribs of a swan or owl, nor the rump of a tame duck, nor the liver of a fowl, nor the kidneys of a wild goose, nor the gizzard of the wild goose without the hind-toe, nor the stomach of the deer.

32. Flesh cut small was made into mince; cut into slices it was made into hash. Some say that the flesh of elks, deer, and fish was pickled; that of muntjacs also, being cut in small pieces; that of fowls and wild pigs, in larger pieces; of hares, the stomach was pickled. Onions and scallions were mixed with the brine to soften the meat.

33. Soup and boiled grain were used by all, from the princes down to the common people, without distinction of degree. Great officers did not regularly have savoury meat, but when seventy they had their cupboards. The cupboards of the son of Heaven were five on the right (of the dining hall), and five on the left; those of dukes, marquises, and earls were five, all in one room; those of Great officers three (in a side chamber), and other officers had one on their buffet.

[. . .]

4. For the Rich Fry, they put the pickled meat fried over rice that had been grown on a dry soil, and then enriched it with melted fat. This was called the Rich Fry.

5. For the Similar Fry, they put the pickled meat fried over the millet grains, and enriched it with melted fat. This was called the Similar Fry.

6. For the Bake, they took a sucking-pig or a (young) ram, and having cut it open and removed the entrails, filled the belly with dates. They then wrapped it round with straw and reeds, which they plastered with clay, and baked it. When the clay was all dry, they broke it off. Having washed their hands for the manipulation, they removed the crackling and macerated it along with rice-flour, so as to form a kind of gruel which they added to the pig. They then fried the whole in such a quantity of melted fat as to cover it. Having prepared a large pan of hot water, they placed in it a small tripod, which was filled with fragrant herbs, and the slices of the creature which was being prepared. They took care that the hot water did not cover this tripod, but kept up the fire without intermission for three days and nights. After this, the whole was served up with the addition of pickled meat and vinegar.

7. For the Pounded Delicacy, they took the flesh of ox, sheep, elk, deer and muntjac, a part of that which lay along the spine, the same in quantity of each, and beat it now as it lay flat, and then turning it on its side; after that they extracted all the nerves. (Next), when it was sufficiently cooked, they brought it (from the pan), took away the outside crust, and softened the meat (by the addition of pickle and vinegar).

8. For the Steeped Delicacy, they took the beef, which was required to be that of a newly killed animal, and cut it into small pieces, taking care to obliterate all the lines in it. It was then steeped from one morning to the next in good wine, when it was eaten with pickle, vinegar, or the juice of prunes.

9. To make the Grill, they beat the beef and removed the skinny parts. They then laid it on a frame of reeds, sprinkled on it pieces of cinnamon and ginger, and added salt. It could be eaten thus when dried. Mutton was treated in the same way as beef, and also the flesh of elk, deer, and muntjac. If they wished the flesh wet, they added water and fried it with pickled meat. If they wished it dry, they ate it as eaten (at first).

10. For the (Soup) Balls, they took equal quantities of beef, mutton and pork, and cut them small. Then they took grains of rice, which they mixed with the finely cut meat, two parts of rice to one of meat, and formed cakes or balls, which they fried.

11. For the Liver and Fat, they took a dog's liver, and wrapped it round with its own fat. They then wet it and roasted it, and took it in this condition and scorched it. No smartweed was mixed with the fat.

12. They took the grains of rice and steeped them in prepared rice-water. They then cut small the fat from a wolf's breast, and with it and the grains of rice made a fry.

TWENTY-FOUR

The Yellow Emperor's Classic of Internal Medicine

HUANGDI

This medical text formed the cornerstone of a medical tradition stretching across several millennia. The Yellow Emperor Huangdi is a semimythical figure said to have lived from 2697 to 2597 B.C. and was regarded as the inventor of Chinese civilization. The text was probably composed somewhere between the Warring States period and the Han Dynasty, which means that it is contemporaneous with the Hippocratic corpus and Galen, and it held a comparable stature in Eastern medicine. It is in the form of a dialogue between the emperor and one of his court physicians. Like the ritual texts above, this was required knowledge for all medical practitioners who were licensed by the state.

1. TREATISE ON THE NATURAL TRUTH IN ANCIENT TIMES

In ancient times when the Yellow Emperor was born he was endowed with divine talents; while yet in early infancy he could speak; while still very young he was quick of apprehension and penetrating; when he was grown up he was sincere and comprehending; when he became perfect he ascended to Heaven.

The Yellow Emperor once addressed T'ien Shih, the divinely inspired teacher: "I have heard that in ancient times the people lived (through the years) to be over a hundred years, and yet they remained active and did not become decrepit in their activities. But nowadays people reach only half of that age and yet become decrepit and failing. Is it because the world

Huangdi. *The Yellow Emperor's Classic of Internal Medicine*. Translated by Ilza Veith. Berkeley: University of California Press, 2002, pp. 97–98, 147–48, 198–207.

changes from generation to generation? Or is it that mankind is becoming negligent (of the laws of nature)?"

Ch'i Po answered: "In ancient times those people who understood Tao [the way of self cultivation] patterned themselves upon the Yin and the Yang [the two principles in nature] and they lived in harmony with the arts of divination.

"There was temperance in eating and drinking. Their hours of rising and retiring were regular and not disorderly and wild. By these means the ancients kept their bodies united with their souls, so as to fulfill their allotted span completely, measuring unto a hundred years before they passed away.

"Nowadays people are not like this; they use wine as beverage and they adopt recklessness as usual behaviour. They enter the chamber (of love) in an intoxicated condition; their passions exhaust their vital forces; their cravings dissipate their true (essence); they do not know how to find contentment within themselves; they are not skilled in the control of their spirits. They devote all their attention to the amusement of their minds, thus cutting themselves off from the joys of long (life). Their rising and retiring is without regularity. For these reasons they reach only one half of the hundred years and then they degenerate."

12. THE DIFFERENT METHODS OF TREATMENT AND THE APPROPRIATE PRESCRIPTIONS

The Yellow Emperor asked: "When the physicians treat diseases, do they treat each disease differently from the others and can they all be healed?"

Ch'i Po answered: "Yes, they can all be healed according to the physical features of the place where one lives.

"Beginning and creation come from the East. Fish and salt are the products of water and ocean and of the shores near the water. The people of the regions of the East eat fish and crave salt; their living is tranquil and their food delicious. Fish causes people to burn within (thirst), and the eating of salt injures (defeats) the blood. Therefore the people of these regions are all of dark complexion and careless and lax in their principles. Their diseases are ulcers, which are most properly treated with acupuncture by means of a needle of flint. Thus the treatment with acupuncture with a needle of flint has its origin in the regions of the East.

"Precious metals and jade come from the regions of the West. The dwellings in the West are built of pebbles and sandstone. Nature (Heaven and Earth) exerts itself to bring a good harvest. The people of these regions live on hills and, because of the great amount of wind, water, and soil, become robust and energetic. The people of these regions wear no clothes other than those of coarse woolen stuff or coarse matting. They eat good and variegated food and therefore they are flourishing and fertile. Hence evil cannot injure their external bodies, and if they get diseases they strike at the inner body. These diseases are most successfully cured with poison medicines. Thus the treatment with poison medicines comes from the West.

"The North is the region of storing and laying by. The country is hilly and mountainous, there are biting cold winds, frost and ice. The people of these regions find pleasure in living in this wilderness, and they live on milk products. The extreme cold causes many diseases. These diseases are most fittingly treated with cauterization by burning the dried tinder of the artemisia (moxa). Hence the treatment with cauterization has its origin in the regions of the North.

"Nourishment and growth come from the South. The Sun makes the life of those who live in the regions of the South plentiful and nourishing. Although there is water beneath the earth, the soil is deficient, (but) it collects dew and mist. The people who live in the regions of the South crave sour food and curd. They are secretive and soft in their ways and attached to the red color. Their diseases are bent and contracted muscles and numbness. These diseases are most fittingly treated with acupuncture with fine needles. Hence the treatment with the nine needles comes from the South.

"The region of the center, the Earth, is level and moist. Everything that is created by the Universe meets in the center and is absorbed by the Earth. The people of the regions of the center eat mixed food and do not (suffer or weary at their) toil. Their diseases are many: they suffer from complete paralysis and chills and fever. These diseases are most fittingly treated with breathing exercises, massage of skin and flesh, and exercises of hands and feet. Hence the treatment with breathing exercises, massage and exercises of the limbs has its origin in the center regions.

"The ancient sages combined these various treatments for the purpose of cure, and each patient received the treatment that was most fitting for him. These treatments were so extraordinary and so different in each case that all diseases were healed. Thus the circumstances and needs of each disease were ascertained and the principle of the art of healing became known."

22. TREATISE ON THE SEASONS AS PATTERNS OF THE VISCERA

The Yellow Emperor said: "In order to bring into harmony the human body one takes as standard the laws of the four seasons and the five elements. This method serves as a regulator to man, [no matter] whether he is obedient or whether he is in opposition (to these laws), whether he is successful or whether he suffers failure. I desire further enlightenment in this matter."

Ch'i Po replied: "The five elements are metal, wood, water, fire, and earth. Their changes, their increasing value, their increasing depreciation and worthlessness serve to give knowledge of death and life and they serve to determine success and failure. They determine the strength of the five viscera, and establish their important division according to the four seasons and their dates of life and death."

The Emperor said: "I desire complete information about all this."

Ch'i Po answered: "The liver rules over Spring. The [region of the] 'absolute Yin' and the lesser Yang within the foot control the treatment and cure. The days of Spring are those of the celestial stems *chia i*. When the liver suffers from an acute attack one should quickly eat sweet (food) in order to calm it down.

"The heart rules over the Summer. The [region of the] lesser Yin and the region of the great Yang control the treatment and cure. The days of Summer are those of the celestial stems *ping ting*. When the heart suffers from tardiness, one should quickly eat sour (food) which has an astringent effect.

"The spleen rules over the long Summer. The regions of the great Yin and the [regions of] 'sunlight' within the foot control the treatment and the cure. The days of the long Summer are those of the celestial stems *wu chi*. When the spleen suffers from moisture one should quickly eat bitter food which has a drying effect.

"The lungs rule over Fall. The [region of the] great Yin and the region of 'sunlight' within the hands control the treatment and cure. The days of Fall are those of the celestial stems *kêng hsin*. When the lungs suffer from the obstruction of the upper respiratory tract, one should quickly eat bitter (food) which will disperse the obstruction and restore the flow.

"The kidneys rule over Winter. The [region of the] lesser Yin and the region of the great Yang control the treatment and cure. The days of Winter are those of the celestial stems *jên kuei*. When the kidneys suffer from dryness, one should quickly eat pungent food which will moisten them. It will open the pores and will bring about a free circulation of the saliva and the fluid secretions.

"Disease of the liver should be healed in Summer. When it is not healed in Summer it will become graver in Fall; when death does not strike in Fall it can be warded off in Winter. But (the disease) will arise again in Spring and then one should strictly avoid exposure to the winds.

"Those who suffer from diseases of the liver should be cured during the period of the celestial stems *ping ting*. When the improvement has not taken place during the period of *ping ting*, it will be the same during the period of the celestial stems *kêng hsin*. When then death does not strike during the period of *kêng hsin*, it can be warded off during the period of the celestial stems *jên kuei*. But the disease arises again during the period of *chia i*.

"Those who have a disease of the liver are animated and quick-witted in the early morning. Their spirits are heightened in the evening and at midnight they are calm and quiet. When the liver (is sick) it has the tendency to disintegrate. Then one should quickly eat pungent food which dispels this tendency. One uses pungent food in connection with the liver in order to supplement its function and to stop leaks, and one uses sour food in order to drain and expel.

"When the disease is located within the heart it should improve during the long Summer. If it does not improve during the long Summer, it becomes graver in Winter. If in Winter death does not follow, it can be warded off in Spring; but the disease will arise again in Summer. Then one should avoid eating hot food and wearing clothes that produce heat.

"Those who suffer from a disease of the heart should be cured during the period of the celestial stems *wu chi*. When the improvement has not taken place during the period of *wu chi*, it will be the same in the period of *jên kuei*; and when death does not strike during the period of the celestial stems *jên kuei*, it can be warded off during the period of the celestial stems *chia i*. But the disease arises again during the period of the celestial stems *ping ting*.

"Those who suffer from a sick heart are animated and quick-witted at noon, around midnight their spirits are heightened, and in the early morning they are peaceful and quiet. A (sick) heart has the tendency to soften and to weaken. Then one should quickly eat salty food to make the heart pliable. One uses salty food in connection with the heart in order to supplement and to strengthen it, and one uses sweet food in order to drain and to dispel.

"When the disease is located within the spleen it should improve during Fall. If it does not improve during Fall it becomes graver in Spring. If in Spring death does not follow, it can be warded off in Summer; but (the disease) will arise again in the period of the long Summer. One should avoid eating warm food and eating to repletion; one should keep off swampy land and one should not wear damp clothing.

"Those who suffer from a disease of the spleen should be cured during the period of the celestial stems *kêng hsin*. If it does not improve during the period of the celestial stems *kêng hsin*, it will be the same in the period of the celestial stems *chia i*. And when death does not strike during the period of *chia i*, it can be warded off during the period of the celestial stems *ping ting*, but then the disease will arise again during the period of *wu chi*.

"Those who suffer from a disease of the spleen are animated and quick-witted around sunset, their spirits are heightened around sunrise and towards evening they become quiet and calm. A (sick) spleen has the tendency to work tardily and lazily; then one should quickly eat sweet food to set it at ease. One uses bitter food to drain the spleen and one uses sweet food to supplement and to strengthen it.

"When the disease is located within the lungs it should improve during Winter. If it does not improve during Winter it will become more serious in Summer. If death does not follow in Summer, it can be warded off during the period of the long Summer evenings, but the disease will again arise in Fall. One should avoid eating and drinking cold things and one should not wear chilly clothing.

"Those who suffer from a disease of the lungs should be cured during the period of the celestial stems *jên kuei*. If the disease does not improve during this period, it will be the same during the period of the celestial stems *ping ting*. And when death does not follow during the period of *ping ting*, it can be warded off during the period of *wu chi*, but the disease will again arise during the period of *kêng hsin*.

"Those who suffer from a disease of the lungs are animated and quick-witted during evening, their spirits are heightened at noon and they are calm and peaceful at midnight. (Sick) lungs have the tendency to close and to bind; then one should quickly eat sour food in order to make them receive what is due to them. One uses sour food to supplement and to strengthen the lungs and one uses pungent food to drain them and to make them expel.

"When the disease is located within the kidneys it should improve during Spring. If it does not improve during Spring it will become more serious during the period of the long Summer evenings. If death does not follow during the period of the long Summer, it can be warded off in Fall, but the disease will arise again in Winter. One should strictly avoid burning fires, hot food, and wearing clothing which is too warm.

"Those who suffer from a disease of the kidneys should be cured during the period of the celestial stems *chia i*. If the disease does not improve during the period of the celestial stems *chia i*, it will become graver during the period of *wu chi*. And if death does not strike during the period of *wu chi*, it can be warded off during the period of *kêng hsin*, but then the disease will arise again during the period of *jên kuei*.

"Those who suffer from a disease of the kidneys are quick-witted and active at midnight, and their spirits are heightened during the entire days of the last months of Spring, Summer, Fall, and Winter, and they become calm and quiet toward sunset. (Sick) kidneys have the tendency to harden; then one should eat bitter food to strengthen them. One uses bitter food to supplement and to strengthen them and one uses salty food to drain them and to make them expel.

"Thus when evil influences visit the body they must be overcome and prevented from increasing. This must be achieved by those who are healthy and whose diseases are consequently curable. This should also be achieved by those who cannot overcome the evil spirits and who consequently become more gravely ill. It also refers to those who are healthy and can ward off the disease by themselves."

TWENTY-FIVE

Qi Min Yao Shu
(Agricultural Text)

JIA SIXIE

Translated roughly as Essential Skills for Common People, this agricultural manual was writ-
ten by an administrator during the Northern Wei Dynasty, in a period of turmoil between
533 and 544. It was intended to help people survive by teaching basic skills. It quotes many
older sources and in many respects is comparable to Geoponika in the Greek section. Com-
pare what was considered essential in these two traditions.

"How to collect (good) seeds (for reproduction) of melons: Gather the 'pen-mu-tzu' (motherly
fruits) fruits every year. Discard both ends, only the middle portion seeds good for reproduction
are taken. 'Pen-mu-tzu' fruits are those which are formed after the first few leaves have expanded;
seeds of these fruits grow to plants bearing fruits earlier. Plants from medium-early fruits bear
fruits only after the vine attaining 3 to 4 ch'ih in length. Melons still later yield seeds which give
rise to individuals bearing no fruits until the vine has attained full length, and the fruits formed
ripen very late. Earlier fruits give offsprings fruiting earlier and smaller; late fruits give offsprings
producing bigger though later fruits. Seeds of the proximal end produce crooked and slender
melons, those from the distal end produce short and wry fruits."

"When eating melons, remember to gather the seeds from the delicious ones. Mix the seeds
with some fine chaff. Sun a little while, and before they are quite dry, rub them between the
hands and winnow. The seeds will be quite clean in a very short time."

Jia Sixie. *A Preliminary Survey of the Book Ch'i Min Yao Shu: An Agricultural Encyclopaedia of the 6th Century.*
    Edited by Shih Sheng-Han. Peking: Science Press, 1962, pp. 51–60, 66–70, 87.

"How to plant melons: Wash the seed with water. Mix with table-salt (treatment with table salt protects the vine from mildew). Slice off the topmost layer of dry soil with shovel. (If not sliced off first, no matter how big the hole is, there is always some dry soil in it, and the seeds will not sprout). Then make a pit as big as a bowl. Place 4 melon-seeds and 3 soya beans in the sunny side of the pit. After several leaves have expanded on the melon vine, pinch off the bean seedlings. (Melon seedlings are too weak to break through the ground, therefore advantage should be taken of the lifting force of sprouting beans. When melon vines have grown somewhat, the bean-stalks must be got rid of so that the vine may not be shadowed to disadvantage.—Bean-stalks when pinched will give out sap to moisten the soil. Never pull, or the ground would be loosened and dry.)"

"In the 9th or 10th month (late October to early December) dig trenches 4 to 5 ch'ih deep at the sunny southern side beneath a wall. Into such trenches pack fresh vegetables in layers (better only one sort in one layer) alternating with layers of earth, until about 1 ch'ih below the ground. Then cover with earth and finally with straw. The stored vegetables will last for the winter. Pick out whatever you like whenever wanted, they will be as fresh and crispy as summer-grown ones."

"To graft: Use crab-apple tree (= *Pyrus phaeocarpa*, *P. betulifolia* etc.) as stocks. (*Pyrus phaeocarpa*, stocks give bigger and finer pears, *P. betulifolia* being only second to the former. Pears on mulberry stocks are very bad. Fruits from grafts on jujube or pomegranate are superior to any other; but out of ten grafts less than 1 or 2 may succeed.) Stocks up to the thickness of the forearm will do. (Better sow the stock seeds one year ahead. Both stock and scion seeds sown the same year will be successful only if all stock seedlings grow well. Scions are useless if stocks are wanting.) Bigger stocks take 5 to 6 scions, smaller stocks, 2 or 3. Slight swelling of leaf-buds indicates the best time for grafting; actual bursting of the buds indicates the last chance. Prepare some hemp-skein to wrap the stock in the middle for a dozen rounds. Saw off the tip so as to leave a stump 5 or 6 ts'un high, Wrapage stops splitting of the bark when the scions are applied. Higher stumps certainly allow better growth of the scions, but then the greater will be the risk of burst of the joint in a wind. (Breakage at the joint caused by wind can be avoided by making a tall encasing of plaited straw around the stock so as to cover the joint and hard-ramming in enough mud. A cage around the scion helps further.) Cut a bamboo stick so as to shape it into a sharp, oblique chisel-like point. Push it down in between the bark and wood of the stock for 1 ts'un or so. Cut a scion twig 5–6 ts'un long from the sunny side of a choice pear-tree. (Shady side twigs used for scion yield less fruits). Cut its lower end chisel-like just the same as the bamboo stick. Gently incise above the oblique point to remove the brown (cutis) layer, and be careful not to injure the green bark beneath or it dies. Pull out the bamboo stick from the stock, and drive the scion-twig in its place. See to it that the bark and wood of the scion and the stock are in good contact. When this is well done, wrap up with silk batting, and seal the wrapping with mud, only the tip of the scion just appearing above the seal. Water on the scion twig. When all water has seeped away, cover with some dry soil. Always see that the earthen-seal on the joint should be moist and pliable. Pear-twigs are exceedingly brittle; so when heaping soil on the joint, be careful not to crush it or the twig may break. If the stock is split lengthwise into four to receive the scions, nice joint will never be obtained—for the exposed wood dies due to loss of sap. After the pear-scions succeed in growing, prune away any leaf or bud formed on the stock—otherwise a division of vigour will retard the growth of the whole tree."

"When grafting pear-trees in an orchard, scions should be inserted sidewise; in a courtyard, insert upwards.—Sidewise scions facilitate fruit-picking while upright growth makes no trouble with the buildings. Scions taken near the stump give better-looking trees, but fruit later. (Forked) crowfoot-like branches fruit in 3 years, but the tree looks untidy."

"Storage of fresh grapes: When fully ripe, pick down in whole clusters. Dig a pit under roof, and make a number of holes at its side. Now insert the grape-clusters by stalks into these holes, and beat in some earth to fasten them. Fill and cover the pit with earth. The grapes will stay fresh for the whole winter."

"Storage of fresh pears: Pick after the first frost,—for exposure to more frost renders the fruits less endurable and so it could not last the summer out. Dig a deep light-proof pit under a roof. See that its bottom is quite dry. Pile up fresh pears into it. There is no need to cover. The fruits will keep to the coming summer. Be careful in receiving the falling fruits when picking from the tree; for any bruise makes fruits perish more easily."

"Keep a sharp lookout at the fair and purchase pregnant animals there. Colts and calves 150 days old, and lambs 60 days old, can live by themselves without sucking. If the dam were good for breeding, keep her; if not, sell her again. The original cost may be recovered sooner or later while young animals are now obtained gratis. With the same sum of money, buy pregnant animals again. Within one year's time, cattle, horses and donkeys can be multiplied 2 times, sheep and goats, 4 times. Lambkins born in the last or the first month of the year should be kept for reproduction; kids of other months may be castrated and sold."

"Lamb or kids born in the first or last months of the year are the best; next, those in the 11th or 2nd months. Litters of other months will have singed pilage and small stature due to the influence of cold and hot seasons. Birth in the 8th, 9th and 10th months certainly coincides with the autumn fattening of the dams; but owing to the incidence of weaning time into late winter when no green fodder is available, the growth of the young animals is handicapped. Therefore the youngs are not very good. In 3rd or 4th months, the pasture is in the best condition, but the sucklings cannot be benefited by the hot milk of the dam while they themselves are not yet able to enjoy the green food. In the 5th, 6th and 7th months, hot weather and hot milk accentuate each other, rendering the youngs the worst of the worse. Birth in 11th and 2nd months means that the dam is fattening herself through the effect of pregnancy, notwithstanding the dry forage, and the youngs will get the best spring pasture at weaning."

"For chicken, always take eggs laid when leaf-fall of the mulberry-trees begins. The birds hatched therefrom are medium-sized, light-plumed, and short-shanked. They are nest-keepers, quiet, domiciliary, good brooders and attentive mothers."

"For geese and ducks, take those which brood twice a year for propagation. One brood a year yields less eggs, while three broods means a long wintry sitting which has the risk of much cold death of nestlings."

"(Piglets) 3 days old, ought to have their tail-tips pinched off, and then be castrated at 60 days old. After pinching off the tail-tip, there is no fear of tetany. Pigs dying from castration are actually (infected) with tetany or 'tail-wind-malady.' Castration without pinching off tip of tail leads to pigs with large head and small buttocks. Castration makes pigs grow less in bone and more in musculature; those not castrated have thicker bones and less flesh. Castrate piglets in the same way as calves, there will be no risk of death by wind (or tetany)."

"Once I myself had a herd of 200 sheep. Wanting of forage and pulses, caused half of them died in starvation. Those survived were ill, lean, scab-covered and miserable-looking, not very different from being dead, with pilage short and light, dry and matted. I thought that probably sheep did not fit in with my household, or that particular year was not good for sheep-keeping. Later I realised it was due to hunger and nothing else. . . . As the classics taught, 'He whose arm has broken thrice, will make a good surgeon,' and 'It is not too late to mend the ranch after you lost some sheep.' Things are more or less like this; how can one not pay attention?"

⚊ ⚊

"Shih is usually made in the 5th to 8th month,—this is the timely season. Take 1 shih (≎ 22 litre) beans, scour them well, and soak over night. Steam it next morning. Rub a grain between fingers, if the skin slips out, it is well done. Spread on the ground to a thickness of 2 ts'un (6 cm.)—or on a mat if the ground is bad. Let stay there and cool down. Cover with rushes, also 5–6 cm. thick. After 3 days, see whether all are yellow. If so, take off the rushes and spread the beans to form a thinner layer. Make grooves with fingers among the layer, shape into 'plots.' Mix up. Spread and make 'plots' again a few hours later. Repeat these thrice a day for three more days. Cook another portion of beans to get a thick syrupy decoction. Take 5 shêng (shêng ≎ 0.22 litre) smaller 'starters' (made of glutinous rice) and 5 shêng good table salt, mix both into the yellowed beans, sprinkle with bean decoction. Knead with both hands, till some juice begin to run out between fingers. Then place in a pottery jar until full,—but don't press! Any empty space left on top should be stuffed with wild mulberry leaves. Tightly seal on with mud. Place in the middle of the courtyard for 27 days. Then pour out, spread and dry in the sunshine. Steam, sprinkle with a decoction of mulberry-leaves. Steam as long as if to steam raw beans; when done, spread and sun again. After steaming and sunning thrice, the finished product is obtained."

TWENTY-SIX
The Classic of Tea

LU YU

Lu Yu lived from 733 to 804 A.D. and was a scholar during the Tang Dynasty. His book is the first solely devoted to tea drinking, which in this period became universal through China, though the text also records many literary references and anecdotes about tea that go back much further. Although short, the book is a work of consummate connoisseurship, explaining the best water, the finest sources for tea, the utensils necessary, and how properly to appreciate the beverage. Perform an online image search for Lu Yu and tea, and you will find many beautiful renditions of the master appreciating tea.

The Brewing of Tea

WHENEVER YOU HEAT TEA, take heed that it not lie between the wind and the embers. The fire can flame out and if it penetrates the brick, the curing operation will be uneven. When that happens, grasp the brick and press it against the fire several times. Then turn it upright until it is roasted. Then pull it out and bank it. When the shape begins to hump like the back of a toad, pull it back five inches from the fire, roll it and let it rest until it assumes its original state. Then heat it again.

When tea is dried by fire, you can tell by the temper of it when it has been cooked enough. When it is sun-dried, its softness will be the test. In cases when the tea is especially young and tender, steam it and then pound it while hot. The buds and shoots will retain their shape but the leaves should be pulpy. In cases in which the leaves are tough, grasp a heavy pestle and pound the

Lu Yu. *The Classic of Tea*. Translated by Francis R. Carpenter. Boston: Little, Brown and Company, 1974, pp. 103–19.

leaves until they are broken like lacquered beads or become like brave soldiers who have received their orders not to halt and go on until there is no strength left in them.

When the tea has been heated until the stems are as tender as a baby's arm, store it in a paper bag while it is still hot. If you do that, then nothing of its original purity or nature will be dissipated. Pulverize it as soon as it is cold. It is best to use charcoal for the fire and failing that, faggots of a very hard wood will do. However, charcoal that has been used before will give off a musty, rank and greasy smell. One must never use an oily wood or worn-out or discarded utensils as fuel.

The ancients placed great store in tea's flavor when it was brewed with firewood that had been cured for a long time.

On the question of what water to use, I would suggest that tea made from mountain streams is best, river water is all right, but well-water tea is quite inferior, (The poem on tea says, When it comes to water, I bow before the pure-flowing channels of the Min.)

Water from the slow-flowing streams, the stone-lined pools or milk-pure springs is the best of mountain water. Never take tea made from water that falls in cascades, gushes from springs, rushes in a torrent or that eddies and surges as if nature were rinsing its mouth. Over usage of all such water to make tea will lead to illnesses of the throat.

Of the many other streams that flow through mountain and valley, there are those that are clear and pure but which sink into the ground and are absorbed before finding an outlet. From the hot season to the time of frost, the dragon may be sequestered and noxious poisons will accumulate within them. One taste of the water will tell you if it is all right. If the evil genius of a stream makes the water bubble like a fresh spring, pour it out.

If you must use river water, take only that which man has not been near; and if it is well water, then draw a great deal before using it.

When the water is boiling, it must look like fishes' eyes and give off but the hint of a sound. When at the edges it chatters like a bubbling spring and looks like pearls innumerable strung together, it has reached the second stage. When it leaps like breakers majestic and resounds like a swelling wave, it is at its peak. Any more and the water will be boiled out and should not be used.

When the boiling water is in its first stage, you may add a measure of salt in accordance with the amount of water. You can tell when to stop by sampling it.

During the second stage of the boiling, draw off a ladle full of water and stir around the center of the boil with your bamboo pincers. If you judge that it is not yet right, lower the pincers into the center of the boil and do it with force. If it still leaps up making waves and splashing into a froth, pour back some of the water you have drawn off. That will stop it from overboiling while encouraging its essential virtue.

Pour it into cups so that it will come out frothy. The frothy patches are the ornamentation to the decoction and are called *mo* if thin, *po* if thick. When they are fine and light, they are called flowers, for they resemble the flowers of the jujube tree tossing lightly on the surface of a circular pool.

They should suggest eddying pools, twisting islets or floating duckweed at the time of the world's creation. They should be like scudding clouds in a clear blue sky and should occasionally overlap like scales on fish. They should be like copper *cash,* green with age, churned by the rapids of a river, or dispose themselves as chrysanthemum petals would, promiscuously cast on a goblet's stand.

To achieve the froth called *po,* heat the remaining water until it boils. Then the fine, light flowery froth will gather and become as silvery and white as drifted snow.

The poem on tea speaks of froth as flaming brilliance, and says that it must be as lustrous as the snowdrift and as sumptuous as the spring lotus.

When you draw off the water during the first boil, allow it to stand. If on the surface of the froth there is a lining like a black cloud, do not drink it, for the flavor will be untrue.

The first cup should have a haunting flavor, strange and lasting. There are those who allow it to continue simmering to nourish the elegance and retain the froth even through a first, second and third cup. After the third cup, one should not drink more than a fourth or fifth cup unless he is very thirsty.

At every brewing, one pint of water should be used for five cups of tea. Take the tea cups one after the other so that the heavy impurities will remain at the bottom and the choicest froths float across the top like patches of thin ice. Then the delicate virtues of the tea will be retained throughout. But when you drink it, sip only. Otherwise, you will dissipate the flavor.

Moderation is the very essence of tea. Tea does not lend itself to extravagance. If a tea is insipid and bland, it will lose its flavor before even half a cup has disappeared. How much more so in the case of extravagance in its use. The vibrance will fade from the color and the perfection of its fragrance will melt away.

When tea has a sweet flavor, it may be called *chia*. If it is less than sweet and of a bitter or strong taste, it is called *ch'uan*. If it is bitter or strong when sipped but sweet when swallowed, it is called *ch'a*.

DRINKING THE TEA

BORN TO THIS EARTH are three kinds of creatures. Some are winged and fly. Some are furred and run. Still others stretch their mouths and talk. All of them must eat and drink to survive.

There are times, nonetheless, when the meaning of "drink" becomes obscure. If one would merely slake his thirst, then he can drink rice and water. Should melancholy, sadness or anger strike, he can turn to wine to drink. But if one would dispel an evening's unproductive lassitude, the meaning of "drink" is tea.

Now tea, used as a drink, was first discovered by the Emperor Shen Nung. Among other great tea drinkers, we have heard that in the State of Lu there was the Duke of Chou while the State of Ch'i had Yen Ying. During the Han Dynasty there were Yang Hsiung and Ssu-Ma Hsiang-ju. During the Wu, there was Wei Yao. During the Chin there were Liu Kun, as well as Chang. Ts'ai, my distant ancestor Lu Na and Hsieh An among others pulled out of memory at random. All of them drank tea.

Tea has been traditionally taken so extensively that it is immersed in our customs and flourishes in the present Dynasty both North and South. From Ching to Yü, it is the common drink of every household.

The beverage that the people take may be from coarse, loose, powdered or cake tea. It can be chopped, boiled, roasted and then tamped down into a bottle or pottery vessel where it awaits only hot water.

Sometimes such items as onion, ginger, jujube fruit, orange peel, dogwood berries or peppermint are boiled along with the tea. Such ingredients may be merely scattered across the top for a glossy effect, or they can be boiled together and the froth drawn off. Drinks like that are no more than the swill of gutters and ditches; still, alas, it is a common practice to make tea that way.

In the ten thousand objects which Heaven nourishes, there is supreme perfection. It is only for ease and comfort that man works at things. He sequesters himself in a house. So the house he refines to the perfection of his own taste. He covers himself with clothing. The clothing he refines to perfection. He consumes to satiety both food and drink. These also he cultivates and refines to the utmost.

Thus with tea. There are nine ways by which man must tax himself when he has to do with tea.

He must manufacture it.
He must develop a sense of selectivity and discrimination about it.
He must provide the proper implements.
He must prepare the right kind of fire.
He must select a suitable water.
He must roast the tea to a turn.
He must grind it well.
He must brew it to its ultimate perfection.
He must, finally, drink it.

There are no short cuts. Merely to pick tea in the shade and dry it in the cool of the evening is not to manufacture it. To nibble it for flavor and sniff at it for fragrance is not to be discriminating. To bring along a musty tripod or a bowl charged with nose-insulting odors is not to provide the proper implements. Resinous firewood and old kitchen charcoal are not the stuff for a seemly fire. Water from turbulent rapids or dammed-up flood water is not a suitable water. Tea cannot be said to be roasted when it is heated on the outside and left raw underneath. Reducing it to jade powder and green dust is not grinding tea. Manipulating the instruments awkwardly and transitions from instrument to instrument that attract attention are not brewing tea. Finally, taking prodigious amounts of tea in summer and none at all in winter are not drinking tea.

For exquisite freshness and vibrant fragrance, limit the number of cups to three. If one can be satisfied with less than perfection, five are permissible. If one's guests number up to five rows, it will be necessary to use three bowls. If seven, then five bowls will be required. If there are six guests or fewer, do not economize on the number of bowls.

But if even one guest is missing from the assemblage, then the haunting and lasting flavor of the tea must take his place.

TWENTY-SEVEN
Yin-Shan Cheng-Yao

HU SZU-HUI

This text was compiled in 1330 toward the end of a long period of Mongol overlordship during the Yuan Dynasty founded by Kublai Khan. It is remarkably international, including traditional Chinese dishes as well as Turkic, Muslim, and Mongolian ones. The overall idea is a guide to health, which likewise draws on many different medical traditions. The author was not a physician, though, but cook to the emperor. Some of these ingredients would have traveled quite far—the mastic, for example, came from Chios, an island in present day Greece. Other ingredients, of course, went the other direction, as did people like Marco Polo. This would come to an end when the Ming Dynasty stopped allowing visitors. Along with the recipes are descriptions of the medicinal virtues of various ingredients.

Mastic Soup

It supplements and increases, warms the center, and accords chi'i. Mutton (leg; bone and cut up) tsaoko cardamoms (five), cinnamon (2 ch'ien), chickpeas [Muslim beans] (one-half sheng; pulverize and remove the skins). Boil the ingredients together to make a soup. Strain broth. [Cut up meat and put aside] add 2 ho of cooked chickpeas, 1 sheng of aromatic non-glutinous rice, 1 ch'ien of mastik. Evenly adjust flavors with a little salt. Add [the] cut up meat and [garnish with] coriander leaves.

Hu Szu-Hui. *A Soup for the Qan: Chinese Dietary Medicine of the Mongol Era as Seen in Hu Szu-Hui's Yin-Shan Cheng-Yao*. Edited and Translated by Paul D. Buell and Eugene N. Anderson. London: Kegan Paul International, 2000, excerpted from throughout text.

Turtle Soup

It is good for a wounded center, and increases ch'i. It supplements [in cases of] insufficiency. Mutton (leg; bone and cut up), tsaoko cardomoms (five). Boil ingredients together into a soup. Strain [broth]. Cook five or six turtles. When done, remove the skin and bones, and cut into lumps [and add to soup]. Use two liang of flour to make fine vermicelli. Roast together with one ho of juice of sprouting ginger, one liang of black pepper. [Add to soup and] adjust flavors with onions, salt, and vinegar.

Carp Soup

It treats jaundice, stops thirst, and pacifies the womb. If a person is ill with chronic abdominal mass he should not eat it. Large young carp (ten, remove the scales and intestines, clean), finely ground Chinese flower pepper (five ch'ien). Marinate ingredients with a combination of five ch'ien of ground coriander, two liang of onions (cut up), a little liquor, salt. Put fish into bouillon. Then add five ch'ien of finely ground black pepper, three ch'ien of sprouting ginger, and three ch'ien of ground long pepper. Adjust flavors with salt and vinegar.

Deboned Chicken Morsels

Fat chickens (ten; pluck; clean; cook and cut up. Debone as morsels); juice of sprouting ginger (one ho), onions (two liang; cut up); finely ground ginger (half a chin), finely ground Chinese flower pepper (four liang) [wheat] flour (two liang; make into vermicelli). (For) the ingredients take the broth used to boil the chickens and fry [cook dry]. Add onions and vinegar. Adjust flavors with the juice of sprouting ginger.

Poppy Seed Buns

White flour (five chin), cow's milk (two sheng), liquid butter (one chin), poppy seeds (one liang. Slightly roasted). [For] ingredients use salt and a little soda and combine with the flour. Make the buns.

Ginseng Puree (Drink in Place of Liquor)

It accords ch'i, opens the diaphragm, controls thirst and brings forth saliva. Korean ginseng (four liang; remove green shoots and cut up); prepared mandarin orange peel (one liang; remove the white), purple perilla leaves (two liang), crude granulated sugar (one chin). [For] ingredients use two tou of water. Boil down to one tou. Remove the dregs. Let clear. Drink when one likes.

Fragrant Orange Aromatic Cakes

They extend the chest, and accord ch'i. They clean and benefit head and eye. New fragrant orange peel (one liang; dry over a fire; remove white), garuwood (five ch'ien). grain of paradise (five ch'ien), cardamom kernel (five ch'ien), cubebs (three ch'ien), southern borax (three ch'ien;

grind separately), baroos camphor . . . (one ch'ien, grind separately), musk deer musk (two ch'ien; grind separately). Make ingredients into a fine powder. Combine into a dose with liquorice paste and cut out into a cake. Eat one cake each time. Let it dissolve slowly in the mouth.

Mr. T'ieh Weng's Red Jade Paste

This paste fills out the essence and is a tonic for the marrow. [It makes] the bowel transform. [It makes] the tendons and the ten-thousand spirits complete and full, the five viscera filled out in excess, marrow [substantial] and full, white hair become black. It reverses old age and restores youth. [It makes] the gait like a running horse. If it is taken repeatedly as the days advance, one will not starve if one does not eat for the entire day. It opens the way for a strong will. One can intone ten-thousand words a day. The spirit and the knowledge will go to great heights. One will be without dreams or visions at night. If one takes the materials [of the paste] when one is not yet aged 27 sui, one can attain the age of 360 sui. If one takes it before the age of 45 sui, one can reach the age of 240 sui. If one takes it before the age of 63 sui, one can reach the age of 120 sui. If one takes it above the age of 64 sui, one can live to 100 sui. If ten doses are taken, it should suppress the passions, and if one cultivates secret merits, I think one could become an earth immortal. If one set of materials is divided into five portions, it can help the abscess diseases of five persons. If divided into ten portions, it can help the debility diseases of ten persons. When you compound it, wash your hands and body, perfect your heart, and do not frivolously show it to others:

Korean ginseng (24 liang; remove the shoots), fresh Chinese foxglove (16 chin; the juice), China root (49 liang; remove the black skin) crystallized honey (10 chin, refine). [For] ingredients, grind the ginseng and China root finely. After using thin silk to strain the honey, take the natural juice of the Chinese foxglove. Do not use a copper or iron vessel to catch the juice when it is pounded. When finished remove the sediment. Take the medicinals and mix together evenly at one time. Put into a mica vessel, or a good porcelain pot and seal. Use 20 or 30 layers of clean paper to seal. Put [i.e., sealed pot] into boiling water. Boil for three days and nights over a mulberry wood fire. When the mixture is removed from the fire, several layers of waxed paper should be used to wrap the mouth of the pot. Put the pot into a well. When the pot has been submerged for a while to remove fire poison, take it out of the well and put it into the old boiled water. Boil for one day to bring out [get rid of] the water ch'i and then remove. Open the seal and take three spoonfuls. Put into three small cups and offer them to heaven, earth, and the hundred spirits. Burn incense, spread out the offerings and worship. Be very sincere and upright of spirit. Take a spoonful each day on an empty stomach, dissolved in liquor.

Paddy Rice is sweetish-bitter in flavor, neutral and lacks poisons. It is good for warming the center. It makes one very heated and constipated. Too much should not be eaten. This is the same as no-mi. (su-men [i.e., Indonesian paddy rice] is best. It is often used to make liquor.

Non-Glutinous Rice is sweetish-bitter in flavor, neutral and lacks poison. It is food for increasing ch'i. It controls irritation and leaking [of ch'i]. It harmonizes stomach ch'i and thickens muscle and flesh. There are various varieties at present. (Aromatic Non-glutinous Rice, Tablet Rice, Snow-white-interior Rice, Aromatic Rice.) These varieties are superior to [plain] non-glutinous rices in aroma and flavor. [Non-glutinous rice] can be milled and the kernel washed to make polished rice. This is also called Dried rice.

Foxtail Millet is salty in flavor, slightly cooling and lacks poison. It is good for nourishing kidney ch'i. It removes [evil] heat of spleen and stomach. It increases ch'i. Old [Foxtail Millet] is best. It is used to regulate [evil] heat of the stomach, and excessive thirst. It benefits urination and controls leaking dysentery. The T'ang-pen chu says "There are many varieties of Foxtail Millets. The kernels are fine like Laing-mi ["millet"]. The Uniform washed grains obtained from fine millet are che-mi."

Soybeans are sweetish in flavor, neutral and lack poison. They decrease demon ch'i, control pain and drive out water. They expel [evil] heat of the stomach, bring down blood stasis, and counteract poisons of various drugs. They are made into tou-fu. [Tou-fu] is cooking and moves the ch'i.

Wheat is sweetish in flavor, slightly cooling and lacks poison. It is good for expelling heat and controlling fidgetiness, diabetes, and dry throat. It benefits the urine and nourishes the liver ch'i and controls pain and blood spitting.

Barley [Hordeum vulgare] is salty-warm in flavor, slightly cooking and lacks poison. It is good for diabetes, expels heat, increases ch'i and harmonizes the center. It makes people very heated and is the best of the five grains. The Yao-hsing lun says "It can digest old food retained in the stomach and intestines and destroy chill ch'i."

Honey is sweetish in flavor, neutral, slightly warming and lacks poison. It is good for evil ch'i of chest and abdomen and the various fright convulsions. It supplements for insufficiency ch'i of the five viscera. It augments the center and controls pain. It counteracts poisons, makes ear and eye sharp, harmonizes the hundred drugs, and expels the host of illnesses.

Vinegar is sour in flavor, warming and lacks poison. It disperses carbuncle swelling and edema. It decreases evil poisons and destroys post-partum faintness. It expels obstructions of the bowl and impacted stool. There are various kinds of vinegar: (Liquor Vinegar, Peach Vinegar, Wheat Vinegar, Grape Wine Vinegar, Rice Vinegar is the best and used medicinally.)

Salt is salty in flavor, warming and lacks poison. It is good for decreasing demon vermin [parasites], evil-possession-poison, exogenous febrile disease, and from bringing up accumulation of phlegm of the thorax center. It controls sudden chest and abdomen pain. If too much is eaten it wounds the lungs. It causes one to cough and lose color.

Mutton is sweetish in flavor, very heating and lacks poison. It is good for warming the center, head wind, severe wind producing sweat, hsu-lao cold evil, supplements the center and augments ch'i. Sheep's Head is cooling. It regulates hectic fever to yin deficiency, brain heat, vertigo and emaciation. Sheep's Heart is used to regulate diaphragm ch'i of depression and rage. Sheep's liver is chilling in nature. It treats liver ch'i deficiency heat and conjunctivitis impaired vision. Sheep's blood is good for regulating female apoplexy and blood deficiency. In cases of post-partum faintness and pressing [chest sensation] that is extreme, one sheng, drunk fresh. The five viscera of sheep supplement the five viscera of people. Sheep's kidneys supplement kidney asthenia and augment the vital medullae. Sheep bone is heating. It controls hsu-lao diseases and cold-evil attack emaciation. Sheep's Medullae are sweetish in flavor and warming. They are good for regulating male and female wounding of the center and insufficiency of yin-ch'i. They benefit the blood vessels and augment essential ch'i. Sheep's brain: A lot should not be eaten. Sheep's Milk Cream regulates diabetes and supplements for exhaustion.

Pig Meat is bitter in flavor and lacks poison. It is good for obstructed pulse. It weakens joint and bone. Persons with depletion or puffiness should not eat pork for an extended time. It moves wind. It is even worse for those suffering from wounds caused by metal weapons. Pig suet is good for supplementing the center and augmenting ch'i. It stops thirst. Boar kidney is chilling. It harmonizes and orders kidney ch'i and penetrates and benefits the bladder. The Four Hooves of a Pig are somewhat cooling. They are good for whip or cudgel injuries and infected wounds, and bring down milk.

Carp is sweetish in flavor, cooling, and lacks poison. It is good for coughing-bringing up ch'i (asthmatic coughing), and for jaundice. It controls thirst and tranquilizes the womb. It regulates edema and evil for ch'i. It should not be eaten after a contagious ailment. Those with chronic asthma cannot eat it.

Persimmons are sweetish in flavor, cooling, and lack poison. They cause ear and nose ch'i to pass, and supplement for hsu-lao, bloody stool insufficiency. They make the stomach ample.

Sweet oranges are sweet-sour in flavor and lack poison. They remove nausea. If a lot are eaten they injure live ch'i. The peel is aromatic and delicate.

Lichee Fruits are sweetish in flavor, neutral, and lack poison. They stop thirst and produce juices. They increase a person's facial glow.

Gingko [Nuts] are sweetish-bitter in flavor and lack poison. They can be eaten roasted or boiled. If eaten green they cause illness.

Garlic is acrid in flavor, warming, and lacks poison. It is good for dissipating tumorous swellings, expels wind evil and destroys poison ch'i.

Bamboo Shoots are sweetish in flavor and lack poison. They are good for diabetes, benefit the water ways and increase ch'i. If too many are eaten they produce illness.

TWENTY-EIGHT

Yin Zhuan Fu Shi Jian (Discourse on Food and Drink)

GAO LIAN

Gao Lian was a playwright of the late sixteenth and early seventeenth century during the Ming Dynasty. He was a contemporary of Shakespeare. But like scholars in China at the time, he wrote about many topics, living a good life in harmony with the seasons, how to avoid disease and live a long life, and of course eating well was just as important. These directions for preserving food show that such topics were not beneath even the most refined of scholars.

Pounded Preserved Pork

Prepare 1 jin of newly-slaughtered and still warm lean pork, cut into 4–5 pieces. Smear 1/2 liang of stir-fried salt on pork and prevent it from permeating the meat. Sun the salted pork until half dry. Measure good wine and water, and put in pork. Add Chinese pepper, fennel and orange peel, and cook with small flame until dry. Pound and crush the cooked pork.

Cure Pork

Prepare 10 jin of meaty and tender castrated pork, cut into 20 pieces. Smear 8 liang of salt with 2 jin of wine on the pork to make it more tender, press with a heavy stone and sun until completely dry. Mix the remaining wine and fermented grain mash, and smear the mixture on the dried pork. Hang the pork on a bamboo fence for air-drying. Alternatively, prepare 10 jin of pork.

Gao Lian. *Yin Zhuan Fu Shi Jian (Discourse on Food and Drink), in Culinary Arts in Late Ming China: Refinement, Secularization, and Nourishment.* Translated by Su Heng-an. Taipei: SMC Publishing, 2008, excerpted from throughout text.

Boil water with 20 liang of salt, cool and draw the clear brine for further use. Immerse the pork in the brine of 20 days. When done, remove from the brine and hang in an airy place.

Another option is to make it in summer. Smear stir-fried salt on pork, age for a night and hang up. Press with a heavy stone whenever the hanged pork drips water. Repeat the process of pressing hanging and airing.

Pickled Fish

Prepare 1 jin of fish, mince and wash. Stir-fry 3 liang of salt, 1 qian of Chinese pepper, 1 qian of fennel, 2 qian of divinity fermentation yeast, 5 qian of red yeast rice and mix with wine. Add and blend in the seasoned mixture, pack in a porcelain bottle and seal for 10 days. Sprinkle with some scallion mince when served.

TIPS FOR THE PREPARATION OF FOODSTUFFS

1. Wash Pork stomach with flour, and wash pork organs and intestines with sugar to eliminate any smelly odors.

2. Add some peppermint and salt or ashes while cooking bamboo shoots to prevent shrinking.

3. Add 1/2 tablet of gleditsia (Chinese horny locust) in pickled crab with fermented grain to mash to prolong its preservation.

4. Wash fish with 1 or 2 drops of raw oil to help eliminate mucilage.

5. Season with incense ash to eliminate smelly odors when cooking fish.

6. Add a few cherry leaves to help soften the meat when cooking a goose.

7. Put a few flaming charcoals in boiling pot when cured meat is almost done. This is to eliminate greasiness and retain favorable fragrance.

8. Add 1 or 2 granules of paper mulberry in a pot and firmly cover when cooking any kind of meat. This is to accelerate softness and enhance fragrance.

9. Cooking meat by adding vinegar can preserve meat for as long as 10 days in summer.

10. Use only boiled water to make dough.

11. Avoid impure firewood when roasting meats.

12. Avoid light while pickling or fermenting live crabs to eliminate their spitting sand.

13. Stir-fry 1 sheng of red mung bean without oil until scorched. Bag it and place in the wine jar where wine is becoming sour.

14. Sun the drained light dyed lime from a dyeing mill, and use it to wrap and preserve cucumber and eggplant. This method will prolong the preserved vegetables until winter.

15. Preserve oranges for 3 or 4 months. Prevent them from becoming dry by wrapping them with pine needles or mung bean.

16. Make pasty porridge from wheat and flour, add a little salt, cool and pour in a jar. Collect fresh red and unripe peaches, put in the jar, seal and preserve until winter. The fruit will remain as fresh as if it were newly picked.

17. Replace honey with asarum to avoid worms when making traditional honey-soaked ripe plums.

18. Soak loquat, Chinese pearleaf crabapple and box myrtle in a handful of wax water and peppermint, and a little alum. The color of these fruits will remain unchanged and their flavor fresh.

Pickled Cucumber and Soybean

Prepare 50 jin of very ripe cucumber and young eggplant and measure 2½ liang of salt per jin of these two ingredients. Use salt to pickle for a night in order to seep out vegetable water. Collect 5 jin or orange peel, 2 jin of newly picked perilla with root, 3 jin of shredded ginger, 2 jin of husked apricot seed, 4 liang of cassia flower, 2 liang of licorice and 1 dou of soybean, cook with 5 jin of wine and blend them in a jar.

Add the cucumber and eggplant into the jar and press. Cover with 5 layers of bamboo leaves, tighten with bamboo slips and seal with mud and bamboo leaves.

Sun the jar for two months. Remove the mixture, add 1/2 jin of each Chinese pepper, fennel, and cardamom, and evenly lay on the ground for sunning. When dried enough, they will taste crispy and delicious. Regarding soybean preparation, choose large grains of bean, cook until soft, and cover with gluten to keep warm. When done remove the gluten and wash the soybean.

TWENTY-NINE

Bencao Gangmu

LI SHIZHEN

This text is a massive botanical reference work first published in 1578. This version is not exactly a translation, but more of an interpretation; nonetheless, it has sections on cakes and congee that are very revealing about food and its medicinal values in this era. Congee, or juk, is a breakfast comfort food made of rice thoroughly boiled until it forms a porridge. These versions suggest that people at home could engage in a degree of self-diagnosis and therapy via food.

SWEET-MEATS are known by the names *I-t'ang* and *Hsing*. They are made of a variety of grains and seeds; but that used medicinally is made of glutinous rice, with that made of maize sometimes employed. It is said to be best in the form of a thick treacle, like the Japanese *midsu ame*. It is often made of malted grain, when it probably much resembles *glucose*. It is regarded as tonic, cooling, strengthening, carminative, and expectorant. It is also regarded as an antidote to aconite poisoning. Externally it is applied to virulent sores and wounds.

⚬⚬⚬

CONGEE.—*Chou, Mi.* When this gruel has been boiled thick it is called *Chan*, and when thin the name is *I*. The number of these gruels is very large, and they are made from any of the cereal grains and other substances, sometimes used alone and sometimes with an admixture of other drugs. The common congee is made of rice or millet, that made of the former being also known

Li Shizhen. *Chinese Medicinal Herbs: A Modern Edition of a Classic Sixteenth-Century Manual.* Translated by Shih-Chen Li. Mineola, NY: Dover, 1973, pp. 469–74.

as *Hsi-fan*. This is almost the universal staple of the Chinese breakfast, being eaten with a relish of salted vegetables or bean curd. It is easily digested and fattening, and as a diet for the sick it is most excellent, being demulcent, cooling, easily digestible, and nourishing. When a demulcent is needed, as in bowel or bladder difficulties, there is nothing better, as it can easily be diluted by adding boiling water, it can be strained, or meat broth, wine, or other substances can be added to it. It readily takes the place of, and excels, barley broth or barley water. To prepare it, a relatively small quantity of rice should be put to boil in a sufficiently large quantity of water, so that no water need be added to make the gruel of the right consistency. For this reason, it is better to use too much water rather than too little, as it rather improves the congee to boil it a long time until the water has sufficiently evaporated. The gruel used for breakfast is usually much thicker than that given to the sick. Two places where this gruel finds very practical use is in the case of nursing mothers, to increase the supply of milk, and in the case of hand-fed infants, as a useful addition to and diluent of cow's milk. It should always be freshly made for this latter purpose.

Wheat Congee, Hsiao-mai-chou, is considered to be cooling and is used in feverish conditions.

Apricot Kernel Congee, called *Han-shih-chou*, is made of apricot or peach kernels and certain flowers. It is recommended for coughs, as a carminative, and stomachic.

Congee made of *glutinous rice*, (*No-mi*), glutinous *Setaria italica* (*Shu-mi*), and glutinous *Panicum miliacum* (*Shu-mi*), is used as a demulcent in diarrhœas, and vomiting, and is employed as a local application in small-pox in children.

Congee made of *ordinary rice* (*Kêng-mi*), Annamese rice (*Shan-mi*), Indian corn (*Su-mi*), and *Sorghum vulgare* (*Liang-mi*), is considered to be diuretic, thirst-relieving, and nutrient.

Congee of *Phaseolus radiatus* beans, *Chih-hsiao-tou-chou*, is diuretic, resolvant in dropsies, and curative in gout.

Congee of *Phaseolus mungo* beans, *Lu-tou-chou*, is cooling and thirst-relieving.

Congee of *poppy seeds, Yü-mi-chou*, relieves vomiting and benefits the large intestine.

Congee of the kernels of *Coix lachryma, I-i-jên-chou*, is considered curative in rheumatism and beneficial to the digestive organs.

Congee of *lotus seed meal, Lien-tzǔ-fên-chou*, is tonic to the spleen and stomach, and astringent in diarrhœa and dysentery.

Congee prepared of the meal made from the seeds of *Euryale ferox, Ch'ien-shih-fên-chou*, also called *Chi-tou-chou*, is regarded as tonic and constructive, improving the vision and hearing.

Congee made of the meal of the *water chestnut, Ling-shih-fên-chou*, is beneficial to the digestive organs, and cooling to the viscera.

Chestnut Congee, Li-tzǔ-chou, is tonic to the kidneys and strengthening to the loins and legs.

Congee of *Dioscorea quinqueloba, Shu-yü-chou*, is strengthening to the kidneys and virile organs, as well as to the digestive organs.

Taro Congee, Yü-chou, is regarded as very nutritious.

Congee made of the flour of *lily bulbs, Pai-ho-fên-chou*, is moistening to the lungs and harmonizing to the centers.

Radish Congee, Lo-po-chou, is digestive and beneficial to the diaphragm.

Carrot Congee, Hu-lo-po-chou, is carminative and peptic.

Purslane Congee, Ma-ch'ih-hsien-chou, is recommended for rheumatism and swellings.

Rape Congee, Yu-ts'ai-chou, is harmonizing to the centers and carminative.

Pond weed Congee, Chün-ta-ts'ai-chou, is strengthening to the stomach and beneficial to the spleen.

Spinach Congee, Po-lêng-ts'ai-chou, is harmonizing and moistening to the viscera.

Shepherd's-purse Congee, Chi-ts'ai-chou, brightens the eye and benefits the liver.

Celery Congee, Ch'in-ts'ai-chou, is cooling in summer and beneficial to the intestines.

Mallow Congee, K'uei-ts'ai-chou, is moistening in feverishness and peptic.

Mustard Congee, Chieh-ts'ai-chou, expels phlegm and prevents evil effluvia.

Leek Congee, Chiu-ts'ai-chou, is warming to the viscera.

Salted onion Congee, Ts'ung-shih-chou, is diaphoretic and lubricating to the muscles.

Congee made of the meal of *Pachyma cocos, Fu-ling-fên-chou*, is a general tonic and nutrient.

Pine-nut kernel Congee, Sung-tzŭ-jên-chou, is moistening to the heart and lungs, and harmonizes the large intestine.

Wild jujube Congee, Suan-tsao-jên-chou, relieves fever and benefits the gall.

Congee made of the seeds of *Lycium sinense, Kou-chi-tzŭ-chou*, is tonic to the blood and beneficial to the kidneys.

Scallion bulb Congee, Hsieh-pai-chou, cures "cold diarrhœa" in the aged.

Ginger Congee, Shêng-chiang-chou, is warming and antiseptic to the viscera.

Red-pepper Congee, Hua-chiao-chou, prevents malaria and cold.

Fennel Congee, Hui-hsiang-chou, harmonizes the stomach and cures hernia.

Congee made with *black pepper* (*Hu-chiao-chou*), *Congee* of *Boymia rutœcarpa* (*Chu-yü-chou*), and *Smart-weed Congee* (*La-mi-chou*), are all carminative, and are recommended for pain in the bowels.

Congee made of *hemp seed* (*Ma-tzŭ-chou*), *sesamum seed* (*Hu-ma-chou*), or the kernels of *Prunus japonica* (*Yu-li-jên-chou*), are all moistening to the intestines and cure rheumatism.

Congee made of the seeds of *Perilla ocymoides, Su-tzŭ-chou*, is carminative and benefits the diaphragm.

Congee with *bamboo-leaf decoction, Chu-yeh-t'ang-chou*, is thirst relieving and purifies the heart.

Congee with *pig's kidney* (*Chu-shên-chou*), *sheep's kidney* (*Yang-shên-chou*), or *deer's kidney* (*Lu-shên-chou*), is thought to be strengthening in all wasting diseases of the kidneys.

Congee with *sheep's liver* (*Yang-kan-chou*), or *chicken's liver* (*Chi-kan-chou*), is similarly used in diseases of the liver.

Congee with *mutton broth* (*Yang-chih-chou*), or *chicken broth* (*Chi-chih-chou*), is recommended in wasting and injuries.

Congee with *duck broth* (*Ya-chih-chou*), or *carp broth* (*Li-yü-chih-chou*), is recommended in dropsy.

Congee with *milk, Niu-ju-chou*, is recommended for the thin and emaciated.

Congee with *milkcurd* and *honey, Su-mi-chou*, is considered beneficial to the heart and lungs.

Congee to which has been added *deer's horn glue, Lu-chio-chiao-ju-chou*, is eaten to benefit the vital principle and as constructive food.

Congee to which *browned flour* has been added, *Ch'ao-mien-ju-chou*, is used to cure "white dysentery."

Congee with *baked salt*, *Shao-yên-ju-chou*, is recommended in the treatment of bloody flux.

Rehmannia glutinosa Congee, *Ti-huang-chou*, is made by boiling the root with rice, and when it is nearly done adding curds and honey and boiling dry. The mixture is afterwards boiled in water and eaten as a tonic to the blood and general constructive.

PART IV

Study Questions

1. In what way do manners and rituals prevent the threat of violence, and why is the dinner table such a volatile place? Compare the Confucian solution to other systems of manners.
2. In what ways is the Chinese system of medicine similar to the Greek? How does it differ?
3. Is appreciation of fine foods and beverages more likely in a society in which patronage is concentrated in the hands of a few wealthy people or spread more evenly among many people? Is great art, culinary or otherwise, possible in a democracy?
4. Consider the state of cooking and preserving technology among the Chinese in various historical periods. What accounts for the sophistication, especially in comparison with the Western tradition?
5. How would the family structure and the idea of filial piety contribute to passing down culinary traditions among the Chinese?

PART FIVE

Ancient India

The original inhabitants of the Indian subcontinent founded the civilization now identified with the Indus River Valley and cities such as Harappa and Mohenjo Daro. We know relatively little about them since their language has not been deciphered, but, like the first agricultural and pastoral peoples elsewhere, they settled into permanent dwellings and developed a level of culture, social stratification, and material wealth comparable to those in other areas and at roughly the same time, from about 2500 to 1500 B.C. Thereafter, they were beset by invasions, as were most ancient cultures at this time. Whether it was climatic change that prompted nomadic invaders to attack their settled neighbors or some other factors, India was invaded by the Aryans. These were an Indo-European people who spoke Sanskrit, an ancient language related to Greek and Celtic. They were primarily cattle-rearing people who ruled over the native people and, similar to many other warrior cultures, sacrificing and eating large animals was an expression of strength and bravado. But it was also central to the religion, as shown in the selection from the great epic *Mahabharata*.

Although the people of this region were at one time eaters of meat, they eventually revered cattle, and some became strict vegetarians. How this came about has been widely debated. One theory posits that eating cows is simply inefficient in a place where traction animals, dung for fuel, and a plentiful supply of milk makes more economic sense. According to this theory, the idea that cows are a reincarnated form of humans developed to give religious sanction to these practices. But, in fact, the idea of reincarnation predates the veneration of cows. Another theory looks closely at the social structure of the Aryans, who were divided into strict castes. There were Brahmin priests at the top, warriors below, then craftsmen, farmers, and so on. During a period of terrible famine, the Brahmins, still eating flesh, were threatened with losing their status and decided to implement the full implications of their doctrine of reincarnation, forbidding cow eating. They could no longer be suspected of consuming all the resources since they were more abstemious than castes below them. Ultimately, the diet was a way to maintain power, through purity.

Whatever the original impetus, the caste system and the veneration of cattle and the practice of ahimsa, or nonviolence, are cornerstones of religious and dietary practice in Hinduism, which evolved from these early events. Some scholars think Buddhism played a major role in spreading vegetarianism throughout the continent. The reverence for all life is, however, contained in the earliest texts in the *Rig Veda* and *Upanishads*. Here it is explained that in the beginning of time there was only Atman, or Self. Atman divided and subdivided, creating all living beings. Thus, all creatures are manifestations of the original Atman and equally divine. Because people are reincarnated after death and the highest form of reincarnation is as a cow, it makes perfect sense to revere cows. Not all Hindus today are vegetarian, though.

Neither are Buddhists strict vegetarians. Although there are texts advocating abstention from meat, such as the sutra excerpted here, the practicalities of daily life sometimes prevent it. For example, a Buddhist monk must never refuse food offered in charity, and one is even allowed to eat meat if the animal was not specifically slaughtered for one's use. To refuse it would be wasteful. Moreover, in some places—especially Tibet—vegetables simply don't grow, and people must use meat to survive. Buddha himself ate meat on occasion. Nonetheless, vegetarianism remained an ideal, and in many places an elaborate vegetarian cuisine developed. For a brief time under the reign of Asoka in the mid-200s B.C., India was largely Buddhist and vegetarian.

India also has a medical system, Ayurveda, still in use today, which is comparable to the Greek system, but in practice very different. The tradition is said to date back over three thousand years, though most of the tests were written down in the first century A.D., around the same time as Galen was writing. There are five elements in this system: air, fire, water, earth, and space. Each in combination with another creates what is called a *dosha*, a force that governs physiologic functions. Space and air combine to create the *vata dosha*—which regulates all movement, such as breathing, circulation, nerve impulses—even ideas. Fire and water combine to form the *pitta dosha*, which is the principle of digestion and metabolism. Water and earth create the *kapha dosha*—which is the structural principle, holding things together. And having too much or too little of each of these forces causes illness. The key here is a balance, and diet is central to maintaining this balance. Each food also has its own unique *guna*, or properties, and role in maintaining health.

The history of Indian cuisine after the Middle Ages is connected with the story of the spread of Islam and will be taken up in that section.

THIRTY

Mahabharata
(Horse Sacrifice Feast)

KRISHNA-DWAIPAYANA VYASA

The Mahabharata *is one the great epics of ancient times, similar to* The Iliad, *though many times longer and more complex. Like* The Iliad, *the* Mahabharata *describes the heroic exploits of princes as well as sacred texts about religion. Traditionally, it is ascribed to Vyasa, the great scribe of the Vedas. The material may date back as far as the eighth or ninth century* B.C., *but it was compiled over the course of many centuries later as well. The text reflects a period when animal sacrifice was still practiced, in this case on an enormous scale with food and drink. Consider the social function of this ritual, who is invited, and what the sacrifice is meant to accomplish. Also note the mention of soma, an intoxicating drug used in the rituals. There are many points of comparison to the Judeo-Christian as well as Greco-Roman traditions. You may wish to search online for images of this and the* Mahabharata, *which has been painted many times.*

When the great sacrifice of Yudhishthira commenced, many eloquent dialecticians started diverse propositions and disputed thereon, desirous of vanquishing one another. The (invited) kings beheld the excellent preparations of that sacrifice, resembling those of the chief himself of the deities, made, O Bharata, by Bhimasena. They beheld many triumphal arches made of gold, and many beds and seats and other articles of enjoyment and luxury, and crowds of men collected at different sports. There were also many jars and vessels and cauldrons and jugs

Krishna-Dwaipayana Vyasa. *The Mahabharata of Krishna-Dwaipayana Vyasa.* Book 1: *Adi Parva.* Translated by Kisari Mohan Ganguli. 1883–1896. Published online at sacred-texts.com, 2003. http://www.sacred-texts.com/hin/m01/m01000.htm.

and lids and covers. The invited kings saw nothing there that was not made of gold. Many sacrificial stakes also were set up, made, according to the directions of the scriptures of wood, and adorned with gold. Endued with great effulgence, these were duly planted and dedicated (with scriptural Mantras). The king saw all animals, again, which belong to land and all those which belong to water, collected there on the occasion. And they also beheld many kine and many buffaloes and many old women, and many aquatic animals, many beasts of prey and many species of birds, and many specimens of viviparous and oviparous creatures, and many that are filth-born, and many belonging to the vegetable kingdom, and many animals and plants that live or grow on mountains. Beholding the sacrificial compound thus adorned with animals and kine and corn, the invited kings became filled with wonder. Large heaps of costly sweet-meats were kept ready for both the Brahmanas and the Vaisyas. And when the feeding was over of a hundred thousand Brahmanas, drums and cymbals were beat. And so large was the number fed that the sounds of drums and cymbals were repeatedly heard, indeed, from day to day those sounds continued.

Thus was performed that sacrifice of king Yudhishthira of great intelligence. Many hills of food, O king, were dedicated on the occasion. Many large tanks were seen of curds and many lakes of ghee. In that great sacrifice, O monarch, was seen the entire population of Jamvud-wipa, with all its realms and provinces, collected together. Thousands of nations and races were there. A large number of men, O chief of Bharata's race, adorned with garlands and wearing bright ear-rings made of gold, taking innumerable vessels in their hands, distributed the food unto the regenerate classes by hundreds and thousands. The attendants of the Pan-davas gave away unto the Brahmanas diverge kinds of food and drink which were, besides, so costly as to be worthy of being eaten and drunk by kings themselves.

O king. Those foremost of Soma-drinkers, O monarch, extracting the juice of the Soma, then performed the Savana rite following the injunctions of the scriptures. Among those that came to that sacrifice none could be seen who was cheerless, none who was poor, none who was hungry, none who was plunged into grief, and none that seemed to be vulgar. Bhimasena of mighty energy at the command of the king, caused food to be ceaselessly distributed among those that desired to eat. Following the injunctions of the scriptures, priests, well-versed in sacrificial rites of every kind, performed every day all the acts necessary to complete the great sacrifice. Amongst the Sadasayas of king Yudhishthira of great intelligence there was none who was not well conversant with the six branches of (Vedic) learning. There was none among them that was not an observer of vows, none that was not an Upadhyaya; none that was not well versed in dialectical disputations. When the time came for erecting the sacrificial stake, O chief of Bharata's race, six stakes were set up that were made of Vilwa, six that were made of Khadira, and six that were made of Saravarnin. Two stakes were set up by the priests that were made of Devadaru in that sacrifice of the Kuru king, and one that was made of Sleshmataka. At the command of the king, Bhima caused some other stakes to be set up, for the sake of beauty only, that were made of gold.

Bulls, possessed of such qualifications as are mentioned in the scriptures, and aquatic ani-mals were properly tied to the stakes after the rites relating to the sacrificial fire had been per-formed. In that sacrifice of the high-souled son of Kunti, three hundred animals were tied to the stakes setup, including that foremost of steeds. That sacrifice looked exceedingly beautiful as if adorned with the celestial Rishis, with the Gandharvas singing in chorus and the diverse tribes of Apsaras dancing in merriment.

Vaisampayana said, "Having cooked, according to due rites, the other excellent animals that were sacrificed, the priests then sacrificed, agreeably to the injunctions of the scriptures, that steed (which had wandered over the whole world)." After cutting that horse into pieces, conformably to scriptural directions, they caused Draupadi of great intelligence, who was possessed of the three requisites of *mantras*, things, and devotion, to sit near the divided animal. The Brahmanas then with cool minds, taking up the marrow of that steed, cooked it duly, O chief of Bharata's race. King Yudhishthira the just, with all his younger brothers, then smelled, agreeably to the scriptures, the smoke, capable of cleansing one from every sin, of the marrow that was thus cooked. The remaining limbs, O king, of that horse, were poured into the fire by the sixteen sacrificial priests possessed of great wisdom. Having thus completed the sacrifice of that monarch, who was endued with the energy of Sakra himself, the illustrious Vyasa with his disciples eulogised the king greatly.

"Hence, I have given away unto the sacrificial priests the Earth conquered by Arjuna. Ye foremost of Brahmanas, I shall enter the woods. Do ye divide the Earth among yourselves. Indeed, do you divide the Earth into four parts according to what is done in the Chaturhotra sacrifice. Ye best of regenerate ones I do not desire to appropriate what now belongs to the Brahmanas. Even this, ye learned Brahmanas, has been the intention always cherished by myself and my brothers." When the king said these words, his brothers and Draupadi also said, "Yes, it is even so." Great was the sensation created by this announcement. Then, O Bharata, an invisible voice was heard in the welkin, saying,—"Excellent, Excellent!" The murmurs also of crowds of Brahmanas as they spoke arose. The Island-born Krishna, highly applauding him, once more addressed Yudhishthira, in the presence of the Brahmanas, saying, "The Earth has been given by thee to me. I, however, give her back to thee. Do thou give unto these Brahmanas gold. Let the Earth be thine." Then Vasudeva, addressing king Yudhishthira the just, said, "It behoveth thee to do as thou art bid by the illustrious Vyasa." Thus addressed, the foremost one of Kuru's race, along with all his brothers, became glad of soul, and gave away millions of golden coins, in fact, trebling the Dakshina ordained for the Horse-sacrifice. No other king will be able to accomplish what the Kuru king accomplished on that occasion after the manner of Marutta. Accepting that wealth, the Island-born sage, Krishna, of great learning, gave it unto the sacrificial priests, dividing it into four parts. Having paid that wealth as the price of the Earth, Yudhishthira, cleansed of his sins and assured of Heaven rejoiced with his brothers.

The son of Pandu, for gratifying his sister Dussala, established her infant grandson in his paternal kingdom. The Kuru king Yudhishthira, having a full control over his senses, then dismissed the assembled kings all of whom had been properly classed and honoured by him. The illustrious son of Pandu, that chastiser of foes, then duly worshipped the high-souled Govinda and Valadeva of great might, and the thousands of other Vrishni heroes having Pradyumna for their first. Assisted by his brothers, he then dismissed them for returning to Dwaraka. Even thus was celebrated that sacrifice of king Yudhishthira the just, which was distinguished by a profuse abundance of food and wealth and jewels and gems, and oceans of wines of different kinds. There were lakes whose mire consisted of ghee, and mountains of food. There were also, O chief of Bharata's race, miry rivers made of drinks having the six kinds of taste. Of men employed in making and eating the sweetmeats called Khandavaragas, and of animals slain for food, there was no end. The vast space abounded with men inebriated with wine, and with young ladies filled with joy. The extensive grounds constantly echoed with the sounds of drums and the blare of conches. With all these, the sacrifice became exceedingly delightful. "Let agreeable things be given away,"—"Let agreeable food be eaten,"—these were the sounds that were repeatedly heard day and night in that sacrifice. It was like a great festival, full of rejoicing and contented men. People of diverse realms speak of that sacrifice to this day. Having showered wealth in torrents, and diverse objects of desire, and jewels and gems, and drinks of various kinds, the foremost one of Bharata's race, cleansed of all his sins, and his purpose fulfilled, entered his capital.

THIRTY-ONE

The Taittiriya Upanishad (I Am Food)

The Upanishads are commentaries upon the sacred revealed texts of the Vedas, written many centuries B.C. to early in the Common Era. This one was written around the sixth or fifth century B.C. and is among the oldest. The term upanishad *in Sanskrit means sitting nearby, as would a student while learning. They are philosophical in nature, asking questions such as the meaning of life, the path to happiness, and, in this case, the nature of eating and being eaten. If you think of the idea of immortality, what is it that truly lasts forever—the soul or the physical material of our bodies being constantly recycled? This selection invites questions such as this.*

SECOND VALLI OR, THE CHAPTER ON ANANDA (BLISS).

Harih, Om! May it (the Brahman) protect us both (teacher and pupil)! May it nourish us both! May we acquire strength together! May our knowledge become bright! May we never quarrel! Peace! Peace! Peace!

First Anuvaka

He who knows the Brahman attains the highest (Brahman). On this the following verse is recorded:

"He who knows Brahman, which is (i.e., cause, not effect), which is conscious, which is without end, as hidden in the depth (of the heart), in the highest ether, he enjoys all blessings, at one with the omniscient Brahman."

Max Müller, trans. *The Taittiriya Upanishad.* 1884. Published online at Wikisource, last modified June 9, 2012. http://en.wikisource.org/wiki/Taittiriya_Upanishad.

From that Self (Brahman) sprang ether (akasa, that through which we hear); from ether air (that through which we hear and feel); from air fire (that through which we hear, feel, and see); from fire water (that through which we hear, feel, see, and taste); from water earth (that through which we hear, feel, see, taste, and smell). From earth herbs, from herbs food, from food seed, from seed man. Man thus consists of the essence of food. This is his head, this his right arm, this his left arm, this his trunk (Atman), this the seat (the support).

On this there is also the following Sloka:

Second Anuvaka

All beings, that exist on earth, are born of food; then they live by food, then again to the food they go at the end. So verily food is the eldest of all creatures. Therefore, it is called the medicament of all. All those who worship food as Brahman obtain all food. Food is indeed the eldest of all creatures. Therefore, it is called the medicine for all. From food all beings are born, having been born they grow by food. Food is eaten by the beings and it also eats them. Therefore, it is called food (Anna). Other than that (soul) made of the essence of food, there is another self within, formed of Prana, By that this is filled. This (Pranamaya) is exactly of the form of man (Purusha). Its human form is according to the human form of the former. Of that, Prana is the head, Vyana its right wing (side), Apana is the left wing (sign), the Akasa is the trunk (body), the earth is the tall, the support.

. . .

"From food are produced all creatures which dwell on earth. Then they live by food, and in the end they return to food. For food is the oldest of all beings, and therefore it is called panacea (sarvaushadha, i.e. consisting of all herbs, or quieting the heat of the body of all beings)."

They who worship food as Brahman, obtain all food. For food is the oldest of all beings, and therefore it is called panacea. From food all creatures are produced; by food, when born, they grow. Because it is fed on, or because it feeds on beings, therefore it is called food (anna).

Different from this, which consists of the essence of food, is the other, the inner Self, which consists of breath. The former is filled by this. It also has the shape of man. Like the human shape of the former is the human shape of the latter. Prana (up-breathing) is its head. Vyana (back-breathing) is its right arm. Apana (down-breathing) is its left arm. Ether is its trunk. The earth the seat (the support).

He perceived that food is Brahman, for from food these beings are produced; by food, when born, they live; and into food they enter at their death.

Seventh Anuvaka

Let him never abuse food, that is the rule.

Breath is food, the body eats the food. The body rests on breath, breath rests on the body. This is the food resting on food. He who knows this food resting on food, rests exalted, becomes rich in food, and able to eat food (healthy), becomes great by offspring, cattle, and the splendour of his knowledge (of Brahman), great by fame.

Eighth Anuvaka

Let him never shun food, that is the rule. Water is food, the light eats the food. The light rests on water, water rests on light. This is the food resting on food. He who knows this food resting on food, rests exalted, becomes rich in food, and able to eat food (healthy), becomes great by offspring, cattle, and the splendour of his knowledge (of Brahman), great by fame.

Ninth Anuvaka

Let him acquire much food, that is the rule. Earth is food, the ether eats the food. The ether rests on the earth, the earth rests on the ether. This is the food resting on food. He who knows this food resting on food, rests exalted, becomes rich in food, and able to eat food (healthy), becomes great by offspring, cattle, and the splendour of his knowledge (of Brahman), great by fame.

Tenth Anuvaka

1. Let him never turn away (a stranger) from his house, that is the rule. Therefore a man should by all means acquire much food, for (good) people say (to the stranger): "There is food ready for him." If he gives food amply, food is given to him amply. If he gives food fairly, food is given to him fairly. If he gives food meanly, food is given to him meanly.

2. He who knows this, (recognises and worships Brahman) as possession in speech, as acquisition and possession in up-breathing (prana) and down-breathing (apana); as action in the hands; as walking in the feet; as voiding in the anus. These are the human recognitions (of Brahman as manifested in human actions). Next follow the recognitions (of Brahman) with reference to the Devas, viz. as satisfaction in rain; as power in lightning;

3. As glory in cattle; as light in the stars; as procreation, immortality, and bliss in the member; as everything in the ether. Let him worship that (Brahman) as support, and he becomes supported. Let him worship that (Brahman) as greatness (mahah), and he becomes great. Let him worship that (Brahman) as mind, and he becomes endowed with mind.

4. Let him worship that (Brahman) as adoration, and all desires fall down before him in adoration. Let him worship that (Brahman) as Brahman, and he will become possessed of Brahman. Let him worship this as the absorption of the gods in Brahman, and the enemies who hate him will die all around him, all around him will die the foes whom he does not love.

He who is this (Brahman) in man, and he who is that (Brahman) in the sun, both are one.

5. He who knows this, when he has departed this world, after reaching and comprehending the Self which consists of food, the Self which consists of breath, the Self which consists of mind, the Self which consists of understanding, the Self which consists of bliss, enters and takes possession of these worlds, and having as much food as he likes, and assuming as many forms as he likes, he sits down singing this Saman (of Brahman): "Havu, havu, havu!"

6. "I am food (object), I am food, I am food! I am the eater of food (subject), I am the eater of food, I am the eater of food! I am the poet (who joins the two together), I am the poet, I am the poet! I am the first-born of the Right (rita). Before the Devas I was in the centre of all that is immortal. He who gives me away, he alone preserves me: him who eats food, I eat as food.

"I overcome the whole world, I, endowed with golden light. He who knows this, (attains all this). This is the Upanishad."

THIRTY-TWO

The Sammadhitti Sutta

This is a Buddhist text in the Pali Canon that discusses the idea of nourishment in a literal and metaphysical sense—what is truly wholesome and what appears to be so. What causes fulfillment, again literally and metaphorically, is not craving and consuming but being detached from such things, and thereby avoiding suffering. It makes for interesting comparison with Greek Stoic and Epicurean ideas as well as the ascetics we will encounter in the chapter on early Christianity.

THE WHOLESOME AND THE UNWHOLESOME

"When, friends, a noble disciple understands the unwholesome, the root of the unwholesome, the wholesome, and the root of the wholesome, in that way he is one of right view, whose view is straight, who has perfect confidence in the Dhamma, and has arrived at this true Dhamma.

"And what, friends, is the unwholesome, what is the root of the unwholesome, what is the wholesome, what is the root of the wholesome? Killing living beings is unwholesome; taking what is not given is unwholesome; misconduct in sensual pleasures is unwholesome; false speech is unwholesome; malicious speech is unwholesome; harsh speech is unwholesome;

Bhikkhu Ñanamoli, trans., and Bhikkhu Bodhi, ed. *The Discourse on Right View: The Sammaditthi Sutta and Its Commentary. The Wheel 377—379.* Kandy, Sri Lanka: Buddhist Publication Society, 1991. http://buddhasutra.com/files/sammaditthi_sutta.htm.

gossip is unwholesome; covetousness is unwholesome; ill will is unwholesome; wrong view is unwholesome. This is called the unwholesome.

"And what is the root of the unwholesome? Greed is a root of the unwholesome; hate is a root of the unwholesome; delusion is a root of the unwholesome. This is called the root of the unwholesome.

"And what is the wholesome? Abstention from killing living beings is wholesome; abstention from taking what is not given is wholesome; abstention from misconduct in sensual pleasures is wholesome; abstention from false speech is wholesome; abstention from malicious speech is wholesome; abstention from harsh speech is wholesome; abstention from gossip is wholesome; non-covetousness is wholesome; non-ill will is wholesome; right view is wholesome. This is called the wholesome.

"And what is the root of the wholesome? Non-greed is a root of the wholesome; non-hate is a root of the wholesome; non-delusion is a root of the wholesome. This is called the root of the wholesome.

"When a noble disciple has thus understood the unwholesome, the root of the unwholesome, the wholesome, and the root of the wholesome, he entirely abandons the underlying tendency to lust, he abolishes the underlying tendency to aversion, he extirpates the underlying tendency to the view and conceit 'I am,' and by abandoning ignorance and arousing true knowledge he here and now makes an end of suffering. In that way too a noble disciple is one of right view, whose view is straight, who has perfect confidence in the Dhamma and has arrived at this true Dhamma."

NUTRIMENT

Saying, "Good, friend," the Bhikkhus delighted and rejoiced in the Venerable Shariputra's words. Then they asked him a further question: "But, friend, might there be another way in which a noble disciple is one of right view . . . and has arrived at this true Dhamma?"—"There might be, friends.

"When, friends, a noble disciple understands nutriment, the origin of nutriment, the cessation of nutriment, and the way leading to the cessation of nutriment, in that way he is one of right view . . . and has arrived at this true Dhamma.

"And what is nutriment, what is the origin of nutriment, what is the cessation of nutriment, what is the way leading to the cessation of nutriment? There are these four kinds of nutriment for the maintenance of beings that already have come to be and for the support of those seeking a new existence. What four? They are physical food as nutriment, gross or subtle; contact as the second; mental volition as the third; and consciousness as the fourth. With the arising of craving there is the arising of nutriment. With the cessation of craving there is the cessation of nutriment. The way leading to the cessation of nutriment is just this Noble Eightfold Path; that is, right view, right intention, right speech, right action, right livelihood, right effort, right mindfulness and right concentration.

"When a noble disciple has thus understood nutriment, the origin of nutriment, the cessation of nutriment, and the way leading to the cessation of nutriment, he entirely abandons the underlying tendency to greed, he abolishes the underlying tendency to aversion, he extirpates the underlying tendency to the view and conceit 'I am,' and by abandoning igno-rance and arousing true knowledge he here and now makes an end of suffering. In that way too a noble disciple is one of right view, whose view is straight, who has perfect confidence in the Dhamma and has arrived at this true Dhamma."

THE FOUR NOBLE TRUTHS

Saying, "Good, friend," the Bhikkhus delighted and rejoiced in the Venerable Shariputra's words. Then they asked him a further question: "But, friend, might there be another way in which a noble disciple is one of right view . . . and has arrived at this true Dhamma?"—"There might be, friends.

"When, friends, a noble disciple understands suffering, the origin of suffering, the cessa-tion of suffering, and the way leading to the cessation of suffering, in that way he is one of right view . . . and has arrived at this true Dhamma.

"And what is suffering, what is the origin of suffering, what is the cessation of suffering, what is the way leading to the cessation of suffering? Birth is suffering; aging is suffering; sick-ness is suffering; death is suffering; sorrow, lamentation, pain, grief and despair are suffering; not to obtain what one wants is suffering; in short, the five aggregates affected by clinging are suffering. This is called suffering.

"And what is the origin of suffering? It is craving, which brings renewal of being, is accom-panied by delight and lust, and delights in this and that; that is, craving for sensual pleasures, craving for being and craving for non-being. This is called the origin of suffering.

"And what is the cessation of suffering? It is the remainder-less fading away and ceasing, the giving up, relinquishing, letting go, and rejecting of that same craving. This is called the cessation of suffering.

"And what is the way leading to the cessation of suffering? It is just this Noble Eightfold Path; that is, right view . . . right concentration. This is called the way leading to the cessation of suffering.

"When a noble disciple has thus understood suffering, the origin of suffering, the cessation of suffering, and the way leading to the cessation of suffering . . . he here and now makes an end of suffering. In that way too a noble disciple is one of right view . . . and has arrived at this true Dhamma."

The Caraka Samhita (Sutra Sthana)—Ayurvedic Medicine and Diet

CARAKA

This is the classic text of Indian medicine, said to date back to Vedic times, but not written down until about 100 A.D. This makes it roughly contemporaneous with the Greek and Chinese dietary selections here. Compare how each culture used the idea of heating and cooking, the speed of digestion and evacuation as well as elemental forces in determining the qualities of food. Here the forces referred to are doshas, *mentioned in the introduction to this section. The text mentions specific recipes, though* rasala *today is a dish made with* paneer *(a kind of pressed fresh cheese) in a sauce made of cashews, tomatoes, and chilies—all of which are New World plants, so it's not clear what the original recipe might have been.*

THE GENERAL QUALITIES OF HONEY

Honey is provocative of Vata, heavy, cooling, curative of hemothermia and Kapha disorders and is synthesizing, dry, astringent and sweet.

ITS INCOMPATABILITY WITH HEAT

Warmed honey causes death unwarmed also, it kills patients suffering from thermal affliction as it is admixed with poisonous matter during the process of accumulation. Being heavy, dry, astringent and cooking, it is wholesome in small doses.

Caraka. "Sutra Sthana." In *The Caraka Samhita*. Vol. 5. Shree Jamanagar, India: Gulabkunverba Ayurvedic Society, 1949.

THE QUALITIES OF THIN GRUEL

Now begins the section on cooked foods. Thin gruel removed hunger, thirst, weariness, weakness, stomach disorder and fever. It causes perspiration, stimulates the gastric fire and regulates the course of flatus and feces.

THE QUALITIES OF THICK GRUEL AND GRUEL-WATER

Thick gruel is nourishing, astringent, light and cordial; gruel water kindles the gastric fire and regulates the downward course of Vata. It softens the channels and causes perspiration. It sustains life on account of its quality of stimulating the gastric fire and of lightness, in those that have undergone the lightening therapy, purificatory procedure, and those who have developed thirst after the unctuous dose has been digested.

THE QUALITIES OF COOKED RICE

The rice that is well cleansed, squeezed out, steam-softened and warm makes light food. In toxicosis and Kapha disorders, fried rice is indicated. Cooked rice uncleansed with the boiled water not pressed out, not properly softened and eaten cold is heavy.

Rice prepared with flesh, vegetables, fat, oil, ghee, marrow or fruit is strengthening, nourishing, cordial, heavy, roborant. Likewise is rice cooked together with black gram [beans] til [sesame], milk and green gram.

THE QUALITIES OF PULSE PREPARATIONS

Preparations of pulses are provocative of Vata, dry and cooling. They must be taken in small quantities with pungent, unctuous and saltish substances.

SUMMARY OF QUALITIES

Preparations that require to be cooked over a low fire for a long time and that are thick and hard are heavy, get slowly digested and impart plumpness and strength.

The heaviness and lightness of preparations must be determined according to the combination of the substances, the nature of preparation and the measure of each substance.

THE QUALITIES OF RASALA PUDDING AND OF CURDS WITH GUR

The preparation called Rasala is roborant, aphrodisiac, unctuous, strengthening and an appetizer. Curds taken with gur increases the unctuous element, is nourishing, cordial and curative of Vata.

THE QUALITIES OF GINGER

Ginger is slightly unctuous, digestive stimulant, aphrodisiac, hot and curative of Vata and Kapha, sweet after digestion, cordial and appetizing.

THE QUALITIES OF BLACK PEPPER

Black pepper is not very hot, in anaphrodisiac, light, appetizer and being depletive and desiccant, it is a digestive stimulant and cures Kapha and Vata.

PART V
Study Questions

1. Why is it that despite very different conceptual frameworks, many of the ancient dietary systems qualify certain foods in the same ways and imagine that they interact with the body in consistent terms?
2. In many traditions, a sacrifice is said to wash away sins. In what way does the horse sacrifice among the Aryans serve this function?
3. In the Buddhist tradition, compassion for other beings is the counterpart to preventing personal suffering by disavowing all cravings. Consider vegetarianism in these terms.
4. Reflect upon the idea that, although in most traditions it is the soul that achieves immortality, the Upanishads seem to suggest that it is our physical molecules that achieve immortality, because they serve as food for other beings in recurring cycles.
5. How does self-denial empower an individual? Compare ascetic traditions across various cultures.

PART SIX

Ancient Hebrews

No other culture through history has been more focused on food than that of the ancient Hebrews. Food provided the material for sacrifice, its consumption was strictly regulated, and ways of eating essentially defined an individual's and the community's relationship to God. The Bible, and the various stages of history described in it, are essentially different dietary phases. Eden, for example, represents God's original intentions for his creation. There is no death there. Adam and Eve are fruitarians, eating only fruits and seeds that involve no killing. This is important for the kosher laws that are elaborated long after. Following the expulsion, as punishment for having eaten forbidden fruit, Adam must earn his bread by the sweat of his brow. In other words, he has become an agriculturalist, while Eve's punishment is subordination and pain in childbirth. Their children, Cain and Abel, are fittingly enough a farmer and a shepherd, reflecting perfectly the new economy of the Middle East following the Neolithic Revolution.

The biggest change, however, comes after the Flood, when God made a concession to human weakness and allows Noah and his descendants to eat anything they want, including meat. It is also here that the first sacrifice is made. The logic of the sacrifice, eventually explained in subsequent books, is that killing (as is necessary when eating meat) is still wrong, and it must be expiated with punishment. That is, justice must be restored in the universe, and someone, or something, must be sacrificed for the transgression. In this case, the animal, or scapegoat, stands in to redress the wrong committed. Later, this sacrifice would become a central and regular part of worship in the Temple in Jerusalem. However, the only other food restriction at this point is blood, which contains the life, and must be poured on the ground rather than consumed. This practice later becomes a formal prohibition under kosher law.

These laws are only given, however, once Moses leads his people out of slavery in Egypt and a new dietary dispensation is framed. Following the same logic of killing being forbidden, animals that kill to survive, because they can't expiate their sin, are considered unclean. Herbivores, on the other hand, are clean because they do not commit murder. Rather than list every possible clean and unclean animal, the Levitical priests devised an easy shorthand way to recognize herbivores: they chew their cud (or, as we would say, they are ruminants) and they have a cloven hoof. This includes cows, sheep, and goats, but not pigs.

There is also a certain logic to the way species were categorized, which probably explains why other creatures were banned. Animals must move in the medium appropriate to their species—meaning that animals on land must walk with four legs, fish with fins must swim, and birds must fly with wings. Taxonomic aberrations, such as shellfish that walk on legs or animals that slither, such as snakes, are unclean. By *unclean* we should not think of dirt or health, though the Levitical priests were concerned with hygiene. The locust is kosher. So it is really a system of thinking that led to these specific rules, and sometimes mistakes were made. Rabbits were probably thought to be carnivores, though they aren't. Having paws makes them unkosher nonetheless.

The importance of these rules in Jewish culture cannot be overstated. They serve to not only bind the community together but keep it distinct from others. One may not eat with non-Jews, and so close relations and marriage outside the faith are rare. More importantly, they constitute a covenant, or promise, made with God to keep the law in return for favor as a chosen people. As the prophets attest, this was not always accomplished easily.

Food rituals span the Hebrew calendar. Passover commemorates the release from bondage in Egypt, recounted in Exodus. During the entire week, no leavened bread is eaten, but rather flat, unleavened matzo, to remember the Jews' hasty escape when they didn't have time to let their bread rise. Special foods are also set on a platter, including bitter herbs, salt water, and a fruit-and-nut paste called *charoset*, which is meant to recall mortar from which bricks were made; a lamb bone recalls sacrifice. Participants in the meal also recline and drink four glasses of wine, and the ceremony may even replicate customs common in the Greek Symposium, since Greek and Jewish thought intermingled in late antiquity.

The fast of Yom Kippur, or the Day of Atonement, is the most important fast, but other fasts took place on emergent occasions, to appease the wrath of God, and to stave off natural disaster or impending enemy armies. Individuals also fasted as an act of penitence, to show God the sincerity of their contrition. This practice would be adopted by early Christians as well.

Judaism changed dramatically after the destruction of the second temple in 70 A.D. Formal ritual sacrifice came to an end, and, because Jews were scattered throughout the Roman Empire due to a series of events known as the Diaspora, worship took place in synagogues. Many rituals also shifted to the household because Jews were usually in the minority.

Genesis

Traditionally ascribed to Moses, modern scholars have recognized four separate authors of the first five books of the Old Testament, though more recently this has been called into question, seeing several revisions upon a central text. Nonetheless, you can note even in the passages below that some parts of the story are told twice and very differently. Scholars disagree about when it was written as well, certainly drawing on an oral tradition, but not perhaps composed until the sixth or fifth century B.C. Although you may be familiar with this text, read it closely to catch all the references to food and how what people eat essentially defines their relationship to God. Consider also how this story is a kind of mythic version of events that really did take place, paralleling in interesting ways the transition from hunting and gathering to agricultural and pastoral life. Yet why is killing missing from Eden, and what function did this vegetarian state serve for the ancient Hebrews? Eden is depicted in images in strikingly different ways throughout history. Compare images of the Renaissance, perhaps by Lucas Cranach or Masaccio, with those of later eras.

CHAPTER 1

The Beginning

[1] In the beginning God created the heavens and the earth. [2] Now the earth was formless and empty, darkness was over the surface of the deep, and the Spirit of God was hovering over the waters.

Genesis 1–3. In *The Holy Bible, New International Version*®. Colorado Springs, CO: Biblica, Inc.

³ And God said, "Let there be light," and there was light. ⁴ God saw that the light was good, and he separated the light from the darkness. ⁵ God called the light "day," and the darkness he called "night." And there was evening, and there was morning—the first day.

⁶ And God said, "Let there be a vault between the waters to separate water from water." ⁷ So God made the vault and separated the water under the vault from the water above it. And it was so. ⁸ God called the vault "sky." And there was evening, and there was morning—the second day.

⁹ And God said, "Let the water under the sky be gathered to one place, and let dry ground appear." And it was so. ¹⁰ God called the dry ground "land," and the gathered waters he called "seas." And God saw that it was good.

¹¹ Then God said, "Let the land produce vegetation: seed-bearing plants and trees on the land that bear fruit with seed in it, according to their various kinds." And it was so. ¹² The land produced vegetation: plants bearing seed according to their kinds and trees bearing fruit with seed in it according to their kinds. And God saw that it was good. ¹³ And there was evening, and there was morning—the third day.

¹⁴ And God said, "Let there be lights in the vault of the sky to separate the day from the night, and let them serve as signs to mark sacred times, and days and years, ¹⁵ and let them be lights in the vault of the sky to give light on the earth." And it was so. ¹⁶ God made two great lights—the greater light to govern the day and the lesser light to govern the night. He also made the stars. ¹⁷ God set them in the vault of the sky to give light on the earth, ¹⁸ to govern the day and the night, and to separate light from darkness. And God saw that it was good. ¹⁹ And there was evening, and there was morning—the fourth day.

²⁰ And God said, "Let the water teem with living creatures, and let birds fly above the earth across the vault of the sky." ²¹ So God created the great creatures of the sea and every living thing with which the water teems and that moves about in it, according to their kinds, and every winged bird according to its kind. And God saw that it was good. ²² God blessed them and said, "Be fruitful and increase in number and fill the water in the seas, and let the birds increase on the earth." ²³ And there was evening, and there was morning—the fifth day.

²⁴ And God said, "Let the land produce living creatures according to their kinds: the livestock, the creatures that move along the ground, and the wild animals, each according to its kind." And it was so. ²⁵ God made the wild animals according to their kinds, the livestock according to their kinds, and all the creatures that move along the ground according to their kinds. And God saw that it was good.

²⁶ Then God said, "Let us make mankind in our image, in our likeness, so that they may rule over the fish in the sea and the birds in the sky, over the livestock and all the wild animals, and over all the creatures that move along the ground."

²⁷ So God created mankind in his own image, in the image of God he created them; male and female he created them.

²⁸ God blessed them and said to them, "Be fruitful and increase in number; fill the earth and subdue it. Rule over the fish in the sea and the birds in the sky and over every living creature that moves on the ground."

²⁹ Then God said, "I give you every seed-bearing plant on the face of the whole earth and every tree that has fruit with seed in it. They will be yours for food. ³⁰ And to all the

beasts of the earth and all the birds in the sky and all the creatures that move along the ground—everything that has the breath of life in it—I give every green plant for food." And it was so.

³¹ God saw all that he had made, and it was very good. And there was evening, and there was morning—the sixth day.

CHAPTER 2

¹ Thus the heavens and the earth were completed in all their vast array.

² By the seventh day God had finished the work he had been doing; so on the seventh day he rested from all his work. ³ Then God blessed the seventh day and made it holy, because on it he rested from all the work of creating that he had done.

Adam and Eve

⁴ This is the account of the heavens and the earth when they were created, when the LORD God made the earth and the heavens.

⁵ Now no shrub had yet appeared on the earth and no plant had yet sprung up, for the LORD God had not sent rain on the earth and there was no one to work the ground, ⁶ but streams came up from the earth and watered the whole surface of the ground. ⁷ Then the LORD God formed a man from the dust of the ground and breathed into his nostrils the breath of life, and the man became a living being.

⁸ Now the LORD God had planted a garden in the east, in Eden; and there he put the man he had formed. ⁹ The LORD God made all kinds of trees grow out of the ground—trees that were pleasing to the eye and good for food. In the middle of the garden were the tree of life and the tree of the knowledge of good and evil.

¹⁰ A river watering the garden flowed from Eden; from there it was separated into four headwaters. ¹¹ The name of the first is the Pishon; it winds through the entire land of Havilah, where there is gold. ¹² (The gold of that land is good; aromatic resin and onyx are also there.) ¹³ The name of the second river is the Gihon; it winds through the entire land of Cush. ¹⁴ The name of the third river is the Tigris; it runs along the east side of Ashur. And the fourth river is the Euphrates.

¹⁵ The LORD God took the man and put him in the Garden of Eden to work it and take care of it. ¹⁶ And the LORD God commanded the man, "You are free to eat from any tree in the garden; ¹⁷ but you must not eat from the tree of the knowledge of good and evil, for when you eat from it you will certainly die."

¹⁸ The LORD God said, "It is not good for the man to be alone. I will make a helper suitable for him."

¹⁹ Now the LORD God had formed out of the ground all the wild animals and all the birds in the sky. He brought them to the man to see what he would name them; and whatever the man called each living creature, that was its name. ²⁰ So the man gave names to all the livestock, the birds in the sky and all the wild animals.

But for Adam no suitable helper was found. ²¹ So the LORD God caused the man to fall into a deep sleep; and while he was sleeping, he took one of the man's ribs and then closed up the place with flesh. ²² Then the LORD God made a woman from the rib he had taken out of the man, and he brought her to the man.

²³ The man said,

"This is now bone of my bones
and flesh of my flesh;
she shall be called 'woman,'
for she was taken out of man."

²⁴ That is why a man leaves his father and mother and is united to his wife, and they become one flesh.

²⁵ Adam and his wife were both naked, and they felt no shame.

CHAPTER 3

The Fall

¹ Now the serpent was more crafty than any of the wild animals the LORD God had made. He said to the woman, "Did God really say, 'You must not eat from any tree in the garden'?"

² The woman said to the serpent, "We may eat fruit from the trees in the garden, ³ but God did say, 'You must not eat fruit from the tree that is in the middle of the garden, and you must not touch it, or you will die.'"

⁴ "You will not certainly die," the serpent said to the woman. ⁵ "For God knows that when you eat from it your eyes will be opened, and you will be like God, knowing good and evil."

⁶ When the woman saw that the fruit of the tree was good for food and pleasing to the eye, and also desirable for gaining wisdom, she took some and ate it. She also gave some to her husband, who was with her, and he ate it. ⁷ Then the eyes of both of them were opened, and they realized they were naked; so they sewed fig leaves together and made coverings for themselves.

⁸ Then the man and his wife heard the sound of the LORD God as he was walking in the garden in the cool of the day, and they hid from the LORD God among the trees of the garden. ⁹ But the LORD God called to the man, "Where are you?"

¹⁰ He answered, "I heard you in the garden, and I was afraid because I was naked; so I hid."

¹¹ And he said, "Who told you that you were naked? Have you eaten from the tree that I commanded you not to eat from?"

¹² The man said, "The woman you put here with me—she gave me some fruit from the tree, and I ate it."

¹³ Then the LORD God said to the woman, "What is this you have done?"

The woman said, "The serpent deceived me, and I ate."

¹⁴ So the LORD God said to the serpent, "Because you have done this,

"Cursed are you above all livestock
and all wild animals!
You will crawl on your belly

and you will eat dust
all the days of your life.
¹⁵ And I will put enmity
between you and the woman,
and between your offspring and hers;
he will crush your head,
and you will strike his heel."

¹⁶ To the woman he said,

"I will make your pains in childbearing very severe;
with painful labor you will give birth to children.
Your desire will be for your husband,
and he will rule over you."

¹⁷ To Adam he said, "Because you listened to your wife and ate fruit from the tree about which I commanded you, 'You must not eat from it,'

"Cursed is the ground because of you;
through painful toil you will eat food from it
all the days of your life.
¹⁸ It will produce thorns and thistles for you,
and you will eat the plants of the field.
¹⁹ By the sweat of your brow
you will eat your food
until you return to the ground,
since from it you were taken;
for dust you are
and to dust you will return."

²⁰ Adam named his wife Eve, because she would become the mother of all the living.

²¹ The LORD God made garments of skin for Adam and his wife and clothed them. ²² And the LORD God said, "The man has now become like one of us, knowing good and evil. He must not be allowed to reach out his hand and take also from the tree of life and eat, and live forever." ²³ So the LORD God banished him from the Garden of Eden to work the ground from which he had been taken. ²⁴ After he drove the man out, he placed on the east side of the Garden of Eden cherubim and a flaming sword flashing back and forth to guard the way to the tree of life.

THIRTY-FIVE

Leviticus and Deuteronomy

In these chapters and the brief selection from Deuteronomy are laid down the ritual laws for sacrifice as well as the rules explaining clean and unclean animals. The Levites were a priestly class, and it is clear that part of the offerings serve to feed them. Consider the function of the sacrifice here: Is it to feed God? Why does he want sacrifice? Is it merely for atonement of sins, or does it serve some other function? Also imagine what the experience of this ritual slaughter would have been like, in many ways much like entering a slaughterhouse today. Why would this be something worthy of witnessing and even making sacred? Finally, what exactly does unclean *mean for the Hebrews?*

CHAPTER 1

The Burnt Offering

¹ The LORD called to Moses and spoke to him from the tent of meeting. He said, ² "Speak to the Israelites and say to them: 'When anyone among you brings an offering to the LORD, bring as your offering an animal from either the herd or the flock.

³ "'If the offering is a burnt offering from the herd, you are to offer a male without defect. You must present it at the entrance to the tent of meeting so that it will be acceptable to the LORD. ⁴ You are to lay your hand on the head of the burnt offering, and it will be accepted

---

Leviticus 1–3, 7, 11, Deuteronomy 14:1–21. In *The Holy Bible, New International Version*®. Colorado Springs, CO: Biblica, Inc.

on your behalf to make atonement for you. ⁵ You are to slaughter the young bull before the LORD, and then Aaron's sons the priests shall bring the blood and splash it against the sides of the altar at the entrance to the tent of meeting. ⁶ You are to skin the burnt offering and cut it into pieces. ⁷ The sons of Aaron the priest are to put fire on the altar and arrange wood on the fire. ⁸ Then Aaron's sons the priests shall arrange the pieces, including the head and the fat, on the wood that is burning on the altar. ⁹ You are to wash the internal organs and the legs with water, and the priest is to burn all of it on the altar. It is a burnt offering, a food offering, an aroma pleasing to the LORD.

¹⁰ "'If the offering is a burnt offering from the flock, from either the sheep or the goats, you are to offer a male without defect. ¹¹ You are to slaughter it at the north side of the altar before the LORD, and Aaron's sons the priests shall splash its blood against the sides of the altar. ¹² You are to cut it into pieces, and the priest shall arrange them, including the head and the fat, on the wood that is burning on the altar. ¹³ You are to wash the internal organs and the legs with water, and the priest is to bring all of them and burn them on the altar. It is a burnt offering, a food offering, an aroma pleasing to the LORD.

¹⁴ "'If the offering to the LORD is a burnt offering of birds, you are to offer a dove or a young pigeon. ¹⁵ The priest shall bring it to the altar, wring off the head and burn it on the altar; its blood shall be drained out on the side of the altar. ¹⁶ He is to remove the crop and the feathers and throw them down east of the altar where the ashes are. ¹⁷ He shall tear it open by the wings, not dividing it completely, and then the priest shall burn it on the wood that is burning on the altar. It is a burnt offering, a food offering, an aroma pleasing to the LORD.'"

CHAPTER 2

The Grain Offering

¹ "'When anyone brings a grain offering to the LORD, their offering is to be of the finest flour. They are to pour olive oil on it, put incense on it ² and take it to Aaron's sons the priests. The priest shall take a handful of the flour and oil, together with all the incense, and burn this as a memorial portion on the altar, a food offering, an aroma pleasing to the LORD. ³ The rest of the grain offering belongs to Aaron and his sons; it is a most holy part of the food offerings presented to the LORD.

⁴ "'If you bring a grain offering baked in an oven, it is to consist of the finest flour: either thick loaves made without yeast and with olive oil mixed in or thin loaves made without yeast and brushed with olive oil. ⁵ If your grain offering is prepared on a griddle, it is to be made of the finest flour mixed with oil, and without yeast. ⁶ Crumble it and pour oil on it; it is a grain offering. ⁷ If your grain offering is cooked in a pan, it is to be made of the finest flour and some olive oil. ⁸ Bring the grain offering made of these things to the LORD; present it to the priest, who shall take it to the altar. ⁹ He shall take out the memorial portion from the grain offering and burn it on the altar as a food offering, an aroma pleasing to the LORD. ¹⁰ The rest of the grain offering belongs to Aaron and his sons; it is a most holy part of the food offerings presented to the LORD.

¹¹ "'Every grain offering you bring to the LORD must be made without yeast, for you are not to burn any yeast or honey in a food offering presented to the LORD. ¹² You may bring

them to the LORD as an offering of the firstfruits, but they are not to be offered on the altar as a pleasing aroma. [13] Season all your grain offerings with salt. Do not leave the salt of the covenant of your God out of your grain offerings; add salt to all your offerings.

[14] " 'If you bring a grain offering of firstfruits to the LORD, offer crushed heads of new grain roasted in the fire. [15] Put oil and incense on it; it is a grain offering. [16] The priest shall burn the memorial portion of the crushed grain and the oil, together with all the incense, as a food offering presented to the LORD.

CHAPTER 3

The Fellowship Offering

[1] " 'If your offering is a fellowship offering, and you offer an animal from the herd, whether male or female, you are to present before the LORD an animal without defect. [2] You are to lay your hand on the head of your offering and slaughter it at the entrance to the tent of meeting. Then Aaron's sons the priests shall splash the blood against the sides of the altar. [3] From the fellowship offering you are to bring a food offering to the LORD: the internal organs and all the fat that is connected to them, [4] both kidneys with the fat on them near the loins, and the long lobe of the liver, which you will remove with the kidneys. [5] Then Aaron's sons are to burn it on the altar on top of the burnt offering that is lying on the burning wood; it is a food offering, an aroma pleasing to the LORD.

[6] " 'If you offer an animal from the flock as a fellowship offering to the LORD, you are to offer a male or female without defect. [7] If you offer a lamb, you are to present it before the LORD, [8] lay your hand on its head and slaughter it in front of the tent of meeting. Then Aaron's sons shall splash its blood against the sides of the altar. [9] From the fellowship offering you are to bring a food offering to the LORD: its fat, the entire fat tail cut off close to the backbone, the internal organs and all the fat that is connected to them, [10] both kidneys with the fat on them near the loins, and the long lobe of the liver, which you will remove with the kidneys. [11] The priest shall burn them on the altar as a food offering presented to the LORD.

[12] " 'If your offering is a goat, you are to present it before the LORD, [13] lay your hand on its head and slaughter it in front of the tent of meeting. Then Aaron's sons shall splash its blood against the sides of the altar. [14] From what you offer you are to present this food offering to the LORD: the internal organs and all the fat that is connected to them, [15] both kidneys with the fat on them near the loins, and the long lobe of the liver, which you will remove with the kidneys. [16] The priest shall burn them on the altar as a food offering, a pleasing aroma. All the fat is the LORD's.' "

CHAPTER 7

The Guilt Offering

[1] " 'These are the regulations for the guilt offering, which is most holy: [2] The guilt offering is to be slaughtered in the place where the burnt offering is slaughtered, and its blood is to be splashed against the sides of the altar. [3] All its fat shall be offered: the fat tail and the fat that

covers the internal organs, [4] both kidneys with the fat on them near the loins, and the long lobe of the liver, which is to be removed with the kidneys. [5] The priest shall burn them on the altar as a food offering presented to the LORD. It is a guilt offering. [6] Any male in a priest's family may eat it, but it must be eaten in the sanctuary area; it is most holy.

[7] "'The same law applies to both the sin offering and the guilt offering: They belong to the priest who makes atonement with them. [8] The priest who offers a burnt offering for anyone may keep its hide for himself. [9] Every grain offering baked in an oven or cooked in a pan or on a griddle belongs to the priest who offers it, [10] and every grain offering, whether mixed with olive oil or dry, belongs equally to all the sons of Aaron.

The Fellowship Offering

[11] "'These are the regulations for the fellowship offering anyone may present to the LORD:

[12] "'If they offer it as an expression of thankfulness, then along with this thank offering they are to offer thick loaves made without yeast and with olive oil mixed in, thin loaves made without yeast and brushed with oil, and thick loaves of the finest flour well-kneaded and with oil mixed in. [13] Along with their fellowship offering of thanksgiving they are to present an offering with thick loaves of bread made with yeast. [14] They are to bring one of each kind as an offering, a contribution to the LORD; it belongs to the priest who splashes the blood of the fellowship offering against the altar. [15] The meat of their fellowship offering of thanksgiving must be eaten on the day it is offered; they must leave none of it till morning.

[16] "'If, however, their offering is the result of a vow or is a freewill offering, the sacrifice shall be eaten on the day they offer it, but anything left over may be eaten on the next day. [17] Any meat of the sacrifice left over till the third day must be burned up. [18] If any meat of the fellowship offering is eaten on the third day, the one who offered it will not be accepted. It will not be reckoned to their credit, for it has become impure; the person who eats any of it will be held responsible.

[19] "'Meat that touches anything ceremonially unclean must not be eaten; it must be burned up. As for other meat, anyone ceremonially clean may eat it. [20] But if anyone who is unclean eats any meat of the fellowship offering belonging to the LORD, they must be cut off from their people. [21] Anyone who touches something unclean—whether human uncleanness or an unclean animal or any unclean creature that moves along the ground—and then eats any of the meat of the fellowship offering belonging to the LORD must be cut off from their people.'"

Eating Fat and Blood Forbidden

[22] The LORD said to Moses, [23] "Say to the Israelites: 'Do not eat any of the fat of cattle, sheep or goats. [24] The fat of an animal found dead or torn by wild animals may be used for any other purpose, but you must not eat it. [25] Anyone who eats the fat of an animal from which a food offering may be presented to the LORD must be cut off from their people. [26] And wherever you live, you must not eat the blood of any bird or animal. [27] Anyone who eats blood must be cut off from their people.'"

The Priests' Share

[28] The LORD said to Moses, [29] "Say to the Israelites: 'Anyone who brings a fellowship offering to the LORD is to bring part of it as their sacrifice to the LORD. [30] With their own hands they are to present the food offering to the LORD; they are to bring the fat, together with the breast, and wave the breast before the LORD as a wave offering. [31] The priest shall burn the fat on the altar, but the breast belongs to Aaron and his sons. [32] You are to give the right thigh of your fellowship offerings to the priest as a contribution. [33] The son of Aaron who offers the blood and the fat of the fellowship offering shall have the right thigh as his share. [34] From the fellowship offerings of the Israelites, I have taken the breast that is waved and the thigh that is presented and have given them to Aaron the priest and his sons as their perpetual share from the Israelites.'"

[35] This is the portion of the food offerings presented to the LORD that were allotted to Aaron and his sons on the day they were presented to serve the LORD as priests. [36] On the day they were anointed, the LORD commanded that the Israelites give this to them as their perpetual share for the generations to come.

[37] These, then, are the regulations for the burnt offering, the grain offering, the sin offering, the guilt offering, the ordination offering and the fellowship offering, [38] which the LORD gave Moses at Mount Sinai in the Desert of Sinai on the day he commanded the Israelites to bring their offerings to the LORD.

CHAPTER 11

Clean and Unclean Food

[1] The LORD said to Moses and Aaron, [2] "Say to the Israelites: 'Of all the animals that live on land, these are the ones you may eat: [3] You may eat any animal that has a divided hoof and that chews the cud.

[4] "'There are some that only chew the cud or only have a divided hoof, but you must not eat them. The camel, though it chews the cud, does not have a divided hoof; it is ceremonially unclean for you. [5] The hyrax, though it chews the cud, does not have a divided hoof; it is unclean for you. [6] The rabbit, though it chews the cud, does not have a divided hoof; it is unclean for you. [7] And the pig, though it has a divided hoof, does not chew the cud; it is unclean for you. [8] You must not eat their meat or touch their carcasses; they are unclean for you.

[9] "'Of all the creatures living in the water of the seas and the streams you may eat any that have fins and scales. [10] But all creatures in the seas or streams that do not have fins and scales—whether among all the swarming things or among all the other living creatures in the water—you are to regard as unclean. [11] And since you are to regard them as unclean, you must not eat their meat; you must regard their carcasses as unclean. [12] Anything living in the water that does not have fins and scales is to be regarded as unclean by you.

[13] "'These are the birds you are to regard as unclean and not eat because they are unclean: the eagle, the vulture, the black vulture, [14] the red kite, any kind of black kite, [15] any kind of raven, [16] the horned owl, the screech owl, the gull, any kind of hawk, [17] the little owl, the

cormorant, the great owl, ¹⁸ the white owl, the desert owl, the osprey, ¹⁹ the stork, any kind of heron, the hoopoe and the bat.

²⁰ " 'All flying insects that walk on all fours are to be regarded as unclean by you. ²¹ There are, however, some flying insects that walk on all fours that you may eat: those that have jointed legs for hopping on the ground. ²² Of these you may eat any kind of locust, katydid, cricket or grasshopper. ²³ But all other flying insects that have four legs you are to regard as unclean.

²⁴ " 'You will make yourselves unclean by these; whoever touches their carcasses will be unclean till evening. ²⁵ Whoever picks up one of their carcasses must wash their clothes, and they will be unclean till evening.

²⁶ " 'Every animal that does not have a divided hoof or that does not chew the cud is unclean for you; whoever touches the carcass of any of them will be unclean. ²⁷ Of all the animals that walk on all fours, those that walk on their paws are unclean for you; whoever touches their carcasses will be unclean till evening. ²⁸ Anyone who picks up their carcasses must wash their clothes, and they will be unclean till evening. These animals are unclean for you.

²⁹ " 'Of the animals that move along the ground, these are unclean for you: the weasel, the rat, any kind of great lizard, ³⁰ the gecko, the monitor lizard, the wall lizard, the skink and the chameleon. ³¹ Of all those that move along the ground, these are unclean for you. Whoever touches them when they are dead will be unclean till evening. ³² When one of them dies and falls on something, that article, whatever its use, will be unclean, whether it is made of wood, cloth, hide or sackcloth. Put it in water; it will be unclean till evening, and then it will be clean. ³³ If one of them falls into a clay pot, everything in it will be unclean, and you must break the pot. ³⁴ Any food you are allowed to eat that has come into contact with water from any such pot is unclean, and any liquid that is drunk from such a pot is unclean. ³⁵ Anything that one of their carcasses falls on becomes unclean; an oven or cooking pot must be broken up. They are unclean, and you are to regard them as unclean. ³⁶ A spring, however, or a cistern for collecting water remains clean, but anyone who touches one of these carcasses is unclean. ³⁷ If a carcass falls on any seeds that are to be planted, they remain clean. ³⁸ But if water has been put on the seed and a carcass falls on it, it is unclean for you.

³⁹ " 'If an animal that you are allowed to eat dies, anyone who touches its carcass will be unclean till evening. ⁴⁰ Anyone who eats some of its carcass must wash their clothes, and they will be unclean till evening. Anyone who picks up the carcass must wash their clothes, and they will be unclean till evening.

⁴¹ " 'Every creature that moves along the ground is to be regarded as unclean; it is not to be eaten. ⁴² You are not to eat any creature that moves along the ground, whether it moves on its belly or walks on all fours or on many feet; it is unclean. ⁴³ Do not defile yourselves by any of these creatures. Do not make yourselves unclean by means of them or be made unclean by them. ⁴⁴ I am the LORD your God; consecrate yourselves and be holy, because I am holy. Do not make yourselves unclean by any creature that moves along the ground. ⁴⁵ I am the LORD, who brought you up out of Egypt to be your God; therefore be holy, because I am holy.

⁴⁶ " 'These are the regulations concerning animals, birds, every living thing that moves about in the water and every creature that moves along the ground. ⁴⁷ You must distinguish

between the unclean and the clean, between living creatures that may be eaten and those that may not be eaten.'"

DEUTERONOMY 14:1–21

Clean and Unclean Food

[1] You are the children of the LORD your God. Do not cut yourselves or shave the front of your heads for the dead, [2] for you are a people holy to the LORD your God. Out of all the peoples on the face of the earth, the LORD has chosen you to be his treasured possession.

[3] Do not eat any detestable thing. [4] These are the animals you may eat: the ox, the sheep, the goat, [5] the deer, the gazelle, the roe deer, the wild goat, the ibex, the antelope and the mountain sheep. [6] You may eat any animal that has a divided hoof and that chews the cud. [7] However, of those that chew the cud or that have a divided hoof you may not eat the camel, the rabbit or the hyrax. Although they chew the cud, they do not have a divided hoof; they are ceremonially unclean for you. [8] The pig is also unclean; although it has a divided hoof, it does not chew the cud. You are not to eat their meat or touch their carcasses.

[9] Of all the creatures living in the water, you may eat any that has fins and scales. [10] But anything that does not have fins and scales you may not eat; for you it is unclean.

[11] You may eat any clean bird. [12] But these you may not eat: the eagle, the vulture, the black vulture, [13] the red kite, the black kite, any kind of falcon, [14] any kind of raven, [15] the horned owl, the screech owl, the gull, any kind of hawk, [16] the little owl, the great owl, the white owl, [17] the desert owl, the osprey, the cormorant, [18] the stork, any kind of heron, the hoopoe and the bat.

[19] All flying insects are unclean to you; do not eat them. [20] But any winged creature that is clean you may eat.

[21] Do not eat anything you find already dead. You may give it to the foreigner residing in any of your towns, and they may eat it, or you may sell it to any other foreigner. But you are a people holy to the LORD your God.

Do not cook a young goat in its mother's milk.

THIRTY-SIX

The Song of Songs

These verses are scattered excerpts dealing with food taken from the love poems traditionally ascribed to King Solomon. Many have interpreted these as an allegorical statement of one's love for God, but it is difficult not to read into these a sensuous and even luxuriant culture that appreciates excellent food, perfumes, and produce of nature. The fact that these products could be obtained from great distances attests to the wealth of this culture at the height of its power.

1:2–3, 7–8, 12–13

She
[2] Let him kiss me with the kisses of his mouth—
   for your love is more delightful than wine.
[3] Pleasing is the fragrance of your perfumes;
   your name is like perfume poured out.
   No wonder the young women love you!
[. . .]
[7] Tell me, you whom I love,
   where you graze your flock
   and where you rest your sheep at midday.
   Why should I be like a veiled woman

The Song of Songs 1, 2, 4–7. In *The Holy Bible, New International Version*®. Colorado Springs, CO: Biblica, Inc.

beside the flocks of your friends?
Friends
[8] If you do not know, most beautiful of women,
follow the tracks of the sheep
and graze your young goats
by the tents of the shepherds.
[. . .]
She
[12] While the king was at his table,
my perfume spread its fragrance.
[13] My beloved is to me a sachet of myrrh
resting between my breasts.

2:3–5, 10–16

She
[3] Like an apple tree among the trees of the forest
is my beloved among the young men.
I delight to sit in his shade,
and his fruit is sweet to my taste.
[4] Let him lead me to the banquet hall,
and let his banner over me be love.
[5] Strengthen me with raisins,
refresh me with apples,
for I am faint with love.
[. . .]
[10] My beloved spoke and said to me,
"Arise, my darling,
my beautiful one, come with me.
[11] See! The winter is past;
the rains are over and gone.
[12] Flowers appear on the earth;
the season of singing has come,
the cooing of doves
is heard in our land.
[13] The fig tree forms its early fruit;
the blossoming vines spread their fragrance.
Arise, come, my darling;
my beautiful one, come with me."
He
[14] My dove in the clefts of the rock,
in the hiding places on the mountainside,
show me your face,

let me hear your voice;
for your voice is sweet,
and your face is lovely.
¹⁵ Catch for us the foxes,
the little foxes
that ruin the vineyards,
our vineyards that are in bloom.
She
¹⁶ My beloved is mine and I am his;
he browses among the lilies.

4:1–16

He
¹ How beautiful you are, my darling!
Oh, how beautiful!
Your eyes behind your veil are doves.
Your hair is like a flock of goats
descending from the hills of Gilead.
² Your teeth are like a flock of sheep just shorn,
coming up from the washing.
Each has its twin;
not one of them is alone.
³ Your lips are like a scarlet ribbon;
your mouth is lovely.
Your temples behind your veil
are like the halves of a pomegranate.
⁴ Your neck is like the tower of David,
built with courses of stone;
on it hang a thousand shields,
all of them shields of warriors.
⁵ Your breasts are like two fawns,
like twin fawns of a gazelle
that browse among the lilies.
⁶ Until the day breaks
and the shadows flee,
I will go to the mountain of myrrh
and to the hill of incense.
⁷ You are altogether beautiful, my darling;
there is no flaw in you.
⁸ Come with me from Lebanon, my bride,
come with me from Lebanon.
Descend from the crest of Amana,

from the top of Senir, the summit of Hermon,
from the lions' dens
and the mountain haunts of leopards.
⁹ You have stolen my heart, my sister, my bride;
you have stolen my heart
with one glance of your eyes,
with one jewel of your necklace.
¹⁰ How delightful is your love, my sister, my bride!
How much more pleasing is your love than wine,
and the fragrance of your perfume
more than any spice!
¹¹ Your lips drop sweetness as the honeycomb, my bride;
milk and honey are under your tongue.
The fragrance of your garments
is like the fragrance of Lebanon.
¹² You are a garden locked up, my sister, my bride;
you are a spring enclosed, a sealed fountain.
¹³ Your plants are an orchard of pomegranates
with choice fruits,
with henna and nard,
¹⁴ nard and saffron,
calamus and cinnamon,
with every kind of incense tree,
with myrrh and aloes
and all the finest spices.
¹⁵ You are a garden fountain,
a well of flowing water
streaming down from Lebanon.
She
¹⁶ Awake, north wind,
and come, south wind!
Blow on my garden,
that its fragrance may spread everywhere.
Let my beloved come into his garden
and taste its choice fruits.

5:1, 5, 11–16

He
¹ I have come into my garden, my sister, my bride;
I have gathered my myrrh with my spice.
I have eaten my honeycomb and my honey;
I have drunk my wine and my milk.

Friends
Eat, friends, and drink;
drink your fill of love.
[. . .]
[She]
⁵ I arose to open for my beloved,
and my hands dripped with myrrh,
my fingers with flowing myrrh,
on the handles of the bolt.
[. . .]
¹¹ His head is purest gold;
 his hair is wavy
 and black as a raven.
¹² His eyes are like doves
by the water streams,
washed in milk,
mounted like jewels.
¹³ His cheeks are like beds of spice
yielding perfume.
His lips are like lilies
dripping with myrrh.
¹⁴ His arms are rods of gold
set with topaz.
His body is like polished ivory
decorated with lapis lazuli.
¹⁵ His legs are pillars of marble
set on bases of pure gold.
His appearance is like Lebanon,
choice as its cedars.
¹⁶ His mouth is sweetness itself;
he is altogether lovely.
This is my beloved, this is my friend,
daughters of Jerusalem.

6: 5–7, 11

[He]
⁵ Turn your eyes from me;
they overwhelm me.
Your hair is like a flock of goats
descending from Gilead.
⁶ Your teeth are like a flock of sheep
coming up from the washing.

Each has its twin,
not one of them is missing.
[7] Your temples behind your veil
are like the halves of a pomegranate.
[. . .]
[11] I went down to the grove of nut trees
to look at the new growth in the valley,
to see if the vines had budded
or the pomegranates were in bloom.

7:1–4, 6–13

[He]
[1] How beautiful your sandaled feet,
O prince's daughter!
Your graceful legs are like jewels,
the work of an artist's hands.
[2] Your navel is a rounded goblet
that never lacks blended wine.
Your waist is a mound of wheat
encircled by lilies.
[3] Your breasts are like two fawns,
like twin fawns of a gazelle.
[4] Your neck is like an ivory tower.
Your eyes are the pools of Heshbon
by the gate of Bath Rabbim.
Your nose is like the tower of Lebanon
looking toward Damascus.
[. . .]
[6] How beautiful you are and how pleasing,
my love, with your delights!
[7] Your stature is like that of the palm,
and your breasts like clusters of fruit.
[8] I said, "I will climb the palm tree;
I will take hold of its fruit."
May your breasts be like clusters of grapes on the vine,
the fragrance of your breath like apples,
[9] and your mouth like the best wine.
She
May the wine go straight to my beloved,
flowing gently over lips and teeth.
[10] I belong to my beloved,

and his desire is for me.

[11] Come, my beloved, let us go to the countryside,
let us spend the night in the villages.
[12] Let us go early to the vineyards
to see if the vines have budded,
if their blossoms have opened,
and if the pomegranates are in bloom—
there I will give you my love.
[13] The mandrakes send out their fragrance,
and at our door is every delicacy,
both new and old,
that I have stored up for you, my beloved.

Study Questions

1. In what ways do food prohibitions promote cohesion among people in a group? How and why do they necessarily exclude others?
2. What other possible reasons could have led the ancient Hebrews to consider pork unclean? What of the other forbidden foods?
3. Explain the meaning of sacrifice in the biblical texts. Why does God want animals dismembered, their blood flung around the altar and fat burned? What does this do for the community and for the class of priests?
4. Judging from the foods mentioned, how has Hebrew culture changed in the era of kings? How far do their trade routes extend?
5. What does the story of transgression and fall from Eden explain to the ancient Hebrews? How does it justify the status quo and the agricultural and pastoral way of life?

PART SEVEN

Early Middle Ages

Christianity began as a reform movement within Judaism at the time Palestine, as the province was called, was under Roman rule. The Jews enjoyed a privileged but precarious position within the empire. They were favored as good taxpayers, but their monotheism would not allow them to worship the official state religion of Rome. They were also known to have revolted against previous rulers—the revolt of the Maccabees during Seleucid Greek rule being only the most memorable. Hanukkah commemorates this revolt.

It was in this milieu that Jesus of Nazareth was born. Although Jesus often told parables that recounted the experience of common people, fishermen, vineyard workers, and other food-related professions, his message was not primarily concerned with food regulations. He did often perform miracles, providing loaves of bread and fish, or plentiful wine at wedding parties. Nonetheless, it was only when Paul opened the religion to non-Jews and began to explain that the laws of the Old Testament were now abrogated did Christians begin to abandon the kosher laws and ritual sacrifice. Early Christians in general deemphasized ritual worship and focused more on charitable acts and moral behavior; thus, they replaced the literal fulfillment of the law with a figurative one. In other words, a new dietary dispensation was ushered in. Jesus's sacrifice on the cross fulfilled and replaced the sacrifice of animals in the Temple—hence the idea that he died for our sins; he became the scapegoat punished to absolve the sins of others.

While kosher laws were abolished—considering it is not what goes into the mouth but what comes out (i.e., words) that defiles a man—the early Christians did have many concerns over food. For example, was it permissible to eat food sacrificed to pagan gods? Technically, yes, was the answer given to the Greek Christians, who wanted to remain loyal to their civic administrations. All the same, it would probably be better to avoid the communal sacrifice and feasts since it might lead others astray into actually believing in paganism.

Another unique attitude toward food stemmed from the practice of monasticism and asceticism. Although there were Jewish hermits—Saint John the Baptist might be included among them—and sometimes entire communities (such as the Essenes) went into the desert to practice purification rituals, the practice of extreme self-mortification is a Christian phenomenon. The idea is partly that being well nourished increases the production of blood and sperm (both in men and women)—an idea taken directly from Greek medicine—and a plethora of sperm incites the libido. Therefore, cutting down or abstaining entirely from nourishing foods such as meat would be an aid to abstinence. Celibacy was especially important for holy men, and thus a variety of vegetarianism was introduced. Fish were eaten, however, because they were categorized as cold and moist and therefore, like vegetables, not very nourishing. Asceticism takes these ideas a step further, insisting that it is a positive good to mortify the flesh not to the point of bodily destruction but to abate the flesh and therefore strengthen the soul. Men and sometimes women performed acts of heroic asceticism, fasting for extended periods, depriving themselves of sleep, and, of course, abstaining from sexual relations—all biological imperatives for survival but culturally valued since individuals could pray for and be penitent for the souls of others.

These values also permeated the secular community, especially insofar as fasts became ritually prescribed. On the vigils of saint's days, and especially during Lent, the forty days between Ash Wednesday and Easter, minus Sundays, meat and meat products were forbidden. This included cheese, butter, and milk. Practice varied widely from place to place, but Saturdays were usually designated as fasts (beginning on Friday night) and sometimes Wednesdays as well. This meant that a large proportion of the calendar was devoted to fast days, despite the near total absence of food regulations from the start. This was merely part and parcel of the entire process of institutionalizing the church, putting in an ecclesiastical hierarchy, defining orthodoxy, and defining ritual practice. Monasticism was also regularized into formal orders, and the Rule of Saint Benedict provided the model for the Western Church. In many cases, these were small islands of culture in a sea of turmoil, preserving not only ancient texts, including manuscripts of Apicius, but maintaining vineyards and herb gardens and sometimes horticultural practices inherited from classical culture.

Although Christianity became the official religion of the Roman Empire, after the fall of the Western half in the fifth century, Germanic tribes swept into Europe. They were not only pagan but brought with them very different food practices and attitudes. They valued hunting wild animals and brewing beer rather than the Roman practice of planting neat rows of wheat, vineyards, grafted orchards, and well-maintained stockyards. The Germanic tribes that eventually came to rule did keep cattle but preferred grazing over open spaces and letting pigs run free in forests. The cuisine they introduced was also much simpler, based more on stews and roasts. The dietary book of Anthimus, visiting the Franks, provides a decent impression of their foodways.

Charlemagne, ruler of the Frankish Empire, and crowned emperor in 800, inherited the three major traditions of medieval food culture. As a German warrior he enjoyed large hunks of flesh and copious drafts of beer. As an emperor modeling his state as best he could on ancient or Byzantine models, he was expected to live a sober and moderate life in the cultivation of virtue. On the other hand, as a Christian, he was expected to fast and be penitent. It must have been very difficult to reconcile these many factors, as his biographer Einhard suggests. The daily administration of his empire, however, and the practicalities of feeding a moving army are recorded in his Capitularies.

THIRTY-SEVEN

Matthew

In this gospel the departure from Levitical law, including food, is first explained. The Pharisees were one among several groups within Judaism who ironically appealed to common people and the spirit of the law rather than the letter of the law and Temple sacrifice, which more closely resembles the ideas of their rivals, the Sadducees. Nonetheless, this is how they were depicted by Matthew, writing long after these events took place. The second selection is about the Last Supper, the origin of the central sacrament of the mass in Christianity.

CHAPTER 15

That Which Defiles

¹ Then some Pharisees and teachers of the law came to Jesus from Jerusalem and asked, ² "Why do your disciples break the tradition of the elders? They don't wash their hands before they eat!"

³ Jesus replied, "And why do you break the command of God for the sake of your tradition? ⁴ For God said, 'Honor your father and mother' and 'Anyone who curses their father or mother is to be put to death.' ⁵ But you say that if anyone declares that what might have been used to help their father or mother is 'devoted to God,' ⁶ they are not to 'honor their father or mother' with it. Thus you nullify the word of God for the sake of your tradition. ⁷ You hypocrites! Isaiah was right when he prophesied about you:

Matthew 15:1–39 and 26:1–39. In *The Holy Bible, New International Version*®. Colorado Springs, CO: Biblica, Inc.

⁸ "'These people honor me with their lips,
but their hearts are far from me.
⁹ They worship me in vain;
their teachings are merely human rules.'"

¹⁰ Jesus called the crowd to him and said, "Listen and understand. ¹¹ What goes into someone's mouth does not defile them, but what comes out of their mouth, that is what defiles them."

¹² Then the disciples came to him and asked, "Do you know that the Pharisees were offended when they heard this?"

¹³ He replied, "Every plant that my heavenly Father has not planted will be pulled up by the roots. ¹⁴ Leave them; they are blind guides. If the blind lead the blind, both will fall into a pit."

¹⁵ Peter said, "Explain the parable to us."

¹⁶ "Are you still so dull?" Jesus asked them. ¹⁷ "Don't you see that whatever enters the mouth goes into the stomach and then out of the body? ¹⁸ But the things that come out of a person's mouth come from the heart, and these defile them. ¹⁹ For out of the heart come evil thoughts—murder, adultery, sexual immorality, theft, false testimony, slander. ²⁰ These are what defile a person; but eating with unwashed hands does not defile them."

The Faith of a Canaanite Woman

²¹ Leaving that place, Jesus withdrew to the region of Tyre and Sidon. ²² A Canaanite woman from that vicinity came to him, crying out, "Lord, Son of David, have mercy on me! My daughter is demon-possessed and suffering terribly."

²³ Jesus did not answer a word. So his disciples came to him and urged him, "Send her away, for she keeps crying out after us."

²⁴ He answered, "I was sent only to the lost sheep of Israel."

²⁵ The woman came and knelt before him. "Lord, help me!" she said.

²⁶ He replied, "It is not right to take the children's bread and toss it to the dogs."

²⁷ "Yes it is, Lord," she said. "Even the dogs eat the crumbs that fall from their master's table."

²⁸ Then Jesus said to her, "Woman, you have great faith! Your request is granted." And her daughter was healed at that moment.

Jesus Feeds the Four Thousand

²⁹ Jesus left there and went along the Sea of Galilee. Then he went up on a mountainside and sat down. ³⁰ Great crowds came to him, bringing the lame, the blind, the crippled, the mute and many others, and laid them at his feet; and he healed them. ³¹ The people were amazed when they saw the mute speaking, the crippled made well, the lame walking and the blind seeing. And they praised the God of Israel.

³² Jesus called his disciples to him and said, "I have compassion for these people; they have already been with me three days and have nothing to eat. I do not want to send them away hungry, or they may collapse on the way."

³³ His disciples answered, "Where could we get enough bread in this remote place to feed such a crowd?"

³⁴ "How many loaves do you have?" Jesus asked.

"Seven," they replied, "and a few small fish."

³⁵ He told the crowd to sit down on the ground. ³⁶ Then he took the seven loaves and the fish, and when he had given thanks, he broke them and gave them to the disciples, and they in turn to the people. ³⁷ They all ate and were satisfied. Afterward the disciples picked up seven basketfuls of broken pieces that were left over. ³⁸ The number of those who ate was four thousand men, besides women and children. ³⁹ After Jesus had sent the crowd away, he got into the boat and went to the vicinity of Magadan.

CHAPTER 26

The Plot against Jesus

¹ When Jesus had finished saying all these things, he said to his disciples, ² "As you know, the Passover is two days away—and the Son of Man will be handed over to be crucified."

³ Then the chief priests and the elders of the people assembled in the palace of the high priest, whose name was Caiaphas, ⁴ and they schemed to arrest Jesus secretly and kill him. ⁵ "But not during the festival," they said, "or there may be a riot among the people."

Jesus Anointed at Bethany

⁶ While Jesus was in Bethany in the home of Simon the Leper, ⁷ a woman came to him with an alabaster jar of very expensive perfume, which she poured on his head as he was reclining at the table.

⁸ When the disciples saw this, they were indignant. "Why this waste?" they asked. ⁹ "This perfume could have been sold at a high price and the money given to the poor."

¹⁰ Aware of this, Jesus said to them, "Why are you bothering this woman? She has done a beautiful thing to me. ¹¹ The poor you will always have with you, but you will not always have me. ¹² When she poured this perfume on my body, she did it to prepare me for burial. ¹³ Truly I tell you, wherever this gospel is preached throughout the world, what she has done will also be told, in memory of her."

Judas Agrees to Betray Jesus

¹⁴ Then one of the Twelve—the one called Judas Iscariot—went to the chief priests ¹⁵ and asked, "What are you willing to give me if I deliver him over to you?" So they counted out for him thirty pieces of silver. ¹⁶ From then on Judas watched for an opportunity to hand him over.

The Last Supper

¹⁷ On the first day of the Festival of Unleavened Bread, the disciples came to Jesus and asked, "Where do you want us to make preparations for you to eat the Passover?"

¹⁸ He replied, "Go into the city to a certain man and tell him, 'The Teacher says: My appointed time is near. I am going to celebrate the Passover with my disciples at your house.'" ¹⁹ So the disciples did as Jesus had directed them and prepared the Passover.

²⁰ When evening came, Jesus was reclining at the table with the Twelve. ²¹ And while they were eating, he said, "Truly I tell you, one of you will betray me."

²² They were very sad and began to say to him one after the other, "Surely you don't mean me, Lord?"

²³ Jesus replied, "The one who has dipped his hand into the bowl with me will betray me. ²⁴ The Son of Man will go just as it is written about him. But woe to that man who betrays the Son of Man! It would be better for him if he had not been born."

²⁵ Then Judas, the one who would betray him, said, "Surely you don't mean me, Rabbi?" Jesus answered, "You have said so."

²⁶ While they were eating, Jesus took bread, and when he had given thanks, he broke it and gave it to his disciples, saying, "Take and eat; this is my body."

²⁷ Then he took a cup, and when he had given thanks, he gave it to them, saying, "Drink from it, all of you. ²⁸ This is my blood of the covenant, which is poured out for many for the forgiveness of sins. ²⁹ I tell you, I will not drink from this fruit of the vine from now on until that day when I drink it new with you in my Father's kingdom."

³⁰ When they had sung a hymn, they went out to the Mount of Olives.

Jesus Predicts Peter's Denial

³¹ Then Jesus told them, "This very night you will all fall away on account of me, for it is written:

" 'I will strike the shepherd,
and the sheep of the flock will be scattered.'

³² But after I have risen, I will go ahead of you into Galilee."

³³ Peter replied, "Even if all fall away on account of you, I never will."

³⁴ "Truly I tell you," Jesus answered, "this very night, before the rooster crows, you will disown me three times."

³⁵ But Peter declared, "Even if I have to die with you, I will never disown you." And all the other disciples said the same.

Gethsemane

³⁶ Then Jesus went with his disciples to a place called Gethsemane, and he said to them, "Sit here while I go over there and pray." ³⁷ He took Peter and the two sons of Zebedee along with him, and he began to be sorrowful and troubled. ³⁸ Then he said to them, "My soul is overwhelmed with sorrow to the point of death. Stay here and keep watch with me."

³⁹ Going a little farther, he fell with his face to the ground and prayed, "My Father, if it is possible, may this cup be taken from me. Yet not as I will, but as you will."

THIRTY-EIGHT
On Fasting

TERTULLIAN

Tertullian lived in Carthage in Northern Africa from about 160 to 225 A.D. He is the first really important Christian author writing in Latin and was mostly concerned with countering heresies. This was a time when the church was still in the process of becoming institutionalized, defining its theology, and actively considering food practices, such as fasting.

CHAPTER 15: OF THE APOSTLE'S LANGUAGE CONCERNING FOOD

The apostle reprobates likewise such as "bid to abstain from meats; but he does so from the foresight of the Holy Spirit, precondemning already the heretics who would enjoin perpetual abstinence to the extent of destroying and despising the works of the Creator; such as I may find in the person of a Marcion, a Tatian, or a Jupiter, the Pythagorean heretic of to-day; not in the person of the Paraclete. For how limited is the extent of our "interdiction of meats!" Two weeks of xerophagies in the year (and not the whole of these,—the Sabbaths, to wit, and the Lord's days, being excepted) we offer to God; abstaining from things which we do not reject, but defer. But further: when writing to the Romans, the apostle now gives you a home-thrust, detractors as you are of this observance: "Do not for the sake of food," he says, "undo the work of God." What "work?" That about which he says, "It is good not to eat flesh, and not to drink wine:" "for he who in these points doeth service, is pleasing and propitiable

Tertullian. *On Fasting*. Whitefish, MT: Kessinger Publishing Reprints, print on demand, pp. 27–34.

to our God." "One believeth that all things may be eaten; but another, being weak, feedeth on vegetables. Let not him who eateth lightly esteem him who eateth not. Who art thou, who judgest another's servant?" "Both he who eateth, and he who eateth not, giveth God thanks." But, since he forbids human choice to be made matter of controversy, how much more Divine! Thus he knew how to chide certain restricters and interdicters of food, such as abstained from it of contempt, not of duty; but to approve such as did so to the honour, not the insult, of the Creator. And if he has "delivered you the keys of the meat-market," permitting the eating of "all things" with a view to establishing the exception of "things offered to idols"; still he has not included the kingdom of God in the meat-market: "For," he says, "the kingdom of God is neither meat nor drink"; and, "Food commendeth us not to God"—not that you may think this said about dry diet, but rather about rich and carefully prepared, if, when he subjoins, "Neither, if we shall have eaten, shall we abound; nor, if we shall not have eaten, shall we be deficient," the ring of his words suits, (as it does), you rather (than us), who think that you do "abound" if you eat, and are "deficient if you eat not; and for this reason disparage these observances.

How unworthy, also, is the way in which you interpret to the favour of your own lust the fact that the Lord "ate and drank" promiscuously! But I think that He must have likewise "fasted" inasmuch as He has pronounced, not "the full"; but "the hungry and thirsty, blessed": (He) who was wont to profess "food" to be, not that which His disciples had supposed, but "the thorough doing of the Father's work"; teaching "to labour for the meat which is permanent unto life eternal"; in our ordinary prayer likewise commanding us to request "bread," not the wealth of Attalus therewithal. Thus, too, Isaiah has not denied that God "hath chosen" a "fist"; but has particularized in detail the kind of fast which He has not chosen: "for in the days," he says, "of your fasts your own wills are found (indulged), and all who are subject to you ye stealthily sting; or else ye fast with a view to abuse and strifes, and ye smite with the fists. Not such a fast have I elected"; but such an one as He has subjoined, and by subjoining has not abolished, but confirmed.

CHAPTER 16: INSTANCES FROM SCRIPTURE OF DIVINE JUDGMENTS UPON THE SELF-INDULGENT; AND APPEALS TO THE PRACTICES OF HEATHENS

For even if He does prefer "the works of righteousness," still not without a sacrifice, which is a soul afflicted with fasts. He, at all events, is the God to whom neither a People incontinent of appetite, nor a priest, nor a prophet, was pleasing. To this day the "monuments of concupiscence" remain, where the People, greedy of "flesh," till, by devouring without digesting the quails, they brought on cholera, were buried. Eli breaks his neck before the temple doors, his sons fall in battle, his daughter-in-law expires in child-birth: for such was the blow which had been deserved at the hand of God by the shameless house, the defrauder of the fleshly sacrifices. Sameas, a "man of God," after prophesying the issue of the idolatry introduced by King Jeroboam—after the drying up and immediate restoration of that king's hand—after the rending in twain of the sacrificial altar,—being on account of these signs invited (home) by the king by way of recompense, plainly declined (for he had been prohibited by God) to touch food at all in that place; but having presently afterwards rashly taken food from another old man, who lyingly professed himself a prophet, he was deprived, in accordance with the word of God then and there uttered over the table, of burial in his fathers' sepulchres. For he was prostrated by the rushing of a lion upon him in the way, and was buried among strangers; and thus paid the penalty of his breach of fast.

These will be warnings both to people and to bishops, even spiritual ones, in case they may ever have been guilty of incontinence of appetite. Nay, even in Hades the admonition has not ceased to speak; where we find in the person of the rich feaster, convivialities tortured; in that of the pauper, fasts refreshed; having—(as convivialities and fasts alike had)—as precep-tors "Moses and the prophets." For Joel withal exclaimed: "Sanctify a fast, and a religious service"; foreseeing even then that other apostles and prophets would sanction fasts, and would preach observances of special service to God. Whence it is that even they who court their idols by dressing them, and by adorning them in their sanctuary, and by saluting them at each particular hour, are said to do them service. But, more than that, the heathens recognise every form of ταπεινοφρόνησις (humble wisdom). When the heaven is rigid and the year arid, barefooted processions are enjoined by public proclamation; the magistrates lay aside their purple, reverse the fasces, utter prayer, offer a victim. There are, moreover, some colonies where, besides (these extraordinary solemnities, the inhabitants), by an annual rite, clad in sackcloth and besprent with ashes, present a suppliant importunity to their idols, (while) baths and shops are kept shut till the ninth hour. They have one single fire in public—on the altars; no water even in their platters. There is, I believe, a Ninevitan suspension of business! A Jewish fast, at all events, is universally celebrated; while, neglecting the temples, through-out all the shore, in every open place, they continue long to send prayer up to heaven. And, albeit by the dress and ornamentation of mourning they disgrace the duty, still they do affect a faith in abstinence, and sigh for the arrival of the long-lingering evening star to sanction (their feeding). But it is enough for me that you, by heaping blasphemies upon our xerophagies, put them on a level with the chastity of an Isis and a Cybele. I admit the comparison in the way of evidence. Hence (our xerophagy) will be proved divine, which the devil, the emulator of things divine, imitates. It is out of truth that falsehood is built; out of religion that superstition is compacted. Hence you are more irreligious, in proportion as a heathen is more conform-able. He, in short, sacrifices his appetite to an idol-god; you to (the true) God will not. For to you your belly is god, and your lungs a temple, and your paunch a sacrificial altar, and your cook the priest, and your fragrant smell the Holy Spirit, and your condiments spiritual gifts, and your belching prophecy.

CHAPTER 17: CONCLUSION

"Old" you are, if we will say the truth, you who are so indulgent to appetite, and justly do you vaunt your "priority": always do I recognise the savour of Esau, the hunter of wild beasts: so unlimitedly studious are you of catching fieldfares, so do you come from "the field" of your most lax discipline, so faint are you in spirit. If I offer you a paltry lentile dyed red with must well boiled down, forthwith you will sell all your "primacies": with you "love" shows its fervour in sauce-pans, "faith" its warmth in kitchens, "hope" its anchorage in waiters; but of greater account is "love," because that is the means whereby your young men sleep with their sisters! Appendages, as we all know, of appetite are lasciviousness and voluptuousness. Which alliance the apostle withal was aware of; and hence, after premising, "Not in drunkenness and revels," he adjoined, "nor in couches and lusts."

To the indictment of your appetite pertains (the charge) that "double honour" is with you assigned to your presiding (elders) by double shares (of meat and drink); whereas the apostle has given them "double honour" as being both brethren and officers. Who, among you, is superior in holiness, except him who is more frequent in banqueting, more sumptuous in catering, more learned in cups? Men of soul and flesh alone as you are, justly do you reject things spiritual. If the prophets were pleasing to such, my (prophets) they were not. Why, then, do not you constantly preach, "Let us eat and drink, for to-morrow we shall die?" just as we do not hesitate manfully to command, "Let us fast, brethren and sisters, lest to-morrow perchance we die." Openly let us vindicate our disciplines. Sure we are that "they who are in the flesh cannot please God"; not, of course, those who are in the substance of the flesh, but in the care, the uffection, the work, the will, of it. Emaciation displeases not us; for it is not by weight that God bestows flesh, any more than He does "the Spirit by measure." More easily, it may be, through the "strait gate" of salvation will slenderer flesh enter; more speedily will lighter flesh rise; longer in the sepulchre will drier flesh retain its firmness. Let Olympic cestus-players and boxers cram themselves to satiety. To them bodily ambition is suitable to whom bodily strength is necessary; and yet they also strengthen themselves by xerophagies. But ours are other thews and other sinews, just as our contests withal are other; we whose "wrestling is not against flesh and blood, but against the world's power, against the spiritualities of malice." Against these it is not by robustness of flesh and blood, but of faith and spirit, that it behoves us to make our antagonistic stand. On the other hand, an over-fed Christian will be more necessary to bears and lions, perchance, than to God; only that, even to encounter beasts, it will be his duty to practise emaciation.

THIRTY-NINE

Early Ascetics

The following selections offer insight into the mentality of early Christian ascetics and their attitudes toward food and the body. Psychologically, they are fascinating readings, and one can clearly see how these people actively made life difficult and excruciating for themselves, in conscious imitation of Christ's suffering on the cross. Consider also what would lead one to acts of self-mortification. Spite against the rest of the world? An attempt to control something—namely, the self—in a world where nothing can be controlled? Or perhaps it was simply a bid to gain attention and even fame? Look at images online of Saint Jerome or the Temptation of Saint Anthony to capture the spirit of these early ascetics.

PART IV

Of Self-control

1. Some brothers from Scete wanted to visit Abba Antony, and embarked in a ship to go there. In the ship they found an old man who also wanted to go to Antony, but they did not know him. During the voyage they talked about the sayings of the Fathers, and the Scriptures, and then the work of their hands. But the old man was silent through it all. When they came to the landing-place, they saw that the old man also was preparing to go up to Abba Antony. When they arrived, Abba Antony said to them: "You found good company on your journey in this old man." And he said to the old man: "You found good companions in these brothers."

Owen Chadwick, ed. *Western Asceticism*. Philadelphia: Westminster Press, 1958, pp. 48–59.

The old man said: "Yes, they are good, but their house has no door. Whoever wants, goes into the stable and steals the donkey." He said this because they uttered the first thing that came into their heads.

2. Abba Daniel said of Abba Arsenius that he used to spend all night watching. He would stay awake all night, and about dawn when nature seemed to force him into sleep, he would say to sleep: "Come, you wicked servant," and he would snatch a little sleep still sitting: and at once rose up.

3. Abba Arsenius said: "An hour's sleep is enough for a monk: that is, if he is a fighter."

4. Abba Daniel said of him: "All the years he stayed with us, we gave him a little enough measure of food for the year. And every time we came to visit him, he shared it with us."

5. He said also, that he only changed the water for the palm-leaves once a year; otherwise he added to it. He would make a plait of the palm-leaves, and weave it till noon. So the elders asked him why he would not change the water for the palm-leaves, which was stinking. And he said to them: "When I was in the world I used incense and sweet-smelling ointments, so now I must profit from this stink."

6. He also said this. When he heard that all the apples were ripe, he said: "Bring them to me." And he took one little mouthful of each kind, giving thanks to God.

7. They said of Abba Agatho that for three years he kept a pebble in his mouth, to teach himself silence.

8. Once Abba Agatho was going a journey with his disciples. And one of them found a tiny bag of green peas on the road, and said to the old man: "Father, if you command, I will take it." The old man gazed at him in astonishment, and said: "Did you put it there?" The brother replied: "No." And the old man said: "How is it that you want to take something which you did not put there?"

9. Once an old man came to Abba Achillas, and saw blood dripping from his mouth: and he asked him: "What is the matter, Father?" And the old man said: "A brother came and spoke a word which grieved me, yet I have been trying with all my might to nurse that grievance. And I prayed God that he would take it away, and the word turned into blood in my mouth. Look, I have spat it out, and am now at rest, and have forgotten my grievance."

10. Once Abba Achillas came to the cell of Abba Isaiah in Scete, and found him eating. He had put salt and water in his vessel. Seeing that he hid the vessel behind the plaits of palm-leaves, Abba Achillas said: "Tell me what you were eating." And he answered: "Forgive me, Abba; but I was cutting palms and began to be on fire with thirst. And so I dipped a piece of bread in the salt, and put it in my mouth. But my mouth was parched, and I could not swallow the bread, so I was forced to pour a little water on the salt and then I could swallow it. But forgive me." And Abba Achillas used to say: "Come and see Isaiah eating broth in Scete. If you want to eat broth, go to Egypt."

11. They said of Abba Ammoi that though he was on a bed of sickness for several years, he never relaxed his discipline; and never went into the store-cupboard at the back of his cell to see what he had. Many people brought him presents because he was sick. But even when his disciple, John, went in and out, he shut his eyes so as not to see what he was doing. He knew what it means to be a faithful monk.

12. Abba Benjamin, who was presbyter in Cellia, said that some brothers went to an old man in Scete and wanted to give him a measure of oil. But the old man said: "Look, there is the little vessel of oil which you brought three years ago. It has stayed there, where you put it." And Abba Benjamin said: "When we heard it, we marvelled at the old man's devotion."

13. They told a story of Abba Dioscorus of Namisias, that his bread was made of barley, and his gruel of lentils. And every year he made one particular resolution: not to meet anyone for a year, or not to speak, or not to taste cooked food, or not to eat any fruit, or not to eat vegetables. This was his system in everything. He made himself master of one thing, and then started on another, and so on each year.

14. Abba Evagrius said that an old man said: "I cut away my fleshly pleasures, to remove the opportunities of anger. For I know that it is because of pleasure that I have to struggle with anger, and trouble my mind, and throw away my understanding."

15. Once Epiphanius the bishop from Cyprus sent a message to Abba Hilarion, and asked him: "Come, that I may see you before I die." And when they had met and greeted each other, part of a fowl was set before them. The bishop took it and gave it to Abba Hilarion. And the old man said to him: "Forgive me, Father. From the time I took my habit, I have eaten nothing that has been killed." And Epiphanius said to him: "From the time I took my habit, I have let none go to sleep who still had something against me, and I have never gone to sleep with an enemy in the world." And the old man said to him: "Forgive me. Your devotion is greater than mine."

16. They said of Abba Helladius that he lived twenty years in Cellia, and did not once lift his eyes upward to see the roof of the church.

17. Once Abba Zeno was walking in Palestine; and when he had finished his work, he sat down to eat near a cucumber plant. And his soul tried to persuade him, saying: "Pick one of those cucumbers for yourself, and eat it. What does it matter?" And he replied to his temptation: "Thieves go down to torment. Test yourself then to see whether you can bear torment." So he rose and stood in the sun for five days, without drinking, and dried himself in the heat. And his soul (so to say) spoke to him: "I cannot bear torment." So he said to his soul: "If you cannot bear torment, do not steal to get a meal."

18. Abba Theodore said: "The monk's body grows weak with eating little bread." But another elder said: "It grows weaker with watching in the night."

19. Abba John the Short said: "If a king wants to take a city whose citizens are hostile, he first captures the food and water of the inhabitants of the city, and when they are starving subdues them. So it is with gluttony. If a man is earnest in fasting and hunger, the enemies which trouble his soul will grow weak."

20. He also said: "As I was climbing up the road which leads to Scete, carrying plaits of palms, I saw a camel-driver who talked to me and annoyed me. And I dropped what I was carrying, and ran away."

21. Said Abba Isaac the presbyter of Cellia: "I know a brother who was harvesting and wanted to eat an ear of wheat. And he said to the owner of the field: 'Will you let me eat one ear?' And when he heard it, he wondered, and said: 'The whole field is yours, Father, why do you ask me?' So scrupulous was that brother."

22. One of the brothers asked Abba Isidore the priest of Scete: "Why are the demons so violently afraid of you?" And the old man said: "Ever since I became a monk, I have been trying not to let anger rise as far as my mouth."

23. He said also that though he felt in his mind impulses towards the sins of concupiscence or anger, he had not consented to them for forty years.

24. Abba Cassian told a story of an Abba John who went to see Abba Paesius who had lived for forty years in the deep desert. And because he had much charity towards him, he asked him with the confidence born of charity: "You have been isolated so long, and cannot easily suffer any trouble from man—tell me, what progress have you made?" And he said: [From the time I began to be a solitary, the sun has never seen me eating." And Abba John said to him: "Nor me angry."]

25. He said also: "Abba Moses told us what Abba Serapion said to him: 'While I was still a lad, I was staying with Abba Theonas; and after each meal I was moved by some demon and stole one of the rolls of bread, and secretly ate it, Theonas knowing nothing of the matter. For some time I went on with this, until the sin began to dominate my mind, and I could not stop myself. Only my conscience judged me, for I was ashamed to say anything to the old man. But by God's mercy it happened that some visitors came to the old man in search of profit to their soul, and they asked him about their own thoughts. The old man replied: ["Nothing harms the monk so much, and gives such happiness to the demons, as when he conceals his thoughts from his fathers in the spirit."] And he also talked to them about self-control. And while he was speaking, I thought to myself that God had revealed to him what I had done. Stricken in my heart, I began to weep: then I pulled the roll of bread out of my dress, threw myself on the floor, and begged forgiveness for what I had done, and for prayer that I might be helped not to do it again.

Then the old man said: "My son, you are freed from your captivity though I have said nothing. You are freed by your own confession. The demon which by your silence you let dwell in your heart, has been killed because you confessed your sin. You let him rule you because you never said him nay, never rebuked him. Henceforth he shall never make a home in you, because you have thrown him out of doors into the open air." The old man had not finished speaking, when his words were visibly fulfilled—something like a flame shot out of my breast and so filled the house with its stench, that the people present thought it was burning sulphur. And the old man said: "My son, see the sign, whereby the Lord has proved that I have spoken truly and you are free."

26. They said of Abba Macarius that if he was called among the brothers, he made a rule for himself thus: if wine could be had, he used to drink it for the brothers' sake: and then, for one cup of wine he would go without water for a whole day. And the brothers, wanting to refresh him, used to give him wine. And the old man took it with joy, so as later to crucify himself. But his disciple, knowing the reason, said to the brothers: "For God's sake, I beg you, do not give it him. In the cell afterwards he tames himself with torments." When the brothers knew it, they gave him no more wine.

27. Abba Macarius the Great said to the brothers in Scete after service in church: "Flee, my brothers." And one of the brothers said to him: "Father, where have we to flee beyond this desert?" And he put his finger upon his lips and said: "I tell you, this you must flee." And so he entered his cell, and shut the door, and dwelt alone.

28. Abba Macarius said also: "If when you want to reprove someone you are stirred to anger, you are pandering to your own passion. Lose not yourself to save another."

29. Said Abba Poemen: "Unless Nebuzaradan the captain of the guard had come, the temple of the Lord would not have been burnt. And unless greed brought idleness into the soul, the mind would not fail in its fight against the enemy."

30. They said of Abba Poemen that when he was invited to eat and did not want to go, he went weeping, and praying that he might obey his brothers and not sadden them.

31. They told Abba Poemen that a certain monk did not drink wine. And he said to them: "Wine is not for monks at all."

31A. Abba Poemen also said: "All rest of the body is an abomination to the Lord."

31B. Abba Poemen also said: "The only way to humble the soul is by eating less bread."

31C. He also said that if a man remembered the word of Scripture "out of thy mouth thou shalt be justified and out of thy mouth shalt thou be condemned" he would more and more choose not to speak.

31D. He also said that a monk asked Abba Pambo if it is good to praise your neighbour. And he answered: "It is a greater good to hold your peace."

31E. A monk asked Abba Poemen: "How should I behave in my common life among the brothers?" The old man said to him: "He who lives among the brothers ought to regard them as though they were but one person, and to keep guard over his mouth and eyes; and so he will be able to win peace of mind."

32. Abba Poemen also said: "They smoke out bees to steal away their honey. And so idleness drives the fear of God from the soul, and steals away good works."

33. One of the old men told this story of Abba Poemen and his brothers, who lived in Egypt. Their mother wanted to see them, and could not. So she looked out for her chance, and presented herself in front of them as they were going to church. The moment they saw her, they turned, went to their cell, and shut the door in her face. But she stood at the door and screamed and besought them in her misery. Abba Anub, hearing her, went to Abba Poemen and said: "What shall we do about the little old woman who is crying outside the door?" Abba Poemen rose up, and went to the door, and stood just inside and heard her beseeching them miserably. And he said: "What are you screaming for, old woman?" When she heard his voice, she cried out the more and implored them: "I want to see you, my sons. Why should I not see you? Am I not your mother? Have I not given you milk at the breast, and now every hair of my head is grey? When I hear your voice, I am in distress." The old man said to her: "Do you want to see us in this world or the next?" She said to him: "If I do not see you in this world, shall I see you in the next, my sons?" He said: "If you can suffer, with a calm spirit, not to see us here, you shall see us there." And so the woman went away happy, and saying: "If I shall truly see you there, I do not want to see you here."

34. They said of Abba Pior that he ate while walking about. And when someone asked him why he ate in this manner, he replied that he did it casually, as if there were no need of it. But when someone else asked the same question, he replied: "So that my soul does not receive bodily pleasure from eating."

35. They said of Abba Peter, named Pyonius, who was in Cellia, that he did not drink wine. And when he grew old, they asked him to take a little wine. When he refused, they warmed

some water, and offered it to him. And he said: ["Believe me, my sons, I drink it as though it was spiced wine." And he declared that he was content with warm water.]

36. Once they celebrated a great service on the mountain of Abba Antony, and a little wine was found there. One of the elders took a small cup, and carried it to Abba Sisois, and gave it him. And he drank it. And a second time Abba Sisois received it, and drank it. And the elder offered it a third time. But he did not receive it, and said: "Stay, brother, do you not know that Satan still exists?"

37. A brother asked Abba Sisois: "What am I to do? When I go to church, out of charity the brothers often make me stay to the meal afterwards." The old man said to him: "That is burdensome."

So Abraham his disciple said to him: "If in the meeting at church on Saturday and Sunday, a brother drinks three cups, is it much?" And the old man said: "If there were no Satan, it would not be much."

38. Often the disciple used to say to Abba Sisois: "Rise, Abba, let us eat." And he would say: "Have we not eaten already, my son?" And the disciple would reply: "No, Father." The old man used to say: "If we have not eaten yet, bring the food, let us eat."

39. Abba Sisois once said with confidence: "Believe me, for thirty years I have not been in the habit of praying to God about sin. But when I pray, I say this: 'Lord Jesus Christ, protect me from my tongue.' And even now, it causes me to fall every day."

40. Once Abba Silvanus and his disciple Zacharias came to a monastery. And the monks made them sup a little before they went on their way. And when they departed, the disciple found a pool by the wayside and wanted to drink. Abba Silvanus said: "Zacharias, today is a fast." And Zacharias said: "Have we not already eaten today, Father?" The old man said to him: "To eat that meal was charity: but as for us, let us keep our fast, my son."

41. The holy Syncletice said: "We who have chosen this holy way ought above all to keep chastity. Even among men of the world chastity is regarded. But in the world they are also stupid about it, and sin with their other senses. For they peep indecently, and laugh immoderately."

42. She said also: "Animal's poison is cured by still stronger antidotes. So fasting and prayer drive sordid temptation from the soul."

43. She also said: "The pleasures of the wealthy world must not seduce you, as if those pleasures were useful. Because of this pleasure they honour the art of cooking. But by rigorous fasting, you should trample on those pleasures. Never be sated with bread, nor want wine."

44. Abba Sisois said: "Our form of pilgrimage is keeping the mouth shut."

45. Said Abba Hyperichius: "Donkeys are terrified of lions. So temptations to concupiscence are terrified of a proved monk."

46. He also said: "Fasting is the monk's rein over sin. The man who stops fasting is like a stallion who lusts the moment he sees a mare."

47. He also said: "When the monk's body is dried up with fasting, it lifts his soul from the depths. Fasting dries up the channels down which worldly pleasures flow."

48. He also said: "The chaste monk shall be honoured on earth, and in heaven shall be crowned in the presence of the Most Highest."

49. He also said: "The monk who cannot control his tongue when he is angry, will not control his passions at other times."

50. He also said: "Let not thy mouth speak an evil word: the vine does not bear thorns."

51. He also said: "It is better to eat flesh and drink wine than to eat the flesh of the brothers by disparaging them."

52. He also said: "The serpent murmured to Eve and cast her out of paradise. The man who rails against his neighbour is like the serpent. He loses the soul of him that listens to him, and he does not save his own."

53. Once there was a feast in Scete, and they gave a cup of wine to an old man. He threw it down, saying: "Take that death away from me." When the others who were eating with him saw this, they also did not drink.

54. Another time a vessel of wine was brought there from the first fruits of the vintage, so that a cup of it could be given to each of the brothers. And a brother came in and saw that they were drinking wine, and fled up on a roof, and the roof fell in. And when they heard the noise, they ran and found the brother lying half-dead. And they began to abuse him, saying: "It has served you right, for you were guilty of vainglory." But an abba embraced him, and said: "Leave my son alone, he has done a good work. By the living Lord, this roof shall not be rebuilt in my time, as a reminder to the world that a roof fell in Scete because of a cup of wine."

55. Once a priest from Scete went up to see the bishop of Alexandria. And when he came back to Scete the brothers asked him: "How goes the city?" But he said to them: "Believe me, brethren, I saw no man's face but the bishop alone." And when they heard this, they wondered, and said: "What do you think has happened to all the population?" They hesitated to believe him. But he cheered them by saying: "I have wrestled with my soul, not to look upon the face of a man." And so the brothers were edified, and kept themselves from lifting up their eyes.

56. Once an old man came to another old man. And the second said to his disciple: "Make us a little lentil broth, my son." And he made it. "Dip the bread in it for us." And he dipped it. And they went on with their godly discourse till noon next day. Then the old man said to his disciple: "Make us a little lentil broth, my son." He replied: "I made it yesterday." And so they rose and ate their food.

57. An old man came to a father, who cooked a few lentils and said: "Let us, worship God and eat afterwards." One of them recited the whole psalter. The other read and meditated upon two of the greater prophets. And in the morning the old man went away, and they forgot to eat their food.

58. A brother felt hungry at dawn, and struggled with his soul not to eat till 9 o'clock. And when 9 o'clock came, he extracted from himself a resolution to wait till noon. At noon he dipped his bread and sat down to eat—but then rose up again, saying: "I will wait till three." And at 3 o'clock he prayed, and saw the devil's work going out of him like smoke; and his hunger ceased.

59. One of the old men was ill, and for many days could not eat. His disciple asked him to take something and restore his strength. So the disciple went away and made some lentil cake. A jar was hanging in the cell containing a little honey: and there was another jar with evil-smelling linseed oil only used for the lamp. The brother took the wrong jar in error and put grease instead of honey into the mixture. The old man tasted it, and said nothing, but quietly ate the mouthful. The disciple forced him to take a second mouthful. The old man

tortured himself and ate it. Yet a third time the disciple pressed it upon him. But he did not want to eat, and said: "Truly, my son, I cannot." But his disciple encouraged him, and said: "It is good, Abba; look, I keep you company." When the disciple tasted it and saw what he had done, he fell flat on his face, and said: "Alas, Father! I have killed you, and you have laid this sin upon me because you did not speak." And the old man said to him. "Be not sad, my son. If God had willed that I should eat honey you would have been given the honey to mix in those buns."

60. They said of one old man that he sometimes longed to eat cucumber. So he took it and hung it in front of him where he could see it. And he was not conquered by his longing, and did not eat it, but tamed himself, and did penitence that he wanted it at all.

61. Once a brother went to visit his sister who was ill in a nunnery. She was a person full of faith. She herself did not consent to see a man: nor did she want to give her brother occasion to come into the midst of women. So she commanded him thus: "Go, my brother, pray for me. For by Christ's grace I shall see you in the kingdom of heaven."

62. On a journey a monk met some nuns and when he saw them he turned aside off the road. The abbess said to him: "If you had been a perfect monk, you would not have looked so closely as to see that we were women."

63. Once some brothers went to Alexandria, invited by Archbishop Theophilus to be present when after prayer he destroyed a pagan temple. And while they were supping with the archbishop, they were served with veal, and ate it without realizing it. And the archbishop took a piece of meat, and gave it to the old man who was reclining next to him, and said: "Look, here is a good piece of meat. Eat it, Abba." But they answered him: "Till now, we thought we were eating vegetables. If this is meat, we do not eat it." And not one of them would take another mouthful.

64. A brother brought some new bread to Cellia and invited his elders to taste. And when they had each eaten two rolls of bread, they stopped. But the brother knew how austere was their abstinence, and humbly began to beg them: "For God's sake eat today until you are filled." And they ate another two rolls. See how these true and self-disciplined monks ate much more than they needed, for God's sake.

65. Once one of the old men lay gravely ill, and was losing a lot of blood from his bowels. And a brother brought him some dry fruit, and made gruel, and offered them to the old man, and asked him: "Eat; perhaps it is good for you." The old man looked at him for a long time, and said: "In truth, I tell you that I have wanted God to leave me in my sickness for thirty years more." And in his weakness he absolutely refused to take even a little food; so the brother took away what he had brought, and returned to his cell.

66. Another old man had lived in the desert for a long time. And it happened that a brother came to him and found him sickening. He washed his face, and made a meal for him out of what he had brought. And when the old man saw it, he said: "Truly, brother, I had forgotten that men found comfort in food." And he offered him a cup of wine as well. And when he saw it, he wept, saying: "I hoped I would never drink wine until I died."

67. An old man made a resolution not to drink for forty days. And if ever he thirsted he washed a vessel and filled it with water and hung it in front of his eyes. And when the brothers asked him why he was doing this, he replied: "So that if I do not taste what I long for and can see, my devotion will be greater and I shall be granted a greater reward by the Lord."

68. On a journey, one brother had with him his mother, who had now grown old. They came to a river, and the old woman could not get across. Her son took off his cloak, and wrapt it round his hands, so as not to touch his mother's body, and carried her across the river. His mother said to him: "Why did you wrap your hands like that, my son?" He said: "Because a woman's body is fire. Simply because I was touching you, the memory of other women came into my soul."

69. One of the fathers said that he knew a brother who fasted in his cell the whole of Easter week. And when at last he came to mass on Saturday, he ran away as soon as he had communicated, to prevent the other brothers forcing him to join in the dinner in the church. In his own cell he only ate a few boiled beetroots, with salt but without bread.

70. At a meeting of the brothers in Scete, they were eating dates. And one of them, who was ill from excessive fasting, brought up some phlegm in a fit of coughing, and unintentionally it fell on another of the brothers. This brother was tempted by an evil thought and driven to say: "Be quiet, and do not spit on me." So to tame himself and restrain his own angry thought he picked up what had been spat and put it in his mouth and swallowed it. And then he began to say to himself: "If you say to your brother what will sadden him, you will have to eat what nauseates you."

FORTY

Sacrifice

CLEMENT OF ALEXANDRIA

This selection from Clement is ostensibly about sacrifices and how they are overturned by Christians, but it rambles from food topic to topic in a way that is very revealing. Titus Flavius Clemens (ca. 150–215) was a Roman living in Egypt, a learned elite familiar with Greek pagan religion, Plato, and Jewish food laws. It describes the many dilemmas people of this generation faced when wondering what to eat.

CHAPTER 6

30. As then God is not circumscribed in place, nor made like to the form of any creature, so neither is he of like passions, nor lacks he anything after the manner of created things, so as from hunger to desire sacrifices for food. Things that are capable of suffering are all mortal; and it is useless to offer meat to that which is in no need of sustenance. The famous comic poet Pherecrates in his *Deserter* wittily represents the gods themselves as finding fault with men for their offerings. "When you sacrifice to the gods, first of all you set apart what is customary for the priests first among you, and then—shame to say—do you not pick the thigh-bones clean to the groin and leave the hip-joint absolutely bare, assigning to us gods nothing but the dogs' portion, a back-bone polished as with a file, which you then cover with thick layers of sacrificial meal to save appearances?" And another comic poet, Eubulus, writes as follows about the sacrifices: "To the gods themselves you offer nothing but the tail and

Clement of Alexandria. "Clement of Alexandria." in *Alexandrian Christianity*. Edited and translated by John Leonard Oulton and Henry Chadwich. Philadelphia: Westminster Press, 1954, pp. 110–15.

the thigh, as though they were enamoured of these." And, where he brings on Dionysus in his *Semele*, he represents him as distinguishing: "First of all, when any sacrifice to me, they sacrifice blood and bladder—don't mention heart or caul—the gall and thigh-bones are no food for me." 31. And Menander has written of "the scrag end of the rump, the gall and dry bones, which," says he, "they set before the gods, while they consume the rest themselves." Why, the smoke of burnt sacrifices is intolerable even to the beasts. If, however, this smoke is really the meed of the gods of Greece, no time should be lost in deifying the cooks also (since they are deemed worthy of the same happiness) and in worshipping the stove itself, when it becomes an altar closely connected with the precious smoke. Hesiod somewhere says that: "Zeus, being outwitted in some division of the flesh of the sacrifice by Prometheus, chose the white bones of the ox craftily concealed in the glistening lard: and from that time the tribes of men on earth burn to the immortals white bones on fragrant altars." Still they altogether deny that God's partaking of nourishment could be explained by the craving which grows out of want. Accordingly they must suppose him nourished without appetite like plants or hibernating bears. At all events they say that these are not impeded in their growth, whether it be that they are nourished from the density of the air, or even from the exhalation arising from their own body. And yet, if they hold that the Deity is nourished without needing it, what is the use of nourishment to one who needs it not? But if the Deity, being by nature exempt from all need, rejoices to be honoured, we have good reason for honouring God by prayer, and for sending up most rightly this sacrifice, the best and holiest of sacrifices when joined with righteousness, venerating him through whom we receive our knowledge, and through him glorifying him (i.e., the Father) whom we have learnt to know. At any rate our altar here on earth is the congregation of those who are devoted to the prayers, having, as it were, one common voice and one mind.

As to the kinds of nutrition received through the sense of smell, though they may be less unworthy of the deity than those received through the mouth, still they witness to respiration. 32. What then is the worshippers' idea as to the breathing of God? Is it by means of transpiration as in the demons? or by inspiration only, as in fishes through the dilatation of their gills? or by circumspiration, as in insects, through the pressure of the membranes on the waist? No, they would not liken God to any of these, if they were in their senses. But as for creatures that live by respiration, they draw in the air by rhythmic beats corresponding to the counter-dilatation of the lungs against the chest. Then if they assign viscera and arteries and veins and sinews and members to God, they will exhibit him as in no respect differing from man. The word "conspiration" is that which is properly used of the Church. For the Church's sacrifice is indeed speech rising, like incense, from holy souls, while every thought of the heart is laid open to God along with the sacrifice. They are fond of talking about the purity of the most ancient altar at Delos, that altar which, we are told, was the only one approached by Pythagoras, because it was unpolluted by slaughter and death: will they then refuse credence to us when we say that the truly hallowed altar is the righteous soul, and the incense which ascends from it, the prayer of holiness? Sacrifices, I believe, are an invention of mankind to excuse the eating of flesh, though, even apart from such idolatry, it was always possible for one who wished it to partake of flesh. The Mosaic sacrifices symbolize Christian piety; for instance the dove and the pigeon offered for sins show that the purging away of the irrational part of the soul is acceptable to God. But if any of the righteous refuses to weigh down his soul by the eating of flesh, he does this on some reasonable ground, not as Pythagoras and his school from some dream as to the transmigration of souls. Xenocrates in a special treatise on animal food and Polemon in his book on Life according to Nature, seem to lay it down clearly that a flesh diet is inexpedient, as it has already passed through a process of digestion and been thus assimilated to the souls of irrational creatures.

33. On this ground especially the Jews abstain from swine's flesh, considering that this animal is unclean because it roots up and destroys the fruits more than any other. But if it is argued that the animals have been given to men, we too agree in this, only we say that they are not given entirely, nor indeed all, for the purpose of eating, but only those that do no work. Wherefore the comic poet Plato in his play *The Feasts* well says: "Hereafter 'twere well to kill no beast but swine, for they are excellent eating, and we get nothing out of them but bristles and mire and squealing." Hence it was well said by Aesop that "the reason why pigs make such an outcry when they are being dragged away is because they are conscious that they are good for nothing but to be sacrificed." And so Cleanthes says that in them the soul takes the place of salt to prevent the flesh from putrefying. Some then eat it because it is useless, and others because it injures the fruits; while others again abstain from eating it because of its immoderate salacity. For the same reason the law never requires the sacrifice of a goat except with a view to banishing evils, since pleasure is the fountainhead of vice. Further, they tell us that the eating of goats' flesh conduces to epilepsy. And they say that the largest amount of nutriment is supplied from pork, for which reason it is of use to those who practise bodily training, but, owing to the sluggishness produced by eating flesh, it is of no use to those who try to encourage the growth of the soul. A gnostic might therefore abstain from flesh, both for the sake of discipline and to weaken the sexual appetite. For, as Androcydes says, "wine and fleshly gorging make the body strong, but the soul more sluggish." Such a diet does not tend to precision of thought. Wherefore also the Egyptians in their purifications forbid their priests to eat flesh, and they themselves live on fowl as the lightest diet and abstain from fish for various fanciful reasons and especially from the idea that such food makes the flesh flabby.

34. Besides this, the life of beasts and birds is supported by breathing the same air as our souls, their soul being akin to the air; but we are told that fishes do not even breathe our air, but that air which was infused into water, as into the other elements, on its first creation, which is also a proof of the fact that air pervades all matter.

"It is not then expensive sacrifices that we should offer to God, but such sacrifices as are dear to him," viz., that composite incense of which the Law speaks, an incense compounded of many tongues and voices in the way of prayer, or rather which is being wrought into the unity of the faith out of divers nations and dispositions by the divine bounty shown in the Covenants, and which is brought together in our songs of praise by purity of heart and righteous and upright living grounded in holy actions and righteous prayer. For (to add the charm of poetry) "what man is there so unwise and beyond measure credulous as to expect that, at the burning of bare bones and gall, which even hungry dogs would refuse, the gods would all rejoice, and accept this as their due meed"; aye, and would show their gratitude to the celebrants, though they might be pirates or robbers or tyrants? The Christian teaching is that the fire sanctifies, not flesh or sacrifice, but sinful souls, understanding by fire not the all-devouring flame of common life, but the discerning flame which pierces through the soul that walks through fire.

FORTY-ONE

Saint Benedict's Rule

BENEDICT OF NURSIA

Saint Benedict of Nursia (ca. 480–543) established a monastery in Monte Cassino, Italy, and wrote a rule for monks that set the pattern for not only for the Benedictine Order, founded later, but all Western monasticism. Unlike the heroic ascetics, he makes concessions for sick brothers, what to serve when visitors arrive, and even who deals with the dirty work, like cleaning the dishes. He is not only practical but moderate, and even makes concessions for monks drinking wine.

35. OF THE WEEKLY OFFICERS IN THE KITCHEN

The brothers are to serve by turns; and no one is exempt from duty in the kitchen, unless he be hindered by ill-health or employed on some business for the good of the monastery. From this service a monk learns charity and gains a greater degree of merit. Notwithstanding they shall provide assistance for the weak, to take away all occasion for grievance; and in general, everyone shall have help, with regard to the circumstances of the community and the situation of the place.

If the community be numerous, the cellarer shall be exempt from the kitchen, as well as those (aforesaid) who are more profitably employed. The others shall serve each other in charity.

Benedict of Nursia. "Benedict Rule." In *Western Asceticism*. Edited by Owen Chadwick. Philadelphia: Westminster Press, 1958, pp. 315–23.

He who has finished his week, on Saturday, shall clean everything, and wash the towels which the brothers have used to dry their hands and feet: and, with his incoming successor of the next week, he shall wash the feet of the whole community. He shall restore to the cellarer the vessels which belong to his office, and restore them clean and undamaged: and the cellarer shall deliver them to the next man, so that he may keep a weekly check upon them.

An hour before meals the weekly officer may be allowed to take a drink and a piece of bread above the usual allowance, and so be able to serve his brothers at meals without complaint or too great hardship. But on great festivals he shall abstain until the end of the office.

On Sundays after Lauds, the weekly officers—ending and beginning—shall kneel down before the whole community in the oratory and ask their prayers. The officer who has ended his week shall say this verse: "Blessed art thou, O Lord, who hast helped me and comforted me"; and after this has been said three times, he shall receive a blessing. Then the officer who is beginning his week shall say the verse: "O God, make speed to save me, O Lord, make haste to help me": and after everyone has repeated this three times, he shall receive his blessing and enter upon his duties.

36. OF THE SICK BROTHERS

The care of the sick is to be put before everything else. They are to be tended as Christ himself, who tells us: "I was sick and you visited me," and "Inasmuch as you have done it unto one of the least of these, you have done it unto me."

The sick on their side are to reflect that the attention paid to them is for the honour of God, and they are not to be a grievance to those that tend them, by demanding too much. Yet even, if they ask too much, they are to be borne with, for thereby they are a means to a greater reward.

The abbot is to take great care that they do not suffer by the negligence of those who look after them. An infirmary, apart, is to be appointed for their care, and one to look after it who fears God and is diligent and solicitous.

The use of baths may be allowed to the sick as often as may be fitting; but for those who are well, and, particularly, young people, only seldom.

The sick who are very weakly are to be allowed to eat meat to help their recovery. But as soon as their health is re-established, they are to abstain like the rest.

The abbot is to take great care that the sick be not neglected by the cellarer or those that look after them. The fault of his disciples is, in some measure, his own fault.

37. OF OLD MEN AND CHILDREN

Although nature of its own accord is inclined to take pity on old men and children, yet it is better they should be provided for by the authority of the Rule. Their weakness is always to be considered, and the rigour of the rule about eating is not to be enforced. They shall be shown tenderness, and given leave to eat before the proper times.

38. OF THE WEEKLY READER

There shall be reading during meals. The reader shall not be anyone, whoever happens to pick up the book: one person shall read for a week, beginning on Sunday. As he enters on his week, after the office and the Communion, he shall ask everyone for their prayers that God may preserve him from the spirit of vanity. In the oratory he shall begin the verse: "O Lord, open thou my lips, and my mouth shall show forth thy praise" and everyone shall repeat it three times. Then he shall receive the blessing, and so enter upon his office.

Complete silence shall be kept during meals. There shall be no whispering: no one is to say anything except the reader. The brothers are to supply each other with what they need in the way of food and drink, so that no one needs to ask for anything. If anything is lacking, they are to ask for it by a sign, not by speaking.

No one is to ask questions about what is read or about any other subject, so that no one will have to answer. The one exception is if the superior wishes to say a few words that are edifying.

The weekly reader may take a little food before he begins to read, so that he may share in the meal with sanctification, and so that he does not find difficulty in fasting a long time. He can eat after the community meal, with the brothers who during that week are serving in the kitchen.

Not all the brothers in turn are to read or to sing; only those whose reading or singing edifies the listener.

39. OF THE QUANTITY OF FOOD

I am of the opinion that for normal nourishment, whether they are eating at noon or 3 o'clock, two dishes will be sufficient at each meal. This is to provide for the weakness of different people, so that the brother who cannot eat one dish may perhaps be able to eat the other. All the brethren are to be content with these two hot dishes: and if fruit or young vegetables can conveniently be had, they may be allowed a third.

A full pound of bread shall suffice for a whole day, whether they dine and sup, or have only one meal. If they sup as well as dine, the cellarer shall keep a third part of the bread for the evening.

Notwithstanding, it shall be in the abbot's power to increase the allowance, if he thinks fit, for those with heavier work. Yet he must take care to avoid excess or sudden temptation to gluttony. For nothing is so contrary to the life of a Christian as overeating: as our Lord said: "Take heed lest at any time your hearts be charged with surfeiting."

The same quantity is not to be given to the younger children: they should be given less than the others, and always be frugal.

Except the very weak, no one shall eat meat at any time.

40. OF THE QUANTITY OF DRINK

"Every man hath his proper gift from God, the one after this manner, and another after that." So it is a nice point to prescribe a certain measure of food and drink for others.

Notwithstanding, having regard to the weakness of the sick, I am of opinion that a hemina of wine every day will suffice. Yet be it known to those whom God has granted the gift of abstinence, that they shall have an especial reward.

If the necessity of the place, or the hard work, or the heat of the summer, makes them need more, it shall be in the power of the superior to add to the allowance: yet always with caution, that they may not fall to the temptations of satiety and drunkenness. Although we read that wine is never for monks, it is hard to persuade modern monks of this. At least we must all agree that we are not to drink to satiety, but with moderation. "For wine makes even wise men to fall into apostasy."

Where the poverty of the place prevents this measure being available, but much less, or even none at all; the monks there are to bless God, and not complain.

I give this especial instruction, that no one shall complain.

41. WHAT HOURS ARE MOST CONVENIENT FOR MEALS?

From Easter to Whitsuntide the community shall dine at noon and sup in the evening. But from Whitsuntide to the end of the summer, if they are not working in the fields or troubled by an excessively hot summer, they shall fast on Wednesdays and Fridays until three in the afternoon. On other days they shall dine at noon. When working in the fields or oppressed by heat, they shall dine at noon every day, if the abbot thinks fit. But he must so moderate and dispose everything that souls may be saved and that the brothers may do their work without having good reason to complain.

From September 14th until the beginning of Lent, the community shall always eat at three in the afternoon. In Lent, and until Easter, they are to eat in the evening, but at such a time that they do not need lamps, and the meal may be finished in daylight. At all times, they must so manage the hour of the meal, whether they dine or sup, that it is in daylight.

42. OF SILENCE AFTER COMPLINE

Monks at all times ought to study silence, but most of all during the night. Throughout the year, whether they are having supper or fasting, a similar rule shall apply. In the time of year when they are having suppers, as soon as they rise from the table, they shall assemble in one place, and one of them shall read the *Conferences* or *The Lives of the Fathers*; or at least some book which will edify the listeners. They are not to read the first seven books of the Bible or the book of Kings, because that part of Scripture is not profitable to weak understandings at such a time: these books are to be read at other times.

If it is a time of year when they are fasting, they are to leave a short interval after Vespers, and assemble as before for the reading of the *Conferences*. The reader shall read four or five pages, or as much as time allows. During this interval, anyone who has been occupied on special duties has time to join the assembled brothers.

When they are all present, they shall say Compline. And after Compline, no one shall be allowed to speak. If any be discovered to break this rule of silence, he shall be gravely punished: unless it be on account of guests and their needs; and even then it must be done with composure and moderation and gentleness.

43. OF THOSE WHO COME LATE TO
THE DIVINE OFFICE OR TO TABLE

As soon as the bell rings, everyone shall leave the work he has upon his hands and hasten to the office, as quickly as he can, though without rudeness and so that there is no place for jesting. Nothing shall be put before the work of God.

If anyone comes to the night office after the *Gloria* of Psalm 94 (a Psalm which, with this in mind, we wish to be recited very slowly), he shall not take his place in the choir, but stand lowest of all, or in a place apart appointed by the abbot for the negligent: so that he may be seen by the abbot and the community, until he do public penance at the end of the divine office.

I have thought it right that they should stand in the lowest place or in a place apart, so that the very shame of being seen by everybody may reform them. For if they remain outside the oratory they may be inclined to return to bed again and sleep or at least to sit down outside and trifle away the time, and so give the evil spirit his opportunity. Therefore they are to enter the oratory, so that they are present for part of the office, and may amend for the future.

He who comes late to the hours of the day office, after the versicle and the *Gloria* of the first psalm, which is said after the versicle, shall stand in the lowest place, as above, and not presume to join in choir till he has made satisfaction; unless the abbot gives him absolution and leave to join in—even so, on condition that he makes amends for his fault.

He who does not come to meals before grace is ended (for all shall say grace together and pray together and all sit down together to table) shall be rebuked twice for his negligence: and if he does not amend, he shall not be admitted to the common table, but shall eat apart from the rest, and his allowance of wine shall be taken from him till he has made satisfaction and mended his ways. The same penalty shall be inflicted on him who is not present at the grace which is said after meals.

Nor shall anyone presume to eat or drink, but at the hour appointed. But if the superior offers him something and he refuses it, he shall receive nothing whatever at the time when he does want what he first refused, or indeed anything else; until he has made atonement.

44. HOW EXCOMMUNICATED PERSONS ARE
TO MAKE SATISFACTION

He who for a great fault is suspended from oratory and table, shall lie prostrate at the door of the oratory during the divine office; saying nothing, but lying there, with his head touching the ground, at the feet of everyone as they come out. This he shall repeat until the abbot declares that he has made satisfaction for his fault. And when he is allowed by the abbot to come into the oratory, he shall throw himself at the feet of the abbot and the whole community, to ask their prayers. Then, if the abbot commands, he shall be received into the choir in a place appointed him; but he is not to lead a psalm or read a lesson or take any other individual part in the office, until further order from the abbot.

At the end of every office, he shall prostrate himself where he stands, until again the abbot judges him to have made satisfaction and bids him desist.

They who for lesser faults are only deprived of the table, shall make satisfaction in the oratory till the abbot commands otherwise. They shall do it until he gives them the blessing and says: "It is enough."

45. OF THOSE WHO MAKE MISTAKES IN THE ORATORY

If anyone, while reciting a psalm, responsory, antiphon, or lesson, make a mistake, unless he humble himself by making reparation before all, he shall incur a greater punishment. For he would not retrieve by humility what he did amiss by neglect.

Boys for this fault shall be chastised.

46. OF THOSE WHO FAIL IN ANY OTHER MATTERS

If anyone, being employed in the kitchen, store, refectory, bakehouse, garden, or anywhere else, commits a fault, breaks or loses anything, or in any way fails in his duty, and does not immediately declare his fault and offer himself of his own accord to make amends before the abbot and the community; when it is discovered by another, he shall be more severely punished.

But if the fault be a hidden matter concerning the soul, he shall only reveal it to his abbot or spiritual elders, who know how to heal their own wounds as well as the wounds of others, and will not disclose and publish them abroad.

47. OF THE DUTY OF RINGING FOR OFFICES

The abbot ought to undertake the charge of ringing to the divine office night and day, or to entrust it to a brother who is punctual, so that everything may be done at the proper times.

The leading of the psalms and antiphons shall be done by those appointed thereto, in their order after the abbot. No one shall presume to sing or read who has not skill enough to do it with edification. It is to be done with humility and composure, and in the fear of God, and by the persons whom the abbot appoints.

48. OF DAILY LABOUR

Idleness is the enemy of the soul. Therefore the brothers must spend a fixed part of their time in sacred reading, and another fixed part in manual labour.

From Easter to September 14th they shall go out and work, at any necessary task, from 7 A.M. until 10 A.M. or thereabouts. From 10 A.M. until about noon, they shall employ their time in reading.

After dinner at noon, they may rest on their beds in silence. If anyone would rather read a book, he may, provided he does not disturb others.

The hour of None is to be advanced, and said about 2.30 P.M. and afterwards they shall return to their work until Vespers. If the circumstances or the poverty of the place require that the monks cut their corn themselves, they must not look upon it as a grievance. For they are truly monks if they live by the work of their hands, as our forefathers and the apostles have done before them. Yet all is to be done with moderation, by reason of weak constitutions.

From September 14th to the beginning of Lent they are to read quietly until 8 o'clock: then Terce shall be said: and from Terce to None they shall work at their appointed tasks. As soon as the first bell for None goes, they are to stop work and get themselves ready in time for the second bell. After the meal they are to apply themselves to reading and to learning the psalms.

In Lent, they are to read from break of day until 9 A.M., and then work at their different tasks until 4 P.M. During Lent they are each to take one book of the Bible, and read the whole of it from beginning to end: these books are to be distributed at the beginning of Lent. Particular care should be taken that one or two of the elders be deputed to go round the monastery, and oversee the monks at the times appointed for reading, to discover if any of them be bored, or idle, or trifling away his time with frivolous talk instead of serious reading, unprofitable to himself and an interruption to others. If (though God forbid) any such person be found, let him be rebuked, twice if necessary; and if he then does not amend, he shall be punished in accordance with the Rule, severely enough to make the others afraid. No one shall converse with another brother at improper times.

On Sundays all shall employ their time in reading, except those who have been given special duties. If there be anyone so negligent and slothful that he neither can nor will meditate or read, he must be employed about some other work which he can do, and must not be idle. Those brothers who are sick or of tender constitutions must receive consideration from the abbot, and be employed in a craft or work suitable to their strength, that they may not be altogether idle, nor burdened with labour beyond their powers and so driven away from the monastery.

49. OF THE OBSERVANCE OF LENT

The whole life of a monk ought to be a continual Lent. But because this perfection is so uncommon, at least I advise everyone, during the holy season of Lent, to practise particular purity of life, and redeem their negligences of other times. This will be rightly performed if we control our faults, and betake ourselves to prayer with tears, to reading, to compunction of heart and to abstinence.

Therefore, in Lent, everyone must of his own accord add something above his usual practice; for example by offering more prayer in private, by taking less than usual in food and drink, so that everyone may, with comfort in the Holy Ghost, make a voluntary sacrifice to God of something beyond what is normally appointed him. This means that each shall deprive his body of something in eating, drinking, sleeping, talking and the little liberties of merriment and discourse; and he is to look forward, with a pure joy of spirit, to the holy feast of Easter.

Each shall make known to the abbot what he is offering up, and so it is to be done with the abbot's prayers and approval. For what is done without the consent of him who is their spiritual father, shall be looked upon as presumption and vanity, and not regarded as gaining merit. Everything must be done with the abbot's approval.

FORTY-TWO

De Observatione Ciborum (On the Observance of Foods)

ANTHIMUS

Anthimus was a Greek physician sent to the Ostrogothic court of Theodoric in Italy in the sixth century before being sent to serve the king of the Franks. Although his overall dietary theory remains in the Greek tradition, it is clear that he is catering to his barbarian audience as well, in recommending such products as raw bacon. The original language is Latin, so it could be understood in Western Europe. It is among the few learned treatises on food of the early Middle Ages.

Here begins the letter of Anthimus, a Distinguished Gentleman, Count and Legate to His Excellency Theuderic, King of the Franks, concerning the observance of food. Or: how all food should be eaten so that it may be properly digested and promote health, rather than cause stomach problems and persistent infirmity of the body.

I have taken care, to the best of my ability, following the directions of medical writers, of a plan of diet for Your Reverence which will be of benefit to you, because in men excellence of health corresponds to the suitability of food. By that I mean: if food has been prepared well, it helps towards good digestion, but if it has not been cooked properly, it causes a heaviness in the stomach and bowels. It can even engender undigestible fluids, together with smelly hiccoughs and violent belching. Following on this, a vapour rises into the head, as a result of which sudden dizziness and unpleasant exhalations can often arise. This type of indigestion can lead to diarrhoea, or at the very least to vomiting, because the stomach is unable to digest

Anthimus. *On the Observance of Foods.* Translated by Mark Grant. Totnes, UK: Prospect, 1996, pp. 47–59.

raw food. But if food has been well prepared, the ensuing digestion is good and agreeable, and useful humours will be nourished. To such a degree does excellent health depend on this, that anyone who is prepared to take care over his food in the way which I shall set out will have need of no other medicine.

Drink should be treated in the same way, for as much should be taken as will harmonise with the food. If too much is drunk and at too a low temperature, the stomach grows chilled and loses its efficacy, so that there ensues diarrhoea and the other conditions that I mentioned above. Let me give you an analogy: if someone is constructing a wall of a house, he should mix the lime and water in the correct proportions to ensure that the mortar is thick, for then it is both useful for the building and it sets; but if too much water is added, then it is no longer useful. In a similar way proportion ought to be observed in food and drink, for as we said above, excellence of health corresponds to food that has been properly cooked and properly digested.

But let us suppose that someone asks how anyone can take this sort of care when engaged in military manoeuvres or a long journey. I would say that if a fire can be lit and if there is time, what has been suggested ought to be possible. However, if force of circumstance compels one to eat meat or anything else raw, then eat sparingly rather than to excess. What I am arguing can be summed up by the ancient motto: 'Everything in excess is harmful.' As far as drink is concerned, if someone drinks too much before riding his horse or hurrying about his business, then he will suffer pain when jolted on his horse, and what will be produced in his bowels will be worse than if he had eaten food.

Perhaps there will be asked the question of how it is that other peoples eat raw and bloody meat and yet are healthy. The answer is that these peoples may not really be healthy, because they make themselves remedies; for when they feel ill, they burn themselves on the stomach and the belly and in other places, in the same way that untamed horses are burned. My explanation for all this is as follows: these people just like wolves eat one sort of food rather than a variety of foods, since they possess nothing but meat and milk, and whatever they have they eat, and they appear to be healthy because of the restricted nature of their diet. Sometimes they have something to drink, and sometimes they do not, and this lack of abundance seems to be responsible for their state of health. By way of contrast, we who excite ourselves with different food and different delicacies have, by necessity, to govern ourselves in such a way as not to be aggravated by excess, so that by living more frugally we may maintain our health. If pleasure is taken from eating food of whatever kind, then the food that is eaten first should have been properly prepared, and anything else taken more sparingly, in order that what is eaten first may not only be of benefit and but also be digested well.

With this in mind, everyone should steadfastly observe what has been put forward by me through the help of Our Divine Majesty and Lord Jesus Christ, by Whose bountifulness we may have a longer life and excellent health. I therefore present, to the best of my knowledge, a scheme of how different foods should be used according to the instructions of a number of writers.

1. To begin with, it is best to eat white bread, not unleavened, but well leavened and, when the situation allows, hot every day, because such bread is better digested. For if the bread is not well risen, it weighs heavily on the stomach.

2. Barley is, by its nature, moist and cold, and the juice from its husk is purgative. You can prove this by toasting unparched barley, and watching the juice oozing out in large quantities.

3. Beef which has been steamed can be used both roasted in a dish and also braised in a sauce, provided that, as soon as it begins to give off a smell, you put the meat in some water. Boil it in as much fresh water as suits the size of the portion of meat; you should not have to add any more water during the boiling. When the meat is cooked, put in a casserole about half a cup of sharp vinegar, some leeks and a little pennyroyal, some celery and fennel, and let these simmer for one hour. Then add half the quantity of honey to vinegar, or as much honey as you wish for sweetness. Cook over a low heat, shaking the pot frequently with one's hands so that the sauce coats the meat sufficiently. Then grind the following: 50 pepper corns, 2 grammes each of costmary and spikenard, and 1.5 grammes of cloves. Carefully grind all these spices together in an earthenware mortar with the addition of a little wine. When well ground, add them to the casserole and stir well, so that before they are taken from the heat, they may warm up and release their flavour into the sauce. Whenever you have a choice of honey or must reduced either by a third or two-thirds, add one of these as detailed above. Do not use a bronze pan, because the sauce tastes better cooked in an earthenware casserole.

4. Mutton is suitable even if eaten often, both braised in a plain sauce or when roasted, provided that it is cooked some way from the fire. For if it is cooked near the fire, the meat burns on the outside whilst the inside remains raw, and it becomes more harmful than beneficial. So cook it, as I have stated, some way from the fire and for a long time; let it become in this way like steamed meat. When it is roasting, salt mixed with wine should be spread over it with a feather.

5. Lamb and kid are both excellent, using whatever method you like, either steamed or boiled in a sauce. They are equally good roasted.

6. Venison can be eaten boiled and steamed, but should be eaten only on occasion. It is good roasted, provided it comes from young deer, because it is rather heavy if it comes from old deer.

7. Fawn and wild goat are also suitable, but they are better when they are young.

8. The fresher the boar, the lighter it is, but it should be eaten boiled. If it is roasted, it should be placed some way from the fire and for a long time, as we explained in the case of mutton.

9. Pork can be eaten both boiled and roasted. In fact, the fresher the pork, the lighter and more digestible it is. Loin of pork is best eaten roasted, because it is a good food and well digested, provided that, while it is roasting, it is spread with feathers dipped in brine. If the loin of pork is rather tough when eaten, it is better to dip in pure salt. We ban the use of fish sauce from every culinary rôle.

10. Sucking-pig is extremely good and agreeable when boiled, or cooked in a sauce, as well as roasted in an oven, provided that the heat is not too great and that it is not burnt too much, but instead prepared so that it becomes like steamed meat. It can then

be dipped in a simple honey and vinegar mixture, made with two parts of honey to one part of vinegar. The meat is dipped into this sauce when it is eaten.

11. Tender ox is suitable if the meat is eaten either boiled or steamed. If you want, you can eat it roasted, on condition that it is roasted some way from the fire, but it is not digested well.

12. Salted beef and ox are not agreeable, unless necessity dictates that they are eaten, because the fat runs out of the meat on account of the salt, and the meat becomes dry and difficult to digest.

13. Hare, if young, can be eaten in a sweet sauce made with pepper, a little clove and ginger, costmary, and spike or leaf of nard.

14. At this point I will explain how bacon may be eaten to the best effect, for there is no way that I can pass over this Frankish delicacy. If it has been simply roasted in the same way as a joint of meat, the fat drains into the fire and the bacon becomes dry, and whoever eats it is harmed and is not benefitted; it also produces bad humours and causes indigestion. But if bacon that has been boiled and cooled is eaten, it is more beneficial, regulating constipated bowels and being well digested. But it should be boiled well; and if of course it is from a ham, it should be cooked more. None of the rind should be eaten, because it is not digested. Bacon fat which is poured over some foods and vegetables when oil is not available is not harmful. But frying brings absolutely no benefit.

As for raw bacon which, so I hear, the Franks have a habit of eating, I am full of curiosity regarding the person who showed them such a medicine as to obviate the need for other medicines. They eat it raw, because it is very beneficial and as a remedy is responsible for their health. Its effect is akin to that of a good medicine for their internal organs, and if they have any difficulties with their bowels or intestines, it cures them. Stomach and gnawing worms are expelled by this medicine as soon as they are born. It regulates the bowels and, what is so good for them, they are healthier than other people because of this food. Let me give a good example so that what I am writing may be believed: thick bacon, placed for a long time on all wounds, be they external or internal or caused by a blow, both cleanses any putrefaction and aids healing. Look at what power there is in raw bacon, and see how with it the Franks heal what doctors try to cure with drugs or with potions.

15. Beer, plain mead and spiced mead are absolutely fine for drinking by almost everyone. Beer that is well brewed possesses goodness and surpasses expectation, as does barley soup, which we make in a different way to beer. Mead that is well brewed is very beneficial, provided that the honey is good.

16. It is not a good idea to eat pigs' kidneys, except for the edges, which are suitable and are well digested. Kidneys of no other animal should be eaten.

17. My sources instruct us to eat cow and mutton belly, except for those which are of a dense texture. They should be boiled, however, and not roasted.

18. Sow's womb is extremely good, but only when boiled.

19. Sow's udder is good both fried and boiled.

20. Calf belly is suitable boiled. I do let people eat on occasion the bacon that is put into the stuffing.

21. Fried pig's liver is not at all suitable for either healthy or sick people. But if those in health wish, they may eat it as follows: when it has been cut up well and placed on a metal gridiron with broad rods, it is coated with oil or with fat, and then grilled over gently burning charcoal. While it is hot, but still underdone, it can be eaten sprinkled with oil, salt and coriander.

22. We now come to fowl. Look out for fattened pheasants and geese, for their breasts are agreeable because they are fed. The parts that consist of white meat only are more suitable. Do not eat their hind parts, because they burden the stomach, since they are the product not of natural but of forced feeding.

23. Hens and plump chickens, so long as they are not fattened, are good provided that in winter they have been killed two days before and in summer the evening before eating. Birds that are prepared while they still give off a suitable smell make for better eating, particularly their breasts and wings, because those parts nourish good humours and blood. The hind parts of all birds are suitable particularly for healthy people, and this applies to these and all the other parts. Medical writers pay attention to those parts which are most important among the different sorts of food available to people living a luxurious life and tasting of a variety of foodstuffs. It is on behalf of these people that this scheme of diet has been written, and especially for those who are weak in body. For if one item mixed among various wholesome ingredients at a meal is raw and not suitable, it ruins all the other good ingredients and prevents the stomach from digesting properly. The fowl just mentioned are suitable both if cooked well in a sauce and if steamed, provided they are cooked immediately after being killed. They are also suitable roasted, so long as they are roasted carefully at a distance from the hearth.

FORTY-THREE
Capitularies

CHARLEMAGNE

Charlemagne (ca. 742–814) was king of the Franks and, after 800, emperor of the Romans; he reigned over an enormous empire covering much of Europe. He initiated what is often called a Carolingian Renaissance, involving rescuing of classic literature and the arts. But he also faced the practical problem of feeding his armies while on campaign. These orders to have various foods planted throughout the empire were an attempt to solve the problem of military provisioning.

15 "DE VILLIS," END OF THE EIGHTH CENTURY

1 It is our wish that those of our estates which we have established to minister to our needs shall serve our purposes entirely and not those of other men.

2 That all our people shall be well looked after, and shall not be reduced to penury by anyone.

3 That the stewards shall not presume to put our people to their own service, and shall not compel them to give their labour or to cut wood or to do any other work for them; and they shall accept no gifts from them, neither a horse nor an ox, nor a cow, nor a pig, nor a sheep, nor a piglet, nor a lamb, nor anything other than bottles of wine, vegetables, fruit, chickens and eggs.

H. R. Loyn and John Percival, eds. *The Reign of Charlemagne.* New York: St. Martin's Press, 1975, pp. 65–73.

4 If anyone of our people does harm to our interests through theft or any other neglect of duty, let him make good the damage in full, and in addition let him be punished by whipping according to the law, except in the case of murder or arson, for which a fine may be exacted. As far as concerns other men, let the stewards be careful to give them the justice to which they have a right, as the law directs. Our people, as we have said, are to be whipped in preference to being fined. Free men, however, who live on our crown lands [*fiscis*] and estates shall be careful to pay for any wrong they may have done, according to their law; and whatever they may give as their fine, whether it be cattle or any other form of payment, shall be assigned to our use.

5 Whenever it falls to our stewards to see that our work is done, whether it be sowing or ploughing, harvesting, haymaking or the gathering of grapes, let each one of them, at the appropriate time and place, supervise the work and give instructions as to how it should be done, so that everything may be successfully carried out. If a steward is not in his district, or cannot get to a particular place, let him send a good messenger from among our people, or some other man who can be trusted, to look after our affairs and settle them satisfactorily; and the steward shall be especially careful to send a reliable man to deal with this matter.

6 It is our wish that our stewards shall pay a full tithe of all produce to the churches that are on our estates, and that no tithe of ours shall be paid to the church of another lord except in places where this is an ancient custom. And no clerics shall hold these churches except our own or those from our people or from our chapel.

7 That each steward shall perform his service in full, according to his instructions. And if the necessity should arise for his service to be increased, let him decide whether he should add to the manpower or to the days spent in performing it [*si servitium debeat multiplicare vel noctes*].

8 That our stewards shall take charge of our vineyards in their districts, and see that they are properly worked; and let them put the wine into good vessels, and take particular care that no loss is incurred in shipping it. They are to have purchased other, more special, wine to supply the royal estates. And if they should buy more of this wine than is necessary for supplying our estates they should inform us of this, so that we can tell them what we wish to be done with it. They shall also have slips from our vineyards sent for our use. Such rents from our estates as are paid in wine they shall send to our cellars.

9 It is our wish that each steward shall keep in his district measures for *modii* and *sextaria*, and vessels containing eight *sextaria,* and also baskets of the same capacity as we have in our palace.

10 That our mayors and foresters, our stablemen, cellarers, deans, tollcollectors and other officials shall perform regular services, and shall give pigs in return for their holdings: in place of manual labour, let them perform their official duties well. And any mayor who has a benefice, let him arrange to send a substitute, whose task it will be to carry out the manual labour and other services on his behalf.

11 That no steward, under any circumstances, shall take lodgings for his own use or for his dogs, either among our men or among those living outside our estates.

12 That no steward shall commend a hostage of ours on our estates.

13 That they shall take good care of the stallions, and under no circumstances allow them to stay for long in the same pasture, lest it should be spoiled. And if any of them is unhealthy, or too old, or is likely to die, the stewards are to see that we are informed at the proper time, before the season comes for sending them in among the mares.

14 That they shall look after our mares well, and segregate the colts at the proper time. And if the fillies increase in number, let them be separated so that they can form a new herd by themselves.

15 That they shall take care to have our foals sent to the winter palace at the feast of St Martin.

16 It is our wish that whatever we or the queen may order any steward, or whatever our officials, the seneschal or the butler, may order them in our name or in the name of the queen, they shall carry out in full as they are instructed. And whoever falls short in this through negligence, let him abstain from drinking from the moment he is told to do so until he comes into our presence or the presence of the queen and seeks forgiveness from us. And if a steward is in the army, or on guard duty, or on a mission, or is away elsewhere, and gives an order to his subordinates and they do not carry it out, let them come on foot to the palace, and let them abstain from food and drink until they have given reasons for failing in their duty in this way; and then let them receive their punishment, either in the form of a beating or in any other way that we or the queen shall decide.

17 A steward shall appoint as many men as he has estates in his district, whose task it will be to keep bees for our use.

18 At our mills they are to keep chickens and geese, according to the mill's importance—or as many as is possible.

19 In the barns on our chief estates they are to keep not less than 100 chickens and not less than 30 geese. At the smaller farms they are to keep not less than 50 chickens and not less than 12 geese.

20 Every steward is to see that the produce is brought to the court in plentiful supply throughout the year; also, let them make their visitations for this purpose at least three or four times.

21 Every steward is to keep fishponds on our estates where they have existed in the past, and if possible he is to enlarge them. They are also to be established in places where they have not so far existed but where they are now practicable.

22 Those who have vines shall keep not less than three or four crowns of grapes.

23 On each of our estates the stewards are to have as many byres, pigsties, sheepfolds and goat-pens as possible, and under no circumstances are they to be without them. They are also to have cows provided by our serfs for the performance of their service, so that the byres and plough-teams are in no way weakened by service on our demesne. And when they have to provide meat, let them have lame but healthy oxen, cows or horses which are not mangy, and other healthy animals; and, as we have said, our byres and plough-teams must not suffer as a result of this.

24 Every steward is to take pains over anything he has to provide for our table, so that everything he gives is good and of the best quality, and as carefully and cleanly prepared as possible. And each of them, when he comes to serve at our table, is to have corn for two meals a day for his service; and any other provisions, whether in flour or in meat, are similarly to be of good quality.

25 They are to report on the first of September whether or not there will be food for the pigs.

26 The mayors are not to have more land in their districts than they can ride through and inspect in a single day.

27 Our houses are to have continuous watch-fires and guards to keep them safe. And when our *missi* and their retinues are on their way to or from the palace, they shall under no circumstances take lodging in the royal manor houses, except on our express orders or those of the queen. And the count in his district, or the men whose traditional custom it has been to look after our *missi* and their retinues, shall continue, as they have done in the past, to provide them with pack-horses and other necessities, so that they may travel to and from the palace with ease and dignity.

28 It is our wish that each year in Lent on Palm Sunday, which is also called Hosanna Sunday, the stewards shall take care to pay in the money part of our revenue according to our instructions, after we have determined the amount of our revenue for the year in question.

29 With regard to those of our men who have cases to plead, every steward is to see to it that they are not compelled to come into our presence to make their plea; and he shall not allow a man to lose, through negligence, the days on which he owes service. And if a serf of ours is involved in a lawsuit outside our estates, his master is to do all he can to see that he obtains justice. And if in a given place the serf has difficulty in obtaining it, his master shall not allow him to suffer as a result, but shall make it his business to inform us of the matter, either in person or through his messenger.

30 It is our wish that from all the revenue they shall set aside what is needed for our purposes; and in the same way they are to set aside the produce with which they load the carts that are needed for the army, both those of the householders and those of the shepherds, and they shall keep a record of how much they are sending for this purpose.

31 That in the same way each year they shall set aside what is necessary for the household workers and for the women's workshops; and at the appropriate time they are to supply it in full measure, and must be in a position to tell us how they have disposed of it and where it came from.

32 That every steward shall make it his business always to have good seed of the best quality, whether bought or otherwise acquired.

33 After all these parts of our revenue have been set aside or sown or otherwise dealt with, anything that is left over is to be kept to await our instructions, so that it can be sold or held in reserve as we shall decide.

34 They are to take particular care that anything which they do or make with their hands— that is, lard, smoked meat, sausage, newly-salted meat, wine, vinegar, mulberry wine, boiled wine, garum, mustard, cheese, butter, malt, beer, mead, honey, wax and flour—that all these are made or prepared with the greatest attention to cleanliness.

35 It is our wish that tallow shall be made from fat sheep and also from pigs; in addition, they are to keep on each estate not less than two fattened oxen, which can either be used for making tallow there or can be sent to us.

36 That our woods and forests shall be well protected; if there is an area to be cleared, the stewards are to have it cleared, and shall not allow fields to become overgrown with woodland. Where woods are supposed to exist they shall not allow them to be excessively cut and damaged. Inside the forests they are to take good care of our game; likewise, they shall keep our hawks and falcons in readiness for our use, and shall diligently collect our dues there. And the stewards, or our mayors or their men, if they send their pigs into our woods to be fattened, shall be the first to pay the tithe for this, so as to set a good example and encourage other men to pay their tithe in full in the future.

37 That they shall keep our fields and arable land in good order, and shall guard our meadows at the appropriate time.

38 That they shall always keep fattened geese and chickens sufficient for our use if needed, or for sending to us.

39 It is our wish that the stewards shall be responsible for collecting the chickens and eggs which the serfs and manse-holders contribute each year; and when they are not able to use them they are to sell them.

40 That every steward, on each of our estates, shall always have swans, peacocks, pheasants, ducks, pigeons, partridges and turtle doves, for the sake of ornament.

41 That the buildings inside our demesnes, together with the fences around them, shall be well looked-after, and that the stables and kitchens, bakeries and wine-presses, shall be carefully constructed, so that our servants who work in them can carry out their tasks properly and cleanly.

42 That each estate shall have in its store-room beds, mattresses, pillows, bed-linen, table-cloths, seat-covers, vessels of bronze, lead, iron and wood, fire-dogs, chains, pot-hangers, adzes, axes, augers, knives and all sorts of tools, so that there is no need to seek them elsewhere or to borrow them. As to the iron tools which they provide for the army, the stewards are to make it their business to see that these are good, and that when they are returned they are put back into the storeroom.

43 They are to supply the women's workshops with materials at the appropriate times, according to their instructions—that is, linen, wool, woad, vermilion, madder, wool-combs, teazles, soap, oil, vessels and the other small things that are needed there.

44 Two thirds of the Lenten food shall be sent each year for our use—that is, of the vegetables, fish, cheese, butter, honey, mustard, vinegar, millet, panic, dry or green herbs, radishes, turnips, and wax or soap and other small items; and as we have said earlier, they are to inform us by letter of what is left over, and shall under no circumstances omit to do this, as they have done in the past, because it is through those two thirds that we wish to know about the one third that remains.

45 That every steward shall have in his district good workmen—that is, blacksmiths, gold- and silver-smiths, shoemakers, turners, carpenters, shield-makers, fishermen, falconers, soap-makers, brewers (that is, people who know how to make beer, cider, perry or any other suitable beverage), bakers to make bread for our use, net-makers who can make good nets for hunting or fishing or fowling, and all the other workmen too numerous to mention.

46 That the stewards shall take good care of our walled parks, which the people call *bro-gili,* and always repair them in good time, and not delay so long that it becomes necessary to rebuild them completely. This should apply to all buildings.

47 That our hunters and falconers, and the other servants who are in permanent attendance on us at the palace, shall throughout our estates be given such assistance as we or the queen may command in our letters, on occasions when we send them out on an errand or when the seneschal or butler gives them some task to do in our name.

48 That the wine-presses on our estates shall be kept in good order. And the stewards are to see to it that no one dares to crush the grapes with his feet, but that everything is clean and decent.

49 That our women's quarters shall be properly arranged—that is, with houses, heated rooms and living rooms; and let them have good fences all round, and strong doors, so that they can do our work well.

50 That each steward shall determine how many horses there should be in a single stable, and how many grooms with them. Those grooms who are free men, and have benefices in the district, shall live off those benefices. Similarly the men of the fisc, who hold manses, shall live off them. And those who have no holding shall receive their food from the demesne.

51 Every steward is to take care that dishonest men do not conceal our seed from us, either under the ground or elsewhere, thus making the harvest less plentiful. Similarly, with the other kinds of mischief, let them see to it that they never happen.

52 It is our wish that the men of the fisc, our serfs, and the free men who live on our crown lands and estates shall be required to give to all men the full and complete justice to which they are entitled.

53 That every steward shall take pains to prevent our people in his district from becoming robbers and criminals.

54 That every steward shall see to it that our people work well at their tasks, and do not go wasting time at markets.

55 It is our wish that the stewards should record, in one document, any goods or services they have provided, or anything they have appropriated for our use, and, in another document, what payments they have made; and they shall notify us by letter of anything that is left over.

56 That every steward in his district shall hold frequent hearings and dispense justice, and see to it that our people live a law-abiding life.

57 If any of our serfs should wish to say something to us about his master in connection with our affairs, he is not to be prevented from coming to us. And if a steward should learn that his subordinates wish to come to the palace to lodge a complaint against him, then that steward shall present his arguments against them at the palace, and give reason why we should not be displeased at hearing their complaint. In this way we wish to find out whether they come from necessity or merely on some pretext.

58 When our puppies are entrusted to the stewards they are to feed them at their own expense, or else entrust them to their subordinates, that is, the mayors and deans, or cellarers, so that they in their turn can feed them from their own resources—unless there should be an order from ourselves or the queen that they are to be fed on our estate at our own expense. In this case the steward is to send a man to them, to see to their feeding, and is to set aside food for them; and there will be no need for the man to go to the kennels every day.

59 Every steward shall, when he is on service, give three pounds of wax and eight *sextaria* of soap each day; in addition, he shall be sure to give six pounds of wax on St Andrew's Day, wherever we may be with our people, and a similar amount in mid-Lent.

60 Mayors are never to be chosen from among powerful men, but from men of more modest station who are likely to be loyal.

61 That each steward, when he is on service, shall have his malt brought to the palace; and with him shall come master-brewers who can make good beer there.

62 That each steward shall make an annual statement of all our income, from the oxen which our ploughmen keep, from the holdings which owe ploughing services, from the pigs, from rents, judgement-fees and fines, from the fines for taking game in our forests without our permission and from the various other payments; from the mills, forests, fields, bridges and ships; from the free men and the hundreds which are attached to our fisc; from the markets; from the vineyards, and those who pay their dues in wine; from hay, firewood and torches, from planks and other timber; from waste land; from vegetables, millet and panic; from wool, linen and hemp; from the fruits of trees; from larger and smaller nuts; from the graftings of various trees; from gardens, turnips, fishponds; from hides, skins and horns; from honey and wax; from oil, tallow and soap; from mulberry wine, boiled wine, mead and vinegar; from beer and from new and old wine; from new and old grain; from chickens and eggs and geese; from the fishermen, smiths, shield-makers and cobblers; from kneading troughs, bins or boxes; from the turners and saddlers; from forges and from mines, that is, from iron- or lead-workings and from workings of any other kind; from people paying tribute; and from colts and fillies. All these things they shall set out in order under separate headings, and shall send the information to us at Christmas time, so that we may know the character and amount of our income from the various sources.

63 With regard to all the things mentioned so far, our stewards should not think it hard of us to make these demands, since it is our wish that they likewise should be able to make demands of their subordinates without giving offence. And all the things that a man ought to have in his house or on his estates, our stewards shall have on our estates.

64 That our carts which go to the army as war-carts shall be well constructed; their coverings shall be well-made of skins, and sewn together in such a way that, should the necessity arise to cross water, they can get across rivers with the provisions inside and without any water being able to get in—and, as we have said, our belongings can get across safely. It is also our wish that flour—12 *modii* of it—should be placed in each cart for our use; and in those carts which carry wine they are to place 12 *modii* according to our measurement, and they are also to provide for each cart a shield, a lance, a quiver and a bow.

65 That the fish from our fishponds shall be sold, and others put in their place, so that there is always a supply of fish; however, when we do not visit the estate they are to be sold, and our stewards are to get a profit from them for our benefit.

66 They are to give an account to us of the male and female goats, and of their horns and skins; and each year they are to bring to us the newly-salted meat of the fattened goats.

67 With regard to vacant manses and newly acquired slaves, if they have any surplus which they cannot dispose of, they are to let us know.

68 It is our wish that the various stewards should always have by them good barrels bound with iron, which they can send to the army or to the palace, and that they should not make bottles of leather.

69 They shall at all times keep us informed about wolves, how many each of them has caught, and shall have the skins delivered to us. And in the month of May they are to seek out the wolf cubs and catch them, with poison and hooks as well as with pits and dogs.

70 It is our wish that they shall have in their gardens all kinds of plants: lily, roses, fenugreek, costmary, sage, rue, southernwood, cucumbers, pumpkins, gourds, kidney-bean, cumin, rosemary, caraway, chick-pea, squill, gladiolus, tarragon, anise, colocynth, chicory, ammi, sesili, lettuces, spider's foot, rocket salad, garden cress, burdock, penny-royal, hemlock, parsley, celery, lovage, juniper, dill, sweet fennel, endive, dittany, white mustard, summer savory, water mint, garden mint, wild mint, tansy, catnip, centaury, garden poppy, beets, hazelwort, marshmallows, mallows, carrots, parsnip, orach, spinach, kohlrabi, cabbages, onions, chives, leeks, radishes, shallots, cibols, garlic, madder, teazles, broad beans, peas, coriander, chervil, capers, clary. And the gardener shall have house-leeks growing on his house. As for trees, it is our wish that they shall have various kinds of apple, pear, plum, sorb, medlar, chestnut and peach; quince, hazel, almond, mulberry, laurel, pine, fig, nut and cherry trees of various kinds. The names of apples are: *gozmaringa, geroldinga, crevedella, spirauca*; there are sweet ones, bitter ones, those that keep well, those that are to be eaten straightaway, and early ones. Of pears they are to have three or four kinds, those that keep well, sweet ones, cooking pears and the late-ripening ones.

FORTY-FOUR
Beowulf

This brief passage from the great Anglo-Saxon poem Beowulf *shows the central role of feasting and drinking in the mead hall, especially as preparatory to a battle, in this case with the monster Grendel. It was written sometime between the eighth and eleventh centuries.*

590 "Proud son, if your hands were as hard, your heart
     As fierce as you think it, no fool would dare
     To raid your hall, ruin Herot
     And oppress its prince, as Grendel has done.
595 But he's learned that terror is his alone,
     Discovered he can come for your people with no fear
     Of reprisal; he's found no fighting, here,
     But only food, only delight.
     He murders as he likes, with no mercy, gorges
600 And feasts on your flesh, and expects no trouble,
     No quarrel from the quiet Danes. Now
     The Geats will show him courage, soon
     He can test his strength in battle. And when the sun
     Comes up again, opening another
605 Bright day from the south, anyone in Denmark
     May enter this hall: that evil will be gone!"
     Hrothgar, gray-haired and brave, sat happily

Burton Raffel, trans. *Beowulf*. New York: Signet Classics, 2008, pp. 28–30.

Listening, the famous ring-giver sure,
At last, that Grendel could be killed; he believed
In Beowulf's bold strength and the firmness of his spirit.
610 There was the sound of laughter, and the cheerful clanking
Of cups, and pleasant words. Then Welthow,
Hrothgar's gold-ringed queen, greeted
The warriors; a noble woman who knew
615 What was right, she raised a flowing cup
To Hrothgar first, holding it high
For the lord of the Danes to drink, wishing him
Joy in that feast. The famous king
Drank with pleasure and blessed their banquet.
620 Then Welthow went from warrior to warrior,
Pouring a portion from the jeweled cup
For each, till the bracelet-wearing queen
Had carried the mead-cup among them and it was Beowulf's
Turn to be served. She saluted the Geats'
Great prince, thanked God for answering her prayers,
625 For allowing her hands the happy duty
Of offering mead to a hero who would help
Her afflicted people. He drank what she poured,
Edgetho's brave son, then assured the Danish
Queen that his heart was firm and his hands
630 Ready:
"When we crossed the sea, my comrades
And I, I already knew that all
My purpose was this: to win the goodwill
Of your people or die in battle, pressed
635 In Grendel's fierce grip. Let me live in greatness
And courage, or here in this hall welcome
My death!"
Welthow was pleased with his words,
His bright-tongued boasts; she carried them back
640 To her lord, walked nobly across to his side.
The feast went on, laughter and music
And the brave words of warriors celebrating
Their delight. Then Hrothgar rose, Healfdane's
Son, heavy with sleep; as soon
645 As the sun had gone, he knew that Grendel
Would come to Herot, would visit that hall
When night had covered the earth with its net
And the shapes of darkness moved black and silent
Through the world. Hrothgar's warriors rose with

650   him.
       He went to Beowulf, embraced the Geats'
       Brave prince, wished him well, and hoped
       That Herot would be his to command. And then
       He declared:
655   "No one strange to this land
       Has ever been granted what I've given you,
       No one in all the years of my rule.
       Make this best of all mead-halls yours, and then
       Keep it free of evil, fight
660   With glory in your heart! Purge Herot
       And your ship will sail home with its treasure-holds full."

PART VII

Study Questions

1. How did Jesus and the apostles explain why the kosher rules were abolished, although perhaps in form rather than substance?
2. Reflect on the time and place that Christian asceticism arises. Why would this be a logical response to persecution?
3. Imagine what an early medieval army ate while on campaign, drawn from the directions given by Charlemagne. What practical difficulties do you think he encountered, and how is war a stimulus to innovation?
4. In the Saxon mead hall scene from *Beowulf*, warriors feast as a form of ritual. How does eating and drinking with others not only cement social bonds but give a sense of common purpose?
5. In all the readings of early Christians describe how various different food traditions interact, clash, and ultimately are reconciled.

Medieval Islam

Islam was founded by the prophet Mohammed as a religion supplanting the earlier pagan religions of the Arabian Peninsula, though inheriting many features of Judaism and Christianity. Islam was said to be the final revelation of the same God of the Old and New Testaments, and therefore other "People of the Book" were not to be persecuted. Food laws as they developed in Islam are a little simpler than the kosher laws, but in many respects they are similar. Pork is considered unclean, and animals must be ritually slaughtered without pain, giving thanks to the animal for sustenance and killing in the name of Allah. There are also fasts, similar to both older religions, but in Islam fasting takes place over the entire month of Ramadan, when people eat or drink absolutely nothing from sunup to sundown. Islam forbids alcohol, though in practice some more secular states have allowed it. A sectarian division among Muslims between Sunni and Shiite has usually determined attitudes toward both the nature of rule, be it more secular or holy, as well as regulations concerning the enforcement of Koranic law.

One feature common to all Arab cultures is the requirement to be hospitable toward strangers. This began most likely as an absolute necessity for survival in the desert, but it became an active command to practice charity. Traditional food is served while seated on the floor. Men sit around common platters and share food scooped with their right hand or with a piece of flat bread. Women traditionally eat after the men.

Islam, as it developed, was in many respects the heir to classical civilization. Despite humble origins in the Arabian Peninsula, Islam spread quickly through the former Byzantine Empire. These were cultured and ancient civilizations, the seat of power first in Syria under the Umayyads and then in Persia under the Abbasids. The latter, centered in Baghdad, was not only the richest and perhaps most opulent city in the world at the time but also among the most learned. The rulers consciously sponsored translation of Greek texts in medicine, philosophy, science, and other fields touching closely upon food. They composed their own gastronomic texts, and, judging by the magnificence of the cuisine, it is not difficult to label this as one of the great gastronomic traditions in world history. It spread as far as India and later beyond toward the east and as far as Spain to the west. One might even argue that the penchant for spicy food prevalent in medieval Europe and ultimately passed on to the New World in the sixteenth century has its roots in Baghdad. There are, for example, similar thick, spicy sauces, forms of fried dough, and drinks across this great expanse and even down to today.

As with all great culinary traditions, adjunct fields developed in food writing. Avicenna, writing about diet based on the Galenic system, is perhaps among the most influential writers in the Western tradition. His works became the foundation of the medical curriculum in medieval universities, and they spread throughout the Muslim world and even to Pakistan and India, where they are still practiced as *Unani* medicine. Unani is a form of the word *Ionian*—that is, Greek. Other scientists, interestingly sometimes Christian or Jewish (such as Maimonides), carried on the tradition of dietary medicine. The three religions flourished side by side, interacted in fruitful ways, and for a time coexisted peacefully.

Agriculture under Muslim rule also reached a high level of sophistication with advanced irrigation techniques, intensive cultivation, and the introduction of new crops. One only has to consider the many Arabic words that made their way into Spanish, and ultimately English, to appreciate the variety of foods introduced to the West in these years. Our words for lemon, rice, artichoke, spinach, almonds, alcohol, and alchemy all come from Arabic.

FORTY-FIVE

A Baghdad Cookery Book

aL-BAGHDADI

This is the most important Arabic cookbook of the Middle Ages, written in the thirteenth century at a time when Baghdad was the cultural center of the Muslim world under the Abbasid caliphate. Muhammad ibn al-Hasan ibn Muhammad ibn Karim al-Katib al-Baghdadi was the author's full name. Many of these dishes survive in the Middle East and especially in Turkey, where this manuscript has been kept.

CHAPTER I

On Sour Dishes and Their Varieties

AMONG the sour dishes are those sweetened with sugar, syrup, honey or date molasses, and those not sweetened or, properly speaking, sour; but everyone has decided that they should be in one chapter.

al-Sikbāj. The way to make it is to cut up fat meat medium and put it in the pot with water to cover it, [a bunch of] green coriander, a stick of cinnamon and the necessary amount of salt. Then, when it boils, remove its scum and froth with a spoon and throw it away. Then put dry coriander on it and remove the green coriander. Then take white onions, Syrian leeks and carrots, if in season, or eggplant (if they are not), and skin them all. Quarter the eggplant lengthwise and half boil it in salt water in another pot, then dry it and leave them in the pot on top of the meat. [Throw the spices on it and adjust its salt in it.] When it is nearly done, take wine vinegar and

al-Baghdadi. *A Baghdad Cookery Book. Petits Proposal Culinaires 79.* Translated by Charles Perry. Totnes, UK: Prospect Books, 2005, pp. 30–44, 86–91.

date molasses—some people prefer to use honey, but date molasses is more appropriate—and mix them, balancing the sweetness and sourness. Then pour them into the pot and boil it for a while. When the fire needs to be cut, take some of the broth and mix it with the necessary amount of saffron. Pour it into the pot. Then take peeled sweet almonds which have been split in half and leave them on top of the pot, with a few jujubes, raisins and dry figs. [And put them on top of the pot.] Cover it awhile to grow quiet on the heat of the fire. Wipe the sides of the pot with a clean cloth and sprinkle rose-water on top. When it grows quiet on the fire, take it up.

Ibrāhīmiyya. The way to make it is to cut up meat medium and put it in the pot with water to cover and the necessary amount of salt. Boil it so that it stews. Put in it a piece of strong linen, tied with pounded coriander, ginger, pepper and finely pounded [galingale] inside it. Then put pieces of cinnamon and mastic on it, and chop up two or three small onions finely and throw them in it. [Pound lean meat and make into meatballs according to the rule, and put them in.] When the ingredients are done, remove that cloth that the spices are in. You make a sauce with the juice of aged mild sour grapes; if there is none, with fresh sour grapes squeezed by hand, without boiling, then strained, [or with filtered vinegar]. Beat sweet almonds, which have been finely pounded to a liquid consistency with water. Pour the sour grape juice on it and sweeten it a little with white sugar; let it not be strongly sour. (Sc. add it to the pot.) Leave it on the fire awhile to grow quiet, and wipe the sides with a clean cloth. Then sprinkle the top of it with a little rose-water, and when it is quiet, take it up.

Jurjāniyya. The way to make it is to cut up meat medium and leave it in the pot, and put water to cover on it with a little salt. Cut onions into dainty pieces, and when the pot boils, put the onions on it, and dry coriander, pepper, ginger and cinnamon, all pounded fine. If you want, add peeled carrots from which the woody interior has been removed, chopped medium. Then stir it until the ingredients are done. When it is done, take seeds of pomegranates and black raisins in equal proportion and pound them fine, [macerate] well in water and strain through a fine sieve. Then throw them into the pot. Let there be a little bit of vinegar with it. Beat peeled sweet almonds pounded fine to liquid consistency with water, then throw them in the pot. When it boils and is nearly done, sweeten it with a little sugar, as much as needed. [That is, enough to make it pleasant, yuʿadhdhibuhā.] Throw [a handful of] jujubes on top of the pot and sprinkle a little rose-water on it. Then cover it until it grows quiet on the fire, and take it up.

Ḥummāḍiyya. The way to make it is to cut up fat meat medium and leave it in the pot with water to cover and a little salt. Then bring it to the boil and throw the spices on it; and they are coriander, ginger, pepper and cloves, pounded fine and tied in a stout piece of linen. Throw in pieces of cinnamon. Then pound lean meat with spices and form it into meatballs, then put them into [the pot] after it has come to the boil. When they are done, remove the bag of spices. Take the pulp of large citrons, clean it of its seeds, and squeeze it well by hand. Then mix it with about a quarter as much sour grape juice and put it on the meat in the pot so that it boils awhile. Then take peeled sweet almonds, beaten to liquid consistency with water after being pounded fine, and add them to it. Then sweeten it with sugar; if you want, use syrup. Leave the pot on the fire to grow quiet. Sprinkle rose-water on top of the pot and wipe the sides of the pot with a clean cloth, then take it up.

Dīkabrīka. The way to make it is to cut up meat medium and leave it in the pot. Throw on a little salt, a handful of peeled chickpeas, dry and fresh coriander and cut-up onions and leeks. Throw on water to cover and bring it to the boil, then take away its scum. Throw on wine vinegar and soy sauce, throw in a bit of finely ground pepper and cook it until its taste is evident. Some people sweeten it with a little sugar. When it is done, throw in some mixed spices, leave it to grow quiet on the fire, and take it up.

Zīrbāj. The way to make it is to cut up fat meat small and put it in the pot, with enough water on it to cover it and pieces of cinnamon, peeled chickpeas and a little salt. When it boils, take away its scum. Then throw on a pound of wine vinegar, a quarter of a pound of sugar and an ounce of peeled sweet almonds, pounded fine. Mix with rose-water and vinegar, then throw them on the meat. Throw on a *dirham* (each) of ground coriander, pepper and sieved mastic, then colour it with saffron. Put a handful of split [peeled] almonds on top of the pot. Sprinkle a little rose-water on it, wipe its sides with a clean cloth, leave it on the fire to grow quiet, and take it up. If you like to put chicken in it, take a plucked hen and wash it and joint it. When the pot comes to the boil, throw it on the meat to become done.

Nīrbāj. The way to make it is to cut up meat small or medium and throw it in the pot with a little salt and water to cover. Then boil it and take its scum away, and put chopped onions on it. If you like to put in carrots, put them. Throw on dry coriander, cinnamon, pepper, mastic, ginger and bunches of mint. When it is done, take pomegranate seeds and a third as much of black [raisins]. Pound them fine, dissolve them in water, strain them and put them in the pot. Take walnuts and pound them fine, then milk them with water and throw them in the pot also. Put whole walnuts on top of it. Take bunches of dried mint, then crumble them into the top of the pot. When the meat stews and the water decreases, sprinkle lean meat with spices and make it into meatballs (sc. and add them to the pot until they are done). Then sprinkle rose-water on the surface of the pot, rub its sides with a clean cloth and leave it on the fire to grow quiet, and take it up.

Ṭabāhaja. The way to make it is to take sliced meat, cutting it up small. Take tail fat, slice it up and put it in the pot, with a little bit of water, half a *dirham* of pounded salt and a *dānaq* of saffron on it. When the tail fat melts and you have removed its cracklings, throw the meat into the pot on the fat. Throw on pieces of onion, bunches of mint and celery leaf, and stir it until its water dries up. Then throw on dry coriander, cumin, caraway, cinnamon and ginger, [all] finely pounded; set half the spices aside to throw on after it is done. Then take wine vinegar, sour grape juice and lemon juice and mix them, and throw some of all the spices on it. If you like to add some sumac juice, do so. Then moisten it with those liquids from time to time until it is completely done. Then take out the vegetables (*buqūl*), sprinkle aged soy sauce on it and add the rest of the spices to it, with a little bit of pepper. Decorate its surface with egg yolks and sprinkle rose-water on it. Wipe the sides of the pot with a clean cloth, and leave it on the fire to grow quiet, and take it up.

Tuffāḥiyya. The way to make it is to take fat meat, cut it into small elongated pieces and throw them in the pot, with a little salt and some dry coriander on them. Boil it until it is nearly done. Remove its scum and throw it away. Then cut onions small and throw them on top of it, with a stick of cinnamon, pepper, mastic, finely pounded ginger and bunches of mint. Then take sour apples, remove their pits and pound them in a stone mortar, and squeeze out their juice and put it on the meat. Then beat some peeled almonds to a liquid consistency for it and throw them on it. Kindle the fire under it until it is done, and leave it on the fire to grow quiet. If you want to put a jointed hen in it, (do so), letting it cook until done, and you take it up.

Ḥiṣrimiyya. The way to make it is to take fat meat, cut it up and throw it in the pot, with a little salt and dry coriander on it. Then cover it with water (sc. and boil), and take away its scum. Cut up onions (sc. and add.) Peel eggplant and half boil it in a separate pot with water and salt, then dry it and leave it in the (first) pot. Throw on bunches of mint and pieces of gourd with their peel and pulp (*shaḥm*) removed, and throw on pepper, mastic and finely pounded cinnamon. Then take fresh sour grapes, squeeze them well by hand and strain them in a fine strainer. Add a tenth as much lemon juice (to the sour grape juice) and put it in the pot. Then beat pounded peeled sweet almonds to a liquid consistency with a little water. Adjust its taste (i.e., the taste of the stew) with water and the desired amount of the almond milk. Then take a little bit of dry mint and crumble it into the top of the pot. Some people put some sourish apples on top of the pot, and it is good. Likewise, put in a jointed hen if you wish, after throwing the meat (in the pot). Then sprinkle the surface of the pot with rose-water, leave it on a quiet fire awhile so that it grows quiet, and take it up.

Ḥulwiyya, which is called *farḫāna*. The way to make it is to cut up fat meat by itself, and tail fat by itself, and leave them in the pot with a little bit of salt, dry coriander and some chopped-up onions and carrots. Cover it with water and boil it until it is nearly done, and take its scum and throw it away. Then throw on pepper, ginger, mastic and finely pounded cinnamon. When is fully done, take wine vinegar and sugar or syrup, adjust its mixture according to desire and colour it with saffron (sc. and add to the pot). When it is nearly done, put split peeled sweet almonds, ju-jubes, peeled pistachios and hazelnuts, red raisins and small pieces of sweet prunes on the surface of the pot. Sprinkle rose-water on the surface of the pot and wipe its sides with a clean cloth, and leave it on a quiet fire, and take it up. If you like, put a jointed hen with it after the meat is half boiled, to cook with it.

Rummāniyya. The way to make it is to cut up fat meat medium and put it in the pot with a little spiced salt, and cover it with water (sc. and cook it) and thoroughly remove its scum. Then take eggplant and remove its black peel and quarter it lengthwise. Peel and quarter onions like-wise, and peel gourds and clean them of their seeds and flesh, and cut them into strips. Throw all these in the pot, after half boiling them in a separate pot. Throw on coriander, cumin, cinnamon, pepper, mastic and bunches of mint, and cook until done. Then take sour pomegranates, strip them by hand and squeeze them well. Then strain (the juice) and throw it in the pot. Then crum-ble dry mint and put it on the surface of the pot. Pound a little bit of garlic and leave it in the pot also. You might put a jointed chicken in the pot to cook with the meat. Then leave it on the quiet fire awhile, then take it up.

Rībāsiyya. It is meat boiled and (then) stewed with the spices. Throw on a little chopped onion, then squeeze rhubarb juice and throw it on. Beat some peeled, finely pounded sweet al-monds to a liquid consistency and throw them in. Then leave it on the fire, its fire being quiet. Then leave it until it is done, then take it up.

Summāqiyya. The way to make it is to cut up fat meat medium, then leave it in the pot. (Sc. Add water.) Then throw a little good salt on it. Then let it come to the boil until it is nearly done. Thoroughly take its scum away. Then throw on it boiled chard, cut in pieces a finger-width long, and carrots. Then take onions and Nabatean leeks, peel them, wash them in water and salt and put them on. If it is the season of eggplant, put it in with its black peel removed; boil it in a separate pot (i.e. before putting them with the meat). Then take sumac and put it in a separate pot, put a little salt and bread crumbs on it, boil it well and strain it. If you want, take a scalded, jointed hen and throw it in the pot. Pound lean meat fine and (sprinkle) the spices on it. Make it into medium-sized meatballs and throw them in the pot also. Put spices on it, namely dry cori-ander, cumin, pepper, ginger, cinnamon, finely mastic and bunches of fresh mint. Then take the mentioned sumac water and put it in the pot. Pound walnuts, beat them to a liquid consistency with water and throw them into the pot. Then crumble dry mint onto its surface, and throw in whole pieces of walnuts without pounding. Pound a little garlic, mix it with a little of the broth and throw it in the pot. Some people put whole raw eggs (sc. in the pot). Leave it on a quiet fire to grow quiet, then take it up.

["*Amīrbārīsiyya*, which is *zirishkiyya*. It is made like *summāqiyya* except that it is with al-monds. The best of it is made with fresh barberries." *Minhāj*.] *Amīrbārīs* and *zirishk* are Persian names for barberry.

Līmūniyya. The way to make it is to cut up meat and tail fat and leave them in the pot with a little salt, and cover them with water and boil until done. Take off its scum. Then take onions, leeks and carrots, if it is their season, or eggplant. Wash the onions and leeks with [warm] water and salt, and half boil [the eggplant] on its own in a separate pot, then leave them in the pot. If it is carrots, they do not need to be boiled separately. Then throw over it finely pounded dry coriander, mastic, pepper, cinnamon, finely pounded ginger and bunches of mint. Take a hen, joint it and put it in the pot, then throw the vegetables (*tawābil*) in it. Take choicest lemon juice, strain it from its sediment and its seeds, then throw it in the pot. Take peeled sweet almonds, pound them fine and beat to a liquid consistency with water, and leave them in the pot. Crumble bunches of dry mint into the pot, sprinkle it with rose-water and wipe the sides of the pot with a clean cloth. Then leave it on the fire to grow quiet, and take it up. Some people sweeten it with sugar. When it is eaten sweetened, omit the mint and eggplant.

Maghmūma, which is called *al-muqaṭṭaʿa*. The way to make it is to take fat meat and cut it up small, and cut tail fat in thin strips and cut them small. Take onions and eggplant, peel them and half boil them; they might not be boiled separately but peeled and cut into the pot of meat. Spread the tail fat in a layer on the bottom of the pot and a layer of meat on top of it. Sprinkle it with finely pounded spices, namely dry coriander, cumin, caraway, pepper, cinnamon, ginger and salt. Then spread a layer of eggplant and onions on the meat. Proceed according to this rule until they remain about four or five finger-widths from the pot (i.e., the ingredients stand four or five finger-widths high). Sprinkle the finely pounded spices on every layer as needed. Then mix excellent vinegar with a bit of water and a little saffron, and put it in to cover the pot—and over that meat and the vegetables (*ḥawāyij*) by two or three finger-widths. Leave it to grow quiet on the fire, then take it up.

Mamqūriyya. The way to make it is to cut up fat meat small and throw it in the pot, along with a little salt. Throw on water to cover, then bring it to the boil and remove its scum. When it is nearly done, throw on the spices coriander, cumin, cinnamon, mastic and pepper, and chopped onions. When it is done, throw on one part wine vinegar and two parts soy sauce. Throw a small handful of whole coriander seeds on the pot, sprinkle it with rose-water and leave it to grow quiet on the fire, and take it up.

Ḥubaishiyya. The way to make it is to cut up fat meat medium, then throw it in the pot with a little salt and water to cover. Boil it and take off its scum. When it is nearly done, throw on chopped-up onions, which you have washed with warm water and salt, and peeled carrots from which you have removed that which is inside them (viz. the woody core). Throw on dry coriander, cumin, cinnamon, mastic and pepper. Then take the necessary amount of black raisins and pound them fine, then macerate them by hand and strain them. Take two parts of their juice and one part of good sharp vinegar, and throw them in the pot. Pound some walnuts and macerate them with the mentioned juice, and throw them on it. Crumble bunches of dried mint onto the pot. Leave the pot on the fire to grow quiet and take it up, after wiping its sides with a clean cloth.

Mishmishiyya. Take fat meat, cut it up small and put it in the pot with a little salt and water to cover. Then boil it and take away its scum. Then cut up onions, wash them and throw them on the meat, and throw on the spices coriander, cumin, mastic, cinnamon, pepper and finely pounded ginger. Take dry apricots and soak them in hot water, then clean them and throw them into another pot. Bring them to a light boil, then take them down, macerate by hand and strain them through a strainer. Take the juice and make sauce (for) the pot with it. Then beat finely pounded sweet almonds to a liquid consistency with some of the apricot juice and throw it on it. Some people colour it with a little saffron. Then sprinkle a little rose-water on top of the pot, wipe its sides with a clean cloth, leave it to grow quiet on the fire and take it up.

Nāranjiyya. The way to make it is to cut up fat meat medium and leave it in the pot [with water to cover] until it boils. When it boils, remove its scum and throw the necessary amount of salt on it. Cut up onions and leeks and wash them with water and salt. Scrape carrots, cut them four finger-widths long and throw them in the pot. Throw on cumin, dry coriander, sticks of cinnamon, pepper, ginger, finely pounded mastic and bunches of mint. Then pound lean meat finely with the spices and make it into medium-sized meatballs. Take oranges, peel them, take the [white] flesh from them and squeeze them; let him who squeezes them not be the one who peeled them. Then strain (the juice) in a filter and throw it in the pot. Take safflower (seeds) which have been soaked in hot water for a while, then clean them and pound them well in a stone mortar; and if there is none, then (in) a copper (mortar). Milk their juice by hand, strain it and throw it in the pot. Then crumble bunches of dry mint on top of the pot, wipe its sides with a clean cloth and leave it on the fire until it settles, and take it up.

Nārsūn. This is a Persian name, and its origin is *anār sirk,* which means pomegranate and vinegar. The way to make this dish is to cut up fat meat medium, then throw it in the pot and cover it with water. Throw some salt on it and boil it, and remove its scum. When it is nearly done, throw on coriander, cumin, pepper, cinnamon and mastic, all finely ground except for the cinnamon; leave it as sticks. Cut up onions, wash them and throw them in the pot with bunches of mint. Put meatballs in the pot, made from lean meat pounded with the spices. Then take pomegranate seeds, pound them finely, mix them with wine vinegar, filter it and throw it into the pot. Take peeled walnuts, pound them fine, mix them with hot water and put them on the dish. Then adjust its flavour according to desire; let there be enough walnut for the stew to have a consistency. Then throw whole pieces of walnut on the pot and crumble bunches of dry mint into it. Sprinkle a little rosewater on it, wipe its sides with a clean cloth and leave it on the fire to grow quiet, and take it up.

Maṣūṣiyya. The way to make it is to cut up fat meat medium and put it in the pot with water to cover and a little salt. When it boils, remove its scum. Throw on a bunch of celery (leaves), cut from their roots and stems and cleaned, and some chopped onions, and the spices coriander, cumin, pepper, mastic and sticks of cinnamon. Then throw on it enough good wine vinegar to cover it, and colour it with a little saffron, and throw whole raw eggs on it. Leave it on a quiet fire awhile, then take it up.

Section on Yogurt and What Is Cooked from It

al-Maḍīra. The way to make it is to cut up fat meat medium, then put it in the pot with a little salt and water to cover, then boil it and remove its scum. When it is nearly done, take large onions and large Nabatean leeks also, peel them, cut off their tails, then wash them in water and salt, dry them and throw them in the pot. Throw on dry coriander, cumin, mastic and finely pounded cinnamon. And when it is done and its water has dried up and nothing remains but the fat, ladle it into a dish. Then take the necessary amount of Persian yogurt, throw it on the pot. Leave it until it comes to the boil. Then reduce the heat from it and stir it. When its boiling subsides, return that meat [and the vegetables] to it. Cover the pot, wipe its sides and leave it to grow quiet on the fire, and take it up.

Buqūliyya. The way to make it is to cut up fat meat medium and throw it in the pot with a little salt and water to cover. When it boils, take its scum away. When it is nearly done, take vegetable leeks, cut them small, pound fine in the mortar and throw them in the pot. Then take lean meat, pound it with the known spices and a little bit of those leeks, make it into meatballs and throw them in the pot. When its liquid has dried up, throw on coriander, cumin, finely pounded pepper and sticks of cinnamon. Then throw the necessary amount of Persian yogurt on it. Crumble bunches of dry mint into its top. Wipe the sides of the pot with a clean cloth, leave it to grow quiet on the fire and take it up.

Labaniyya. The way to make it is to cut up meat and throw it in the pot with a little salt and water to cover [and boil it] until it is nearly done. When it stews in its fat and most of the water has dried up, throw chopped, washed onions and leeks on it, and eggplant, quartered lengthwise and half boiled in a separate pot; and afterward, dry coriander, pounded cumin, mastic, sticks of cinnamon and bunches of mint. Then boil it in the remainder of its liquid until it is completely done. Throw Persian yogurt on it in which you have put pounded garlic. Crumble bunches of dry mint into the top of the pot. Wipe the sides of the pot with a clean cloth, leave it on the fire to grow quiet for awhile, then take it up.

Buqūliyya [Mukarrara]. The way to make it is to cut fat meat medium and throw it in the pot with a little salt and water to cover. When it boils, take its scum away. When it is nearly done, throw the known spices on it. Then take green coriander [and bunches of mint], strip their leaves and throw them in the pot. Take vegetable leeks which have been cut small with the knife, then pound them in a stone mortar and throw them in the pot. Pound lean meat with the spices and mix a little of those pounded leeks with it, make it into meatballs, and throw them in the pot. And when its liquid has dried up, (sc. throw into the pot) a little finely ground pepper, ginger and mastic. Then throw the necessary amount of Persian yogurt on it. Crumble bunches of dry mint into its top, wipe the sides of the pot with a clean cloth, leave it on the fire awhile to grow quiet, then take it up.

Mujazzaᶜa. The way to make it is to cut fat meat medium, throw it in the pot with a little salt and cover it with water. When it boils, remove its scum. Cut up two or three onions and throw them on. Then take two or three bunches of chard for the pot of meat and wash them, after cutting them (in pieces) four finger-widths long, and throw them in the pot. Throw on dry coriander, cumin, mastic, cinnamon and pepper. When it is done, throw on Persian yogurt in which you have put a sufficient quantity of pounded garlic. Then when the pot grows quiet on the fire, sprinkle a little nigella on top of the pot. Wipe its sides and take it up.

ᶜUkaika. The way to make it is to take fresh tail fat, cut it small and melt it, and take its cracklings out. Then take fat meat, cut it small and throw it on the melted fat, stirring until it is browned. Then put on enough water to cover (the meat) and a little salt, and leave it until it is done and it dries up (sc. and nothing is left) except for the fat. Throw on dry coriander and cumin, both finely pounded, and cinnamon, ground pepper and mastic. Then take a sufficient quantity of Persian yogurt, put pounded garlic in it, throw it on the pot and leave it until it boils. Then cut the fire under the pot and leave it [on] a quiet fire until the yogurt thickens. Throw away the fat on its surface. Then sprinkle a little finely ground cinnamon on it, wipe the sides of the pot with a clean cloth and take it up.

Maṣliyya. The way to make it is to cut up fat meat and boil it as usual, and remove the scum. When it is done, throw on a handful of chopped onion, a little [salt,] ground dry coriander, cumin, pepper, sticks of cinnamon and mastic. When its liquid has dried up and the fat appears, take dried whey, pound it fine, throw hot water on it and macerate it well by hand until it becomes like sour yogurt (in appearance) and of the same consistency, then throw it in the pot. Grind a little garlic and throw it in the pot with bunches of fresh mint. Sprinkle some finely ground cinnamon on the surface. Then wipe the sides of the pot with a clean cloth, leave it on the fire awhile to grow quiet and take it up.

CHAPTER VII

On Pickles, Relishes and Condiments

THERE are many kinds which are served among dishes, to cleanse their greasiness from the mouth, to improve the appetite, to aid the digestion of food and to make food palatable. We shall mention a preferred selection, briefly, as we have said.

━━ ～ ━━

Section on Vinegar Pickles

Naʿnaʿ Mukhallal. Take large-leaved fresh mint and clean the leaves from the stalks, then wash them and dry them in the shade. Sprinkle aromatic herbs on them. If you like, add celery leaves and peeled cloves of garlic. Put it in a clean glass jug, cover it with good vinegar and colour it with a little saffron. Leave it until the leaves absorb the sourness of the vinegar and its sharpness is cut; and use it.

Bādhinjān Mukhallal. Take medium eggplants and cut off half their stems and their leaves. Then half boil them in water and salt, take them up and dry them off. Then quarter them lengthwise and stuff them with fresh celery leaves, a few bunches of mint and peeled cloves of garlic, and pack them one on another in a glass jug. Sprinkle a little of the herbs and finely ground mixed spices on them, cover them with good vinegar and leave them until they are thoroughly mature, and use them.

Lift Mukhallal Muḥallā. Take medium turnips and peel them, then cut them in small pieces. Then sprinkle a little salt on them, and afterward sprinkle them with some mixed spices and the herbs, and rub them well into those (turnips) with the hand. Then take the necessary amount of vinegar, and put two ounces of honey in every pound, and colour it with a little saffron. Put enough vinegar and honey on the turnips to cover them. Put them in a glass jug, and stopper its top until they mature, and use them. As for (the kind) that is not sweetened, cut them up and boil lightly in water and salt, and sprinkle a little mixed spices on them. Cover them with vinegar, and when they are mature, use them.

Bādhinjān Maḥsī. The way to make it is to take eggplant, cut its stems and leaves off and boil it lightly in water and salt. Then take it out and dry it off, and cut it into small pieces. Sprinkle a little salt and some of the herbs and mixed spices on them. Then take good, well-pounded pomegranate seeds, macerate them in good vinegar, filter them and throw their dregs away. Put that vinegar on the mentioned eggplant and mix it with it. Then take walnuts and almonds and pound them [coarsely]. Put peeled sesame seeds with them and toast them. Then put a little sesame oil in a copper *dist*. When it boils, put the almonds, walnuts and sesame in it and stir them. Then put them on that eggplant with the sesame oil, and put it in a glass jug, and put some finely ground mixed spices on it. Then use it after (some) days.

As for smooth cucumbers, ridged cucumbers, onions and other (vegetables) which you want to pickle, put them in vinegar alone until they soften and mature, and use them.

Bādhinjān bi-Laban. Take medium eggplant, cut off its leaves and half its stems, and half boil it in water and salt. Then take it out, dry it well and throw it in yogurt and garlic. Refine fresh sesame oil with a bit of cumin and coriander and throw it on it. Sprinkle a bit of mixed spices and nigella on it, and use it.

Qarʿ bi-Laban. Take gourds, peel them, throw away their pith and seeds and cut them small. Then boil them in water and salt until they are done. Take them out of the water and dry them. When they are dry, put them in Persian yogurt with which well-pounded garlic has been mixed. Sprinkle nigella on it, and use it.

Silq bi-Laban. Take chard with large ribs, cut off the edges of its leaves and cut it into pieces the length of a span. Wash it, then boil it in water and salt until it is done. Then dry it and put it in Persian yogurt and garlic, and sprinkle a little nigella on it, and use it.

Shīrāz bi-Buqūl. It is a good relish which stimulates the appetite and benefits (the digestion). The way to make it is to take mint, celery and vegetable leeks. Strip the leaves of the celery and mint, cut everything small with the knife and pound it in the mortar. Then mix it well with *shīrāz*. Sprinkle it with a little salt, as much as necessary, and finely pounded mustard, and scatter coarsely pounded walnut meats on its surface, and use it. If there is no *shīrāz,* then renneted yogurt (*al-laban al-mās*) which has been strained from the water which is in it will be its substitute. A little sour yogurt is mixed with it, and it is used.

Isfānākh Muṭajjan. Take spinach, cut off the bottom of its stems and wash it. Then boil it lightly in water and salt, and dry it. Then refine sesame oil, throw it (the spinach) in it (the oil), and stir it until it gives off its fragrance. Then pound a little garlic and put in it, and sprinkle cumin, dry coriander and finely pounded cinnamon on it, and take it up.

Section on Condiments

Among them:

Kāmakh Rījāl. Several kinds of it are made according to one principle; they differ according to the flavourings (*hawāyij*) that are left in them. The way to make it is first to take the shell of a large [dry] gourd, from which you have cleaned all the pulp and seeds which are inside it, and soak it in water for two hours. Then dry it [well], and leave five pounds of sour yogurt, ten pounds of sweet milk and a pound and a half of finely ground salt in it, and stir it. Then cover its top and leave it in the hot sun for several days. The making of it starts in June (*Ḥuzairān*), at the beginning of the hot season. Then throw three pounds of sweet milk on it in the morning of every day, and stir it morning and evening. Whenever it decreases, add milk, until the beginning of August (*Āb*). Take mint leaves, nigella and peeled cloves of garlic and throw them in it, and stir it. Add sweet milk when it decreases, as usual, until the middle of September (*Ailūl*), and cover its top until the beginning of October (*Tishrīn*). Then take it out of the sun until it congeals, and use it.

As for its varieties, one of them is the plain, into which no flavourings at all are put. One of them is another variety into which you put nigella and garlic. Dry red rose petals, cut from the stems, are put in another variety.

Zaitūn Mubakhkhar. Take olives when they are ripe. If you like, take them green, and if you like, take them black; the green is [better] for smoking. Bruise them, put the necessary amount of salt on them and turn them over every day until their bitterness goes away. Then put them on a tray woven of sticks for a day and a night until the moisture which is in them dries up. Then pound peeled garlic and dry thyme finely, and take a *dirham* of it, and an olive pit, a piece of cotton dipped in sesame oil and a *dirham* of walnut meats, and leave them on a quiet fire. Put that on it. Then put the woven tray holding the olives on a stove (*kānūn*) into which you have thrown this described incense (*bukhūr*). Close its door, and cover the olives with a cup or a bowl so that the smoke from it does not get out. Stir them several times so that the smoke moves around in them, and leave it for whole day. Then take it up and throw on sesame oil, coarsely pounded walnut meats, toasted peeled sesame, garlic and finely pounded thyme. Then mix all of that well, and leave it covered in a glass or greased pottery jug for days. Then use it.

Khall wa-Khardal. Take sweet almonds, peel them, pound them fine, then beat them to a liquid consistency with sharp vinegar until they are thin (of a thin consistency). Pound mustard fine and mix it with the desired amount of it (i.e. of the almonds and vinegar) along with some mixed spices, and use it.

Milḥ Muṭayyab. Take big crystals of Andarani salt, put them in a new earthenware jar and seal its top. Then leave it in a hot tandoor for a whole day, and take it out. When it is cold, grind it fine. Then take coriander, sesame, nigella, hemp seeds, poppy seeds, cumin, fennel (seeds), asafoetida leaves and anise, and toast everything, and mix it with it. The salt might be coloured after grinding by putting it into water in which there is saffron for a day and a night; then dry it and grind it again. It might be coloured the same way with sumac juice or water of vermillion (*asrīqūn*). If you want it green, (dye it) with chard water.

Bāqillā bi-Khall. Take green broad beans as soon as they are rough. Remove their external husks, then boil them in water and salt until done, and dry them off. Sprinkle a little caraway and finely pounded cinnamon on them. Pour a bit of sesame oil on them. Put good vinegar to cover on them, and use them.

FORTY-SIX

On Manners

aL-GHAZALI

al-Ghazali (1058–1111) was probably the most influential Muslim theologian and philosopher of all time, in particular in turning Islamic thought away from Plato and Aristotle and more toward Sufi mysticism. This selection comes from Book XI on the revival of the religious sciences, and shows how important eating behavior was in this period.

THE PRESENTATION OF FOOD AND EATING

As regarding the presentation of food, there are five rules of good conduct. The first is that the food be served quickly, for this honours the guest. The Emissary of God (may God bless him and grant him peace) said, "He who believes in God and the Last Day let him be generous to his guest." When the majority of the guests have arrived, but one or two are absent, being late for the appointed time, those who are present have a greater right to be served quickly than those who are late [have a right] for the meal to be delayed; unless the person who is late is poor or will be greatly distressed by it, in which case there is no harm in delaying. One of the two meanings is found in God's words: "*Has the story of Abraham's honoured guests reached you?*" They were honoured by being served food quickly, as indicated by His words "*and he soon brought a fatted calf*"; and his words "*and he hastened to his family and brought a fatted calf.*" It was said that he brought a leg of meat and it was called ʿijl [calf] because he brought it quickly without tarrying.

al-Ghazali. *On the Manners Relating to Eating (Kitāb Ādāb al-Akl).* Translated by D. Johnson-Davies. Cambridge, UK: Islamic Texts Society, 2000, pp. 38–45.

Ḥātim al-Aṣamm said, "Haste is from the devil except in five cases of the Emissary's *Sunna*: feeding one's guest, preparing the dead for burial, marrying a virgin, paying back a debt and repenting a sin." Making haste to a banquet is desirable. It has been said that [a wedding] banquet on the first day is *Sunna,* on the second a courtesy, on the third hypocrisy.

The second [rule of good conduct] is that, regarding the order of the foods, precedence should first be given to fruit, if there be any, for that is medically fitting. Since fruit is more quickly transmuted, it should lie at the bottom of the stomach. The Qur'ān enjoins the serving of fruit first—in God's words, *"and fruit of their choosing"*; after which He says *"and the meat of birds they desire."* Thus, the best thing to be served after fruit is meat and *tharīd*. The Emissary of God (may God bless him and grant him peace) said, "The superiority of ʿĀisha over [other] women is like the superiority of *tharīd* over the rest of food." And if after this a person were brought sweetmeats, [everything] good will have been brought together.

Honouring with meat is indicated in God's words about Abraham, who brought a fatted calf to his guest—namely, calf which has been well cooked. This is one of the two things meant by honouring [a guest], by which I mean serving meat. In His description of good things, God has said: *"We have brought down to you manna and quail."* Manna is honey and *salwā* [quail] is meat. It was called *salwā* because one takes more pleasure in it than in all the forms of *idām* and nothing can replace it. Thus the Emissary of God (may God bless him and grant him peace) said, "The chief *idām* is meat." And after mentioning manna and quails, God said: *"Eat of the good things We have provided you with"*—meat and sweetmeats being among the good things.

Abā Sulaymān al-Dārānī (may God be pleased with him) said, "Eating good things brings contentment with God." These good things are completed by drinking cold water and pouring tepid water over the hand when washing. al-Ma'mūn said, "Drinking water with ice makes sincere one's thanks to God."

A man of letters once said, "If you invite your brethren and feed them *haṣramiyya* and *būrāniyya* and give them cold water to drink, you will have perfected your hospitality."

One person spent [many] dirhams on hospitality, and a wise man told [him], "We had no need of this: if your bread is good, your water cold and your vinegar sour, that is enough." Another said, "[Serving] sweetmeats after the food is better than an abundance of dishes; being comfortable at table is better than increasing [the meal] by two dishes." It is said that angels are present at a table on which there are vegetables, for that too is desirable because they are graced with greenness.

Tradition has it that the table which was sent down to the Israelites had on it all the vegetables except leeks; it had on it a fish with vinegar at its head and salt at its tail, and seven loaves of bread with olives and pomegranate seeds on each loaf. When these are brought together, compatibility is achieved.

The third [rule of good conduct] is to serve the choicest dishes first, so that whoever wishes may have his full share of them and not eat too much afterwards. The practice of those who indulge in luxurious living is to serve coarse food first and to rekindle the appetite by offering delicate food only afterwards; this is contrary to the *Sunna,* for it is a device for increasing the intake of food. It used to be the *Sunna* of the people of old to serve all the courses at one and the same time, and to line up the dishes of food on the table for each person to eat of that which he fancied. If [the host] has only one type of food he should mention this, to allow [his guests] their fill of it without having to wait for something better. It is said that a virtuous person used to write out a list of dishes he had asked to be prepared and would show it to his guests. A *shaykh* said, "A *shaykh* served me a type of food known in Syria and I told him, 'In Iraq we serve this only at the end.' He said, 'It is the same with us in Syria.' He had no other sort of food and I was embarrassed for him."

Another said, "We were a group at an invitation, and we were presented with various kinds of fried heads, cooked and preserved. We did not eat but waited for some [other] course or a lamb. Then [the host] brought us the basin [to wash our hands after the meal] without anything else being served. We looked at each other and one of the *shaykhs* said in jest, 'God (Exalted be He!) is capable of creating heads without bodies.' We spent that night hungry and we asked for crumbled bread for *suḥūr*." It is thus desirable that everything be served [together] or that he notify [his guests] of the kinds of food he has.

The fourth [rule of good conduct] is that a person should not hurry to remove the dishes before [the guests] have had their fill and ceased to eat. For one of them may have found the remainder of that course more appetising than what had previously been presented, or there remained in him a need to eat and he may be put off by the hasty [withdrawal of the food]. This is what is meant by "being comfortable at table," and it is said to be better than two [more] courses of food. It is likely that the purpose of this is to avoid things being done in a hurry, although it is equally likely that its purpose is to make space [at table].

It is related that al-Sutūrī, a Sufi with a predilection for humour, was present at the table of a worldly man and a lamb was served to them. The man at whose table he ate was somewhat niggardly. When he saw that people had torn the lamb completely to pieces, he was irritated and said, "Lad, take it to the children." So the lamb was taken inside the house, but al-Sutūrī, having risen to his feet, ran after the lamb. Someone said to him, "Where are you going?" He said: "I'm off to eat with the children." The man, feeling ashamed, ordered the lamb to be brought back. From this example it is shown that the host should not raise his hand before others have done so, lest they be embarrassed. On the contrary, he should be the last [to stop] eating.

A hospitable man used to inform people of all the dishes [to be served] and to let them have their fill. When they had almost finished, he would squat down and stretch out his hand to the food and eat, saying, "In the name of God, help me, may God bless you." The *salaf* found this commendable about him.

The fifth [rule of good conduct] is that a sufficient quantity of food be served, for to serve less indicates lack of good manners. But that to have [food] in excess is affectation and hypocrisy; this is especially so when a person does not intend that [his guests] eat everything. However, if he serves [food] in abundance, and rejoices when people eat it all, his intention being to seek a blessing from the food that remains, then, according to the Tradition, he is not held to account for it.

Ibrāhīm ibn Adham once brought plenty of food to his table and Sufyān [al-Thawrī] said to him, "O Abū Isḥāq, do you not fear that this is extravagant?" Ibrāhīm replied, "There is no extravagance in food unless the intention is to be extravagant; abundant provision would [then] be an affectation." Ibn Mas‘ūd said, "We have been forbidden to accept the invitation of someone who boasts about his food." A group of the Companions disliked eating food that had been boasted about.

No leftovers were ever removed from before the Emissary of God (may God bless him and grant him peace), because they used to serve only the necessary quantity, for they did not eat to repletion.

The portion allotted to the members of the household must first be set aside, to prevent their eyes from avidly expecting that some of it will be returned [from the guests]; for maybe it will not be returned and they would feel frustrated and their tongues give vent to feelings against the guests. This would mean that feeding the guests results in [them] being disliked by others and this would be a disloyalty to them.

Whatever remains of the food is not for the guests to take away, but is what the Sufis call *zalla*, unless the person providing the food has clearly and with a consenting heart given [his guests] permission to take it; or this has been understood through indications and circumstances, and he is happy about it. If, however, there is a suspicion that he might be disinclined, then it must not be taken. If his approval is known, fairness and impartiality must be exercised among the company, for none may take more than what pertains to him or that which his companion consents to, willingly rather than through shyness.

TAKING LEAVE

There are three rules of good conduct for taking leave. The first is that the host should accompany the guest to the door of the house. This is *Sunna* and a show of respect to the guest, and we have been commanded to show him respect. The Emissary of God (may God bless him and grant him peace) said, "Let him who believes in God and the Last Day respect his guest." And he said, "It is proper behaviour towards a guest that he be accompanied to the door of the house."

Abū Qatāda said, "The delegation from the Negus came to the Emissary of God (may God bless him and grant him peace) and he himself served them. His Companions said to him: 'There are enough of us to make it unnecessary for you to do this, O Emissary of God.' He said: 'No, they honoured my Companions and I wish to repay them.'"

A full show of respect consists of being of cheerful countenance and pleasant conversation when entering or leaving, and also at table. al-Awzā‘ī was asked, "What is showing respect to a guest?" He answered, "A cheerful countenance and pleasant conversation." Yazīd ibn Abī Zayyād said, "I never entered upon ‘Abd al-Raḥmān ibn Abī Layla without him conversing with us pleasantly and providing us with good food."

The second [rule of good conduct] is that the guest make his departure in good spirits, even if he had not been fully treated as is his right—this being a matter of good character and of modesty. The Emissary of God (may God bless him and grant him peace) said, "A man attains with good character the degree of someone who fasts and who prays at night."

A messenger was sent to invite one of the *salaf*, but could not find him. When [the man] heard [of the invitation] he went, but everyone had already dispersed, having finished and left. The owner of the house went out to him and said, "The people have left." He said, "Is there anything left?" The owner said, "No." He said, "A piece of bread only, if there is any left." The owner said, "There is nothing left." He said, "Then the pot for me to wipe clean." "I have washed it," said the owner. So the man went away giving praise to God. He was asked about that and said, "The man invited us with good intention and he turned us away with good intention—this is what humility and good disposition mean."

It is related that a young boy had given his father's invitation to the teacher of Abū Qāsim al-Junayd four times, and [when the teacher of al-Junayd came] the father turned [him] away on the four occasions. On each occasion the latter returned in order to delight the boy's heart by attending and the father's heart by turning [him] away. Such are the souls of those who have effaced themselves in humility to God (Exalted be He!), contented with the belief in the unity of God and who see in every rejection and acceptance an indication of their relationship with their Lord. They are not broken by the humiliation that comes from God's servants, nor do they rejoice in any honour from them. To them everything comes from the One, the Subduer. Thus one of them said, "I only accept an invitation because it reminds me of the food of Paradise—that is to say, good food that relieves us of toiling for it, supplying it and being made to account for it."

The third [rule of good conduct] is that he should not go out without the consent and permission of the owner of the house, and he should examine his heart for the amount of time he may stay. If he comes as a guest, his stay should not exceed three days, since [the host] may become bored with him and will need to evict him. The Emissary of God (may God bless him and grant him peace) said, "Hospitality is for three days; anything more is charity." Certainly, if the owner were to press him with a sincere heart, he may then stay on. It is desirable that one should have a bed for a guest who is staying. The Emissary of God (may God bless him and grant him peace) said, "A bed for the man, a bed for the wife, a bed for the guest—and the fourth is for Satan."

FORTY-SEVEN

Canon

AVICENNA

This is the most important medical work of the entire Middle Ages, not only among Muslims but among Christians as well, because it was a cornerstone of the university medical curriculum in Europe. Avicenna, or Ibn Sina, was a philosopher and physician, born in Bukhara, modern-day Uzbekistan. His dietary theory follows humoral physiology inherited from Galen, but the details of his advice can be quite different. It was through Avicenna and other Arabic authors that Europe first adopted these dietary theories.

759. In seeking to maintain health care must be taken that the essential basis of the meal is not in medicinal nutrients like potherbs, fruits, and such-like. For things which are tenuous in character over-oxidize the blood, and those which are dense render the blood phlegmatic, and the body heavy.

The meal should include: (1) flesh, especially kid of goats, veal, and year-old lamb; (2) wheat, which is cleaned of extraneous matter, and gathered during a healthy harvest without ever having been exposed to injurious influences; (3) sweets of appropriate temperament; (4) fragrant wine of good quality. Any other kinds of food can only be regarded as a sort of medicament or preservative.

The more nutritious fruits are: figs, grapes (ripe and sweet), dates from countries and regions in which they are indigenous. But if superfluity arises after partaking of these fruits, speedy evacuation should be procured.

Avicenna. *A Treatise on the Canon of Medicine of Avicenna Incorporating a Translation of the First Book.* Translated by O. Cameron Gruner. London: Luzac, 1930. Reprint by New York: Augustus M. Kelley, 1970, pp. 394–408.

760. In winter the food should be hot; in summer cold or only slightly warm. A food should not be served either hot or cold if it is likely to be spoiled thereby.

761. A person should not eat unless hungry. Nor should he delay his meal until the appetite has passed off. This rule does not apply in the case of the fictitious appetite met with in drunkards, or the subjects of nausea. If fasting be continued, the stomach will fill up with putrescent humours.

Nothing is worse than to eat to repletion during a time of plenty after having been in a state of starvation during a time of famine, and vice versa. But the transition period is the worse. For we often see many people who lack food at a time of famine, and eat to repletion when a fertile year comes, with fatal result. Great repletion is very dangerous in any case, whether in regard to food or to drink. For how often do not people over-eat, and perish from the consequent choking of the channels of the body?

762. An error in eating or drinking any of the medicinal nutrients is to be corrected according to the digestion and maturation thereof, and the person must be protected from the intemperament which is likely to arise. To effect this, one takes the contrary substance until the digestion is completed. Thus, if the aliment was cold (e.g. cucumber, gourd), temper it with its opposite (e.g. onions, leek). If the aliment was hot, temper it with the opposite (e.g. cucumber, purslane). If the aliment is binding, take some food which will open and evacuate, and then fast for a suitable period. A person in this state—and this is true for all who wish to maintain their health—should not partake of food until there is a definite appetite, and unless the stomach and upper small intestine have emptied themselves of the previous meal. For there is nothing more harmful to the body than to superpose aliment upon incompletely digested food. There is also nothing worse than nauseative indigestion, especially when this is the result of bad foods. For if these are gross, the following symptoms and illnesses arise: pains in the joints, in the kidneys; dyspnoea, podagra, indurative enlargement of the spleen and liver, illnesses in which the serous or atrabilious humours are concerned. If the foods were attenuated, then acute fevers, malignant fevers, and grave acute inflammatory disturbances would develop.

However, it is sometimes really necessary to give a food or a substance like food, on the top of another food, by way of medicine. For example, if one has taken sharp and salty nutrients, one may further take humectant aliments which have no flavour, before the former have digested completely. The chyme by which the body is nourished is then rectified. This is a suitable measure for cases of this kind, and the use of exercise is not indicated.

The contrary holds good in the case of those who partake of gross foodstuffs and afterwards admix with them something which is speedily digested and acrid in taste.

763. A small amount of movement or *activity after a meal* allows the food to descend to the fundus of the stomach, especially if after this there is a desire to sleep. Mental excitement or emotion; vigorous exercise; these hinder digestion.

764. In *winter*, feebly nutrient foods, like pot-herbs, are not to be partaken of. The aliments should be stronger and more solid in texture—such as cereals, legumes, and the like. In summer, the contrary is true.

765. The *quantity of food* taken at a meal.—No meal should be bulky enough to completely satisfy the appetite. One should rise from the table while some appetite or desire for food is still present. For such remnants of hunger will disappear in the course of an hour. Custom is to be regarded in this regard, for a meal is injurious when it brings heaviness to the stomach, and wine is injurious when it exceeds moderation, and swims in the stomach.

If one ate to excess one day, one should fast the next, and a longer sleep should be taken in some place which is neither hot nor cold. If sleep refuse to come, one should take gentle walking exercise and allow neither rest nor recumbent position. A little pure wine should be taken. Rufus says, "Walking after a meal is grateful to me, for it gives a good preparation for the evening meal."

A short sleep after a meal is useful; one should lie first on the right side, then on the left, and finally turn back again to the right side. If the body be covered with a number of wraps and the neck be raised, this will aid digestion. The limbs should slope downwards and not upwards.

The standard *size of the meal* depends on usage and vigour. A normally robust person should take as much as will not produce a sense of heaviness, or a sense of tightness of the hypochondria. There should be no subsequent rumbling in the stomach, or splashing of the food on bodily movement. Nausea should not be experienced, nor a canine appetite, nor loss of appetite, nor great disinclination for exertion, nor sleeplessness. The taste of the food should not repeat in the eructations. If the taste of food lingers in the mouth a very long time after the meal, it shows that the latter was too heavy.

766. Indications that the meal was moderate: the pulse does not become full; the breathing does not become shallow. The latter only occurs if the stomach is compressing the diaphragm, thus making the inspirations shallow and short. The pressure to be met by the heart increases after a large meal, and as the force of the heart does not diminish, the pulse becomes large and full.

A person who experiences a sense of heat and flushing after a meal should not take a whole meal at one sitting, but partake of the food in small portions at short intervals to avoid the effects of repletion—such as shivering followed by a sense of heat like that in a sthenic fever. This is due to the heating effect of the food.

A person who cannot digest the amount of food appropriate for him should increase the number of articles of diet, but diminish the quantity.

A person of atrabilious constitution needs a diet which is very humectant but not very heating.

A person of choleric constitution needs a diet which is humectant and infrigidant.

A person who generates hot inflammable blood needs feebly nutritious articles of food, which are cold. One who generates phlegmatic blood needs feebly nutritious articles of diet which are hot and attenuant.

767. The order in which the components of a meal are to be taken.—A person who is desirous of maintaining his health needs to be watchful of this matter. Thus, one should not take a tenuous food, which is rapidly digested, after taking a very nutritious dish which is slowly digested. An exception to this rule has been named above. The reason is that the first article of food will be digested first and therefore float over the other, unable to enter the blood. Consequently it ferments and decomposes, and in addition sets up decomposition of the food next taken. The reverse order, therefore, is the one to adopt, so that the labile food will pass on with the other into the intestine, and then undergo complete digestion.

Fish and similar articles of food should not be taken after laborious work (or exercise), because they undergo decomposition and then decompose the humours.

Some persons may be allowed to eat an article of food in which there is a styptic property as a preparatory to the actual meal.

768. *Idiosyncrasies.* Some persons have an idiosyncrasy of the stomach in which the foods leave it very rapidly, and do not stay in it long enough to undergo gastric digestion. This explains the necessity for taking the idiosyncrasy of the stomach and its temperament, into consideration [along with other factors when drawing up a dietary].

There are some persons in whom tenuous food, instead of being digested quickly as it should, undergoes decomposition in the stomach, whereas less rapidly digestible foods are digested more readily. The stomach of such a person is designated igneous. But other persons are exactly the opposite. Therefore the rules to be given must be adapted to the peculiarity of each (patient).

769. The countries in which people live have also their own natural properties, which are distinct from the ordinary rule. This must also be borne in mind, and a test must be made to ascertain what the rule should be. Thus, a food which is often used, though injurious to a certain degree, may be more appropriate for a given individual than a food which he does not often take, though its character is good.

770. Then again, there is a food which is to be regarded as appropriate to everyone's physique and temperament. To change from such a diet would prove injurious and detrimental to him.

Good and laudable foods may be injurious to some. They should therefore avoid them. But persons who are able to digest "bad" foods should not be deceived, because (for all they know) they will some day give rise to bad humours and the consequent obstinate ailments.

Good food may often be allowed liberally in the case of persons in whom the humours are unhealthy, so long as diarrhœa from intestinal weakness does not supervene in consequence. But if the person be of spare habit, and liable to have the motions loose, the diet should consist of moist aliments, because they are digested quickly, even though it is a fact that such persons can tolerate various heavy foods, and are less liable to be affected adversely by intrinsic noxae, and are more susceptible to the antagonistic influence of extraneous noxae.

771. An active person accustomed to take much flesh-meat needs frequent bleeding. A person inclined to be frigid in temperament should drink substances which cleanse the stomach, intestines and the (mesenteric) veins—including confections of spices and myrobalan electuary.

772. It is a bad practice to combine nutrients of diverse character in one meal and so prolong it. For by the time the last portion has entered the stomach, the first portion is already digested, and therefore the various contents of the stomach are not all at the same stage of digestion.

773. *Palatability.* One should remember too that aliment is best which has the most agreeable flavour, for the walls of the stomach and the retentive faculty jointly apply themselves better to a food of good substance, and the efficiency of the retentive power is assisted when the principal members all mutually concur—the temperament of one being not more divergent from that of another than natural. That is the requisite condition. The conditions

are not fulfilled, for instance, if the temperaments are not normal, or alike in the respective members. Thus, the temperament of the liver may differ to an unnatural extent from that of the stomach.

Among noxious influences arising from the taste of aliments is that if very gross aliments are tasty, a person may be tempted to eat too freely of them.

774. In taking successive satiating meals, it is best for a person to take only one on one day and two on the next (morning and evening). But one must not be too strict in this rule, for if a person is accustomed to have two meals a day, and then takes only one, he will be weakened and his (digestive) faculty will suffer. A person of weak digestion should take two meals a day, lessening the amount partaken. On occasion he may eat once a day. A person who is accustomed to take one good meal a day will, on resuming the habit of two meals a day, suffer from weakness, lack of energy, slackness. If he should take no food at bedtime, he will feel weak; and if he should take a late meal he will not be able to digest it, and will have acid eructations, nausea, bitter taste in the mouth, loose bowels and become moody, or irritable. This is because he has put into the stomach something to which it is not accustomed, and so he is liable to show some of the symptoms which befall a person whose aliment is not fully digested.—And these you are now acquainted with.

775. Among the symptoms arising when a person does not take a late meal are: subjective sensations at the cardiac orifice of the stomach, gnawing pains, a sensation of a void in the stomach so that all the interior organs and intestines feel as if they were suspended, and therefore all clumped together. He passes scalding urine, and the faeces produce a burning sensation as they are passed. There may be a feeling of cold in the extremities owing to the bilious humour being poured out into the stomach and irritating it and making it congested. This is more likely in persons of bilious temperament, and in those who have bilious humour in the stomach but not to an undue extent in the rest of the body; these suffer from loss of sleep, and keep turning over from one side to the other [in bed].

776. Persons then in whom the bilious humour is apt to accumulate in the stomach should take their meals divided, thereby taking the food quickly; the meal is taken before bathing. In other persons exercise should be taken first, then the bath, and then the meal. The meal should not precede the bath in these cases. If circumstances demand that the meal be taken before the exercise, the food should consist of bread only, and to an amount no greater than can be easily digested. As it is necessary that the exercise should not be gentle if taken *before* food, so it is necessary that the exercise should be mild and gentle if it is taken *after* the meal.

When the appetite is depraved so that it prefers sharp-tasting things to sweet or unctuous things, nothing is better than to procure emesis with such as oxymel with radish after fish.

777. A person who is stout should not eat at once after a bath, but should wait and take a little nap. He is best advised to take only one meal in the day.

778. One should not go to sleep immediately after a meal, with the food still swimming in the stomach, and one should, as much as possible, abstain from much exercise after a meal, lest the food pass into the blood before it is sufficiently digested, or glide out of the stomach without being digested at all, or undergoes decomposition, since the exercise disturbs the gastric temperament.

779. Nor should much water be drunk after a meal, for it causes the food to leave the coats of the stomach and float about. One should wait, and not drink fluids until the food has left the stomach—which is evidenced by the sensation of lightness in the upper part of the abdomen. However, if there were urgent thirst one may take a modicum of cold water through a straw, and the colder it is the less one will require. Such an amount would soothe the stomach and keep the food together.

780. To sum up—if a person must drink, it is better only to take so small an amount, at the end of the meal (not during the meal), as will spread over and moisten the food, and therefore not be injurious.

To go to sleep while thirsty, is beneficial to cold and moist temperaments, but is injurious to those in whom the temperament is too warm, because of the bilious humour (being too plentiful). The same is true as regards going to sleep while fasting.

Bilious humour comes to predominate in persons who fast, and therefore flows into the stomach. Therefore when they eat any food it decomposes, and the same symptoms occur in them, whether asleep or awake, as when, food corrupts. And, furthermore, there is loss of desire for food.

781. When there is *loss of appetite for food* something needs to be given to counteract this and relax the bowels. For this purpose something mild, like prune, should be given, or something which does not suggest nausea, like a laxative fruit-juice (manna). Meals may be resumed after the appetite has returned. Those whose tissues are moist in virtue of natural humidity are liable to speedy aperient action, and are in consequence not able to fast as long as those whose tissues are dry in virtue of only a small (degree of natural) humidity:—unless the latter should be rich in humidities other than those inherent to the substance of the tissues, for these are proper, good and receptive, and in consequence the natural faculty is able to change them completely into (true) nutriment.

782. To take wine after a meal is very unsatisfactory, for it is rapidly digested and enters the blood quickly and carries food on into the blood before it is properly digested. Obstructions and decompositions [in this imperfectly digested aliment ultimately] arise.

Sweet things readily produce obstructions [in the channels of the body] because the attractive faculty draws them into the blood before they have been properly digested. Obstructions culminate in various diseases, of which dropsy is one.

Heaviness of the air or water, especially that of summertime, favours the decomposition of food. In this case, then, it is not harmful to take a tempered wine after a meal, or hot water in which xylaloes and mastic have been boiled.

783. If a person whose alimentary tract is "hot" and strong, should eat *heavy food,* it will give rise to flatulence in the stomach and fermentative ailments.

When a person takes a *tenuous* article of *food* upon an empty stomach, the latter contracts on it, and if he then takes something heavy, the stomach abandons the tenuous food and ceases digesting it, and it undergoes putrescence in consequence. This would be avoided by allowing an interval of time to elapse between the two kinds of food. Under these circumstances it is best to take the heavy food slowly, because then the hold which the stomach has on the tenuous food is not broken.

784. When a state of over-repletion exists in regard to some meal, whether as a result of exercise (which causes undue hunger), or because a draught has been taken as well, then there will be a need for rapid emesis. If this should fail, or one cannot vomit, the person should sip hot water until the repletion is displaced and sleep supervenes. The person should therefore lie down and (compose himself to) sleep. Let him sleep as long as he will.—But should this not suffice, or should he be unable to go to sleep, reflect whether the natural course of events is likely to save you from procuring emesis. If so, good. If not, assist the natural power by any gentle laxative, such as myrobalan electuary, confection of roses, or origanum prepared with sugar or honey; or by the use of such things as cumin, spiced candies, asphodel and cabbage ptisan.

It is not as bad to be repleted with wine as with solid food.

785. Among the (aperient) remedies which are suitable after food are: aloes to the bulk of three chick-peas; or half a drachm of aloes, half a drachm of mastic, and a sixth of a dram of nitre. Mild remedies are: turpentine resin to the amount of two or three chick-peas; nitre in equal quantity, or less, if necessary. Another much praised remedy is to use an epitheme with wine.

If none of these remedies succeed, let the patient sleep for a long time, and abstain from food for a whole day. Then, if he feels better, let him bathe, and place a hot blanket over the abdomen, and see that the aliments are tenuous.

If the food is still not properly digested, in spite of all these measures, and heaviness, distension, and lack of energy are experienced, you may know that the veins are already overcharged with effete matters. Bulky and unneeded nutriment, even were it digested in the stomach, would hardly undergo the proper changes in the veins, and so would remain "crude" within them, and stretch them, even to bursting point. This is the explanation of the lack of energy, the heaviness, the desire to stretch oneself and the yawnings. The treatment in such a case consists in securing the release of the superfluities from the blood vessels.

If these are not the symptoms, but there is only a transient weariness, followed later by another form of weariness, this should be treated in the manner to be described.

786. If a person should be very advanced in years, and his body does not derive as much benefit from the food as it did when he was young, and if his aliments become simply effete matters, then he should not eat as much as he used to do.

787. If a person is accustomed to a heavy diet and then lightens it by the use of attenuant foods, the new food material is unable to keep the channels (of the body) as full as before. So, on resuming the heavy foods, obstructions are brought about.

788. *Heating foods.* The injurious effects of heating or calefacient foods can be corrected by the use of syrup containing acetic acid, especially when made with seeds, for then the syrup is more efficient. If honey is used however, the simple syrup will suffice. The injurious effect of "cold" foods is corrected by the use of hydromel, and its syrup, and caraway.

789. *Heavy and light foods.* To correct aliments which are heavy, a person having a hot temperament should use acetous syrup made of strong seeds; a person with a cold temperament should use a little capsicum or peppermint.

Tenuous foods are better for the health, but less valuable for the vegetative faculties and strength. Heavy foods have the opposite value. Hence, for a person in need of a tonic, aliments which make strong chyme are necessary, and such as antagonize the hunger-feeling. But they should not be taken in greater quantity than can be digested. Heavy foods are better borne by those who take plenty of exercise or are accustomed to heavy work. Probably the deep sleep which this favours helps the digestion. But on the other hand they lose much by sweating. And as their livers seize whatever of the aliment has not yet digested fully, this paves the way for fatal illnesses towards the end of life, or at the beginning of life, the more so because they trust in their digestive powers too much. This power is really due to the deep sleep which is customary, and that is lost by old age.

790. *Fruit.* Fresh fruit is only good for those who carry out hard work, or take much exercise, or for persons with plenty of bilious humour, or during the height of summer. Fruit should be taken before a meal,—namely, for instance, chrysomela, mulberries, melons, peaches, and prunes. But it is better to regulate oneself by using other articles of food than these, for they render the blood too watery, and so it is apt to ferment. Hence the juices of fruits, unless taken at a seasonable time, pave the way for putrefactive processes. So, too, any food which comes to burden the blood with "crude" humour has this effect, though it is true that sometimes such a food may be beneficial (e.g., cucumber; c. anguinalis). That is why people who make use of such aliments, even though they are primarily infrigidant, are likely to develop febrile diseases.

You will also realize that it is when watery humour is not dispersed, but lingers in the blood-vessels, that it usually becomes toxic. However, when exercise is taken before such aquosities have become aggregated, and exercise is taken immediately after eating the fruit, these aquosities will disperse and the noxious effect of the fruits is thereby lessened.

Note too that the presence of "crude" serous humour or of wateriness in the blood prevents the nutrient part of the food from adhering to the tissues, some of the nutritive value of the food being lost in consequence.

A person who partakes of fruit must (therefore) take walking exercise afterwards, and then eat something which will cause the (aquosities) to flow out.

791. Aliments which give rise to (1) wateriness; (2) "crude," raw, immature humour; (3) gross humour, and bilious humour, give rise to febrile diseases. This is because (1) the watery parts permit putrescence to occur in the blood; (2) viscous gross substances close the orifices (of the juice-canals); and (3) the (increase of) bilious humour adds to the heat of the body, and renders the blood sharp.

Bitter pot-herbs are sometimes very advantageous in winter-time, just as tasteless herbs are beneficial in summer-time.

792. *Correctives of unwholesome foods.* If a person is bound to partake of unwholesome aliments, he should do so seldom and sparingly, and should counteract their action by combining with them something of contrary effect. Thus, if a certain sweet food is injurious, he may counteract it by a sour aliment like vinegar, and pomegranate, and an acetous syrup prepared with sour wine and quince and the like, and also by procuring evacuation. Should it be a sour aliment that is injurious to him, he may follow it up with honey, or old wine, taking this before the maturation and digestion of the former are complete. If it be an oily aliment that is injurious, this can be corrected by (a) pungent articles, like chestnut, myrtle-seeds, carob bean of Syria, the fruit of the sidr tree, medlar; (b) bitters, such as conserved elecampane;

(*c*) salt and sharp substances, like capers, onions, garlic [that is, articles usually belonging to the second course of a meal], and other contraries.

793. If the body is in a state of repletion by unhealthy humours, this state may be counteracted by a liberal allowance of commendable attenuant aliments. If the body is one which is easily purged, moist and easily digested food should be made use of.

Galen says that a humid article of food is nutrient when it is separated from all other qualities, and is as it were tasteless—being neither sweet nor sour, bitter nor acrid, pungent nor salt.

794. A heavy food which is divided up into small portions will be better borne than one which is taken solid.

If dry aliments be taken plentifully, the strength will fail and the colour will fade, and the "nature" become dry.

Fatty food produces lack of energy and vim, and creates a false appetite. "Cold" food produces lack of vim and is infrigidative (or, attenuant). Sour food has the same effect as old age; it dries the body and makes it lean. Sharp and salt food is injurious to the stomach. Salt food is bad for the eyesight.

If an appropriate aliment is oily, and is followed by an uncommendable aliment, the latter will decompose it.

Viscous aliment experiences delay in passing through the intestine. Citrul [a species of cucumber] passes down the intestine more rapidly if the rind is taken as well than if first peeled. Bread also passes down more quickly if the crust be taken as well than if it be deprived thereof by crumbling it through a sieve.

If a fatigued person, who is accustomed to a mild regimen, should take heavy foods—as for instance, a dish of rice with soured milk—after a long fast, it will come about that his blood becomes sharp in quality and as if ebullient. Hence reducing regimen would be indicated (e.g., blood-letting), though only to a moderate extent. A similar remedy is applicable when a person is angry.

Note too, that sweet aliment accelerates the "nature" before the food is matured and digested, and the blood is tainted in consequence.

795. *Incompatibilities between foods.* Certain rules must be noted in regard to combining various articles of food. Indian observers and others have long taught that (1) milk must not be taken with sour foods; (2) fish must not be taken with milk—for in that case chronic ailments such as leprosy may develop; (3) pulse must not be taken with cheese or radishes or with the flesh of flying birds; (4) a polenta of barley-meal should not follow on a dish of rice made with soured milk; (5) eatables should not have oil added, or oil which has stood in a brass vessel; (6) fleshmeat should not be taken when it has been roasted over live coals (with certain herbs).

796. *Courses of a meal.* To have several courses to a meal is injurious in two directions: (*a*) the rate of digestion is diverse, for the part that digests more speedily is admixed with a part which is not yet digested; (*b*) a person may eat too much of one dish. Already in ancient times, too, persons who had been exercising themselves avoided this error, being satisfied to partake of meat alone in the morning, and bread alone at supper-time.

During the summer it is best to take the (main) meal at an hour when the temperature is cooler.

During a period of fasting the stomach sometimes fills with unhealthy humours.

Note further that when meat is roasted, and taken with onions and eggs, it is very nutritious; but it is slow in passing through the intestines, and lingers in the caecum. White soup [a Syrian dish containing rice, honey, onions] is nourishing, and when onion is added it dispels flatulencies; if onions are omitted, borborygmi arise.

Some people consider that grapes are good to take after roasted meats; but the contrary is really the case; they are very bad indeed. So too, is a dish containing dates, figs, and the like. But (dry) pomegranate seeds are good.

Fowl.—The flesh of partridge is dry and constipating; but that of chicken is moist and relaxing to the bowels. Roast fowls are better if they have been prepared (stuffed) in the belly of a kid or lamb because that preserves their moisture. Chicken-broth tempers the humours strongly; more so than fowl-broth, though the latter is more nutritious.

Kid of the goats is better when cold than when warm because the steam quiesces it. The flesh of lamb is better when hot because its unsatisfactory odour is thereby dispersed.

Meat boiled in water and vinegar [a Persian dish] should be served hot, and then needs no saffron in it. But if served cold saffron must be introduced.

Honey confections may be made with dates or wheat flour (sweetmeats); but they are unhealthy because they cause obstructions and evoke thirst.

Bread is an unsatisfactory food when it does not digest, more so than (flesh-food) when it does not digest.

FORTY-EIGHT

Regimen of Health

MOSES MAIMONIDES

Maimonides (1135–1204) was a Jewish philosopher and rabbi born in Cordoba, Spain, but he left for Morocco and eventually traveled to Egypt when a dynasty came to power unfavorable to the Jews. His thought is exemplary of the last phase of fruitful interchange among all three monotheistic faiths in Spain. This brief excerpt shows that his thought is still in the Greek tradition, as was Avicenna's thousands of miles away.

Physicians all agree, that taking a little food of bad quality is less harmful than taking much good and laudable food. This is because when a man takes bad foods and does not overeat, they are digested well, and the organs derive from them all that is beneficial. The expulsive faculty is strengthened and expels their evil superfluities, and no damage at all occurs, or if any occurs, it is not serious. But in repletion, even if it is with well prepared bread and laudable meat, the digestion will in no wise progress well; we have already mentioned the cause of this.

To guard against repletion, physicians have warned against eating many dishes and recommended limiting each meal to one dish, so that one does not overeat, and the appetite subsides before surfeit occurs. He will also be saved from a diversity of digestions, for different dishes are digested in different digestions, each dish according to its nature.

The view of this Servant regarding the determination of the quantity of food for anyone who wishes to conserve his health, is to take in the temperate season an amount that does not

Moses Maimonides. "Two Treatises on the Regimen of Health: Fī Tadbīr al-Sihhah and Maqālahfi Bayān Ba'd al-A'rād wa-al-Jawāb 'anhā'." *Transactions of the American Philosophical Society* (New Series) 54, no. 4. Translated by Ariel Bar-Sela, Hebbel E. Hoff, and Elias Faris. 1964, 3–50.

distend the stomach, or burden it and impede the digestion. When it becomes clear that this is a good measure, inasmuch as it does not cause evil eructation or arouse thirst, but is pleasant and light, making the stools moderate, continuous and tending slightly toward softness, then this is the proper measure to keep on taking.

When the weather becomes warmer, one should reduce the amount of food, since in the summer the digestions are feeble because of the dispersal of the natural heat. When the weather turns cooler, the amount should be increased, for in the winter the digestions are strong because of the increase of the natural heat in the interior of the body, owing to the constriction of the pores, and satiety will not be reached.

This Servant says: If man were to conduct himself as he manages the animal he rides, he would be safeguarded from many ailments. That is, you find no one who throws fodder to his animal haphazardly, but rather he measures it out to her according to her tolerance. Yet he himself eats indiscriminately, without measure. Moreover, he takes into consideration the activity of his animal and exercises her, so that she does not stand still forever and be ruined. Yet he does not do this for himself, or pay attention to the exercise of his own body, which is the cornerstone of the conservation of health and the repulsion of most ailments.

FORTY-NINE

The Rubaiyyat

OMAR KHAYYAM

Omar Khayyam (1048–1131) was one of the great Persian mathematicians of the Middle Ages, writing the most important book on algebra. His poetry became known in the West through Edward Fitzgerald's nineteenth-century translation, which was rich and evocative. "A Jug of Wine, A Loaf of Bread—and Thou" is probably the most famous quote from this version. But it may do injustice to Omar's original intentions, which might have been allegorical, wine symbolizing a kind of ecstatic, all-consuming love of God. This more recent translation perhaps captures the original spirit better, though it is not entirely clear that Omar wasn't really just praising wine. The illustrations to Fitzgerald's edition are beautiful and can be found online.

Should our day's portion be one wheaten loaf,
A haunch of mutton and a gourd of wine
Set for us two alone on the wide plain,
No Sultan's bounty could evoke such joy.

A gourd of red wine and a sheaf of poems—
A bare subsistence, half a loaf, not more—
Supplied us two alone in the free desert:
What Sultan could we envy on his throne?

Greedily to the bowl my lips I pressed
And asked how might I sue for green old age.

Omar Khayyam. *The Rubaiyyat of Omar Khayyam.* Translated by Robert Graves and Omar Ali-Shah. London: Cassell, 1967, pp. 51, 57–60, 64–65, 73.

Pressing its lips to mine it muttered darkly:
"Drink up! Once gone, you shall return no more!"

This jug was, ages past, a doleful lover
Like me—who had pursued a dream, like me.
This handle at its neck was once an arm
Entwined about some neck he loved too well.

Yesterday in the market stood a potter
Pounding relentlessly his batch of clay.
My inner ear could hear it sigh and groan:
'Brother, I once was like you. Treat me gently!"

In the potter's workroom, shadowed by the wheel,
I pondered, watching how the Master made
Handles and covers for his jugs and pitchers
From clay—from hands of kings, from beggars' feet.

I wandered further down the Potters' Row.
Continuously they tried new skills on clay;
Yet some, devoid of vision, never noted
The ancestral dust on every turning wheel.

Each drop of wine that Saki negligently
Spills on the ground may quench the fires of grief
In some sore heart. All praise to Him who offers
Such medicine to relieve its melancholy!

Raise the bowl high, like tulip-cups at Nauroz,
And if the moon-faced one has time to spare
Drink gloriously deep, for brutal Time
Will strike you down with never a warning yell.

Avoid all greed and envy, unperturbed
By permutations, foul succeeding fair;
Possess your bowl, play with your loved one's curls;
Soon the whole scene must vanish past recourse.

Khayyam, should you be drunk with love, rejoice!
Or bedded with your heart's delight, rejoice!
Your end is no more than the whole world's end.
Fancy yourself no longer there; then smile.

Oppose all resurrections of your past,
Resent no anguish still prepared for you,
Dwell lightly on your entrance and your exit—
Drink, never cast your essence to the winds.

This vast, unmeasured, universal vault
Offers one bowl for all mankind to drink.
When your turn comes, refrain from tears, be merry,
Lift high the bowl, then drain it to its lees!

I shall possess myself of a great goblet
With pipes of wine for its replenishment,
Annulling former ties to Faith and Reason
By marriage with this daughter of the Vine.

As one familiar with all exoterics
Of being and not-being, who has plumbed
The abyss of shame, how can I greet as valid
Any condition short of drunkenness?

Misguided foes call me philosopher—
God knows this is the one thing I am not.
I am even less: in such a nest of sorrows
I cannot tell you even who I am.

In drink this evening, as I passed the tavern,
A fellow toper met me with a flask.
Cried I: "Old man, have you no awe of God?"
"Come," he said, "God is bountiful! Come, drink!"

Banish your crowding griefs with wine, disperse
Your memories of the two-and-seventy sects
And praise wine's alchemy that still can banish
With one red draught more than a thousand spites.

I drink wine as my fellow-topers drink.
How much I drink can seem of small concern
To God, who knows well that I drink. Abstention
From drink would make God's knowledge ignorance.

They say: "Be sober, lest you die of drink
And earn Hell fire on God's Last Judgement Day."
Nevertheless my blaze of drunkenness
Outshines both worlds: your Now and your Hereafter.

Should I fall dead, wash my poor corpse in wine;
Read it into the grave with drinking songs.
On Judgement Day, if you have need of me,
Delve in the soil beneath our tavern door.
Take heed to pamper me with bowls that change
A pasty-coloured cheek to ruby red.

When I fall dead, I say, wash me in wine
And use the vine's own slats for coffin-wood.

So lovingly I drink, the wine's bouquet
Will scent the air where I lie underground;
A toper treading past my grave will pause
To sniff, and find himself ignobly drunk.

FIFTY
Kitāb al-Filāha (Islamic Agriculture)

ABŪ 'L-KHAYR ASH-SHAJJĀR aL-ISHBĪLĪ

This agricultural text was written around 1070–1075. Its author was from Seville, Spain, which at the time was under Muslim rule by the Umayyad Dynasty in a period of intense cultural and economic prosperity. Abū 'l-Khayr wrote the most important botanical and medicinal text of the era. His knowledge of soil types, irrigation systems, and pruning techniques is typical of the innovations introduced to Spain in this era.

THE CULTIVATION OF THE OLIVE

Propagation

Olives may be propagated in three different ways.

The first, by cuttings, is carried out as follows. In October one takes from a young, vigorous, well-grown olive tree offshoots about ten to twelve spans long and about as thick as a man's leg [sic], removing some of the mature wood from the trunk of the stock-tree along with the cutting. Having done this dig a hole where you want the tree to grow, about five spans deep and three in diameter, and place the cutting so that its lower end rests on the bottom of the hole. Place some small stones around the base of the cutting to keep it fresh, then proceed to fill the hole, though not completely, leaving a depression so that rainwater can collect there. Filling-in should be done carefully, in equal and regular layers pressed down lightly with the foot. For the tree to develop properly and achieve its full potential, the cuttings should be spaced at least twenty cubits part, as recommended by the Greek

Abū 'l-Khayr ash-Shajjār al-Ishbīlī. *Kitāb al-Filāha ou Le Livre de la Culture*. Edited by Henri Pérès. Translated by Auguste Cherbonneau. Algiers: Editions Carbonel, 1946. English translation by A. H. Fitzwilliam-Hall. Published online by Editions Carbonel, 2010. http://filaha.org/khayr_final_translation_revised.html.

Casthos. This provision allows the tree to grow without restriction and reach a great size, producing abundant crops.

Dry calcareous land, and poor, crumbly soils containing some gravel, as well as deep black, sandy lands are best for growing olives. Lowlands with a basically hot climate are not suitable.

The second method of propagating olives is by layering. This is the art of detaching suckers that usually grow around the foot of the main trunk and transplanting them individually, to form new plants. To this end one encourages, to the exclusion of all others, five or six good shoots at the foot of an old tree, then, when these shoots have grown for two years one lays them in the soil, without separating them from the main trunk, so that only their tips emerge above the surface. Once the covered section of the layer is considered to be adequately equipped with roots, it is carefully detached from the mother-tree and removed together with the soil that surrounds it so as not to disturb the young roots, which are still too delicate to be exposed. The depth of hole dug to receive the new tree should be proportionate to its size. This mode of propagation is the most common because it is the most successful in terms of results.

The third method is that of sowing, or propagation by stone or pit. For this one chooses olive stones that have the best appearance and which have not been subject to the corrosive action of salt. Then one takes a suitable pot and fills it with *terre blanche* [chalky clay], slightly stiff, taken from the mountains, mixed with well-rotted compost or manure. Plant the seeds in this mixture, taking care to cover them sufficiently so that they are not disturbed by watering nor affected by the air. It is important that this layer of soil is not too loose, nor likely to absorb too much water. This operation is carried out in October. It can be done later but then one must hasten and facilitate germination by slitting the stone before planting it, taking care not to damage the embryo. This method is very effective. It will give you, in less than four years, plants with stems as thick as the forefinger, which bear fruit. We know this from our own experience.

If you want to further hasten fruiting take the young stem of an olive obtained by seed and graft it onto an old tree of another species. If the graft takes, it will not be long before it produces. If you take the precaution of planting *djoulnars* and pomegranates nearby, the new tree will give you flowers and fruits that do not drop.

[. . .]

Grafting

The olive is grafted in the last two weeks of March. A scion of this tree grafted onto a vine stock produces sweet fruit, and vines planted between olive-trees give grapes that taste of olives.

Harvesting the Crop

Olives should be gathered before it gets cold and as soon as they take on a bluish tint. One should choose a mild day for this. Olives are harvested by hand, not with a pole, which bruises them, and then piled carefully in small heaps at the foot of the tree. They are harvested only as and when they are to be delivered, on the same day, to the press. In this way excellent oil is obtained. If, instead, they are left lying in a heap they will take on a bad smell which is passed on to the oil.

It may be, however, that one has to wait a few days between harvesting and pressing. In this case the olives should be sprinkled with salt in order to prevent fermentation. It also helps to place the olives in small heaps on a slight slope so that any oil which exudes can easily run off. Piled in this way and suitably salted they can keep, without deteriorating, for five or six days before pressing. A longer wait would render them unfit for the production of oil. They would yield a thick liquid with a strong and unpleasant smell.

Properties of the Olive

The learned al-Majūsī contends that olives produce an oil that is nutritious, strengthening and aphrodisiac. There are two types of olives: dry and oily (this difference depending perhaps on whether they are preserved in brine or in oil). Ibn al-Ḥabīb observes that the olive is cold, astringent and dry when it is not quite mature but possesses emollient properties at the peak of maturity. He advises chewing the leaves of the tree to get rid of phlegm and cure irritation of the gums and scorbutic ulcers. The doctor al-Manātiqī says that the green olive is astringent and that it refreshes and fortifies. The black olive, he says, is benign and mild. It contains warming properties that are very favourable to weak stomachs. However, over-consumption causes pains in the stomach and headaches. He reports that over-ripe olives are anti-digestive and advises against their use. The reddish olive (yākoutī) combines, according to him, the properties of both the green and the black olive. Preserved with honey and the zest of citron (utrunj), it constitutes a very substantial food for the elderly.

Purification of the Oil

When olives intended for the production of oil have become soft and spoilt to the point of resembling soap they should only be sent to the press after being mixed with olive or fig leaves, or after being subjected to the heat of a blazing fire. The oil from this process of trituration comes out of the press thick and impure. It is clarified in the following way: Leave it to settle in a receptacle for five or six days, then slowly pour the mixture into another container into which you have placed a mixture of olive, citron and bay leaves crushed together. Soon the oil will clarify and lose its unpleasant odour. When olives have not reached perfect maturity they should be left to ferment in small piles for eight or ten days before being pressed, in order to bring the flesh to the point of softness that indicates ripeness.

Clarification of Thick Oil

Thick oil can be clarified by two different methods. The first is to boil the liquid in pots with a certain amount of salt; the second is to expose it to the sun, in jars, during the hottest weather, adding salt that has been crushed to a powder. In both cases one carefully removes, as and when it clarifies, the upper layer of oil, which always clarifies first.

If the oil has an unpleasant smell, this can be corrected by dropping in some boiling pitch which precipitates first to the bottom of the receptacle then comes up to the surface where it hardens. In its sinking and rising this substance rids the oil of its bad taste. In the absence of pitch one can use either green olives, slightly crushed, or pulverized olive leaves.

The various methods of purification given above are based on the principle that to clarify a fatty substance all you have to do is mix in some salt and then subject it to heat.

Regarding oil whose flavour is unpleasant, this calls for a little more care. If the process that we have recommended above does not produce a satisfactory result, the oil should be left to settle for two or three days in a receptacle containing a sachet of cumin. One can use coriander instead, dried in the shade and pulverized. Five or six days of treatment will suffice to rid the oil of any bad smell.

When olives are of poor quality, the oil is extracted as follows: once the fruits are picked they are taken to the press and laid, alternately, between beds of leaves taken from the same tree. The pressing of this mixture produces a tasty and pleasant oil.

Preparation of Olives in Brine

Take green olives that have been lightly crushed and scald them with boiling water. Then put them in a container with well-salted water and cover them with the leaves of bay, fennel and citron. A few days after this, add a little salt and a bundle of thyme.

Another method is to take olives in autumn and pit them with a pointed reed. Then wash them with plenty of water. Then put the fruit in a jar with leaves of thyme, mountain balm, bay, citron and mint. Fill with a liquid composed of one third drinking water and two thirds vinegar, well mixed, then seal the container until the olives are preserved.

A third method: gather good white olives in October and wash them as described above. Put them in a jar and sprinkle with salt, then with oil, then flavour with leaves of mint, thyme, coriander, fennel, citron and bay. Complete the process by covering the olives with a syrup of honey and vinegar. Finally, stuff the opening of the receptacle with the leaves of sumach and fennel and seal it tightly.

Preserving Black Olives

After washing the olives allow them to dry until the pulp begins to shrivel and wrinkle. Place them in a container layer by layer, pressing them down lightly with the hand and alternating with a layer of paste made from the following mixture: bay leaves, citron leaves, mountain balm, *za'tar*, and thyme with olives, all pounded together with vinegar and reduced to a soft paste that is easy to spread. When you have filled the receptacle with successive layers of fruit and paste, wet the preserve with a well-beaten mixture of: 1 part vinegar, 2 parts oil, and 5 parts fresh water. Finally, cover the container with the leaves of bay and citron, and some quarters of quince. After 20 days the olives are ready to eat.

PART VIII
Study Questions

1. Why is Muslim cookery so complex and luxuriant? Why are spices used in such profusion, and where do they come from?
2. In what ways does the Arabic medical tradition both draw from but also depart from its Greek roots? Why, ultimately, was it the Arabic tradition that was passed on to medieval Europe?
3. Does Omar Khayyam's *The Rubaiyat* contain a deep philosophy of life, or does his poem merely extol the virtues of hedonism and wine drinking?
4. Why was the olive so important to so many ancient cultures of the Middle East? What effect did trade in olives and oil have on these societies and their world outlook, and especially on Islam?
5. If eating customs were not ritualized in Muslim society to a great extent, why were rules for dining written? Who were they intended for, and what do they reveal about the nature of hospitality in this culture?

PART NINE

Late Medieval and Renaissance Europe

After the year 1000, the European population began to rise dramatically. Viking raids had begun to subside, there was greater political stability, and, most importantly, a general warming trend resulted in an extended growing season and greater supplies of food. Agricultural innovations included improved plows, the horse collar, and crop rotation systems. Technological advances such as the water wheel–driven mill also increased the food supply. All of these factors in turn demanded more sophisticated methods of governance, more complex laws, and professional services. Cities grew, as did trade routes both within Europe and beyond to the East. While the Crusades are usually given too much credit for introducing medieval Europe to the culture of the Middle East and its cuisine, it is nonetheless true that aristocrats and townspeople alike grew fond of spices, sugar, dried fruits, nuts, and other imports from the eastern Mediterranean. Medieval cuisine was richly colored and often combined sweet and sour flavors in finely pounded sauces, including many spices mixed together. It was closer aesthetically to modern Indian cuisine than anything you might find in Europe today.

The fasts established in the early Middles Ages continued, though individuals or sometimes whole towns could purchase dispensations from various requirements—for example, being allowed to eat butter for a fee. Naturally, the period leading up to the Lenten ban on meat was raucous, especially the final days of Carnival and Mardi Gras (Fat Tuesday). During this time people would eat and drink and engage in great licentiousness, but they also went about masked and took the opportunity to mock their superiors, holding mock trials, mock weddings, and so on. Carnival, it has been suggested, served a vital social function, allowing underlings one day to blow off steam and vent their frustrations with immunity. Yet the next day, everything went back to normal and the social order was maintained. Only when real violence began to become a threat in the sixteenth century were celebrations like these banned, considered by both Protestant and Catholic reformers to be indecorous.

The economy of the late Middle Ages was entirely different from previous centuries of growth. In the early fourteenth century there were serious famines, but these were nothing compared to the onslaught of bubonic plague in the second half of the century. Approximately one-third of Europeans perished. Apart from the immediate dislocation, ironically survivors fared comparatively well. Property was divided up, the demand for labor drove up wages, and feudalism—which tied serfs to the land—was gradually replaced with other forms of tenancy and rents with better terms. Guild restrictions on manufacturing jobs were also loosened, though not without violence and numerous revolts. In the end, it is safe to say that the lot of the average person improved; they ate more meat and enjoyed a higher standard of living. People's higher expendable incomes stimulated trade and consumption of goods, including, of course, food. This greater wealth allowed the middling ranks of society to imitate their superiors, and especially in urban areas in northern Italy and the Netherlands and in cities like Paris and London, late medieval culture was remarkably vibrant. Venice became wealthy from profits in the spice trade and built a maritime empire stretching down the Dalmatian coast toward the Levant. Because the spices changed hands so many times in their journey from Asia, they were fabulously expensive and a marker of status, used liberally in cooking. The cuisine of this era was magnificent, and a spate of cookbooks were written; selections from many are included here. Many of the recipes appear in cookbooks all across the continent, showing that this style, much like gothic architecture, was very international.

The Renaissance, which was primarily an intellectual and cultural movement, also had a major impact on the culture of food, although Renaissance cuisine is not very different from late medieval. Greek medicine remained the dominant force in dietary theory, though in the Middle Ages it had largely been translated from Arabic sources. The Renaissance returned to the original Greek texts of Galen and Hippocrates, and there was a general revival that sought to extirpate the Arabic texts and replace them with the original sources. The invention of printing was crucial to this process, which in turn, stimulated a great deal of debate, new discoveries, and, in the long run, scientific investigations that overturned the humoral system. The humanistic urge to recover and understand classical antiquity also led to the publication of Apicius's cookbook and one might even argue to the birth of food history as an academic discipline. Understanding ancient food habits became a serious topic of inquiry.

FIFTY-ONE

De Miseria Condicionis Humanae (On Gluttony)

POPE INNOCENT III

Pope Innocent III was born Lotario dei Conti di Segni in 1160 or 1161, became pope in 1198, and died in 1216. He is famous for having called crusades, not only in the Holy Land but against heretics at home—most notably the Albigensians. This work was written before he became pope and is representative of standard clerical attitudes toward gluttony as well as denigration of the body and the human condition in general. Good images of gluttony to accompany this text can be found by searching online for Taddeo di Bartolo at San Gimignano.

[17] OF GLUTTONY

"The beginning of man's life is water and bread and clothing and a house to cover shame." But now the fruits of trees are not sufficient for gluttons, nor the varieties of vegetables, nor the roots of plants, nor the fish of the sea, nor the beasts of the earth, nor the birds of the sky, but they seek for paints, compare aromas, nurse fattened birds, catch the plump ones, which are carefully prepared by the skill of the cooks, which are splendidly presented by the ceremony of the waiters. One grinds and strains, another mixes and prepares, turns substance into accident, changes nature into art, so that satiety turns into hunger, squeamishness recovers an appetite; to stimulate gluttony, not to sustain nature; not fill a need, but to satisfy a desire. Yet the pleasure of gluttony is so brief that as to the size of the place it is scarcely four inches, as to

Pope Innocent III. *De Miseria Condicionis Humanae*. Edited by Robert E. Lewis. Athens: University of Georgia Press, 1978, pp. 165–70.

length of time scarcely as many moments. Moderation is condemned, and superfluity is pursued. The appetite knows no limit in diversity of foods and variety of tastes, and greediness exceeds measure. But then the stomach is weighed down, the mind is disturbed, the intellect is overcome; thence not prosperity and health, but sickness and death. Hear the opinion of the wise man on this: "Be not greedy in any feasting, and pour not out thyself upon any meat; for in many meats there will be sickness, and by surfeiting many have perished." "Meat for the belly and the belly for the meats: but God shall destroy both it and them."

[18] EXAMPLES AGAINST GLUTTONY

Gluttony demands a costly tribute, but it returns the smallest value, because the more delicate the foods are, the more stinking the excrements are. What goes in vilely comes out vilely, expelling a horrible wind above and below, and emitting an abominable sound. Gluttony closed paradise, sold the birthright, hanged the baker, beheaded the Baptist. Nabuzardan, chief of cooks, burned the temple and destroyed all Jerusalem. At the banquet Baltasar saw the hand writing against him: "Mane, Thecel, Phares," and he was killed by the Chaldeans the same night. "The people sat down to eat and drink, and they rose up to play," but "yet their meat was in their mouth, and the wrath of God came upon them." "They that were feeding delicately died in the streets." The rich man who "feasted sumptuously every day" "was buried in hell."

[19] OF DRUNKENNESS

What is more unsightly than a drunkard, in whose mouth is a stench, in whose body a trembling; who utters foolish things, betrays secrets; whose reason is taken away, whose face is transformed? "For there is no secret where drunkenness reigneth." "Whom have the well filled cups not made well spoken?" Then wine does not suffice, nor cider, nor beer, but mead, syrup, spiced wine are eagerly prepared with great labor, with not a little care, with the greatest expense. But after that there are fights and brawls, disputes and quarrels. "For wine drunken with excess," as the wise man says, "raiseth quarrel and wrath and many ruins." And see: "Fornication and wine and drunkenness take away the understanding." Therefore the Apostle says: "Avoid wine, wherein is luxury." And Solomon: "Wine is an inebriating thing and drunkenness riotous." The son of Rechab and the son of Zachary did not drink wine or cider or anything that could inebriate.

[20] EXAMPLES AGAINST DRUNKENNESS

Drunkenness exposed the private parts, committed incest, killed the son of the king, strangled the head of the army. What Solomon says is therefore true: "They that give themselves to drinking and that club together shall be consumed." And Isaias: "Woe to you that rise up early in the morning to follow drunkenness and to drink till the evening in order to be inflamed with wine. The harp and the lyre and the timbrel and the pipe and wine are in your feasts." "Woe to you that are mighty at drinking wine and stout men at mixing drunkenness." "Behold joy and gladness, killing calves and slaying rams, eating flesh and drinking wine. Let us eat and drink, for tomorrow we die. And it will be revealed to my ears, says the Lord of Hosts, 'if this iniquity shall be forgiven you till you die.'" "Woe to the crown of pride of Ephraim." "The priests and the prophets have been ignorant of judgment." O shame, when the blessing was asked of a certain father at the reciting of the gospel reading, he is reported to have said in a high voice, belching forth the inebriation of the day before and the drunkenness of the night: "May the King of the Angels bless the drink of his servants."

[21] OF LUST

A foul mother produces a fouler daughter. For it is just that "he that is filthy may be filthy still." "They are all adulterers, like an oven heated by the baker. The princes began to be mad with wine." "For a richly filled belly willingly embraces Venus." O extreme foulness of desire, which not only weakens, but debilitates the body; not only defiles the soul, but pollutes the person. "For every sin that a man doth is without his body, but he that committeth fornication sinneth against his own body." Desire and wantonness always precede it, stench and filth always attend, sorrow and repentance always follow. "For the lips of a harlot are like a honeycomb dropping, and her throat is smoother than oil; but her end is as bitter as wormwood and sharp as a two-edged sword."

FIFTY-TWO

Libellus de Arte Coquinaria

This is the oldest European cookbook of the Middle Ages, and it exists in four manuscript versions in Danish, Low German, and Icelandic. All were probably translated from an earlier work in Latin going back perhaps to the twelfth century, since the recipe headings remain in Latin, or perhaps it came from the French. It is evidence that in Northern Europe and as far as Iceland recipes with exotic ingredients were of interest and could probably be made. Medieval cuisine was extremely international, and similar recipes are found everywhere at the time. The logic of almond butter is that it was allowed during Lent, and it is a real solidified fat, not merely crushed almonds as we make today. Almond milk is made by pounding blanched almonds, soaking them in hot water, and draining. Images of this manuscript can be found online by searching for the title.

How to Make Almond Butter

One should take almond kernels and make milk from them, and add water, and place it in a pot and heat it up over the embers and add saffron well crushed and salt and vinegar to taste, and heat it until it thickens. When it has become sufficiently thick, place it in a cloth sewn together as

Rudolf Grewe and Constance B. Hieatt, eds. *Libellus de Arte Coquinaria: An Early Northern Cookery Book*. Medieval and Renaissance Texts and Studies, Vol. 222. Tempe: Arizona Center for Medieval and Renaissance Studies, 2001, pp. 29, 31, 37.

a bag and hang it on a wall until the liquid has drained off, and then take it out, and make beaten butter of it.

How to Prepare a Sauce for the Lords and How Long It Lasts

One takes cloves and nutmeg, cardamom, pepper, cinnamon—that is canel—and ginger, all in equal amounts, except that there should be as much canel as all the other spices, and add twice as much toasted bread as of everything else, and grind it all together, and blend with strong vinegar, and place it in a case. This is a lordly sauce, and it is good for half a year.

How to Prepare a Chicken Pasty

One should cut a young chicken in two and cover it with whole leaves of sage, and add diced bacon and salt. And wrap this chicken with dough and bake it in an oven like bread. In the same way one can make all kinds of pasties of fish, of fowl, and of other meats.

FIFTY-THREE

The Viandier of Taillevent

GUILLAUME TIREL

Taillevent was perhaps the first superstar chef, who cooked for King Charles V of France. He was ennobled and even given a coat of arms with stew pots on it. His given name was Guillaume Tirel; his nickname means "Slice-wind." Many of the recipes in his cookbook weren't actually written by him, though, and versions appear in earlier manuscript collections—but then again, how many recipes are really original? The recipes do work, and for good reason it was the most popular cookbook of the era. For some beautiful dining and farming scenes, look online at the Limbourg Brothers' Très Riches Heures.

⌐⌐   ⌐⌐

27. Rappé: Rappé. *Sear your meat on the spit, then* fry your meat in bacon grease; steep bread in beef broth, strain and throw it over your meat; grind ginger, infuse it in verjuice and wine, and put it over your meat; then get currants or verjuice grapes *boiled in water* and set the meat in this (*var.: use these as a garnish when the meat is served in bowls*).

28. Civé de veel: Veal Stew. Roasted on a spit or on the grill, without overcooking, cut up into pieces and fried in grease with chopped onions; steep burnt toast in wine and beef broth or in pea puree, and boil your meat with this; then add ground ginger, cinnamon, cloves, grains of paradise, and saffron for colour, infused in verjuice and vinegar. It should be thick, there should be enough onions, the bread should be dark and sharp with vinegar, and it should be yellowish.

29. Civé de lievres: Hare Stew. It should be black and the bread well burnt in order to give it colour; it is made of the same ingredients as Veal Stew, and the hare should not be washed.

Guillaume Tirel. *The Viandier of Taillevent*. Edited by Terence Scully. Ottawa, Canada: University of Ottawa Press, 1988, pp. 283–90.

30. Civé de connins: Rabbit Stew. It should be strong and not quite so dark as the Hare Stew, nor so yellow as the Veal Stew, but between the two; and it should be made of the same ingredients as the Veal Stew.

Here Follow Roast Meats

31. Porc rosti: Roast Pork. Eaten with verjuice. And some people put garlic, onions, wine and verjuice in the pan with the drippings from the roast and make a sauce with it. Also, in a pasty *with saffron and spice powder*, eaten with verjuice.

32. Veel rosti: Roast Veal. Strongly parboiled, larded *and roasted*; it is eaten with Cameline Sauce. In a pastry, with spice powder, bacon fat and saffron; it is eaten with verjuice.

33. Fraise de veel: Calf's Tripe, called Charpie. Take your cooked meat, cut it up small and fry it in bacon grease; then grind ginger and saffron, mix with beaten raw eggs and pour this on your meat in the frying pan; serve garnished with spice powder or green verjuice.

34. Mouton rosti: Roast Mutton. Eaten with fine salt, with Cameline Sauce, or with verjuice.

35. Chevreaux, aigneaux: Roast Kids, Lambs. Plump them briefly in boiling water and sear them a little on the spit and then lard them; eat them with Cameline Sauce.

36. Oyes: Roast Geese and Goslings. *Pluck them dry, then plump them in hot water and cut off the wings, neck and feet; roast them without larding*; they are eaten with white or green Garlic Sauce, with black Pepper Sauce or with Jance *or with boiled Garlic Sauce*; and some people eat them with Saint Merry Sauce, that is with garlic steeped in the broth of the goose offal or in any other greasy water; and some gourmets take the goose or gosling, when it is roasted, to the goose butchers of Saint Merry or Saint Severin or the Baudés Gate to be cut up into pieces and slices in such a way that in each piece there is skin, flesh and bone; and they do it very neatly. (*Var.: And the offal should be washed once or twice in salted water, and set it about the goose—that is the liver, head, wings, feet and the other offal; this should be put to cook in a pot with salt meat, and then let cool; it is eaten with vinegar and parsley before the goose is roasted because it is the first thing to be eaten of the goose, and is called "goose giblets".*)

37. Poulés rostis: Roast Pullets (var.: *Hens*) and Chicks. *They should be plucked in water, larded and roasted*; they are eaten with Cold Sage Sauce *or with Cameline Sauce or with verjuice*. In a pasty with *spice powder and pieces of bacon fat*, they are eaten with green verjuice in the summer or without sauce in the winter.

38. Chappons, gelines, hetoudeaux: Roast Capons, Hens and Cockerels. Eaten with Must Sauce in summer, or with Poitevin Sauce or Jance in the winter: this latter sauce is made in the winter like Must Sauce, that is with wine and sugar boiled together.

39. Connins rostis: Roast Rabbits. They should be parboiled, larded and set to roast; they are eaten with Cameline Sauce. In a pasty they should be parboiled and larded and set either whole or in large pieces in the pastry with spice powder; they are eaten with Cameline Sauce or with verjuice.

40. Chappons de haulte gresse: Fat Capons in a Pasty. Without larding; empty the grease into a dish and make the Dodine Sauce out of this grease boiled in a metal pan, with parsley, wine and verjuice; and then make sops, long or flat or small, untoasted.

41. Lievres en rost: Roast Hare. Without washing, *seared on the spit*, larded *and roasted*; eat with Cameline Sauce or with Saupiquet Sauce that is made out of the grease that falls into the dripping pan, chopped onions, wine, verjuice and a little vinegar; this is poured over the hare when it has roasted, or set out in bowls. *And as it is roasting some people baste it with a sauce as* *for a Bourbier of Boar.* In a pasty, large pieces of hare are parboiled and larded; eaten with Cameline Sauce *or sprinkled with spice powder.*

42. Bourbier de sanglier: Bourbier of Fresh Wild Boar. The breast should first be put into boiling water and quickly withdrawn and set to roast *on a spit*, and baste it with a sauce made of spices—that is, ginger, cinnamon, cloves, and grains of paradise of the best variety—and toast that has been moistened in wine, verjuice and vinegar *and strained*; then, when it has cooked, baste it all together (*var.: when it has cooked, cut it into pieces and set it to boil in your sauce*). It should be clear and dark.

43. Toute venoison fresche: *Note that* fresh venison generally is not basted; *it is eaten* with Cameline Sauce.

44. Pijons rostis: Pigeons. Roasted with their heads and without their feet; eaten with fine salt. In a pasty, eaten with fine salt or wine or shallots, with the grease of the pasty.

45. Menus oiseaux: Roasted Small Birds, such as larks, quail, thrush, and others. Plucked dry without water *then remove the gizzards and the viscera*, then boil them a little (*var.: sear them in a clear flame*), and mount them on a spit with their heads and feet, sideways and not lengthwise, and put between every two of them slices or rashers of bacon or slices of sausage *and bay leaves; and fill the bellies of the birds with a mixture of good rich cheese and beef marrow;* they are eaten with fine salt *and they are served at table between two bowls or between two plates.* In a pasty, with cream cheese in their bellies.

46. Plouviers, videcoqs: Roast Plovers and Woodcocks. Pluck them dry, *sear them*, and leave their heads and feet on, mount them lengthwise on the spit; they are eaten with fine salt, and some people prefer Cameline Sauce. In a pasty, with fine salt without putting in any cheese.

47. Perdris: Roast Partridge. Pluck them dry, *remove their gizzards*, cut off their heads and feet, plump them in boiling water, *eviscerate and wash them*, then lard them (*var.: interlard them*); eaten with fine salt. For some people, in a pasty, with fine salt. And some people cut them up and slice them into small pieces and put them between two dishes with water and salt and set them to heat over a low fire until the water boils; then they eat them, and they say that that is a very good sauce.

48. Turturelles: Roast Turtle-Doves. Pluck them dry and plump them in boiling water without larding; eat them with fine salt. In a pasty with the head removed.

49. Cygnes: *Roast Swan. It is plucked dry like a goose, mounted on a spit and roasted with its feet still on; when being killed, its throat should be slit from its head to its shoulders; optionally it may be glazed; it is eaten with yellow Pepper Sauce.*

50. Paons: Roast Peacock. It is killed as a goose (*var.: swan*), the head and the tail are left on; it is larded and mounted on a spit and glazed as it roasts; it should be eaten with fine salt. *It is better eaten cold than warm, and can be kept for a long time.* It lasts well for a month after being cooked, and if it should be mouldy on the surface, just remove the mouldiness and you will find it white, good and sound underneath. *Peacock offers three types of meat: one similar to beef, another similar to hare, and a third much like partridge.*

51. Faisans: Roast Pheasant. Pluck dry, interlard, mount on a spit, and optionally plump it in hot water; the bird should be roasted without plucking its head or tail, which are wrapped in damp cloths to prevent their burning. Alternatively, remove the head, tail and wings and roast the bird without larding, if it is good and fat; when serving it, attach the head, tail and wings in their places with sticks *the neck and tail should not be roasted.* Eat it with fine salt.

52. Cigognes: Roast Storks. They should be plucked like a goose, *plumped in boiling water, the wings cut off*, and the feet, tail and head left on, and they should be set to roast on a spit, and singed *thoroughly*; eaten with fine salt.

53. Herons: Roast Heron. It should be bled or (*var.*: *and*) its throat slit down to the shoulders, as is done for a swan and a peacock, and it should be prepared as a stork; *or pluck dry and plump it in hot water, cut off its wings, feet and head* (*var.*: *leave on its feet and head*) *mount it on a spit and singe it*; eaten with fine salt or Cameline Sauce.

54. Malars de riviere: Roast River Mallards. Pluck them dry, and mount them on a spit without head or feet *or wings*, and catch the grease in order to make the Dodine Sauce. This is made from milk or wine or verjuice *from bacon fat, verjuice, onions, wine* and parsley *and spice powder*; and make long, thin, toasted sops *over which the Dodine is poured, or else boil the quartered birds in the Dodine*; it should be eaten with fine salt.

55. Outardes, gentes, grues: Roast Bustards, *Wild Geese, Cranes.* As with a stork; eaten with fine salt.

56. Butors: Roast Bittern. As with a stork; eaten with fine salt.

57. Cormorans: Roast Cormorant. As with a heron; eaten with fine salt.

58. Poches . . . : Roast Spoonbills and similar river birds. As with a heron.

59. Sarcelle: Roast Teal. Just the same as with a river mallard.

60. Pourcelet farci: Roast Stuffed Suckling Pig or Piglet. It should be scalded, washed well and put on the spit. The stuffing is made from the viscera of the piglet, from cooked pork, *cooked* egg yolks, a rich cheese, cooked, peeled chestnuts, and good spice powder (*var.*: *and salt*); all of this is *ground together and* put into the belly of the piglet, and the cut is sewn up; then put it to roast *basting it* with vinegar and good boiling grease *and salt*; eat it with hot yellow Pepper Sauce—some lazy persons eat it with Cameline Sauce.

Here Follow the *Entremets*

61. Faux grenon: Faulxgrenon. Cook poultry livers and gizzards, or veal, then chop them up very fine and fry them in bacon grease; grind ginger, cinnamon, cloves and grains of paradise and infuse these in wine, verjuice and beef broth, and (*var.*: *or*) in that broth of the livers, gizzards and veal; add a great quantity of egg yolks, pour this over your meat and boil everything thoroughly together. Some people add a little bread and some saffron. It should be quite thick, yellowish, and sharp with verjuice. When serving in bowls, sprinkle cinnamon powder over top.

62. Menus drois: Pettitoes: feet, livers and gizzards. Set them to cook thoroughly in wine and water, and put them on a plate with parsley and vinegar over them *or, instead of parsley and vinegar, put on milk thickened with egg yolks and bread, spice powder and a little saffron; and serve it in bowls without parsley and vinegar.*

63. Formentee: Frumenty. Clean grains of wheat *in warm water, wrap it in a cloth and beat heavily on this with a pestle until all the chaff has separated*, and wash it well and cook it in water; when it has cooked, mash it; bring cow's milk to a boil, put the wheat into it and bring it to a boil again *stirring frequently*; remove this from the fire and stir frequently and add a great quantity of *well beaten* egg yolks, *and it should not be too hot when they are added*; and some people add spices and *a little* saffron and venison water (*var.*: *and a good quantity of sugar added into the pot*). It should be yellowish and quite thick.

64. Garlins/Taillis: Taillis. Take figs, grapes, boiled almond milk, cracknels, *galettes* and white bread crusts cut into small cubes and boil these last items in your milk, with saffron to give it colour, and sugar, and then set all of this to boil until it is thick enough to slice. Set it out in bowls.

65. Millet: Millet. Soak it in three changes of hot water, then put it into simmering cow's milk—and do not put a spoon into this until it has boiled; then remove it from the fire *and beat it* *with the back of the spoon*, put in a little saffron and then set it to boil until it has boiled enough *is very thick*. Then set it out in bowls.

66. Poullaille farcie: Stuffed Poultry. Take your hens, cut their neck, scald and pluck them, and be careful that the skin remains undamaged and whole, and do not plump the birds; then take some sort of straw and push it between the skin and the flesh, and blow; then cut the skin between the shoulders, not making too large a hole, and leave the legs *with the feet*, wings, and neck *with the head* still attached to the skin.

To make the stuffing, take mutton, veal, pork and the *cooked* dark meat of chickens, and chop up all of this raw, and grind it in a mortar, together with *a great quantity of* raw eggs, *cooked chestnuts*, a good rich cheese, good spice powder and a little saffron, and salt to taste. Then stuff your chickens and sew up the hole again. With any leftover stuffing make *hard* balls, using a great deal of saffron, the size of packets of woad, and cook them in beef broth and boiling water gently, so they do not fall apart. Then mount your chickens and the balls on very slender iron spits.

To glaze them or cover them with green or yellow: for the yellow, take a great quantity of egg yolks, beat them well with a little saffron, and set this glazing in a dish of some sort; and should you want a green glazing, grind the greenery with the eggs *without saffron, and put this through the strainer and apply it*: after your poultry and your balls of stuffing are cooked, place your spit in the dish with the glazing mixture two or three times and cast your glazing the full length of the spit, then put it back on the fire so that your glazing will take; and watch that your glazing does not have so hot a fire that it burns.

67. [Unnamed] *Quarter chickens and sautee them in a pot with rashers of bacon, stirring frequently and keeping the lid tight; then, after frying, take beef broth and cook them in it; then add beaten egg yolks, verjuice and saffron. It should be quite thick. Serve the quarters on plates, and on each plate place a rasher of bacon and then pour your broth over top.*

68. Gelee de poisson . . . : Fish and Meat Jelly. *Take any fish whose skin is covered with a natural oil, or any meat, and* cook it in wine, verjuice and vinegar—and some people add a little water (*var.: a little bread*); then grind ginger, cinnamon, cloves, grains of paradise, long pepper, *nutmegs, saffron and chervil [?]* and infuse this in your bouillon, strain it (*var.: tie it in a clean cloth*), and put it to boil with your meat; then take bay leaves, spikenard, galingale and mace, and tie them in your bolting cloth, without washing it, along with the residue of the other spices, and put this to boil with your meat; keep the pot covered while it is on the fire, and when it is off the fire keep skimming it until the preparation is served up; and when it is cooked, strain your bouillon into a clean wooden vessel and let it sit. Set your meat on a clean cloth; if it is fish, skin it and clean it and throw your skins into your bouillon until it has been strained for the last time. Make certain that your bouillon is clear and clean *and do not wait for it to cool before straining it*. Set out your meat in bowls, and afterwards put your bouillon back on the fire in a bright clean vessel and boil it *constantly skimming*, and pour it boiling over your meat; and on your plates or bowls in which you have put your meat and broth sprinkle ground cassia buds and mace, and put your plates in a cool place to set. Anyone making jelly cannot let himself fall asleep. If your bouillon is not quite clear and clean, filter it through two or three layers of a white cloth. *And salt to taste*. On top of your meat put crayfish necks and legs; and cooked loach, if it is a fish dish.

69. Lamproie fresche a la saulce chaude: Fresh Lamprey in a Hot Sauce. The lamprey should be bled by its mouth, and its tongue removed; you should shove a skewer into it to help bleed it, and keep the blood because that is the grease *and scrape the inside of the mouth with a knife*, then scald it as you would an eel and roast it on a very slender spit inserted through it sideways once or twice. Then grind ginger, cinnamon, cloves, grains of paradise, nutmegs and a little burnt toast moistened in the blood together with vinegar and, if you wish, a little wine; infuse all of this together and bring it to a boil, and then put your lamprey whole into it. The sauce should not be too dark—that is, when the sauce is thin, but when the sauce is thick, and is called "mud," it should be dark. Also, it is not necessary for the lamprey to be boiled with the sauce; rather the lamprey is brought dry to the table and the thin sauce, or the "mud," is poured over the lamprey or is served in bowls; and the lamprey should be cut into pieces lengthwise and sent to the table on plates; nevertheless, some gourmets insist on having it dry with the sauce, made of the drippings and fine salt, served in the same plate in which it is brought.

70. **Lamproie a la galentine:** Lamprey in Galantine. Bleed a lamprey as previously, keeping the blood, then set it to cook in vinegar and wine and a little water; and when it is cooked, set it to cool on a cloth; steep burnt toast in your bouillon, strain it, and boil it with the blood, stirring to keep it from burning; when it is well boiled, pour it into a mortar or a clean *wooden* bowl and keep stirring until it has cooled; then grind ginger, cassia buds, cloves, grains of paradise, nutmegs and long pepper and infuse this in your bouillon and put it, and your fish with it, in a bowl as was said; and put it in either a wooden or pewter vessel, and you will have good gelatine.

71. **Ris engoulé:** Fancy Rice for Meat-Days. Cull the rice and wash it thoroughly in hot water and set it to dry by the fire, then cook it in simmering cow's milk; then add ground saffron infused in your milk, to lend it a russet colour, and greasy *beef* broth from the pot.

72. **Cigne resvestu:** An *Entremets* of a Swan Redressed in its Skin with all its Plumage. Take the swan and inflate it between its shoulders *as with Stuffed Poultry* and slit it along its belly, then remove the skin together with the neck cut off at the shoulders, and with the legs remaining attached to the body; then fix it on a spit *interlarded as poultry*, and glaze it; and when it is cooked, it should be redressed in its skin, with the neck either straight or flat; it should be eaten with yellow Pepper Sauce.

73. **Froide sauge:** A Cold Sage. Cook your poultry in water, then set it to cool; grind ginger, cassia buds (*var.*: *cinnamon*), grains of paradise and cloves, and do not strain them; then grind bread, parsley and sage, with, if you wish, a little saffron in this greenery to make it a bright green, and sieve this; and some people add strained, hard-cooked egg yolks steeped in vinegar; *do not boil*. Break your poultry apart into halves, quarters or members, set it out on plates with the sauce over *and hard-cooked egg whites on top*. If you used hard eggs, cut them up with a knife rather than breaking them by hand.

74. **Soux de pourcelet:** Soux of Piglet. *Take the feet, tail, ears and snout of the piglet and cook them thoroughly with salt, wine and water, and then* proceed as for a Cold Sage, but without using any saffron or eggs, and with less sage than parsley; *and as soon as your meat has cooled, put your sauce over it.*

Thick Meatless Pottages

75. **Comminee de poisson:** Cuminade of Fish. The fish are cooked in water or fried in oil; grind almonds *infused* in your broth, in pea puree or in boiled water, and make almond milk *and set it to boil*; grind ginger and cumin, infused in wine and verjuice, and put it to boil with your milk. If this is to be a sick-dish, there must be sugar in it.

76. **Brouet vergay d'anguilles:** Bright-Green Brewet of Eels. Skin them or scald them, cook them in wine and water; grind bread and parsley, with a very little saffron in the green to make it yellowish green, and steep this in your broth; then grind ginger that is infused in verjuice, and boil everything together. If you wish, little cubes of a good cheese can be used.

77. Gravé de loche: Gravy of Loach. Take toast, wine and either pea puree or boiled water, put all of this through the strainer and set it to boil; then add ground ginger, cinnamon, cloves, grains of paradise, and saffron for colour, infused in vinegar, and chopped onions fried in oil, and boil everything together; and fry your loach *in oil* without flouring it, and do not boil it but set it out in bowls with your broth over top; *and it should be thoroughly washed of the natural oil on its skin before all else.* It should be of a yellow colour.

78. Chaudumet a becquet/beschet: Chaudumel of Pike *or Pickerel.* Roast your fish *on the grill*; then grind bread, ginger and saffron, and steep this in pea pure or boiled water, wine and verjuice, strain, and boil; then pour this on your fish and, if you wish, a very little vinegar. It should be yellowish.

79. Une soringne/soringue: A Soringue. Scald or skin the eel, then slice it across and set it to sautee in oil *in a covered pot over a low fire* with sliced onions and parsley leaves; take toast, pea puree or boiled water, and wine—with the wine predominating—strain it and put it with the other to boil; then add ground ginger, cinnamon, cloves, grains of paradise, and saffron for colour, infused in verjuice; boil all of this. Season it with vinegar.

80. Brouet sarrasinois: Saracen Brewet. *Skin eels, cut them across and fry the slices in oil without having (var.: after having) dredged them in salt*; grind *ginger*, cinnamon, *cloves, grains of paradise, galingale*, long pepper, and saffron for colour, infuse these in wine and verjuice and then boil it all together with your eels. It should not be too thick because it thickens by itself.

81. *Lemprions: Lamprill. Take your lamprill and scald and clean them thoroughly, then fry them in oil; take good bastard wine and mustard, or any other good red wine with sugar—though with bastard wine sugar is unnecessary because it is sweet by nature—and add to it ginger and, in greater quantity, cassia buds, sieved together; and pour this over the lamprill without boiling.*

82. Civé d'oistres: Oyster Stew. Scald oysters and wash them well, *parboil them a little* and fry them in oil *together with chopped onions*; take toast, pea puree or the water in which the oysters were scalded, or any other hot, boiled water, and a generous proportion of wine *and verjuice*, and strain this; then add in ground cinnamon, ginger, cloves, grains of paradise, and saffron for colour, infused in vinegar, and onions fried in oil, and boil all of this together. It should be stiff *and yellowish, and salted to taste.* Some people do not boil the oysters in this.

83. Soupe en moustarde: Mustard Sops. Take the oil in which you fried or poached your eggs *without shells*, with wine and water *and chopped onions fried in oil*, and boil everything in an iron pan; then take crusts of bread, toast them on the grill, cut them into square pieces and add them to boil with the other; then strain your bouillon, and drain your sops and drop them on a plate (*var.: bowl*); then put a little very thick mustard into your bouillon pan and boil everything *and pour it on top of the sops.*

84. Civé d'oeufs: Egg Stew. Poach eggs in oil, fry sliced onions in oil and set them both to boil with wine, verjuice and vinegar; and when you serve your bouillon, set it out poured over your meat. It should not be thick. Then make Mustard Sops as above.

85. Brouet d'Alemagne d'oeufs: German Egg Brewet. Boil together eggs poached in oil, boiled almond milk and sliced onions fried in oil; then grind ginger, cinnamon, cloves, grains of paradise and a little saffron infused in verjuice, and add these to the other ingredients without boiling too much. It should be quite thick and not too yellow. With Mustard Sops *as above*, if you wish.

86. Lait de prouvance/Lait lié: Thickened Cow's Milk *Provençal Milk.* Cow's milk should be brought to a boil and then removed from the fire, then *when it has cooled a little* add in a large quantity of egg yolks either directly or after having put them through the strainer. It should be quite thick and somewhat yellowish, though not too much. Then poach eggs in water and put them with this without boiling.

87. Brouet vert d'oeufs et de fromage: Green Brewet of Eggs and Cheese. Take parsley and a little sage, with a very little saffron in this green, and bread steeped in *pea* puree or boiled water; then add in *ground* ginger, infused in wine, and set it to boil; then add in cheese, and eggs after they have been poached in water. It should be thick and bright green. Some people do not put in any bread, but they do add almond milk.

88. Une saulce jaunette de poisson: A Yellowish Sauce for Fried *Cold or Warm* Fish. *Pickerel or perch are skinned and* fried in oil without being dredged in flour; grind almonds, steep them in a mixture of wine and a little verjuice, strain them and boil; then add ground ginger, *cinnamon,* cloves, grains of paradise and a little saffron, infused in your broth, and boil all of this well together with sugar. It should be quite thick.

89. Gravé de perche: Gravy of Perch. Perch, or any other fish *such as loach*, should be cooked, skinned and fried without flour; the dish is prepared as Gravy of Loach. It is not so yellow but rather russet-coloured, and quite thick.

FIFTY-FOUR

Ménagier de Paris

This household guide was written in Paris in the late 1300s by an elderly businessman, or perhaps lawyer, for his young bride. His assumption was that he would die and she would need to remarry, an unlikely prospect without basic household skills, so he wrote this book to help her. It covers a broad range of topics on the theme of wifely obedience and includes a whole section on cooking. Many of the recipes come from Taillevent, which is decent evidence that cooking techniques and taste preferences were trickling down from the court to the middling ranks of society.

2.5 Recipes

This is now the place to explain the preparation of the foods named in the above menus.

1. But *primo* you must know several general terms, and you will be able to assemble a complete list by adding others that are here and there throughout this book, that is, regarding the thickener for all pottages, such as bread, eggs, starch, flour, etc.

2. *Item*, to prevent your pottage from burning, you must stir down to the bottom of the pot and watch that the burning logs do not touch the pot. If it has already begun to burn, immediately switch it into another pot. *Item*, to keep milk from turning. *Item*, so that the pot does not boil over onto the fire.

3. You must put well-ground, and not strained, spices into pottage, and only at the last moment. In sauces and in aspic, *secus*.

Gina L. Greco and Christine M. Rose, ed. and trans. *The Good Wife's Guide (Le Ménagier de Paris): A Medieval Household Book*. Ithaca, NY: Cornell University Press, 2009, pp. 271–82.

4. Know your spices, as explained previous to this fifth article.

5. *Item*, to kill pigs. It is said that the season males should be slaughtered is the month of November, and the females in December, as for example when people say "February hens."

6. *Item,* to make boudin, collect the blood of a pig in a suitable basin or pan. When the pig has been butchered and the haslet washed thoroughly and set to cook, while it is cooking, remove the clots of blood from the bottom of the basin and discard them. Next, mix peeled and minced onions, about half the amount as there is blood, with about half as much *entrecerele*— that is, the fat found between the intestines—minced as small as dice. Add some ground salt, and stir the mixture into the blood. Grind together ginger, cloves, and a little pepper. Take the small intestines, wash them well, turn them inside out, and rinse well in running water. To remove the odor, place them in a pan on the fire and stir; then add salt, and do it a second and a 3rd time and then wash them. Turn them, this time outer side out, wash them, and set them to dry on a towel, rubbing and wringing them to remove moisture. (What are called the entrecerele are the large intestines, which have fat inside that is pulled out with a knife.) After you have measured and put in equal portions and quantities (half as much onions as blood and a quarter as much fat), and when your boudins have been filled with this mixture, cook them in a pan with the haslet broth, and prick them with a pin when they swell; otherwise they will burst. *Nota* that the blood keeps well for two, indeed even 3, days, once the spices are added. Some may use as spices pennyroyal, savory, hyssop, and marjoram, gathered when they are in flower and then dried and ground. As for the haslet, put it in a copper pot to cook on the fire, whole and without salt, and skim the pot along the edges, for haslet will foam. When it is cooked, take it out and save it to make pottage.

To make liver boudin. Take two pieces of liver, two pieces of lung, a piece of fat and put it in an intestine along with some blood, and for the rest do as above.

Nota that good boudin can be made with goose blood, provided that the goose is thin, for thin geese have larger intestines than fat ones.

Queritur: how are the intestines turned inside out to be washed? *Responsio*: by a linen thread and a brass wire as long as a gauger's rod.

7. *Nota* that some folks hang their pigs during the Easter season and the air yellows them; for this reason it is best to keep them in salt as they do in Picardy, although it seems that the flesh is then not as firm. Nonetheless, it is much nicer to serve fair and white lard than yellow, for no matter how good the yellow is, its unappealing color condemns it and discourages its use.

8. To make andouille sausage. *Nota* that andouille sausages are made from rectal guts and other large intestines, which are stuffed full of the other entrails to make sausage. These small intestines, when you want to put them in andouille sausages, are split lengthwise into 4 parts. *Item*, you can make andouille from thinly sliced stomach. *Item*, from the meat beneath the ribs. *Item*, from sweetbreads and other things that are around the "small haste" when you do not wish to use the small haste intact. But first these entrails are deodorized in a pot with salt two or three times, as described above for boudin. The other things explained above, that is, the lower and other guts that must be filled to make andouille sausage, are first pricked and sprinkled with a half ounce of powdered pepper and a sixth of fennel, ground, with a dash of finely ground salt sparingly added to the spices. When each andouille is thus stuffed and filled, you place them to be preserved in salt with lard, on top of the lard.

9. Freshly salted-ribs, roasted on the grill.

10. Chines and hams are salted 3 days and nights with peas.

11. *Nota* that if a ham is cured for a long time in salt, such as for a month, you must soak it in cold water the evening before, and the next day scrape it and wash it in hot

water before cooking it; *primo*, cook in water and wine, then throw out this first liquid and cook it in fresh water.

12. Hereafter follow the names of all the parts of a pig, which are sold at the tripe shop for seven blancs.

Primo, when the pig is butchered, the blood and clots come out first, and if you choose you can make boudin from them. *Item*, the viscera include: *primo* the fat, *secundo* the small haste, 3rd the offal. The fat is that fat between the intestines and the small haste; the haslet are the liver, the lungs, the heart, and the tongue; the small haste is the spleen, and to this is tightly connected half of the liver and the kidneys; the other half of the liver is connected to the entrails between the lungs and the heart. The offal are the bowels called the entrecerele of the intestines, and these include the small intestines from which boudin and sausages are made, and also the stomach.

13. The viscera of sheep include the stomach and the rennet stomach, the 4 feet and the head, and it all costs two parisis at the tripe shop.

14. The entrails extracted from calves include the head and the innards, the belly and the 4 feet and costs two blancs at the tripe shop. *Nota*, the innards are the rennet stomach, the belly, and the bowels, which the tripe merchants sell cleaned, washed, and prepared, soaked in clear, clean water. But those who purchase them do not rely only on the tripe seller to prepare this material for them. Rather they themselves wash the stuff in hot water 2 or 3 times and then wash them out again with salt, putting it all to cook in water without salt until the water boils off, then adding some mutton broth. Put herbs, some of the cooking water, and saffron on a platter with these innards, eating them like tripe with salt and verjuice.

15. *Nota* here the great variety of terms: what one calls viscera of a pig are liver, lungs, and heart; what one calls the viscera of sheep are the head, the stomach, the rennet stomach, and the 4 feet; and what we call the viscera of a calf are the head, the guts, the stomach, and the 4 feet; and what we call the viscera of a cow are the stomach, the omasum, the rennet stomach, the spleen, the lungs, and the liver and the four feet. And for venison, different parts, different names. *Queritur* the cause of this diversity concerning this one word "viscera."

16. Venison of stag or any other. If you wish to salt it in the summer, you must salt it in a washtub or a bathtub with coarsely ground salt and then dry it in the sun. The croup, *id est*, the hindquarters, that has been salted must be boiled first in water with wine to remove the salt. Then throw away the water and wine and set it to finish cooking in meat broth with turnips. Serve the venison on a platter sliced thinly, with its broth. *Item*, if you have young, small turnips, cook them in water without wine for the first boiling, then throw away that water and continue cooking them in water and wine with chestnuts—or if there are no chestnuts, use sage. Serve as above.

17. In June and July, salted beef and mutton pieces should be well boiled in water with scallions and salted from morning to evening, or a day at most.

18. The butchers of Paris hold that, according to their way of speaking, a cow has only 4 principal members: that is, the two shoulders and the two thighs, and the front and back of the body. The shoulders and thighs being removed, the cow is split from the side, making one piece of the front and another of the rear. In this manner the cow's carcass is transported to the market stall, if the cow is small or medium-sized. But if it is large, the front quarters would be split down the back, and the hind piece also, to be carried more easily. Thus we now have 6 pieces of beef, of which the two briskets are removed first, and then the two plates underneath that hold them, which are three good feet long and a half foot wide, coming from below and not from above. And then the front quarter is cut, and next the sirloin, which is hardly more than 2 or 3 fingers thick. Then the tenderloin, which is closest to the spine, as thick as a large fist. Next, the cut called the numbles, which is a good foot long and no more and stretches from the neck at one end to

the kidney. This section belongs rightfully to the one who holds the cow's feet during the skinning. He sells it in a small stall that is below the Grande-Boucherie, and it is of little value. *Item*, according to the size of the cows, they are cut into more or fewer portions and sold at the Porte de Paris. I don't know how the bourgeois' tally can justly proportion itself in measure with the butchers'. For one good cow costs 20 pounds, but another costs only 12. *Item*, the beef extractions cost 8 sols at the tripe shop—that is, the viscera, in which are the belly, the omasum, the rennet stomach, the spleen, the lungs, the liver, and the 4 feet.

19. *Item*, in Béziers, as of the feast of St. Andrew, which is before Christmas, sheep are salted in quarters, by rubbing and rerubbing more and more, and then placing the quarters one upon another for 8 days and then setting them in the fireplace.

20. If you want to salt beef or mutton flesh in the winter, use coarse salt. Dry the meat very well in the pan, then grind it finely and salt it. *Nota* that in June and July mutton must be soaked before salting.

21. Salted beef tongue. In the proper season for salting, take a quantity of beef tongues and boil them a little; then scrape and peel them. Salt them one atop the other and leave them in salt for 8 or 9 days. Then hang them in the chimney and leave them there for the winter. After that, hang them in a dry place for one or 2 or 3 years.

22. Goose must be salted for 3 days and nights.

23. Coot salted for 2 days are good with cabbage. Wood pigeons also; *nota* that they return every 3 years.

24. If a hare is caught 15 days or three weeks before Easter, or at another time when you want to preserve it, split it and remove the entrails; then slit the skin on the head, tear it, and make an opening in the head to remove the brain. Fill that cavity with salt and sew up the skin. It will keep for a month if it is hung by the ears.

25. *Nota* that one of the best morsels or prime pieces of beef, whether for roasting or for stewing, is the noyau. And *nota* that the noyau of beef is the piece below the neck and shoulders. Additionally, this piece is supremely good sliced and put in pasties. After the pasty is cooked, pour on some lamprey sauce.

26. Eel. Let it die in salt and leave it there for 3 entire days and nights. Then scald it and remove the slime; cut it in slices and salt it, then boil in water with scallions. If, instead, you want to salt it from Vespers until the morning, skim off the foam and gut the eel, then cut it into slices and salt it, rubbing each slice well with coarse salt. And if you wish to expedite it even more, grind some salt and rub the cut sides of the pieces and toss it in salt between two bowls. Cook as above and eat with mustard.

27. Herring *caqué* should be soaked in a large quantity of fresh water for 3 days and 3 nights. At the end of 3 days, the herring need to be washed and the water changed; then soak for another 2 days, changing the water twice each day. Some herrings, due to their nature or small size, require less soaking than others.

28. Smoked herring. Good smoked herring is thin with a thick back, round and green, while the inferior kind is fat and yellow or has a flat and dry back.

Ordinary Pottages, Unthickened and without Spices:

29. *Primo*, old pea pottage. First you must sort and cull the peas and find out from the people of that region the nature of the peas. (For peas commonly do not cook in well water; and in some places they cook just fine in spring water or river water, as in Paris, yet in others they do not cook in spring or river water, as in Béziers.) Once you know the character of the regional peas, wash them in warm water, then put them in a pot of water on the fire and boil them till they burst.

Drain off the stock and set it aside; refill the pot of peas with warm water. Set it on the fire to boil, and drain off the cooking water a second time, if you want to have more stock. Then put them back on the fire without water, for they will release enough and will cook in that. Do not put the spoon into the pot once they have been drained, but instead shake the pot and the peas together and little by little add warm or fairly hot water, certainly not cold, and bring them to a boil and cook them thoroughly before you add anything other than hot water, whether meat or something else. Do not include salt or bacon fat or a seasoning until they are fully cooked. You can add bacon stock or meat stock, but do not salt or stir with the spoon until they are well cooked. Nonetheless you can swirl them around in the pot.

On a meat day, after the peas have been drained, enhance the dish with bacon or meat broth, adding it when they are nearly cooked. When you remove the bacon from the peas, rinse it in meat broth, so that it will be more attractive when set in thin slices on the meat and not appear encrusted with peas.

On a fish day, while the peas are cooking, have a pot of onions cooking for just as long and, as with the bacon stock, add the onion broth to the peas and serve them. In a similar way on a fish day, when you have put the peas on the fire in a pot, put the sliced onions separately in another pot, and use the onion water to add to the peas; and when all is cooked, fry the onions and mix half of them into the peas and add the other half to the broth, which is mentioned below, and then some salt. If on this fish day or in Lent there is salted whale meat, substitute it for the bacon used on a meat day.

30. As for new peas, sometimes they are cooked on a meat day with meat stock, with minced parsley to make green pottage for a meat day; and on a fish day, they are cooked in milk with ginger and saffron; and sometimes for a crétonnée, as will be explained below [95].

31. With all these peas, whether old or new, you can make a thin strong coulis using a flour sieve, straining cloth, or sackcloth; but you must yellow old peas with ground saffron. The saffron water should boil the peas, and the saffron is cooked with the pea stock.

32. There are other peas that are prepared in their pods with bacon added.

33. *Item,* new pea crétonnée, you will find in the next chapter.

34. On a meat day, you need not worry about the pea stock. On a fish day and in Lent, fry onions as is spoken of above, and mix the fried onions and the oil in which they were fried with breadcrumbs, ginger, cloves, and grains of paradise that have been ground and moistened with vinegar and wine. You then add a little saffron; then prepare sops in the bowl.

Item, with the stock you can make a stew on a fish day; so do not stir it at all, and remove it quickly from the fire and put it into another pot. *Item,* thin a chard purée with the stock, and this will make a very good Lenten pottage, provided that you do not add any other water.

35. *Nota* that all pottages on the fire will overflow and spill over onto the fire until you add salt and fat to the pot, and then they will not.

36. *Item, nota* that the best bouillon is from beef cheeks washed in hot water 2 or three times, then boiled and well skimmed.

37. *Nota,* if you notice that your pottage is burning, add some liquid (it burns because it is too thick) and stir constantly whatever is burning in the bottom of the pot before you add anything else. Before your pottage sticks to the pan and burns, and so that it does not scorch, stir it often, scraping your spoon on the bottom to keep the pottage from sticking. Keep in mind that peas or beans rarely stick to the pan if the burning logs do not touch the bottom of the pot while it is over the fire.

38. Here is how onions are cooked: boil in water quite a while before adding the peas, and in such a way that the water completely evaporates. Then you add the pea stock to complete the cooking and remove the taste of the water.

39. Similarly, oysters are first washed in warm water, then boiled so that their flavor remains in the stock, but they are not skimmed. Then remove the oysters and fry them, if you wish, and place some of them in the bowls and with the rest make another dish.

40. Old beans that are to be cooked in their pods must be soaked and placed on the fire in a pot the evening before and left all night. Then toss out the water, add clean water, and cook them. Drain as for peas to remove that first strong flavor; then boil in meat stock with lard, as is described above in the pea stock recipe, or on a fish day use fresh water, adding afterward some oil. Or cook in onion stock, with the onions, and if you want to make a coulis, do as with the peas.

Item, beans are shelled in this way at Easter: you must sort and wash them, but not soak them. Place the beans in their shells in water to simmer on the fire, and let them boil until the shell wrinkles and bursts. Then push them to the back of the fire and scoop them up with a spoon. Skin and shell them one spoonful at a time while they are hot, then bathe them in cold water. After this wash them in warm water as for peas and cook in cold water, and when they have boiled until they split, pour off the liquid and fill the pot with meat stock if it is a meat day, or another liquid if it is a fish day. Season the beans with oil and well-cooked onions, then fry, or dress them with butter. They can be made green again using fresh ground-up bean leaves, soaked in hot water and strained. Next proceed as with the other peas, either with bacon on a meat day or as on a fish day.

41. *Item*, crétonnée of new beans is prepared as you find in the next chapter.

42. *Item*, if you care to eat beans all year that have the scent and flavor of new beans: plant beans each month, and take a handful of the most tender as they grow up from the soil, grind them, and add them to your other beans. The beans will lighten and will have the color and flavor of new beans.

43. *Item*, new beans must first be cooked until they split, then drained, and afterward in their stock boil large sops of brown bread, two fingers thick; then put in each bowl of beans two of these sops and add salt.

Item, once the beans have split and are strained, they can be fried in bacon grease, then sprinkled lightly with spices.

44. You can recognize bog beans because they are flat, whereas field beans are round. *Item*, they are soft to the tooth, and their pod is tender, unlike the others.

45. *Item*, if you want to shell new beans, you must first cut them lengthwise with a knife, and once everything is cut, peel them by hand.

46. *Nota*, in August one begins to eat coulis of beans and peas with salted meat.

47. *Nota* that a ham must be salted for three days and nights, and then it is at its best.

48. *Nota* also, regarding beans and peas, that crétonée of beans and peas is in the chapter on thick pottages.

49. Porée. Cooks designate three kinds of porée: white porée, green porée, and black porée.

50. White porée is so named because it is made from the white of leeks, pork chine, andouille or ham, in autumn or winter for a meat day. Understand that no other fat besides pork tastes right in it. First, you select, mince, wash, and blanch the leeks—that is, in summertime when the leeks are young, but in the winter when the leeks are older and tougher, they should be boiled instead of just blanched. On a fish day, after doing all that, place them in a pot of hot water, and cook them thus. Likewise, cook minced onions and then fry them. Next, fry the leeks with those onions, then mix together to stew in a pot, with cow's milk if it is a meat day. On a fish day and during Lent, use almond milk. If it is a meat day, when the leeks are blanched in summer, or boiled in the winter, as explained, set them to cook in a pot of salted meat or pork stock and add lard. *Nota*, this leek porée is sometimes thickened with bread.

Item, white porée of chard is made as above, in a stock of mutton and beef, but not with pork; and on a fish day with milk, from almonds or cows.

Item, garden cress during Lent with almond milk. Take the cress and set it to boil with a handful of chopped chard, and then fry it all in oil. Then boil it in almond milk. When meat is allowed, fry it in lard and butter until done, then moisten with meat broth or with cheese, and serve immediately; otherwise it will scorch. However, should you decide to add parsley to it, do not blanch the parsley first.

A variety of greens called spinach has longer leaves, thinner and greener than the ordinary porée. It can also be called *epinoche*, and it is eaten at the beginning of Lent. To cook this, select the new and tender leaves and pick over them, removing the large ribs as one does for cabbage. Without chopping, put the porée in a simmering pot of clear water or broth, with salt. Serve by pouring olive oil or verjuice into the bowl, but no parsley. Sometimes, and most frequently, you fry the spinach, completely raw, and when well fried, add a little water as you do for sops with oil.

Another porée of new chard. Either quickly blanched in the summer when young, or boiled in winter for older greens, depending upon their age. Porée of chard that has been washed then cut up and boiled stays greener than that which is first boiled and then chopped. But still greener and better is that which has been sorted, then washed and cut up very small, then blanched in cold water. You then change the water and soak it all in the fresh water. Then squeeze out the water and shape the greens into little balls and boil in a pot with bouillon of bacon fat and mutton stock. When it has boiled a little and you are ready to serve it, add some parsley, carefully picked, washed, and minced, with a little bit of young fennel, and bring it to a boil once only. Everything considered, the less you boil porée, the greener it stays. Parsley should not be boiled, or for only the briefest time, for in boiling it loses its flavor.

51. Green porée on a fish day. Sort, cut up, and wash the greens in cold water without boiling, then cook with verjuice and a little water, and add some salt, then serve it boiling hot and very thick, without liquid. In the bottom of the serving bowl, underneath the porée, put salted or fresh butter, or cheese, or old verjuice.

Porée of cabbage sprouts is in season from January until Easter and even later.

And *nota* that when preparing porée with almond milk, the milk must not be passed through a sieve, although you do sieve it for some other pottages, and to drink.

52. Black porée is made including slices of grilled salted bacon. Namely, the porée is sorted, washed, then cut up and blanched in boiling water, then fried in bacon fat; then thinned with simmering water. Some say that if it is washed in cold water, it will be blacker and uglier. To serve, place two pieces of bacon on each platter.

53. There are five types of cabbage. The best are those that have been touched by the frost; they are tender and cook quickly; and in frosty weather they must not be boiled, although in rainy weather they should be. And this list begins with these because they are the first to grow in the year, *scilicet* from April, and then it proceeds in order, descending toward vine harvest, Christmas, and then Easter.

White cabbages come at the end of August. Cabbage heads are ready at the end of the vine harvest. And after you pick the head of cabbage from the center of the plant, pull up the rest of the cabbage plant and transplant it to new soil, and from it will grow big leaves that spread out. Cabbage takes a lot of space, and such cabbages are called Roman cabbages and are eaten in the winter. If the stumps are replanted, little cabbages called sprouts develop; they are eaten with raw herbs in vinegar. If they are plentiful, they are tasty when sorted, washed in warm water, and boiled whole in a little water. When they are cooked, add some salt and oil and serve them very thick, without broth. In Lent, drizzle olive oil over them. Other cabbages are called Easter cabbages, because they are eaten at Easter time, yet they are sown in August. After these have grown up half a foot, uproot them and transplant them elsewhere. They need to be watered frequently. Indeed, all the cabbages spoken of above are first sown, then transplanted when they are about half a foot in height.

And first concerning cabbage heads, you need to know that once the leaves are stripped off, picked over, and chopped, they need to be boiled very well and long—longer than the other cabbages. The green leaves of Roman cabbages need to be torn into pieces and the yellow, that is the rib or veins, crushed in a mortar; then all blanched together in hot water, then drained well and put in a pot of warm water, if you do not have enough meat bouillon. Serve with the fattiest meat stock. Some cooks add ground bread.

Also recognize that cabbages must be put on the fire quite early in the morning and cooked for a stretch of time, much longer than any other pottage, and over a robust fire. All varieties of cabbage—heads or leaves—should be soaked in beef fat, and no other sort, except for sprouts. Note also that stock of beef and mutton is proper, never pork stock, which is good only with leeks.

If you prepare cabbage on a fish day, boil it, cook it in warm water, and add oil and salt. *Item*, some add meal. *Item*, instead of oil, some put butter in. On a meat day you might add pigeons, sausages and hare, coots and plenty of bacon.

54. Turnips are firm and difficult to cook until they have been through the cold and frost. Cut off the head and tail and other whiskery rootlets or roots. After peeling them, wash in two or three changes of good, hot water; then cook them in steaming meat stock of either pork, beef, or mutton. *Item*, in Beauce after cooking them, they slice them up and fry them in a pan and sprinkle them with spices.

55. Little delicacies. Take gizzards and livers and cook them in wine and water—first the gizzards and afterward the livers. Then place in a dish with minced parsley and pour vinegar over them. *Item,* the feet of beef, mutton, and kid.

56. *Gramose* is made with the household's cold meat left over from dinner and with stock made from this leftover meat, in the following manner: *Primo*, beat 4 or 6 eggs (both yolk and white) until they reach the consistency of water, for otherwise they will curdle; add the same amount of verjuice as eggs, and boil it with meat stock. While it cooks, cut the meat into thin slices and put 2 pieces in a bowl. Then pour the soup over it.

57. Impromptu sops. Take parsley and fry it in butter, then pour boiling water over it and bring it all to a boil. Add salt, and prepare sops as with any vegetable stock.

Aliter, if you have cold beef, slice it thinly and then grind a little bread moistened with verjuice and strain through cloth and set it in a dish and sprinkle it with powdered spices. Warm it over the coals. It serves three.

Aliter, on a fish day, simmer some almonds in water; then peel and grind them, moistening with warm water. Strain them and boil them with ginger powder and saffron. Serve with a slice of fried fish in each dish.

Aliter, on a meat day, take broth from the meat cauldron and bread soaked in degreased meat broth, then grind it with 6 eggs, strain, and put in a pot with fatty stock, spices, verjuice, vinegar, and saffron. Bring it to a boil once and serve in bowls.

Item. If you are in a hurry and should you find meat bouillon at an inn and decide to make pottage with it, add spices and bring it to a boil, then trickle in beaten eggs and serve.

Aliter, on a fish day, grind some bread and soak it in water, verjuice, and vinegar; set it on the fire. When it simmers, take it off the fire and add egg yolks. Replace it on the fire and warm it at low heat until it comes to a boil; add powdered spices and make your sops.

Aliter, boil a little bacon in a pot. When it is half done, slice a fresh mackerel and cook it with the bacon. Remove it from the fire and add minced parsley, then bring to a brisk boil and serve.

58. How to recognize a good cheese. Good cheese has six qualities: *Non Argus, nec Helena, nec Maria Magdalena, sed Lazarus, et Martinus, respondens pontifici:*

Not white like Helen,
Nor weeping, like Magdalen,
Not like Argus, but rather all blind,
And also heavy as an ox.
It stands up to the thumb's pressure,
And it should have a scaly rind.
Eyeless and tearless, and not white,
Crusted, firm, and heavy.

FIFTY-FIVE
Libre de Sent Soví

This is an anonymous Catalan cookbook written in 1324. At the time, before the plague, Catalonia not only dominated the western Mediterranean economically and politically but was a cultural leader for much of Europe. These dishes were often imitated elsewhere, and, of course, many also still exist in modern forms.

V

Half-Roast

If you want to make half-roast, put chicken on a spit. Then make broth of other chickens, or of the innards of those on the spit, and make it a good broth with salt pork; then take peeled almonds and make milk with them. Take out the livers and blend them with the milk. Set it to boil with good spices: pepper and ginger, cloves, cinnamon, and verjuice, flavor and white sugar; and let it boil a lot. When the roast chickens should be cooked, quarter them and let them boil in the sauce enough so you know they are cooked; and distribute into bowls with the chicken.

If you serve white dish, you can serve with this sauce the remaining [parts of] chickens, that is, heads, thighs, wings, and legs. However, fry them beforehand in the casserole dish with salt pork grease, before they are put into the sauce.

XIII

If You Want to Make Fish in Vinegar Sauce

If you want to make fish in vinegar sauce out of fried fish, make fish broth, put in onions, oil, salt and parsley, and cook it in a pot. Take almond milk made with the broth. Then take the fried

Joan Santanach, ed. *The Book of Sent Soví: Medieval Recipes from Catalonia*. Translated by Robin Vogelzang. Barcelona and Woodbridge, VA: Barcino Tamesis, 2008, pp. 53, 69, 83, 111, 115, 147, 179.

fish—and boiled fish, if you have any—and mince it with toasted bread soaked in vinegar; and if you have pine nuts, grind some. Set it to boil in a pot with good spices, verjuice and sweetening. After that take round onions that are four fingers thick and slice them thin, and fry them with oil that is scarcely boiling. Then, when the onion is fried, when it crunches a bit, put it in with the sauce when it boils, and some of the oil from frying, so it is not too noticeable; and flavor it with sweetening, verjuice, salt and spices. You can put in raisins ground with wine or vinegar, and put it on top of the hot fried fish. It should be cooled before it is served.

I have seen that with the seasonings, they ground toasted almonds and hazelnuts and toasted bread soaked in vinegar, and that they mixed it with wine and vinegar.

XX

Green Sauce

If you want to make green sauce, take parsley leaves, and wash the tender parts, and dry them in the sun, or without sun. Grind them well with cinnamon and ginger and cloves, pepper and toasted hazelnuts. Put in a good measure of each ingredient and taste it, and if you see one thing is more evident than another, balance it to be equal. And mix it with vinegar, so that the vinegar is more evident. And one can put in bread, toasted and soaked in vinegar. Put in honey or sugar for a delicate or sick person.

XXXIV

Almond Milk

If you want to make milk of boiled almonds, take a bowl of peeled almonds, and grind them, and then take the same amount of water as the almonds. Strain them with a good cloth, firmly, until no more liquid comes out. Put it in a pot to cook; put in white sugar. It should cook until it is quite thick.

If you want to serve it to a healthy man, put in salt and whole ginger roots.

XXXVI

Aubergines

If you want to make aubergines, boil them with salt and water. First, however, one cuts them into three or four parts lengthwise. When it has boiled a lot, take them out; choose those that you find are not as well boiled and press them firmly between two wooden plates. And then take those that are more cooked, and onion, parsley, mint, and marjoram, and chop it all together on a plate. Put eggs and grated cheese on a plate; then take raisins and cooked garlic. Grind it all together and mix in good spices. Then stuff each one [of the aubergine slices] with this [mixture]. Take an onion, and put it on the bottom of a casserole dish. The head of the aubergine goes at the bottom and the tail at the top. Take almond milk made with good broth, a little oil, and a little grease, and pour it over top. And it goes in the oven.

LII

Tender Chickpeas

If you want to prepare tender chickpeas, wash them well. Take almond milk, and cook them with the milk and oil and salt; and put in one or two onions scalded with boiling water. When they should be cooked, put in parsley, basil, marjoram and other good herbs, and a little ground ginger and a little sour grape juice. This is the way to cook them when they are tender, but not among the first.

If you want to prepare the most tender ones, boil the almond milk with oil, salt, and new onions, and the herbs listed above and ginger and sour grape juice. Put in the chickpeas, washed with hot water, and they'll be done right away.

In this way you can also prepare young broad beans; you can put in green coriander with some good spices, pepper, ginger, cinnamon and saffron.

LXVIII

Spinach

If you want to make spinach without water, take the spinach [leaves] and clean them well, and then wash them and make two or three pieces of them. Take a pot, and put in a large spoon of oil, or according to the number of those you will serve it to. Then squeeze them well and put them in the pot, and put in a little salt, but in a way so it is not too much, until they have melted, and cut them up.

FIFTY-SIX

De Honesta Voluptate

PLATINA (BARTOLOMEO SACCHI)

Platina was a humanist scholar and first librarian of the Vatican Library. This work was the first printed cookbook, appearing about 1470 in an undated edition. It is not entirely a cookbook, nor entirely by Platina. It is a book about the qualities of food drawn mostly from classical authorities into which is added an earlier manuscript cookbook by Maestro Martino of Como. The recipes sometimes clash with the medical advice, but otherwise it is a remarkable work of gastronomy. The recipes are also superb. Do look online at the excellent portrait of Platina by Melozzo da Forli as well as images of the first printed cookbook.

11. ON THE COOK

One should have a trained cook with skill and long experience, patient with his work and wanting especially to be praised for it. He should lack all filth and dirt and know in a suitable way the force and nature of meats, fish and vegetables so that he may understand what ought to be roasted, boiled, or fried. He should be alert enough to discern by taste what is too salty or too flat; if possible, he should be completely like the man from New Como [Martino], the prince of cooks of our age, from whom I have learned the art of cooking food. He should not be gluttonous or greedy, as was the Frenchman Marisius, so as not to appropriate and devour what his master was supposed to eat.

Platina (Bartolomeo Sacchi). *Platina: On Right Pleasure and Good Health*. Translated by Mary Ella Milham. Medieval and Renaissance Texts and Studies, Vol. 168. Tempe: Arizona Center for Medieval and Renaissance Studies, 1998, pp. 119–21, 157, 293.

12. ON SETTING A TABLE

One must set a table according to the time of year: in winter, in enclosed and warm places; in summer, in cool and open places. In spring, flowers are arranged in the dining room and on the table; in winter, the air should be redolent with perfumes; in summer, the floor should be strewn with fragrant boughs of trees, of vine, and of willow, which freshen the dining room; in autumn, let the ripe grapes, pears and apples hang from the ceiling. Napkins should be white and the tablecloths spotless, because, if they were otherwise, they would arouse squeamishness and take away the desire to eat. Let a servant scrub the knives and sharpen their edges so that diners will not be delayed by dullness of iron. The rest of the dishes should be scrubbed clean, whether they are earthen or silver, for this meticulous care arouses even a sluggish appetite.

13. ON SALT

The table needs salt so that the food will not seem bland, from which we call fatuous men stolid and insipid because they have no salt, that is, wit. The word for salt [*sal*] comes from the Greek word *hals* with the rough breathing *h* turned into *s*. The force of salt is fiery so that it contracts, dries and binds whatever bodies it touches. If dead flesh is salted in time, it is very well preserved, as we can see in hams and other salted meats. It is especially effective against certain ills, since it burns, combats, diminishes, and dissolves; however, it is not good for the stomach except for arousing the appetite. Its immoderate use also harms the liver, blood, and eyes very much. When it is daubed on certain sores or poison bites, it is effective. Salt which is going to be used on the table ought to be white and clean, like that from Volterra in Tuscany.

14. ON BREAD

Among the fruits of earth discovered for man's use, grain is the most useful. According to Celsus, its kinds are considered spelt, rice, pearl barley, starch, wheat, winter wheat, and the kind of spelt which the ancients called *adoreum,* from which we get the word "adore," so called because offerings of cakes made from *adoreum* were proffered to the gods. Nothing is more productive and pleasant or more nourishing than wheat, which nourishes much more if it is grown in the hills and not on the plain.

Barley is considered the noblest grain of all because it wants to be sown in dry, loose earth, because it matures quickly, and because of the slenderness of its stalk, it is cut before all other grains. Polenta and a sweetened broth are more advantageously made from it than from bread for those who are ill. I do not believe that the African winter wheat whose bread the ancients praised was in any way like that which our own age eats, because there is no kind of bread more unpalatable than this, and because it represses the appetite to no purpose.

Anyone, therefore, who does baking should use flour [*farina*] which is well-ground from wheat, although *farina* is so-called from *far,* ground grain. From this, he should separate the bran and the inferior flour with a very fine flour sieve, then put the flour, with warm water and some salt, on a baker's table closed in at the sides, as the people at Ferrara in Italy are accustomed to do. If you live in damp places and a bit of leaven is used, [the baker], with help from his associates, kneads to that consistency at which bread can be made fairly easily. Let the baker be careful not to put in too much or too little leaven, for, from the former, bread can acquire a sour taste, and, from the latter, it can become too heavy to digest and too unhealthy, since it binds the bowels. Bread should be well-baked in an oven and not used the same day, nor is it especially nourishing when made from very fresh wheat and if it is digested slowly.

15. ON SUGAR

Sugar comes not only from Arabia and India but also from Crete and Sicily. Pliny calls it the honey collected from cane. It is really fine when it is ground up, or even ground by the teeth. Surely, the whiter it is, the better, which it becomes through a long purification, whence we say it needs probably three or more days uncooked. Its force is warm and damp so that it is of good nourishment, is good for the stomach, and soothes whatever discomforts there are, if any. In persons who are choleric, however, it is easily converted into the dominant humor.

I think the ancients used sugar merely for medicinal purposes, and for that reason no mention is made of it among their foods. They were surely missing a great pleasure, for nothing given us to eat is so flavorless that sugar does not season it. Hence arose that proverb of frequent use: no kind of food is made more tasteless by adding sugar. By melting it, we make almonds (softened and cleaned in water), pine nuts, hazelnuts, coriander, anise, cinnamon, and many other things into sweets. The quality of sugar then almost crosses over into the qualities of those things to which it clings in the preparation.

41. Blancmange

Blancmange [*cibarium album*], which is more properly called *leucophagum,* you make in this way for twelve guests. Pound well in a mortar two pounds of almonds, soaked overnight in water and skinned; do this by sprinkling with a bit of water so they do not produce oil. Then grind in the same mortar the boned breast of capon, and add bread crust after it has been softened with verjuice or thin juice. Besides, add an ounce of ginger and a half-pound of sugar. Mix this all together and when it has been mixed, pass it through a meal sifter into a clean pot. Then let it boil on coals on a slow fire and stir often so it will not stick to the pot. When it has cooked, put in three ounces of rose water, and put it on the table either in the dishes where the meat is or separately, but in smaller dishes. If you decide to pour it over the capons so it may seem more elegant, sprinkle pomegranate seeds on top. But if you really want this divided into a double dish, color part with an egg yolk and saffron mixed together with a bit of verjuice, which I call broom from its color. Serve the remaining part, as it is white, as I have said, to your guests.

I have always preferred this to Apician condiments, nor is there any reason why the tastes of our ancestors should be preferred to our own, for even if we are surpassed by them in nearly all arts, nevertheless in taste alone we are not vanquished, for in the whole world there is no incentive to taste which has not been brought down, as it were, to the modern cooking school, where there is the keenest of discussion about the cooking of all foods. What a cook, oh immortal gods, you bestowed in my friend Martino of Como, from whom I have received, in great part, the things of which I am writing. You would say he is another Carneades if you were to hear him eloquently speaking ex tempore about the matters described above.

PART IX

Study Questions

1. Why did medieval people favor spices so much and dense flavor combinations of sweet, sour, and savory? Can you think of dishes like these we still enjoy?
2. How did an ingredient like almonds get to Iceland in the Middle Ages? What does it suggest about trade routes and the dispersion of cooking preferences in this period?
3. Why is it significant that the royal recipes of Taillevent appear in the bourgeois book of Le Menagier? In what way does this kind of social emulation drive the evolution of cooking?
4. What impact did the plague have on the European economy, and in what ways did it impact the culinary literature?
5. Are health and pleasure readily reconcilable when it comes to food? Does Platina succeed in his Renaissance program?

PART TEN

The Americas

On the eve of discovery by Europeans, two great civilizations flourished in the Americas, the Aztecs in Central Mexico and the Inca along the west coast of South America. There were many earlier great civilizations whose cultures were largely inherited by these two and, of course, dozens of other peoples throughout the two continents as well, but it was these two that had the greatest impact on world history and cuisine, primarily because of the ingredients they gave to the rest of the world. But we can also get a sense of what the cuisine of these people was like before contact through the few surviving written texts and, more importantly, through the accounts of the Spanish conquistadors. Of course, we must keep in mind that these accounts are biased and sometimes intentionally negative. The Spanish intended to rule and destroy indigenous religion and culture. But American cuisine survived for the most part, even when it adopted Old World plants and animals.

The capital of the Aztec Empire, Tenochtitlan, was a teeming metropolis boasting many markets, canals, and distribution of food on a scale comparable to any European city. Much food also came from afar as tribute from subject states. The staple grain here was maize (corn) processed in such a way that it provided a fairly complete nutritional package, especially when combined with beans and green vegetables. Processing, called *nixtamalization*, involved soaking the dried kernels in lye made from ashes or lime (calcium hydroxide), which caused the seed coat to swell. It could then be rubbed off by hand. The grains were then crushed on a saddle-shaped metate and made into dough, which could be flattened into tortillas or wrapped in corn husks and steamed for tamales. This is difficult work, but this wet processing meant that kitchen labor took place at home and by women, not in large-scale mills. Another interesting contrast to the Old World is the absence of large domesticated cattle. Some scholars have speculated that this left the Aztecs protein deficient and may have even led to cannibalism. In fact, cannibalism was a ritual practice, intended to feed the God Huitzilo-pochtli, and almost certainly not a major source of food. Moreover, the Aztecs had a bountiful supply of other animals for food, not least of which was the turkey.

Many other foods of world importance are native to America: starchy roots such as the sweet potato and potato, which come from the Andes. Amaranth was also a crucial staple, though banned by the Spanish because of the role it played in the Aztec religion. Not until the twentieth century would it gain widespread attention globally. Tomatoes, tomatillos, and chili peppers were and still are a major flavoring. The rapid spread of chilies across the globe in the early sixteenth century, from Sichuan to Hungary, from India to West Africa, is due partly to the fact that they are grown easily from seed without very specific requirements and therefore provide a universal and inexpensive flavoring—unlike pepper and other tropical spices.

Aztec society was highly stratified, with the emperor at the top, warriors and priests below, and common people ranged beneath. That customs filtered from the top down is suggested by accounts of the emperor's dining habits compared to those of merchants and other people. For example, the emperor was said to drink chocolate from a golden cup all day long. Other people drank as much as they could afford. At banquets they also followed hand-washing rituals and smoking tobacco at the end of the meal, much as did the emperor. In this respect, Aztec and European society were quite similar, and conquistador Bernal Díaz said the city reminded him of Venice.

The Aztecs were also quite abstemious, and, ideally, pulque (an alcoholic beverage made from agave) was only meant to be drunk on special occasions. One snippet of advice suggested, "You are to be prudent in drink, in food, for many things pertain to it. You are not to eat excessively . . . when you are eating you are not to be hasty, you are not to take excessively nor break up your tortillas. You are not to put a large amount in your mouth; you are not to swallow it unchewed. You are not to gulp like a dog." Actually, it was excessive eating and drinking of spirits, which the Spanish introduced, that the Aztecs believed led to widespread disease and destruction.

FIFTY-SEVEN

Popol Vuh

The Popol Vuh is a holy text of the Maya from the K'iche' Kingdom in Guatemala, which flourished before the Spanish conquest. It was handed down orally but written, possibly from a phonetic manuscript in the original language, in the eighteenth century by a Dominican friar, Francisco Ximénez. In it is a creation myth, though the gods get it wrong twice, first with people made of mud, then a second race made of wood, but without souls. They decide to destroy the second attempt. The method of their destruction, by the animals and implements they used in life, has a strange culinary form of revenge to it. In the final successful attempt, people are made from corn. This is a literal translation from K'iche' by Allen J. Christenson.

Spoke all their maize grinders,
Their griddles,

Their plates,
Their pots,

Their dogs,
Their grinding stones,

However many things,
All crushed their faces.

Allen J. Christenson, trans. *Popol Vuh: Literal Translation*. Alresford, UK, and New York: 2004. Published online by Mesoweb Publications, 2007. http://www.mesoweb.com/publications/Christenson/PV-Literal.pdf.

"Pain you did to us.
You ate us,

You now therefore,
We will eat you now,"

Said the their dogs,
Their turkeys to them.

This therefore the grinding stones:
"We were ground fine by you,

Every day,
Every day,

In the evening,
  At dawn,
Always,

Holi!
Holi!

Huki!
Huki!

Our faces
  By you.
  This then the first our service before your faces
You when first people.

This day therefore you shall try
Our strength.

We shall grind you like maize,
We shall grind also your flesh,"

Said the their grinding stones to them.
This therefore the their dogs said again when they spoke:

"Why because not you will give our food?
"Merely we look,

Merely also you throw us out hither,
You throw us also hither.

Raised up thither,
Our beating with sticks by you

When you eat.
Only thus you spoke to us.

Not we speak,
Not then therefore we received of you.

How not you understood?
You understood then therefore.

Behind you then therefore we were lost.
This day therefore you shall try

Our teeth
That are in our mouths.

We shall eat you,"
They said the dogs to them.

Then were crushed their faces.

This now therefore the their griddles,
Their pots, spoke again to them:

"Pain this
You did to us.

Sooty our mouths,
Sooty our faces.

Always we are thrown on its top fire.
  You burn us.
  Not pain we felt, you shall try it therefore.
We shall burn you," said the their pots.

All of them,
Were crushed their faces.

These the stones,
The their hearthstones,

Would flatten them,
Would come from fire,

Landed on their heads,
Pain was done to them.

FIFTY-EIGHT
Journal

CHRISTOPHER COLUMBUS

Christopher Columbus was first and foremost a merchant, not an explorer. He was trying to get to China and East Asia to trade for spices and other goods. His original journal was lost; but an edited version was made by Bartolome de las Casas, who was generally sympathetic with the admiral but later went on to champion Native American rights against the cruelties of the Spanish. In any case, it is clear that Columbus was desperate to find spices, and one wonders how he could have been so mistaken about some of them. He may have expected his report to make it back to Queen Isabella, and, of course, he did not want to return empty-handed.

FRIDAY, 2ND OF NOVEMBER

The Admiral decided upon sending two Spaniards, one named Rodrigo de Jerez, who lived in Ayamonte, and the other Luis de Torres, who had served in the household of the Adelantado of Murcia, and had been a Jew, knowing Hebrew, Chaldee, and even some Arabic. With these men he sent two Indians, one from among those he had brought from Guanahani, and another a native of the houses by the river-side. He gave them strings of beads with which to buy food if they should be in need, and ordered them to return in six days. He gave them specimens of spices, to see if any were to be found. Their instructions were to ask for the king of that land, and they were told what to say on the part of the Sovereigns of Castille, how they had sent the Admiral with letters and a present, to inquire after his health and establish friendship, favouring him in what he might desire from them. They were to collect

Christopher Columbus. *The Journal of Christopher Columbus*. Translated by Clements R. Markham. N.p.: Hakluyt Society, 1893.

information respecting certain provinces, ports, and rivers of which the Admiral had notice, and to ascertain their distances from where he was.

This night the Admiral took an altitude with a quadrant, and found that the distance from the equinoctial line was 42 degrees. He says that, by his reckoning, he finds that he has gone over 1,142 leagues from the island of Hierro. He still believes that he has reached the mainland.

SATURDAY, 3RD OF NOVEMBER

In the morning the Admiral got into the boat, and, as the river is like a great lake at the mouth, forming a very excellent port, very deep, and clear of rocks, with a good beach for careening ships, and plenty of fuel, he explored it until he came to fresh water at a distance of two leagues from the mouth. He ascended a small mountain to obtain a view of the surrounding country, but could see nothing, owing to the dense foliage of the trees, which were very fresh and odoriferous, so that he felt no doubt that there were aromatic herbs among them. He said that all he saw was so beautiful that his eyes could never tire of gazing upon such loveliness, nor his ears of listening to the songs of birds. That day many canoes came to the ships, to barter with cotton threads and with the nets in which they sleep, called *hamacas*.

SUNDAY, 4TH OF NOVEMBER

At sunrise the Admiral again went away in the boat, and landed to hunt the birds he had seen the day before. After a time, Martin Alonso Pinzon came to him with two pieces of cinnamon, and said that a Portuguese, who was one of his crew, had seen an Indian carrying two very large bundles of it; but he had not bartered for it, because of the penalty imposed by the Admiral on anyone who bartered. He further said that this Indian carried some brown things like nutmegs. The master of the *Pinta* said that he had found the cinnamon trees. The Admiral went to the place, and found that they were not cinnamon trees. The Admiral showed the Indians some specimens of cinnamon and pepper he had brought from Castille, and they knew it, and said, by signs, that there was plenty in the vicinity, pointing to the S.E. He also showed them gold and pearls, on which certain old men said that there was an infinite quantity in a place called *Bohio*, and that the people wore it on their necks, ears, arms, and legs, as well as pearls. He further understood them to say that there were great ships and much merchandise, all to the S.E. He also understood that, far away, there were men with one eye, and others with dogs' noses who were cannibals, and that when they captured an enemy they beheaded him and drank his blood.

The Admiral then determined to return to the ship and wait for the return of the two men he had sent, intending to depart and seek for those lands, if his envoys brought some good news touching what he desired. The Admiral further says: "These people are very gentle and timid; they go naked, as I have said, without arms and without law. The country is very fertile. The people have plenty of roots called *zanahorias* (yams), with a smell like chestnuts; and they have beans of kinds very different from ours. They also have much cotton, which they do not sow, as it is wild in the mountains, and I believe they collect it throughout the year, because I saw pods empty, others full, and flowers all on one tree. There are a thousand other kinds of fruits which it is impossible for me to write about, and all must be profitable." All this the Admiral says.

MONDAY, 5TH OF NOVEMBER

This morning the Admiral ordered the ship to be careened, afterwards the other vessels, but not all at the same time. Two were always to be at the anchorage, as a precaution; although he says that these people were very safe, and that without fear all the vessels might have been careened at the same time. Things being in this state, the master of the *Niña* came to claim a reward from the Admiral because he had found mastick, but he did not bring the specimen, as he had dropped it. The Admiral promised him a reward, and sent Rodrigo Sanchez and master Diego to the trees. They collected some, which was kept to present to the Sovereigns, as well as the tree. The Admiral says that he knew it was mastick, though it ought to be gathered at the proper season. There is enough in that district for a yield of 1,000 *quintals* every year. The Admiral also found here a great deal of the plant called aloe. He further says that the *Puerto de Mares* is the best in the world, with the finest climate and the most gentle people. As it has a high, rocky cape, a fortress might be built, so that, in the event of the place becoming rich and important, the merchants would be safe from any other nations. He adds: "The Lord, in whose hands are all victories, will ordain all things for his service. An Indian said by signs that the mastick was good for pains in the stomach."

TUESDAY, 6TH OF NOVEMBER

"Yesterday, at night," says the Admiral, "the two men came back who had been sent to explore the interior. They said that after walking 12 leagues they came to a village of 50 houses, were there were a thousand inhabitants, for many live in one house. These houses are like very large booths. They said that they were received with great solemnity, according to custom, and all, both men and women, came out to see them. They were lodged in the best houses, and the people touched them, kissing their hands and feet, marvelling and believing that they came from heaven, and so they gave them to understand. They gave them to eat of what they had. When they arrived, the chief people conducted them by the arms to the principal house, gave them two chairs on which to sit, and all the natives sat round them on the ground. The Indian who came with them described the manner of living of the Christians, and said that they were good people. Presently the men went out, and the women came sitting round them in the same way, kissing their hands and feet, and looking to see if they were of flesh and bones like themselves. They begged the Spaniards to remain with them at least five days." The Spaniards showed the natives specimens of cinnamon, pepper, and other spices which the Admiral had given them, and they said, by signs, that there was plenty at a short distance from thence to S.E., but that there they did not know whether there was any. Finding that they had no information respecting cities, the Spaniards returned; and if they had desired to take those who wished to accompany them, more than 500 men and women would have come, because they thought the Spaniards were returning to heaven. There came, however, a principal man of the village and his son, with a servant. The Admiral conversed with them, and showed them much honour. They made signs respecting many lands and islands in those parts. The Admiral thought of bringing them to the Sovereigns. He says that he knew not what fancy took them; either from fear, or owing to the dark night, they wanted to land. The ship was at the time high and dry, but, not wishing to make them angry, he let them go on their saying that they would return at dawn, but they never came back. The two Christians met with many people on the road going home, men and women with a half-burnt weed in their hands, being the herbs they are accustomed to smoke. They did not find villages on the road of more than five houses, all receiving them with the same reverence. They saw many kinds of trees, herbs, and sweet-smelling flowers; and birds of many different kinds, unlike those of Spain, except the partridges, geese, of which there are many, and singing nightingales. They saw no quadrupeds except the dogs that do not bark. The land is very fertile, and is cultivated with yams and several kinds of beans different from ours, as well as corn. There were great quantities of cotton gathered, spun, and worked up. In a single house they saw more than 500 *arrobas,* and as much as 4,000 *quintals* could be yielded every year. The Admiral said that "it did not appear to be cultivated, and that it bore all the year round. It is very fine, and has a large boll. All that was possessed by these people they gave at a very low price, and a great bundle of cotton was exchanged for the point of a needle or other trifle. They are a people," says the Admiral, "guileless and unwarlike. Men and women go as naked as when their mothers bore them. It is true that the women wear a very small rag of cotton-cloth, and they are of very good appearance, not very dark, less so than the Canarians. I hold, most serene Princes, that if devout religious persons were here, knowing the language, they would all turn Christians.

FIFTY-NINE

Montezuma's Banquet

BERNAL DÍAZ

Bernal Díaz was a conquistador who accompanied Cortes in his conquest of Mexico in 1521. This book is an eyewitness account by a man who took part in the story. This excerpt describes a banquet of the Aztec emperor Montezuma (or Motecusuma, as it is spelled in the account), just at the point when the Spaniards arrive in Tenochtitlan, present-day Mexico City. The most curious aspect of the account is that it sounds very much like the banquets Díaz would have been familiar with back in Europe, especially the ritual formalities, but also the entertainment with dwarves, the variety of dishes, and especially the account keeping by a steward. Either Díaz was projecting his own ideas and expectations onto the scene he witnessed, or remarkable similarities exist between these two disparate cultures.

Above 300 kinds of dishes were served up for Motecusuma's dinner from his kitchen, underneath which were placed pans of porcelain filled with fire, to keep them warm. Three hundred dishes of various kinds were served up for him alone, and above 1000 for the persons in waiting. He sometimes, but very seldom, accompanied by the chief officers of his household, ordered the dinner himself, and desired that the best dishes and various kinds of birds should be called over to him. We were told that the flesh of young children, as a very dainty bit, was also set before him sometimes by way of a relish. Whether there was any truth in this we could not possibly discover; on account of the great variety of dishes, consisting in fowls, turkeys,

Bernal Díaz. *The Memoirs of the Conquistador Bernal Diaz del Castillo.* Vol. 1. Translated by John Ingram Lockhart. London: J. Hatchard and Son, 1844, pp. 229–31. Published online by Project Gutenberg, 2010. http://www.gutenberg.org/files/32474/32474-h/32474-h.htm.

pheasants, partridges, quails, tame and wild geese, venison, musk swine, pigeons, hares, rabbits, and of numerous other birds and beasts; besides which there were various other kinds of provisions, indeed it would have been no easy task to call them all over by name. This I know, however, for certain, that after Cortes had reproached him for the human sacrifices and the eating of human flesh, he issued orders that no dishes of that nature should again be brought to his table. I will, however, drop this subject, and rather relate how the monarch was waited on while he sat at dinner. If the weather was cold a large fire was made with a kind of charcoal made of the bark of trees, which emitted no smoke, but threw out a delicious perfume; and that his majesty might not feel any inconvenience from too great a heat, a screen was placed between his person and the fire, made of gold, and adorned with all manner of figures of their gods. The chair on which he sat was rather low, but supplied with soft cushions, and was beautifully carved; the table was very little higher than this, but perfectly corresponded with his seat. It was covered with white cloths, and one of a larger size. Four very neat and pretty young women held before the monarch a species of round pitcher, called by them Xicales, filled with water to wash his hands in. The water was caught in other vessels, and then the young women presented him with towels to dry his hands. Two other women brought him maise-bread baked with eggs. Before, however, Motecusuma began his dinner, a kind of wooden screen, strongly gilt, was placed before him, that no one might see him while eating, and the young women stood at a distance. Next four elderly men, of high rank, were admitted to his table; whom he addressed from time to time, or put some questions to them. Sometimes he would offer them a plate of some of his viands, which was considered a mark of great favour. These grey-headed old men, who were so highly honoured, were, as we subsequently learnt, his nearest relations, most trustworthy counsellors and chief justices. Whenever he ordered any victuals to be presented them, they ate it standing, in the deepest veneration, though without daring to look at him full in the face. The dishes in which the dinner was served up were of variegated and black porcelain, made at Cholulla. While the monarch was at table, his courtiers, and those who were in waiting in the halls adjoining, had to maintain strict silence.

After the hot dishes had been removed, every kind of fruit which the country produced was set on the table; of which, however, Motecusuma ate very little. Every now and then was handed to him a golden pitcher filled with a kind of liquor made from the cacao, which is of a very exciting nature. Though we did not pay any particular attention to the circumstance at the time, yet I saw about fifty large pitchers filled with the same liquor brought in all frothy. This beverage was also presented to the monarch by women, but all with the profoundest veneration.

Sometimes during dinner time, he would have ugly Indian humpbacked dwarfs, who acted as buffoons and performed antics for his amusement. At another time he would have jesters to enliven him with their witticisms. Others again danced and sung before him. Motecusuma took great delight in these entertainments, and ordered the broken victuals and pitchers of cacao liquor to be distributed among these performers. As soon as he had finished his dinner the four women cleared the cloths and brought him water to wash his hands. During this interval he discoursed a little with the four old men, and then left table to enjoy his afternoon's nap.

After the monarch had dined, dinner was served up for the men on duty and the other officers of his household, and I have often counted more than 1000 dishes on the table, of the kinds above mentioned. These were then followed, according to the Mexican custom, by the frothing jugs of cacao liquor; certainly 2000 of them, after which came different kinds of fruit in great abundance.

Next the women dined, who superintended the baking department; and those who made the cacao liquor, with the young women who waited upon the monarch. Indeed, the daily expense of these dinners alone must have been very great!

Besides these servants there were numerous butlers, house-stewards, treasurers, cooks, and superintendents of maise-magazines. Indeed there is so much to be said about these that I scarcely knew where to commence, and we could not help wondering that everything was done with such perfect order. I had almost forgotten to mention, that during dinner-time, two other young women of great beauty brought the monarch small cakes, as white as snow, made of eggs and other very nourishing ingredients, on plates covered with clean napkins; also a kind of long-shaped bread, likewise made of very substantial things, and some pachol, which is a kind of wafer-cake. They then presented him with three beautifully painted and gilt tubes, which were filled with liquid amber, and a herb called by the Indians tabaco. After the dinner had been cleared away and the singing and dancing done, one of these tubes was lighted, and the monarch took the smoke into his mouth, and after he had done this a short time, he fell asleep.

About this time a celebrated cazique, whom we called Tapia, was Motecusuma's chief steward: he kept an account of the whole of Motecusuma's revenue, in large books of paper which the Mexicans call *Amatl*. A whole house was filled with such large books of accounts.

SIXTY

General History of the Things of New Spain

BERNARDINO DE SAHAGÚN

Bernardino de Sahagún was a priest among the second wave of clerics sent to the New World in the early sixteenth century. His job was to convert the Aztecs and gain sympathy for the process of conversion, but he also made meticulous records of their festivals and religious practices. They are so complete that many people regard him as the first ethnographer. His report was so thorough that when it reached the hands of King Philip II of Spain, the king feared it might be published and used to revive pagan worship and so he had it carefully locked up, where the book remained for several centuries. It wasn't published until the nineteenth century. Note in Bernardino de Sahagún's description of festivals among ordinary people how they mirror the feasts of the emperor described by Díaz.

The fourth month was called Veytocoztli (according to Clavijero Huytozoztli). On the first day of this month they celebrated the feast in honor of the god Cinteutl, who was regarded as the god of corn (maize). To honor him they fasted four days previous to the festival.

Veytocoztli

For this festival they put branches of reed-mace by the doors of their houses and sprinkled them with blood from their ears or from the shin-bone. (This might also mean the blackheads which draw blood when dug out). The nobles and also the wealthy adorned

Bernardino de Sahagún. *A History of Ancient Mexico: Anthropological, Mythological, and Social, 1547–1577.* Translated by Fanny R. Bandelier. Nashville, TN: Fisk University Press, 1932. Reprint by Detroit: Blaine Ethridge Books, 1971, pp. 53–54, 74–75, 175–76, 244–46.

their whole houses besides the reed-mace with branches or wreaths which are called acxoatl, and likewise they placed wreaths around the gods each one had in his house, and put flowers before them.

After this they went into the cornfields and brought back some cornstalks (which were still small), arranged them with flowers, and then went to put them in front of their gods in the oratory they call Calpulli. They also put food before them.

After having done this in the different city districts (wards) they went to the Cú (temple) of the goddess whom they called Chicomecoatl and there, in front of her, they represented sham battles, and all the girls carried ears of corn of the previous year on their backs and walked in procession up to the goddess to present them to her; then they took them back home with them as blessed objects. From this corn they gathered the seed for the following year's sowing. They also used such ears of corn as "hearts" of the corn bins, because they had been blessed. Of the dough called azoalli they made the image of this goddess in the court-yard of her Cú, and in front of this they placed as offerings all the different kinds of corn, of beans and of chian, the leaves of which are eaten as vegetable and the seeds are used for flavouring, like sesame, because they believed her to be the creator and giver of these things, which are the food-staples of these people.

The Ceremonies and Sacrifices Celebrated in the Second Month Called Tlacaxipeoaliztli

On the last day of the said month they celebrated a very solemn feast in honor of the god called Xippetototec, as well as in honor of Vitzilopuchtli. During this festival they killed all the captives they had, men, women and children. Before killing them, however, they celebrated a great many ceremonies, which were as follows: on the eve of the feast after midday they began a very solemn dance, and during the entire night they watched over the captives who were to die, in the house called Calpulco. Here they pulled their hair off the top of the head. This ceremony was performed close to the fire at midnight, when they also drew blood from their own ears to offer it to the gods, a thing they always did at that hour. At daybreak they took their captives to where they were to die, which was in the temple of Vitzilopuchtli. They were killed by the ministers (priests) of the temple in the manner told before, then they flayed them all, and for that reason this festival was called Tlacaxipeoalizcli, which means "skinning of men who, in turn, were called xipeme, or by another name tototecti; the first one of these names means "skinned" or "flayed," the second "dead in honor of the god Totec." The owners of the captives delivered them to the priests at the foot of the Cú, who then dragged them up the steps, each priest his own prisoner, holding them by the hair, toward the sacrificial stone where they were to be killed, tearing out the heart of each one, which then was offered to the sun, as stated before. They then threw them down the steps, where subsequently, other priests flayed them. This all was done in the Cú (temple) of Vitzilopuchtli. The hearts they had thus torn out of the bodies and had offered to the sun and the other gods were thrown into a wooden bowl; these hearts were called quauhnoctli, and those who died after having their hearts torn out were called quauhteca; after the bodies had been flayed by the old men who were called quauquacuilli, they carried them to the calpulco, where the owner of each captive had made his promise or vow, and the body was divided (cut up), and a thigh sent to Mochtecuzoma for him to eat, the rest being distributed to other chieftains or relatives, who went to eat it in the house of the man who had captured the victim. They cooked that meat with corn and gave each one a piece of it with its broth in a bowl with the cooked corn; they called that stew tlacatlaolli; after the meal followed general drunkenness.

How They Honored Vitzilopuchtli as a God

Likewise, they say that the day they venerated him by celebrating the festival of Panquetzaliztli, they took wild amaranth-seeds and cleaned them very well, picking out the straws and separating other seeds from them, which are called petzicatl and tezcaoauhtli; then they ground them very carefully. When the flour was very light, they mixed a dough, and with this formed the body of Vitzilopuchtli. On the following day a man, called Quetzalcoatl, shot a dart with a stone point (arrow-head) at the body of this said Vitzilopuchtli, and this (stone arrow-point) stuck in his heart, the king or chieftain being present (at this ceremony), and also a favorite (or intimate) of Vitzilopuchtli, who was called Teuoa. There were also present four high priests, furthermore four teachers of young men who were in charge of the instruction of youth, its school being called Telpuchtlotoque. All these (personages) were present when the body of Vitzilopuchtli was killed; after having killed it, they broke it into pieces, since it had been made of dough of wild amaranth-seeds. The heart of Vitzilopuchtli was taken for (to give to) the chief or king, and the whole body and some pieces that were like the (mouth and) lips of Vitzilopuchtli they divided in equal parts among the natives of Mexico and Tlaltelulco. Those of Mexico who were the priests of the said Vitzilopuchtli and were called Calpules, took four pieces of the body and an equal amount was taken by those of Tlaltelulco for the men of the same calling (order, i.e., priests). In this manner they divided among them the four pieces of the body of Vitzilopuchtli; they belonged to the Indians of two city districts (wards) and to the priests of the idols who were called Calpules, all of whom, every year, ate the body of Vitzilopuchtli in the order and custom they had. Every one ate a piece of the body of this god, and those who ate it were unmarried men (bachelors), and they said that it was the body of god called Teuqüalo, and those who received and ate the body of Vitzilopuchtli were called the ministers (priests) of god.

CHAPTER XXXVI

About the Festivity Celebrated on Account of Christenings, the Order of Service, and the Hard Drinking Done on Such Occasions.

We continue the description of such baptismal feasts. On the day of the feast the guests gathered in the house of their host and were seated in their order; that is, each one had his place according to his rank. At once those who were in charge began to serve the food that had been selected for the occasion. With the plates they first put smoke-sticks (canes) in front of each of the guests, gave them flowers to hold in their hands, placed wreaths on their heads and garlands of roses around their necks. At once all the guests began to inhale the smoke of the canes and to smell the perfume of the flowers, then the servants entered with the food and served each one according to his appetite, placing it in front of him wherever he sat. The first order was a sort of willow baskets containing various kinds of bread, and next to these chiquihuites as many little square boxes (generally of paper), with different kinds of meat- or fishstews. Before the guests began to eat the food placed before them, each one took a mouthful to throw into the fire (of the hearth) in honor of the god Tlaltecutli; after this they all ate. At the end of the dinner they gave the left-overs to their own servants as also the little paper boxes and the baskets, called chiquivites (or chiquihuites). Then came those who served the cocoa or chocolate, placing before each guest a xicara (bowl) of it, and at the same time they gave each a little stick, which they call aquavitl. The left-over cocoa was also given to their servants (by the guests).

After having satiated themselves with the cocoa, they remained a little while seated, resting, but some, displeased with the food and drink offered, would rise at once in anger and, murmuring against the feast and their host, would go home cross (angry). If anyone on the part of the host noticed it he would tell the latter at once, and he would then invite these people to dinner on the next day in order to appease them. This second day invitation was called apealo because this was the end of the feast.

The women, who were eating in another part of the house, were not given cocoa to drink, but a certain kind of gruel powdered over with various kinds of chilmolli. The old men and women gathered (again) that night to drink pulque and they got drunk. In order to produce this drunkenness, they placed before them a large pitcher or jar of pulque, and the one who served them poured from it into a jicara and gave each one according to his rank until there was none left. Sometimes they served the kind of pulque called iztacuctli, which means white pulque, which is (made of) the sap of maguey; at other times they served imitation pulque of water and honey boiled with the root of maguey and which they called ayuctli, meaning pulque made with water, and this the host had prepared and in readiness several days before the feast. When the servant found that his charges (the old men and women) did not become intoxicated, he began to serve again, this time from the left or opposite side on, beginning with those lowest in rank. Once they were all intoxicated they began to sing; some sang and cried, others sang to give pleasure. Each one would sing whatever he liked and in the key he fancied best, and none of them harmonized; some sang out loud, others softly, merely humming to themselves. There were some who, instead of singing, talked and laughed, told funny stories, and they would laugh out loud if they heard a good joke.

In this manner private festivities were celebrated upon invitation from a host, for one reason or another.

CHAPTER XXXVII

About the Celebration of Baptismal Festivities of Today Which Are Very
Similar to the Ancient Customs, About the Way Banquets Were Offered in Ancient Times
and in Our Era, among Chieftains, Prominent Men and Merchants. Also About the Rest
of the Days of the Sign Cequauhtli.

The manner in which today christenings are celebrated is the same as it was in ancient times with the exception that then the chiefs, prominent men, merchants and the wealthy people made their invitations each one after his own taste and fashion. All, however, invited a great many guests, and they had head waiters and servants to serve their guests; the first named were to see to it that all were honored according to their rank, in giving them flowers as well as in serving the meal and presenting them with blankets and belts. For this purpose a large amount of food was prepared, a great number of blankets, of belts, flowers and smoke-canes were assembled, so that all the guests would be provided plentifully with everything. No guest was to be insulted or affronted, neither was the host to be ashamed of his banquet, but rather be praised and honored on account of the order in which it was conducted and the great abundance of viands and presents offered his guests. As these latter knew this, they had hopes that they would partake of all the things at the banquet, but they also wished that there would be no lack of anything, so that their host might not fall into disgrace, and that nobody would have cause for complaint of the host nor of the banquet itself.

As the day of the banquet approached, all the servants and the overseers and head stewards hired for this occasion were solicitously preparing all the necessary items, adorning the courts and roads with reed-mace and flowers, sweeping and levelling the said courts and entrances to the house where the banquet was to be held. Some carried water, some swept and sprinkled the grounds or strew them with sand; some hung up the reed-mace where the dance was to be held. Many were busy dressing chickens or killing and singeing dogs, some roasted and others boiled chickens, still others filled the little canes with perfume (for the so-called smoke-canes). Old women and girls were busy making the many varieties of tamales, for some of these were made of bean-flour, others with meat. Some of the women washed the boiled corn, others peeled off the eye of it which is hard, in order to make finer bread. Still others carried water or cracked cocoa beans or ground them and mixed the cooked maize with the cocoa, and many were cooking soups and stews. As soon as the day dawned they spread petates (mats) everywhere and also seats, and they also piled hay on the floor entwining the edges of it so that they looked like blankets of soft herbs. Thus they prepared everything as required and it was not even necessary for the master to give orders or to see what they were doing, for it was all done by the servants, or rather, waiters and their officials (head waiters), who were also the ones who distribute the smoke-canes, the flowers and the food. Also by those who make the cocoa and lift it in the air (to cool it?) and serve it to those who are (entitled) to drink it. There were also special people detailed to personal service of the guests customary among chiefs, prominent men, merchants and the wealthy in general. The poorer classes made their feasts as they were best able, in a poor, rustic way, for they have little and do not know much about manners. They give flowers that cost little, and the smoke-canes they give their guests usually have served once.

SIXTY-ONE
Utopia

THOMAS MORE

Thomas More (1478–1535) was a scholar and statesman, who lost his head for his allegiance to the Catholic Church in the reign of Henry VIII during the English Reformation. Utopia, meaning nowhere, was an ideal society modeled after an account of Native Americans in what is today Venezuela, written by Amerigo Vespucci. As a Christian Humanist, More's intention was moral reform, to get Europeans to examine themselves by comparison with a simple and pure people living without property and in peace, much as had Jesus and his disciples. More's solutions for eating communally, ironically influenced real Utopian experiments, even one in South America.

They have in the country in all parts of the shire, houses or farms builded, well appointed and furnished with all sorts of instruments and tools belonging to husbandry. These houses be inhabited of the citizens, which come thither to dwell by course. No household or farm in the country hath fewer than forty persons, men and women, beside two bondmen, which be all under the rule and order of the good-man and the good-wife of the house, being both very sage and discreet persons. And every thirty farms or families have one head ruler, which is called a Phylarch, being as it were a head bailiff. Out of everyone of these families or farms cometh every year into the city twenty persons which have continued two years before in the country. In their place so many fresh be sent thither out of the city, which of them that have been there a year already, and be therefore expert and cunning in husbandry, shall be instructed and taught; and they the next year shall teach others. This order is used, for fear

---

Thomas More. *Sir Thomas More's Utopia*. London: Chatto & Windus, 1908, pp. 108–11, 129–38, 158–71.

that either scarceness of victuals or some other like incommodity should chance through lack of knowledge, if they should be altogether new and fresh and unexpert in husbandry. This manner and fashion of yearly changing and renewing the occupiers of husbandry, though it be solemn and customably used, to the intent that no man shall be constrained against his will to continue long in that hard and sharp kind of life, yet many of them have such a pleasure and delight in husbandry, that they obtain a longer space of years. These husbandmen plough and till the ground, and breed up cattle, and make ready wood, which they carry to the city, either by land or by water, as they may most conveniently. They bring up a great multitude of pullets and that by a marvellous policy. For the hens do not sit upon the eggs; but by keeping them in a certain equal heat they bring life into them, and hatch them. The chickens, as soon as they be come out of the shell, follow men and women instead of the hens.

They bring up very few horses; nor none but very fierce ones; and that for none other use or purpose, but only to exercise their youth in riding and feats of arms. For oxen be put to all the labour of ploughing and drawing. Which they grant to be not so good as horses at sudden brunt, and (as we say) at a dead lift; but yet they hold opinion, that oxen will abide and suffer much more labour and pain than horses will. And they think that they be not in danger and subject unto so many diseases, and that they be kept and maintained with much less cost and charge; and finally that they be good for meat when they be past labour.

They sow corn only for bread. For their drink is either wine made of grapes, or else of apples or pears, or else it is clear water; and many times mead made of honey or liquorice sodden in water, for thereof they have great store. And though they know certainly (for they know it perfectly indeed), how much victuals the city with the whole country or shires round about it doth spend; yet they sow much more corn, and breed up much more cattle, than serveth for their own use; and the overplus they part among their borderers. Whatsoever necessary things be lacking in the country, all such stuffs they fetch out of the city; where without any exchange they easily obtain it of the magistrates of the city. For every month many of them go into the city on the holiday. When their harvest day draweth near and is at hand, then the Phylarchs, which be the head officers and bailiffs of husbandry, send word to the magistrates of the city what number of harvest men is needful to be sent to them out of the city. The which company of harvest-men, being there ready at the day appointed, almost in one fair day despatcheth all the harvest work.

OF THEIR LIVING AND MUTUAL CONVERSATION TOGETHER

But now will I declare how the citizens use themselves one towards another; what familiar occupying and entertainment there is among the people; and what fashion they use in the distribution of everything. First, the city consisteth of families; the families most commonly be made of kindreds. For the women, when they be married at a lawful age, they go into their husbands' houses. But the male children, with all the whole male offspring, continue still in their own family and be governed of the eldest and ancientest father, unless he dote for age; for then the next to him in age, is put in his room.

But to the intent the prescribed number of the citizens should neither decrease, nor above measure increase, it is ordained that no family, which in every city be six thousand in the whole, besides them of the country, shall at once have fewer children of the age of fourteen years or thereabout than ten, or more than sixteen, for of children under this age no number can be appointed. This measure or number is easily observed and kept, by putting them that in fuller families be above the number into families of smaller increase. But if chance be that in the whole city the store increase above the just number, therewith they fill up the lack of other cities. But if so be that multitude throughout the whole Island pass and exceed the due number, then they choose out of every city certain citizens, and build up a town under their own laws in the next land where the inhabitants have much waste and unoccupied ground, receiving also of the inhabitants to them, if they will join and dwell with them. They, thus joining and dwelling together, do easily agree in one fashion of living, and that to the great wealth of both the peoples. For they so bring the matter about by their laws, that the ground, which before was neither good nor profitable for the one nor for the other, is now sufficient and fruitful enough for them both. But if the inhabitants of that land will not dwell with them, to be ordered by their laws, then they drive them out of those bounds, which they have limited and appointed out for themselves. And if they resist and rebel, then they make war against them. For they count this the most just cause of war, when any people holdeth a piece of ground void and vacant to no good nor profitable use, keeping other from the use and possession of it, which notwithstanding by the law of nature ought thereof to be nourished and relieved. If any chance do so much diminish the number of any of their cities, that it cannot be filled up again without the diminishing of the just number of the other cities (which they say chanced but twice since the beginning of the land through a great pestilent plague), then they make up the number with citizens fetched out of their own foreign towns; for they had rather suffer their foreign towns to decay and perish than any city of their own Island to be diminished.

But now again to the conversation of the citizens among themselves. The eldest (as I said) ruleth the family. The wives be ministers to their husbands, the children to their parents, and, to be short, the younger to their elders. Every city is divided into four equal parts. In the midst of every quarter there is a market place of all manner of things. Thither the works of every family be brought in to certain houses. And every kind of thing is laid up several in barns or store-houses. From hence the father of every family or every householder fetcheth whatsoever he and his have need of, and carrieth it away with him without money, without exchange, without any gage or pledge. For why should anything be denied unto him; seeing there is abundance of all things, and that it is not to be feared lest any man will ask more than he needeth? For why should it be thought that man would ask more than enough, which is sure never to lack? Certainly, in all kinds of living creatures, either fear of lack doth cause covetousness and ravine, or in man only pride, which counteth it a glorious thing to pass and excel other in the superfluous and vain ostentation of things. The which kind of vice among the Utopians can have no place.

Next to the market places that I spake of stand meat-markets, whither be brought not only all sorts of herbs, and the fruits of trees, with bread, but also fish, and all manner of four-footed beasts, and wild fowl that be man's meat. But first the filthiness and ordure thereof is clean washed away in the running river, without the city, in places appointed, meet for the same purpose; from thence the beasts brought in killed, and cleaned washed by the hands of their bondmen. For they permit not their free citizens to accustom themselves to the killing of beasts; through the use whereof they think that clemency, the gentlest affection of our nature, doth by little and little decay and perish. Neither they suffer anything that is filthy, loathsome, or uncleanly, to be brought into the city, lest the air by the stench thereof infected and corrupt, should cause pestilent diseases.

Moreover every street hath certain great large halls set in equal distance one from another, every one known by a several name. In these halls dwell the Syphogrants. And to every one of the same halls be appointed thirty families, of either side fifteen. The stewards of every hall at a certain hour come into the meat-markets, where they receive meat according to the number of their halls.

But first and chiefly of all, respect is had to the sick that be cured in the hospitals. For in the circuit of the city, a little without the walls, they have four hospitals; so big, so wide, so ample, and so large, that they may seem four little towns; which were devised of that bigness, partly to the intent the sick, be they never so many in number, should not lie too throng or strait, and therefore uneasily and incommodiously; and partly that they which were taken and holden with contagious diseases, such as be wont by infection to creep from one to another, might be laid apart far from the company of the residue. These hospitals be so well appointed, and with all things necessary to health so furnished; and moreover so diligent attendance through the continual presence of cunning physicians is given, that though no man be sent thither against his will, yet notwithstanding there is no sick person in all the city, that had not rather lie there than at home in his own house. When the steward of the sick hath received such meats as the physicians hath prescribed, then the best is equally divided among the halls, according to the company of every one, saving that there is had a respect to the Prince, the bishop, the Tranibores, and to ambassadors, and all strangers, if there be any, which be very few and seldom. But they also, when they be there, have certain houses appointed and prepared for them.

To these halls at the set hours of dinner and supper cometh all the whole Syphogranty or ward, warned by the noise of a brazen trumpet; except such as be sick in the hospitals, or else in their own houses. Howbeit, no man is prohibited or forbid, after the halls be served, to fetch home meat out of the market to his own house; for they know that no man will do it without a cause reasonable. For though no man be prohibited to dine at home, yet no man doth it willingly, because it is counted a point of small honesty. And also it were a folly to take the pain to dress a bad dinner at home, when they may be welcome to good and fine fare so nigh hand at the hall. In this hall all vile service, all slavery and drudgery, with all laboursome toil and business, is done by bondmen. But the women of every family by course have the office and charge of cookery, for seething and dressing the meat, and ordering all things thereto belonging. They sit at three tables or more, according to the number of their company. The men sit upon the bench next the wall, and the women against them on the other side of the table; that if any sudden evil should chance to them, as many times happeneth to women with child, they may rise without trouble or disturbance of anybody, and go thence into the nursery.

The nurses sit several alone with their young sucklings in a certain parlour appointed and deputed to the same purpose, never without fire and clean water, nor yet without cradles; that when they will, they may lay down the young infants, and at their pleasure take them out of their swathing-clothes and hold them to the fire, and refresh them with play. Every mother is nurse to her own child, unless either death or sickness be the let. When that chanceth, the wives of the Syphogrants quickly provide a nurse. And that is not hard to be done. For they that can do it do proffer themselves to no service so gladly as to that. Because that there this kind of pity is much praised; and the child that is nourished ever after taketh his nurse for his own natural mother. Also among the nurses sit all the children that be under the age of five years. All the other children of both kinds, as well boys as girls, that be under the age of marriage, do either serve at the tables, or else if they be too young thereto, yet they stand by with marvellous silence. That which is given to them from the table they eat, and other several dinner-time they have none. The Syphogrant and his wife sitteth in the midst of the high table, forasmuch as that is counted the most honourable place, and because from thence all the whole company is in their sight. For that table standeth overthwart the over end of the hall. To them be joined two of the ancientest and eldest; for at every table they sit four at a mess. But if there be a church standing in that Syphogranty or ward, then the priest and his wife sitteth with the Syphogrant, as chief in the company. On both sides of them sit young men, and next unto them again old men. And thus throughout all the house equal of age be set together, and yet be mixt with unequal ages. This they say was ordained, to the intent that the sage gravity and reverence of the elders should keep the youngers from wanton licence of words and behaviour; forasmuch as nothing can be so secretly spoken or done at the table, but either they that sit on the one side or on the other must needs perceive it. The dishes be not set down in order from the first place, but all the old men (whose places be marked with some special token to be known) be first served of their meat, and then the residue equally. The old men divide their dainties, as they think best, to the younger that sit of both sides them. Thus the elders be not defrauded of their due honour, and nevertheless equal commodity cometh to every one.

They begin every dinner and supper of reading something that pertaineth to good manners and virtue. But it is short, because no man shall be grieved therewith. Hereof the elders take occasion of honest communication, but neither sad nor unpleasant. Howbeit they do not spend all the whole dinnertime themselves with long and tedious talks, but they gladly hear also the young men; yea and do purposely provoke them to talk, to the intent that they may have a proof of every man's wit and towardness or disposition to virtue, which commonly in the liberty of feasting doth shew and utter itself. Their dinners be very short; but their suppers be somewhat longer; because that after dinner followeth labour; after supper sleep and natural rest; which they think to be of no more strength and efficacy to wholesome and healthful digestion. No supper is passed without music; nor their banquets lack no conceits nor junkets. They burn sweet gums and spices for perfumes and pleasant smells, and sprinkle about sweet ointments and waters; yea they leave nothing undone that maketh for the cheering of the company. For they be much inclined to this opinion: to think no kind of pleasure forbidden, whereof cometh no harm.

Thus therefore and after this sort they live together in the city; but in the country they that dwell alone, far from any neighbours, do dine and sup at home in their own houses. For no family there lacketh any kind of victuals, as from whom cometh all that the citizens eat and live by. They think: that all our actions, and in them the virtues themselves, be referred at the last to pleasure, as their end and felicity.

Pleasure they call every motion and state of the body or mind, wherein man hath naturally delectation. Appetite they join to nature, and that not without a good cause. For like as not only the senses, but also right reason, coveteth whatsoever is naturally pleasant; so that it may be gotten without wrong or injury, not letting or debarring a greater pleasure, nor causing painful labour; even so those things that men by vain imagination do feign against nature to be pleasant (as though it lay in their power to change the things as they do the names of things), all such pleasures they believe to be of so small help and furtherance to felicity, that they count them great let and hindrance; because that, in whom they have once taken place, all his mind they possess with a false opinion of pleasure: so that there is no place left for true and natural delectations. For there be many things, which of their own nature contain no pleasantness: yea, the most part of them much grief and sorrow, and yet through the perverse and malicious flickering enticements of lewd and unhonest desires, be taken not only for special and sovereign pleasures, but also be counted among the chief causes of life.

In this counterfeit kind of pleasure they put them that I spake of before; which, the better gown they have on, the better men they think themselves; in the which thing they do twice err. For they be no less deceived in that they think their gown the better, than they be in that they think themselves the better. For if you consider the profitable use of the garment, why should wool of a finer spun thread be thought better, than the wool of a coarse spun thread? Yet they, as though the one did pass the other by nature, and not by their mistaking, advance themselves and think the price of their own persons thereby greatly increased. And therefore the honour, which in a coarse gown they durst not have looked for, they require as it were of duty for their finer gown's sake. And if they be passed by without reverence, they take it angrily and disdainfully.

And again, is it not a like madness to take a pride in vain and unprofitable honours? For what natural or true pleasure dost thou take of another man's bare head or bowed knees? Will this ease the pain of thy knees, or remedy the frenzy of thy head? In this image of counterfeit pleasure, they be of a marvellous madness, which for the opinion of nobility rejoice much in their own conceit, because it was their fortune to come of such ancestors, whose stock of long time hath been counted rich (for now nobility is nothing else), specially rich in lands. And though their ancestors left them not one foot of land, or else they themselves have pissed it against the walls, yet they think themselves not the less noble therefore of one hair.

In this number also they count them that take pleasure and delight (as I said) in gems and precious stones and think themselves almost gods, if they chance to get an excellent one; specially of that kind which in that time of their own countrymen is had in highest estimation. For one kind of stone keepeth not his price still in all countries, and at all times. Nor they buy them not but taken out of the gold and bare; no, nor so neither, before they have made the seller, to swear that he will warrant and assure it to be a true stone and no counterfeit gem. Such care they take lest a counterfeit stone should deceive their eyes in the stead of a right stone. But why should'st thou not take even as much pleasure in beholding a counterfeit stone, which thine eye cannot discern from a right stone? They should both be of like value to thee, even as to a blind man.

What shall I say of them that keep superfluous riches, to take delectation only in the holding, and not in the use or occupying thereof? Do they take true pleasure, or else be they deceived with false pleasure? Or of them that be in a contrary vice, hiding the gold which they shall never occupy, nor peradventure never see more; and whilst they take care lest they shall lose it, do lose it indeed? For what is it else, when they hide it in the ground, taking it both from their own use, and perchance from all other men's also? And yet thou, when thou hast hid thy treasure, as one out of all care, hoppest for joy. The which treasure if it should chance to be stolen, and thou, ignorant of the theft, shouldst die ten years after; all that ten years' space that thou livedst, after thy money was stolen, what matter was it to thee whether it had been taken away, or else safe as thou leftst it? Truly both ways like profit came to thee.

To these so foolish pleasures they join dicers, whose madness they know by hearsay and not by use; hunters also, and hawkers. For what pleasure is there (say they) in casting the dice upon a table; which thou hast done so often, that if there were any pleasure in it, yet the oft use might make thee weary thereof? Or what delight can there be, and not rather displeasure, in hearing the barking and howling of dogs? Or what greater pleasure is there to be felt, when a dog followeth an hare, than when a dog followeth a dog? For one thing is done in both; that is to say, running; if thou hast pleasure therein. But if the hope of slaughter, and the expectation of tearing in pieces the beast doth please thee, thou shouldst rather be moved with pity to see a silly innocent hare murdered of a dog; the weak of the stronger; the fearful of the fierce; the innocent of the cruel and unmerciful. Therefore all this exercise of hunting, as a thing unworthy to be used of free men, the Utopians have rejected to their butchers; to the which craft (as we said before) they appoint their bondmen. For they count hunting the lowest, vilest, and most abject part of butchery; and the other parts of it more profitable and more honest, as which do bring much more commodity; and do kill beasts only for necessity. Whereas the hunter seeketh nothing but pleasure of the silly and woeful beast's slaughter and murder. The which pleasure in beholding death, they think, doth rise in the very beasts, either of a cruel affection of mind, or else to be changed in continuance of time into cruelty, by long use of so cruel a pleasure. These therefore and all suchlike, which is innumerable, though the common sort of people doth take them for pleasures, yet they, seeing there is no natural pleas- antness in them, do plainly determine them to have no affinity with true and right pleasure. For as touching that they do commonly move the sense with delectation (which seemeth to be a work of pleasure) this doth nothing diminish their opinion. For not the nature of the thing, but their perverse and lewd custom is the cause hereof; which causeth them to accept bitter or sour things for sweet things; even as women with child in their vitiate and corrupt taste, think pitch and tallow sweeter than any honey. Howbeit no man's judgment, depraved and corrupt, either by sickness or by custom, can change the nature of pleasure, more than it can do the nature of other things.

They make divers kinds of true pleasures. For some they attribute to the soul, and some to the body. To the soul they give intelligence, and that delectation that cometh of the contem- plation of truth. Hereunto is joined the pleasant remembrance of the good life past.

The pleasure of the body they divide into two parts. The first is when delectation is sensibly felt and perceived: which many times chanceth by the renewing and refreshing of those parts, which our natural heat drieth up: this cometh by meat and drink, and sometimes whiles those things be voided, whereof is in the body over-great abundance. This pleasure is felt when we do our natural easement, or when we be doing the act of generation, or when the itching of any part is eased with rubbing or scratching. Sometimes pleasure riseth, exhibiting to any member nothing that it desireth, nor taking from it any pain that it feeleth; which for all that tickleth and moveth our senses with a certain secret efficacy, but with a manifest motion, and turneth them to it; as is that which cometh of music.

The second part of bodily pleasure they say is that which consisteth and resteth in the quiet and upright state of the body. And that truly is every man's own proper health, intermingled and disturbed with no grief. For this, if it be not letted nor assaulted with no grief, is delectable of itself, though it be moved with no external or outward pleasure. For though it be not so plain and manifest to the sense, as the greedy lust of eating and drinking, yet nevertheless many take it for the chiefest pleasure. All the Utopians grant it to be a right great pleasure, and as you would say the foundation and ground of all pleasures; as which even alone is able to make the state and condition of life delectable and pleasant; and it being once taken away, there is no place left for any pleasure. For to be without grief, not having health, that they call insensibility and not pleasure. The Utopians have long ago rejected and condemned the opinion of them, which said that steadfast and quiet health (for this question also hath been diligently debated among them) ought not therefore to be counted a pleasure, because they say it cannot be presently and sensibly perceived and felt by some outward motion. But, of the contrary part, now they agree almost all in this, that health is a most sovereign pleasure. For seeing that in sickness (say they) is grief, which is a mortal enemy to pleasure, even as sickness is to health, why should not then pleasure be in the quietness of health? For they say it maketh nothing to this matter, whether you say that sickness is a grief, or that in sickness is grief; for all cometh to one purpose. For whether health be a pleasure itself, or a necessary cause of pleasure, as fire is of heat, truly both ways it followeth, that they cannot be without pleasure that be in perfect health. Furthermore, whiles we eat (say they), then health, which began to be appaired, fighteth by the help of food against hunger. In the which fight whilst health by little and little getteth the upper hand, that same proceeding, and (as ye would say) that outwardness to the wonted strength ministereth that pleasure, whereby we be so refreshed. Health therefore, which in the conflict is joyful, shall it not be merry when it hath gotten the victory? But as soon as it hath recovered the pristine strength, which thing only in all the fight it coveted, shall it incontinent be astonished? Nor shall it not know nor embrace that own wealth and goodness? For that it is said health cannot be felt, this, they think, is nothing true. For what man waking, say they, feeleth not himself in health, but he that is not? Is there any man so possessed with stonish insensibility, or with the sleeping sickness, that he will not grant health to be acceptable to him and delectable? But what other thing is delectation than that which by another name is called pleasure?

They embrace chiefly the pleasures of the mind. For them they count the chiefest and most principal of all. The chief part of them they think doth come of the exercise of virtue, and conscience of good life. Of these pleasures that the body ministereth they give the pre-eminence to health. For the delight of eating and drinking, and whatsoever hath any like pleasantness, they determine to be pleasures much to be desired, but no otherwise than for health's sake.

For such things of their own proper nature be not pleasant, but in that they resist sickness privily stealing on. Therefore, like as it is a wise man's part rather to avoid sickness, than to wish for medicines, and rather to drive away and put to flight careful griefs, than to call for comfort; so it is much better not to need this kind of pleasure, than in feeling the contrary grief to be eased of the same. The which kind of pleasure if any man take for his felicity, that man must needs grant, that then he shall be in most felicity, if he live that life which is led in continual hunger, thirst, itching, eating, drinking, scratching, and rubbing. The which life how not only foul it is, but also miserable and wretched, who perceiveth not? These doubtless be the basest pleasures of all, as impure and imperfect. For they never come but accompanied with their contrary griefs. As with the pleasure of eating is joined hunger, and that after no very equal sort. For of these two, the grief is both the more vehement, and also of longer continuance. For it riseth before the pleasure, and endeth not until the pleasure die with it.

Wherefore such pleasures they think not greatly to be set by, but in that they be necessary. Howbeit they have delight also in these, and thankfully knowledge the tender love of mother nature, which with most pleasant delectation allureth her children to that, which of necessity they be driven often to use. For how wretched and miserable should our life be, if these daily griefs of hunger and thirst could not be driven away, but with bitter potions, and sour medicines; as the other diseases be, wherewith we be seldomer troubled? But beauty, strength, nimbleness, these as peculiar and pleasant gifts of nature, they make much of. But those pleasures that be received by the ears, the eyes, and the nose, which nature willeth to be proper and peculiar to man (for no other kind of living beasts doth behold the fairness and the beauty of the world, or is moved with any respect of savours, but only for the diversity of meats, neither perceiveth the concordant and discordant distances of sounds and tunes) these pleasures (I say) they accept and allow, as certain pleasant rejoicings of life. But in all things this cautel they use, that a less pleasure hinder not a bigger, and that the pleasure be no cause of displeasure; which they think to follow of necessity, if the pleasure be un-honest. But yet to despise the comeliness of beauty, to waste the bodily strength, to turn nimbleness into sluggishness, to consume and make feeble the body with fasting, to do injury to health, and to reject the other pleasant motions of nature (unless a man neglect these his commodities, whilst he doth with a fervent zeal procure the wealth of others, or the common profit, for the which pleasure forborne he is in hope of a greater pleasure of God): else for a vain shadow of virtue, for the wealth and profit of no man, to punish himself, or to the intent he may be able courageously to suffer adversity, which perchance shall never come to him: this to do they think it a point of extreme madness, and a token of a man cruelly minded towards himself, and unkind towards nature, as one so disdaining to be in her danger, that he renounceth and refuseth all her benefits.

This is their sentence and opinion of virtue and pleasure. And they believe that by man's reason none can be found truer than this, unless any godlier be inspired into man from heaven. Wherein whether they believe well or no, neither the time doth suffer us to discuss, neither it is now necessary. For we have taken upon us to shew and declare their lores and ordinances, and not to defend them.

But this thing I believe verily: howsoever these decrees be, that there is in no place of the world neither a more excellent people, neither a more flourishing commonwealth. They be light and quick of body, full of activity and nimbleness, and of more strength than a man would judge them by their stature, which for all that is not too low. And though their soil be not very fruitful, nor their air very wholesome, yet against the air they so defend them with temperate diet, and so order and husband their ground with diligent travail, that in no country is greater increase and plenty of corn and cattle, nor men's bodies of longer life, and subject or apt to fewer diseases. There, therefore, a man may see well and diligently exploited and furnished, not only those things which husbandmen do commonly in other countries; as by craft and cunning to remedy the barrenness of the ground; but also a whole wood by the hands of the people plucked up by the roots in one place and set again in another place. Wherein was had regard and consideration not of plenty but of commodious carriage; that wood and timber might be nigher to the sea, or the rivers, or the cities. For it is less labour and business to carry grain far by land than wood. The people be gentle, merry, quick, and fine witted, delighting in quietness, and, when need requireth, able to abide and suffer much bodily labour. Else they be not greatly desirous and fond of it; but in the exercise and study of the mind they be never weary.

PART X

Study Questions

1. Think about how many foods you eat regularly were introduced in the Old World from America in this period.
2. What was Columbus really intending to accomplish in his voyage of 1492? Where did he think he was going, and what did he bring back to Spain to impress Queen Isabella?
3. Judging from the accounts of the conquistadors and early colonists, what do the food ways of the Aztecs reveal about their social structure?
4. Why were the records of Aztec festivals and foods they ate, in particular amaranth, hidden from both Aztecs and Spaniards after the conquest?
5. What kinds of medicinal plants did Aztecs use, and how did their system of medicine differ from the Spanish?

PART ELEVEN

Era of Nation-States 1500–1650

Several factors—all of which relate directly to the history of food—denote the beginning of the modern era: first, the discovery of the New World by Columbus; second, the Protestant Reformation; and third, the development of the modern nation-state. We might add other developments as well such as a resurgence of the population in Europe, growth of the economy, and direct trade to the East.

The original motive for exploration was, in fact, to reach China and the Spice Islands. Portugal took the lead, first heading down the coast of West Africa, venturing to the southernmost tip and out into the Indian Ocean. Eventually the Portuguese created a direct trade route to India as well as the Moluccas in what is now Indonesia, the source of nutmeg and cloves. They also traded directly with China and Japan and set up small trading posts throughout the area. Thus, they ultimately cut out the Venetians and Arab middlemen. Not that the price of spices lowered, though. The Portuguese maintained a monopoly and kept the price high, though spices arrived in much greater volume. This allowed people of middling ranks to imitate their superiors and use spices lavishly, and, of course, the cookbooks of the sixteenth century reflect this. In the long run, because of their ubiquity, spices lost their role as a marker of status, and by the latter seventeenth century they were increasingly marginalized in cuisine. The same goes for sugar, which was banished to the dessert course.

Spices were, of course, the original impetus for Columbus to seek a westerly route to Asia, along with gold and other luxuries he expected to find there. To his dying day, he believed that he had found land adjacent to Asia, not a separate continent thousands of miles away. His journal is very revealing, and many passages indicate that he was almost desperate to find botanical specimens he could bring back to impress the monarchs of Spain. He could not, however, have imagined the stupendous impact some of the foods he found would have.

Tomatoes and corn did not catch on for quite some time in Europe but eventually became foundational ingredients. American species of beans—navy beans, pinto beans, and black beans—however, were adopted immediately, primarily because a bean-eating tradition was already established. Quite the opposite was the case with the potato, which derived from the Andes and wasn't eaten much in Europe for several centuries. The impact of European plants, animals, and diseases was just as dramatic. Wheat, cattle, pigs, and countless Old World plants were introduced to the Americas. The diseases brought by the conquistadors were devastating and, in fact, made the conquest possible in the first place.

The Protestant Reformation is the next factor that designated this period as early modern. This was not merely the splintering of the universal Catholic Church into numerous denominations, but equally a food story. The Swiss Reformation was actually incited by eating sausages in Lent, which was defended by the Zurich prelate Ulrich Zwingli, who insisted that the New Testament contained no food prohibitions at all. Moreover, he criticized the doctrine of the Eucharist, in which the bread and wine are miraculously transformed into the flesh and blood of Jesus. If this were true, then communion would be a kind of cannibalism. Zwingli insisted, as is clear from the metaphorical language Jesus always used, that in the Last Supper he was merely asking his disciples to remember him when they eat and drink, and the phrase "this is my body" should not be taken literally. The Reformation, begun by Luther, was also important for breaking down the complex fasting rules and what were deemed quasi-pagan festivals. Monasticism was abolished in Protestant countries, as was the celibate priesthood. The liturgy was also translated into the vernacular. Most importantly, especially in the Calvinist or Reform tradition, a new austere attitude toward food proliferated. Pleasures of the flesh, and especially the extremes of fasting and feasting, were to be replaced with eating merely to maintain the body, without superfluous enticements.

Finally, political and demographic changes at the turn of the sixteenth century had a broad impact on the history of food. The nation-state as we know it—with contiguous borders, plenipotentiary jurisdiction, and the ability to set nationwide policies—came into being. Not that medieval states were unable or unwilling to institute food regulations such as fixed prices and wages, but the early modern state was able to do it more effectively, and there was greater need to do so since the swelling population grew increasingly dangerous and unruly. In general, as the population grew, demand for food rose, prices rose, and the poor became poorer. Peasant food became stigmatized, and ways of eating according to class became more sharply pronounced. Different ways of eating to match the stratification of society were also articulated: eating to maintain health, eating to express power and opulence, and eating—or not eating—to fortify the spirit. In other words, eating habits were divided not merely into rich and poor but into many different eating cultures in between. The culinary literature of this period reflects these divergent cultures, and it also reflects distinctively national recipes and eating habits.

For this entire section, images of market scenes such as those by Vincenzo Campi or Joachim Beuckelaer are particularly apt. Giuseppe Arcimboldo is also very amusing.

SIXTY-TWO

De Civilitate Morum Puerilium (On Good Manners for Boys)

DESIDERIUS ERASMUS

Desiderius Erasmus was the most famous scholar of the early sixteenth century, a humanist, Christian translator, commentator, and correspondent with everyone of interest in his day. This little tract was written for young boys' proper behavior, this selection specifically about table manners. Much has been made of the appearance of guidebooks like this, and presumably a growing demand for them matched the social mobility of the day and the increasing numbers of people having to pass at court. Perhaps there was also, as has been argued, an overall pervasive influence of the nation-state in curbing violence through polite behavior.

4 / ON BANQUETS

At banquets there should be joviality but no wantonness. Never sit down without having washed and without first trimming your nails lest any dirt stick to them and you are called ῥυποκόνδυλος "dirty-knuckled"; before sitting down you should have urinated in private, or defecated if need be; and if your belt happens to be too tight it is prudent to slacken the buckle little—an action that would be inelegant at table. When wiping your hands, wipe away at the same time whatever troubles your mind, for it is bad manners to be sad at a banquet or to sadden anyone else. If bidden to say grace, compose your expression and hands as befits the solemn office, looking towards either the one first in order of precedence at the banquet

Desiderius Erasmus. "De Conscribidendis Episotlis Formula de Civilitate" [On Good Manners for Boys]. In *Collected Works of Erasmus*. Vol. 25. *Literary and Educational Writings 3*. Edited by J. K. Sowards. Toronto: University of Toronto Press, 1985, pp. 280–86.

or the image of Christ, if one should be there, genuflecting at the name of Jesus and the Virgin Mary. If this duty has been delegated to someone else, listen and make your responses with no less reverence. Gladly yield precedence in seating to another, and decline courteously when invited to a place of greater honour. If, however, someone in authority should make repeated and pressing demands for this, comply modestly, so that you do not, through courtesy, appear intransigent. When sitting down have both hands on the table, not clasped together, nor on the plate. It is bad manners to have one or both hands on one's lap as some do. It is permissible for the elderly and convalescent to lean one or both elbows on the table; but this, as practised by some affected courtiers who consider their every action elegant is something to be avoided, not imitated. Meanwhile, be careful not to be a nuisance by nudging the person beside you with your elbow or kicking the person opposite you. Fidgeting in one's seat, shifting from side to side, gives the appearance of repeatedly breaking wind or of trying to do so. The body should, therefore, be upright and evenly balanced. If given a napkin, put it over either the left shoulder or the left forearm. When you are at table with persons of note, comb your hair and take off your cap, unless the custom of the area decrees otherwise, or one whose rank it would be impolite not accede to requests it. It is the custom among some peoples for boys to stand bareheaded and take their food at the end of the table of their elders. In such societies a boy should not approach the table unless bidden nor should remain until the end of the banquet, but having satisfied his hunger and removed his plate, he should bow and salute the guests, especially the most distinguished among them. The cup and small eating knife, duly cleaned, should be on the right-hand side, the bread on the left. Grasping the bread in the palm of the hand and breaking it with the fingertips is an affected practice which should be left to certain courtiers. You should cut it properly with your knife, not tearing off the crust or cutting it away from both sides as this smacks of affectation. The ancients were in the habit at every banquet of piously treating bread as something sacred and it is from this that the present custom has derived of kissing the bread if it happens to fall on the ground.

To begin a meal with drinking is the hallmark of a drunkard who drinks not from need but from habit. Such a practice is not only morally degrading but also injurious to bodily health. One should not start drinking as soon as one has a spoonful of soup, much less so after taking some milk. For a boy to drink more than twice or at most three times in the course of a banquet is neither seemly nor healthful. He should have his first drink at some time during the second course of the meal, especially if it is a dry one; his second, towards the close of the banquet. He should take it in moderate sips, and not gurgle it down sounding like a horse. Both wine and beer (which is no less intoxicating than wine) are as injurious to a boy's health as they are harmful to his character. Water is suitable for the vigour of youth, or if the nature of the region or some other reason prevents his drinking water a boy should drink a light beer, or nonpotent wine diluted with water. Otherwise the wages of addiction to undiluted wine are decaying teeth, bloated cheeks, impaired eyesight, mental dulness—in short, premature old age. Chew your food before you drink and do not raise the cup to your lips without first wiping them with a napkin or cloth, especially if someone offers you his cup or when drinking from the common cup. It is discourteous to look askance at others while you are drinking, just as it is impolite to turn your neck round like a stork lest a drop remain at the bottom of the cup. You should courteously acknowledge someone toasting you with his cup, and touching your own cup with your lips sip a little and pretend to drink: this will satisfy a polite man simply playing the buffoon. When someone boorishly presses you to drink, promise to reply when you have grown up.

Some people have scarcely seated themselves comfortably before they thrust their hands into the dishes. That is the behaviour of wolves or of those who, as the proverb puts it, devour meat from the pot before the sacrifices are made. Do not be the first to touch food set on the table, not only because that convicts you of greed, but because it does, on occasion, involve danger, since someone who takes a mouthful of burning hot food without first testing it is forced either to spit it out, or, if he swallows it, to scald his gullet—in either event appearing both foolish and pitiful. Some degree of delay is necessary so that a boy becomes accustomed to controlling his appetite. With such an end view, Socrates never let himself drink from the first wine bowl of the evening even when he was an old man. If seated with his elders, a boy should be the last to reach for his plate—and only when he has been invited to do so. It is boorish to plunge your hands into sauced dishes. You should take what you want with a knife or fork; nor should you select from the entire dish as epicures do but should take whatever portion is in front of you—as you may learn from Homer who frequently employs this line: Οἱ δ' επ' ονε ίαθ' ετοίμα προκείμενα χειραζ ιαλλον ί "They put forth their hands to the dishes lying ready before them." But if that portion also is extremely choice, then you should leave it for someone else and take the next piece. Just as it is, therefore, a sign of intemperance to thrust your hand into every part of the dish, so it is equally impolite to turn the dish so that the choicer morsels come to you. If someone else offers you a choicer portion of food, you should demur a little before accepting, but after cutting off a small portion for yourself you should offer the remainder to the giver or share it with your neighbour. What cannot be taken with the fingers should be taken on your plate. If someone offers you a piece of cake or pie take it on a spoon or plate or take what is offered on a spoon and, placing the food on your plate, return the spoon. If what is given is rather fluid, take it on a spoon for tasting and return the spoon after wiping it on a napkin. It is equally impolite to lick greasy fingers or to wipe them on one's tunic: you should wipe them with a napkin or cloth. To consume whole pieces of food at a gulp is for storks and buffoons. If a portion is cut by someone else, it is impolite to hold out your hand or plate before the carver has offered the portion, lest you appear to be snatching what has been prepared for someone else. What is offered should be taken in three fingers or by holding out your plate. If what is offered does not agree with you be careful not to use the comic character Clitophon's words: "I cannot, sir!" but rather thank him courteously. For this is the most polite form of refusal. If the person persists in urging it on you, say respectfully either that it does not agree with you or that you want nothing more.

The technique of carving should be learnt from the earliest years, and not performed over-elaborately as some do, but politely and properly. For the shoulder is carved in one way, the haunch in another, the neck in another the ribs in another; a capon in one way, a pheasant in another, a partridge in another, and a duck in another; so that to teach them one by one would be time-consuming and not worth the trouble. The following can be given as a general guide: it is excessively fastidious to carve off from every portion what is pleasing to your palate. It is rude to offer someone what you have half eaten yourself; it is boorish to redip half-eaten bread into the soup; just as it is disgusting to spit out chewed food and put it on your plate: if you happen to have eaten something that cannot be swallowed, you should discreetly turn away and toss it somewhere. It is discourteous to pick up again half-eaten food or bones once these have been deposited on the plate. Do not throw bones or similar left-overs under the table to litter the floor, or toss them onto the table cloth, or replace them in the serving dish, but put them at the side of your plate or in the dish which some people provide as a receptacle for left-overs. To offer food from the table to other people's dogs is put down to a lack of tact; it is even more tactless to stroke them at the banquet. It is ridiculous to pick an eggshell clean with finger-nails or thumb, to do so by inserting one's tongue is even more ridiculous; the polite way is to use a small knife. To gnaw bones is for a dog; good manners requires them to be picked with a small knife. Three fingers thrust into the salt-cellar is, by common jest, said to be the sign of the boor. The salt you require should be taken on a small knife. If the salt-cellar is some distance away, the plate should be held out to obtain some. To lick a plate or dish to which some sugar or other sweet substance has adhered is for cats, not for people. One should first cut up one's meat into small portions on the plate and then add some bread and chew them for some time before swallowing. That is conducive not only to good manners but also to good health. Some rend rather than eat their food, just like those who, as the saying goes, are shortly to be marched off to prison. Such gorging should be left to brigands. Some stuff so much at one time into their mouth that their cheeks swell like a pair of bellows. Others open their jaws so widely in chewing that they produce a noise like pigs. Some in their voracity, breathe heavily through the nose as if they were being strangled. It is neither polite nor safe to drink or speak with one's mouth full. Continuous eating should be interrupted now and again with stories. Some people eat or drink without stopping not because they are hungry or thirsty but because they cannot otherwise moderate their gestures, unless they scratch their head, or pick their teeth, or gesticulate with their hands, or play with their dinner knife, or cough, or clear their throat, or spit. Such habits, even if originating in a sort of rustic shyness, have the appearance of insanity about them. When you have to listen to the conversations of others and you are not given an opportunity to speak, you should conceal any sign of boredom. It is impolite to sit at table rapt in thought. You may, however, observe some people so withdrawn into their private thoughts that they neither hear what others are saying nor are aware that they are eating, and if you call them by name they give the appearance of being roused from sleep—so completely absorbed are they in the dishes. It is bad manners to let your eyes roam around observing what each person is eating, and it is impolite to stare intently at one of the guests. It is even worse to look shiftily out of the corner of your eye at those on the same side of the table; and it is the worst possible form to turn your head right round to see what is happening at another table. It is bad taste for anyone, but much more so for a boy, to gossip about an indiscretion of word or deed some-one has committed when in his cups. When seated with his elders a boy should never speak unless the occasion demands it or someone invites him to do so. He should laugh moderately at wittiness but never at improprieties; he should not frown, however, if the person who has uttered them is of superior rank, but so control his expression that he appears either not to have heard them or at least not to have understood them. Silence is becoming in women but even more so in boys.

Some people reply before the speaker has finished what he has to say, so that their unrelated response makes them a laughing-stock and gives rise to the old proverb, "I was looking for sickles but they said they did not have any spades." This is taught by the wisest of kings who makes it a sign of stupidity to answer before you hear: he who has not understood does not listen. If he has not fully grasped what a person is saying he should keep silent for a time until the speaker offers to repeat what he has said. Should he fail to do so and presses for a reply, the boy should politely beg his pardon and ask him to repeat what he has said. When a question has been understood he should pause for a moment and then answer briefly and agreeably. Nothing should be blurted out at a banquet that might cloud the spirit of merriment. It is wrong to defame the character of those not present; nor should one's personal sorrow be unburdened to another on such an occasion. It is impolite and shows ingratitude toward your host to find fault with what is set before you. If the banquet is being given at your expense, while it is polite to apologize for the humble quality of the fare, to praise or recall the cost of each item takes the edge off the guests' appetite at once. Finally, if someone through inexperience commit some *faux pas* at a banquet, it should be politely passed over rather than mocked. One should feel at ease during a party. It is a base act, as Horace says, to expose to the light of day something that someone lets slip at dinner without thinking. Pay no heed to what is done or said there, putting it down to the wine: μισῶ μνάμονα συμπόταν "I detest a drinking companion who remembers all." If the banquet goes on later than is suitable for a boy and seems to be slipping into debauchery, as soon as you fully satisfy your needs, take yourself off either surreptitiously or after begging to be excused. Those who compel boys to fast are, in my opinion, no better than those who stuff them with too much food. For fasting undermines the growth of a young body, while too much food destroys the vigour of the mind. Moderation, however, must be learnt right from the start. A boy's body should be replenished without being filled to satiety, through frequent rather than heavy meals. Some do not realize that they are full unless their belly is so distended that they are in danger of bursting or unless they discharge their burden by vomiting. Those who habitually allow the very young to sit at banquets that last far into the night show a complete disregard for the well-being of children. If, therefore, you have to rise from a banquet that has gone on for too long, take up your plate with its left-overs and bow to the man who seems to be the most distinguished of the guests, then to the others as a group, and take your leave, but promise to return shortly lest you appear to have left frivolously or out of impoliteness. On your return, wait to see if anything is required or sit respectfully at the table waiting to see if someone asks for something. If you place anything on the table or remove it make sure you do not soak someone's clothing with sauce. When you are going to snuff out a candle, first remove it from the table and immediately dip the wick in sand or stamp it with your shoe to prevent any distasteful smell assailing the nostrils. If offering or pouring something see that you do not do it with your left hand. When called to give a vote of thanks compose your expression showing that you are ready until the guests finally fall silent and the chance to speak presents itself. Meanwhile your gaze should be respectfully and firmly directed towards the master of ceremonies.

SIXTY-THREE
Food Laws

ULRICH ZWINGLI

Zwingli was a clergyman in Zurich when the fasting laws were openly broken by a printer and his workmen by eating sausages during Lent. Zwingli defended the printer with this sermon, citing biblical passages that show there are no food regulations in Christianity. With the Bible as his guide, he would be a leader of the Swiss Reformation as well as other churches that followed this theological tradition, the Dutch, Scots, and Puritans in England and New England. Look at images online of Pieter Brueghel's depiction of The Battle of Carnival and Lent.

To all pious Christians at Zurich, I, Huldreich Zwingli, a simple herald of the Gospel of Christ Jesus, wish the grace, mercy, and peace of God.

DEARLY Beloved in God, after you have heard so eagerly the Gospel and the teachings of the holy Apostles, now for the fourth year, teachings which Almighty God has been merciful enough to publish to you through my weak efforts, the majority of you, thank God, have been greatly fired with the love of God and of your neighbour. You have also begun faithfully to embrace and to take unto yourselves the teachings of the Gospel and the liberty which they give, so that after you have tried and tasted the sweetness of the heavenly bread by which man lives, no other food has since been able to please you. And, as when the children of Israel were led out of Egypt, at first impatient and unaccustomed to the hard journey, they sometimes in vexation wished themselves back in Egypt, with the food left there, such as garlic, onions, leeks, and flesh-pots, they still entirely forgot such complaints when they had come into the promised land and had tasted its luscious fruits: thus also some among us leapt and jumped

---

Ulrich Zwingli. *Ulrich Zwingli, Early Writings*. Edited by Samuel Macauley Jackson. Eugene, OR: Wipf and Stock, 1999, pp. 71–76.

unseemly at the first spurring—as still some do now, who like a horse neither are able nor ought to rid themselves of the spur of the Gospel;—still, in time they have become so tractable and so accustomed to the salt and good fruit of the Gospel, which they find abundantly in it, that they not only avoid the former darkness, labour, food, and yoke of Egypt, but also are vexed with all brothers, that is, Christians, wherever they do not venture to make free use of Christian liberty. And in order to show this, some have issued German poems, some have entered into friendly talks and discussions in public rooms and at gatherings; some now at last during this fast—and it was their opinion that no one else could be offended by it—at home, and when they were together, have eaten meat, eggs, cheese, and other food hitherto unused in fasts. But this opinion of theirs was wrong; for some were offended, and that, too, from simple good intentions; and others, not from love of God or of his commands (as far as I can judge), but that they might reject that which teaches and warns common men, and they might not agree with their opinions, acted as though they were injured and offended, in order that they might increase the discord. The third part of the hypocrites of a false spirit did the same, and secretly excited the civil authorities, saying that such things neither should nor would be allowed, that it would destroy the fasts, just as though they never could fast, if the poor labourer, at this time of spring, having to bear most heavily the burden and heat of the day, ate such food for the support of his body and on account of his work. Indeed, all these have so troubled the matter and made it worse, that the honourable Council of our city was obliged to attend to the matter. And when the previously mentioned evangelically instructed people found that they were likely to be punished, it was their purpose to protect themselves by means of the Scriptures, which, however, not one of the Council had been wise enough to understand, so that he could accept or reject them. What should I do, as one to whom the care of souls and the Gospel have been entrusted, except search the Scriptures, particularly again, and bring them as a light into this darkness of error, so that no one, from ignorance or lack of recognition, injuring or attacking another come into great regret, especially since those who eat are not triflers or clowns, but honest folk and of good conscience? Wherefore, it would stand very evil with me, that I, as a careless shepherd and one only for the sake of selfish gain, should treat the sheep entrusted to my care, so that I did not strengthen the weak and protect the strong. I have therefore made a sermon about the choice or difference of food, in which sermon nothing but the Holy Gospels and the teachings of the Apostles have been used, which greatly delighted the majority and emancipated them. But those, whose mind and conscience is defiled, as Paul says [Titus, i., 15], it only made mad. But since I have used only the above-mentioned Scriptures, and since those people cry out none the less unfairly, so loud that their cries are heard elsewhere, and since they that hear are vexed on account of their simplicity and ignorance of the matter, it seems to me to be necessary to explain the thing from the Scriptures, so that every one depending on the Divine Scriptures may maintain himself against the enemies of the Scriptures. Wherefore, read and understand; open the eyes and the ears of the heart, and hear and see what the Spirit of God says to us.

First, Christ says, Matthew xv., 17, "What goes in at the mouth defileth not the man," etc. From these words any one can see that no food can defile a man, providing it is taken in moderation and thankfulness. That this is the meaning, is showed by the fact that the Pharisees became vexed and angry at the word as it stands, because according to Jewish law they took great account of the choice of food and abstinence, all of which regulations Christ desired to do away with in the New Testament. These words of Christ, Mark speaks still more clearly, vii., 15: "There is nothing from without a man, that entering into him can defile him; but the things which come out from him, those are they that defile the man." So the meaning of Christ is, all foods are alike as far as defilement goes: they cannot defile at all.

Secondly, as it is written in the Acts of the Apostles, x., 10, when Peter was in Joppa (now called Jaffa), he went one day upon the housetop at the sixth hour, and desired to pray. He became hungry and wished to eat; and when the servants were making ready, he fell into a trance and saw heaven opened and a vessel descending as it were a great linen cloth held together by the four corners and let down upon earth, in which cloth were all four-footed animals, wild beasts, and creeping and flying creatures. Then a voice spoke to him, saying: "Arise, Peter, kill and eat." But Peter said, "No, Lord, for I have never eaten forbidden or un- clean food." Then again the voice spoke to him, saying: "What God has purified, shalt thou not consider forbidden or unclean." Now, God has made all things clean, and has not forbid- den us to eat, as his very next words prove. Why do we burden ourselves wilfully with fasts? Here answer might be made: This miracle, shown to Peter, meant that he should not avoid the heathen, but them also should he call to the grace of the Gospel, and therefore material food should not be understood here. Answer: All miracles that God has performed, although symbolical in meaning, were still real occurrences and events. As when Moses struck the rock with his staff and it gave forth water, it was symbolical of the true Rock of Christ, from which flowed, and ever shall flow for us all, the forgiveness of sins and the blessings of heavenly gifts, but none the less was the rock really smitten and gave forth water. And so here, although this miracle was symbolical, still the words of God's voice are clear: What God hath cleansed, shalt thou not consider unclean. Until I forget these words I shall use them.

Thirdly, Paul writes to the Corinthians (I., vi., 12): "All things are lawful unto me, but all things are not expedient: all things are lawful for me, but I will not be brought under the power of any. Meats for the belly and the belly for meats: but God shall destroy both it and them." That is, to me are all things free, although some things are rather to be avoided, in case they offend my neighbour too much. (About the troubling of one's neighbour, I shall speak specially later on). And therefore no one can take from me my freedom and bring me under his authority. Food is taken into the belly to sustain life. As now the belly and the food are both to be destroyed, it makes no difference what one eats or wherewith one nourishes his mortal body.

Fourthly, Paul says, I. Corinthians viii., 8: "But meat commendeth us not to God: for nei- ther, if we eat, are we the better; nor, if we eat not, are we the worse." This word Paul speaks of the food which was offered to the idols, not now of daily food. Notice this, however, to a clearer understanding. At the time when Paul wrote the epistle, there were still many unbe- lievers, more indeed, it seems to me, than Christians. These unbelievers offered to their idols, according to custom, animals, such as calves, sheep, and also other forms of food; but at these same offerings, a great part, often all, was given to eat to those that made the offerings. And as unbelievers and Christians lived together, the Christians were often invited to partake of food or meat, that had been sacrificed to the honour of the idols. Then some of the Christians were of the opinion, that it was not proper to eat this food; but others thought that, if they ate the food of the idols, but did not believe in them, such food could not harm them, and thought themselves stronger in their belief, because they had been free to do this thing, than those who from faint-heartedness and hesitation did not venture to eat all kinds of food. To settle this difference, Paul uses the above words: "No kind of food commends us to God." Even if one eats the food of the idols, he is not less worthy before God, nor yet more worthy, than one who does not eat it; and whoever does not eat it is no better. Indeed that will seem very strange to you, not only that meat is not forbidden, but also that even what has been offered to idols a Christian may eat.

Fifthly, Paul says in the First Epistle to the Corinthians, x., 25: "Whatsoever is sold in the shambles, that eat, asking no questions for conscience' sake." These words are clear and need no explanation, except that they are among other words about the offence caused by the food of idols. But do not let yourself err. From the pulpit I shall speak sufficiently of giving offence, and perhaps more clearly than you have ever heard.

Sixthly, Paul also says, Colossians ii., 16: "No man shall judge you in meat or in drink, or in respect of a holy day." Again you hear that you are to judge no man either as good or bad from his food or drink; he may eat what he please. If one will, let him eat refuse. Here it should be always understood that we are speaking not of amount but of kind. As far as kind and character of food are concerned, we may eat all foods to satisfy the needs of life, but not with immoderation or greediness.

Seventhly, Paul says again, I. Timothy iv., i: "Now the Spirit speaketh expressly, that in the latter times some shall depart from the faith, giving heed to seducing spirits, and doctrines of devils; speaking lies in hypocrisy; having their consciences seared with a hot iron; forbidding to marry and commanding to abstain from meats, which God hath created to be received with thanksgiving of them which believe and know the truth. For every creature of God is good, and nothing to be refused, if it be received with thanksgiving: for it is sanctified by the word of God and of prayer." These are all the words of Paul. And what could be more clearly said?

SIXTY-FOUR

Opera

BARTOLOMEO SCAPPI

Scappi worked his way up through the papal kitchens to eventually become personal chef to Pope Pius V, a man noted for his asceticism. One can only guess that the appointment may have led directly to the chef's retirement and perhaps even the composition of what is without doubt the largest and most important cookbook written until that time, his Works. *It is encyclopedic, including recipes for every imaginable dish, full menus, and shopping instructions, and it is the first cookbook to be illustrated. We actually get a glimpse into the kitchens in action as well as cookware and utensils of the era. His cookbook is the pinnacle of culinary arts of this era. Images in the* Opera *can be found online.*

[45.]1 I shall not go on to mention various stamps and moulds that Master Cooks and pastry chefs normally use, of brass, lead and white metal, such as small tubes for pouring jelly, and implements for engraving pastry, with various other wax and wood moulds, because all that will depend on whether the cook cares and can be bothered. It seems to me, though, that it would all be incomplete and open to criticism if I did not review the furnishings and facilities appropriate for a conscientious and competent Master Cook, along with his assistants and scullions; likewise, were I not to deal with what procedure is proper should it happen that more than one Master were in the kitchen, as is the case at great courts where it is usual for cooks to alternate weekly. I say, therefore, that when there are several Masters both have to be equal and have the same authority of that Office. If the one whose turn it is to serve that

Bartolomeo Scappi. *The Opera of Bartolomeo Scappi: L'arte et prudenza d'un maestro Cuoco (The Art and Craft of a Master Cook)*. 1st Italian ed. 1570. Translated by Terence Scully. Toronto: University of Toronto Press, 2008, pp. 130–32, 228–30.

week does not need the help of his fellow Master, he will enjoy all of the prerogatives and perquisites; but if his companion is helping him, they will both share those prerogatives and perquisites in a brotherly way, recognizing, though, his assistants and scullions according to their station. Should there be a formal contract with the Master of the Household and the Master Steward, then to comply with it they will have to observe the prerogatives and perquisites of the household. As for salary, I shall not speak of it, referring you to the contracts of both parties. With regard to living arrangements, though, I say that the cook shall have his chamber with the pallet furnished, candles and brooms, and firewood in winter just as gentlemen receive. With regard to his food, three pounds of bread per day and four litres of wine of at least the same quality as is set on the gentlemen's board. I say nothing of the food allowance because that will depend on the contract; however, at noble courts (excepting those of the Pope, the Emperor and the King, which are free) it is usual to give every Master, per day, two and a half pounds of veal or wether mutton, and a capon or hen, taken as the dish is being proved in the kitchen; on lean days he will receive eight eggs and during Lent two and a half pounds of fish, apart from the assortment of foods taken when dishes are proved. As well as that, for each of his assistants, half of the things listed above. Moreover, he will be allowed his expenses for any mount that must be used for any trip the Master Cook undertakes in the service of his Lord. The assistants, scullions and pastry workers, apart from their furnished room and pallet, should get for their allowance three pounds of bread per day and five and a third litres of ordinary table wine and a pound and a half of meat; on lean days, six eggs with the *hors-d'oeuvres,* and during Lent a pound and a half of fish. This arrangement is allowed so they will serve the Lord more faithfully and will endure greater toil submissively. Moreover, the Master Cook should have full authority—without, however, prejudicing the authority of the Master of the Household or of the Chief Steward—to engage and dismiss assistants, pastry workers and scullions, and any other person who is under his orders. Should it become necessary for him—who is deemed of use and service to a Lord—to go travelling, he should be able with authority and propriety to select skilled and reliable men and, while still appropriate for the Office, the lightest and most functional equipment, not overlooking mounts for his assistants, scullions and pastry workers, who have to go on ahead with the first kitchen; and mounts likewise for those who have to remain behind with the second one, and he has to arrange that the scullions who will follow on foot will not lack shoes and other things normally given to them, nor the porters who accompany such kitchens, loading and unloading the packs, not forgetting wind-proof torches and their windvane, when the kitchen sets out on a journey.

There remain the perquisites to speak about, those that are accorded Master Cooks and that it has always been the custom to accord them. It should therefore be known that by right they receive all the ashes produced in the kitchen, with the obligation, though, of keeping all the coarse cloths, fine cloths and other fabrics clean that are needed in the kitchen; likewise, all the hides of quadrupeds that are consigned to the kitchen and that are skinned, or ordered skinned, by those Masters; likewise, all the feathers of fowls that they pluck or order plucked; likewise, all the feet, necks and heads of quadrupeds that are consigned to the kitchen and skinned, along with all the offal of animals and fish; likewise, all the viscera and gizzards of every fowl, and all the grease that drips from roasts along with whatever is in excess on large cuts of meat; likewise, they receive all the oils and fried grease, with pork rinds and rank bacon. And at least once a year, the Masters, along with their assistants and scullions, receive clothing.

174. To Prepare a Thick Macaroni Soup in the Roman Style

Make up a dough with a pound of flour, four ounces of white breadcrumb which has soaked in warm goat's milk, four egg yolks and two ounces of sieved sugar. When it is ready and not too moist, and has been kneaded on a table for half an hour, make a sheet of it with a rolling pin, leaving that sheet a little thicker than the previous one. Let the sheet dry. With an iron or wooden roller, cut macaroni. When they are made, let them dry out. If you want to cook them in plain water, do that in a large pot with a good lot of water and enough salt; put the macaroni in when the water is boiling because, put into cold water, they will sink to the bottom. That is a dough for making every sort of drawn pasta. When they have boiled for half an hour, see if they are tender enough; if they are not, let them boil until they are thoroughly done. When done, have at hand a silver, pewter or earthenware platter broadly sprinkled with grated cheese, sugar and cinnamon, and set with slices of fresh provatura. Put some well drained macaroni onto that and on it in turn sprinkle cheese, sugar and cinnamon, with slices of provatura and lumps of butter. In that way make up three layers. Splash rosewater over it all, cover it with another platter and let it sit on hot coals or in a moderately hot oven for half an hour. Serve it hot.

175. To Prepare a Thick Macaroni Soup with an Iron Rod

Make up a dough similar to the one above but firmer, and sweeter with sugar; colour it with saffron. Spread the dough out, making sheets the thickness of the spine of a knife. Let it dry up—that is, dry out—and cut it in strips half a finger wide and four fingers long. Get an iron stiletto—that is, a needle a handswidth long, like what is used to make birettas—and put it on the strips so that it lies over the full length of the strip, and with the palm of your hand give it the shape of macaroni, so that the dough goes right around the iron stiletto; then draw out the stiletto. Let the macaroni, now hollow, dry. When making that macaroni, make sure that the sheet of dough is lightly floured so it will not stick to the iron rod. When they are dry they can be cooked and served like the ones above. Note that these as well as the ones above can be cooked in a fat meat broth or else in milk and butter.

176. To Prepare a Thick Soup with Macaroni Called "Gnocchi"

Get two pounds of flour and a pound of grated and sieved white bread; make a dough of that with a fat broth that is boiling, or with water, adding in four beaten egg yolks as you knead the dough. When it is done in such a way that it is neither too firm nor too runny, but has been made exactly right, take a walnut's amount of it. Sprinkle the back of a cheese grater with flour, put the dough on the grater and make the gnocchi with it. If you do not have a cheese grater, make them on a table, drawing the gnocchi out nicely with three fingers. Put in as little flour as possible so they stay soft, and be careful not to handle the dough because it will get too runny. When they are made up, let them sit awhile, then cook them in a fat broth that is boiling, or in water, in a big pot. When they are done, set them out in dishes with cheese and provatura—both grated and not too salted—sugar, cinnamon and lumps of fresh butter the way macaroni are set out in Recipe 174. And let those, too, stew between two dishes on hot coals.

177. To Prepare Tortellini with Capon Flesh

In a mortar grind the flesh of two capon breasts that have first been boiled with a pound of boneless beef marrow, three ounces of chicken fat, and three ounces of boiled veal udder; when everything is ground up, add in a pound of creamy cheese, eight ounces of sugar, one ounce of cinnamon, half an ounce of pepper, enough saffron, half an ounce of cloves and nutmeg together, four ounces of very clean currant raisins, a handful of mint, sweet marjoram and other common aromatic herbs together, four fresh egg yolks and two with their whites. When the mixture is so made up that it is not too salty, get a rather thin sheet of dough made of flour, rosewater, salt, butter, sugar and warm water, and out of that dough, with a cutting wheel or dough cutter, cut out large or small tortellini. Cook them in a good fat broth of chicken or some other meat. Serve them with cheese, sugar and cinnamon over top. In the same way you can do it with the flesh of spit-roasted turkey hens and peacocks, and of pheasants and partridges and other commonly eaten fowl, and also of veal loin roasted on a spit with kidney-fat.

SIXTY-FIVE

English Recipes

GERVASE MARKHAM AND ROBERT MAY

This selection of English recipes runs the gamut from simple, homely meals to elegant dishes meant for the wealthiest of patrons. It will be easy to tell which is which, but do note the use of exotic ingredients and spices and how they were used progressively down the social scale. The author of the first cookbook is unknown. The second is from Gervase Markham, an early seventeenth-century hack who wrote on just about every possible topic, usually for country houses of middling wealth. Robert May was a chef to aristocrats, and his is one of the most comprehensive and thorough cookbooks ever written, revealing both exotic procedures and homespun English fare. Look online for images of Hans Eworth's portrait William Brooke and Family *as well.*

GOOD HUSWIFES HANDMAIDE FOR THE KITCHEN

To Make Paste, and to Bake Chickens

Take water, and put in a good piece of butter, and let it seeth as hot as you can blow off your Butter into your flower, and break two yolkes of Egges, and one white, and put in a good peece of Sugar, and collour your paste with Saffron, athen shall it be short. Then take your Chickens,

Stuart Peachy, ed. *The Good Huswifes Handmaide for the Kitchen.* 1588. Reprint by Bristol, UK: Stuart Press, 1992, p. 25.
Gervase Markham. *The English Housewife.* 1615. Edited by Michael R. Best. Reprint by Toronto: McGill-Queen's University Press, 1986, pp. 176–77.
Robert May. *The Accomplisht Cook.* London: Obadiah Blagrave, 1685.

Raisons, Clove, Mace, Corrans, Prunes and Dates, then close them up, and make a litle hole in the midst of the lid. Then set it in the Oven, and to make syrrope for the same pie, take Malmsey, Cream, and two yolkes of Egges, and beat them together, and put in Synamon and Sugar, and when the Pie is almost baked, then put in the syrrop, and let them bake together.

THE ENGLISH HOUSEWIFE

To make a new milk or morning milk cheese, which is the best cheese made ordinarily in our kingdom; you shall take your milk early in the morning as it comes from the cow, and sile it into a clean tub, than take all the cream also from the milk you milked the evening before, and strain it into your new milk; then take a pretty quantity of clean water, and, having made it scalding hot, pour it into the milk also to scald the cream and it together, then let it stand, and cool it with a dish till it be no more than lukewarm; then go to the pot where your earning bag hangs, and draw from thence so much of the earning, without stirring of the bad, and will serve for your proportion of milk, and strain it therein very carefully; for if the least more of the curd of the earning fall into the cheese, it will make the cheese rot and mould; when your earning is put in you shall cover the milk, and so let it stand half an hour or thereabouts; for if the earning be good it will come in that space; but if you see that it doth not, then you shall put in more: being come, you shall with a dish in your hand break and mash the curd together, possing and turning it about diversely: which done, with the flats of yours hands very gently press the curd down into the bottom of the tub; then with a thin dish take the whey from it as clean as you can, and so having prepared your cheese vat answerable to the proportion of your curd, with both your hands joined together put your curd therein and break it and press it down hard into the vat till you have filled it; then lay upon the top of the curd your flat cheese board, and a little small weight thereupon, that the whey may drop from it into the under vessel; when it hath done dropping take a large cheese cloth, and having wet it in cold water lay it on the cheese board, and then turn the cheese upon it; then lay the cloth into the cheese-vat; and so put the cheese therein again, and with a thin slice thrust the same down close on every side; then laying the cloth also over the top, lay on the cheese board, and so carry it to your great press, and there press it under a sufficient weight; after it hath been there pressed half an hour, you shall take it and turn it into a dry cloth, and put it into the press again, and thus you shall turn it into dry press again, not taking it therefrom till the next day in the evening at soonest, and the last time it is turned you shall turn it into the dry vat without any cloth at all.

THE ACCOMPLISHT COOK

To Make Mackeroons

Take a pound of the finest sugar, and a pound of the best Jordan-almonds, steep them in cold water, blanch them and pick out the spots: then beat them to a perfect paste in a stone mortar, in the beating of them put rose-water to them to keep them from oyling, being finely beat, put them in a dish with the sugar, and set them over a chafing-dish of coals, stir it till it will come clean from the bottom of the dish, then put in two grains of musk, and three of ambergriese.

SIXTY-SIX

Of Experience

MICHEL DE MONTAIGNE

Michel de Montaigne (1533–1592) essentially invented the modern essay form, and his personal anecdotes and perambulations about himself make him one of the most engaging authors of all time. As a skeptic he also challenged received wisdom and posed important questions with freshness and a sense of humor. Here he talks about medicine, food, and his own weird tastes. We rarely get so close a glimpse of a person's food preferences until recent times.

The art of physic is not so fixed, that we need be without authority for whatever we do; it changes according to climates and moons; according to Fernel and to Scaliger. If your physician does not think it good for you to sleep, to drink wine, or to eat such and such meats, never trouble yourself; I will find you another that shall not be of his opinion; the diversity of medical arguments and opinions embraces all sorts of forms.

[. . .]

I hardly ever choose my dish at table, but take the next at hand, and unwillingly change it for another. A confusion of meats and a clutter of dishes displease me as much as any other confusion; I am easily satisfied with few dishes; and am an enemy to the opinion of Favorinus that in a feast they should snatch from you the meat you like, and set a plate of another sort before you; and that 'tis a pitiful supper, if you do not sate your guests with the rumps of various fowls, the beccafico only deserving to be all eaten. I usually eat salt meats, and yet I love bread that has no salt in it; and my baker never sends up other to my table, contrary to the custom of the country. In my infancy, what they had most to correct in me was the refusal

Michel de Montaigne. "Of Experience." In *1575 Essays*. Translated by Charles Cotton. http://oregonstate.edu/instruct/phl302/texts/montaigne/montaigne-essays-8.html#XXI.

of things that children commonly best love, as sugar, sweetmeats, and march-panes. My tutor contended with this aversion to delicate things, as a kind of overnicety; and indeed 'tis nothing else but a difficulty of taste, in anything it applies itself to. Whoever cures a child of an obstinate liking for brown bread, bacon, or garlic, cures him also of pampering his palate. There are some who affect temperance and plainness, by wishing for beef and ham among pheasant and partridge; 'tis all very fine; this is delicacy upon delicacies; 'tis the taste of effeminacy that disrelishes ordinary and accustomed things.

[. . .]

The ancient Greeks and Romans had more reason than we in sitting apart for eating, which is a principal action of life, if they were not prevented by other extraordinary business, many hours and the greatest part of the night; eating and drinking more deliberately than we do, who perform all our actions post-haste; and in extending this natural pleasure to more leisure and better use, intermixing with their meals pleasant and profitable conversation.

They whose concern it is to have a care of me, may very easily hinder me from eating anything they think will do me harm; for in such matters I never covet nor miss anything I do not see; but withal, if it once comes in my sight, 'tis in vain to persuade me to forbear; so that when I design to fast, I must be kept apart from the supper-table, and must have only so much given me, as is required for a prescribed collation; for if I sit down to table, I forget my resolution. When I order my cook to alter the manner of dressing any dish, all my family know what it means, that my stomach is out of order, and that I shall not touch it.

I love to have all meats, that will endure it, very little boiled or roasted, and prefer them very high, and even, as to several, quite gone. Nothing but hardness generally offends me (of any other quality I am as patient and indifferent as any man I have known); so that, contrary to the common humor, even in fish it often happens that I find them both too fresh and too firm: not for want of teeth, which I ever had good, even to excellence, and which age does but now begin to threaten: I have always been used every morning to rub them with a napkin, and before and after dinner.

[. . .]

I am not very fond either of salads or fruits, except melons. My father hated all sorts of sauces; I love them all. Eating too much hurts me; but, as to the quality of what I eat, I do not yet certainly know that any sort of meat disagrees with my stomach; neither have I observed that either full moon or decrease, spring or autumn, have any influence upon me. We have in us notions that are inconstant and for which no reason can be given: for example, I found radishes first grateful to my stomach, since that nauseous, and now again grateful. In several other things, I find my stomach and appetite vary after the same manner; I have changed again and again from white wine to claret, from claret to white.

I am a great lover of fish, and consequently make my fasts feasts, and feasts fasts: and I believe what some people say, that it is more easy of digestion than flesh. As I make a conscience of eating flesh upon the fish-days, so does my taste make a conscience of mixing fish and flesh; the difference between them seems to me too remote.

From my youth, I have sometimes kept out of the way at meals; either to sharpen my appetite against the next morning (for, as Epicurus fasted and made lean meals to accustom his pleasure to make shift without abundance, I, on the contrary, do it to prepare my pleasure to make better and more cheerful use of abundance); or else I fasted to preserve my vigor for the service of some action of body or mind; for both the one and the other of these is cruelly dulled in me by repletion; and, above all things, I hate that foolish coupling of so healthful and sprightly a goddess with that little belching god, bloated with the fumes of his liquor; or to cure my sick stomach, or for want of fit company; for I say, as the same Epicurus did, that one is not so much to regard what he eats, as with whom; and I commend Chilo, that he would not engage himself to be at Periander's feast till he first was informed who were to be the other guests; no dish is so acceptable to me, nor no sauce so appetizing, as that which is extracted from society. I think it more wholesome to eat more leisurely and less, and to eat oftener; but I would have appetite and hunger attended to; I should take no pleasure to be fed with three or four pitiful and stinted repasts a day, after a medicinal man-ner; who will assure me, that, if I have a good appetite in the morning, I shall have the same at supper? But, we old fellows especially, let us take the first opportune time of eating, and leave to almanac makers hopes and prognostics. The utmost fruit of my health is pleasure; let us take hold of the present and known. I avoid the invariable in these laws of fasting; he who would have one form serve him, let him avoid the continuing it; we harden ourselves in it, our strength is there stupefied and laid asleep; six months after, you shall find your stomach so inured to it, that all you have got is the loss of your liberty of doing otherwise but to your prejudice.

[. . .]

For what concerns our affairs and pleasures, it is much more commodious, as the an-cients did, to lose one's dinner, and defer making good cheer till the hour of retirement and repose, without breaking up a day; and so was I formerly used to do. As to health, I since by experience find, on the contrary, that it is better to dine, and that the digestion is better while awake. I am not very used to be thirsty, either well or sick; my mouth is, indeed, apt to be dry, but without thirst; and commonly I never drink but with thirst that is created by eating, and far on in the meal; I drink pretty well for a man of my pitch; in summer, and at a relishing meal, I do not only exceed the limits of Augustus, who drank but thrice, precisely; but not to offend Democritus' rule who forbade that men should stop at four times as an unlucky number, I proceed at need to the fifth glass, about three half-pints; for the little glasses are my favorites, and I like to drink them off, which other people avoid as an unbecoming thing. I mix my wine sometimes with half, sometimes with the third part water; and when I am at home, by an ancient custom that my father's physician prescribed both to him and himself, they mix that which is designed for me in the buttery, two or three hours before 'tis brought in. 'Tis said, that Cranaus, king of Athens, was the inventor of this custom of dashing wine with water; whether useful or no, I have heard disputed. I think it more decent and wholesome for children to drink no wine till after sixteen or eighteen years of age. The most usual and common method of living is the most becoming; all particularity, in my opinion, is to be avoided; and I should as much hate a German who mixed water with his wine, as I should a Frenchman who drank it pure. Public usage gives the law in these things.

[. . .]

'Tis indecent, besides the hurt it does to one's health, and even to the pleasure of eating, to eat so greedily as I do; I often bite my tongue, and sometimes my fingers, in my haste. Diogenes meeting a boy eating after that manner, gave his tutor a box on the ear. There were men at Rome that taught people to chew, as well as to walk, with a good grace. I lose thereby the leisure of speaking, which gives great relish to the dinner-table, provided the discourse be suitable, that is, pleasant and short.

SIXTY-SEVEN

Spanish Recipes

RUPERT OF NOLA, DIEGO GRANADO, DOMINGO HERNANDEZ DE MACERAS,
FRANCISCO MARTINÉZ MONTIÑO, AND JUAN DE ALTAMIRAS

The following recipes illustrate the development of the cuisine of Spain from the time of Ferdinand and Isabella to the early seventeenth century, when Spain took the lead in culinary fashion in Europe. A distinctively national cooking style is evident here. The recipes are taken from several disparate works. Rupert of Nola (Mestre Robert) was working in Catalonia, and his was the first cookbook published in Catalonian in 1520 and shortly thereafter in Castilian Spanish. Nothing is known of Diego Granado except that most of his book was pirated from Bartolomeo Scappi without attribution. Domingo Hernandez de Maceras was chef for a college refectory in Valladolid and reflects perhaps the tastes of middling ranks, while Francisco Martinéz Montiño cooked for King Philip III in the era of Don Quixote. Altamiras was a pseudonym for Brother Raimundo Gómez, and the work was reprinted many times into the nineteenth century. Many Spanish painters' works make a nice accompaniment to these selections. Start with Juan Sanchez Cotan and make your way to Velasquez, especially An Old Woman Cooking Eggs *and* Los Borrachos.

Rupert of Nola. "Recipe 63." In *Libre del Coch*. Fifteenth century. Translated by Ken Albala. Reprint by Barcelona: 1568.

Diego Granado. *Libro del Arte de Cozina*. Translated by Ken Albala. Madrid: Luis Sanchez, 1599, pp. 184–85.

Domingo Hernandez de Maceras. *Libro del Arte de Cozina*. 1607. Translated by Ken Albala. Reprint by Salamanca: Ediciones Universidad de Salamanca, 1999, pp. 73, 85–86.

Francisco Martinéz Montiño. *Arte de Cocina, Pastelería, Vizcochería, y Conservería*. 1611. Translated by Ken Albala. Reprint by Barcelona: Maria Angela Marti, 1763, p. 202.

Juan de Altamiras. *Nuevo Arte de Cocina*. Translated by Ken Albala. Barcelona: Juan de Bezares, 1758.

LIBRO DE COCH

Madam's Broth

Take almonds that are not peeled, and pine nuts that are clean and white, and pound everything together and when it is all pounded, add a good chicken broth, and strain it through a sieve. After that place it in a clean pot to boil and add these spices: ginger, long pepper, and galingale, all pounded. Put it in the pot with parsley, and oregano, and a bit of pennyroyal, and boil everything together with much saffron. When it is well boiled, you know that it should be lifted from the fire, take a dozen eggs beaten with vinegar and put them in the pot. Make it so that the broth will be a little sour, but not much. When you put them into the broth, be careful that it is not very hot so that the eggs do not cook at once. Stir it constantly with a spoon when the eggs are in the broth, so they don't curdle.

LIBRO DEL ARTE DE COZINA

To Fry and Marinate Sardines

Take fresh sardines, scale and wash them and lay them on a table. Mix them with a bit of white salt for a while, then flour them and fry in olive oil, which is always better than fat, and being fried serve with orange juice, or slices of lemon, or fried parsley on top. After they are fried conserve them in bay leaves, or myrtle, and if you want to marinate them place them after they are fried in vinegar, in which sugar helps, or wine cooked with saffron, and conserve in this escaveche until you want to serve it. In summer in place of vinegar you can serve it with verjuice incorporated with egg yolks, or the soft insides of bread, or also after frying you can cover it with green sauce.

LIBRO DEL ARTE DE COZINA

How to Make Rice with Milk

After washing the rice in four changes of water, you must drain the water, and for twelve bowls of rice, you pour out a pound and a half of rice. After it's drained pour it to cook in an açumbre [two quarts] of water with salt and let it cook until it's well dried. Then add an açumbre of milk, and a pound of sugar and let it cook on a low fire, because you don't stir it, shake it so it doesn't stick, and let it soak up the milk. Cover it and let it rest, and fill the bowls, and pour on top sugar and cinnamon. If you want, make it with almond milk. From one pound of almonds you draw out an açumbre of milk, and to be good you shouldn't draw out more. And add the sugar to be good.

How to Make Eggplants

You must cook the eggplants in water and salt, and being cooked discard the water, you mince them well and put them in a casserole to fry with much oil. Add grated cheese and bread, and six or eight maravedis of spices, and one garlic clove, totally smashed, and cook everything carefully. Add eggs and let them solidify, placing the fire on top. This is called a *caçuela mongil* (monk's casserole) of eggplant, but you can also cook them with fat in a pot, and serve them with fatty salt pork, pepper or parsley. Eggplants can also be kept all year in a conserve having made them in this manner, cook them in the conserve, and adding cloves and cinnamon when you cook it, and put it in a glazed pot, in which you keep it.

ARTE DE COCINA, PASTELERÍA, VIZCOCHERÍA, Y CONSERVERÍA

Pork Chorizos

Take pork meat that is more lean than fat, and put it in a marinade of just wine with a touch of vinegar. The meat should be cut into little radish-sized knobs and the marinade should be sparing, no more than to cover. Season with spices and salt and let it sit for twenty-four hours. Fill up the chorizos. They should be a bit plump. Cook them in water. These can be kept all year. Eating them cooked, there should be so little vinegar that you can't sense it before eating them.

NUEVO ARTE DE COCINA

Stew with Pepper Sauce

Meat from the leg is best for stew; cut it in bits the size of a nut, place it in a pot with salt, bay leaves and bacon between fat and lean cut up as large as dice. Fry it in the pot. Crush some garlic with pepper and loosen it with a bit of water and put it all in the stew, add oil, and place the pot on the embers so that it browns. When it seems right, add enough hot water, season it with salt and all the spices, always get parsley or tomato to throw in, and you can smack your lips if you're not polite.

SIXTY-EIGHT

Cruz and Rada in China

GASPAR DA CRUZ AND MARTÍN DE RADA

These selections are drawn from the accounts of two clergymen who visited China. Gaspar da Cruz (1520–1570) was sent by the Portuguese, and Martín de Rada (1533–1578) went representing the Spanish via the Philippines. Both were extraordinarily observant about Chinese eating habits, and often it does take an outsider to notice what is obvious to someone within a culture. Compare these with contemporary habits as described by Erasmus, or indeed what the Chinese themselves said in earlier selections in Part IV.

GASPAR DA CRUZ

The Chinese are very courteous men. The common courtesy is, the left hand closed, they enclose it within the right hand, and they move their hands repeatedly up and down towards the breast, showing that they have one another enclosed in their heart; and to this motion of the hands, they join words of courtesy, though the words of the common sort is to say one to another, *chifã mesão*, which is to say "Have you eaten or no," for all their good in this world is resolved in eating.

The particular courtesies between men who have some breeding, and who have not seen one another for some days, are the arms bowed and the fingers clasped one within another, they stoop and speak with words of great courtesy, each one labouring to give the hand to the other to make him rise; and the more honourable they are the longer they stand in these courtesies. The honourable and noble people do use also many courtesies at the table, the

---

Gaspar da Cruz and Martín de Rada. *South China in the Sixteenth Century*. Edited by C. R. Boxer. Bangkok: Orchid Press, 2004, pp. 138–42, 287–90.

one giving drink to the other, and each one laboureth to give the hand to the other in their drinking, for at the table there is no other service than that of drinking.

If there come any guest newly to his friend's or to his kinsman's house, if the master of the house be not apparelled in holiday clothes, when the guest cometh in, he maketh no account of him nor any mention, till he commandeth to bring his festival apparel and foot-wear; and after he is so apparelled, he goeth to the guest, and receiveth him with many compliments, and courtesies. For they hold it not convenient that a new-come guest and of reverence be received with common apparel, but clothed in festive apparel, for in this he showeth him that his entering into his house is a feast-day to him.

Whatsoever person or persons come to any man of quality's house, it is customary to offer him on a fair tray in a porcelain cup (as or many cups as there are persons) a kind of warm water which they call *cha*, which is somewhat red and very medicinal, which they use to drink, made from a concoction of somewhat bitter herbs; with this they commonly welcome all manner of persons that they do respect, be they acquaintances or be they not, and to me they offered it many times.

The Chinas are great eaters and they use many dishes. They eat at one table fish and flesh, and the base people dress it sometimes all together. The dishes which are to be eaten at one table, are set all together on the board, that every one may eat which he liketh best. The noble and gentle folk have much polity in their dealings, conversation and apparel. The common people have some gross things.

Certain noble Portugals went to show me on a day at Cantam a banquet which a rich merchant made, which was worth the sight. The house where it was made was storied and very fair, with many fair windows and casements, and it was all great sport. The tables were set in three places of the house, for every guest invited there was a table and a chair very fair and gilt, or with silver, and every table had before it a cloth of damask down to the ground. On the tables was neither cloth nor napkins, as well because the tables were very fine, as because they eat so cleanly that they need none of these things. The fruit was set along the edges of every table, all set in order, which was, roasted chestnuts and peeled, and nuts cracked and shelled, and sugar-canes clean and cut in slices, and the fruit we spoke of before called Lichias, great and small, but they were dried. All the fruit was set in small heaps like turrets very well made, crossed between with certain small sticks very clean, whereby all the tables in a circle were very fairly adorned with these little turrets. Presently after the fruit, all the services were placed in fine porcelain dishes, all very well dressed and neatly carved, and every thing set in good order; and although the sets of dishes were set on top of the other, all were beautifully set; in such sort that he who sat at the table might eat what he would without any need of stirring or removing any of them. And presently there were two small sticks, very fine and gilt, for to eat with, holding them between the fingers; they use them like a pair of pincers, so that they touch nothing of that which is on the board with their hand. Yea, though they eat a dish of rice, they do it with those sticks, without any grain of the rice falling.

And because they eat so cleanly, not touching with the hand their meat, they have no need of cloth or napkins. All comes carved and well ordered to the table. They have also a very small porcelain cup gilt, which holdeth a mouthful of wine, and only for this is there a waiter at the table. They drink so little because at each mouthful of food they must take a sip of drink, and therefore the cup is so small. There are some Chinas who wear very long finger-nails, from half a span to a span long, which they keep very clean; and these finger-nails do serve them instead of the chop-sticks for to eat withal.

8. OF THEIR MANNER OF EATING, AND OF THEIR BANQUETS (MARTÍN DE RADA)

The principal food of all Chinos is rice, for although they have wheat and sell bread kneeded therefrom, yet they do not eat it save as if it were a fruit. Their chief bread is cooked rice, and they even make a wine from it which is comparable with a reasonable grape-wine and might even be mistaken for it. They eat seated at tables, but they do not use table-cloths or napkins; for they do not touch with their fingers anything that they are going to eat, but they pick up everything with two long little sticks. They are so expert in this, that they can take anything, however small, and carry it to their mouth, even if it is round, like plums and other such fruits. At the beginning of a meal they eat meat without bread, and afterwards instead of bread they eat three or four dishes of cooked rice, which they likewise eat with their chop-sticks, even though somewhat hoggishly. At banquets, a table is placed for each guest, and when the banquet is a formal one, each guest gets many tables, and to explain this I would like to recount what sort of banquets they offered us, and the way in which they were served.

In a large room, at the top of the hall, they placed seven tables in a row for each one of the Religious, and along the side-walls five tables for each of the Spanish laymen who were there, and three tables for each of the Chinese captains who accompanied us. And next to the doors of the hall, opposite the Religious, sat the captains who had invited us, each one at his own table. In our room they had arranged on one side three tables bearing the covers for each one of us. All these tables were loaded as much as they could be with plates and dishes of food, save that only the principal table contained cooked meats, and all the uncooked food was on the other tables which were for grandeur and display. There were whole geese and ducks, capons and hens, gammons of bacon and other chops of pork, fresh pieces of veal and beef, many kinds of fish, a great quantity of fruits of all kinds, with elegant pitchers and bowls and other knicknacks all made of sugar, and so forth. All this which was put upon the tables, when we got up therefrom, was put into hampers and carried to our lodgings. In sort that everything which is put there for display all belongs to the guests.

Outside the door of the house where the banquet was held, was arrayed the whole bodyguard of our host, with their weapons, drums and musical instruments which they began to play when we arrived. The captains who were to be present at the banquet came out halfway into the court-yard to receive us, and without making any courtesy or bow we went together to a reception-room which was in front of the banqueting-hall, where we made our bows one by one according to their custom. With many ceremonies we seated ourselves there, each on a chair, and they forthwith brought the hot water [tea] which I have described above. When we had drunk this, we conversed for a short space, and then went to the banqueting-hall, where, after many ceremonies and cour-tesies which I omit to avoid tediousness, they conducted each one of us individually to the table where we were to sit. On this table the captains placed the first dish and a little cup full of wine. When everyone was seated, the music began to play, consisting of tamborets, gitterns, rebecks, lutes with a big arch, and they played continuously for as long as the banquet lasted.

Other persons in the middle of the hall acted a play, and what we saw were elegant representations of old stories and wars, whose plot was explained to us beforehand, so that although we did not understand the words yet we well understood what was happening. In Hocchiu [Foochow], besides the plays, there was a tumbler who did fine tricks, both on the ground and on a stick. Although the table be full of food, there is never any pause in the flow of broths and dressed meats. As long as the banquet lasts they drink healths heartily, although not with goblets but, as it were, in little saucers. In drinking they are a temperate people as far as we could see. They do not drink wine continually but only water; and when they drink wine they drink it very hot, and they sip it like a broth, although they gave it us cold, as they knew that we did not drink it hot. They think it mean of the host to rise first from the table, but on the contrary as long as the guests are there, more and more dainties are continually served until they wish to get up. Even after we got up, they asked us to sit down again, begging us to wait for another one or two dishes, and this they did two or three times. Their manner of acting is with chanting, and they also usually act puppet-plays which go through all their motions, and men behind the scenes say what has to be spoken.

In their food they are not great meat-eaters, but on the contrary in our experience their principal food is fish, eggs, vegetables, broths and fruit. The things which we saw like unto our own (apart from many other different kinds) were fish, wheat, barley, rice, beans, millet and *borona*. There were kine and buffaloes, and they say that there are also sheep the land inward; and we also saw pigs, goats, and hens like ours and others which have black flesh and are more tasty, and likewise capons and godwits. We did not see any game, because in the region where we were there was no waste-land for them, but they say there is some the land inward. We saw birds of prey, likewise geese and royal ducks, and great store of doves and turtle-doves. Of fruits, there are white and black grapes in vines, although we did not see any wine made therefrom, and I do not believe they know how to make it. Also oranges and lemons of many kinds, and large citrons, pears, apples, wild pears, peaches, plums, mulberries, nuts, chestnuts, jujubes, pumpkins, cucumbers, water-melons, cabbages, cole-worts, turnips, radishes, garlick, onions, and many other fruits and vegetables peculiar to the country. They have much sugar and they make many and very good conserves. Even in the squares and streets they have dwarf trees in pots and tubs, and I do not know with what ingenuity they grow them that though so small they can yet bear fruit, because we saw them laden with fruit. They also have a kind of tree from the fruit of which they take something like tallow, whereof throughout the whole country they make candles to give light, and which anyone would think was animal fat. They have coconut-palms in the southern provinces but not in Hocquien [Fukien] nor north thereof. They have horses although small ones, and asses, mules and donkeys. We saw good ones and droves of them.

PART XI
Study Questions

1. What does it reveal about the cooking profession if detailed introductory directions are written in a book such as Scappi's? Is printing the important factor here, or is a new kind of reader using these texts?
2. What does it reveal that common table manners needed to be taught in a book? Is it that medieval people had no manners, or are these written for a different class of reader?
3. Why does Montaigne examine his eating habits in detail, and what does he expect it will reveal about his character to his readers? Are his self-observations always flattering?
4. Consider whether Europeans, when first encountering eating habits in China, considered them elegant or not. What did the Europeans think of these strange, exotic foods, and what impact has this fascination had on global eating habits?
5. Judging from the recipes in this section, did early modern people like spices any less than their predecessors? Why does Spanish cuisine seem simpler among these, even though it was arguably the wealthiest and most powerful country in this era?

The Mercantile Era
1650–1800

This period witnessed the emergence of three new powers on the international scene: England, France, and the Netherlands, each of which built a formidable global empire largely designed to supply luxury foods. Plantation economies provided sugar and spices; new drinks such as coffee, tea, and chocolate; not to mention tobacco. Slaves were brought from Africa to the Caribbean and Brazil to supply labor, while in Asia dominance was asserted through independent companies like the Dutch East India Company. The Dutch had essentially stolen the Indonesian spice colonies from the Portuguese. The new caffeinated drinks, it has been argued, matched the work ethic of northern European Protestant nations perfectly—they would keep people awake and alert and ready to do business. In fact, coffee houses became prime sites for making business deals and discussing politics or literature.

The dominant economic theory of this era, mercantilism, also stipulated that nation-states should take a direct interest in framing policies to the advantage of their own citizens. Thus, monopolies were granted giving individual companies so much power that they could effectively beat out foreign competitors. High import duties on food and manufactured goods encouraged exports, under the assumption that this would draw money into the country, which could then be taxed efficiently to swell the royal coffers. The idea was that there is a fixed volume of trade and the only way to generate profit is to steal trade routes from other nations; thus, the royal reserves were spent on purely mercantile wars to snatch colonies or secure trading posts. It was in the conclusion of one of these wars, for example, that the Dutch traded New Amsterdam with the English in exchange for the Island of Run in the Moluccas.

This period also witnessed the birth of what is known as classic French haute cuisine. The court of Louis XIV, and in particular the cookbook of La Varenne, is said to have turned the tide definitively away from heavily spiced and sweetened recipes toward elegance and refinement, flavorings based on the main ingredient via stocks and reductions, and the rationalization of the meal into progressive courses. Culinary innovations such as the roux—a combination of flour and butter cooked together as a thickener—are said to have been introduced by La Varenne. In fact, La Varenne was quite conservative and anything but revolutionary. Even one generation later he was ridiculed by another cookbook writer for including dishes such as larks in hippocras and veal hocks *à l'épigramme,* which still uses medieval flavorings. The transition to modern taste preferences took many years, but many of the changes are discernible in this period, when French cuisine and other arts dominated the continent.

Eighteenth-century English cookbooks were, for the most part, quite different from their French counterparts. They were usually not written for male professionals serving at court or for aristocrats, but rather for women running the kitchens of landed estates. The English were also somewhat schizophrenic, at times being attracted to French cuisine and at others violently defending native foodways. Of course, wars with France had much to do with this, as they did in cultivating a taste for Spanish sherry and Portuguese port, since there were official embargoes against French wine. Cookbooks in the American colonies were at first reproductions of English works, but by the end of the century works appeared using native ingredients and cooking methods and reflected American practice. Amelia Simmons's cookbook, excerpted below, is simply the first of these.

The late eighteenth century witnessed the invention of the modern restaurant. Although the French Revolution and the demise of aristocratic patrons probably played a minor role, the abolition of guild restrictions certainly facilitated the proliferation of new dining establishments, as did the opportunity to dine out for bourgeois patrons, who wanted to flaunt their newfound wealth with fanciful meals. Not coincidentally, modern gastronomy was also born here—both in the sense of food writing, as in the work of Jean Anthelme Brilliat-Savarin in the early nineteenth century and with restaurant reviews, food criticism, and eventually all branches of food journalism. Celebrity chefs such as Careme and Soyer also made restaurateurship glamorous, and their cookbooks were best-sellers.

Suggested images to accompany this section are Dutch still-life paintings; those of Aertsen and Claesz are especially magnificent.

SIXTY-NINE

Le Cuisinier François

FRANÇOIS PIERRE LA VARENNE

François Pierre de la Varenne (1615–1678) is widely credited for having ushered in not only classical French haute cuisine but the modern idea of having foods taste of themselves, separating sweets and spices to the end of a meal, techniques such as thickening sauces with a roux made of butter and flour, and using fresh herbs. But his contribution is not so straightforward, and these were a few culinary innovations that took place over the course of several decades among many cookbook writers. His is among the first of a large crop of classical texts in the era of Louis XIV. Some of his recipes were still somewhat medieval, such that authors only a few decades later could make fun of him, precisely for young turkey with raspberries and veal epigram. Look online for images of Abraham Bosse's engraving of the feast of the Chevaliers of Saint-Esprit.

1. Young Turkey with Raspberries

After a young turkey is dressed, remove its brisket and its meat, which you chop up with fat and a little veal; mix that with egg yolks and squab, all of it well seasoned with salt, pepper, capers and ground cloves. Stuff your young turkey with that. Then mount it on a spit and turn it gently. When it is almost done, take it down and put it in a terrine with bouillon, mushrooms and a bouquet of herbs. To thicken the sauce, get a little cut-up lard and put it into a frying pan; when it has melted, draw it off and mix it with a little flour and let it brown, and dilute it with a little bouillon and vinegar; then put it into your terrine with lemon juice. Serve. If it is in raspberry season, put a handful of them on top.

François Pierre La Varenne. *La Varenne's Cookery*. Translated by Terence Scully. Totnes, UK: Prospect Books, 2006, pp. 156–57, 260–62.

2. Cardinal's Leg of Mutton

Get a leg of mutton, beat it and lard it with coarse pieces of lard, then skin it. Flour the mutton and sauté it in a frying pan in lard. Cook it with some bouillon and a bouquet of parsley, thyme and chives bound with mushrooms, truffles and tidbits. The sauce should be thick. Then serve.

3. Veal Hocks *à l'épigramme*

When veal hocks are blanched in cool water, flour them and sauté them in a frying pan in melted or clarified lard. Then break them apart and put them into a pot seasoned with salt, pepper, cloves and a bouquet of herbs; add in an onion, a little bouillon and capers. Then coat them in batter and braise them with the pot's lid on; cook them gradually covered like that for three hours. After that you uncover them; reduce your sauce until everything is the better for it; add in some mushrooms if you have any. Then serve.

CHAPTER XVI

Entrées for Lean Days outside of Lent

1. Sole in Ragout

Get your sole, scrape and gut them, set them to drain and dry them; flour them and put them into a pan to half-cook by frying. Then open them up and remove their backbone. After that you stuff them with capers, mushrooms, truffles, milt, a little bread crust, a scallion, only a little verjuice and bouillon; simmer everything together. Serve with the juice of a little lemon on top.

2. Pike in Ragout

Cut it up and put it [to cook] with white wine, a bouquet of herbs and very fresh butter; season that well with capers and mushrooms. Then, with the sauce much reduced and thickened, serve with slices of lemon and pomegranate seeds.

3. Tench in Ragout

Scald and dress them, cut them into rounds and wash them carefully; then set them to boil in a skillet with salt, pepper and onion; add in a cup of white wine and a little chopped parsley. When the sauce is very reduced, thicken it with egg yolks. Serve.

4. Stuffed Tench in Ragout

Scald and debone them; then with their flesh and hard-boiled egg yolks make a stuffing which you season and with which you stuff your tench. Then set them to simmer in a dish in a little bouillon and white wine, with a few bread crust crumbs, mushrooms if you have any, asparagus, milt and truffles. Serve.

5. Fried and Marinated Tench

When the tench have been dressed, split them in half; then set them to marinate in salt, pepper, onion and lemon peel. When they have marinated, take them out, dry them and flour them; alternatively, mix a little flour into two or three eggs and salt; fry them in clarified butter. When done, set them to come to a boil in their marinade. Serve, garnishing them with whatever you have.

6. Stewed Carp

Dress your carp, scale them and cut them up according to their size. Set them to cook in a pot, cauldron or skillet, in white or claret wine, and season them well with salt, cloves, pepper, chopped onion, scallions, capers and a few crusts of bread; cook everything together. When they are done and the sauce is quite thick and reduced, serve them.

7. Stuffed Carp in Ragout

With your carp carefully scaled, gut them and split them along the backbone; remove their skin, and their flesh which you chop up very small and season with parsley, fresh butter, salt, pepper, egg yolks, milk and milt. Then make a ragout of bouillon, verjuice, fresh butter, mushrooms, asparagus and scallions. When the stuffed fish are well cooked, and the sauce quite thickened with crust crumbs and capers, serve.

8. Fried Carp in Ragout

The carp has to be scaled and gutted; then split it and remove its backbone. Sprinkle it with salt, flour it and fry it in clarified butter. When it is done, serve it dry, with orange juice on top.

9. Roast Carp in Ragout

Gut it as it comes out of the water; cut it open on top, butter it and set it on the grill. When it has roasted, make a sauce of fresh butter browned in a pan, parsley and chives, both finely chopped, verjuice, vinegar and a little bouillon; season all that; cook it with capers. If you like, serve it with Green Sauce as soon as you have set it out.

10. Carp in a Half Court-Bouillon

Get your carp straight out of the water, gut it and cut it up according to its size; then put it with vinegar, very little salt, pepper and chopped onion, then put with it capers and very fresh butter. Then cook it in a cauldron with your mixture. As soon as the sauce has thickened, put it into a dish for fear that your cauldron may give a brass taste. Serve.

11. Carp Hash

Get carp, scale and gut them; remove their skin by cutting it by the gills and pulling it downwards. When they are skinned, remove their flesh and chop it up with parsley; then mix in a little bouillon and very fresh butter; season it well; cook it with a bouquet of herbs. When it is done, add in some cream or milk, with egg yolks if you like. Serve them well garnished with asparagus stalks and carp milt.

SEVENTY
Coffee Advertisement

*This ad is a broadsheet printed in the 1650s in London, right at the time coffee was intro-
duced to the country. Note how the seller used a variety of angles, including medicinal, to sell
the new drink. Many beverages begin as medicines and gradually are drunk for mere pleasure.
Interestingly, many of coffee's qualities the author gets quite right. The advertisement is held
by the British Library; the ellipses note where the text is frayed and missing. Also, look online
at any image of a seventeenth-century coffee house; they are usually pictured as riotous.*

THE VERTUE OF THE COFFEE DRINK

First Publiquely Made: and Sold in England, by Pasqua Rosee

The Grain or Berry called Coffee, groweth upon little Trees, only in the Deserts of Arabia. It
is brought from thence, and drunk generally throughout all the Grand Seigniors Dominions.
It is a simple innocent thing, composed into a Drink, be being dryed in an Oven, and ground
to Powder, and, boiled up with Spring water, and about half a pint of it to be drunk, fasting an
hour before, and not eating an hour after, and to be taken as hot as possibly can be endured;
the which will never fetch the skin off the mouth, or raise any Blisters, by reason of that Heat.

The Turks drink at meals and other times, is usually Water, and their Dyet consists much of
Fruit, the Crudities whereof are very much corrected by this Drink. The quality of this Drink is
cold and Dry, and though it be a Dryer, yet it neither heats, nor inflames more then hot Posset. It
so closeth the Orifice of the Stomack, and fortified the heat with . . . its very good to help digestion, and therefore of great use to be . . . bout 3 or 4 a Clock afternoon, as well as in the morning.

. . . ven quickens the Spirits, and makes the Heart Lightsome . . . is good against sore Eys, and the better if you hold your Head over it and take in the Steem that way. It supresseth Fumes exceedingly, and therefore good against the Head-ach, and will very much stop any Defluxion of Rheums, that distil from the Head upon the Stomack, and so prevent and help Consumptions and the Cough of the Lungs.

It is excellent to prevent and cure the Dropsy, Gout, and Scurvy. It is known by experience to be better then any other Drying Drink for People in years, or Children that have any running humors upon them, as the Kings Evil, &c. It is very good to prevent Mis-carrying on Child-bearing Women, It is a most excellent Remedy agains the Spleen, Hypocondriack Winds, or the like.

It will prevent Drowsiness, and make one fit for business, if one have occasion to Watch, and therefore you are not to Drink of it after Supper, unless you intend to be watchful, dot it will hinder sleep for 3 or 4 hours. It is observed in Turkey, where this is generally drunk, that they are not trobled with the Stone, Gout, Dropsie, or Scurvey, and that their Skins are exceeding cleer and white. It is neither Laxative nor Restringent.

Made and Sold in St. Michaels Alley in Cornhill, by Pasqua Rosee at the Signe of his own Head.

SEVENTY-ONE
Two Treatises of Government

JOHN LOCKE

The great English philosopher John Locke (1632–1704) uses an apt analogy of food process-ing to explain the origin of property—which he believed was a natural human right and the cornerstone of a stable society with a legitimate government. But by the same logic he also condoned taking land from others if they did not improve it with efficient agriculture; at least this was how the English justified settling in North America and removing the Indians, whose methods of cultivation were presumably seen as backward. The following selection is from Essay Two, "Concerning the True Original Extent and End of Civil Government."

CHAPTER V: OF PROPERTY

[. . .]

25. God, who hath given the world to men in common, hath also given them reason to make use of it to the best advantage of life and convenience. The earth and all that is therein is given to men for the support and comfort of their being. And though all the fruits it natu-rally produces, and beasts it feeds, belong to mankind in common, as they are produced by the spontaneous hand of Nature, and nobody has originally a private dominion exclusive of the rest of mankind in any of them, as they are thus in their natural state, yet being given for the use of men, there must of necessity be a means to appropriate them some way or other before

John Locke. *Two Treatises of Government (A New Edition, Corrected).* Vol. 5. London: Thomas Tegg; London: W. Sharpe and Son; London: G. Offor; G. and J. Robinson; London: J. Evans and Co.; Glasgow: R. Griffin and Co.; Dublin: J. Gumming, 1823. Prepared by Rod Hay. Published online by McMaster University Archive of the History of Economic Thought. http://socserv.mcmaster.ca/~econ/ugcm/3ll3/locke/government.pdf.

they can be of any use, or at all beneficial, to any particular men. The fruit or venison which nourishes the wild Indian, who knows no enclosure, and is still a tenant in common, must be his, and so his—i.e., a part of him, that another can no longer have any right to it before it can do him any good for the support of his life.

26. Though the earth and all inferior creatures be common to all men, yet every man has a "property" in his own "person." This nobody has any right to but himself. The "labour" of his body and the "work" of his hands, we may say, are properly his. Whatsoever, then, he removes out of the state that Nature hath provided and left it in, he hath mixed his labour with it, and joined to it something that is his own, and thereby makes it his property. It being by him removed from the common state Nature placed it in, it hath by this labour something annexed to it that excludes the common right of other men. For this "labour" being the un-questionable property of the labourer, no man but he can have a right to what that is once joined to, at least where there is enough, and as good left in common for others.

27. He that is nourished by the acorns he picked up under an oak, or the apples he gathered from the trees in the wood, has certainly appropriated them to himself. Nobody can deny but the nourishment is his. I ask, then, when did they begin to be his? when he digested? or when he ate? or when he boiled? or when he brought them home? or when he picked them up? And it is plain, if the first gathering made them not his, nothing else could. That labour put a distinction between them and common. That added something to them more than Nature, the common mother of all, had done, and so they became his private right. And will any one say he had no right to those acorns or apples he thus appro-priated because he had not the consent of all mankind to make them his? Was it a robbery thus to assume to himself what belonged to all in common? If such a consent as that was necessary, man had starved, notwithstanding the plenty God had given him. We see in com-mons, which remain so by compact, that it is the taking any part of what is common, and removing it out of the state Nature leaves it in, which begins the property, without which the common is of no use. And the taking of this or that part does not depend on the express consent of all the commoners. Thus, the grass my horse has bit, the turfs my servant has cut, and the ore I have digged in any place, where I have a right to them in common with others, become my property without the assignation or consent of anybody. The labour that was mine, removing them out of that common state they were in, hath fixed my property in them.

28. By making an explicit consent of every commoner necessary to any one's appropriating to himself any part of what is given in common. Children or servants could not cut the meat which their father or master had provided for them in common without assigning to every one his peculiar part. Though the water running in the fountain be every one's, yet who can doubt but that in the pitcher is his only who drew it out? His labour hath taken it out of the hands of Nature where it was common, and belonged equally to all her children, and hath thereby appropriated it to himself.

29. Thus this law of reason makes the deer that Indian's who hath killed it; it is allowed to be his goods who hath bestowed his labour upon it, though, before, it was the common right of every one. And amongst those who are counted the civilised part of mankind, who have made and multiplied positive laws to determine property, this original law of Nature for the

beginning of property, in what was before common, still takes place, and by virtue thereof, what fish any one catches in the ocean, that great and still remaining common of mankind; or what ambergris any one takes up here is by the labour that removes it out of that common state Nature left it in, made his property who takes that pains about it. And even amongst us, the hare that any one is hunting is thought his who pursues her during the chase. For being a beast that is still looked upon as common, and no man's private possession, whoever has employed so much labour about any of that kind as to find and pursue her has thereby removed her from the state of Nature wherein she was common, and hath begun a property.

SEVENTY-TWO

The Compleat Housewife

E. SMITH

This cookbook was first published in England in 1727 and reprinted many times, includ-ing in Williamsburg, Virginia, in 1742. It is, as it advertises, a complete compendium for running a household and cooking from scratch. Many of the recipes were taken from other cookbooks, and this seems to have been a common practice among them all.

To Make Asparagus Soup

Take twelve pounds of lean beef, cut in thin slices; then put a quarter of a pound of butter in a stew-pan over the fire, and put your beef in; let it boil up thick till it begins to brown, then put in a pint of brown ale, and a gallon of water; cover it close, and let it stew gently for an hour and a half; put in what spice you like in the stewing, and strain out the liquor, and skim off all the fat; then put in some vermicelly, some celery wash'd and cut small, half a hundred of asparagus cut small, and palates boiled tender and cut; put all these in, and let them boil gently till tender; just as it is going up fry a handful of spinach in butter, and throw in a French roll.

E. [Eliza?] Smith. *The Compleat Housewife*. 1758. Facsimile, London: Studio Editions, 1994, p. 89.

SEVENY-THREE
Emile

JEAN-JACQUES ROUSSEAU

Rousseau (1712–1778) was one of the great French philosophers of the Enlightenment, but he did not share their faith in progress. In fact, he thought we were best in the state of nature and that property and civilization in general ruined us. This selection is from his educational guidebook called Emile, *in which he attempts to raise a boy "naturally," and that includes natural foods. Consider how every generation has a very different idea of what it means to eat naturally.*

We should die of hunger or poison if we were compelled to wait in order to choose the food that is best for us, till experience had taught us to know and to choose it; but the Supreme Goodness which has caused the pleasure of sensitive beings to be the instrument of their conservation shows us, from what pleases our palate, what is best for our stomach. Naturally, there is no safer physician for a man than his own appetite, and, taking him in his primitive condition, I doubt not that the food which he found most agreeable was also the most wholesome.

The farther we depart from the state of Nature the more we lose our natural tastes; or, rather, habit becomes to us a second nature, which we substitute so completely for the original that none of us longer know what our original is.

Those who say that children must be accustomed to the aliments which they will use when grown, do not seem to me to reason correctly. Why ought their nurture to remain the same while their manner of living is so different? A man exhausted by labor, care, and trouble,

Jean-Jacques Rousseau. *Emile*. Translated by William H. Payne. New York: Appleton & Co., 1909, pp. 117–20.

needs succulent food, which brings new energy to the brain; while the child who has just been playing, and whose body is growing, needs a copious diet which produces an abundance of chyle. Moreover, the grown man already has his station in life, his occupation and his home; but who of us can be sure of what Fortune has in reserve for the child? In no particular let us impose on him so determinate a form that it will cost him too much to change it when necessity requires. Let us not cause him to die of hunger in foreign countries, if he does not keep a French cook with him wherever he goes, nor to say, one day, that people know how to eat only in France. This, by the way, is a fine compliment! For myself I would say, on the contrary, that it is only the French who do not know how to eat, since such a peculiar art is required in order to render their food palatable.

Gluttony is the vice of natures which have no substance in them. The soul of a glutton is all in his palate—he is made only for eating; in his stupid incapacity, he is himself only at table, he is able to judge only of dishes. Leave him to this employment without regret; both for ourselves and for him, this employment is better for him than any other.

The fear that gluttony may take root in a child of any capacity is a narrow-minded precaution. The child thinks of nothing but eating; but in adolescence we no longer think of it; for everything tastes good, and we have many other things to occupy our thoughts. However, I would not have an indiscreet use made of so low a motive, nor support the honor of doing a noble deed on the promise of some toothsome morsel. But as the whole of childhood is, or ought to be, devoted only to sports and gay amusements, I see no reason why exercises purely corporeal should not have a material and sensible reward. When a little Majorcan, seeing a basket on the top of a tree, brings it down by the use of his sling, is it not very proper that he should profit by the feat? When a young Spartan, at the risk of a hundred blows of the whip, cleverly slips into a kitchen and there steals a live fox, and while carrying him off in his frock is scratched, bitten, and covered with blood; and when, for fear of being caught, the child allows his bowels to be lacerated without a scowl and without uttering a single cry—is it not just that he finally profit by his booty, and that he eat it, after having been eaten by it? A good dinner never ought to be a reward; but why should it not sometimes be the effect of the pains we have taken to procure it? Émile never regards the cake which I put on the stone as a reward for having run well; he knows merely that the only means of getting the cake is to be the first to reach it.

This does not at all contradict the maxims which I lately stated concerning simplicity of diet; for, in order to sharpen the appetite of children, it is not necessary to excite their gustatory pleasure but only to satisfy their hunger; and this will be accomplished by the most common things in the world if we do not set ourselves at work to refine their taste. Their continual appetite, excited by the need of growth, is a sure condiment which takes the place of many others. Fruits, milk, some piece of cookery more delicate than ordinary bread, and, above all, the art of dispensing all this with moderation—this is the way to lead armies of children through the world without giving them a taste for exciting savors or running the risk of blunting their palates.

Whatever diet you give your children, provided you accustom them only to common and simple dishes, let them eat, run, and play as much as they please, and you may be sure that they will never eat too much, and will never be troubled by indigestion; but if you starve them half the time, and they find the means of escaping your vigilance, they will make up for what they have lost with all their might: they will eat to repletion, almost to bursting. Our appetite is inordinate only because we give it other rules than those of Nature; always regulating, prescribing, adding and retrenching, we do nothing save with the balance in hand; but this balance is governed by our fancies and not by our stomachs. I am always recurring to my illustrations. Among peasants the cupboard and the fruit-room are always open, and neither children nor men know what indigestion is.

If it should happen, however, that a child eat too much—a thing which I do not believe possible, according to my method—it is so easy to distract him with amusements which he likes that we might finally exhaust him with inanition without his thinking of it. How is it that means so sure and easy escape all our teachers? Herodotus relates that the Lydians, sore pressed by an extreme famine, bethought themselves of inventing games and other amusements, by which they diverted attention from their hunger and passed whole days without thinking of eating. Your wise tutors have perhaps read this passage a hundred times without seeing the application that might be made of it to children. Some of them will say to me that a child does not willingly leave his dinner in order to study his lesson. Master, you are right. I was not thinking of that sort of amusement.

SEVENTY-FOUR

American Cookery

AMELIA SIMMONS

This was not the first cookbook published in the United States; the earliest were merely reprints of English titles. But this is the first that reflects uniquely American ingredients and recipes. There is still a veneer of English taste and refinements, but also simple preparations based on corn and pumpkins. Little is known about the author except that she was an orphan, and perhaps even illiterate. The work was reprinted and pirated many times after the first edition of 1798.

To Stuff and Roast a Turkey, or Fowl

One pound soft wheat bread, 3 ounces beef suet, 3 eggs, a little sweet thyme, sweet marjoram, pepper and salt, and some add a gill of wine; fill the bird therewith and sew up, hand down to a steady solid fire, basting frequently with salt and water, and roast until a steam emits from the breast, put one third of a pound of butter into the gravy, dust flour over the bird and baste with the gravy; serve up with boiled onions and cranberry-sauce, mangoes, pickles or celery.

2. Others omit the sweet herbs, and add parsley done with potatoes.

3. Boil and mash 3 pints potatoes, wet them with butter, add sweet herbs, pepper, salt, fill and roast as above.

To Dress a Turtle

Fill a boiler or kettle, with a quantity of water sufficient to scald the callapach and Callapee, the fins, &c. and about 9 o'clock hang up your Turtle by the hind fins, cut off the head and save the blood, take a sharp pointed knife and separate the callapach from the callapee, or the back

---

Amelia Simmons. *American Cookery*. Hartford, CT: Simeon Butler, 1798, pp. 18–19, 20–22, 26, 28.

from the belly part, down to the shoulders, so as to come to the entrails which take out, and clean them, as you would those of any other animal, and throw them into a tub of clean water, taking great care not to break the gall, but to cut it off from the liver and throw it away, then separate each distinctly and put the guts in another vessel, open them with a small pen-knife end to end, wash them clean, and draw them through a woolen cloth, in warm water, to clear away the slime and then put them in clean cold water till they are used with the other parts of the entrails, which must be cut up small to be mixed in the baking dishes with the meat; this done, separate the back and belly pieces, entirely cutting away the fore fins by the upper joint, which scald; peal off the loose skin and cut them into small pieces, laying them by themselves, either in another vessel, or on the table, ready to be seasoned; then cut off the meat from the belly part, and clean the back from the lungs, kidneys, &c. and that meat cut into pieces as small as a walnut, laying it likewise by itself; after this you are to scald the back and belly pieces, pulling off the shell from the back, and the yellow skin from the belly, when all will be white and clean, and with the kitchen cleaver cut those up likewise into pieces about the bigness or breadth of a card; put those pieces into clean cold water, wash them and place them in a heap on the table, so that each part may lay by itself; the meat being thus prepared and laid separate for seasoning; mix two thirds part of salt or rather more, and one third part of cayenne pepper, black pepper, and a nutmeg, and mace pounded fine, and mixt altogether; the quantity to be proportioned to the size of the Turtle, so that in each dish there may be about three spoonfuls of seasoning to every twelve pound of meat; your meat being thus seasoned, get some sweet herbs, such as thyme, savory, &c. let them be dryed and rub'd fine, and having provided some deep dishes to bake it in, which should be of the common brown ware, put in the coarsest part of the meat, put a quarter pound of butter at the bottom of each dish, and then put some of each of the several parcels of meat, so that the dishes may be all alike and have equal portions of the different parts of the Turtle, and between each laying of meat strew a little of the mixture of sweet herbs, fill your dishes within an inch and half, or two inches of the top; boil the blood of the Turtle, and put into it, then lay on forcemeat balls made of veal, highly seasoned with the same seasoning as the Turtle; put in each dish a gill of Madeira Wine, and as much water as it will conveniently hold, then break over it five or six eggs to keep the meat from scorching at the top, and over that shake a handful of shread parsley, to make it look green, when done put your dishes into an oven made hot enough to bake bread, and in an hour and half, or two hours (according to the size of the dishes) it will be sufficiently done.

A Nice Indian Pudding

No. 1. 3 pints scalded milk, 7 spoons fine Indian meal, stir well together while hot, let stand till cooled; add 7 eggs, half pound raisins, 4 ounces butter, spice and sugar, bake one and half hour.

No. 2. 3 pints scalded milk to one pint meal salted; cool, add 2 eggs, 4 ounces butter, sugar or molasses and spice q: s: it will require two and half hours baking.

No. 3. Salt a pint of meal, wet with one quart milk, sweeten and put into a strong cloth, brass or bell metal vessel, stone or earthen pot, secure from wet and boil 12 hours.

Pompkin

No. 1. One quart stewed and strained, 3 pints cream, 9 beaten eggs, sugar, mace, nutmeg and ginger, laid into paste No. 7 or 3, and with a dough spur, cross and chequer it, and baked in dishes three quarters of an hour.

No. 2. One quart of milk, 1 pint pompkin, 4 eggs, molasses, allspice and ginger in a crust, bake 1 hour.

Johnny Cake, or Hoe Cake

Scald 1 pint of milk and put to 3 pints of indian meal, and half pint of flower—bake before the fire. Or scald with milk two thirds of the indian meal, or wet two thirds with boiling water, add salt, molasses and shortening, work up with cold water pretty stiff, and bake as above.

Indian Slapjack

One quart of milk, 1 pint of indian meal, 4 eggs, 4 spoons of flour, little salt, beat together, baked on gridles, or fry in a dry pan, or baked in a pan which has been rub'd with suet, lard or butter.

SEVENTY-FIVE

The Physiology of Taste

JEAN ANTHELME BRILLAT-SAVARIN

Jean Anthelme Brillat-Savarin (1755–1826) is regarded as the father of modern gastron-omy. This book in many respects set the stage for professional food writing for the next two centuries. The best known and most overused passage, "Tell me what you eat and I will tell you what you are," comes from this work. Brillat-Savarin was by profession a lawyer and had to escape to the United States during the French Revolution, but he returned to become a magistrate. Look online at the images of Louis-Léopold Boilly's The Gourmand, *and Jehan Vibert's* The Marvelous Sauce.

APHORISMS. I. The universe without life would be nothing, and all that lives must be fed. II. Animals feed; man eats; the man of intellect alone knows how to eat. III. The fate of na-tions depends upon how they are fed. IV. Tell me what you eat, I will tell you what you are. V. The Creator in making it obligatory on man to eat to live, invites him thereto by appetite, and rewards him by the pleasure he experiences. VI. Good living is an act of our judgment, by which we give a preference to things agreeable to taste, to those which do not possess that quality. VII. Pleasures of the table are for all ages, all conditions, all countries, and of great variety; they are the concomitants of all other pleasures, and when all the rest are gone, they remain to console us for their loss. VIII. The dinner-table is the only place where men are not bored during the first hour. IX. The discovery of a new dish does more for the happiness of mankind, than the discovery of a new planet. X. Men who eat hastily or get drunk do not

Jean Anthelme Brillat-Savarin. *The Handbook of Dining*. Translated by Leonard Francis Simpson. London: Longman Green, 1864, pp. 5–8, 53–64.

know how to eat or drink. XI. Comestibles vary from the most substantial to the most light. XII. Beverages range from the mildest to the strongest and most delicately flavoured. XIII. To say that a man ought not to vary his wine is heresy: the palate becomes deadened; after the third glass the finest wine in the world becomes insipid. XIV. A dinner without cheese is like a pretty woman with only one eye. XV. Cookery is a science. No man is born a cook. XVI. The most indispensable qualification of a cook is punctuality. The same must be said of guests. XVII. To wait too long for a guest is a breach of politeness towards all who have arrived punctually. XVIII. A man who invites friends to dinner, and takes no personal interest in his dinner, is not worthy of friendship. XIX. The lady of the house should always take care that the coffee is excellent; and the master of the house should be sure that the liqueurs are of the first quality. XX. When you invite a man to dinner, never forget that during the short time he is under your roof his happiness is in your hands.

ON TASTE

Another method was ordained for the preservation of the animals of the earth, of which man is incontestably the most perfect. A peculiar instinct advises him to get food; he looks around him, he seizes upon the objects in which he fancies there is property to satisfy his wants; he eats, feels restored, and thus fulfils the career pointed out for him. Taste appears to have two principal functions:—1. It invites us by pleasure to repair the continual losses we incur by the action of life. 2. It aids us to select amongst the various substances which nature offers us those most suitable for food. In this selection, taste is powerfully aided by smell, as we shall see further on; for it may be asserted as a general maxim that nutritious substances are not repulsive either to taste or smell. The number of flavours is infinite, for every substance capable of solution has a peculiar flavour of its own. The sense of smell has a great influence on taste. I am inclined to believe that taste and smell are one and the same sense, the laboratory of which is the mouth, and the nose the chimney. The nose is a sentinel, and is always on the alert to cry, Who's there? Take away the sense of smell, and that of taste goes with it. This principle once put, I maintain that there are three distinct orders of taste: viz. direct sensation; complete sensation; and the sensation of judgment. Direct sensation is the first impression from the contact of the food with the organs of the mouth whilst on the point of the tongue. Complete sensation consists of the first sensation and the impression arising from it when the morsel of food leaves the first position, passes to the back of the mouth, and strikes the whole organ with its taste and perfume. Finally, the sensation of judgment is that of the mind, which reflects upon the impression transmitted by the organ. Let us have an example:—The man who eats a peach is first agreeably struck by its fragrance; he puts a slice in his mouth, and experiences a sensation of freshness and acidity, which induces him to continue; but it is only at the moment he swallows that the real perfume of the peach is revealed: this is the complete sensation caused by a peach. Finally, it is only when he has swallowed the morsel that he can exclaim, "That was delicious!" The same may be said of a man who drinks a good glass of wine. As long as the wine is in his mouth he experiences an agreeable, but not a perfect impression. It is only when he has swallowed the liquid that he really can taste, appreciate, and discern the particular perfume of the wine; and then a few minutes must be allowed to the gourmet to give vent to his feelings by: *"Peste, c'est du Chambertin!"* or, *"Mon Dieu! c'est du Surêne!"* This will suffice to prove that your real connoisseur sips his wine; at every sip he takes he has the sum total of the pleasure which another man enjoys when he swallows a whole glass. Let us take an opposite example. A doctor orders a man to take a black draught. His nose, a faithful sentinel, warns him of the treacherous liquor he is about to imbibe. His eyes become globular, as at the approach of danger; disgust is on his lips; his stomach rises. He is encouraged by the doctor, he gargles his throat with brandy, pinches his nose, and drinks. As long as the detestable beverage fills his mouth, the sensation is confused and supportable; but when the last drop disappears, the sickening flavours act, and the patient makes a grimace which the fear of death alone would warrant. If it is a glass of water, there is no taste; he drinks, swallows, and that is all. Taste is not so richly endowed as hearing; the latter sense can compare divers sounds at the same time; taste, on the contrary, is simple in actuality, that is to say, it cannot be impressioned by two flavours at the same time. But it may be double and even multiplied by succession; that is to say, in the same act of gutturation, a second and even a third sensation may be experienced, which gradually lessens, and which is designated as arriere-gout, perfume or fragrance; in the same manner as, when a key-note is struck, a practised ear discerns one or more sonances, the number of which has not yet been accurately ascertained. Hasty and careless eaters do not discern the impressions in the second degree; they are the exclusive property of a small body of elect; and it is by their means that they can classify, in order of excellence, the various substances submitted to their examination. These fugitive nuances of flavour remain for some time on the palate; the professors assume, without being aware of it, an appropriate position, and it is always with an elongated neck and a twist of the nose that they pronounce their judgment. Let us now take a philosophical glance at the pleasure or unpleasantness taste may occasion. We first find the application of that, unhappily, too general truth, that man is more organised for suffering than for experiencing pleasure. In fact, the injection of very bitter, acid, or tart substances may cause us the sensation of excruciating pain. It is even supposed that hydrocyanic acid only kills so rapidly because it causes such excruciating agony that the vital powers cannot support it. Agreeable sensations, on the contrary, are on a limited scale; and though there is a marked difference between what is insipid and what is palatable, there is no great interval between what is admitted to be good and what is reputed excellent; for example: 1st term, hard-boiled beef; 2nd term, a piece of veal; 3rd term, a pheasant roasted to a turn. Yet taste, such as nature has awarded it to us, is still that sense which, well considered, procures us the greatest degree of enjoyment.

1st. Because the pleasure of eating is the only one which, done in moderation, is not followed by fatigue. 2nd. Because it is of all times, all ages, all conditions. 3rd. Because it returns necessarily, at least once a day, and may be repeated without inconvenience two or three times within the same period of time. 4th. Because it may be enjoyed with other enjoyments, and even console us for their absence. 5th. Because its impressions are more durable and more dependent on our will; and, 6th, and finally. Because in eating we experience a certain indescribable sensation of pleasure, by what we eat we repair the losses we have sustained, and prolong life. This subject is more amply developed in that Chapter in which we discuss "the pleasures of the table" in the point of view of the present state of civilisation. We were brought up in the flattering belief that of all creatures that walk, swim, crawl, or fly, man was the one whose taste was most perfect. This faith is threatened with being upset. Dr. Gall, on what grounds I know not, pretends that there are animals whose organ of taste is much more developed and perfect than is that of man. Such doctrine smacks of heresy. Man, by divine right, king of all he surveys, for whose benefit the earth was covered and peopled, must necessarily be provided with an organ to place him in contact with all that is sapid amongst his subjects. The tongue of animals is in proportion to their intelligence; in fishes it is simply a movable bone; in birds, generally speaking, a membraneous cartilage; in quadrupeds it is often covered with scales or points, and moreover has no circumflex movement. The tongue of man, on the contrary, by the delicacy of its conformation and of the diverse membranes by which it is surrounded, or which are close to it, denotes the operations to which it is destined. I have, moreover, discovered at least three movements unknown to animals, and which I call movements of spication, rotation, and verrition.* The first takes place when the tongue leaves the lips which compress it: the second, when the tongue makes a circular movement round the space comprised between the interior of the cheeks and the palate; the third, when the tongue, turning over or under, picks up the atoms which may remain in the semicircular canal formed by the lips and gums. Animals are limited in their tastes: some live exclusively upon vegetables; others only eat flesh; others feed upon grain; not one understands a combined flavour. Man, on the contrary, is omnivorous; everything eatable becomes a prey to his vast appetite; which at once implies digestive powers proportionate to the general use he puts them to. In fact, the machinery of taste in man is of rare perfection, and to be convinced of the fact let us see it act. As soon as an esculent substance is introduced into the mouth it is confiscated, gas and juices, irretrievably. The lips prevent its leaving; the teeth seize upon it and crush it; the saliva absorbs it; the tongue bruises it and turns it round; the breath forces it towards the gullet; the tongue again rises to make it slip down; the sense of smell enjoys it as it glides past, and it is precipitated into the stomach to undergo ulterior transformations without, during the whole of this operation, the slightest atom, particle, or drop being lost, which has not been submitted to the appreciating power. And a consequence of this perfection is that gourmandise is the exclusive apanage of man. This gourmandise is even contagious; and we transmit it promptly to the animals we have in our service, and which become, in a certain measure, our companions, as elephants, dogs, cats, and even parrots. If some animals have a larger tongue than others, a more developed palate, a wider swallow, it is because that tongue, as a muscle, is meant to move heavier morsels, to press and swallow larger portions; but no logic can prove that the sense of taste is more perfect. Moreover, as taste can only be esteemed by the nature of the sensation it procures to the common centre, the impression received by an animal cannot be compared to that received by a man; the latter impression, being more clear and more precise, naturally implies a superior quality in the organ which transmits it. Finally, what greater refinement of taste can be desired, when a Roman bon-vivant could at once tell whether a fish had been caught above or below bridge? And, in our own days, a real good eater discovers at once the superior flavour of the leg of the partridge upon which it has slept. And do we not know gourmets who can tell in what latitude a grape has ripened

*From the Latin verb verro, I sweep.

from the wine they sip, with as much preciseness as Arago would predict an eclipse? And what results herefrom? Let us render to Caesar that which is Caesar's, proclaim man the great gourmand of nature, and not be astonished if Gall, like Homer, sometimes "sleeps." Hitherto we have examined taste only in the light of its physical constitution, and we have kept to the level of science. But our task does not end here, for it is especially in the moral history of this repairing sense that its importance and its glory ought to be sought. We have therefore arranged, according to analytical order, the theories and facts which constitute this history, that instruction may result without fatigue. Thus, in the chapters which follow, we shall endeavour to show how sensations from repetition and reflection have perfected the organ, and extended the sphere of its powers; how the want of eating, at first only an instinct, became a passion of influence which has assumed a marked ascendency over everything else connected with society. We will also point out how all branches of science, which have reference to the composition of substances, act in concert to place apart those which are appreciable to taste, and how travellers have worked towards the same end by submitting to our examination substances which nature seemingly never meant to bring together. We will follow chemistry from the moment it entered our subterraneous laboratories to enlighten our cooks, lay down principles, create methods, and reveal causes which have hitherto remained secret. Finally, we shall see how by the combined power of time and experience a new science arose, which nourishes, restores, preserves, persuades, consoles, and, not satisfied with strewing flowers by handfuls along the path of man, contributes also powerfully to the strength and prosperity of empires. If in the midst of these grave lucubrations a piquant anecdote, an amiable souvenir, some adventure of an agitated career, should drop from our pen, let it pass to give a zest to our readers' attention, whose number does not alarm us, and with whom we are always glad to chat; for if they are men, we feel convinced they are as indulgent as they are well informed; if they are ladies, they cannot be otherwise than charming.

PART XII

Study Questions

1. How does French taste differ from English in this period? Does this have anything to do with the type of reader these texts address? Does English antagonism for French fussiness have anything to do with it?
2. Consider why gastronomic literature arises at the end of this period? What does the advancement of science have to do with it, and are Brillat-Savarin's pretensions to scientific inquiry really justified?
3. Think about how Locke's conception of the invention of property coincides with real events. How does he use it to justify taking land from those he considered less advanced?
4. This era has often been called the first consumer society. What new goods were sold, and how were they different from goods available in previous eras? Why was caffeine so attractive to people?
5. Can you notice any similarities between Simmons's taste preferences and those of modern Americans? What accounts for these differences, apart from available ingredients?

PART THIRTEEN

Nineteenth-Century Industrial Era

The Industrial Revolution changed people's lives so dramatically that it should be considered as ushering in the second most important shift in human foodways since the Neolithic Revolution. Before the era of machines, most people grew and processed food for a living; thereafter, those who made their living that way were a minority; and today food growers and processors are a tiny minority. It was all made possible by an initial revolution in agriculture. Although historians argue about how and when this happened—and sometimes even whether it happened at all—there is no doubt that farming became so efficient and so highly capitalized that Britain and the other industrial nations that soon followed in its wake—Belgium, northern France, western Germany, northern Italy—were among the first places ever to overcome recurrent subsistence crises. Efficient crop rotation systems, plants and animals specially bred for increased yields, and eventually the use of machines such as Jethro Tull's seed drill and the McCormick Reaper—and, later in the century, chemical fertilizers—all made agriculture remarkably productive. This led directly to increased population, the growth of cities, and naturally industry itself.

In the short run, working-class diets actually deteriorated, primarily because there were no minimum wages or labor standards. There also were no food regulations, so a whole variety of additives and poisons found their way into the food supply. Instead of beer, bread, cheese, and perhaps a little meat as the regular staples, people began to live on bread and tea, or simply potatoes. The Irish potato famine was the worst calamity of the century, caused mostly by dependence on a single crop. Crowded slums, polluted water, and children working in factories all contributed to widespread disease, cholera epidemics, and malnutrition. The worker's relationship to his job also changed. Karl Marx suggested that, unlike other animals, humans can work beyond meeting our daily needs and actually derive pleasure from labor and work beyond what is necessary to feed ourselves. When one owns the tools and has creative free-dom to make what one likes, work is an outlet for self-expression. On the other hand, in a factory, where one simply obeys orders, makes what one is told on a soulless machine, and never owns the means of production, the worker is estranged from his work. In fact, the labor is sold to someone else, and all the excess profit that congeals in the manufactured object goes to someone else. Marx believed that this was a fundamental problem with capitalism and it would inevitably be overturned when workers revolted.

There were, of course, many violent revolutions; whether any implemented Marx's ideas is another question entirely. But it is true that in the latter nineteenth century both agriculture and industry permanently changed the way people eat. Increasingly, food was mass manufac-tured and shipped farther distances by train or later by truck. With the advent of efficient new technologies such as pasteurization, canning, refrigeration, and freezing, as well as steamships that could bring tropical fruit out of season or meat raised thousands of miles away, the human diet was radically transformed. Food corporations also became extremely powerful and able to influence public policy.

The strangest effect of corporate power is that in corporations' search for new sources of raw materials and new markets to sell manufactured goods, an entirely new wave of colo-nialism was ushered in. There was a mad scramble to gobble up every remaining part of the world—especially Africa and Asia. The industrial nations often conquered an area without even knowing what benefits it might yield, or simply to prevent another nation from taking it. Thus, the interests of the industrial nations displaced subsistence farming all over the globe with production of cash crops for export—whether they be bananas in Central America, pineapples in Hawaii, coffee in Java, sugar in the Caribbean, or other crops throughout Africa and Asia.

Not everyone was pleased with these developments, though, and a number of countercul-ture movements attempted to reject modern industrial feeding. These ranged from utopian communities whose members fled the cities and provided their own sustenance to religiously inspired diets and natural/health food movements that introduced whole grains, alcohol, and meat-free diets. Or, ironically, as is the case with companies such as Kellogg and Post, new breakfast cereals were introduced for health and soon become the most industrial of foods, mass produced and sold widely as convenience foods.

SEVENTY-SIX

Treatise on Adulterations of Food

FRIEDRICH ACCUM

Friedrich Accum (1769–1838) was a German chemist who moved to Britain for work. In Britain he was outraged by the extent of adulteration of common foods, and conducted chemical tests to discover what had been put into various products. He published his discoveries in this treatise in 1820. It gained him many enemies who sued him, forcing him to leave the country. In the spirit of free trade, food safety laws were not put in place for many years.

PRELIMINARY OBSERVATIONS

Of all the frauds practised by mercenary dealers, there is none more reprehensible, and at the same time more prevalent, than the sophistication of the various articles of food.

This unprincipled and nefarious practice, increasing in degree as it has been found difficult of detection, is now applied to almost every commodity which can be classed among either the necessaries or the luxuries of life, and is carried on to a most alarming extent in every part of the United Kingdom.

It has been pursued by men, who, from the magnitude and apparent respectability of their concerns, would be the least obnoxious to public suspicion; and their successful example has called forth, from among the retail dealers, a multitude of competitors in the same iniquitous course.

Friedrich Accum. *A Treatise on Adulterations of Food, and Culinary Poisons*. London: Longman, 1822, pp. 1–13.

To such perfection of ingenuity has this system of adulterating food arrived, that spurious articles of various kinds are every where to be found, made up so skilfully as to baffle the discrimination of the most experienced judges.

Among the number of substances used in domestic economy which are now very generally found sophisticated, may be distinguished—tea, coffee, bread, beer, wine, spirituous liquors, salad oil, pepper, vinegar, mustard, cream, and other articles of subsistence.

Indeed, it would be difficult to mention a single article of food which is not to be met with in an adulterated state; and there are some substances which are scarcely ever to be procured genuine.

Some of these spurious compounds are comparatively harmless when used as food; and as in these cases merely substances of inferior value are substituted for more costly and genuine ingredients, the sophistication, though it may affect our purse, does not injure our health. Of this kind are the manufacture of factitious pepper, the adulterations of mustard, vinegar, cream, &c. Others, however, are highly deleterious; and to this class belong the adulterations of beer, wines, spirituous liquors, pickles, salad oil, and many others.

There are particular chemists who make it a regular trade to supply drugs or nefarious preparations to the unprincipled brewer of porter or ale; others perform the same office to the wine and spirit merchant; and others again to the grocer and the oilman. The operators carry on their processes chiefly in secrecy, and under some delusive firm, with the ostensible denotements of a fair and lawful establishment.

These illicit pursuits have assumed all the order and method of a regular trade; they may severally claim to be distinguished as an *art and mystery*; for the workmen employed in them are often wholly ignorant of the nature of the substances which pass through their hands, and of the purposes to which they are ultimately applied.

To elude the vigilance of the inquisitive, to defeat the scrutiny of the revenue officer, and to ensure the secrecy of these mysteries, the processes are very ingeniously divided and subdivided among individual operators, and the manufacture is purposely carried on in separate establishments. The task of proportioning the ingredients for use is assigned to one individual, while the composition and preparation of them may be said to form a distinct part of the business, and is entrusted to another workman. Most of the articles are transmitted to the consumer in a disguised state, or in such a form that their real nature cannot possibly be detected by the unwary. Thus the extract of *coculus indicus*, employed by fraudulent manufacturers of malt-liquors to impart an intoxicating quality to porter or ales, is known in the market by the name of *black extract*, ostensibly destined for the use of tanners and dyers. It is obtained by boiling the berries of the coculus indicus in water, and converting, by a subsequent evaporation, this decoction into a stiff black tenacious mass, possessing, in a high degree, the narcotic and intoxicating quality of the poisonous berry from which it is prepared. Another substance, composed of extract of quassia and liquorice juice, used by fraudulent brewers to economise both malt and hops, is technically called *multum*.

The quantities of coculus indicus berries, as well as of black extract, imported into this country for adulterating malt liquors, are enormous. It forms a considerable branch of commerce in the hands of a few brokers: yet, singular as it may seem, no inquiry appears to have been hitherto made by the officers of the revenue respecting its application. Many other substances employed in the adulteration of beer, ale, and spirituous liquors, are in a similar manner intentionally disguised; and of the persons by whom they are purchased, a great number are totally unacquainted with their nature or composition.

An extract, said to be innocent, sold in casks, containing from half a cwt. to five cwt. by the brewers' druggists, under the name of *bittern*, is composed of calcined sulphate of iron (copperas), extract of coculus indicus berries, extract of quassia, and Spanish liquorice.

It would be very easy to adduce, in support of these remarks, the testimony of numerous individuals, by whom I have been professionally engaged to examine certain mixtures, said to be perfectly innocent, which are used in very extensive manufactories of the above description. Indeed, during the long period devoted to the practice of my profession, I have had abundant reason to be convinced that a vast number of dealers, of the highest respectability, have vended to their customers articles absolutely poisonous, which they themselves considered as harmless, and which they would not have offered for sale, had they been apprised of the spurious and pernicious nature of the compounds, and of the purposes to which they were destined.

For instance, I have known cases in which brandy merchants were not aware that the substance which they frequently purchase under the delusive name of *flash*, for strengthening and clarifying spirituous liquors, and which is held out as consisting of burnt sugar and isinglass only, in the form of an extract, is in reality a compound of sugar with extract of capsicum; and that to the acrid and pungent qualities of the capsicum is to be ascribed the heightened flavour of brandy and rum, when coloured with the above-mentioned matter.

In other cases the ale-brewer has been supplied with ready-ground coriander seeds, previously mixed with a portion of *nux vomica* and quassia, to give a bitter taste and narcotic property to the beverage.

The retail venders of mustard do not appear to be aware that mustard seed alone cannot produce, when ground, a powder of so intense and brilliant a colour as that of the common mustard of commerce. Nor would the powder of real mustard, when mixed with salt and water, without the addition of a portion of pulverised capsicum, keep for so long a time as the mustard usually offered for sale.

Many other instances of unconscious deceptions might be mentioned, which were practised by persons of upright and honourable minds.

It is a painful reflection, that the division of labour which has been so instrumental in bringing the manufactures of this country to their present flourishing state, should have also tended to conceal and facilitate the fraudulent practices in question; and that from a correspondent ramification of commerce into a multitude of distinct branches, particularly in the metropolis and the large towns of the empire, the traffic in adulterated commodities should find its way through so many circuitous channels, as to defy the most scrutinizing endeavour to trace it to its source.

It is not less lamentable that the extensive application of chemistry to the useful purposes of life, should have been perverted into an auxiliary to this nefarious traffic. But, happily for the science, it may, without difficulty, be converted into a means of detecting the abuse; to effect which, very little chemical skill is required; and the course to be pursued forms the object of the following pages.

SEVENTY-SEVEN

A Plain Cookery Book
for the Working Classes

CHARLES ELMÉ FRANCATELLI

Charles Elmé Francatelli (1805–1876) was a professional chef and even was briefly hired to serve Queen Victoria. This inexpensive little book shows that there was a general spirit of charity in trying to help the working masses, who were paid little, often lived in deplorable conditions, and, most importantly, cooked very little or poorly. Francatelli believed that some basic kitchen skills could improve their condition and health.

INTRODUCTION

MY object in writing this little book is to show you how you may prepare and cook your daily food, so as to obtain from it the greatest amount of nourishment at the least possible expense; and thus, by skill and economy, add, at the same time, to your comfort and to your comparatively slender means. The Recipes which it contains will afford sufficient variety, from the simple every-day fare to more tasty dishes for the birthday, Christmas-day, or other festive occasions.

In order to carry out my instructions properly, a few utensils will be necessary. Industry, good health, and constant employment, have, in many instances, I trust, enabled those whom I now address to lay by a little sum of money. A portion of this will be well spent in the purchase of the following articles:—A cooking-stove, with an oven at the side, or placed under the grate, which should be so planned as to admit of the fire being open or closed at will; by this contrivance much heat and fuel are economized; there should also be a boiler at the back

Charles Elmé Francatelli. *A Plain Cookery Book for the Working Classes*. London: Bosworth and Harrison, 1861. Reprint by Whistable, UK: Pryor Publications, 1993, pp. 9–11, 13–16, 100–101.

of the grate. By this means you would have hot water always ready at hand, the advantage of which is considerable. Such poor men's cooking-stoves exist, on a large scale, in all modern-built lodging-houses. Also, a three-gallon iron pot with a lid to it, a one-gallon saucepan, a two-quart ditto, a frying-pan, a gridiron, and a strong tin baking-dish.

Here is a list of the cost prices at which the above-named articles, as well as a few others equally necessary, may be obtained of all ironmongers:—

	£	s.	d.
A cooking-stove, 2 ft. 6 in. wide, with oven only	1	10	0
Ditto, with oven and boiler	1	18	0
A three-gallon oval boiling pot	0	4	6
A one-gallon tin saucepan, and lid	0	2	6
A two-quart ditto	0	1	6
A potato steamer	0	2	0
An oval frying-pan, from	0	0	10
A gridiron, from	0	1	0
A copper for washing or brewing, twelve gallons	1	10	0
A mash-tub, from	0	10	0
Two cooling-tubs (or an old wine or beer cask cut in halves, would be cheaper, and answer the same purpose), each 6s.	0	12	0
	£6	12	4

To those of my readers who, from sickness or other hindrance, have not money in store, I would say, strive to lay by a little of your weekly wages to purchase these things, that your families may be well fed, and your homes made comfortable.

And now a few words on baking your own bread. I assure you if you would adopt this excellent practice, you would not only effect a great saving in your expenditure, but you would also insure a more substantial and wholesome kind of food; it would be free from potato, rice, bean or pea flour, and alum, all of which substances are objectionable in the composition of bread. The only utensil required for bread-baking would be a tub, or trough, capable of working a bushel or two of flour. This tub would be useful in brewing, for which you will find in this book plain and easy directions.

I have pointed out the necessity of procuring these articles for cooking purposes, and with the injunction to use great care in keeping them thoroughly clean, I will at once proceed to show you their value in a course of practical and economical cookery, the soundness and plainness of which I sincerely hope you will all be enabled to test in your own homes.

COOKERY BOOK

No. 1. Boiled Beef

This is an economical dinner, especially where there are many mouths to feed; and consequently comes within the reach of your means. Buy a few pounds of either salt brisket, thick or thin flank, or buttock of beef; these pieces are always to be had at a low rate. Let us suppose you have bought a piece of salt beef for a Sunday's dinner, weighing about five pounds, at 6½d. per pound, that would come to 2s. 8½d.; two pounds of common flour, 4d., to be made into suet pudding or dumplings, and say 8½d. for cabbages, parsnips, and potatoes; altogether 3s. 9d. This would produce a substantial dinner for ten persons in family, and would, moreover, as children do not require much meat when they have pudding, admit of there being enough left to help out the next day's dinner, with potatoes.

No. 2. How to Boil Beef

Put the beef into your three or four gallon pot, three parts filled with cold water, and set it on the fire to boil; remove all the scum that rises to the surface, and then let it boil gently on the hob; when the meat is about half done, which will take an hour, add the parsnips in a net, and at the end of another half hour put in the cabbages, also in a net. A piece of beef weighing five or six pounds will require about two hours' gentle boiling to cook it thoroughly. The dumplings may, of course, be boiled with the beef, etc. I may here observe that the dumplings and vegetables, with a small quantity of the meat, would be all-sufficient for the children's meal.

No. 3. Economical Pot Liquor Soup

A thrifty housewife will not require that I should tell her to save the liquor in which the beef has been boiled; I will therefore take it for granted that the next day she carefully removes the grease, which will have become set firm on the top of the broth, into her fat pot, and keeps it to make a pie-crust, or to fry potatoes, or any remains of vegetables, onions, or fish. The liquor must be tasted, and if it is found to be too salt, some water must be added to lessen its saltness, and render it palatable. The pot containing the liquor must then be placed on the fire to boil, and when the scum rises to the surface it should be removed with a spoon. While the broth is boiling, put as many piled-up tablespoonfuls of oatmeal as you have pints of liquor into a basin; mix this with cold water into a smooth liquid batter, and then stir it into the boiling soup; season with some pepper and a good pinch of allspice, and continue stirring the soup with a stick or spoon on the fire for about twenty minutes; you will then be able to serve out a plentiful and nourishing meal to a large family at a cost of not more than the price of the oatmeal.

No. 4. Potato Soup for Six Persons

Peel and chop four onions, and put them into a gallon saucepan, with two ounces of dripping fat, or butter, or a bit of fat bacon; add rather better than three quarts of water, and set the whole to boil on the fire for ten minutes; then throw in four pounds of peeled and sliced-up potatoes, pepper and salt, and with a wooden spoon stir the soup on the fire for about twenty-five minutes, by which time the potatoes will be done to a pulp, and the soup ready for dinner or breakfast.

No. 5. Pea Soup for Six Persons

Cut up two and a-half pounds of pickled pork, or some pork cuttings, or else the same quantity of scrag end of neck of mutton, or leg of beef, and put any one of these kinds of meat into a pot with a gallon of water, three pints of split or dried peas, previously soaked in cold water over-night, two carrots, four onions, and a head of celery, all chopped small; season with pepper, but *no* salt, as the pork, if pork is used, will season the soup sufficiently; set the whole to boil very gently for at least three hours, taking care to skim it occasionally, and do not forget that the peas, etc., must be stirred from the bottom of the pot now and then; from three to four hours' gentle boiling will suffice to cook a good mess of this most excellent and satisfying soup. If fresh meat is used for this purpose, salt must be added to season it. Dried mint may be strewn over the soup when eaten.

No. 6. Onion Soup for Six Persons

Chop fine six onions, and fry them in a gallon saucepan with two ounces of butter or dripping fat, stirring them continuously until they become of a very light colour; then add six ounces of flour or oatmeal, and moisten with three quarts of water; season with pepper and salt, and stir the soup while boiling for twenty minutes, and when done, pour it out into a pan or bowl containing slices of bread.

No. 7. Broth Made from Bones for Soup

Fresh bones are always to be purchased from butchers at about a farthing per pound; they must be broken up small, and put into a boiling-pot with a quart of water to every pound of bones; and being placed on the fire to boil, must be well skimmed, seasoned with pepper and salt, and a few carrots, onions, turnips, celery, and thyme, and boiled very gently for six hours; then to be strained off, and put back into the pot, with any bits of meat or gristle which may have fallen from the bones (the bones left are still worth a farthing per pound, and can be sold to the bone-dealers). Let this broth be thickened with peasemeal or oatmeal, in the proportion of a large table-spoonful to every pint of broth, and stirred over the fire while boiling for twenty-five minutes, by which time the soup will be done. It will be apparent to all good housewives that, with a little trouble and good management, a savoury and substantial meal may thus be prepared for a mere trifle.

No. 240. How to Prepare a Large Quantity of Good Soup for the Poor

It is customary with most large families, while living in the country, to kill at least some portion of the meat consumed in their households; and without supposing for a moment that any portion of this is ever wasted, I may be allowed to suggest that certain parts, such as sheep's heads, plucks, shanks, and scrag-ends, might very well be spared towards making a good mess of soup for the poor. The bones left from cooked joints, first baked in a brisk oven for a quarter of an hour, and afterwards boiled in a large copper of water for six hours, would readily prepare a gelatinized foundation broth for the soup; the bones, when sufficiently boiled, to be taken out. And thus, supposing that your copper is already part filled with the broth made from bones (all the grease having been removed from the surface), add any meat you may have, cut up in pieces of about four ounces weight, garnish plentifully with carrots, celery, onions, some thyme, and ground all-spice, well-soaked split peas, barley, or rice; and, as the soup boils up, skim it well occasionally, season moderately with salt, and after about four hours' gentle and continuous boiling, the soup will be ready for distribution. It was the custom in families where I have lived as cook, to allow a pint of this soup, served out with the pieces of meat in it, to as many as the recipients' families numbered; and the soup was made for distribution twice every week during winter.

No. 241. Another Method for Making Economical Soup

In households where large joints of salt beef, or pork, are cooked almost daily for the family, the liquor in which they have been boiled should be saved, all grease removed therefrom, put into the copper with a plentiful supply of carrots, parsnips, celery, and onions, all cut in small pieces, the whole boiled and well skimmed till the vegetables are done; the soup is then to be thickened with either oatmeal, pease-meal, or Indian corn meal, seasoned with pepper and ground allspice, and stirred continuously until it boils up again; it must then be skimmed, and the best pieces of meat selected from the stock-pot should be kept in careful reserve, to be added to the soup, and allowed to boil therein for half an hour longer.

No. 242. How to Make Fish Soup in Large Quantities for Distribution to the Poor

This kind of soup, it will be easily understood, is applicable only on the sea-coast, and wherever fish is to be had very cheap. Chop fine a dozen onions, some thyme, and winter savory, and put these in a copper, or some large pot, with about six gallons of water, one pound of butter, pepper and salt enough to season; allow the whole to boil for ten minutes, then thicken the broth with about four pounds of oatmeal, pease-meal, or flour; stir the soup continuously until it boils, and then throw in about fifteen pounds of fish cut up in one-pound size pieces, and also some chopped parsley; boil all together until the fish is done, and then serve out the soup to the recipients. All kinds of fish, except sprats, herrings, and pilchards, are equally well adapted for making fish soup, but codfish, cod's heads, skate, eels, etc., and all glutinous fish, suit the purpose best.

SEVENTY-EIGHT

A Treatise on Bread, and Bread Making

SYLVESTER GRAHAM

Sylvester Graham (1794–1851) was a dietary reformer whose name is familiar in the eponymous cracker and graham flour. He believed in the virtues of whole wheat for regularity and spoke out against chemical additives in food. He was also a vegetarian, abstained from alcohol, and had an enormous impact on health food movements in the United States. John Harvey Kellogg was deeply influenced by Graham's food philosophies.

No;—it is the wife, the mother only—she who loves her husband and her children as woman ought to love, and who rightly perceives the relations between the dietetic habits and physical and moral condition of her loved ones, and justly appreciates the importance of good bread to their physical and moral welfare—she alone it is, who will be ever inspired by that cordial and unremitting affection and solicitude which will excite the vigilance, secure the attention, and prompt the action requisite to success, and essential to the attainment of that maturity of judgment and skilfulness of operation, which are the indispensable attributes of a perfect bread-maker. And could wives and mothers fully comprehend the importance of good bread in relation to all the bodily and intellectual and moral interests of their husbands and children, and in relation to the domestic and social and civil welfare of mankind, and to their religious prosperity, both for time and eternity, they would estimate the art and duty of bread-making far, very far more highly than they now do. They would then realize that, as no one can feel so deep and delicate an interest for their husbands' and children's happiness as they do, so no one can be so proper a person to prepare for them that portion of their aliment, which

Sylvester Graham. *A Treatise on Bread, and Bread Making.* Boston: Light and Stearns, 1837, pp. 105–11, 123–26.

requires a degree of care and attention that can only spring from the lively affections and solicitude of a wife and mother.

But it is a common thing to hear women say—"We cannot always have good bread, if we take ever so much pains;—it will sometimes be heavy, and sometimes be sour, and sometimes badly baked, in spite of all our care."

It may be true that such things will sometimes happen, even with the best of care;—but I believe that there is almost infinitely more poor bread than there is any good excuse for. The truth is, the quality of bread is a matter of too little consideration; and therefore too little care is given to the making of it. Moreover, the sense of taste is so easily vitiated, that we can very easily become reconciled to the most offensive gustatory qualities, and even learn to love them; and it is a very common thing to find families so accustomed to sour bread, that they have no perception of its acid quality.

"It is very strange," said a lady to me one day at her dinner table, "that some folks always have sour bread, and never know it." She then went on to name a number of families in the circle of her acquaintance, who, she said, invariably had sour bread upon their tables when she visited them—"and they never," continued she, "seem to have the least consciousness that their bread is not perfectly sweet and good."

Yet this very lady, at the very moment she was thus addressing me, had sour bread upon her own table; and although I had for many months been very frequently at her table, I had never found any but sour bread upon it. Still she was wholly unconscious of the fact.

Difficult however as most women think it is, to have good bread always, yet there are some women who invariably have excellent bread. I have known such women. The wife of Thomans Van Winkle, Esq. of the beautiful valley of Booneton, New Jersey—peace to her ashes!—was deservedly celebrated throughout the whole circle of her acquaintance for her excellent bread. Few ever ate at her hospitable board once that did not desire to enjoy the privilege again. I know not how often it has been my good fortune to sit at her table; but the times have not been few; and though long past, and she who presided there has slept for years in her grave, yet the remembrance of those times and of those hospitalities, awakens in my bosom a deep and fervent sentiment of gratitude while I write.

Never at the table of Mrs. Van Winkle did I eat poor bread;—and of my numerous acquaintances who had sat at her table, I never heard one say he had eaten poor bread there. Her bread was invariably good. Nay, it was of such a quality that it was impossible for any one to eat of it, and not be conscious that he was partaking of bread of extraordinary excellence.

Mrs. Van Winkle, said I to her one day, while I was feasting on her delicious bread, tell me truly, is there either a miracle or mystery in this matter of bread-making, by which you are enabled to have such excellent bread upon your table at all times, while I rarely ever find bread equally good at any other table, and at ninety-nine tables in a hundred, I almost invariably find poor bread? Is it necessarily so? Is it not possible for people by any means to have good bread uniformly?

"There is no necessity for having poor bread at any time, if those who make it will give proper care and attention to their business," replied Mrs. Van Winkle, confidently. "The truth is," continued she, "most people attach very little importance to the quality of their bread; and therefore they give little care to the preparation of it. If every woman would see that her flour is sweet and good, that her yeast is fresh and lively, that her bread trough is kept perfectly clean and sweet, that her dough is properly mixed and thoroughly kneaded, and kept at a proper temperature, and at the proper time moulded into the loaf, and put into the oven, which has been properly heated, and there properly baked, then good bread would be as common as poor bread now is. But while there is such perfect carelessness and negligence about the matter, it is not surprising that bread should be generally poor."

Mrs. Van Winkle was undoubtedly correct. If anything like the care were given to bread-making that its real importance demands, a loaf of poor bread would rarely be met with. Indeed, if the same degree of care were given to bread-making, that is devoted to the making of cakes and pastry, we should far more generally be blessed with good bread.

If a lady can ever find a good excuse for having poor bread, she certainly can find none, except perhaps extreme poverty, for setting her poor bread on the table the second time. Yet, too generally, women seem to think that, as a matter of course, if they, by carelessness or any other means, have been so unlucky as to make a batch of poor bread, their family and friends must share their misfortune, and help them eat it up; and, by this means, many a child has had its health seriously impaired, and its constitution injured, and perhaps its moral character ruined—by being driven, in early life, into pernicious dietetic habits.

It was observed many years ago, by one of the most eminent and extensive practitioners in New England, that, during a practice of medicine for thirty years, he had always remarked that, in those families where the children were most afflicted with worms, he invariably found poor bread; and that, as a general fact, the converse of this was true; that is, in those families where they uniformly had heavy, sour, ill-baked bread, he generally found that the children were afflicted with worms.

A careful and extensive observation for a few years, would convince every intelligent mind that there is a far more intimate relation between the quality of the bread and the moral character of a family, than is generally supposed.

"Keep that man at least ten paces from you, who eats no bread with his dinner, said Lavater, in his "Aphorisms on Man." This notion appears to be purely whimsical at first glance; but Lavater was a shrewd observer, and seldom erred in the moral inferences which he drew from the voluntary habits of mankind; and depend upon it, a serious contemplation of this apparent whim, discloses a deeper philosophy than is at first perceived upon the surface.

Whatever may be the cause which turns our children and ourselves away from the dish of bread, and establishes an habitual disregard for it, the effect, though not perhaps in every individual instance, yet, as a general fact, is certainly, in some degree, unfavorable to the physical, and intellectual, and moral, and religious, and social, and civil and political interests of man.

Of all the artificially prepared articles of food which come upon our table, therefore, bread should be that one which, as a general fact, is uniformly preferred by our children and our household,—that one, the absence of which they would notice soonest, and feel the most,—that one which—however they may enjoy for a time the little varieties set before them—they would be most unwilling to dispense with—and which, if they were driven to the necessity, they would prefer to any other dish, as a single article of subsistence.

To effect this state of things, it is obvious that the quality of the bread must be uniformly excellent; and to secure this, I say again, there must be a judgment, an experience, a skill, a care, a vigilance, which can only spring from the sincere affections of a devoted wife and mother, who accurately perceives and duly appreciates the importance of these things, and, in the lively exercise of a pure and delicate moral sense, feels deeply her responsibilities, and is prompted to the performance of her duties.

Would to God that this were all true of every wife and mother in our country—in the world!—that the true relations, and interests, and responsibilities of life were understood and felt by every human being, and all the duties of life properly and faithfully performed!

SEVENTY-NINE

The Book of Household Management

ISABELLA BEETON

This is a massive text that covers every possible thing a woman running a house could possibly need to know. It first appeared in serial form between 1857 and 1861, issued by Mrs. Beeton's husband, who ran a publishing business. It is all the more remarkable given Mrs. Beeton's age; she died at twenty-eight from complications after delivering her fourth child. Much of the material was borrowed from other texts, but still the accomplishment was extraordinary.

THE HOUSEKEEPER

It is not given to us all to become famous, but in this busy world there are few who, metaphorically speaking, need "waste their sweetness on the desert air," or, in less poetical language, lead a useless life. Specially does this apply to women, who, though, perhaps, less gifted with brain power than the sterner sex, have yet a greater versatility of talent, and who, if they seek it, can always find a vocation.

Far from the humblest or the least dignified one is that of a housewife, in whom, if she faithfully fulfil her duties, will centre all the home interests and cares; while to her and to her alone is given the power of making her house, however humble, the embodiment of our ideal, "Home, sweet Home."

Isabella Beeton. *The Book of Household Management*. 2nd. ed. London: Ward, Lock & Co., 1895, pp. 1–12.

Surely there was never a happier title for a song, even if only for the reason that the word, fraught with so much meaning to us, finds no synonym in any other language.

The young housekeeper should never deem any of her duties ignoble ones. "The daily round, the common task," call for the exercise of virtues that would hold but a poor place in pleasure or gaiety. Unselfishness, industry, patience, perseverance and thoughtful care for others are most needful qualities for the good housekeeper to possess, for with her rest many responsibilities.

Take a very homely illustration that may serve to show what we mean.

It falls to the lot of the housewife to prepare the dinner. Does she, grudging the time and disliking the task, get this over in the quickest possible manner, caring but little *how* the food is cooked or whether it is likely to please those for whom it is intended, the result is in nine cases out of ten an unsatisfactory meal. Now, an unsatisfactory meal is not only a meal wasted, but it may be one that has done harm to someone. An infinitesimal injury, it may be said; but, as bricks go one by one to build a house, and by their good or bad qualities determine its stability or instability, so do the meals of a life-time, one by one, according to their suitability and nourishment, help to build up a sound constitution or the reverse. We shall have to introduce this subject again in our remarks on the science of cookery; so to return to the housekeeper and her duties. One of the first we should think of is early rising, to which, in many households, sufficient importance is not attached. It is allowed to be necessary where there are no servants or only one, and where the first duties and the first meal of the day depend upon one pair of hands, but where there are several servants it is thought a small matter for the mistress of the house to be late in the morning. Yet this should not be except in cases of illness or infirmity.

To begin with, few query the truth of "Poor Richard's" maxim, "Early to bed and early to rise makes a man healthy and wealthy and wise," or at any rate will allow that the practice reversed is an injurious one to health; but there are other things to be considered. We are all creatures of example, servants and children being no exception to the rule, and it seldom happens that a late mistress does not make a late household.

There is no work like morning work, particularly household tasks, and those we take up early in the day, fresh from a night's rest and a good breakfast, are "trifles light as air" in comparison with the same dragged or hurried through later in the day when there is not time for their proper performance.

Later, we detail the ordinary routine of domestic work in a small household, which can only be accomplished satisfactorily when early rising and method are the order of the day.

Where there is a large staff of servants or a number proportionate to the work that is to be done in the house, there should be no need for the mistress to give any assistance; her duty should be only to supervise or see that the servants each thoroughly does his or her own work. We cannot approve of the system of being always looking after servants. Those who need their mistress at their elbows to see that they do their work are not worth keeping. Let them know exactly what they have to do and the way and order in which it is to be done, being quite sure that they have *time* for the performance of their daily duties, show them anything they have to learn, then exact the strict carrying out of each day's programme. Do not gloss over faults or carelessness and never allow one day's work to be left for the next. Be firm, strict yet kind and thoughtful for your servants, and they should respect you and carry out your wishes. If they will not do so after a fair trial it is better to part with them rather than have any discomfort in the household. A far less easy task is it to manage where there is but one servant to do all the work. We say all the work, but no general servant can thoroughly do *all* that is to be done, unless it be in a very small house, with perhaps only two in family. The question of how to help in these cases is rather a vexed one. Some say the mistress should do all the cooking, but this we think a grand mistake, for should she be unavoidably prevented from going into the kitchen the servant may not be able to take her place.

If the servant is inexperienced, her mistress should be able to show her how to do all that is necessary in plain cooking, and let her do that part of it every day, reserving for herself the task of making pastry or any other troublesome or fanciful dish that a general servant would not have time to undertake.

There are many ways in which a mistress can help without being much in the kitchen. Say in the turning out of a room. The hard work may be the sweeping and scrubbing, but the time absorbed is in the preparation, of the room for sweeping and the dusting and arranging afterwards. Leaving the harder part to the servant, the mistress might well do the other; also she might lay the cloth and do very many other little tasks that vary in every household, only remembering that her servant should know how to do all that she herself undertakes, in case of accident.

Independent of *necessary* household duties, such as keeping a house clean and tidy and having the food properly cooked and served, there are others that no good housekeeper should neglect. In every household these vary, but there is one rule that may be equally applied to all, that of making the home as attractive and pretty as possible.

One need not be rich to have pretty surroundings, particularly in these times, when there are so many ways of adding to the decoration of our rooms at a small cost, and when we can have advice gratis from experienced persons as to how we can improve and make the best of the furniture we possess. With determination to have her house as elegant as it should be clean, the young housewife will find that, with her heart in her work, a certain amount of labour and a very small outlay of money will achieve wonderful results.

As a good heart and sweet disposition will shine out of and glorify the plainest, homeliest face, so will a few artistic touches, a little labour given to improve and beautify even a humble home, give to it that charm that is found in beauty less seen than felt.

COOKERY

Necessity for Cooking

IN all ages and in all countries the pleasures of the table have been appreciated and cultivated. They are those that we taste the oftenest, and the first and last that we enjoy. In spite of all that is said in favour of our being content without luxuries and taking only what is absolutely necessary in the way of food and brink, the majority of us are quite ready to accept the fact that the good things of this earth were sent for our *use* (not abuse); and the more carefully and pleasantly these good things are prepared for our delectation the better.

It is a great mistake to think that our great men do not appreciate good cooking as well as dainty fare. *Apropos* of them, we recall the saying of Descartes, the French philosopher. One of the French noblesse, whose rank was superior to his brains, seeing the philosopher engaged upon an epicurean repast, exclaimed: "What! do you philosophers eat dainties?" and received the rebuff from Descartes, "Do you think that God made all the good things for fools?"

Dr. Johnson used to hold in contempt those who did not, or pretended not to care for good eating and drinking, and used to consider the consumption of good food a pleasurable part, but still a part of his work.

He was perfectly right, for it may be said the stomach is the mainspring of our system, and unless sufficient nourishment is given to it in the shape of good and digestible food, it cannot support either nerves or circulation.

Animal and intellectual organs are more nearly connected than many would believe. A well nourished person is not only capable of better work, either mental or bodily, but is less liable to temptations of drink or excess of any kind than one who is badly fed. French people are proverbially light-hearted and temperate, and this we think might well be attributed to the fact that, no matter to what rank they belong, they eat heartily at few meals of *well cooked* food.

Quantities and even qualities are secondary considerations compared with the cooking of our food. It is possible to eat a large meal of well prepared food and digest it perfectly, whereas a much smaller quantity, indifferently cooked, would disagree with us; and while a meal of the lightest description may afford nourishment for hours, a heavy one may be as equally unsatisfactory.

No better motto could be found for a cook than to "make the best of everything," and that is where the science of cookery comes in, teaching us, as it does, the constituents and properties of foods, looking upon them in the light of medicines and blending them accordingly, so that out of the minimum of material we may get the maximum of good.

The Science of Cookery

Till lately, chemistry has not been in active growth, but day by day it is now adding to our physiological knowledge, and is fast becoming a more popular science. With it and by its aid, advances the science of cookery.

A dietary cure is now as common, if not more so, than a medicinal one for even the greatest disorders, particularly in cases of mental aberration; and to this reason may be partly owing the giant strides that cookery has taken during the last few years.

It is argued by some who object to the term "science of cookery" that people lived as long before such a thing was heard of. So they did, just as they lived before they knew the laws of gravitation or elementary mathematics, before the days of wonderful machinery or steam. But as we are ready to acknowledge the fact that these discoveries have done much good, specially that science applied to agriculture enables us to support a larger population in greater comfort, why should we not be ready to say whether science in cookery will not aid us in the feeding of our starving millions, inasmuch as its very backbone is economy—economy in the use of the digestive organs as well as in the preparation of the food itself.

We venture to assert that gradually but surely our methods of cooking and our combinations of foods will be based upon the most carefully tested scientific discoveries, and that from laboratory to kitchen, through, it may be, treatise or lecture, the information will be handed down.

It stands to reason that we should study and learn for ourselves the properties of the foods we consume every day of our lives, even before we know those of the medicines we occasionally take, and not test them, at the expense of our bodily health, as we may do, not knowing of what they are composed.

Reasons for Cookery

We may say there are five good reasons for cooking: to make it pleasant to taste, to render mastication easy, to facilitate digestion, to combine foods, and to economise them by eating them warm.

To take the first reason. No one can enjoy and many cannot even be healthily nourished by a monotonous diet. Tasteless food is not simply unpleasant; it is not healthful; and the same food taken day after day, although it may contain all the necessary constituents, looking at it from the point of view of chemical analysis, does not give the requisite sustaining power.

It has been actually pointed out how a great improvement has been effected in the inmates of large public institutions by a change in the dietary.

We cannot give too much importance to this reason for good cooking, which is never monotonous, for it affects so materially the *health* as well as the comfort of us all.

The second reason, that of making mastication easier, is apparent without much consideration. The act may be said to be that of dividing and subdividing the food so that it exposes a greater surface to the action of the digestive juices with which it afterwards comes in contact; and it can easily be seen how the sufficient cooking of food facilitates this. Some of our greatest and strongest animals, chiefly carnivorous ones, can swallow their food raw and without mastication, but their digestion is very different from our human one, and we should require to devote a great deal longer time to our meals had we to accomplish all the grinding and subdividing by our teeth alone.

By cooking fibre is softened, starch hydrated, dough vesiculated, albumen coagulated, and a very large portion of indigestible matter, or matter difficult of mastication, removed; so half our work is done for us in the kitchen.

To the action of heat upon food may be ascribed the most important results of cookery. Cooking may not alter the chemical constitution of food, but it may utterly change its value, turning it from indigestible to digestible matter as well as rendering it pleasant to the taste. Some of the changes wrought by heat are easily explained: whether fibre is shrivelled or swelled, whether gelatine is brittle or dissolved, we do not require science to discover, but science tells us why these things are, and so enables us to more easily bring our food into the conditions we require it.

The fourth reason we have for cooking is the combination of foods, which should be carefully done in the right proportions, so that by supplying deficiencies and counteracting superabundant qualities in various foods, we may materially help digestion and supply the body with *all* its needs.

In many cases this has been done from an early period in cookery by natural instinct. Such as that which prompts us to serve peas with bacon, egg sauce with salt fish, or butter and milk with rice; but this has probably been done long before we could give the reasons, not knowing the constituents of the foods—that peas contain the starch, or floury matter, necessary to combine with fat bacon, or that egg sauce would supply the lack of nourishment in salt fish. Daily, cooks learn these things, but there is still a wide field for their discoveries.

The fifth reason for cooking is the economising of our food by heating it. Part of what we eat is heat-giving food to keep the heat of our bodies at a certain point. So long as we are in health we should be always 98° on a Fahrenheit thermometer—warm but not hot, a higher or lower temperature shows that something is amiss.

A simple illustration may serve to show why warm food is more nourishing than cold. When we put fresh coals on the fire the temperature of the room is lowered at once, because some of the heat from the live coals is absorbed into the fresh coals. This is just the case with the cold food, for some of the heat of our bodies must be employed to heat it.

There are gas burners that give a brilliant light and are yet economical, because the spare heat of the flame is used to heat the gas that will be presently burnt, and we warm our food on the same principle, the coals saving the heat of our bodies. It should be a known fact that whereas hot food is not wholesome, warm food is not only more nourishing than cold, but it goes farther, and is, therefore, as we have said, more economical.

VARIOUS FOODS

The most abundant and the cheapest are the starch and floury foods. Bread, potatoes, rice, barley and other floury foods, contain a large proportion of starch, while cornflour, arrow-root, sago and tapioca contain but very little else.

There is starch in beans and peas, but they also contain a large amount of casein, and are, therefore, usually spoken of as albuminoids, or flesh-forming foods.

There is no starch in milk, but it is, nevertheless, as a single food the most perfect, and said to sustain life alone longer than any other.

Sugar is a good food and replaces starch, but it is apt to produce acidity if used too freely.

Fats, starches and sugars are called heat-givers because they are oxydised in the body to keep it up to its proper temperature. From the starch and sugars fat is deposited, if more is consumed than is required to burn, therefore those who wish to get thin should eat little or none of these, or take sufficient exercise to burn them up.

Fat is a very necessary element in food, and should be eaten in some form or other by everyone. By fat we mean not only the fat of meat, but butter, cream, oil or dripping. Of these the most easily digested are cream and oil; hence the ordering of these for delicate or consumptive persons who have often a very great dislike to, or who cannot digest the fat of fresh meat or bacon.

Fat and starch, to a certain extent, replace one another. Carbonate and salts include besides common salt, potash, phosphates of lime and iron.

Iron is generally looked upon as a medicine rather than a food, but all others are necessary foods. Lime is wanted to make bone, and should be found in milk for the young. When it has been absent we often see weak and rickety limbs and broken and decayed teeth. Potash salt is found in all fresh vegetables and fruits; and a common defect in diet is the lack of these. Common salt, being used for dried fish and flesh, finds too large a place in the diet of the poorer classes.

Albuminoids, or flesh formers, are supplied by lean meat, poultry, game, fish, cheese, eggs, gelatine, gluten in flour, fibrine in oats, and in beans, peas and lentils. Albumen, which exists most largely in eggs, is also found in meat, the blood of animals containing it also. It may be discovered in vegetable juices as well as in seeds and nuts.

Flesh formers being as a rule more expensive than the starchy foods, the poor often suffer from the want of them.

It is reckoned that a good diet for a healthy man, doing a moderate amount of work, should consist of 22½ oz. in the following proportions by avoirdupois.

Albuminoids	3
Fats, starch, sugar, &c.	14
Salts	1
Water	4½
	22½

For a woman the ration should be about 3 oz. smaller, but the proportions the same. The various constituents of a healthy diet being yielded alike by both the animal and the vegetable world, it is clear that we can draw our supplies from either; and those who prefer what is termed a vegetarian diet need not find it less nourishing than another in which animal food enters.

FRESH PROVISIONS AND THEIR COST

Under the head of "Times when things are in Season," we give a list of all the fresh provisions to be obtained in each month; but as to many of us a more important question is the cost of the article, we give the following price list in addition.

Table of Seasons & Prices of Fresh Provision

Meat
Meat varies but little in price the year round, with the exception of early lamb.

SEASONS AND PRICES OF BEEF, DIFFERENT JOINTS AND PARTS.

Part.	In Season.	Best.	Average price.
Aitchbone	All the Year	During Winter	7*d.* per lb.
Brisket	"	"	7*d.* per lb.
Buttock	"	"	9½*d.* per lb.
" in Steaks	"	"	1*s.* per lb.
Leg of Mutton Piece	"	"	9*d.* per lb.
Neck	"	"	6*d.* per lb.
Rump	"	"	9*d.* per lb.

" in Steaks	"	"	1s. 1d. per lb.
Silver Side or Round	"	"	9d. per lb.
Sirloin	"	"	10d. per lb.
Cheek	"	"	5d. per lb.
Heart	"	"	2s. each.
Kidney	"	"	10d. each.
Tail	"	"	2s. 6d. each.
Tongue	"	"	3s. 6d. each.

SEASONS AND PRICES OF VEAL, DIFFERENT JOINTS AND PARTS.

Part.	In Season.	Best.	Average Price.
Breast	Feb. to Nov.	Summer	8d. per lb.
Cutlet	"	"	1s. 2d. per lb.
Fillet	"	"	1s. per lb.
Knuckle	"	"	6d. per lb.
Loin	"	"	9½d. per lb.
Shoulder	"	"	8½d. per lb.
Head	"	"	4s. 6d. to 6s. 6d. each.
Heart	"	"	8d. to 1s. each.
Sweetbread	"	"	From 1s.

SEASONS AND PRICES OF MUTTON, DIFFERENT JOINTS AND PARTS.

Part.	In Season.	Best.	Average Price.
Breast	All the Year	Sept. to April	6d. per lb.
Haunch	"	"	11d. per lb.
Leg	"	"	10d. per lb.
Loin	"	"	9½d. per lb.
Neck (best end)	"	"	9½d. per lb.
" (scrag end)	"	"	7d. per lb.
Saddle	"	"	10d. per lb.
Shoulder	"	"	9d. per lb.
Head	"	"	9d. to 1s. each.
Heart	"	"	4d. to 5d. each.
Kidney	"	"	3d. each.
Chops	"	"	1s. per lb.

SEASONS AND PRICES OF LAMB, DIFFERENT JOINTS AND PARTS.

Part.	In Season,	Best.	Average Price.
Breast	March to Sept.	May to July	9*d.* per lb.
Fore Quarter	"	"	10*d.* per lb.
Hind Quarter	"	"	11*d.* per lb.
Leg	"	"	1*s.* 1*d.* per lb.
Loin	"	"	1*s.* per lb.
Neck (best end)	"	"	11*d.* per lb.
" (scrag end)	"	"	8*d.* per lb.
Shoulder	"	"	10*d.* per lb.
Fry	"	"	About 8*d.* per lb.

SEASONS AND PRICES OF PORK, DIFFERENT JOINTS AND PARTS.

Part.	In Season.	Best.	Average Price.
Belly	Sept. to April	Nov. to March	8*d.* per lb.
Hand	"	"	7½*d.* per lb.
Fore Loin	"	"	9*d.* per lb.
Hind Loin	"	"	9*d.* per lb.
Leg	"	"	8½*d.* per lb.
Spare Rib	"	"	8*d.* per lb.

SEASONS AND PRICES OF FISH OF VARIOUS KINDS.

Name of Fish.	In Season.	Best & Cheapest.	Average Price.
Bloaters	Sept. to April	Sept. to Feb.	1*s.* to 2*s.* per doz.
Bream	All the Year	Autumn	8*d.*
Brill	"	Aug. to April	1*s.* to 6*s.* each.
Carp	Nov. to March	Jan. and Feb.	2*d.* to 6*d.* per lb.
Cockles	All the Year	Summer	2*d.* to 4*d.* per quart.
Cod	Nov. to March	Feb. to March	4*d.* to 1*s.* per lb.
Chub	June to Dec.	Summer	4*d.* to 6*d.* per lb.
Crabs	April to Oct.	"	6*d.* to 3*s.* each.
Cray Fish	All the Year	Summer	1*s.* to 3*s.* per doz.
Dace	June to Dec.	July to Sept.	4*d.* to 6*d.* per lb.
Dory	All the Year	Winter	1*s.* to 5*s.* each.
Eels	June to March	Sept. to Nov.	8*d.* to 1*s.* per lb.
Flounders	All the Year	August to Nov.	2*d.* to 4*d.* each.
Haddocks	August to Feb.	Winter	4*d.* to 1*s.* each.
Halibut	All the Year	Nov. to Jan.	4*d.* to 1*s.* per lb.
Herrings	May to Jan.	June to Sept.	9*d.* to 1*s.* 6*d.* per doz.

Ling	All the Year	Nov. to March	4*d*. to 6*d*. per lb.
Lobsters	"	Summer	6*d*. to 4*s*. each.
Mackerel	Nearly all Year	April to July	4*d*. to 9*d*. each.
Mullet (Grey)	All the Year	Winter	4*d*. to 1*s*. 6*d*. each.
" (Red)	"	April to Oct.	4*d*. to 1*s*. 6*d*. each.
Mussels	Sept. to April	Winter	1*d*. to 2*d*. per quart.
Plaice	All the Year	May to Nov.	6*d*. to. 1*s*. per lb.
Prawns	"	May to Dec.	6*d*. to 1*s*. 6*d*. per doz.
Salmon	Feb. to Sept.	Spring, Summer	9*d*. to 4*s*. per lb.
Shad	"	May to Aug.	6*d*. to 9*d*. per lb.
Shrimps	All the Year	April to Nov.	3*d*. to 6*d*. per pint.
Skate	Sept. to April	Oct. to March	4*d*. to 1*s*. per lb.
Scallops	Jan. to June	March to May	6*d*. to 1*s*. per doz.
Smelts	Oct. to May	Winter	6*d*. to 2*s*. per doz.
Soles	All the Year	April to July	1*s*. to 2*s*. per lb.
Sprats	Nov. to March	Nov. and Dec.	1*d*. to 3*d*. per lb.
Sturgeon	April to Sept.	Summer	6*d*. to 1*s*. per lb.
Trout	Feb. to Sept.	April to July	1*s*. to 2*s*. per lb.
Turbot	All the Year	Spring, Summer	3*s*. to 15*s*. each.
Whitebait	Jan. to Sept.	Feb. to May	1*s*. 6*d*. to 2*s*. 6*d*. per qt.
Whiting	All the Year	Spring, Summer	3*d*. to 9*d*. each.

SEASONS AND PRICES OF POULTRY OF VARIOUS KINDS.

Poultry.	In Season.	Best & Cheapest.	Average Price.
Chickens	Feb. to Oct.	July to Oct.	2*s*. to 3*s*. 6*d*. each.
Ducklings	Feb. to Aug.	May to July	2*s*. 6*d*. to 3*s*. 6*d*. each.
Ducks	Aug. to Feb.	Sept. and Oct.	2*s*. 6*d*. to 4*s*. each.
Fowls	All the Year	June to Oct.	2*s*. 6*d*. to 3*s*. 6*d*. each.
Geese	Sept. to Feb.	Sept. to Nov.	6*s*. to 10*s*. each.
Green Geese	May to Aug.	June	6*s*. to 10*s*. each.
Guinea Fowl	Feb. to Aug.	Summer	3*s*. to 4*s*. each.
Larks	Oct. to Dec.	November	2*s*. to 3*s*. per doz.
Pigeons	Aug. to April	Winter	9*d*. to 1*s*. each.
" (Bordeaux)	All the Year	"	1*s*. to 1*s*. 4*d*. each.
Rabbits	"	Oct. to Feb.	6*d*. to 8*d*. per lb.
" (Ostend)	"	"	7*d*. and 8*d*. per lb.
Turkeys	Oct. to March	Nov. to Jan.	10*s*. to 21*s*. each.

SEASONS AND PRICES OF GAME OF VARIOUS KINDS.

Game.	In Season.	Best & Cheapest.	Average Price.
Black Cook	Aug. to Nov.	Sept. and Oct.	3*s*. to 4*s*. per brace.

Ducks (Wild)	Oct. to Dec.	Nov. and Dec.	3s. to 4s. per brace.
Grouse	Aug. to Nov.	September	3s. 6d. to 5s. per brace.
Hares	Sept. to March	October	3s. 6d. to 5s. each.
Leverets	Aug. to Sept.	August	3s. to 4s. each.
Partridges	Sept. to Feb.	Oct. and Nov.	3s. to 5s. per brace.
Pheasants	Oct. to Feb.	Winter	5s. to 7s. per brace.
Plovers	"	"	1s. to 1s. 6d. each.
Ptarmigan	Sept. to April	September	1s. to 1s. 6d. each.
Quail	Sept. to Feb.	Sept. and Oct.	1s. to 1s. 6d. each.
Snipes	Oct. to Feb.	Oct. and Nov.	2s. 6d. to 3s. 6d. per brace.
Teal	"	Winter	1s. to 1s. 6d. each.
Venison	Sept. to Jan.	Sept. and Oct.	1s. to 2s. per lb.
Widgeon	Oct. to Feb.	Oct. and Nov.	1s. to 1s. 6d. each.
Wood Cock	"	"	3s. 6d. to 5s. per brace.

BUTTER, CHEESE, BACON, & C., AVERAGE PRICES.

Article.	Average Price.	Article.	Average Price.
Butter (Fresh)	1s. 5d. to 1s. 8d. per lb.	Eggs (Geese's)	3s. to 4s. per doz.
" (Dorset)	1s. 2d. to 1s. 6d. per lb.	" (Guinea Fowls')	1s. to 2s. per doz.
" (Salt)	1s. to 1s. 2d. per lb.	" (Plovers')	3s. to 5s. per doz.
Margarine	10d. per lb.	" (Turkeys')	3s. to 4s. per doz.
Cheese (American)	7d. to 9d. per lb.	Milk	4d. a quart.
" (Cheddar)	10d. per lb.	" (Separated)	2d. a quart.
" (Cheshire)	10d. per lb.	Cream	1s. to 3s. a pint.
" (Cream)	6d. each.	Whey	2d. a pint.
" (Dutch)	7d. per lb.	Bacon (Best Parts)	11d. per lb.
" (Gorgonzola)	1s. per lb.	Ham (English)	11d. per lb.
" (Gruyère)	11d. per lb.	" (American)	8d. per lb.
" (Stilton)	1s. per lb.	Lard	10d. per lb.
Eggs (Hens')	1s. to 2s. 6d. per doz.	Pickled Pork	3d. per lb.
" (Ducks')	1s. to 3s. per doz.	Sausages	10d. per lb.

SEASONS AND PRICES OF VEGETABLES OF VARIOUS KINDS.

Vegetables.	In Season.	Best & Cheapest.	Average Price.
Artichokes	July to Oct.	August	3d. to 6d. each.
" (Jerusalem)	Nov. to Feb.	December	1½d. to 2d. per lb.
Asparagus	Jan. to July	April and May	1s. 6d. to 4s. 6d. bun.
Beans (French)	May to Nov.	Sept. and Oct.	2d. to 4d. per lb.
" (Broad)	July and Aug.	August	6d. to 9d. per peck.

" (Runner)	July to Oct.	Aug. and Sept.	2*d*. to 4*d*. per lb.
Beetroot	All the Year	Autumn	1*d*. to 3*d*. each.
Broccoli (Different kinds)	"	"	2*d*. to 6*d*. each.
Sprouts	Jan. to May	April	1*d*. to 2*d*. per lb.
" (Brussels)	Sept. to Feb.	Oct. to Dec.	2*d*. to 4*d*. per lb.
Cabbage	All the Year	Spring, Summer	1*d*. to 2*d*. each.
" (Red)	Oct. to Feb.	Nov. and Dec.	4*d*. to 6*d*. each.
Carrots	All the Year	Autumn	4*d*. to 6*d*. per bunch.
Cauliflower	May to Aug.	July	2*d*. to 6*d*. each.
Celery	Oct. to March	Nov. and Dec.	1*d*. to 4*d*. per stick.
Endive	Sept. to March	Oct. and Nov.	1*d*. to 6*d*. each.
Horseradish	All the Year	Winter	1*d*. to 2*d*. per stick.
Leeks	Oct. to May	Oct. and Nov.	4*d*. to 6*d*. per bunch.
Lettuces	May to Nov.	July and Aug.	1*d*. to 2*d*. each.
Onions	All the Year	Sum. & Autumn	1*d*. to 2*d*. per lb.
Parsnips	Oct. to April	Winter	1*d*. and 2*d*. each.
Peas	June to Sept.	July and Aug.	6*d*. to 2*s*. per peck.
Potatoes	All the Year	Autumn	1*d*. per lb.
" (New)	May to August	July	3*d*. to 8*d*. per lb.
Radishes	May to Sept.	June to Aug.	1*d*. per bunch.
Seakale	Jan. to May	Feb. and March	1*s*. to 2*s*. 6*d*. per baskt.
Savoys	Oct. to March	Nov. to Jan.	1*d*. to 4*d*. each.
Spinach	All the Year	Summer	2*d*. to 4*d*. per lb.
Tomatoes	June to Dec.	Sept. and Oct.	4*d*. to 8*d*. per lb.
Vegetable Marrow	June to Oct.	July and Aug.	1*d*. to 6*d*. each.
Watercress	All the Year	Summer	1*d*. per bunch.

SEASONS AND PRICES OF FRUIT OF VARIOUS KINDS.

Fruit.	In Season.	Best & Cheapest.	Average Price.
Apples	Oct. to March	Oct. to Dec.	3*d*. to 6*d*. per lb.
Apricots	June to Sept.	August	1*s*. 6*d*. to 3*s*. 6*d*. doz.
Bullaces	Autumn	October	2*d*. to 3*d*. per lb.
Cherries	June to August	July	4*d*. to 8*d*. per lb.
Currants	July to Sept.	August	3*d*. to 8*d*. per lb.
Damsons	Sept. and Oct.	October	1*d*. to 4*d*. per lb.
Figs	"	"	2*s*. to 3*s*. per box.
Gooseberries	July to Sept.	August	4*d*. to 8*d*. per quart.
" (Green)	May to July	June	3*d*. to 6*d*. per quart.
Grapes (Foreign)	All the Year	Autumn	4*d*. to 8*d*. per lb.
" (Hot-house)	Sept. to Dec.	October	2*s*. per lb. upwards.
Greengages	Aug. and Sept.	August	3*d*. to 6*d*. per lb.

Medlars	Oct. to Jan.	Oct. and Nov.	4d. to 8d. per lb.
Melons	June to Nov.	October	1s. to 5s. each.
Nectarines	Sept. and Oct.	"	3s. to 4s. per doz.
Oranges	All the Year	Winter	From 4d. per doz.
Peaches	Sept. and Oct.	October	4s. to 8s. per doz.
Pears	Oct. to March	Oct. and Nov.	1d. to 6d. each.
Pines (Foreign)	Aug. to Nov.	September	1s. to 3s. each.
" (English)	Sept. to Dec.	October	5s. to 15s. each.
Plums	Aug. to Oct.	Sept. and Oct.	2d. to 6d. per lb.
Quinces	Sept. to Oct.	October	2s. to 3s. per doz.
Rhubarb	Jan. to June	March and April	4d. to 8d. per bunch.
Strawberries	June to Sept.	July	4d. to 1s. per lb.

These prices are the ordinary ones charged at good shops in London and other large towns for the best provisions. Cheaper and inferior ones are to be purchased, as, for example, American meat, and that and poultry, which is imported in a frozen state; also French eggs, but the articles named in our lists, with the exception of some of the cheeses, are fresh home produce. In our chapter on "marketing" will be found instructions for choosing all sorts of fresh provisions, how to judge of their quality and freshness, and other hints for getting the best value for our money.

INVALID COOKERY

There is no form of cookery that requires more thought and care than that intended for the diet of the sick.

The choice of the food alone is a difficult question—to select what will nourish each particular individual in each particular case, for what is good for one person is not necessarily good for another, even if they be suffering from the same complaint.

It would be well for those who nurse the sick, whether amateur or professional, to know for themselves the value and the constituents of the food they have to administer.

A sick person's diet is as important as his physic, in fact, in many cases it is his physic—in the dietary cures of which we have before spoken. It should, therefore, be prepared as carefully as medicine would be mixed, and administered with the greatest consideration and punctuality.

A sick-room diet, particularly in the case of long and serious illness, should be one that will give the least possible work to that part of the digestive canal that is least able to bear it; to compensate for the waste and drain upon the system. To ensure this, the doctor will prescribe the diet as well as the medicine, and his instructions should be faithfully carried out. It is cruel kindness to give whatever a sick person craves for, in defiance of doctors' opinions. For example, after a fever a person may develop an abnormal appetite which it would be dangerous to gratify.

A much more common difficulty in dealing with the sick is to get them to take enough food; but this is sometimes the fault of the nurse. With the kindest intentions, she will bring a plateful of jelly or a basin of beef-tea to her patient, and he will reject it with disgust, because, in his weak state, the sight of so much food is most distasteful to him; whereas, did she but bring a few spoonfuls at a time, he might rouse himself to make the slight exertion that the swallowing of a small quantity would entail.

Give little food and often. What is taken willingly and with relish, if even a very little, does more good than double the amount swallowed with disgust.

In some cases it is absolutely essential that to get the patient to take any food at all, it must be only given exactly when he chooses to take it, but as a rule, there are times and hours dictated. In these cases, punctuality is of the utmost importance. Never let the patient wait for a meal or even a spoonful beyond the appointed time, unless asleep and it is undesirable to wake him. Most essential is this in the small hours of the morning, when the patient's strength is at its lowest ebb. This is the most trying time for the amateur nurse, but, feeling as she will probably feel then, weak and worn out, she must remember that so will her patient be, and be careful that both food and medicine be punctually given. If kept waiting, most patients lose their desire to eat, and will reject the food when brought. When there is no appetite, give such food as affords the most nourishment with the least amount of exertion either to teeth or digestion. Put the greatest amount of nourishment into the smallest space, and let the food, if solid, be divided.

Never leave food in a sick-room. If the patient cannot eat it, take it away out of the room, and bring it again after a due interval.

Miss Nightingale says, "To leave the patient's untasted food by his side from meal to meal, in hopes that he will take it in the interval, is simply to prevent him taking food at all. I have known patients literally incapacitated from taking any one article of food after another from this piece of ignorance. Let the food come at the right time, and be taken away, eaten or uneaten, at the right time; but never let a patient have 'something always standing by him,' if you don't wish to disgust him with everything."

When disease is infectious no one should take any of the food that comes from the sick-room, anything that remains should be burnt. In acute disease the diet is generally limited to liquids, such as milk and beef-tea. The former is the best food of any in such cases, and it is a most fortunate thing if the patient is able to take it. If he cannot digest it as it is, he may possibly be able to do so if it be boiled and given warm, or if it be mixed with lime-water or soda-water.

When every preparation of fresh milk has been used in vain, whey is sometimes found useful, also koumis, or fermented milk, may be tried. In many illnesses the patient suffers from sickness and nausea, when all food should be given iced or as cold as possible. Milk may be stood on ice for a long time, and if no ice is at hand it is a good plan to wrap a wet cloth round the jug containing it and stand it outside window or door in a draught; it can also be made cooler by setting the jug in a pan of salt and water.

There is often a difficulty in keeping food hot in a sick-room. The best thing we know to do this is a Norwegian cooking apparatus, a box thickly padded with a non-conducting material containing a double tin receptacle, the outer for the hot water and the inner for the food that has to be kept hot. In this, beef-tea or other preparations may be kept hot for some hours.

A word about beef-tea may not be out of place. It is the most common of all invalid food, but it is really not a very nourishing one, for there is not more than half an ounce of solid in a whole pint of beef-tea; yet it is something of a stimulant and is very generally prescribed by medical men. If it can be varied, and given alternately with other food, it is better. We give recipes for beef-tea, but we may remark here that it should never be made in an iron saucepan; nor should milk be heated in one. The best beef-tea is that made in the oven. For patients suffering from acute disease it is better to omit the salt or other flavouring, for if the tea be made as strong as possible it will, in all probability, when the organs of taste are in an extremely sensitive condition, taste too salt from the presence of the saline matter in the meat. A nourishing food can be made of raw beef scraped free from fibre—seasoned with a little pepper and salt and served as sandwiches between thin bread and butter, or, if for very young children it may have a little sugar or jam instead of the savoury flavouring. A quickly prepared beef-tea can be made by rubbing raw beef through a sieve and warming it in a little Liebig's extract.

It is generally considered right to skim off every particle of fat from beef-tea, but if the patient does not object to a little being left, it aids in the digestion of the food.

In convalescence, invalid diet is comparatively easy to manage, though it may take longer to prepare the food from the fact that it should be as *varied* as possible.

Never make a large quantity of anything at one time, thinking that what the invalid has liked he may continue to like, for in nine cases out of ten his appetite will be very capricious. Never let him get tired of any food.

In convalescence eggs are valuable, and are easily digested if beaten to a froth with a little sugar, if liked, and a spoonful of brandy, if desirable. If they are cooked, they should be done very lightly. Sago, tapioca and bread puddings are generally acceptable to the invalid after a long course of beef-tea, broth, arrowroot and jelly. The next step is generally to fish, of which the first should be whiting, as it is of all fish the easiest of digestion. It is condemned by many as tasteless, but this can be remedied if a nice sauce be served with it, the foundation of which may be melted butter.

Mutton is generally the first meat an invalid is allowed to take; but, if in season, lamb is more delicate. Whichever meat it is, it should not be fat, nor should it be fried for the first meat meal. The most digestible way of cooking it is by stewing. We give a very nice recipe for an invalid's outlet in our recipes for invalid cookery. In everything prepared for a sick-room the greatest attention must be paid to cleanliness. If the kitchen utensils are not scrupulously clean, some disagreeable flavour may be imparted to the preparation. A flavour, it may be, imperceptible to the healthy palate, but perfectly obvious to the sick person, whom it will disgust. It is safer to use china or earthenware than metal for very delicate cookery.

A good nurse will always serve a patient's food in the most dainty and tempting way possible, and will see that everything the invalid uses is exquisitely clean. Glass will be bright, silver burnished, napkin uncoiled, saucers free from slops. Although the sick person may not be able to comment upon the way his food is served, he will most likely notice every detail; and, in a weak state, there is actual pain or pleasure in them to him. Let the food itself be made to look as tempting as possible—garnished as prettily as taste may devise. In health we like to see our food nicely and daintily served, but in sickness it is absolutely necessary that it should be so, and while we do not grudge the trouble of cooking the food, we need not mind that of arranging it as carefully as possible to suit the tastes of our invalids.

One or two little things in connection with serving invalid's food we must not forget to mention. In the first place see that his position is as comfortable as it can be made to partake of the meal or draught; take care that there be nothing spilt in a saucer from which he has to lift a cup, so that sheet or dress may not be soiled, also be careful that no crumbs are left in the bed.

EIGHTY

Principles of Nutrition

WILBUR O. ATWATER

Wilbur Atwater (1844–1907) was a chemist who introduced to the public the idea of measuring foods' caloric value, and he formed a habit of calorie counting that we continue to this day. With a respiration calorimeter he conducted experiments that set the stage for the modern science of nutrition; shortly after his work, vitamins were discovered.

FOOD AS BUILDING MATERIAL AND FUEL

The Body as a Machine

Blood and muscle, bone and tendon, brain and nerve—all the organs and tissues of the body—are built from the nutritive ingredients of food. With every motion of the body and with the exercise of feeling and thought as well, material is consumed and must be resupplied by food. In a sense, the body is a superior machine. Like other machines, it requires material to build up its several parts, to repair them as they are worn out, and to serve as fuel. In some ways it uses this material like a machine; in others it does not. The steam engine gets its power from fuel; the body does the same. In the one case coal or wood, in the other food, is the fuel. In both cases the energy which is latent in the fuel—the potential energy, as it is called in scientific language—is transformed into power and heat.

Wilbur O. Atwater. "Food as Building Material and Fuel." In *Principles of Nutrition and Nutritive Value of Food*. Washington, DC: U.S. Government Printing Office, 1910, pp. 8–14.

From the time foods are taken into the body until they are digested, absorbed, utilized, and finally converted largely into the carbon dioxid and water vapor of the breath and the nitrogenous and other excretory products of the urine and feces, they undergo great chemical changes, very many of which liberate heat as a result of oxidation or some closely related process. It is through these complex chemical processes that the body derives the energy for internal and external muscular work. Heat is evolved by such chemical changes and also results from the muscular work of the body, and there is reason to believe that within wide limits the heat thus produced is sufficient for maintaining body temperature. The amount of heat produced in the body must, of course, vary with the amount of food eaten, the work done, and other circumstances. However, the body is such a perfect piece of mechanism that the loss of heat by radiation, etc., is so adjusted to heat production that body temperature remains fairly constant.

One important difference between the human machine and the steam engine is that the former is self-building, self-repairing, and self-regulating. Another is that the material of which the engine is built is very different from that which it uses for fuel, but part of the material which serves the body as a source of energy also builds it up and keeps it in repair. Furthermore, the body can use its own substance for this purpose. This the steam engine cannot do. The steam engine and the body are alike in that both convert the fuel into mechanical power and heat. They differ in that the body uses the same material for fuel as for building and also consumes its own material for fuel. In the use of its source of power the body is much more economical than any engine.

But the body is more than a machine. It has not simply organs to build and keep in repair and supply with energy; it has a nervous organization; it has sensibilities; and there are the higher intellectual and spiritual faculties. The right exercise of these depends upon the right nutrition of the body.

The chief uses of food, then, are two: (1) To form the material of the body and repair its wastes, and (2) to furnish muscular and other power for the work the body has to do and yield heat to keep the body warm. In forming the tissues and the fluids of the body the food serves for building and repair. In yielding power and heat it serves as fuel.

If more food is eaten than is needed, more or less of the surplus may be and sometimes is stored in the body, chiefly in the form of fat. The fat in the body forms a sort of reserve supply of fuel and is utilized in the place of food. When the work is hard or the food supply is low the body draws upon this store of fat and grows lean.

Protein as Building Material

The principal tissue formers are the protein compounds, especially the albuminoids. These make the framework of the body. They build up and repair the nitrogenous materials, as the muscles and tendons, and supply the albuminoids of the blood, milk, and other fluids.

The albuminoids of food are transformed into the albuminoids and gelatinoids of the body. Muscle, tendon and cartilage, bone and skin, the corpuscles of the blood, and the casein of milk are made of the albuminoids of food. The albuminoids are sometimes called "flesh formers" or "muscle formers," because the lean flesh, the muscle, is made from them, though the term is inadequate, as it leaves out of account the energy-furnishing function of protein. The gelatinoids of food, such as the finer particles of tendon and the gelatin, which are dissolved out of bone and meat in soup, though somewhat similar to the albuminoids in composition, are not believed to be tissue formers; but they are valuable in protecting the albuminoids from consumption. That is, when the food contains gelatinoids in abundance less of albuminoids is used.

The proteids can be so changed in the body as to yield fats and carbohydrates, and such changes actually occur to some extent. In this and other ways they supply the body with fuel.

Protein as Fuel for the Body

The protein compounds are not only used for building and repairing tissue, but are also burned directly in the body like the carbohydrates, and thus render important service as fuel. A dog can live on lean meat. He can convert its material into muscle and its energy into heat and muscular power. Man can do the same; but such a one-sided diet would not be best for the dog and it would be still worse for man. The natural food for carniverous animals, like the dog, supplies fats and some carbohydrates, and that for omnivorous animals, like man, furnishes fats and carbohydrates in liberal amounts along with protein. Herbivorous animals, like horses, cattle, and sheep, naturally require large proportions of carbohydrates.

Fats and Carbohydrates as Fuel

Fats and carbohydrates are the chief fuel ingredients of food. Sugar and the starch of bread and potatoes are burned in the body to yield heat and power. The fats, such as the fat of meat and butter, serve the same purpose, only they are a more concentrated fuel than the carbohydrates.

The body can also transform carbohydrates of food into fat. This fat, and with it that stored from the food, is kept in the body as reserve fuel in the most concentrated form.

The different nutrients can to a greater or less extent do one another's work. If the body has not enough of one kind of fuel it can use another. But, while protein can be burned in the place of fats and carbohydrates, neither of the latter can take the place of the albuminoids in building and repairing the tissues. At the same time the gelatinoids, fats, and carbohydrates, by being consumed themselves, protect the albuminoids from consumption.

Value of Food for Supplying Energy

Heat and muscular power are forms of force or energy. The energy latent in the food is developed as the food is consumed in the body. The process is more or less akin to that which takes place when coal is burned in the furnace of the locomotive. For the burning of the food in the body or the coal in the furnace, air is used to supply oxygen.

When the fuel is oxidized, be it meat or wood, bread or coal, the latent energy becomes active, or, in technical language, the potential energy becomes kinetic; it is transformed into power and heat. As various kinds of coal differ in the amount of heat given off per ton, so various kinds of food and food ingredients give off different amounts of energy; that is, have different values as fuel in the body.

Heat of Combustion

The processes of oxidation of material and transformation of energy in the body are less simple than in the engine and less clearly understood. Late research, however, has given us ways of measuring the energy latent in coal, wood, and in food materials as well. This is most generally done in the chemical laboratory by an apparatus called the bomb calorimeter. The amount of heat given off in the oxidation of a given quantity of any material is called its "heat of combustion," and is taken as a measure of its latent or potential energy. The unit commonly used is the calorie, the amount of heat which would raise the temperature of 1 kilogram of water 1° C., or, what is nearly the same thing, 1 pound of water 4° F. Instead of this unit of heat a unit of mechanical energy may be used—for instance, the foot-ton, which represents the force required to raise 1 ton 1 foot. One calorie is equal to very nearly 1.54 foot-tons; that is to say, 1 calorie of heat, when transformed into mechanical power, would suffice to lift 1 ton 1.54 feet.

The Conservation of Energy in the Body

The amounts of energy transformed in the body when food and its own material are burned within it are measured with the respiration calorimeter. It is well known that the food is not completely oxidized in the body. These experiments have shown that the material which is oxidized yields the same amount of energy as it would if burned with oxygen outside the body, e. g., in the bomb calorimeter. The experiments show also that when a man does no muscular work (save, of course, the internal work of respiration, circulation, etc.), all the energy leaves his body as heat; but when he does muscular work, as in lifting weights or driving a bicycle, part of the energy appears in the external work thus done, and the rest is given off from the body as heat. The most interesting result of all is that the energy given off from the body as heat when the man is at rest, or as heat and mechanical work together when he is working, exactly equals the latent energy of the material burned in the body. This is in accordance with the law of the conservation of energy. It thus appears that the body actually obeys, as we should expect it to obey, this great law which dominates the physical universe.

We may make practical application of this principle of the conservation of energy in the body in measuring the actual value of food as fuel to the body, i. e., its "fuel value," by use of the bomb and respiration calorimeters. To do this we have to take into account the chemical composition of the food, the proportions of the nutrients actually digested and oxidized in the body, and the proportion of the whole latent energy of each which becomes active and useful to the body for warmth and work. Taking our common food materials as they are used in ordinary diet, the following general estimate has been made for the energy furnished to the body by 1 gram or 1 pound of each of the classes of nutrients:

Protein, fuel value, 4 calories per gram, or 1,820 calories per pound.
Fats, fuel value, 9 calories per gram, or 4,040 calories per pound.
Carbohydrates, fuel value, 4 calories per gram, or 1,820 calories per pound.

It will be seen that when we compare the nutrients in respect to their fuel value, their capacities for yielding heat and mechanical power, a pound of protein of lean meat or albumen of egg is just about equivalent to a pound of sugar or starch, and a little over 2 pounds of either would be required to equal a pound of the fat of meat or butter or of body fat.

The fuel value of food obviously depends upon the amounts of actual nutrients, and especially upon the amount of fat it contains. Thus a pound of wheat flour, which consists largely of starch, has an average fuel value of about 1,625 calories, and a pound of butter, which is mostly fat, about 3,410 calories. These are only about one-eighth water. Whole milk, which is seven-eighths water, has an average fuel value of 310 calories per pound; cream, which has more fat and less water, 865 calories, and skim milk, which is whole milk after the cream has been removed, 165 calories.

This high fuel value of fat explains the economy of nature in storing fat in the body for use in case of need. Fat is the most concentrated form of body fuel.

We have been considering food as a source of heat and muscular power. There is no doubt that intellectual activity, also, is somehow dependent upon the consumption of material which the brain has obtained from the food; but just what substances are consumed to produce brain and nerve force, and how much of each is required for a given quantity of intellectual labor, are questions which the physiological chemist has not yet answered.

How the Functions and Nutritive Value of Food Are Learned

The principles above explained are based upon a great deal of experimenting and observation. The experimenting is of many kinds, but of especial importance is the work with the respiration apparatus and respiration calorimeter.

Various forms of respiration apparatus have been devised within the last fifty years. Among the most important are those invented by Pettenkofer and Voit in Munich. They consist of metal-walled chambers large enough for the subject (sometimes a man, sometimes a dog, sheep, or other animal) to live in comfortably for several days, and are furnished with devices for pumping air through and measuring and analyzing it as it enters and leaves the chamber. With such an apparatus it is possible not only to measure all the food and excreta, but also the materials given off from the lungs in the breath, and to make accurate determinations of the matter entering and leaving the body.

A still more elaborate apparatus, by which not only all the matter passing in and out of the body may be measured, but also all the heat given off from it, is called a respiration calorimeter—that is, a machine for measuring both the respiratory products and the heat given off by the body. It is like the respiration apparatus, except that it is furnished with devices for measuring temperatures. Several have been built in Europe within the last twenty years, among the most successful being those by Rubner and Rosenthal. Investigations in cooperation with the United States Department of Agriculture are now being carried on in one recently built by the author and Professor Rosa at Wesleyan University. Its main feature is a copper-walled chamber 7 feet long, 4 feet wide, and 6 feet 4 inches high. This is fitted with devices for maintaining and measuring a ventilating current of air, for sampling and analyzing this air, for removing and measuring the heat given off within the chamber, and for passing food and other articles in and out. It is furnished with a folding bed, chair, and table, with scales and with appliances for muscular work, and has telephone connection with the outside. Here the subject stays for a period of from three to twelve days, during which time careful analyses and measurements are made of all material which enters the body in the food and of that which leaves it in the breath and excreta. Record is also kept of the energy given off from the body as heat and muscular work. The differences between the material taken into and that given off from the body is called the balance of matter, and shows whether the body is gaining or losing material. The difference between the energy of the food taken and that of the excreta and the energy given off from the body as heat and muscular work, is the balance of energy, and if correctly estimated should equal the energy of the body material gained or lost.

With such apparatus it is possible to learn what effect different conditions of nourishment will have on the human body. In one experiment, for instance, the subject might be kept quite at rest, and in the next do a certain amount of muscular or mental work, with the same diet as before. Then by comparing the results of the two the use which the body makes of its food under the different conditions could be determined. Or the diet may be slightly changed in one experiment and the effect of this on the balance of matter and energy observed. Such methods and apparatus are very costly in time and money, but the results are proportionately more valuable than those from simpler experiments.

EIGHTY-ONE

The Boston Cooking-School Cook Book

FANNIE MERRITT FARMER

Fannie Farmer is widely credited with having introduced standard measurements in recipes. While that's not quite true, she did popularize the idea of level measurements, as can be seen in this passage. More importantly, this was a cooking guide for women rather than for professionals; it was for women who did not learn basic procedures from their mothers or relatives, who might have been out working. This reflects enormous social change that would be characteristic of the twentieth century and meant that cookbooks like this would remain in demand.

HOW TO MEASURE

Correct measurements are absolutely necessary to insure the best results. Good judgment, with experience, has taught some to measure by sight; but the majority need definite guides.

Tin measuring-cups, divided in quarters or thirds, holding one half-pint, and tea and table spoons of regulation sizes,—which may be bought at any store where kitchen furnishings are sold,—and a case knife, are essentials for correct measurement. Mixing-spoons, which are little larger than tablespoons, should not be confounded with the latter.

Measuring Ingredients. Flour, meal, powdered and confectioners' sugar, and soda should be sifted before measuring. Mustard and baking-powder, from standing in boxes, settle, therefore should be stirred to lighten; salt frequently lumps, and these lumps should be broken. A *cupful* is measured level. To measure a cupful, put in the ingredient by spoonfuls or from a scoop, round slightly, and level with a case knife, care being taken not to shake the cup. *A tablespoonful is measured level. A teaspoonful is measured level.*

Fannie Merritt Farmer. *The Boston Cooking-School Cook Book*. Boston: Little, Brown, 1896, pp. 27–29.

To measure tea or table spoonfuls, dip the spoon in the ingredient, fill, lift, and level with a knife, the sharp edge of knife being toward tip of spoon. Divide with knife lengthwise of spoon, for a half-spoonful; divide halves crosswise for quarters, and quarters crosswise for eighths. Less than one-eighth of a teaspoonful is considered a few grains

Measuring Liquids. A cupful of liquid is all the cup will hold.

A tea or table spoonful is all the spoon will hold.

Measuring Butter, Lard, etc. To measure butter, lard, and other solid fats, pack solidly into cup or spoon, and level with a knife.

When dry ingredients, liquids, and fats are called for in the same recipe, measure in the order given, thereby using but one cup.

HOW TO COMBINE INGREDIENTS

Next to measuring comes care in combining,—a fact not always recognized by the inexperienced. Three ways are considered,—stirring, beating, cutting and folding.

To stir, mix by using circular motion, widening the circles until all is blended. Stirring is the motion ordinarily employed in all cookery, alone or in combination with beating.

To beat, turn ingredient or ingredients over and over, continually bringing the under part to the surface, thus allowing the utensil used for beating to be constantly brought in contact with bottom of the dish and throughout the mixture.

To cut and fold, introduce one ingredient into another ingredient or mixture by two motions: with a spoon, a repeated vertical downward motion, known as cutting; and a turning over and over of mixture, allowing bowl of spoon each time to come in contact with bottom of dish, is called folding. These repeated motions are alternated until thorough blending is accomplished.

By stirring, ingredients are mixed; *by beating*, a large amount of air is inclosed; *by cutting and folding*, air already introduced is prevented from escaping.

EIGHTY-TWO

Fletcherism

HORACE FLETCHER

Fletcher, known as "The Great Masticator" (1849–1919), was a wealthy socialite who decided that chewing food dozens of times until it dissolved and slipped down the throat was the way to health and longevity—and perhaps most importantly, to weight loss. He paid for research and got the backing of professional scientists and many testimonials. He became enormously popular as well and is perhaps indicative of the fad diets that proliferate to the present.

CHAPTER I: HOW I BECAME A FLETCHERITE

My Turning Point—How I Had Ignored My Responsibility—What Happens during Mastication—The Four Principles of Fletcherism

OVER twenty years ago, at the age of forty years, my hair was white; I weighed two hundred and seventeen pounds (about fifty pounds more than I should for my height of five feet six inches); every six months or so I had a bad attack of "influenza"; I was harrowed by indigestion; I was afflicted with "that tired feeling." I was an old man at forty, on the way to a rapid decline.

It was at about this time that I applied for a life-insurance policy, and was "turned down" by the examiners as a "poor risk." This was the final straw. I was not afraid to die; I had long ago learned to look upon death with equanimity. At the same time I had a keen desire to live, and then and there made a determination that I would find out what was the matter, and, if I could do so, save myself from my threatened demise.

Horace Fletcher. *Fletcherism: What Is It?* New York: Frederick A. Stockes, 1913, pp. 1–11.

I realised that the first thing to do was, if possible, to close up my business arrangements so that I could devote myself to the study of how to keep on the face of the earth for a few more years. This I found it possible to do, and I retired from active money-making.

The desire of my life was to live in Japan, where I had resided for several years, and to which country I was passionately devoted. My tastes were in the direction of the fine arts. Japan had been for years my Mecca—my household goods were already there, waiting until I should take up my permanent residence; and it required no small amount of will-power to turn away from the cherished hope of a lifetime, to continue travelling over the world, and concentrate upon finding a way to keep alive.

I turned my back on Japan, and began my quest for health. For a time, I tried some of the most famous "cures" in the world. Here and there were moments of hope, but in the end I was met with disappointment.

The Turning Point

It was partly accidental and partly otherwise that I finally found a clue to the solution of my health disabilities. A faint suggestion of possibilities of arrest of decline had dawned upon me in the city of Galveston, Texas, some years before, and had been strengthened by a visit to an Epicurean philosopher who had a snipe estate among the marshlands of Southern Louisiana and a truffle preserve near Pau, in France. He was a disciple of Gladstone, and faithfully followed the rules relative to thorough chewing of food which the Grand Old Man of England had formulated for the guidance of his children. My friend in Louisiana attributed his robustness of health as much to this protection against overeating as to the exercise incident to his favourite sports. But these impressions had not been strong enough to have a lasting effect.

One day, however, I was called to Chicago to attend to some unfinished business affairs. They were difficult of settlement, and I was compelled to "mark time" in the Western city with nothing especially to do. It was at this time, in 1898, that I began to think seriously of eating and its effect upon health. I read a great many books, only to find that no two authors agreed; and I argued from this fact that no one had found the truth, or else there would be some consensus of agreement. So I stopped reading, and determined to consult Mother Nature herself for direction.

How I Had Ignored My Responsibility

I began by trying to find out why Nature required us to eat, and how and when. The key to my search was a firm belief in the good intentions of Nature in the interest of our health and happiness, and a belief also that anything less than good health and high efficiency was due to transgressions against certain good and beneficent laws. Hence, it was merely a question of search to find out the nature of the transgression.

The fault was one of nutrition, evidently.

I argued that if Nature had given us personal responsibility it was not hidden away in the dark folds and coils of the alimentary canal where we could not control it. The fault or faults must be committed before the food was swallowed. I felt instinctively that here was the key to the whole situation. The point, then, was to study the cavity of the mouth; and the first thought was: "What happens there?" and "What is present there?" The answer was: Taste, Smell (closely akin to taste and hardly to be distinguished from it), Feeling, Saliva, Mastication, Appetite, Tongue, Teeth, etc.

I first took up the careful study of Taste, necessitating keeping food in the mouth as long as possible, to learn its course and development; and, as I tried it myself, wonders of new and pleasant sensations were revealed. New delights of taste were discovered. Appetite assumed new leanings. Then came the vital discovery, which is this: I found that each of us has what I call a food-filter: a discriminating muscular gate located at the back of the mouth where the throat is shut off from the mouth during the process of mastication. Just where the tongue drops over backward toward its so-called roots there are usually five (sometimes seven, we are told) little teat-like projections placed in the shape of a horseshoe, each of them having a trough around it, and in these troughs, or depressions, terminate a great number of taste-buds, or ends of gustatory nerves. Just at this point the roof of the mouth, or the "hard palate," ends; and the "soft palate," with the uvula at the end of it, drops down behind the heavy part of the tongue.

During the natural act of chewing the lips are closed, and there is also a complete closure at the back part of the mouth by the pressing of the tongue against the roof of the mouth. During mastication, then, the mouth is an airtight pouch.

After which brief description, please note, the next time you take food.

What Happens during Mastication

Hold the face down, so that the tongue hangs perpendicularly in the mouth. This is for two reasons: one, because it will show how food, when properly mixed with saliva, will be lifted up in the hollow part in the middle of the tongue, against the direct force of gravity, and will collect at the place where the mouth is shut off at the back, the food-gate.

It is a real gate; and while the food is being masticated, so that it may be mixed with saliva and chemically transformed from its crude condition into the chemical form that makes it possible of digestion and absorption, this gate will remain tightly shut, and the throat will be entirely cut off from the mouth.

But as the food becomes creamy, so to speak, through being mixed with saliva, or emulsified, or alkalised, or neutralised, or dextrinised, or modified in whatever form Nature requires, the creamy substance will be drawn up the central conduit of the tongue until it reaches the food-gate.

If it is found by the taste-buds there located around the "circumvalate papillae" (the teat-like projections on the tongue which I mentioned above) to be properly prepared for acceptance and further digestion, the food-gate will open, and the food thus ready for acceptance into the body will be sucked back and swallowed unconsciously—that is, without conscious effort.

I now started to experiment on myself. I chewed my food carefully until I extracted all taste from it there was in it, and until it slipped unconsciously down my throat. When the appetite ceased, and I was thereby told that I had had enough, I stopped; and I had no desire to eat any more until a real appetite commanded me again. Then I again chewed carefully—eating always whatever the appetite craved.

The Five Principles of Fletcherism

I have now found out five things; all that there is to my discovery relative to optimum nutrition; and to the fundamental requisite of what is called Fletcherism.

First: Wait for a true, earned appetite.

Second: Select from the food available that which appeals most to appetite, and in the order called for by appetite.

Third: Get all the good taste there is in food out of it in the mouth, and swallow only when it practically "swallows itself."

Fourth: Enjoy the good taste for all it is worth, and do not allow any depressing or diverting thought to intrude upon the ceremony.

Fifth: Wait; take and *enjoy as much as possible* what appetite approves; Nature will do the rest.

For five months I went on patiently observing, and I found out positively in that time that I had worked out my own salvation. I had lost upwards of sixty pounds of fat: I was feeling better in all ways than I had for twenty years. My head was clear, my body felt springy, I enjoyed walking, I had not had a single cold for five months, "that tired feeling" was gone!

Study Questions

1. Why do you suppose officials in the nineteenth century were so reluctant to regulate food safety? Is this related somehow to free-market ideas central to capitalism or the power of food industries?
2. What accounts for the meteoric popularity of health and dieting fads in the nineteenth century? Was this merely a reaction to abundance and the ability of many people for the first time to overeat?
3. What impression do you get about the average middle-class Victorian household from the advice given by Mrs. Beeton? Why was this book so popular, and why weren't young women learning these things from their mothers?
4. Why were cooking and household duties presented scientifically in the nineteenth century? Did this affect the status of women?
5. From these readings can you reconstruct an approximation of the working-class diet? Why did it deteriorate so dramatically?

The Twentieth Century

The industrialization of agriculture and food processing continued apace in the twentieth century but was given further impetus by the demands of war, both in transporting food quickly and also in making it imperishable and easy to prepare. Thus, canning technology, freeze-drying, and novel packaging began as military innovations but soon spread to civilian life. These new products were marketed as being quick and convenient, and with new advertising acumen they were sold to a populace eager for innovation and novelty. War also directly prompted scientific research into basic dietary needs. Vitamins were discovered, and increasingly foods were sold with explicit health claims on the label. The government began to set agricultural and nutritional policy, regulate the food supply, and make dietary recommendations.

The Great Depression brought an end to the free-market economy as the government was forced to intervene by providing agricultural subsidies to farmers, supporting works projects to create jobs, and providing relief in the form of welfare checks and food stamps to the needy. Foreign aid, partly to further political agendas but also to relieve the war-stricken and impoverished parts of the world, also became a regular budgetary item.

New ways of retailing food emerged—in particular, the supermarket. What distinguished these establishments was the prepackaged food arranged neatly in aisles that required no weighing or help from sales staff. Shopping carts could simply be filled and brought directly to the checkout. Smaller grocery stores and those specializing in fruits, fish, or meat gradually disappeared. Consumers could stock up on a whole weeks' worth of food, and refrigerators grew in size to accommodate these new shopping habits. All these developments were dependent on being able to drive to the store and the suburbanization of U.S. culture.

Car culture was also responsible for the appearance of fast food. A radically simplified menu sped up the ordering time. Disposable paper plates and plastic cutlery made dishwashers unnecessary, nor was there a need for table service or waiters. The real innovation, however, was the mechanization of the cooking process, which meant labor was largely unskilled and expendable. A part-time student could learn the process quickly, and if he or she quit, the worker was easily replaced. The franchising of fast-food chains also meant that advertising could be on a massive scale, and the product could be relatively homogeneous all across the country. Brand loyalty and having set expectations sent people in droves to McDonald's, Burger King, Kentucky Fried Chicken, and Taco Bell—the same major outlets since the mid-twentieth century. Giving away toys, often connected to motion picture releases, and consciously targeting children increased sales exponentially, as did opening outlets abroad. There is scarcely a place on earth that one can't find some form of fast food.

The prevalence of junk food also changed modern foodways, and many people persuasively argue that obesity is a distinctly modern epidemic catered to directly by the food industries. Snack foods; candy; sweet, carbonated soft drinks; and convenience foods such as frozen TV dinners and ready-made meals all contributed to what many critics have called the culinary deskilling of modern times. People simply never learned basic kitchen procedures. It is ironic that this all occurred at the same time that cooking magazines and TV shows flourished, and a massive wave of what were called "foodies" made food a hot topic. Cooking may have been a leisure activity for the privileged, but the percentage of people actually cooking at home or eating together as families drastically diminished.

Food also became a major political issue. The farm bill subsidies to support growing corn and soybeans were directly connected to the promotion of industrial junk foods and indirectly were the cause of the obesity problem the government claimed to be trying to solve. Concern over animal welfare and the brutality of modern rearing and slaughter practices quickened a fast-growing vegetarian and vegan movement. Concern for the environment led to organic labeling, and the fear of genetically modified organisms in the food supply strengthened an alternative food movement. Locavores criticized the waste in fuel and pollution caused by shipping food across the country or globe when food could be grown locally and sustainably. Food-borne pathogens, several outbreaks of E. coli and salmonella, and the specter of mad cow disease all prompted the serious reevaluation of the food supply. The drastic inequalities of food distribution causing poverty and starvation around the world were perhaps the greatest challenge to the modern food system, even in advanced, industrial nations.

EIGHTY-THREE
The Jungle

UPTON SINCLAIR

The Jungle is the classic of early-twentieth-century muckraking, and it was instrumental in passing food safety laws in the United States. Sinclair had intended the work to be a diatribe about labor practices, but, as he said "I aimed at the public's heart and by accident hit its stomach." The scene in this passage takes place in the Chicago meatpacking industry, the labor mostly immigrant, and the conditions brutal. The socialist leanings of the author met with scant approval among those in power, but his account of the industry led to the Pure Food and Drug Act of 1906, which later led to the Food and Drug Administration.

With one member trimming beef in a cannery, and another working in a sausage factory, the family had a first-hand knowledge of the great majority of Packingtown swindles. For it was the custom, as they found, whenever meat was so spoiled that it could not be used for anything else, either to can it or else to chop it up into sausage. With what had been told them by Jonas, who had worked in the pickle rooms, they could now study the whole of the spoiled-meat industry on the inside, and read a new and grim meaning into that old Packingtown jest—that they use everything of the pig except the squeal.

Jonas had told them how the meat that was taken out of pickle would often be found sour, and how they would rub it up with soda to take away the smell, and sell it to be eaten on free-lunch counters; also of all the miracles of chemistry which they performed, giving to any sort of meat, fresh or salted, whole or chopped, any color and any flavor and any odor they chose. In the pickling of hams they had an ingenious apparatus, by which they saved time and increased the capacity of the plant—a machine consisting of a hollow needle attached to a pump; by plunging this needle into the meat and working with his foot, a man could fill a ham with pickle in a few seconds. And yet, in spite of this, there would be hams found spoiled, some of them with an odor so bad that a man could hardly bear to be in the room with them. To pump into these the packers had a second and much stronger pickle which destroyed the odor—a process known to the workers as "giving them thirty per cent." Also, after the hams had been smoked, there would be found some that had gone to the bad. Formerly these had been sold as "Number Three Grade," but later on some ingenious person had hit upon a new device, and now they would extract the bone, about which the bad part generally lay, and insert in the hole a white-hot iron. After this invention there was no longer Number One, Two, and Three Grade—there was only Number One Grade. The packers were always originating such schemes—they had what they called "boneless hams," which were all the odds and ends of pork stuffed into casings; and "California hams," which were the shoulders, with big knuckle joints, and nearly all the meat cut out; and fancy "skinned hams," which were made of the oldest hogs, whose skins were so heavy and coarse that no one would buy them—that is, until they had been cooked and chopped fine and labeled "head cheese!"

It was only when the whole ham was spoiled that it came into the department of Elzbieta. Cut up by the two-thousand-revolutions-a-minute flyers, and mixed with half a ton of other meat, no odor that ever was in a ham could make any difference. There was never the least attention paid to what was cut up for sausage; there would come all the way back from Europe old sausage that had been rejected, and that was moldy and white—it would be dosed with borax and glycerine, and dumped into the hoppers, and made over again for home consumption. There would be meat that had tumbled out on the floor, in the dirt and sawdust, where the workers had tramped and spit uncounted billions of consumption germs. There would be meat stored in great piles in rooms; and the water from leaky roofs would drip over it, and thousands of rats would race about on it. It was too dark in these storage places to see well, but a man could run his hand over these piles of meat and sweep off handfuls of the dried dung of rats. These rats were nuisances, and the packers would put poisoned bread out for them; they would die, and then rats, bread, and meat would go into the hoppers together. This is no fairy story and no joke; the meat would be shoveled into carts, and the man who did the shoveling would not trouble to lift out a rat even when he saw one—there were things that went into the sausage in comparison with which a poisoned rat was a tidbit. There was no place for the men to wash their hands before they ate their dinner, and so they made a practice of washing them in the water that was to be ladled into the sausage. There were the butt-ends of smoked meat, and the scraps of corned beef, and all the odds and ends of the waste of the plants, that would be dumped into old barrels in the cellar and left there. Under the system of rigid economy which the packers enforced, there were some jobs that it only paid to do once in a long time, and among these was the cleaning out of the waste barrels. Every spring they did it; and in the barrels would be dirt and rust and old nails and stale water—and cartload after cartload of it would be taken up and dumped into the hoppers with fresh meat, and sent out to the public's breakfast. Some of it they would make into "smoked" sausage—but as the smoking took time, and was therefore expensive, they would call upon their chemistry department, and preserve it with borax and color it with gelatine to make it brown. All of their sausage came out of the same bowl, but when they came to wrap it they would stamp some of it "special," and for this they would charge two cents more a pound.

EIGHTY-FOUR

The Use and Need of the Life of Carry A. Nation

CARRY A. NATION

Carry Nation was a Prohibition activist inspired by religion and by her sense of moral duty to prevent drinking as the root of society's evils. She eventually resorted to violence, wielding a hatchet and smashing up saloons; being quite tall, she was a formidable foe for saloon keepers. The following snippet of her autobiography relates an early story of how she began to see her calling. The Volstead Act, prohibiting the manufacture or sale of alcohol in the United States became law in 1919 and was not repealed until 1933. It was among the most disastrous social experiments of the era, mostly because it was unenforceable and increased organized crime.

A MOTHER'S CRY

Yes I represent the mothers. "Rachel wept for her children and would not be comforted because they were not." So I am crying for help, asking men to vote for what their forefathers fought for—their firesides. Republican and Democratic votes mean saloons. There is not one effort in these parties to do ought but perpetuate this treason. Yes, it is treason, to make laws to prohibit crime and then license saloons, that prohibit laws from prohibiting crime. There is not a lawful or legalized saloon. Any thing wrong can not be legally right. "Law commands that which is right and prohibits that which is wrong." Saloons command that which is wrong and prohibit that which is right. This is anarchy. There is another grievous wrong. The loving moral influence of mothers must be put in the ballot box. Free men must be the sons of free women. To elevate men you

Carry A. Nation. *The Use and Need of the Life of Carry A. Nation.* Rev. ed. Topeka, KS: F. M. Steves & Sons, 1905.

must first elevate women. A nation can not rise higher than the mothers. Liberty is the largest privilege to do that which is right, and the smallest to do that which is wrong. Vote for a principle which will make it a crime to manufacture, barter, sell or give away that which makes three-fourths of all the crime and murders thousands every year, and the suffering of the women and children that can not be told. Vote for our prohibition president and God will bless you. Pray for me that I may finish my course with joy, the ministry which I have received of the Lord Jesus.

Carry A. Nation,
Your Loving Home Defender.

I was Jail Evangelist at this time for the W. C. T. U. and I learned that almost everyone who was in jail was directly or indirectly there from the influence of intoxicating drinks. I began to ask why should we have the result of the saloon, when Kansas was a prohibition state, and the constitution made it a crime to manufacture, barter, sell or give away intoxicating drinks? When I went to Medicine Lodge there were seven dives where drinks were sold. I will give some reasons why they were removed. I began to harass these dive-keepers, although they were not as much to blame as the city officials who allowed them to run. Mart Strong was a noted joint-keeper. He and his son, Frank, were both bad drinking characters, and would sell it every chance they got. Mart had a dive and I was in several times to talk to him, and he would try to flatter me and turn things into a joke. When he saw I did not listen to such talk, treated me very rude. One Saturday I saw quite a number of men into his place, and I went in also. Saloons in Kansas generally have a front room to enter as a precaution, then a back room where the bar is. I didn't get farther than the front, for Mart came hastily, taking me by the shoulders and said: "Get out of here, you crazy woman." I was singing this song:

Who hath sorrow? Who hath Woe?
They who dare not answer no;
They whose feet to sin incline,
While they tarry at the wine.

Chorus:

They who tarry at the wine cup
They who tarry at the wine cup.
They who tarry at the wine cup.

Who hath babblings, who hath strife?
He who leads a drunkard's life;
He whose loved ones weep and pine,
While he tarries at the wine.

Who hath wounds without a cause?
He who breaks God's holy laws;
He who scorns the Lord divine,
While he tarries at the wine.

Who hath redness at the eyes?
Who brings poverty and sighs?
Unto homes almost divine,
While he tarries at the wine?

Touch not, taste not, handle not:
Drink will make the dark, dark blot,
Like an adder it will sting,
And at last to ruin bring,
They who tarry at the drink."

I continued to sing this, with tears running down my face. When I finished the song there was a great crowd; some of the men had tears in their eyes as well.

EIGHTY-FIVE

The Italian Cookbook

MARIA GENTILE

From the tenor of the directions in this passage, it is apparent that most Americans did not know the proper way to cook pasta or make sauce, despite the fact that they had been introduced by immigrants long before. But knowing the right way, and being able to distinguish authentic Italian cuisine from Italian American cuisine, would be a mark of distinction throughout the century, until the latter was eventually recognized as a cuisine in its own right.

At this point in the reader, look at this excellent collection of First World War U.S. Food Administration posters as well as any food advertisements of the early twentieth century. Many can be found on the following websites:

http://www2.coloradocollege.edu/library/specialcollections/historicalcollections/wwi/ FA001-042.html,

http://www.digitaldeliftp.com/LookAround/advertspot_kelloggs.htm,

http://www.vintageadbrowser.com/food-ads.

Paste Spaghetti, Macaroni etc

(Pasta Asciutta)

The Italians serve the spaghetti or macaroni at the beginning of the meal, in place of soup, and they give it the name of Minestra Asciutta or "dry" soup. Besides the familiar spaghetti, the paste is served in many other forms and with different seasoning. This is by far the most popular Italian dish, and it seems to have pleased the taste of all the peoples of the earth. The highly

Maria Gentile. *The Italian Cook Book*. New York: Italian Cookbook Company, 1919, pp. 14–15, 17. http://digital. lib.msu.edu/projects/cookbooks/html/books/book_71.cfm.

nutritive qualities of spaghetti and of cheese, their indispensable condiment, have been recognized by all diet authorities and, as for its palatableness, the lovers of spaghetti are just as enthusiastic and numerous outside of Italy as within the boundaries of that blessed country. The most popular seasoning for spaghetti, are tomato sauce, brown stock and anchovy sauce.

Tomato Sauce

(Salsa di Pomidoro)

Chop together, fine, one quarter of an onion, a clove of garlic, a piece of celery as long as your finger, a few bay leaves and just enough parsley. Season with a little oil, salt and pepper, cut up seven or eight tomatoes and put everything over the fire together. Stir it from time to time and when you see the juice condensing into a thin custard strain through a sieve, and it is ready for use.

When fresh tomatoes are not available the tomato paste may be used. This is a concentrated paste made from tomatoes and spices which is to be had, at all Italian grocers', now so numerous in all American cities. Thinned with water, it is a much used ingredient in Italian recipes. Catsup and concentrated tomato soup do not make satisfactory substitutes as they are too sweet in flavor. Of course canned tomatoes seasoned with salt and a bit of bay leaf, can always be used instead of fresh tomatoes.

This sauce serves many purposes. It is good on boiled meat; excellent to dress macaroni, spaghetti or other pastes which have been seasoned with butter and cheese, or on boiled rice seasoned in the same way (see Risotto). Mushrooms are a fine addition to it.

When using concentrated paste the following recipes will be found to give good results:

Chop one onion, one carrot and a celery stalk: form a little bunch of parsley and other aromatic greens and put everything to brown in a saucepan together with a piece of butter. Add a reasonable portion of tomato paste while cooking, stir and keep on a low fire until the sauce assumes the necessary consistency.

Spaghetti or Macaroni with Butter and Cheese

(Pasta al Burro e Formaggio)

This is the simplest form in which the spaghetti may be served, and it is generally reserved for the thickest paste. The spaghetti are to be boiled until tender in salted water, taking care to remove them when tender, and not cooked until they lose form. They should not be put into the water until this is at a boiling point.

Take as much macaroni as will half fill the dish in which it is to be served. Break into pieces two and a half to three inches long if you so desire. The Italians leave them unbroken, but their skill in turning them around the fork and eating them is not the privilege of everybody. Put the macaroni into salted boiling water, and boil twelve to fifteen minutes, or until the macaroni is perfectly soft. Stir frequently to prevent the macaroni from adhering to the bottom. Turn it into a colander to drain; then put it into a pudding-dish with a generous quantity of butter and grated cheese. If more cheese is liked, it can be brought to the table so that the guests can help themselves to it.

The macaroni called "Mezzani" which is a name designating size, not quality, is the preferable kind for macaroni dishes made with butter and cheese.

EIGHTY-SIX

How to Cook a Wolf

M.F.K. FISHER

MFK Fisher (1908–1992) was one of the great American food writers. This selection was written during World War II, when hunger was a real threat, but Fisher managed to keep a sense of humor and upheld gastronomic principles nonetheless. It was first published in 1942.

HOW TO PRAY FOR PEACE

Pray for peace and grace and spiritual food, For wisdom and guidance, for all these are good, But don't forget the potatoes.

—*Prayer and Potatoes*, J. T. PETTEE

IT IS easy to think of potatoes, and fortunately for men who have not much money it is easy to think of them with a certain safety. Potatoes are one of the last things to disappear, in times of war, which is probably why they should not be forgotten in times of peace.

They can be bought, until things change even more radically than the pessimists predict, in sacks at almost any market. There are various names for them, and nice ones too: Idaho Russet, White Rose, Late Beauty of Hebron. They are a vegetable, white inside and shirted in a fine silky brown coat which is like a thin layer of cork, but much more delicious when washed and cooked with the rest.

Potatoes, like most other vegetables and animals, soon die when their skins are removed, so that it is better to boil or bake them entire, and then remove the delicate coat if you prefer to eat them peeled.

M.F.K. Fisher. "How to Cook a Wolf." In *The Art of Eating*. 1942. Reprint by New York: Macmillan, 1990, pp. 286–88, 320–22.

If your tastebuds are truly civilized, however, one of the best meals in the world is a pot of medium-sized unpeeled potatoes, boiled briskly in hot water until they are done, and then drained and "shook" over the flame for a minute until the brown coverings split. Either throw in a handful of chopped fresh herbs like parsley and marjoram and chives (or green onions), and some butter, and shake it all around [A celestial variation is to add to fresh green peas, cooked rapidly in a little chicken broth or water and then drained and tossed generously in sweet butter, half their amount of small new potatoes, cooked and of course unpeeled, and half *their* amount of little braised white onions.] or pour the vegetables straightway into a hot bowl and eat them the way the Swiss do, with a good nubbin of cheese and a good gout of sweet butter and coarse salt and pepper for each biteful. This, with a glass of milk or some white wine and fruit, is a fit supper for Lucullus.

If your oven is going at about 300 to 350°, wash a few even-sized potatoes, dry them, and rub them with a little oil or butter. You can split them if you are in a hurry, buttering their cut sides, of course. As soon as they are tender [. . . or better yet, I now know, when you first put them in the oven] pierce them with a fork to keep them from growing soggy, and then eat them, if you are hungry, with plenty of butter and salt and fresh-ground pepper, not forgetting the delicate nut-like brown skin.

Or hollow them gently, stir the white part briskly with an egg and some seasoning, and put it back in the shells, with a little cheese or a couple of baby sausages on top to brown under the broiler. (These last potatoes can be made several hours before they are to be broiled, and are especially good in winter.)

[It is too bad that so many people have either not yet acquired a healthy acquaintanceship with good potato soup, or have had it shocked out of them by early exposure to a pasty and unreasonable facsimile. Most people I know fall into one of these categories, until I give them, for a winter lunch or a Sunday-night supper or some such loose-jointed feast, a steaming tureen of soup based, just as loose-jointedly, on the following rule:

Quick Potato Soup

(Referred to Sardonically by My Father as Poor Man's Potage . . .)

1/4 pound good butter   2 quarts whole milk
4 large potatoes   salt, pepper, minced parsley if agreeable
4 large onions

Melt the butter in large kettle, or in fireproof casserole in which the soup can be served. Grate the clean potatoes into it. (I like to leave them unpeeled, but the soup is not so pretty unless chopped fresh herbs, added at the last, change its natural whiteness enough to hide the bits of brown skin . . .) Grate the peeled onions into it . . . or slice them very thin. Heat the mixture to bubble-point, stirring well. Then reduce the heat, and cover closely for about ten minutes or until the vegetables are tender but not mushy, shaking the pot now and then to prevent sticking. Add more butter (or chicken-fat) if it seems wise. Heat the milk to boiling point but not beyond, add slowly to the pot, season, and serve. Variations of this recipe are obvious. One of my father's favorites is the last-minute addition of a cup or so of cooked minced clams. A half-pound of grated fresh mushrooms, added to the vegetables just before pouring in the hot milk, is fine. And so on and so on.]

HOW TO BE A WISE MAN

A wise man always eats well.

—*Chinese proverb*

EVERY now and then a sensitive intelligent thoughtful person feels very mournful about this country and, deciding with Brillat-Savarin that "The destiny of nations depends upon what and how they eat," he begins to question.

Why, he asks, are we so ungastronomic as a nation?

Why do we permit and even condone the feeble packaged bread that our men try to keep strong on? [And women . . . and, worst of all, *children*!]

Why do we let our millers rob the wheat of all its goodness, and then buy the wheat germ for one thousand times its value from our druggists so that our children may be strong and healthy?

Why do we go on eating cakes and puddings after good meals, because we always did when we were children?

Why do we talk longingly of the honest beef stew our Aunt Matilda used to make while we spend a dollar or two eating third-rate steamed chicken dipped in batter and fried in a shameful pot of synthetic grease in some roadside hashery?

It is because we are sentimental, probably, and loyal to what we want to remain sweet memories of our younger years. It is because we are proud, and vain, and unwilling to admit our own weaknesses. And most of all it is because we, and almost all American Anglo-Saxon children of the second generation, have been taught when we were young not to mention food or enjoy it publicly.

If we have liked a meringue, or an artful little curl of pastry on a kidney pie, or a toasted walnut placed as only a child would like it right in the middle of a chocolate blanc-mange, we have not been allowed to cry out with pleasure but instead have been pressed down, frowned at, weighted with a heavy adult reasoning that such display was unseemly, and vulgar, and almost "foreign."

Once when young Walter Scott, who later wrote so many exciting books, was exceptionally hungry and said happily, "*Oh*, what a fine soup! Is it not a *fine* soup, dear Papa?," his father immediately poured a pint of cold water into what was already a pretty thin broth, if the usual family menu was any sample. Mr. Scott did it, he said, to drown the devil.

For too many nice ordinary little Americans the devil has been drowned, so that all their lives afterwards they eat what is set before them, without thought, without comment, and, worst of all, without interest. The result is that our cuisine is often expensively repetitive: we eat what and how and when our parents ate, without thought of natural hungers.

It is not enough to make a child hungry; if he is moderately healthy he will have all the requisites of a normal pig or puppy or plant-aphis, and will eat when he is allowed to, without thought. The important thing, to make him not a pig or puppy, nor even a delicate green insect, is to let him eat from the beginning with thought.

Let him choose his foods, not for what he likes as such, but for what goes with something else, in taste and in texture and in general gastronomic excitement. It is not wicked sensuality, as Walter Scott's father would have thought, for a little boy to prefer buttered toast with spinach for supper and a cinnamon bun with milk for lunch. It is the beginning of a sensitive and thoughtful system of deliberate choice, which as he grows will grow too, so that increasingly he will be able to choose for himself and to weigh values, not only sensual but spiritual.

He will remember, some time when he is a man, that once he decided not to eat a chocolate bar, but to let the taste of a stolen apple ride an hour or two longer on his appreciative tongue. And whatever decision he must make as a man will probably be the solider for that apple he ate so long since.

The ability to choose what food you must eat, and knowingly, will make you able to choose other less transitory things with courage and finesse. A child should be encouraged, not discouraged as so many are, to look at what he eats, and think about it: the juxtapositions of color and flavor and texture . . . and indirectly the reasons why he is eating it and the results it will have on him, if he is an introspective widgin. (If not, the fact that what he eats is not only good but pretty will do him no harm.)

If, with the wolf at the door, there is not very much to eat, the child should know it, but not oppressively. Rather, he should be encouraged to savor every possible bite with one eye on its agreeable nourishment and the other on its fleeting but valuable esthetic meaning, so that twenty years later, maybe, he can think with comfortable delight of the little brown toasted piece of bread he ate with you once in 1942, just before that apartment was closed, and you went away to camp.

It was a nice piece of toast, with butter on it. You sat in the sun under the pantry window, and the little boy gave you a bite, and for both of you the smell of nasturtiums warming in the April air would be mixed forever with the savor between your teeth of melted butter and toasted bread, and the knowledge that although there might not be any more, you had shared that piece with full consciousness on both sides, instead of a shy awkward pretense of not being hungry.

[I feel, even more strongly than I did in 1942, that one of the most important things about a child's gastronomical present, in relation to his future, gastronomical and otherwise, is a good *respect* for food. In horrifies me to see contemporary mothers numbly cooking and then throwing away uneaten lamb chops, beans, toast; mussed but unsavored puddings; deliberately spilled or bedabbled milk. I think children should be given small portions of food, according to their natures, and allowed to cope with them at their own speeds, but *finish* them, before more is trotted out in the currently fashionable pediatric pattern. . . . They learn their capacities. They learn good manners. Above all, they learn to respect the food so many other children cry for.]

All men are hungry. They always have been. They must eat, and when they deny themselves the pleasures of carrying out that need, they are cutting off part of their possible fullness, their natural realization of life, whether they are poor or rich.

It is a sinful waste of human thought and energy and deep delight, to teach little children to pretend that they should not care or mention what they eat. How sad for them when they are men! Then they may have to fight, or love, or make other children, and they won't know how to do it fully, with satisfaction, completely, because when they were babies they wanted to say, "*Oh,* what a fine soup!" and instead only dared murmur, "More, please, Papa!"

EIGHTY-SEVEN

Grinding it Out: The Making of McDonald's

RAY KROC

Although not the founder of McDonald's, Ray Kroc made it the empire it became. His key to success was franchising, and in these passages he relates many of the business principles that led to success, among which was extensive advertising and thinking big.

Somewhere in the course of our loan discussions, the idea emerged that we should build and operate ten or so stores as a company. This would give us a firm base of income in the event the McDonald brothers claimed default on our contract (I had yet to receive a single registered letter from them authorizing our buildings to be constructed with basements and furnaces). If worse came to worst, the thinking went, we could always retrench and operate our company stores under some other name. The germ of this idea, too, might have sprung from our dealings with Clem Bohr, in which case I thank him in the same spirit one thanks the robber who at least spared his life.

Establishing company stores, of course, would require a truly massive infusion of capital. But Harry said he thought he could arrange it with the help of his friend Lee Stack.

The proposition that Harry finally brought to me was for three insurance companies to lend us $1.5 million in exchange for about 22-1/2 percent of our stock. Harry introduced me to Fred Fideli, who represented State Mutual Life Assurance, and John Gosnell of the Paul Revere Life Insurance Company. These two men explained how they had arranged with their firms and the Massachusetts Protective Association to make the loan. I was intrigued by the proposal, and I was impressed with Fideli and Gosnell. The only problem seemed to be how we would

Ray Kroc. *Grinding It Out: The Making of McDonald's*. New York: St. Martin's Press, 1992, pp. 108–14.

handle the deal among ourselves. My Bohemian frugality fought with the idea of giving up any part of the stock in the company I had struggled so desperately to build; yet the appeal of $1.5 million was irresistible. The arrangement we came up with, after a lot of discussion, was that I would contribute 22½ percent of my remaining stock (leaving me with 54½ percent), Harry would put in 22½ percent and June Martino would give up 22½ percent of hers.

It turned out to be the best deal those three insurance companies ever made. They sold their stock a few years later for between $7 and $10 million. That is one hell of a return on investment. (However, if they'd waited until 1973 to sell, they could have gotten over five hundred million dollars!)

That loan could be called the lift-off of McDonald's rocketlike growth in the sixties. It took a lot more financial thrust to put us into orbit, but we would never have gotten off the ground without it. Our first McOpCo (McDonald's Operating Company) store was purchased from an operator in Torrence, California. A short time later, in the summer of 1960, we opened our first company-built store in Columbus, Ohio.

I took my hat off to Harry Sonneborn then for negotiating that loan, and I still do today. Yet the results of it, in terms of the posture Harry was giving the company, contained the seeds of a philosophical clash that eventually would split Harry and me and nearly destroy McDonald's. It was then that Harry's view of the corporation as just a real estate business, rather than a hamburger business, began to crystalize. As he had set it up, we would not take a mortgage for more than ten years, even on a subordinated basis. We had twenty-year leases on all the property. This meant, of course, that after ten years when our mortgages were paid off, we would have all the income from a store free and clear to the corporation. That was fine. But Harry's line of thought had this annex: Since we were not obliged to renew licenses, at the expiration of the licenses the company could wind up operating all of the stores. I would not agree with that. I never did and I never will. It can't happen so long as my influence and that of Fred Turner enforce the view that the corporation is in the hamburger restaurant business, and its vitality depends on the energy of many individual owner-operators. The corporation has purchased stores—many of them, as I will show in later chapters. But our procedures for doing so are clearly spelled out to franchisees. We bend over backward to be fair in every case. We recognize that it would be unwieldy and counterproductive for the corporation to own more than about thirty percent of all stores. Our slogan for McDonald's operators is "In business for yourself, but not by yourself," and it is one of the secrets of our success.

A curious circumstance developed for the company in the momentum generated by the loan from the three insurance companies. We could show that we were making a profit now. At the same time, we had no cash flow.

The reason for this was simply that the accounting regulations were weak in the area of deferred expenses you could carry on your books. We were capitalizing all the real estate overhead and all the construction overhead for a period of eighteen months. We called this "Developmental Accounting," and it allowed us to show a bottom line profit. But it was distorting our profit and loss statements.

We hired a regular parade of people in the late fifties. We sold them a dream and paid them as little as possible. I don't feel bad about that, because I wasn't making much myself, and those who stayed with us are now very well off, indeed.

Bob Papp was hired as a draftsman to assist Jim Schindler. He later became a vice-president in charge of construction. John Haran came into the company to help Harry with real estate. These added people meant that we needed more space, of course, so we kept moving around in the area where I had had my original two-room office, knocking down walls and expanding.

One day Harry came in and told me he was going to hire a young fellow named Dick Boylan to help him with finances. "He's a lawyer and accountant, and he's our kind of guy, Ray," Harry said. "Let me tell you what he did. He and his partner, whose name is Bob Ryan, are selling insurance, see? They know they have about as much chance as a snowball in hell of getting to see me with that act. But it happens that they both used to work for the Internal Revenue Service, so they tell my secretary they are from the IRS. Naturally, I think, 'Holy Christ, what now?' And I call June in to listen to what they have to say. Boylan gives me this kind of sheepish grin and says, 'With our background of working for the IRS, Mr. Sonneborn, we know we can design an insurance plan that will help you. . . .' Well, that breaks June up, and I have a hard time keeping a straight face myself.

"Their insurance proposal was pretty good, too. It was a hell of a presentation. June was very impressed, and she's the one who suggested hiring him."

Dick Boylan is now senior executive vice-president and chief financial officer of the company. Some time after he joined us we also hired his former partner, Bob Ryan, and he's a vice-president and treasurer. I could go on and on listing people who joined us at this time, many of whom are now officers of McDonald's or wealthy operators. One of our fine old-timers, Morris Goldfarb from Los Angeles, said at the 1976 operator's convention in Hawaii that he was certain research would show that Ray Kroc has made millionaires of more men than any other person in history. I don't know about that; I appreciate Morrie's view, but I would put it another way. I'd rather say I gave a lot of men the opportunity to become millionaires. They did it themselves. I merely provided the means. But I certainly do know a powerful number of success stories.

McDonald's doesn't confer success on anyone. It takes guts and staying power to make it with one of our restaurants. At the same time, it doesn't require any unusual aptitude or intellect. Any man with common sense, dedication to principles, and a love of hard work can do it. And I have stood flatfooted before big crowds of our operators and asserted that any man who gets a McDonald's store today and works at it relentlessly will become a success, and many will become millionaires—no question.

There are hazards and pitfalls, of course, just as there are in any small business. And some locations go along for years with a very modest volume. But, almost without exception, these stores will catch on at some point and begin to grow, as Morrie Goldfarb himself can testify. He was one of my very first franchisees. His store on La Tijera Boulevard in Los Angeles opened a year after my place in Des Plaines. I went out to look at his location, and it was excellent. I congratulated him on it. But for some reason it turned out to be a real turtle. Morrie had sold a little restaurant he'd scrimped by with for years to go into McDonald's with his son, Ron. He thought that now he was going to get out of the woods at last. But his previous place had been a cakewalk compared to this. He couldn't build enough volume to hire a full crew, and he and Ron were working their heads off handling two stations apiece all day long.

Morrie called me on the telephone and raised hell.

"Ray, I am averaging $5,000 a month here," he said. "If I have a real good month it's $7,000. Now that place called Peak's across town is doing $12,000 a month, and they have an inferior location!"

Peak's happened to be a misfit McDonald's, one of the franchises sold by the McDonald brothers before I came into the picture. I suggested to Morrie that he ask the McDonald boys for some guidance. He said O.K., that was a good idea, he'd do it. A few days later he was back on the phone more upset than before.

"This is ridiculous!" he moaned. "I had Maurice and Richard come down from San Bernardino, and they spent most of the day here poking around. They get ready to leave, Ray, and you know what they tell me? They say, 'You are doing everything just right. All you have to do is continue this way and the business will come.' Hellfire, they were no help at all!"

I told Morrie that I would come out again and see if I could figure it out. It was baffling. I studied that place from every angle without coming up with an answer.

Morrie's volume problem continued for about five years. After he got his equipment paid off he had a little breathing space. Then I moved out and opened our California office. We built a lot of new stores and started a local advertising campaign, and that really got things rolling for Morrie. In 1975, his La Tijera store grossed close to a million dollars. He has torn the old store down now and replaced it with a beautiful new building.

I get furious all over again just thinking about that California situation during the first five years we were in business. It was aggravation unlimited. In many ways it was a parallel to the frustrations I faced at home with my wife. The McDonald brothers were simply not on my wavelength at all. I was obsessed with the idea of making McDonald's the biggest and best. They were content with what they had; they didn't want to be bothered with more risks and more demands. But there wasn't much I could do about it, California was simply too far away for me to deal with effectively from Chicago.

At one point I sent Fred Turner out to report on the McDonald brothers' California operations. He came back appalled at the haphazard situation he'd found. The brothers' own store in San Bernardino was virtually the only "pure" McDonald's operation. Others had adulterated the menu with things like pizza, burritos, and enchiladas. In many of them the quality of the hamburgers was inferior, because they were grinding hearts into the meat and the high fat content made it greasy. The McDonald boys just turned their backs on such poor practices. Their operators refused to cooperate with mine in volume purchasing and advertising. We asked them to contribute one percent of their gross toward an advertising campaign that would benefit our stores and all of them as well, but they would have nothing to do with it. All I could do for the time being was to live with it. I am bitter about the experience; not for myself alone, but for fine operators like Morrie Goldfarb and many others who lost five years' growth as a result.

In our business there are two kinds of attitudes toward advertising and public relations. One is the outlook of the begrudger who treats every cent paid for ad programs or publicity campaigns as if they were strictly expenditures. My own viewpoint is that of the promoter; I never hesitate to spend money in this area, because I can see it coming back to me with interest. Of course, it comes back in different forms, and that may be the reason a begrudger can't appreciate it. He has a narrow vision that allows him to see income only in terms of cash in his register. Income for me can appear in other ways; one of the nicest of them is a satisfied smile on the face of a customer. That's worth a lot, because it means that he's coming back, and he'll probably bring a friend. A child who loves our TV commercials and brings her grandparents to a McDonald's gives us two more customers. This is a direct benefit generated by advertising dollars. But the begrudger has a hard time appreciating this—he wants to have his cake and eat it too.

EIGHTY-EIGHT

Diet for a Small Planet

FRANCES MOORE LAPPÉ

Frances Moore Lappé was born in 1944 and is still an active writer on food and environmental issues, having won many awards and honorary doctorates. This book revolutionized the way people thought about the food supply and inequalities of distribution. Her solution was essentially to switch from inefficient cattle rearing to growing plants, which provide more food that can be eaten directly and shared more equally around the world. This is an indicative selection from the revised edition of her first of many books.

WHO ASKED FOR FRUIT LOOPS?

AT A PARTY not long ago I was talking with a man I hardly knew about the ideas in this edition—how I was struggling to grasp the forces *behind* these eight radical and risky changes in the American diet. "Well, don't blame the corporations," he told me. "If people are stupid enough to eat junk food, they deserve to get sick. Naturally corporations are going to make what sells best."

I think he summed up pretty well how most Americans view these changes in our diet. They are seen as the more or less inevitable consequences of combining the corporate profit motive with human weakness. And since you can't change either, why stew about it?

I'm convinced that this view is popular because while it *appears* to assign responsibility (to the gullible individual), it is really a way to evade responsibility for our economic ground

---

Frances Moore Lappé, ed. *Diet for a Small Planet*. 1971. 2nd rev. ed. New York: Ballantine, 1982, pp. 140–46.

rules. Once accepted, these ground rules justify such practices as feeding 145 million tons of grain to livestock. And they make the expensive, energy-consuming, life-threatening changes in our national diet inevitable.

To understand corporate logic, pretend for a few minutes that you are the chief executive of Conglomerated Foods, Inc.

From the Point of View of Conglomerated Foods, Inc.

Get off the elevator on the top floor. Enter the executive suite. Say hello to your secretary, settle down in your big leather chair, and gaze for a moment out the picture window. Think. How would *you* make Conglomerated Foods prosper? Even if you don't have a degree from Harvard Business School, I think you'll find that certain obvious strategies come to mind.

Ah, yes . . . first *expand sales*. But how?

The "Takeover" Strategy

Your most obvious step in expanding sales is to squeeze out, or buy out, smaller, often regional, producers. (As Proctor & Gamble did when they bought a small southwest coffee company called J.A. Folger about ten years ago.) Then you launch an advertising blitz and a deluge of coupons and even reduce the price of your product below your cost. (You can follow International Telephone & Telegraph's example—it sold its Wonder, Fresh Horizons, and Home Pride breads at a loss to drive smaller bakeries out of the market.) Since you're a conglomerate selling many different products, you can make up for any losses simply by raising prices in your other product lines. And why not expand your sales overseas through takeovers? (As Borden did when it bought Brazil's biggest pasta manufacturer.)

THE IMPACT OF YOUR STRATEGY

Walking into the supermarket, customers still see Aunt Nellie's Pickles and Grandma's Molasses. This illusion of diversity hides the reality that your strategy has succeeded making the food industry one of the most tightly controlled in America. In the scramble to capture national markets, *half* of American food companies have been bought out or closed down during my lifetime. Most of them were not inefficient producers; they simply could not withstand the financial muscle of the cash-laden conglomerates.

Take Beatrice Foods, for example, a company whose name is unknown to most Americans. This one company has bought out more than 400 others. Names like Tropicana, Milk Duds, Rosarita, La Choy, Swiss Miss, Mother's, and Aunt Nellie's, and even Samsonite and Airstream—all these should really be called "Beatrice."

As a result of the surge of takeovers, 50 of the remaining 20,000 companies have emerged at the pinnacle. These 50 corporations now own two-thirds of the industry's assets. Based on present trends, these 50 firms—one-quarter of 1 percent of them all—will control virtually *all* the food industry's assets in another 20 years.

By the 1970s the supergiants had begun to gobble up the giants. In what *Business Week* called the "great takeover binge," Pillsbury plunked down $152 million for Green Giant (frozen vegetables). For $621 million, R.J. Reynolds seized Del Monte's vast fruit and vegetable empire. Nabisco merged with Standard Brands (Chase & Sanborn coffee, Blue Bonnet margarine, Planter's peanuts, etc.).

Now, in most food lines—such as breakfast cereals, soups, and frozen foods—four or fewer firms control at least half of the sales. (See Figure 7.) Economists call that a "shared monopoly"—and with it come monopoly prices, an estimated $20 billion in overcharges to consumers each year. Anticompetitive practices cost consumers a 15-cent "monopoly overcharge" on every dollar's worth of cereal, according to a four-year study by the Federal Trade Commission.

And who's to resist? The combined budget of the antitrust divisions of the Justice Department and the Federal Trade Commission is $20 million a year, the sum that a corporate food giant can put into promoting just one "new" processed food. Spending only $20 million to counter the monopoly abuses in a trillion-dollar economy is what Ralph Nader calls a "charade."

The "Grab a Bigger Market Share" Strategy

But now where are you? In most major food categories, a few giants now make over half the sales. Proctor & Gamble (Folger's) and General Foods (Maxwell House, Sanka) together control nearly 60 percent of the ground-coffee market. Kellogg's, General Foods, and General Mills divvy up 90 percent of the dry-cereal market. Campbell's alone controls nearly 90 percent of the soup market. And on it goes. Industry studies show us that at least half of the shoppers in a supermarket buy mainly the top two brands, even though they usually cost more. So you've got to become number one, or at least number two. You'll have to lure some customers away from the other Big Food companies. But you can't compete in ways that hurt your long-term profits—like offering better quality or lowering prices. Hmmm. Why not up the advertising budget? And you can come up with some eye-catching "new'" products in some eye-catching new packages. If you can't compete in price or quality, you must compete in visibility—and the more snazzy the packaging, the more visible. With more products, you can squeeze your competitors off the supermarket shelf.

FIGURE 7. CONTROL OF OUR FOOD BY SHARED MONOPOLIES*

Industry	Percent of Sales Controlled by Top Four Companies
Coffee, ground	51
Oil, salad and cooking	51
Peanut butter	51
Baked goods, dry cookies	52
Fish and seafood, canned	58
Cigars	59
Beans, canned and dry	65
Corn, wet milling	65
Grain mill products, mixes, and prepared flours	70
Milk, canned	70
Spice	70

FIGURE 7. (*Continued*)

Baked goods, dry crackers	71
Chocolate and cocoa	71
Milk, dried	73
Cereal, to be prepared	80
Cigarettes	80
Coffee, instant	81
Tomato products, catsup	81
Baking powder and yeast	86
Dessert mixes	86
Grain mill products, refrigerated doughs	87
Soft drinks, bottling	89
Soft drinks, syrup	89
Cereal, ready to eat	90
Gum	90
Soup	92
Baby food	95

Source: Food Price Investigation, Senate Hearings, 1973.
* When as few as four firms control in excess of 50 percent of the sales of a given food line, economists usually find "oligopolistic" practices, such as overcharging, in comparison to prices under more competitive conditions.

To create consumer loyalty, you have to have brand names. And that's a lot easier with processed foods. (You did stick labels on bananas, but lettuce and mushrooms were a lot more trouble.) And since you want to sell the products from your giant assembly lines all over the country, you'll need to add such delicacies as BHT and polysorbate for indefinite "freshness."

THE IMPACT OF YOUR STRATEGY

Food advertising costs shot up from about $2 billion a year in 1950 to a record $13 billion in 1978. "On the average, six cents of every dollar we spend on processed foods will go directly to buy ad time on television and 'other promotion'," says food researcher and writer Daniel Zwerdling. "But when we buy one of industry's hot-selling brands, we pay far, far more. In a recent year, breakfast eaters who bought Kellogg's Country Morning, a so-called 'natural cereal' that better resembled crumbled cookies, paid 35 cents of every dollar merely to finance Kellogg's ads. . . ." But the costs of the ads themselves are only a fraction of what the consumer ends up paying for advertising. Because advertising is power, people are willing to pay more for a highly advertised brand-name item than they would for exactly the same product sold under a less well-known or store brand name. (See Figure 8.)

Since launching just one new item nationwide can cost as much as $20 million, only the corporate giants can afford to play this game.

Because of the huge expense of advertising, Zwerdling concludes, the advertising strategy and the takeover strategy are closely tied: "Food corporations merge in part to amass the financial power they need to launch massive advertising campaigns." Other studies confirm that the more any industry relies on advertising, the faster the concentration of market power.

More eye-catching packaging was also part of your strategy. What has this done for us? Well, by 1980 the cost of the package exceeded the cost of the food ingredients for a fourth of the food and beverage product industry. (Soft drink containers cost two times as much as their contents; beer containers five times as much!) Over the last decade packaging costs have gone up 50 percent faster than the labor costs in our food. Today one out of every 11 dollars we spend on food and drink goes to pay for packaging.

And the impact of your new product strategy? "In the beginning, there was just Campbell's chicken rice soup," quips journalist A. Kent MacDougall. "Today, besides chicken with rice soup, Campbell Soup makes chicken gumbo, chicken noodle, chicken noodle-Os, curly noodles with chicken, cream of chicken, creamy mushroom" plus five others. That's what economists call "product proliferation." ("To grow dramatically you have to introduce new products," says General Foods' Peter Rosow, general manager of the company's dessert division.) It's the battle of the giants for supermarket shelf space. And it works. Today, just five companies use 108 brands of cereal to control over 90 percent of cereal sales.

Such product proliferation requires more and more shelf space. Just since the early 1970s, shelf space devoted to candy and chewing gum has gone up 75 percent; that for dog and cat food, 80 percent. All this means bigger stores, more clerks—costs which must mean rising prices.

FIGURE 8. THE PRICE OF A BRAND NAME

	Price of House Brand	Price of Name Brand	Percent Higher
Flour, all-purpose, 10 lb.	$1.35	$2.75 Gold Medal, Pillsbury	104
Salt, iodized, 26 oz.	.22	.33 Morton	50
Sugar, granulated, 5 lb.	1.89	2.49 Domino	32
Corn oil, 1 qt.	1.99	2.25 Mazola	13
Spaghetti, 1 lb.	.59	.85 Mueller's	44
Rice, enriched, parboiled, 32 oz.	1.05	1.69 Uncle Ben's	61
Nonfat dry milk, ten 1-qt. envelopes	3.79	4.49 Carnation	18
Cut green beans, 16-oz. can	.30	.50 Libby's	67
Raisin bran, 20 oz.	1.19	1.63 Kellogg's	37
Orange juice, frozen concentrate, 16 oz.	1.04	1.49 Minute Maid	43
Graham crackers, 16 oz.	.79	1.09 Nabisco	38
Peanut butter, smooth, 12 oz.	.83	1.15 Jif, Peter Pan	39
Coffee, instant, 6 oz.	3.19	3.99 Nescafé, Folger's	25

Source: Center for Science in the Public Interest, 1980.

EIGHTY-NINE

Recipes for Hummus and Spanakopetes

CRAIG CLAIBORNE

Craig Claiborne was one of the most influential food writers of the latter twentieth century, primarily as food critic for the New York Times. *He is often credited for championing regional American cuisine, but his greater legacy seems to have been broadening the palate of Americans to include exotic cuisines and inspiring them to cook it themselves. These were brand-new dishes to most Americans when they were introduced. Consider who would have made these dishes and for what kind of occasions.*

Hummus

About 3 cups, or 8 to 10 servings
2 cups cooked or canned chick-peas, drained
2/3 cup taheeni (sesame paste)
3/4 cup lemon juice
2 cloves garlic
1 teaspoon salt
Italian parsley leaves

   Place the chick-peas, taheeni, lemon juice, garlic and salt in a blender and blend until smooth. Alternatively, the chick-peas may be sieved and mashed along with the remaining ingredients. Pile into a small bowl and garnish with the parsley leaves. Serve as an appetizer.

Craig Claiborne. *The New York Times International Cookbook*. New York: Harper & Row, 1971, pp. 391, 645.

Spanakopetes (Spinach Cheese Puffs)

About 4 dozen
1 medium onion, minced
2 tablespoons butter
1 pound fresh spinach, washed and chopped
1/2 pound feta cheese, crumbled
6 ounces pot cheese
3 eggs, lightly beaten
Salt and freshly ground black pepper
Nutmeg
1/4 cup fresh bread crumbs
1/2 pound phyllo pastry sheets
1 cup melted butter

1. Preheat the oven to 425 degrees.
2. Sauté the onion in the two tablespoons butter until golden. Add the spinach and cook over low heat, stirring occasionally, until the spinach is wilted and most of the moisture has evaporated. Stir in the feta cheese, eggs, salt, pepper, and nutmeg to taste, and the bread crumbs.
3. Cut the phyllo pastry sheets into long strips two inches wide. Brush one strip at a time with melted butter. Keep the phyllo not being used covered at all times with waxed paper and a lightly dampened towel. Put one teaspoon of the spinach mixture at one end of each strip and fold over and over into a small triangle. With each fold, make sure that the bottom edge is parallel with the alternate edge.
4. After all the filling is used arrange the triangles on a baking sheet and brush with melted butter. Bake fifteen to twenty minutes, or until golden. Serve hot.

NINTY

Slow Food Manifesto

FOLCO PORTINARI

The Slow Food international movement officially began when delegates from 15 countries endorsed this manifesto, written by founding member Folco Portinari, on December 10, 1989.

Our century, which began and has developed under the insignia of industrial civilization, first invented the machine and then took it as its life model.

We are enslaved by speed and have all succumbed to the same insidious virus: *Fast Life*, which disrupts our habits, pervades the privacy of our homes and forces us to eat Fast Foods.

To be worthy of the name, *Homo Sapiens* should rid himself of speed before it reduces him to a species in danger of extinction.

A firm defense of quiet material pleasure is the only way to oppose the universal folly of *Fast Life*.

May suitable doses of guaranteed sensual pleasure and slow, long-lasting enjoyment preserve us from the contagion of the multitude who mistake frenzy for efficiency.

Our defense should begin at the table with *Slow Food*.

Let us rediscover the flavors and savors of regional cooking and banish the degrading effects of *Fast Food*.

In the name of productivity, *Fast Life* has changed our way of being and threatens our environment and our landscapes. So *Slow Food* is now the only truly progressive answer.

Folco Portinari. 1989. Published online by Slow Food, 2013. http://www.slowfood.com/about_us/eng/manifesto. lasso.

That is what real culture is all about: developing taste rather than demeaning it. And what better way to set about this than an international exchange of experiences, knowledge, projects?

Slow Food guarantees a better future.

Slow Food is an idea that needs plenty of qualified supporters who can help turn this (slow) motion into an international movement, with the little snail as its symbol.

Study Questions

1. In what ways do these readings show the complete transformation of foodways in the twentieth century? How have our taste preferences changed?
2. How is the modern dieting phenomenon different from or similar to those of past generations? Is weight loss a modern form of asceticism, or are the goals completely different so that no comparison is possible?
3. Has the development of nutritional science and thinking about calories improved the way modern people eat? If not, why? Do you think we are better nourished or worse than in the past? What evidence can you provide for either position, and consider why you think the way you do.
4. Consider the ways in which the battle between fast food and slow food has shaped the way we think about what is natural, good for us, and delicious.
5. Is the way we eat today any more cosmopolitan than in the past? If so, why did this happen? Do you eat the same way your grandparents did?

GLOSSARY

ahimsa—the doctrine of nonviolence, which, when extended to animals, means vegetarianism

allspice—*Pimenta dioica*, a spice native to the Caribbean, where it was seen by Columbus

almond milk—blanched and ground almonds, soaked in hot water and strained, popular in medieval cookery, especially as a substitute for dairy products during Lent

amaranth—a seed widely used by Aztecs for food and a central part of their religion, gaining much attention today because easy to cultivate and very high in protein

ambergris—a waxy substance regurgitated from a whale's stomach that mellows while floating in the ocean, taking on an exotic perfumed scent, once used widely in cooking but extremely expensive

amia—probably a type of bonito, a small tuna fish

amphora—a ceramic vessel with a narrow pointed base and a wide hip with handles, ideal for carrying and storing in the hulls of vessels, as the preferred shipping container for wine and oil in ancient times

asafoetida—in Greek, meaning "stinking hay," among the most pungent and aromatic flavorings on earth, common in Indian cuisine, which some find offensive

ascetic—denying the body through regular exercises in fasting, sleep deprivation, and avoiding all luxuries as a way to strengthen the soul

aubergine—the British word for eggplant, linguistically related to the Spanish *berenjena*, which may ultimately come from Arabic and before that Sanskrit as the eggplant is native to India

Bodhisattva—an enlightened person who remains on earth to help humans with compassion and teaching

bouquet garnis—a small bundle of herbs such as parsley, thyme, bay leaf, and often other herbs, tied into a bundle to flavor a stock or stew, which can be removed before serving

Brahmin—the highest priestly caste in Hindu society

carob—a woody pod from a Mediterranean tree with a sweet flavor, also called St. John's bread because he ate them in the desert; used as a chocolate substitute today

cassava—see manioc

cassia buds—the dried buds of a close relative of the cinnamon plant, once used in medieval cooking in Europe but now almost completely unknown there

ch'i (or xi)—the life-promoting energy force that can be increased by eating certain foods and following certain regimens, in traditional Chinese medicine

cockscombs—the red squiggly bit on top of a chicken's head, formerly eaten as a delicacy

colocynth—a small round yellow fruit, extremely bitter, used as a laxative, whose seeds are also used to make oil

corn—a generic term for all grains used in Britain, refers to maize exclusively only in the United States

cubebs—a spice popular in the Middle Ages, recognizable as a round grain similar to pepper but with a small spike protruding from one side

cud, chewing of—this is the predigested bolus of food that is regurgitated and chewed again by ruminants such as cows, sheep, and goats

cuneiform—an ancient method of writing that uses a small wedge-shaped stylus impressed into soft clay

dharma (dhamma)—law, duty, proper behavior, according to class, age, and gender

domestication—consciously altering the characteristics of plants and animals to benefit humans through selective breeding or seed selection and reproducing them from stock kept near permanent settlements

dormouse—a small rodent especially fattened in small clay vessels (*gliraria*) by the ancient Romans, considered a delicacy

dosha—three energy forces (*vata, pitta, kapha*) that regulate bodily functions in Ayurvedic medicine

emmer—an ancient ancestor of wheat (*Triticum dicoccum*) used to make bread, especially in the Near East and Egypt

entheogen—a drug, the taking of which entails bringing the body of the deity into one's own, as with wine in Catholicism and devotees of Dionysus, soma among the ancient Aryans, and peyote among Native Americans

fruitarian—one who kills no creature for sustenance, including plants, and thus can only eat fruits, grains, and leaves without killing the plant

galangal—a root similar to ginger but harder and hotter to the taste, popular in the Middle Ages and still popular in Southeast Asian cuisine

garum—an ancient sauce of fermented whole fish, not unlike Southeast Asian fish sauces

ghee—clarified butter that keeps well in the hot climate of India, also considered a sacred substance because made from cow's milk

ginseng—an aromatic medicinal root, often taking the appearance of a human, thought to be a universal healing plant in Chinese medicine

grains of paradise—*Amomum melegueta*, a spice commonly used in the Middle Ages with a nutty slightly hot flavor

halal—the dietary regulations of Islam, similar to those of Judaism but somewhat simpler and forbidding alcohol

humoral physiology—the system of medicine originating in ancient Greece that imagines health as the balance of four bodily fluids or humors (blood, phlegm, choler, and black bile)

jujube—*Zizyphus*, a small, sweet, date-like fruit, not to be confused with the modern candy of the same name

kosher—the food laws of the ancient Hebrews, still observed by orthodox Jews today

kottabos—a drinking game in ancient Greece wherein the last bit of wine in a flat *kylix*, or drinking cup, would be flung at a target on a stand

kowtow—kneeling and bowing so the head touches the ground; a sign of respect and deference toward superiors

laganum—a thin dried sheet of dough used for thickening in ancient Greece and Rome, possibly an ancestor of lasagna

laser—see silphium

Lent—The forty-day period between Ash Wednesday and Easter when Christians would fast, with the exception of Sundays

malmsey—a sweet white wine made with the Malvasia grape, grown mostly in Madeira

manioc—or cassava, a starchy tuber native to South America, very important as a staple; also the source of tapioca. There are sweet and bitter versions; the latter must be shredded and soaked to remove cyanide poison.

mastic—an aromatic gum drawn from the *lentisk* tree that grows on the Isle of Chios in the Aegean Sea, used in confections, to line clay amphorae, and to chew as gum

metheglin—a lightly alcoholic drink based on honey, usually flavored with herbs, similar to mead

millet—a tiny round grain, most familiar as birdseed, but very nutritious and tasty

mulsum—a mixture of wine and honey, used for cooking in ancient Rome

muntjac—a species of small deer native to South Asia and China

murri—a fermented barley-based liquid used much in medieval Persian cooking, not unlike soy sauce

musk—a highly aromatic perfume taken from the scent glands of a deer, formerly used in cookery

nigella—a small black seed used as a flavoring in Middle Eastern and Indian cookery, known mostly in the West as the flower Love in a Mist, which bears globular seed capsules containing the seeds

nixtamalization—a process of soaking corn in lime or lye to remove seed coats before processing, increasing nutritional value

panacea—a drug to cure all ailments and promote health in general

papyrus—a reedy aquatic plant that when pounded forms a mucilaginous glue that holds thin strips together forming paper

passum—a thick, sweet raisin wine used for cooking in ancient Rome

pâté de foie gras—a smooth spread made from the fattened livers of force-fed geese or sometimes ducks

perilla *(shiso)*—an aromatic leaf in the mint family used in cooking and for decoration with sushi

posset—a thick, hot drink made with milk and ale that curdles

pulque—a thick, white fermented drink made from maguey plant, sacred in Aztec society but in the colonial period and even today considered common

Pythagorean—the term for vegetarians before the nineteenth century, named for the Greek philosopher and mathematician who believed in reincarnation and did not eat meat

sacrifice—killing an animal as an offering to the gods or God, or foodstuffs offered in replacement, sometimes completely destroyed, but often eaten by people eventually

sapa—a sweet syrup made from grape must boiled down to one-third. Other varieties include *defrutum*, reduced to half, and *caroenum*, reduced to one-third. All were regular ingredients in ancient Roman cooking.

scald—to heat very quickly to the boiling point and then remove from the heat, often done with milk before using in a recipe

silphium—an aromatic herb much used in ancient Rome, imported from Libya, which went extinct in ancient times, its resin was called *laser* or *laserpicium*

spikenard—an aromatic spice from the Himalayas used as incense and flavoring, mentioned many times in the Bible

Sufi—a mystical sect of Islam that stresses deep emotional devotion rather than intellectualism

taro—a root vegetable native to Southeast Asia whose root and leaves are eaten; among the earliest cultivated plants

vegan—one who avoids eating all animals as well as their products such as butter, milk, eggs, and even honey

vegetarian—a term encompassing a wide variety of food practices, usually meaning avoidance of animal flesh and fish

verjuice—the juice of unripe grapes, used as a souring agent in medieval cooking

wheatear—a tiny bird similar to a thrush, sometimes eaten roasted whole

xerophagy—eating "dry" food—meaning made of vegetables cooked not in oil but in water—along with bread, nuts, and simple foods during Lent, but also used in a secular sense for dieting

za'atar—a combination of thyme, sumac, and sesame seeds used as a spice mixture in Middle Eastern cooking; it can also include oregano and savory

WEB RESOURCES

Bibliographies and Time Lines

Food and Culture Bibliography. http://www.utexas.edu/courses/stross/bibliographies/foodbib.htm.
The Food Time Line. http://www.foodtimeline.org/.
Library of Congress Food History Bibliography. http://www.loc.gov/rr/scitech/tracer-bullets/
    foodhistorytb.html.
Medieval Cookbooks: An Annotated Bibliography. http://www.pbm.com/~lindahl/articles/food_
    bibliography.html.
The Stewpot: Bibliography of Books on Medieval and Renaissance Cooking. http://home.earthlink.
    net/~smcclune/stewpot/plibrary.html.
World Food Habits: English-Language Resources for the Anthropology of Food and Nutrition. http://
    lilt.ilstu.edu/rtdirks/.

Primary Sources

Feeding America: The Historic American Cookbook Project. http://digital.lib.msu.edu/projects/
    cookbooks/.
Fons Grewe Historic Cookbooks On Line. http://www.bib.ub.edu/?id=348.
Google Books Advanced Book Search. http://books.google.com/advanced_book_search.
Hearth: Home Economics Archive, Cornell University. http://hearth.library.cornell.edu/.
Medieval and Renaissance Food: Sources, Recipes, and Articles. http://www.pbm.com/~lindahl/food.
    html.
Project Gutenberg. http://www.gutenberg.org/.
Thomas Gloning's Corpus of Culinary and Dietetic Texts of Europe from the Middle Ages to 1800.
    http://www.uni-giessen.de/gloning/kobu.htm.

Links and Other Resources

Acanthus Books Historic Cookbooks. http://www.acanthus-books.com/index.html.
Association for the Study of Food and Society. http://food-culture.org/.
Culinary History, New York Public Library. http://www.nypl.org/node/5629.
Department of Nutrition, Food Studies, and Public Health, Steinhardt School of Culture, Education, and Human Development, New York University. http://steinhardt.nyu.edu/nutrition/food/.
Food Books, Food and Culinary History Links. http://www.foodbooks.com/foodlink.htm.
Food Culture and Society (journal). http://www.bloomsbury.com/us/journal/food-culture-and-society/.
Food History News by Sandy Oliver. http://foodhistorynews.com/linkmain.html.
Food Studies, University of Adelaide. http://www.adelaide.edu.au/food-studies/.
Henry Notaker's Old Cookbooks and Food History. http://www.notaker.com/old_cbks.htm.
Historic Food: The Website of Food Historian Ivan Day. http://www.historicfood.com/.
Master of Liberal Arts in Gastronomy, Boston University. http://www.bu.edu/met/programs/graduate/gastronomy/.Prospect Books. https://prospectbooks.co.uk/.

BIBLIOGRAPHY

Surveys of Food History

These books introduce food history and might serve well as textbooks in a food history course. Some (like Civitello) are specifically geared toward beginning students; others are popular (such as Tannahill's classic); and yet others (such as Parasecoli) are for a more professional audience. The price point will be a good indication of the targeted reader.

Civitello, Linda. *Cuisine and Culture*. Hoboken, NJ: Wiley, 2011.
Fernández-Armesto, Felipe. *Food: A History*. Oxford, UK: Macmillan, 2001.
Flandrin, Jean-Louis, and Massimo Montanari. *Food: A Culinary History*. New York: Columbia University Press, 1999.
Fletcher, Nicola. *Charlemagne's Tablecloth: A Piquant History of Feasting*. New York: St. Martin's Press, 2004.
Freedman, Paul, ed. *Food: The History of Taste*. Berkeley: University of California Press, 2007.
Higman, B. W. *How Food Made History*. Malden, MA: Wiley, 2012.
Kiple, Kenneth. *A Moveable Feast: Ten Millennia of Food Globalization*. Cambridge, UK: Cambridge University Press, 2007.
Parasecoli, Fabio, and Peter Scholliers, general eds. *A Cultural History of Food*. 6 vols. London: Berg, 2012.
Pilcher, Jeffrey. *Food in World History*. New York: Routledge, 2006.
Smith, Andrew F. *Eating History*. New York: Columbia University Press, 2009.
Strong, Roy. *Feast: A History of Grand Eating*. London: Jonathan Cape, 2002.
Tannahill, Reay. *Food in History*. New York: Crown Publishers, 1998.
Toussaint-Samat, Maguelonne. *History of Food*. Oxford, UK: Basil Blackwell, 1992.

Encyclopedias and Reference Works

Achaya, K. T. *A Historical Dictionary of Indian Food*. New York: Oxford University Press, 2002.
Adamson, Melitta, and Francine Segan, eds. *Entertaining: From Ancient Rome to the Superbowl*. Westport, CT: Greenwood, 2008.

Albala, Ken. *Food Cultures of the World Encyclopedia*. Santa Barbara, CA: ABC-CLIO, 2011.

Arndt, Alice. *Culinary Biographies*. Austin, TX: Yes Press, 2006.

Clarkson, Janet. *Menus from History*. Westport, CT: Greenwood, 2009.

Davidson, Alan. *The Oxford Companion to Food*. Oxford, UK: Oxford University Press, 1999.

Katz, Solomon H., ed. *Encyclopedia of Food and Culture*. New York: Charles Scribner's Sons, 2003.

Kiple, Kenneth, ed. *The Cambridge World History of Food*. Cambridge, UK: Cambridge University Press, 2000.

Riley, Gillian. *Italian Food*. Oxford, UK: Oxford University Press, 2007.

Sauer, Jonathan D. *Historical Geography of Crop Plants*. Boca Raton, FL: CRC Press, 2004.

Smith, Andrew F. *Fast Food and Junk Food: An Encyclopedia of What We Love to Eat*. Santa Barbara, CA: Greenwood, 2012.

Smith, Andrew F. *Oxford Encyclopedia of Food and Drink in America*. Oxford, UK and New York: Oxford University Press, 2004.

van Wyk, Ben-Erik. *Food Plants of the World*. Portland, OR: Timber Press, 2005.

Culinary Bibliographies

These are some of the standard reference works for identifying historic cookbooks and culinary literature. They are normally consulted at a research library, and the books they refer to are often old and rare and can only be accessed in archives and rare book rooms. They are nonetheless absolutely indispensable for the food historian. Merely for seeing what kind of books were published at a particular time, they can be very useful, and increasingly these sources are appearing online.

Bitting, Katherine Golden. *Gastronomic Bibliography*. Mansfield Centre, CT: Martino Publishing, 2004. 1st ed. 1939.

Feret, Barbara L. *Gastronomical and Culinary Literature: A Survey and Analysis of Historically-Oriented Collections in the U.S.A.* Metuchen, NJ: Scarecrow Press, 1979.

Lowenstein, Eleanor. *Bibliography of American Cookery Books, 1742–1860*. 3rd ed. Worcester, MA: American Antiquarian Society, 1972.

Notaker, Henry. *Printed Cookbooks in Europe, 1470–1700*. Newcastle, DE: Oak Knoll Press, 2010.

Vicaire, George. *Bibliographie Gastronomique*. Paris: Roquette et fils, 1890.

Food Anthologies

Most of the food anthologies listed here are meant for a popular audience rather than scholars, but they still can be very useful.

Allen, Brigit, ed. *Food, An Oxford Anthology*. Oxford, UK: Oxford University Press, 1995.

Curtin, Deane W., and Lisa Heldke, eds. *Cooking, Eating, Thinking: Transformative Philosophies of Food*. Bloomington: Indiana University Press, 1992.

Digby, Joan, and John Digby, eds. *Food for Thought: An Anthology of Writings Inspired by Food*. New York: William Morrow, 1987.

Gigante, Denise, ed. *Gusto: Essential Writings in Nineteenth-Century Gastronomy*. New York: Routledge, 2005.

Golden, Lilly, ed. *A Literary Feast*. New York: Atlantic Monthly Press, 1993.

Kurlansky, Mark, ed. *Choice Cuts*. New York: Ballantine, 1992.

Levy, Paul, ed. *Penguin Book of Food and Drink*. London: Penguin, 1996.
Spencer, Colin, and Claire Clifton, eds. *Faber Book of Food*. London: Faber and Faber, 1993.

Primary Sources

This list includes sources for food history that are easily accessible and available in English. It is not a bibliography of the works excerpted in the reader, but rather suggestions for students working on a term paper or research assignment. The list is also not exhaustive, especially since a massive number of historic cookbooks are available online, in Google Books, the Gutenberg Project, Gallica, and, if your institution subscribes, Early English Books Online—which are increasingly available on Amazon through print on demand as well. With a little effort spent in an advanced search, historic cookbooks are easy to find. The Feeding America site at Michigan State University has a huge collection online (http://digital.lib.msu.edu/proj ects/cookbooks/).

Anthimus. *On the Observance of Foods*. Translated by Mark Grant. Totnes, UK: Prospect Books, 1996.
Archestratus. *The Life of Luxury*. Translated by John Wilkins and Shaun Hill. Totnes, UK: Prospect Books, 1994.
Athenaeus. *Deipnosophists*. Translated by Charles Burton Gulick. Cambridge, MA: Harvard University Press, 2011.
Austin, Thomas, ed. *Two Fifteenth Century Cookery-Books*. London: Oxford University Press, 2000.
al-Baghdadi. *A Baghdad Cookery Book. Petits Proposal Culinaires* 79. Translated by Charles Perry. Totnes, UK: Prospect Books, 2005.
Beeton, Isabella. *Mrs. Beeton's Book of Household Management*. Oxford, UK: Oxford University Press, 2000.
Bottéro, Jean, ed. and trans. *The Oldest Cuisine in the World*. English translation by Teresa Lavender Fagan. Chicago: University of Chicago Press, 2004.
Brillat-Savarin, Jean Anthelme. *The Physiology of Taste*. Translated by M.F.K. Fisher. New York: Knopf, 2009.
Chadwick, Owen, ed. *Western Asceticism*. Philadelphia: Westminster Press, 1958.
Dawson, Thomas. *The Good Huswife's Jewell*. Edited by Maggie Black. Lewes, UK: Southover, 1996.
Escoffier, Auguste. *Memories of My Life*. New York: International Thompson Publishing 1997.
Francatelli, Charles Elmé. *A Plain Cookery Book for the Working Classes*. Whitstable, UK: Pryor Publications, 1993.
Galen. *On the Properties of Foodstuffs*. Translated by Owen Powell. Cambridge, UK: Cambridge University Press, 2003.
Grewe, Rudolf, and Constance B. Hieatt, eds. *Libellus de Arte Coquinaria: An Early Northern Cookery Book*. Medieval and Renaissance Texts and Studies, Vol. 222. Tempe: Arizona Center for Medieval and Renaissance Studies, 2001.
Grocock, Christopher, and Sally Graingers, trans. *Apicius*. Totnes, UK: Prospect Books, 2006.
Heiatt, Constance B., and Sharon Butler, eds. *Curye on Inglysch*. London: Oxford University Press, 1985.
Heiatt, Constance, Brenda Hosington, and Sharon Butler. *Pleyn Delit*. Toronto: University of Toronto Press, 1996.
Hess, Karen, ed. *Martha Washington's Book of Cookery*. New York: Columbia University Press, 1995.
Marinetti, Fillipo. *The Futurist Cookbook*. San Francisco: Bedford Arts, 1989.
Markham, Gervase. *The English Housewife*. Edited by Michael R. Best. Montreal and Kingston: McGill-Queens University Press, 1986.
May, Robert. *The Compleat Cook*. Totnes, UK: Prospect Books, 2000.

Pouncy, Carolyn Johnston, trans. *The Domostroy: Rules for Russian Households in the Time of Ivan the Terrible*. Ithaca, NY: Cornell University Press, 1994.

Santanach, Joan, ed. *The Book of Sent Soví: Medieval Recipes from Catalonia*. Translated by Robin Vogelzang. Barcelona and Woodbridge, VA: Barcino Tamesis, 2008.

Scappi, Bartolomeo. *The Opera of Bartolomeo Scappi: L'arte et prudenza d'un maestro Cuoco (The Art and Craft of a Master Cook)*. Translated by Terence Scully. Toronto: University of Toronto Press, 2008.

Simmons, Amelia. *American Cookery*. Bedford MA: Applewood, 1996.

Smith, E. [Eliza?]. *The Compleat Housewife*. London: Studio Editions, 1994.

Soyer, Alexis. *A Shilling Cookery for the People*. Whistable, UK: Pryor Publications, 1999.

Tirel, Guillaume. *The Viandier of Taillevent*. Edited by Terence Scully. Ottawa, Canada: University of Ottawa Press, 1988.

Secondary Sources

This is not meant to be an exhaustive list of all that has been written about food by modern historians, but rather suggestions for further reading that resonate with the themes of this reader and food history as I teach it. It is fairly representative of the best recent work in food history as well.

Adamson, Melitta. *Food in Medieval Times*. Westport, CT: Greenwood, 2004.

Adamson, Melitta. *Regional Cuisines of Medieval Europe*. New York: Routledge, 2002.

Albala, Ken. *The Banquet: Dining in the Great Courts of Late Renaissance Europe*. Urbana: University of Illinois Press, 2007.

Albala, Ken. *Beans: A History*. Oxford, UK: Berg, 2007.

Albala, Ken. *Cooking in Europe, 1250–1650*. Westport, CT: Greenwood 2006.

Albala, Ken. *Eating Right in the Renaissance*. Berkeley: University of California Press, 2002.

Anderson, E. N. *Everyone Eats: Understanding Food and Culture*. New York: New York University Press, 2005.

Anderson, E. N. *The Food of China*. New Haven, CT: Yale University Press, 1988.

Atkins, Peter J., Peter Lummel, and Derek J. Oddy. *Food and the City in Europe since 1800*. Aldershot, UK: Ashgate, 2007.

Avakian, Arelen Voski, and Barbara Haber, eds. *From Betty Crocker to Feminist Food Studies: Critical Perspectives on Women and Food*. Amherst: University of Massachusetts Press, 2005.

Belasco, Warren. *Appetite for Change: How the Counterculture Took on the Food Industry, 1966–1988*. New York: Pantheon, 1989.

Belasco, Warren, and Phillip Scranton, eds. *Food Nations: Selling Taste in Consumer Society*. New York: Routledge, 2000.

Bell, Rudolph A. *Holy Anorexia*. Chicago: Chicago University Press, 1985.

Bennett, Judith M. *Ale, Beer, and Brewsters in England: Women's Work in a Changing World, 1300–1600*. New York: Oxford University Press, 1996.

Bentley, Amy. *Eating for Victory: Food Rationing and the Politics of Domesticity*. Urbana: University of Illinois Press, 1998.

Bober, Phyllis Pray. *Art, Culture and Cuisine*. Chicago: University of Chicago Press, 1999.

Bobrow-Strain, Aaron. *White Bread*. Boston: Beacon Press, 2012.

Bourdieu, Pierre. *Distinction: A Social Critique of the Judgement of Taste*. Cambridge, MA: Harvard University Press, 1984.

Bower, Anne, ed. *Recipes for Reading: Community Cookbooks, Stories, Histories*. Amherst: University of Massachusetts Press, 1992.

Braudel, Fernand. *Mediterranean and the Mediterranean World in the Age of Philip II.* Translated by Siân Reynolds. New York: Harper & Row, 1972.

Brears, Peter. *Cooking and Dining in Medieval England.* Totnes, UK: Prospect Books, 2008.

Brothwell, Don, and Patricia Brothwell. *Food in Antiquity.* Baltimore: Johns Hopkins University Press, 1998.

Burnett, John. *Liquid Pleasures: A Social History of Drinks in Modern Britain.* London: Routledge, 1999.

Burnett, John. *Plenty and Want: A Social History of Diet in England from 1815 to the Present Day.* London: Nelson, 1979.

Burke, Peter. *Popular Culture in Early Modern Europe.* 3rd ed. Farnham, UK: Ashgate, 2009.

Bynum, Caroline W. *Holy Feast and Holy Fast: The Religious Significance of Food to Medieval Women.* Berkeley: University of California Press, 1987.

Camporesi, Piero. *Bread of Dreams.* Cambridge, UK: Polity Press, 1989.

Cappatti, Alberto, and Massimo Montanari. *Italian Cuisine.* New York: Columbia University Press, 1999.

Carney, Judith A. *Black Rice: The African Origins of Rice Cultivation in the Americas.* Cambridge, MA: Harvard University Press, 2001.

Carney, Judith, and Richard Nicholas Rosomoff. *In the Shadow of Slavery: Africa's Botanical Legacy in the Atlantic World.* Berkeley: University of California Press, 2011.

Chang, K. C. *Food in Chinese Culture: Anthropological and Historical Perspectives.* New Haven, CT: Yale University Press, 1977.

Clarkson, Leslie A., and E. Margaret Crawford. *Feast and Famine: Food and Nutrition in Ireland, 1500–1920.* Oxford, UK: Oxford University Press, 2002.

Coe, Sophie. *America's First Cuisines.* Austin: University of Texas Press, 1994.

Coe, Sophie D., and Michael D. Coe. *The True History of Chocolate.* New York: Thames and Hudson, 2007.

Collingham, Lizzie M. *A Taste of War: World War Two and the Battle for Food.* London: Allen Lane, 2011.

Colquhoun, Kate. *Taste: The Story of Britain through Its Cooking.* London: Bloomsbury, 2007.

Cooper, John. *Eat and Be Satisfied: A Social History of Jewish Food.* Northvale, NJ: Jason Aronson, 1993.

Counihan, Carol M. *Food in the USA: A Reader.* New York: Routledge, 2002.

Cowan, Brian. *The Social Life of Coffee: The Emergence of the British Coffeehouse.* New Haven, CT: Yale University Press, 2007.

Crosby, Alfred W. *The Columbian Exchange: Biological and Cultural Consequences of 1492.* Westport, CT: Greenwood, 1972.

Crosby, Alfred W. *Ecological Imperialism: The Biological Expansion of Europe, 900–1900.* Cambridge, UK: Cambridge University Press, 1986.

Cwiertka, Katarzyna. *Modern Japanese Cuisine.* London: Reaktion, 2006.

Dalby, Andrew. *Dangerous Tastes.* Berkeley: University of California Press, 2002.

Dalby, Andrew. *Siren Feasts: A History of Food and Gastronomy in Greece.* London: Routledge, 1996.

Darby, William Jefferson, Paul Galioungui, and Louis Grivetti. *Food: The Gift of Osiris.* London: Academic Press, 1977.

David, Elizabeth. *Harvest of the Cold Months.* New York: Viking, 1994.

Davidson, James N. *Courtesans and Fishcakes: The Consuming Passions of Classical Athens.* New York: St. Martin's Press, 1997.

De la Peña, Carolyn. *Empty Pleasures: The Story of Artificial Sweeteners.* Chapel Hill: University of North Carolina Press, 2010.

de Silva, Cara, ed. *In Memory's Kitchen: A Legacy from the Women of Terezín.* Northvale, NJ: Jason Aronson, 1996.

Denker, Joel. *The World on a Plate.* Boulder, CO: Westview Press, 2003.

Diamond, Jared. *Guns, Germs and Steel.* New York: W. W. Norton, 1997.

Diner, Hasia R. *Hungering for America: Italian, Irish, and Jewish Foodways in the Age of Migration*. Cambridge, MA: Harvard University Press, 2001.

Douglas, Mary. *Purity and Danger*. London: Routledge, 2002.

Drummond, J.C., and Anne Wilbraham. *The Englishman's Food: A History of Five Centuries of English Diet*. London: J. Cape, 1939.

DuPuis, E. Melanie. *Nature's Perfect Food: How Milk Became America's Drink*. New York: New York University Press, 2002.

Eden, Trudy. *The Early American Table*. DeKalb: Northern Illinois University Press, 2008.

Elias, Norbert. *The Civilizing Process*. Translated by Edmund Jephcott. Oxford, UK: Blackwell, 2000.

Faas, Patrick. *Around the Roman Table*. New York: Palgrave, 2003.

Feeley-Harnik, Gillian. *The Lord's Table: Eucharist and Passover in Early Christianity*. Philadelphia: University of Pennsylvania Press, 1981.

Ferguson, Priscilla Parkhurst. *Accounting for Taste: The Triumph of French Cuisine*. Chicago: University of Chicago Press, 1984.

Ferrières, Madeleine. *Sacred Cow, Mad Cow: A History of Food Fears*. New York: Columbia University Press, 2006.

Fisher, Carol. *The American Cookbook: A History*. Jefferson, NC: McFarland, 2006.

Flandrin, Jean-Louis. *Arranging the Meal*. Berkeley: University of California Press, 1997.

Floyd, Janet, and Laurel Forster. *The Recipe Reader: Narratives, Contexts, Traditions*. Aldershot, UK: Ashgate, 2003.

Forster, Robert, and Orest Ranum, eds. *Food and Drink in History: Selections from the Annales, économies, sociétiés, civilizations*. Vol. 5. Translated by Elborg Forster and Patricia Ranum. Baltimore: Johns Hopkins University Press, 1979.

Fraser, Eva D.G., and Andrew Rimas. *Empires of Food*. New York: Free Press, 2010.

Freedman, Paul. *Out of the East: Spices and the Medieval Imagination*. New Haven, CT: Yale University Press, 2008.

Freidberg, Suzanne. *Fresh: A Perishable History*. Cambridge, MA: Harvard University Press, 2009.

Freidenreich, David M. *Foreigners and Their Food: Constructing Otherness in Jewish, Christian and Islamic Law*. Berkeley: University of California Press, 2011.

Fussell, Betty. *The Story of Corn*. New York: North Point, 1992.

Gabbaccia, Donna R. *We Are What We Eat*. Cambridge, MA: Harvard University Press, 1998.

Gentilcore, David. *Pomodoro*. New York: Columbia University Press, 2010.

Gigante, Denise. *Taste: A Literary History*. New Haven, CT: Yale University Press, 2005.

Glanville, Phillipa, and Hilary Young, eds. *Elegant Eating*. London: V&A Publications, 2002.

Glasse, Hannah. *The Art of Cookery Made Plain and Easy*. Bedford, MA: Applewood, 1997.

Gold, Carol. *Danish Cookbooks*. Seattle: University of Washington Press, 2007.

Good Huswife's Handmaide for the Kitchen. Bristol, UK: Stuart Press, 1992.

Gratzer, Walter. *Terrors of the Table: The Curious History of Nutrition*. New York: Oxford University Press, 2005.

Greenspoon, Leonard J., Ronald A. Simkins, and Gerald Shapiro. *Food and Judaism*. Omaha, NE: Creighton University Press, 2005.

Griffith, R. Marie. *Born Again Bodies: Flesh and Spirit in American Christianity*. Berkeley: University of California Press, 2004.

Grimm, Veronika E. *From Feasting to Fasting, The Evolution of A Sin: Attitudes to Food in Late Antiquity*. London: Routledge, 1996.

Guerrini, Anita. *Obesity and Depression in the Age of Enlightenment*. Norman: University of Oklahoma Press, 2000.

Haber, Barbara. *From Hardtack to Homefries: An Uncommon History of American Cooks and Meals*. New York: Free Press, 2002.

Harris, Jessica B. *High on the Hog*. New York: Bloomsbury, 2011.

Harris, Marvin. *Cows, Pigs, Wars and Witches*. New York: Vintage, 1974.

Harrison, Brian. *Drink and the Victorians: The Temperance Question in England, 1815– 1872*. London: Faber, 1971.

Hartog, Adel P. den, ed. *Food Technology, Science, and Marketing: European Diet in the Twentieth Century*. East Linton, UK: Tuckwell Press, 1995.

Helstosky, Carol. *Garlic and Oil*. Oxford, UK: Berg, 2004.

Henisch, Bridget Anne. *Fast and Feast*. State College: Penn State University Press, 1976.

Henisch, Bridget. *The Medieval Cook*. Woodbridge, UK: Boydell Press, 2009.

Higman, B. W. *Jamaican Food*. Kingston, Jamaica: University of the West Indies Press, 2008.

Hill, Susan E. *Eating to Excess: The Meaning of Gluttony and the Fat Body in the Ancient World*. Santa Barbara, CA: Praeger, 2011.

Holt, Mack, ed. *Alcohol*. Oxford, UK: Berg, 2006.

Humble, Nicola. *Culinary Pleasures: Cookbooks and the Transformation of British Food*. London: Faber and Faber, 2005.

Innes, Sherrie A. *Dinner Roles: American Women and Culinary Culture*. Iowa City: University of Iowa Press, 2001.

Innes, Sherrie, ed. *Kitchen Culture in America*. Philadelphia: University of Pennsylvania Press, 2001.

Ishige, Naomichi. *The History and Culture of Japanese Food*. New York: Kegan Paul, 2001.

Jacobs, Marc, and Peter Schollers, eds. *Eating Out in Europe*. Oxford, UK: Berg, 2003.

Jeanneret, Michael. *A Feast of Words*. Chicago: University of Chicago Press, 1991.

Johnston, Josée, and Shyon Bauman. *Foodies*. New York: Routledge, 2010.

Jones, Martin. *Feast: Why Humans Share Food*. Oxford, UK: Oxford University Press, 2007.

Kamminga, Harmke, and Andrew Cunningham, eds. *The Science and Culture of Nutrition, 1840–1940*. Amsterdam: Rodopi, 1995.

Kamp, David. *The United States of Arugula*. New York: Broadway Books, 2006.

Kaplan, Steven L. *The Bakers of Paris and the Bread Question, 1700–1775*. Durham, NC: Duke University Press, 1996.

Katz, Solomon H., ed. *Encyclopedia of Food and Culture*. New York: Charles Scribner's Sons, 2003.

Kaufman, Frederick. *A Short History of the American Stomach*. Orlando, FL: Harcourt, 2008.

Keay, John. *The Spice Route: A History*. Berkeley: University of California Press, 2006.

Kelly, Ian. *Cooking for Kings: The Life of Antonin Careme*. New York: Walker, 2003.

Koeppel, Dan. *Banana: The Fate of the Fruit That Changed the World*. New York: Hudson Street, 2008.

Korsmeyer, Carolyn. *Making Sense of Taste: Food and Philosophy*. Ithaca, NY: Cornell University Press, 1999.

Krondl, Michael. *The Taste of Conquest*. New York: Ballantine, 2007.

Kurlansky, Mark. *Cod*. New York: Penguin, 1998.

Kurlansky, Mark. *Salt*. New York: Walker, 2002.

Laszlo, Pierre. *Citrus*. Chicago: University of Chicago Press, 2007.

Lehmann, Gilly. *The British Housewife*. Totnes, UK: Prospect Books, 2002.

Levenstein, Harvey. *Fear of Food. A History of Why We Worry about What We Eat*. Chicago: University of Chicago Press, 2012.

Levenstein, Harvey A. *Paradox of Plenty: A Social History of Eating in Modern America*. New York: Oxford University Press, 1993.

Levenstein, Harvey A. *Revolution at the Table: The Transformation of the American Diet*. New York: Oxford University Press, 1988.

Martin, A. Lynn. *Alcohol, Violence and Disorder in Traditional Europe*. Kirksville, MO: Truman State University Press, 2009.

McAvoy, Liz Herbert, and Teresa Walters, eds. *Consuming Narratives: Gender and Monstrous Appetites in the Middle Ages and Renaissance*. Chicago: University of Chicago Press, 2002.

McFeeley, Mary. *Can She Bake a Cherry Pie? American Women and the Kitchen in the Twentieth Century*. Amherst: University of Massachusetts Press, 2001.

McGovern Patrick. *Uncorking the Past*. Berkeley: University of California Press, 2009.

McNeil, Cameron, ed. *Chocolate in Mesoamerica*. Gainesville: University Press of Florida, 2006.

Mehdawy, Magda, and Amr Hussein. *The Pharaoh's Kitchen*. Cairo: American University in Cairo Press, 2010.

Mendelson, Ann. *Stand Facing the Stove: The Story of the Women Who Gave America The Joy of Cooking*. New York: Henry Holt, 1996.

Mennell, Stephen. *All Manners of Food: Eating and Taste in England and France from the Middle Ages to the Present*. Oxford, UK: Basil Blackwell, 1985.

Mintz, Sidney W. *Sweetness and Power: The Place of Sugar in Modern History*. New York: Viking, 1985.

Mintz, Sidney. *Tasting Food, Tasting Freedom*. Boston: Beacon Press, 1996.

Montanari, Massimo. *The Culture of Food*. Translated by Carl Ipsen. Oxford, UK: Blackwell, 1994.

Montanari, Massimo. *Food Is Culture*. Translated by Albert Sonnenfeld. New York: Columbia University Press, 2006.

Mudry, Jessica J. *Measured Meals: Nutrition in America*. Albany: State University of New York Press, 2009.

Murray, Sarah. *Moveable Feasts: From Ancient Rome to the 21st Century, the Incredible Journeys of the Food We Eat*. New York: St. Martin's Press, 2007.

Norton, Marcy. *Sacred Gifts, Profane Pleasures: A History of Tobacco and Chocolate in the Atlantic World*. Ithaca, NY: Cornell University Press, 2008.

Oddy, Derek J. *From Plain Fare to Fusion Food: British Diet from the 1890s to the 1900s*. Woodbridge, UK: Boydell Press, 2003.

Oddy, Derek, Peter Atkins, and Virginie Amilien, eds. (2009) *The Rise of Obesity in Europe: A Twentieth Century Food History*. Farnham, UK: Ashgate, 2009.

Oddy, Derek J., and Lydie Petránová, eds. *The Diffusion of Food Culture in Europe from the Late Eighteenth Century to the Present Day*. Prague: Academia, 2005.

Offer, Avner. *Epidemics of Abundance: Overeating and Slimming in the USA and Britain since the 1950s*. Oxford, UK: Oxford University Press, 1998.

Oliver, Sandra L. *Food in Colonial and Federal America*. Westport, CT: Greenwood, 2005.

Opie, Frederick Douglass. *Hog and Hominy: Soul Food from Africa to America*. New York: Columbia University Press, 2010.

Ortiz de Montellano, Bernard R. *Aztec Medicine, Health and Nutrition*. New Brunswick, NJ: Rutgers University Press, 1990.

Palmatier, Robert Allen. *Food: A Dictionary of Literal and Nonliteral Terms*. Westport, CT: Greenwood, 2000.

Paston-Williams, Sara. *The Art of Dining*. London: National Trust, 1993.

Pendergast, Mark. *Uncommon Grounds: The History of Coffee and How It Transformed Our World*. New York: Basic Books, 1999.

Pilcher, Jeffrey M. *Que Vivan los Tamales! Food and the Making of Mexican Identity*. Albuquerque: University of New Mexico Press, 1998.

Pilcher, Jeffrey M. *The Sausage Rebellion: Public Health, Private Enterprise, and Meat in Mexico City 1890–1917*. Albuquerque: University of New Mexico Press, 2006.

Pillsbury, Richard. *No Foreign Food: The American Diet in Time and Place*. Boulder, CO: Westview Press, 1998.

Pleij, Herman. *Dreaming of Cockaigne*. New York: Columbia University Press, 2001.

Pollan, Michael. *The Botany of Desire: A Plant's Eye View of the World*. New York: Random House, 2001.

Pollan, Michael. *The Omnivore's Dilemma*. New York: Penguin, 2006.

Preece, Rod. *Sins of the Flesh: A History of Ethical Vegetarian Thought*. Vancouver: University of British Columbia Press, 2008.

Randolf, Mary. *The Virginia Housewife*. Columbia: University of South Carolina Press, 1984.

Rath, Eric. *Food and Fantasy in Early Modern Japan*. Berkeley: University of California Press, 2010.

Rath, Eric, and Stephanie Assmann, eds. *Japanese Foodways Past and Present*. Urbana: University of Illinois Press, 2010.

Reader, John. *Potato: A History of the Propitious Esculent*. New Haven, CT: Yale University Press, 2009.

Rosenblum, Jordan. *Food and Identity in Early Rabbinic Judaism*. Cambridge, UK: Cambridge University Press, 2010.

Rosenblum, Mort. *Olives*. New York: North Point, 1996.

Sack, Daniel. *Whitebread Protestants: Food and Religion in American Culture*. New York: Palgrave, 2000.

Santich, Barbara. *The Original Mediterranean Cuisine*. Chicago: Chicago Review Press, 1995.

Salaman, Redcliffe N. *The History and Social Influence of the Potato*. Cambridge, UK: Cambridge University Press, 1985.

Schaefer, Edward H. *The Golden Peaches of Samarkand*. Berkeley: University of California Press, 1985.

Schivelbusch, Wolfgang. *Tastes of Paradise: A Social History of Spices, Stimulants, and Intoxicants*. Translated by David Jacobson. New York: Pantheon, 1992.

Schlosser, Eric. *Fast Food Nation*. Boston: Houghton Mifflin, 2001.

Schwartz, Hillel. *Never Satisfied: A Cultural History of Diets, Fantasies and Fat*. New York: Anchor, 1986.

Scully, Terence. *The Art of Cookery in the Middle Ages*. Woodbridge, UK: Boydell Press, 1995.

Serventi, Silvano, and Francoise Sabban. *Pasta*. New York: Columbia University Press, 2002.

Shapiro, Laura. *Perfection Salad: Women and Cooking at the Turn of the Century*. New York: Farrar, Straus and Giroux, 1986.

Shaw, Teresa M. *The Burden of the Flesh: Fasting and Sexuality in Early Christianity*. Minneapolis: Fortress Press, 1998.

Siegers, Yves, Jan Bieleman, and Erik Buyst, eds. *Exploring the Food Chain: Food Production and Food Processing in Western Europe, 1850–1990*. Turnhout, Belgium: Brepols, 2009.

Sim, Alison. *Food and Feast in Tudor England*. New York: St. Martin's Press, 1997.

Simoons, Frederick J. *Eat Not This Flesh*. Madison: University of Wisconsin Press, 1994.

Simoons, Frederick J. *Food in China: A Cultural and Historical Inquiry*. Boca Raton, FL: CRC Press, 1991.

Smith, Andrew F. *American Tuna*. Berkeley: University of California Press, 2012.

Smith, Andrew F. *Peanuts*. Urbana: University of Illinois Press, 2002.

Smith, David F., ed. *Nutrition in Britain: Science, Scientists, and Politics in the Twentieth Century*. London: Routledge, 1995.

Smith, David F., and Jim Phillips, eds. *Food, Science, Policy and Regulation in the Twentieth Century: International and Comparative Perspectives*. London: Routledge, 2000.

Sokolov, Raymond. *Why We Eat What We Eat*. New York: Touchstone, 1993.

Spang, Rebecca. *The Invention of the Restaurant: Paris and Modern Gastronomic Culture*. Cambridge, MA: Harvard University Press, 2000.

Spencer, Colin. *British Food*. London: Grub Street, 2002.

Spencer, Colin. *The Heretic's Feast: A History of Vegetarianism*. Hanover, NH: University Press of New England, 1995.

Stearns, Peter N. *Fat History: Bodies and Beauty in the Modern West*. New York: New York University Press, 1997.

Stuart, Tristram. *The Bloodless Revolution: A Cultural History of Vegetarianism from 1600 to the Present*. New York: HarperPress, 2006.

Symonds, Michael. *History of Cooks and Cooking*. Urbana: University of Illinois Press, 2000.

Swislocki, Mark. *Culinary Nostalgia: Regional Food Culture and the Urban Experience in Shanghai*. Stanford, CA: Stanford University Press, 2009.

Tannahill, Reay. *Food in History*. New York: Crown Publishers, 1998.

Teuteberg, Hans Jürgen, ed. *European Food History: A Research Review*. Leicester, UK: Leicester University Press, 1992.

Theophano, Janet. *Eat My Words: Reading Women's Lives through the Cookbooks They Wrote*. New York: Palgrave, 2002.

Thirsk, Joan. *Food in Early Modern England: Phases, Fads, Fashions, 1500–1760*. London: Hambledon Continuum, 2006.

Trubeck, Amy. *How the French Invented the Culinary Profession*. Philadelphia: University of Pennsylvania Press, 2000.

Turner, Jack. *Spice: The History of a Temptation*. New York: Knopf, 2004.

Unger, Richard W. *Beer in the Middle Ages and the Renaissance*. Philadelphia: University of Pennsylvania Press, 2004.

Valenze, Deborah. *Milk: A Local and Global History*. New Haven, CT: Yale University Press, 2011.

Van Winter, Johanna Maria. *Spices and Comfits: Collected Papers on Medieval Food*. Totnes, UK: Prospect Books, 2007.

Vernon, James. *Hunger: A Modern History*. Cambridge, MA: Harvard University Press, 2007.

Vileisis, Anne. *Kitchen Literacy*. Washington, DC: Island Press, 2008.

Visser, Margaret. *Much Depends on Dinner: The Extraordinary History and Mythology, Allure and Obsession, Perils and Taboos, of an Ordinary Meal*. New York: Grove, 1986.

Warde, Alan. *Consumption, Food and Taste: Culinary Antinomies and Commodity Culture*. London: Sage, 1997.

Warman, Arturo. *Corn and Capitalism: How a Botanical Bastard Grew to Global Dominance*. Translated by Nancy L. Westrate. Chapel Hill: University of North Carolina Press, 2003.

Watts, Sydney. *Meat Matters: Butchers, Politics, and Market Culture in Eighteenth-Century Paris*. Rochester, NY: University of Rochester Press, 2006.

Wheaton, Barbara Ketchum. *Savoring the Past: The French Kitchen and Table from 1300 to 1789*. New York: Simon & Schuster, 1983.

Willan, Anne. *Great Cooks and Their Recipes*. London: Pavilion, 2000.

Wilson, Bee. *Swindled: The Dark History of Food Fraud, from Poisoned Candy to Counterfeit Coffee*. Princeton, NJ: Princeton University Press, 2008.

Wilson, C. Anne. *Food and Drink in Britain*. Chicago: Academy Chicago Publishers, 1991.

Witt, Doris. *Black Hunger*. Minneapolis: University of Minnesota Press, 1999.

Woloson, Wendy. *Refined Tastes*. Baltimore: Johns Hopkins University Press, 2002.

Woolgar, C. M. *The Great Household in Late Medieval England*. New Haven, CT: Yale University Press, 1999.

Wrangham, Richard. *Catching Fire: How Cooking Made Us Human*. New York: Basic Books, 2009.

Young, Carolin C. *Apples of Gold in Settings of Silver*. New York: Simon & Schuster, 2002.

Zaouali, Lilia. *Medieval Cuisine of the Islamic World*. Berkeley: University of California Press, 2007.

Ziegelman, Jane. *97 Orchard*. New York: HarperCollins, 2010.

Zohary, Daniel, and Maria Hopf. *Domestication of Plants in the Old World*. Oxford, UK: Clarendon Press, 1993.

Zubaida, Sami, and Richard Tapper. *A Taste of Thyme*. London: Taurus Parke, 2000.

Zuckerman, Larry. *Potato*. New York: North Point 1998.

Zweiniger-Bargielowska, Ina, Rachel Duffett, and Alain Drouard, eds. *Food and War in Twentieth-century Europe*. Farnham, UK: Ashgate, 2011.

APPENDIX OF SOURCES

Grateful acknowledgement is made to the following sources for permission to reproduce material for this volume.

Part One: Sumer and Egypt

1. Jean Bottéro, ed. and trans. *The Oldest Cuisine in the World*. English translation by Teresa Lavender Fagan. Chicago: University of Chicago Press, 2004, pp. 26–35. Reprinted with permission from University of Chicago Press.

2. E. A. Wallis Budge, ed. and trans. *The Book of the Dead: The Papyrus of Ani*. 1895. Reprint by New York: Dover, 1967, excerpted from throughout text. Article is in the public domain.

3. Cyril P. Bryan, trans. *Ancient Egyptian Medicine: The Papyrus Ebers*. 1930. Reprint by Chicago: Ares, 1974, pp. 50–58. Reprinted with permission.

4. Herodotus. *The History of Herodotus*. Book 2. Translated by George Rawlinson. 1858–1860. Available at http://en.wikisource.org/wiki/History_of_Herodotus/Book_2 under a Creative Commons Attribution/Share-Alike License.

5. A. S. Hunt and C. C. Edgar, trans. *Papyri on Food in Daily Life—Select Papyri*. London: William Heinemann, 1956, pp. 229, 377–79, 455–57. Article is in the public domain.

Part Two: Ancient Greece

6. Homer. *The Iliad*. Book 7. Translated by Samuel Butler. 1898. Available at http://en.wikisource.org/wiki/The_Iliad_%28Butler%29/Book_VII under a Creative Commons Attribution/Share-Alike License.

7. Hesiod. "Works and Days." In *The Homeric Hymns and Homerica*. Translated by Hugh G. Evelyn-White. Cambridge, MA: Harvard University Press; London: William Heinemann, 1914. http://www.perseus.tufts.edu/hopper/text?doc= Perseus%3Atext%3A1999.01.0132%3Acard%3D109. Article is in the public domain.

8. Hippocrates. *Hippocrates*. Vol. 4. Loeb Classical Library, Vol. 150. Translated by W.H.S. Jones. Cambridge, MA: Harvard University Press, 1967, pp. 329, 331, 333, 335, 337, 339. Reprinted by permission of Harvard University Press and the Trustees of the Loeb Classical Library. Loeb Classical Library® is a registered trademark of the President and Fellows of Harvard College.

9. Plato. *Gorgias*. Translated by Benjamin Jowett. 1871. Available at http://en.wikisource. org/wiki/Gorgias under a Creative Commons Attribution/Share-Alike License.

10. Xenophon. *Memorabilia and Oeconomicus*. Vol. 4. Loeb Classical Library, Vol. 168. Translated by E. C. Marchant. Cambridge, MA: Harvard University Press, 1923, pp. 511, 513, 515, 517, 519, 521. Reprinted by permission of Harvard University Press and the Trustees of the Loeb Classical Library. Loeb Classical Library® is a registered trademark of the President and Fellows of Harvard College.

11. Archestratus. *The Life of Luxury*. Translated by John Wilkins and Shaun Hill. Totnes, UK: Prospect Books, 1994, pp. 41–45, 72–73, 93–97. Reprinted with permission.

12. Epicurus. *Epicurus: Letters, Principal, Doctrines, and Vatican Sayings*. 1st ed. Translated by Russell M. Geer. New York: Macmillan, 1964, pp. 55–57. Reprinted by permission of Pearson Education, Inc., Upper Saddle River, NJ.

13. Athenaeus. *The Deipnosophists*. Translated by C. D. Yonge. London: Bohn, 1854, pp. 455–60, 593–603. Article is in the public domain.

14. Porphyry. *On Abstinence from Animal Food*. Translated by Thomas Taylor. 1823. Published online by the Tertullian Project, 2007. http://www.tertullian.org/fathers/ porphyry_abstinence_01_book1.htm. Article is in the public domain.

15. Andrew Dalby, trans. *Geoponika: Farm Work*. Totnes, UK: Prospect Books, 2011, pp. 194–95, 252–53, 303–6, 348–49. Reprinted with permission.

Part Three: Ancient Rome

16. Marcus Porcis Cato. *Roman Farm Management. The Treatises of Cato (De Agricultura) and Varro (Rerum Rusticarum Libri Tres)*. Translated by a Virginia Farmer [Fairfax Harrison]. New York: Macmillan, 1918, pp. 19–26, 48–49. Article is in the public domain.

17. Petronius. "The Feast of Trimalchio." In *The Satyricon*. Translated by William Burnaby. Harmondsworth, UK: Penguin, 1984. http://www.gutenberg.org/dirs/ etext04/7pasw10a.txt. Article is in the public domain.

18.   Apicius. *De Re Coquinaria*. Translated by Ken Albala. 2013.

19.   Juvenal. "Satires V and XI." In *The Satires of Juvenal, Persius, Sulpicia and Lucius*. Translated by Lewis Evans. London: George Bell & Sons, 1904, pp. 33–39, 123–35. Article is in the public domain.

20.   Aelius Lampridius. *The Scriptores Historiae Augustae*. Vol. 2. Translated by David Magie. Loeb Classical Library, Vol. 140. Cambridge, MA: Harvard University Press, 1924, pp. 143, 145, 147, 149, 151, 153, 155, 157, 159, 161, 163, 165, 167, 169, 171, 173. Reprinted by permission of Harvard University Press and the Trustees of the Loeb Classical Library. Loeb Classical Library® is a registered trademark of the President and Fellows of Harvard College.

21.   Galen. *Galen on Food and Diet*. Translated by Mark Grant. London: Routledge, 2000, pp. 82–85, 132–34, 188–90. Reproduced by permission of Taylor & Francis Books UK.

Part Four: Imperial China

22.   John Steele, trans. *The I-Li or Book of Etiquette and Ceremonial*. London: Probsthain, 1917, pp. 122–49.

23.   Li Ji. *Li Chi: Book of Rites*. Hyde Park, NY: University Books, 1964, pp. 59–64, 468–707. Article is in the public domain.

24.   Huangdi. *The Yellow Emperor's Classic of Internal Medicine*. Translated by Ilza Veith. Berkeley: University of California Press, 2002, pp. 97–98, 147–48, 198–207. Copyright © 2002 by Ilza Veith. Reprinted with permission.

25.   Jia Sixie. *A Preliminary Survey of the Book Ch'i Min Yao Shu: An Agricultural Encyclopaedia of the 6th Century*. Edited by Shih Sheng-Han. Peking: Science Press, 1962, pp. 51–60, 66–70, 87.

26.   Lu Yu. *The Classic of Tea*. Translated by Francis R. Carpenter. Boston: Little, Brown and Company, 1974, pp. 103–19. Copyright © 1974 by Francis R. Carpenter. Reprinted by permission of Little, Brown and Company. All rights reserved.

27.   Hu Szu-Hui. *A Soup for the Qan: Chinese Dietary Medicine of the Mongol Era as Seen in Hu Szu-Hui's Yin-Shan Cheng-Yao*. Edited and Translated by Paul D. Buell and Eugene N. Anderson. London: Kegan Paul International, 2000, excerpted from throughout text. Reprinted with permission from the authors, Paul D. Buell and Eugene N. Anderson.

28.   Gao Lian. *Yin Zhuan Fu Shi Jian (Discourse on Food and Drink), in Culinary Arts in Late Ming China: Refinement, Secularization, and Nourishment*. Translated by Su Heng-an. Taipei: SMC Publishing, 2008, excerpted from throughout text.

29.   Li Shizhen. *Chinese Medicinal Herbs: A Modern Edition of a Classic Sixteenth-Century Manual*. Translated by Shih-Chen Li. Mineola, NY: Dover, 1973, pp. 469–74. Reprinted with permission.

Part Five: Ancient India

30.   Krishna-Dwaipayana Vyasa. *The Mahabharata of Krishna-Dwaipayana Vyasa*. Book 1:
       Adi Parva. Translated by Kisari Mohan Ganguli. 1883–1896. Published online at
       sacred-texts.com, 2003. http://www.sacred-texts.com/hin/m01/m01000.htm. Article
       is in the public domain.

31.   Max Müller, trans. *The Taittiriya Upanishad*. 1884. Published online at Wikisource,
       last modified June 9, 2012. http://en.wikisource.org/wiki/Taittiriya_Upanishad. Text
       is in the public domain.

32.   Bhikkhu Ñanamoli, trans., and Bhikkhu Bodhi, ed. *The Discourse on Right View:
       The Sammaditthi Sutta and Its Commentary*. *The Wheel* 377–379. Kandy,
       Sri Lanka: Buddhist Publication Society, 1991. http://buddhasutra.com/files/
       sammaditthi_sutta.htm. Copyright © 1991 by the Buddhist Publication Society.
       Reprinted with permission.

33.   Caraka. "Sutra Sthana." In *The Caraka Samhita*. Vol. 5. Shree Jamanagar, India:
       Gulabkunverba Ayurvedic Society, 1949.

Part Six: Ancient Hebrews

34.   Genesis 1–3. In *The Holy Bible, New International Version*®. Colorado Springs,
       CO: Biblica, Inc. Copyright © 1973, 1978, 1984, 2011 by Biblica, Inc. All rights
       reserved worldwide. Used by permission.

35.   Leviticus 1–3, 7, 11, Deuteronomy 14:1–21. In *The Holy Bible, New International
       Version*®. Colorado Springs, CO: Biblica, Inc. Copyright © 1973, 1978, 1984, 2011
       by Biblica, Inc. All rights reserved worldwide. Used by permission.

36.   The Song of Songs 1, 2, 4–7. In *The Holy Bible, New International Version*®.
       Colorado Springs, CO: Biblica, Inc. Copyright © 1973, 1978, 1984, 2011 by
       Biblica, Inc. All rights reserved worldwide. Used by permission.

Part Seven: Early Middle Ages

37.   Matthew 15:1–39 and 26:1–39. In *The Holy Bible, New International Version*®.
       Colorado Springs, CO: Biblica, Inc. Copyright © 1973, 1978, 1984, 2011 by
       Biblica, Inc. All rights reserved worldwide. Used by permission.

38.   Tertullian. *On Fasting*. Whitefish, MT: Kessinger Publishing Reprints, print on
       demand, pp. 27–34. Article is in the public domain.

39.   Owen Chadwick, ed. *Western Asceticism*. Philadelphia: Westminster Press, 1958,
       pp. 48–59. Copyright © 1958 by SCM Press. Used by permission of Hymns
       Ancient and Modern Ltd (rights@hymnsam.co.uk) and Westminster John Knox Press.

40. Clement of Alexandria. "Clement of Alexandria." in *Alexandrian Christianity*. Edited and translated by John Leonard Oulton and Henry Chadwich. Philadelphia: Westminster Press, 1954, pp. 110–15. Copyright © 1954 by SCM Press. Used by permission of Hymns Ancient and Modern Ltd (rights@hymnsam.co.uk) and Westminster John Knox Press.

41. Benedict of Nursia. "The Rule of Saint Benedict." In *Western Asceticism*. Edited by Owen Chadwick. Philadelphia: Westminster Press, 1958, pp. 315–23. Copyright © 1958 by SCM Press. Used by permission of Hymns Ancient and Modern Ltd (rights@hymnsam.co.uk) and Westminster John Knox Press.

42. Anthimus. *On the Observance of Foods*. Translated by Mark Grant. Totnes, UK: Prospect, 1996, pp. 47–59. Reprinted with permission.

43. H. R. Loyn and John Percival, eds. *The Reign of Charlemagne*. New York: St. Martin's Press, 1975, pp. 65–73. Article is in the public domain.

44. Burton Raffel, trans. *Beowulf*. New York: Signet Classics, 2008, pp. 28–30. Copyright © 1963, renewed © 1991 by Burton Raffel. Used by permission of Dutton Signet, a division of Penguin Group (USA) LLC.

Part Eight: Medieval Islam

45. al-Baghdadi. *A Baghdad Cookery Book. Petits Proposal Culinaires* 79. Translated by Charles Perry. Totnes, UK: Prospect Books, 2005, pp. 30–44, 86–91. Reprinted with permission.

46. al-Ghazali. *On the Manners Relating to Eating (Kitāb Ādāb al-Akl)*. Translated by D. Johnson-Davies. Cambridge, UK: Islamic Texts Society, 2000, pp. 38–45. Reprinted with permission.

47. Avicenna. *A Treatise on the Canon of Medicine of Avicenna Incorporating a Translation of the First Book*. Translated by O. Cameron Gruner. London: Luzac, 1930. Reprint by New York: Augustus M. Kelley, 1970, pp. 394–408.

48. Moses Maimonides. "Two Treatises on the Regimen of Health: Fī Tadbīr al-Sihhah and Maqālahfi Bayān Ba'd al-A'rād wa-al-Jawāb 'anhā'." *Transactions of the American Philosophical Society* (New Series) 54, no. 4. Translated by Ariel Bar-Sela, Hebbel E. Hoff, and Elias Faris. 1964, 3–50. Reprinted with permission.

49. Omar Khayyam. *The Rubaiyyat of Omar Khayyam*. Translated by Robert Graves and Omar Ali-Shah. London: Cassell, 1967, pp. 51, 57–60, 64–65, 73. Reprinted by permission of United Agents on behalf of the Trustees of the Robert Graves Copyright Trust and the estate of Syed Omar Ali-Shah.

50. Abū 'l-Khayr ash-Shajjār al-Ishbīlī. *Kitāb al-Filāha ou Le Livre de la Culture*. Edited by Henri Pérès. Translated by Auguste Cherbonneau. Algiers: Editions Carbonel, 1946. English translation by A. H. Fitzwilliam-Hall. Published online by Editions Carbonel, 2010. http://filaha.org/khayr_final_translation_revised.html.

Part Nine: Late Medieval and Renaissance Europe

51.   Pope Innocent III. *De Miseria Condicionis Humanae*. Edited by Robert E. Lewis. Athens: University of Georgia Press, 1978, pp. 165–70. Reprinted with permission.

52.   Rudolf Grewe and Constance B. Hieatt, eds. *Libellus de Arte Coquinaria: An Early Northern Cookery Book*. Medieval and Renaissance Texts and Studies, Vol. 222. Tempe: Arizona Center for Medieval and Renaissance Studies, 2001, pp. 29, 31, 37. Copyright © by Arizona Board of Regents for Arizona State University. Reprinted with permission.

53.   Guillaume Tirel. *The Viandier of Taillevent*. Edited by Terence Scully. Ottawa, Canada: University of Ottawa Press, 1988, pp. 283–90. Reproduced with permission from the University of Ottawa Press.

54.   Gina L. Greco and Christine M. Rose, ed. and trans. *The Good Wife's Guide (Le Ménagier de Paris): A Medieval Household Book*. Ithaca, NY: Cornell University Press, 2009, pp. 271–82. Copyright © 2009 by Cornell University. Used by permission of Cornell University Press.

55.   Joan Santanach, ed. *The Book of Sent Soví: Medieval Recipes from Catalonia*. Translated by Robin Vogelzang. Barcelona and Woodbridge, UK: Barcino Tamesis, 2008, pp. 53, 69, 83, 111, 115, 147, 179. Published by Editorial Barcino. Reprinted with permission from the editor, Joan Santanach i Suñol.

56.   Platina (Bartolomeo Sacchi). *Platina: On Right Pleasure and Good Health*. Translated by Mary Ella Milham. Medieval and Renaissance Texts and Studies, Vol. 168. Tempe: Arizona Center for Medieval and Renaissance Studies, 1998, pp. 119–21, 157, 293. Copyright © by Arizona Board of Regents for Arizona State University. Reprinted with permission.

Part Ten: The Americas

57.   Allen J. Christenson, trans. *Popol Vuh: Literal Translation*. Alresford, UK, and New York: 2004. Published online by Mesoweb Publications, 2007. http://www.mesoweb.com/publications/Christenson/PV-Literal.pdf. Reprinted with permission from the author, Allen J. Christenson.

58.   Christopher Columbus. *The Journal of Christopher Columbus*. Translated by Clements R. Markham. N.p.: Hakluyt Society, 1893. Article is in the public domain.

59.   Bernal Díaz. *The Memoirs of the Conquistador Bernal Diaz del Castillo*. Vol. 1. Translated by John Ingram Lockhart. London: J. Hatchard and Son, 1844, pp. 229–31. Published online by Project Gutenberg, 2010. http://www.gutenberg.org/files/32474/32474-h/32474-h.htm. Article is in the public domain.

60.   Bernardino de Sahagún. *A History of Ancient Mexico: Anthropological, Mythological, and Social, 1547–1577*. Translated by Fanny R. Bandelier. Nashville,

TN: Fisk University Press, 1932. Reprint by Detroit: Blaine Ethridge Books, 1971, pp. 53–54, 74–75, 175–76, 244–46. Reprinted with permission from Fisk University Franklin Library Special Collections.

61.   Thomas More. *Sir Thomas More's Utopia.* London: Chatto & Windus, 1908, pp. 108–11, 129–38, 158–71. Article is in the public domain.

Part Eleven: Era of Nation-States 1500–1650

62.   Desiderius Erasmus. "De Conscribidendis Episotlis Formula de Civilitate" [On Good Manners for Boys]. In *Collected Works of Erasmus.* Vol. 25. *Literary and Educational Writings 3.* Edited by J. K. Sowards. Toronto: University of Toronto Press, 1985, pp. 280–86. Copyright © 1986 by University of Toronto Press. Reprinted with permission of University of Toronto Press.

63.   Ulrich Zwingli. *Ulrich Zwingli, Early Writings.* Edited by Samuel Macauley Jackson. Eugene, OR: Wipf and Stock, 1999, pp. 71–76. Used by permission of Wipf and Stock Publishers (www.wipfandstock.com).

64.   Bartolomeo Scappi. *The Opera of Bartolomeo Scappi: L'arte et prudenza d'un maestro Cuoco (The Art and Craft of a Master Cook).* 1st Italian ed. 1570. Translated by Terence Scully. Toronto: University of Toronto Press, 2008, pp. 130–32, 228–30. Copyright © 2008 by University of Toronto Press. Reprinted with permission of University of Toronto Press.

65.   Stuart Peachy, ed. *The Good Huswifes Handmaide for the Kitchen.* 1588. Reprint by Bristol, UK: Stuart Press, 1992, p. 25. Article is in the public domain. Gervase Markham. *The English Housewife.* 1615. Edited by Michael R. Best. Reprint by Montreal and Kingston: McGill-Queen's University Press, 1986, pp. 176–77. Article is in the public domain. Robert May. *The Accomplisht Cook.* London: Obadiah Blagrave, 1685. Article is in the public domain.

66.   Michel de Montaigne. "Of Experience." In *1575 Essays.* Translated by Charles Cotton. http://oregonstate.edu/instruct/phl302/texts/montaigne/montaigne-essays-8.html#XXI. Article is in the public domain.

67.   Rupert of Nola. "Recipe 63." In *Libre del Coch.* Translated by Ken Albala. Reprint by Barcelona: 1568. Diego Granado. *Libro del Arte de Cozina.* Translated by Ken Albala. Madrid: Luis Sanchez, 1599, pp. 184–85. Domingo Hernandez de Maceras. *Libro del Arte de Cozina.* 1607. Translated by Ken Albala. Reprint by Salamanca: Ediciones Universidad de Salamanca, 1999, pp. 73, 85–86. Francisco Martínez Montiño. *Arte de Cocina, Pastelería, Vizcochería, y Conservería.* 1611. Translated by Ken Albala. Reprint by Barcelona: Maria Angela Marti, 1763, p. 202. Juan de Altamiras. *Nuevo Arte de Cocina.* Translated by Ken Albala. Barcelona: Juan de Bezares, 1758.

68.   Gaspar da Cruz and Martín de Rada. *South China in the Sixteenth Century.* Edited by C. R. Boxer. Bangkok: Orchid Press, 2004, pp. 138–42, 287–90. Reproduced by kind permission of Orchid Press.

Part Twelve: The Mercantile Era 1650–1800

69. François Pierre La Varenne. *La Varenne's Cookery*. Translated by Terence Scully. Totnes, UK: Prospect Books, 2006, pp. 156–57, 260–62. Reprinted with permission.

70. Coffee Advertisement. Printed 1650s in London. Article is in the public domain.

71. John Locke. *Two Treatises of Government (A New Edition, Corrected)*. Vol. 5. London: Thomas Tegg; London: W. Sharpe and Son; London: G. Offor; G. and J. Robinson; London: J. Evans and Co.; Glasgow: R. Griffin and Co.; Dublin: J. Gumming, 1823. Prepared by Rod Hay. Published online by McMaster University Archive of the History of Economic Thought. http://socserv.mcmaster.ca/~econ/ugcm/3ll3/locke/government.pdf. Article is in the public domain.

72. E. [Eliza?] Smith. *The Compleat Housewife*. 1758. Facsimile, London: Studio Editions, 1994, p. 89. Article is in the public domain.

73. Jean-Jacques Rousseau. *Emile*. Translated by William H. Payne. New York: Appleton & Co., 1909, pp. 117–20. Article is in the public domain.

74. Amelia Simmons. *American Cookery*. Hartford, CT: Simeon Butler, 1798, pp. 18–19, 20–22, 26, 28. Article is in the public domain.

75. Jean Anthelme Brillat-Savarin. *The Handbook of Dining*. Translated by Leonard Francis Simpson. London: Longman Green, 1864, pp. 5–8, 53–64. Article is in the public domain.

Part Thirteen: Nineteenth-Century Industrial Era

76. Friedrich Accum. *A Treatise on Adulterations of Food, and Culinary Poisons*. London: Longman, 1822, pp. 1–13. Article is in the public domain.

77. Charles Elmé Francatelli. *A Plain Cookery Book for the Working Classes*. London: Bosworth and Harrison, 1861. Reprint by Whistable, UK: Pryor Publications, 1993, pp. 9–11, 13–16, 100–101. Reprinted with permission from Pryor Publications.

78. Sylvester Graham. *A Treatise on Bread, and Bread Making*. Boston: Light and Stearns, 1837, pp. 105–11, 123–26. Article is in the public domain.

79. Isabella Beeton. *The Book of Household Management*. 2nd. ed. London: Ward, Lock & Co., 1895, pp. 1–12. Article is in the public domain.

80. Wilbur O. Atwater. "Food as Building Material and Fuel." In *Principles of Nutrition and Nutritive Value of Food*. Washington, DC: U.S. Government Printing Office, 1910, pp. 8–14. Published by U.S. Government Printing Office. Article is in the public domain.

81. Fannie Merritt Farmer. *The Boston Cooking-School Cook Book*. Boston: Little, Brown, 1896, pp. 27–29. Article is in the public domain.

82. Horace Fletcher. *Fletcherism: What Is It?* New York: Frederick A. Stockes, 1913, pp. 1–11. Article is in the public domain.

Part Fourteen: The Twentieth Century

83. Upton Sinclair. "Chapter 14." In *The Jungle*. 1906. Reproduced online by Page by Page Books. http://www.pagebypagebooks.com/Upton_Sinclair/The_Jungle/Chapter_14_p1.html. Copyright © 1906 by Upton Sinclair. Reprinted with Permission of McIntosh and Otis, Inc.

84. Carry A. Nation. *The Use and Need of the Life of Carry A. Nation*. Rev. ed. Topeka, KS: F. M. Steves & Sons, 1905. Article is in the public domain.

85. Maria Gentile. *The Italian Cook Book*. New York: Italian Cookbook Company, 1919, pp. 14–15, 17. http://digital.lib.msu.edu/projects/cookbooks/html/books/book_71.cfm. Article is in the public domain.

86. M.F.K. Fisher. "How to Cook a Wolf." In *The Art of Eating*. 1942. Reprint by New York: Macmillan, 1990, pp. 286–88, 320–22. Copyright © 1954, renewed 1982 by M.F.K. Fisher. Reprinted by permission of Houghton Mifflin Harcourt Publishing Company. All rights reserved.

87. Ray Kroc. *Grinding It Out: The Making of McDonald's*. New York: St. Martin's Press, 1992, pp. 108–14. Copyright © 1992 by Ray Kroc. Reprinted by permission of St. Martin's Press. All rights reserved.

88. Frances Moore Lappé, ed. *Diet for a Small Planet*. 1971. 2nd rev. ed. New York: Ballantine, 1982, pp. 140–46. Reprinted with permission from the author's institute, Small Planet Institute.

89. Craig Claiborne. *The New York Times International Cookbook*. New York: Harper & Row, 1971, pp. 391, 645. Copyright © 1961 by Craig Claiborne, renewed © 1989 by Craig Claiborne. Reprinted by permission of HarperCollins Publishers.

90. Folco Portinari. 1989. Published online by Slow Food, 2013. http://www.slowfood.com/about_us/eng/manifesto.lasso. Reprinted with permission from Slow Food International.

Every effort has been made to trace copyright holders and to obtain their permission for the use of copyrighted material. The publisher apologizes for any errors or omissions in the above list and would be grateful if notified of any corrections that should be incorporated in future reprints or editions of this book.

INDEX